Maryknoll
in China

CHINA'S WELCOME TO MARYKNOLL.

(This quaint engraving, sent by a Canadian friend in China, is well worth a few moments of study.)

The Field Afar
July 1916, p. 103

Maryknoll In China

A History, 1918–1955

Jean-Paul Wiest

M. E. Sharpe, Inc.
Armonk, New York
London, England

Available in the United Kingdom and Europe from M. E. Sharpe, Publishers, 3 Henrietta Street, London WC2E 8LU.

Library of Congress Cataloging-in-Publication Data

Wiest, Jean-Paul.
    Maryknoll in China: a history, 1918–1955 / by Jean-Paul Wiest.
        p. cm.
    Bibliography: p.
    Includes index
    1. Catholic Foreign Mission Society of America—Missions—China—History—20th century. 2. Maryknoll Sisters—Missions—China—History—20th century. 3. China—Church history—20th century. I. Title.
BV3415.2.W44   1988   87-32068
266'.251—dc19   CIP
ISBN 0-87332-418-8

Printed in the United States of America

DEDICATED TO
THE CATHOLIC CHURCH
IN CHINA

"Go the whole way for God. Do not turn back. Do not be discouraged by a little difficulty. Nor by big difficulties either. You will have problems to solve, hardships to beat, sometimes, but that is part of our vocation. Progress requires effort. And sometimes it involves pain."

James E. Walsh
(May 1971)

Contents

Preface   xiii

A Note on Romanization and Missioners' Names   xvii

Abbreviations   xix

Chronologies
The Catholic Church in China Until 1952   xxi
Maryknoll in Relation to China   xxii

Introduction   3

Part I: Maryknoll in Context

The Historical Context of the Word "Missions"   9

1. The Coming of Age of American Foreign Missions   11

The Origin of Maryknoll   11
The Making of a Maryknoller   30
Conclusion   42

2. Maryknoll in the Chinese Environment   45

The Catholic Church Prior to the Arrival of Maryknoll   45
The Search for a Mission Territory in China   47
The Five Maryknoll Mission Territories   52
Mission Work in Non-Maryknoll Territories   60
The Physical Environment   64

Part II: The Evangelization of the Non-Christians

The Priority of the Rural Apostolate   73

3. The Direct Apostolate   77

Emphasis on Local Catechists   77
The Wuchow Method   88
The Kaying Method   99
Wuchow and Kaying Methods Merge   114
The Lay Apostolate   119
Conclusion   126

4. Corporal Works of Mercy   131

Expressing God's Concern for the Poor
   and the Afflicted   131
Maryknoll's Medical Mission   132
Maryknoll Orphanages   138
The Hospital in Toishan   152
The Shanghai Mercy Hospital   157
Leper Colony   162
Relief Work   173
Cooperatives   180
Maryknoll Schools   186
Conclusion   199

Part III: The Building of the Native Church

Tensions Surrounding the Emergence of the
   Chinese Church   203

5. The Indigenization of the Clergy and Sisterhoods   207

The Training of Native Priests   207
The Training of Native Sisters   223
Relationships with the Native Clergy and Sisterhoods   241
Proposals for a Chinese Bishop   252
Conclusion   258

6. Adaptation and Accommodation   261

Life-style of Maryknollers: Degrees of
   Personal Adjustment   262
Language   268
Adaptation of the Message   281
Adaptation of Christian Practices   308
Conclusion   313

7. Maryknoll and Politics   318

Attitude toward the Local Wars of South China,
    1920–1930   318
Attitude toward Chinese Nationalism, 1925–1932   327
Involvement during the Japanese Invasion, 1931–1945   342
Maryknoll and Chinese Communism, 1925–1960   380
Conclusion   403

Part IV: Introducing China to North America

8. Maryknoll's Influence on American Catholics   409

The Use of Mass Media   410
The Impact of China Missioners on Maryknoll Vocations   423
Images of China Presented by Maryknoll   426
Conclusion   448

Concluding Remarks: "Souls Are People"   453

Appendices

    I. Methodology of the Maryknoll China
           History Project   457
   II. Sources and the Retrieval System at Maryknoll   459
  III. Maryknoll Sisters with Medical Training Who
           Served in China   461
   IV. Mission Statistics: Catholics and Mission Personnel   462
    V. Maryknoll Mission Works   468
   VI. Maryknoll Personnel in China   473

Notes   479

Glossary of Locations in China   541

Glossary of Chinese Terms and Personal Names   553

Working Bibliography   559

Index   577

Preface

Since the pioneer work of Kenneth Scott Latourette (*A History of Christian Missions in China*) appeared in 1929, numerous scholarly books have been published on twentieth-century North American mission history in China. Most of these studies consider the missioner as a religious manifestation of the broader socio-economic and political impact of the West on China. This growing awareness of the importance of the mission factor for the interpretation of past relationships between China and the West was strengthened by the discovery of the richness of the resources within mission archives. Scholars like Paul Varg approached the subject of missions as "curious investigators anxious to know more about what happens when representatives of one society seek to solve the problems of another society" (*Missionaries, Chinese and Diplomats, the American Protestant Missionary Movement in China, 1890–1952*, p. ix).

In the 1950s and 1960s, research on this topic increased substantially when Professors John K. Fairbank and Liu Kwang-ching encouraged their students at Harvard University to investigate the writings of American missioners in China and the Chinese response. As some of these young scholars matured and pursued their interests in Christian missions, they wrote monographs and held symposia in which they discussed various aspects of the secular contributions of American and British missioners to China. Since 1985, with generous funding from the Henry Luce Foundation, The History of Christianity in China Project at the University of Kansas has provided further support "to significantly advance the understanding of Chinese Christianity and of those aspects of Chinese culture and society which have interacted with Christianity."

However, these studies on American missions in China have had two significant shortcomings. They have drawn mostly on Protestant mission archives, with only a handful of scholarly writings on North American Catholic missions in China. Moreover, only a few timid attempts have been made at evaluating the *religious* content of the missionary work and message in the Chinese context.

I believe that treating mission history like any other secular history deprives it of a very important dimension. As theologian Walbert Bühlmann says in *God's Chosen Peoples*, "Purely profane methods will never sound the deepest essence of the Church. From its foundation to the *parousia*—hence, in all its history—the Church is an object of faith" (p. 62). Therefore any thorough study on the missionary aspect of the Church should be conducted at two levels, the historical as well as the meta-historical or theological.

The Maryknoll China History Project, launched in April 1980, followed that path. Focused on two Catholic groups—the Maryknoll Fathers and Brothers and the Maryknoll Sisters—its goal was to gather and to study all primary source materials, both oral and written, and to produce a critical history of the work of Maryknoll in China. However, these two missionary societies wanted even more than a critical history and further defined their goal so that the project would also provide guidelines for future mission work:

> The primary intent of the project is to seek to understand the past history of the mission work of the two Maryknoll societies in China through objective and critical scholarly research, as a guide for the future service of the two societies. (Joint Advisory Board, February 14, 1980)

Understanding the history of the Catholic Church in China requires examining not only the methods of the missioners, but also their theology and their understanding of mission—in sum, the spiritual legacy of the China missioners.

The Maryknoll China History Project was run by four researchers, Donald MacInnis, Sister Joanna Chan, Susan Perry, and myself. As a team, we combined academic training in Church history, mission studies, theology, Chinese history, and Chinese religions with field experience in mission service, an inside knowledge of Maryknoll, and fluency in the Chinese language as well as expertise in conducting oral history, gathering missionary records, organizing research projects, and developing and using a computerized data retrieval system.

We divided the project into four phases. The first was devoted to defining the project, setting guidelines, and establishing a methodology. The second phase concentrated on oral interviews. Altogether 256 American missioners and Chinese Catholics were interviewed, resulting in over 10,000 pages of transcribed materials which were indexed into a computerized retrieval system. The third stage dealt with archival sources. We studied over 6,000 old photographs from Maryknoll's Photo Library and selected 200 of them to produce a photographic history of Maryknoll in China. Some of the pictures appear in this study. At the same time we surveyed 90,000 pages of materials on China in the Maryknoll archives. To facilitate further research and the writing of the history of Maryknoll in China, about 38,000 pages of documents comprising the diaries of many mission stations and the correspondence and reports of many missioners were also indexed into the retrieval system.*

The fourth stage, the actual writing of the history of Maryknoll in China, was entrusted to me. While I take responsibility for the mistakes and discrepancies this book may contain, I would like to share the credit with a number of persons. Above all, I am indebted to my three colleagues in the Maryknoll China History Project who read the chapters and volunteered valuable ideas for improvement. Among them, however, my deepest gratitude goes to Susan Perry for her precious assistance during every phase of the writing of this book. At the start of each chapter, she developed printouts arranged around selected topics, locations, and groups of persons from our computerized retrieval system. At the same time, she often lent me a hand in lifting from the data the most appropriate and significant materials. She also entered the draft of every chapter into our word processor and played an active part in bringing each to its final form by displaying excellent editorial skills and by helping me with the selection of illustrations and the drawing of maps.

Among the Maryknollers who provided comments and editorial suggestions—but never tried to impose their views on me—I am particularly grateful to Sisters Luise Ahrens, Janet Carroll, Patricia Jacobsen, and Virginia Therese Johnson, and to Fathers Robert Sheridan, John Casey, John Kaserow, John Cioppa, and Peter Barry. I owe more than a customary thanks to Maryknoll's present archivists, Sister Dolores Rosso, Sister William Eugene Cashin, and Father John Harrington, and to those who have already passed away, Mother Mary Coleman and Father James Logues. They always gave me their full cooperation and assisted me in tracking down documents which were thought to have been lost. I am also much obliged to Penny Sandoval of the Maryknoll Photo Library for letting me peruse her fine collection of photographs and to Pat Pasquarella of the Maryknoll Photo Laboratory for his excellent work in copying or restoring the old photographs selected for this book.

I wish I could personally thank each of the 200 missioners and the 56 Chinese individuals who agreed to be interviewed. Their testimony gave this book its human dimension by telling the story of people who have

---

*For more information on the methodology, sources, and retrieval system used in the Maryknoll China History Project, see Appendices 1 and 2.

reached into their past to help us understand today's situation and face tomorrow's challenges.

Finally I must register my debt to scholars who read part of the draft, gave me encouragement, and assisted me in finding a publisher, especially Dr. Donald W. Treadgold of the University of Washington, Dr. C. Martin Wilbur of Columbia University, and Dr. Françoise Aubin of the Centre National de la Recherche Scientifique and the Centre d'Etudes et de Recherches Internationales in Paris.

Although I have pursued this study objectively as a trained historian and theologian, I cannot claim to be a completely dispassionate observer as I have had previous personal experience in the field with missioners. I believe that my understanding of missioners gives my critical analysis of Maryknoll an element of warmth and humanness which is sometimes lacking in scholarly works; nonetheless I have striven for utmost objectivity. It is also my hope that this book will help Maryknoll in some way to become more aware of its own identity, its own history, and its own mission, not only within its own nation and religious family, but in its work abroad as well.

Jean-Paul Wiest

Ossining, New York
February 25, 1987

A Note on Romanization and Missioners' Names

I have attempted to solve the problem of the romanization of Chinese names for people, places, and published materials by adopting the spelling most commonly used by Maryknollers in China. This allowed me to retain some of the flavor of China's linguistic variations at a time when the "national" or "common" language was not as prevalent as it is today. Chinese characters, when available, are provided at the end of the book together with the *pinyin* romanization for place names.

In the 1960s, many Maryknoll Sisters discontinued using religious names and returned to their baptismal names. In the text, the initial occurrence of a Sister's name includes her former religious name in parentheses.

Abbreviations

C.M.   Congregation of the Mission (Lazarists or Vincentians)
C.N.R.R.A. China National Relief and Rehabilitation Administration
C.W.C.C.   Catholic Welfare Committee of China
E.C.A.   Economic Cooperation Administration
FA   *The Field Afar*
FARC   Maryknoll Fathers & Brothers Archives
M.E.P.   Société des Missions Etrangères de Paris
M.M.   Maryknoll Missioner
SACO   Sino-American Cooperation Organization
S.J.   Society of Jesus—the Jesuits
SARC   Maryknoll Sisters Archives
TC   Transcript of oral interview with non-Maryknoll Chinese
TF   Transcript of oral interview with Maryknoll Fathers and
                    Brothers
TF*   Transcript of oral interview with non-Maryknoll priests who
                    worked in China during the period
TS   Transcript of oral interview with Maryknoll Sisters
U.N.R.R.A. United Nations Relief and Rehabilitation Administration

Chronologies

The Catholic Church in China Until 1952

1279   *The Mongols conquer China*
        Khubilai Khan starts the Yüan dynasty

1294   First Catholic missioners establish the Church in China
        Franciscan John of Montecorvino becomes the first archbishop of
          Peking

1368   *The Mongol dynasty topples and is replaced by the Chinese Ming*
          dynasty
        The Catholic Church collapses

1552   Francis Xavier, S.J., dies on Sancian Island off the coast of Kwangtung

1582   Matteo Ricci, S.J., arrives with Jesuit missioners
        Catholic Church reappears

1644   *The Manchus take over China and found the Ch'ing dynasty*

1724   Rites controversy; Rome condemns the Chinese Rites
        Chinese Catholics are persecuted; missioners are expelled

1840–42 *The Opium War; the first unequal treaty is imposed on China*

1860   French Protectorate established over Catholic missions
        Missioners openly reenter China

1900   *Boxer Rebellion*; many Christians are massacred

1911   *Sun Yat-sen founds the Chinese Republic*

1916   *A decade of warlordism begins*

1919   Apostolic letter MAXIMUM ILLUD of Pope Benedict XV

1921   *Founding of the Chinese Communist Party in Shanghai*

1922   Archbishop Celso Costantini, first apostolic delegate to China

1923   The prefecture apostolic of Puchi in Hupeh becomes the first
        ecclesiastical territory entrusted to the Chinese clergy

1924   First Plenary Council of China held in Shanghai

1926   Encyclical letter RERUM ECCLESIAE of Pope Pius XI
        Ordination of six Chinese bishops in Rome

1928   *Chiang Kai-shek assumes the presidency of the Chinese Republic*

1931   *Japan occupies Manchuria; name changed to Manchukuo*

1934   *The Long March begins*

1937–45 *Sino-Japanese War*

1939   Instruction PLANE COMPERTUM EST of Propaganda authorizing the
        practice of Chinese Rites

1940   Death of Father Vincent Lebbe in China

1942   *Abolition of unequal treaties between China and Western nations*

1945–49 *Civil War*

1946   Rome establishes the episcopal hierarchy in China: dioceses
        replace vicariates apostolic
        Archbishop Antonius Riberi, first papal internuncio to China

1949   *Founding of the People's Republic of China*
        Chiang Kai-shek withdraws to Taiwan

1950–53 *Korean War*

1950–55 Missioners are forced out
        End of the missionary period

Maryknoll in Relation to China

1911   Fathers James A. Walsh and Thomas F. Price found the Maryknoll
        Fathers & Brothers

1912   Mary Josephine Rogers assumes the leadership of the "secretaries,"
        the future Maryknoll Sisters

1917   "Field found! Yeungkong!" French Bishop J. B. de Guébriant offers
        James A. Walsh part of his vicariate in Kwangtung province

1918	First four Maryknoll Fathers arrive in China
1919	Father Price, co-founder, is the first Maryknoller to die in China
1920	Rome approves the Maryknoll Sisters as a religious congregation Wuchow in Kwangsi province becomes Maryknoll's second mission territory
1922	First Maryknoll Sisters arrive in Yeungkong
1923	Father Francis Ford starts training seminarians in Yeungkong Sister Gertrude Moore is the first Maryknoll Sister to die in China
1924	Maryknoll mission at Yeungkong is enlarged and becomes the Kongmoon prefecture apostolic
1925	Kaying in eastern Kwangtung becomes a Maryknoll mission
1926	Maryknoll Sisters in Hong Kong receive the first applicant for a Chinese sisterhood for Kongmoon Fushun in Manchuria becomes a Maryknoll mission
1927	James E. Walsh, first Maryknoll missioner, ordained bishop
1936	Maryknoll Sisters start work at Mercy Hospital in Shanghai
1938	Kweilin in Kwangsi becomes a prefecture apostolic under Maryknoll
1941–42	Maryknollers in Manchuria and Hong Kong are interned by the Japanese and repatriated
1941–44	Most Maryknollers in South China are able to avoid the Japanese and stay in their mission stations
1947	Communists control Manchuria; Maryknollers leave Fushun diocese
1950–55	Maryknollers, with all other foreign missioners, are gradually forced out of China
1951	Bishop Francis Ford dies in a Canton prison
1958	Bishop James E. Walsh is arrested and sentenced to 20 years in prison in Shanghai
1970	Bishop James E. Walsh released by the Chinese government

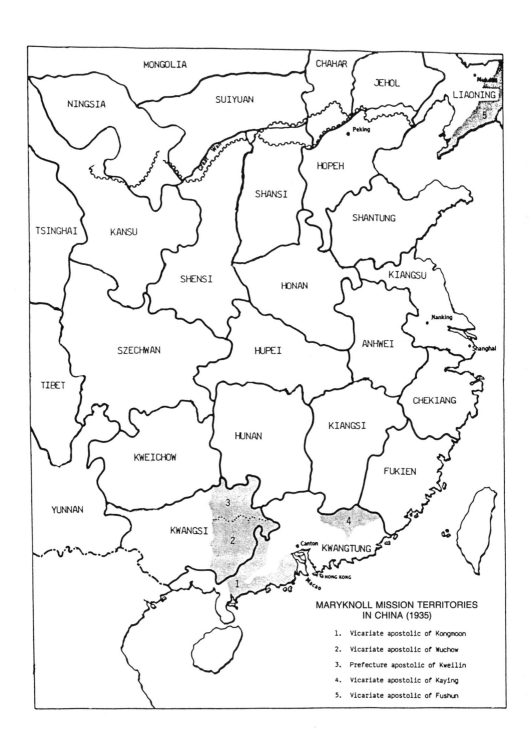

MONGOLIA

NINGSIA

SUIYUAN

CHAHAR

JEHOL

LIAONING
Mukden
5

TSINGHAI

KANSU

SHENSI

SHANSI

HOPEH
Peking

SHANTUNG

KIANGSU
Nanking

HONAN

SZECHWAN

HUPEI

ANHWEI

Shanghai

TIBET

CHEKIANG

HUNAN

KIANGSI

FUKIEN

KWEICHOW

YUNNAN

KWANGSI

3

2

1

Canton
KWANGTUNG
HONG KONG
Macao

4

MARYKNOLL MISSION TERRITORIES
IN CHINA (1935)

1. Vicariate apostolic of Kongmoon

2. Vicariate apostolic of Wuchow

3. Prefecture apostolic of Kweilin

4. Vicariate apostolic of Kaying

5. Vicariate apostolic of Fushun

Maryknoll
in China

Introduction

Early in the twentieth century, a group of men and women banded together to realize their common dream: to send American Catholics to the foreign missions. They had no American precedent or model to show them how to proceed or succeed. In the fall of 1912, this pioneer group established its headquarters outside of Ossining, New York, on a hillside above the Hudson River which it dedicated to the Mother of God and named "Maryknoll." Since then, some 3,000 Maryknoll missioners have descended that hill to become heralds of the good news of Jesus Christ in many parts of the world.

Although sharing the same spirit and the same heritage, the Maryknoll missioners, men and women, belong to two distinct organizations. About one year prior to the move to the "Knoll," the Fathers and Brothers' organization was approved by Rome under the title of the Catholic Foreign Mission Society of America.[1] The concept of American Catholic women missioners took longer to be accepted by the Church both in the United States and in Rome. In February 1920, after many vicissitudes, the status of the women at Maryknoll finally changed from that of supporting lay staff for the Fathers and Brothers to that of an independent and separate missionary organization officially named the Foreign Mission Sisters of St. Dominic.

Of course not all American Catholic missioners were or are Maryknollers. When Maryknoll opened in 1912, 130 years had already elapsed since the United States' first Catholic missioner, Leonard Neale, went to what is now Guyana.[2] Since then, more than ten thousand Catholic American men and women representing a wide array of religious societies and congregations have gone to the foreign missions. Nonetheless, by becoming the Catholic institution in the United States designated by the American hierarchy to specialize in the recruitment and training of foreign missioners, Maryknoll became a beacon for the American Catholic missionary endeavor. Since 1920, the Maryknoll Fathers, Brothers and Sisters have been the largest overseas mission sending group from Catholic America. There is no doubt that when Americans think of Catholic foreign missions, they think first of Maryknoll. As the well-known professor of American Catholic history, Father James Hennesey, S.J., put it: "Maryknoll by itself symbolizes American Catholic mission work. . . . Maryknoll is like the Notre Dame of the Catholic mission societies in America."[3]

The Three Purposes of Maryknoll in the Pre-Vatican II Context

When the first group of men and women settled at the Knoll in the fall of 1912, they had decided to devote their lives to the foreign missions. The newly founded Catholic Foreign Mission Society of America had three clearly defined goals: at home, to educate American Catholics about foreign missions; in non-Christian lands, to send missioners to convert the non-Christians and to train a native clergy.

Its first rule (or provisional constitutions) approved by Rome on July 15, 1915, clearly emphasized the two types of activities the Society would perform in non-Christian territories:

> §1. The Catholic Foreign Mission Society of America is a society of secular priests [and Brothers] formed to spread the Gospel of our Savior Jesus Christ among pagan people living outside of the United States.
> §2. It will aim to form at the earliest opportunity a native clergy as the most efficacious means of perpetuating its work of conversion, and will be always ready to withdraw its membership to work elsewhere when this object shall have been obtained.
> §19. . . . It will strive to give to the missions the form and constitutions of regularly established dioceses.[4]

As the women moved to form a religious congregation, they closely patterned their goals on those of the Maryknoll Fathers and Brothers. In 1917 the earliest draft of the constitutions of the future Maryknoll Sisters already called for full "cooperation with the work of the Catholic Foreign Mission Society of America."[5]

From Maryknoll's earliest days, these three purposes were embedded in the traditional pre-Vatican II concept of the Church and mission. Through the centuries, the Church's missionary and civilizing activities within Europe had produced a Church that was relatively uniform in worship, ritual, and belief. Starting with the Age of Discovery in the fifteenth century, missioners generally exported this pattern of a Church inseparably linked to Western culture without questioning its appropriateness.

This Western-centered vision of the world was still prevalent among most missioners at the time Maryknoll sent its first missioners to China. Moreover, it was reinforced by a theology of evangelization which emphasized the conversion of individual souls rather than the evangelization of a community of people with their own particular culture. Salvation for each person was dependent on his/her knowledge of Jesus Christ and conversion to Him, formally ratified by baptism and enrollment into the Catholic Church. Established in this manner, the Church was basically a foreign body with only shallow roots in the local community. The new Catholics had to live with this dichotomy; more often than not they were accused of having sold out to foreigners.[6]

China, Maryknoll's first mission field, was typical of this situation. In the midst of the political and social turmoil which shook China during the first half of the twentieth century, Maryknoll and the Chinese Church developed a complicated relationship, colored by cultural misunderstandings, successes, and failures.

It is important to describe this context. The first part of this study focuses on the American Catholic religious scene of the late nineteenth and the early twentieth centuries in which Maryknoll was conceived. It also presents the mission climate which existed in China at the time of the arrival of the American missioners. Parts 2, 3, and 4 analyze each of the three purposes of Maryknoll in light of changes which took place—in China, in America, and within the Church—from the time Maryknollers first set foot in China in 1918 until 1955 when they had practically all withdrawn.

In this book, China refers only to the continental China of that time, inclusive of Manchuria or Manchukuo. Maryknoll's presence in Hong Kong and on the island of Taiwan is for the most part outside the scope of this study. In Chapter 2, however, some of the accomplishments of Maryknoll in Hong Kong are described briefly because they tangentially affected the apostolates on the mainland; for instance, schools run by the Maryknoll Sisters in Hong Kong provided financial support for work on the mainland.

The Purpose of This Study

This study does not pretend to prove or disprove any hypothesis concerning American Catholic missioners prior to 1955, but rather seeks to investigate some of the important roles they played in the Church and the society in general, in the United States as well as abroad. The fact that

Maryknoll developed primarily as an American group for the China missions offers a definite field of observation over a period of almost 45 years. The history of Maryknoll in China during this period incorporates vital aspects not only of the establishment of Maryknoll as a mission-sending group, but also of the growth and development of the Catholic Church in America and the emergence of the Catholic Church in China.

This study highlights some of the circumstances which led to the awakening of the Church of the United States to the idea of foreign missions. It focuses on the people and experiences which shaped the young Society and Congregation of Maryknoll. It analyzes the images of China that Maryknollers projected to the American society. It probes into various aspects of Maryknoll's political or nonpolitical involvement at home and in China. It considers nearly all facets of Maryknoll's missionary work in China, pointing to shortcomings as well as to pioneering methods. It explores the ways in which a small part of the present Catholic Church in China was established through the work of Maryknoll missioners.

This study, however, is not just a history of how structures, hierarchy and official theology were established; it is also a history of encounters between people of two different cultures.[7] The front stage is not only occupied by the policy-makers of Maryknoll or the Church in China, but also by "average" missioners and Chinese Catholics. Through the lives of these people we can sense the ups and downs of intercultural relationships and transcultural evangelization. Intermeshed with the necessary scholarly analysis and statistics are the flesh-and-blood stories of idealistic young Americans who went to convert the people of China and often found themselves transformed in the process. Equally important are the narratives of the Chinese people who were convinced by the missioners to embrace the Catholic religion, as well as the written accusations of those who rejected them or turned against them. Inclusion of these Chinese views contributes to a more nuanced and less Western-centered evaluation of Maryknoll in relation to the Church and the society in the United States as well as in China.

The Special Meaning of This Study for Maryknoll: To Assess the Present Reality and Prepare for the Future

The days of cultural absolutism are over. Nations and Churches are in constant evolution, thus making cultural certitudes, traditions, and even value systems relative. Four hundred years ago, the Jesuit Matteo Ricci and his companions, unknowingly perhaps, began to break down cultural barriers and to challenge autocratic thinking as well as one-nation self-sufficiency. They were bridge-builders and agents of dialogue. They fore-shadowed today's movement toward genuine pluralism based on mutual respect, equality, and intercultural exchange. Today the words of Vatican II in the Document on Missionary Activity continue to exhort missioners to "be familiar with the national and religious traditions of peoples, gladly and reverently laying bare the seed of the Word which lies hidden in them."[8]

China has played a unique role in the history of Maryknoll. Its earliest roots are planted in Chinese soil and many of its cherished charisms and traditions were nurtured there. The very architecture of the Maryknoll seminary in New York reflects the thoughts and intentions of its founders and, through the years, China has remained close to the hearts of Mary-knollers. For groups like Maryknoll, direct missionary efforts in China are not possible today; however, it behooves them to reflect on the experience of China and, in association with others, to relate in whatever ways they can to China and the Church in China.

As Father John Cioppa, former assistant to the superior general of the Maryknoll Fathers and Brothers, said:

> Maryknoll as a missionary organization owes it to itself to seek adequate explanations for the termination of the largest missionary enterprise in the history of Christianity. The Chinese experience is moving Maryknoll to seek out its theological implications, thus to probe more deeply for a better understanding of Maryknoll faith and missionary endeavors.[9]

PART I

Maryknoll in Context

The Historical Context of the Word "Missions"

From the beginning it is important to realize that the missioners and the Chinese alike possessed the typical traits of their own cultural and religious background. They were also embedded in a very unique period of time which saw great changes occur in China and in the Catholic Church. Between 1918 and 1949, China hardly knew the meaning of peace and stability. The Chinese have an expression to describe the situation: "Nei luan, wai huan" (disorder from within and turmoil from without). Within China, the Confucian order continued to decay with no strong ideology or government to take its place. The Republic was a sham; warlords carved out their spheres of influence; social unrest and economic difficulties were endemic. From without, Western nations continued to take advantage of China's weaknesses by securing favors and privileges and by interfering in its internal affairs. Japan, with its expansionist politics, posed the most dangerous threat of all.

When Maryknollers arrived in China, they had "American" written all over them and carried with them many of the prejudices of the West. It was intriguing, therefore, to discover why many of them were able to successfully enter into the Chinese culture and share the spirit of the people with whom they lived.

Maryknollers were also generally representative of the "supremacist model" of the Catholic Church which had existed since the dawn of the great missionary era in the late fifteenth century. Ecclesiatically the world

9

was divided in two: the countries of the established Church and the countries with missions. The Church was the center and the missions were on the periphery. This concept had its roots in the medieval notion that Christendom was the source of faith, light, and culture. Beyond was a place of unbelief, darkness, and barbarism where pagans or heathens lived, enslaved by the devil.[1]

At the time of the founding of Maryknoll and during much of the period covered in this book, the American Catholic Church and its missioners shared this Western-centered or Church-centered view of the world. The Maryknoll missions were portions of territory within the foreign missions entrusted specifically to Maryknoll by the Sacred Congregation for the Propagation of the Faith in Rome.[2] Yet at the time Maryknoll was in China, missions as an historical form were seeing their last days: the Church was being established everywhere; former missions became local Churches.

Since Vatican II, the Catholic Church has used the word "mission" almost exclusively in the singular form. It is understood as the ongoing process of evangelization which does not end when missioners leave a given country or when leadership is handed over to the local Church. The local Church, too, has to carry on the missionary task in order to remain faithful to its vocation. In China, for example, evangelization is still taking place today—but the work is in the hands of Chinese Christians, without the help of Western missioners.

It is fascinating to uncover the role played by missioners in the evolution of *missions* from a geographical concept to the rediscovery of *mission* as the deepest identity of the whole Church: the Church's vocation is to evangelize—which means to proclaim the Good News to all people.[3] It cannot be attempted seriously, however, without understanding the home environment which nurtured these missioners as well as the new environment which waited for them in China.

1

The Coming of Age of American Foreign Missions

The Origin of Maryknoll

The Three Founders

The Maryknoll family owes its existence to the collaboration of three persons who shared the same desire to prepare and send American missioners abroad to convert non-Christians: Father Thomas F. Price, Mother Mary Joseph Rogers, and Father James A. Walsh.

Father James A. Walsh's interest in missions was awakened and cultivated by two Sulpician priests on the faculty of St. John's Seminary in Brighton, Massachusetts, where he studied until his ordination in May 1892. The rector, Father John Baptist Hogan, had been ordained at Notre Dame in Paris in June 1852 at the same time as Théophane Vénard, a priest from the Société des Missions Etrangères de Paris who died ten years later as a martyr in Indochina. In his spiritual lectures, Hogan frequently quoted the letters and diaries of Vénard which made a deep impression on Walsh; the first book he published was a biography of the French martyr.

The second Sulpician with a profound influence on Walsh was Father Gabriel André. André corresponded with missioners all over the world; teacher and seminarians spent many hours together perusing these dispatches. One such letter remained so strongly imprinted in Walsh's memory that he quoted it more than 30 years later during a conference to the Maryknoll Sisters.

> I am writing to you, my classmate. It is sixteen years since I left the seminary, with the fervor of youth and the strong desire to shed my blood for Christ. These sixteen years have passed in hard work, with very poor re-

sults. I have accomplished little and have come to the conclusion that nothing can be done in this district until some man's blood has been spilled; and I tell you in all sincerity, as friend to friend, coldly, far from that fervor of the young apostle—that if tomorrow I were called upon to meet death for Christ and souls, I should be the happiest of men.[1]

In 1903, Walsh became the archdiocesan director of the Society for the Propagation of the Faith in Boston. While working to persuade his fellow American Catholics to shoulder their mission responsibilities, James A. Walsh encountered a person with similar desires in a twenty-year-old zoology instructor at Smith College, Mary Josephine Rogers, the future Mother Mary Joseph, foundress of the Maryknoll Sisters.

In October 1906, Miss Rogers decided to start a mission study class in response to a request from her school to organize religious activities for Catholic students. She wrote to Walsh for resource materials, clearly stating her objectives:

> The particular motive of these classes is to inspire the girls to do actual work when they leave school. . . . By giving them what formation we can get, we hope to show how great the work of the Church is, to make them want to keep in touch with that work and give it their hearty support whenever an opportunity affords, now or later.

In her letter to Walsh, she also enumerated key topics for her class to concentrate on: "1. the preparation of priests and nuns for the work; 2. missionary orders and the field of work; 3. nature of the work done; 4. collection and distribution of funds."[2]

Walsh was impressed by the letter in which Miss Rogers had asked in a rhetorical but prophetic way: "Who knows but that the little work we do here may be the beginning of greater efforts in later life?" He promptly sent her materials with some words of advice and invited her to call at his office at the Society for the Propagation of the Faith in Boston. When they met the following December, Walsh showed her the galleys of the first issue of *The Field Afar*, a new missionary magazine he and some colleagues had decided to launch. Miss Rogers realized how much she shared the vision and purpose of that priest who had set out to capture the interest and imagination of American Catholics. She made up her mind to help him pursue that goal.[3]

When she left, Walsh knew that he had gained a valuable friend and partner. He decided to use her letter of October in the May editorial of *The Field Afar* for the "edification of the readers." Their meeting began a life-long association which led in 1920 to the official founding of the Foreign

Mission Sisters of St. Dominic, known more familiarly as the Maryknoll Sisters.[4]

The third founder was Father Thomas F. Price, the first North Carolinian ever to reach the priesthood. Ordained in 1886, he rapidly became a pioneer in evangelizing non-Catholics in the rural districts of his native state. In 1897 he began a magazine called *Truth* to reach more of the primarily Protestant population of North Carolina. He also founded Regina Apostolorum, a seminary which opened in the fall of 1902 with 25 students, to train priests for the rural districts of North Carolina and the other southern states.

Although Price's mission experience was in the southern United States, his vision of mission encompassed the world. In 1901 he presented a paper on his 15 years of missionary experience at the First Conference of the Catholic Missionary Union, an organization to promote mission work in the United States. His address showed that he was already conceptualizing a foreign mission apostolate to stimulate interest in home missions:

> There is no one who is acquainted with our clergy who will not say that our missionary spirit is painfully, even woefully, lacking. The Church's energies have been directed into other channels. Indeed, up to the present, and taken as a whole, we might be said to have no mission spirit at all.
>
> We have confined ourself [sic] almost entirely to our own people. It was publicly thrown into our teeth, time and again during the Chinese trouble (the Boxer Rebellion), that we possessed not a single foreign missioner. The amount of money contributed to the Propagation of the Faith, to the Indian and Negro Fund, and the Catholic Missionary Union, is so insignificant compared to our own resources, and the contributions of our Protestant missionary-minded neighbors for their mission work, that we are the laughing stock of the world. . . . Our American clergy work hard—perhaps there is no clergy on earth more busily employed, but the work is confined wholly to our own people.[5]

Three years later, Price was invited to speak at the Second Conference held in Washington during Easter week. One of the other features of the meeting was a plea for foreign mission activities by Father James A. Walsh. The veteran missioner was surprised to hear the younger priest from Boston present a paper on "Catholic Foreign Missions" which echoed his own thesis:

> While conscious of the need of priests in many parts of our own country, I believe [said Walsh] that to send some of our own young men and women to more remote districts would stimulate vocations for home needs and especially for the more difficult missions of the United States.[6]

Following Walsh's presentation, the two met and began a friendship which ripened through correspondence. Father Price recorded his own feelings in the June 1904 edition of *Truth*:

> Missionary work, both at home and abroad, is the great work of the Church, and no heart is truly Catholic that does not sympathize with it. The work has only to be presented properly to our people, and we are sure that there will be a great outpouring of beneficial aid. May God speed the efforts of . . . Father Walsh!

The two men, nevertheless, continued to go their separate ways. However, when they met again six years later on the occasion of the Eucharistic Congress of Montreal, they were ready to join forces. For all practical purposes, the Catholic Foreign Mission Society of America was conceived at that meeting in Montreal on September 10, 1910.

The Encouragement from England: Herbert Cardinal Vaughan

The origins of Maryknoll, however, go beyond the three personalities of Father Walsh, Miss Rogers and Father Price. Several other forces gave impetus to the awakening need for foreign missions. Although the American Catholic Church was officially classified as a mission Church itself until 1908, it had been urged to produce missioners by the Catholic Church in England since the 1870s.

The original proposal to open an American seminary for foreign missions came as a challenge to the American Church from Bishop Herbert Vaughan, future cardinal archbishop of Westminster. Since he was a young priest, Vaughan had been preoccupied with the idea of foreign missions. He found ardent and powerful supporters in Bishop William Ullathorne of Birmingham and in his two predecessors in the seat of Westminster, Cardinals Nicholas Wiseman and John Manning. In 1866 he opened a foreign mission seminary in the suburbs of London which later became the headquarters of the Mill Hill Foreign Mission Society. In late 1871, the Society was assigned by Rome to work among the black population of the United States. Vaughan accompanied his first four missioners to their new mission field in Baltimore and spent part of the following year touring in the United States and Canada. Noting the gigantic task which faced the Church in America, he offered the same remedy he had suggested for England—send priests to the foreign missions.

His appeal was heard by a young bishop, James Gibbons, who later became cardinal archbishop of the premier see of the United States, Baltimore.[7] In the early fall of 1889, Gibbons invited Vaughan to attend the centennial of the American hierarchy in Baltimore on November 10 through 12 and the inauguration of the Catholic University of America in Washington, D.C., on November 13. Vaughan, who could not attend, wrote to apologize. After a brief excuse, however, he changed the topic and wrote several pages urging the cardinal of Baltimore and the American hierarchy not to delay participation of the American Church in foreign missions. Although his letter is too long to be reproduced in entirety, some of the most important passages are quoted verbatim because of their profound impact on the American Church:

> Hitherto you have been occupied & engrossed with gathering together and ministering to the emigrants who all through this century have been landing upon our shores, not only in units & tens & twenties, but as it were in flights & flocks, which have in turn scattered themselves over your vast States. Your attention has also been given to the Indian & the Negro. You have not indeed compassed your aim, or wholly achieved your mission to the American Continent; but your public records & statistics prove how well you are on your way. . . .
>
> O my Lord! what high hopes may not the Church entertain in beholding your progress at home! How she impatiently looks to the time when you will turn your eyes to the heathen & send forth your Apostles into the missionary lands abroad!
>
> Everything seems to awaken & justify a high expectation. First, the whole of the East, from Constantinople to Jerusalem, China & Japan, & the islands of the Pacific, are at present overrun with Protestant American Missionaries. For energy, self-sacrifice, skill & intelligence, they are generally represented as outstripping the agents of all the great English Protestant missionary Societies. They surpass them through the traits of the national character; but this national character is equally yours, and a fair contribution from it is due to the Apostolic work of the Catholic Church. But more than this. Your Church must be heir to something beyond your natural & national gifts: it must be heir also to the great missionary spirit of S. Patrick. With the enterprise, therefore, the courage, skill & adaptability of the American, conjoined with the Catholic & Apostolic spirit of the Missioner—permit me to say it—your Church ought to produce a race of foreign missioners which should take the lead during the next century in the evangelisation of the heathen world. . . . The Apostles of the American Church cannot refuse to cooperate with Peter in sending forth heralds of the true Faith.
>
> I know that some will meet these proposals with the poor excuse that much remains to be done at home—that your Negro population remains unconverted, that the aboriginal lord of the soil, the Indian, claims your care—and above all, that you cannot overtake the growing demands of your population of European descent. I answer the objection, as applied to America, in the words with which Cardinal Manning replied to it, when it was

urged against us in England, now more than twenty years ago. I quote from the printed report of the Cardinal's speech: "It is quite true we have need of men & of means at home: and it is *because* we have need of men & of means at home and of more men & of more means by a great deal than we as yet possess, that I am convinced that we ought to send both men & means abroad. I am entirely convinced that if we desire to find the surest way to multiply immensely our own material means in this country for our works at home, it is by not limiting the expansion of Charity, & by not paralysing the zeal of self-denial. . . ."

Finally, my Lord Cardinal . . . while you & your colleagues are celebrating the centenary of your Church & worthily marking the epoch by the erection of a Catholic University, would it not be possible to give expression to some determination on the part of the Catholics of America, to participate to the full in the sufferings & martyrdoms, the triumphs & conquests of the Church's Apostolate throughout the world, during the second centenary of the American Episcopate?[8]

Cardinal Gibbons took Vaughan's challenge most seriously. Until his death 32 years later, he was one of the most influential members of the American hierarchy in transforming the American Catholic Church into one of the largest mission-supporting and mission-sending bodies.

The Support of Cardinal Gibbons

Bishop Vaughan's direct influence on Gibbons is most apparent in the circumstances which led to the creation of the Catholic Foreign Mission Society of America. Between 1904 and 1910, rumors circulated periodically about the forthcoming opening of a seminary to train priests for foreign mission work, but nothing actually developed. When Father Thomas Price went to Baltimore in early 1911 to consult Cardinal Gibbons about opening a national seminary for foreign missions, the cardinal gave full approval to the plan of Fathers Price and Walsh.

To rally the hierarchy behind him in support of the proposed "American Foreign Mission Seminary," Gibbons wrote to all the archbishops in the United States commending the plan of the two organizers. He advised the archbishops to discuss it with their suffragan bishops and to be ready to vote on it a month later at their annual meeting. The first part of the cardinal's letter stressed the necessity of more missionary involvement on the part of the Church of the United States. Relying heavily on Vaughan's letter of 1889, Gibbons urged his fellow American bishops to heed the warning of his English colleague:

The priests of the United States number more than 17,000, but I am informed there are hardly 16 on the foreign missions. This fact recalls a warning which the late Cardinal Vaughan gave in a kindly brotherly letter to me 20 years ago, urging us American Catholics not to delay participation in foreign missions, *lest our own faith should suffer.*[9]

As for the argument that America should first attend to mission work at home, Gibbons dismissed it, borrowing from Vaughan's letter a quote of Cardinal Manning:

It is quite true that we have need of men and means at home; and it is *because* we have need of more men and more means, by a great deal, than we as yet possess, that I am convinced we ought to send both men and means abroad. If we desire to find the surest way to multiply immensely our own material means for works at home, it is by not limiting the expansion of Charity and by not paralyzing the zeal of self-denial.[10]

At their meeting in Washington, D.C., on April 27, 1911, the archbishops unanimously passed a resolution to "heartily approve the establishment of an American seminary for foreign missions" and to "warmly commend to the Holy Father the two priests mentioned as organizers."[11] Catholic America had finally answered the challenge raised by Vaughan.

Cardinal Vaughan's Influence on Father Walsh

In addition to influencing the American hierarchy, Vaughan had also inspired one of the founders of Maryknoll, James A. Walsh. After he became the archdiocesan director of the Society for the Propagation of the Faith of Boston in 1903, Walsh went to Europe to visit some of the foreign mission seminaries. Unfortunately, when Walsh reached the Mill Hill Seminary, Vaughan was dying and the two never met. Instead Walsh was received by Father Francis Henry, who had succeeded Vaughan as superior general of Mill Hill. At once the two men became good friends. Walsh learned about Vaughan's "ardent wish" for a foreign mission seminary in America and he began to think about how to make Vaughan's dream a reality.[12]

It seems very likely that Walsh saw a copy of the 1889 letter of Vaughan to Gibbons during his stay at Mill Hill. Upon returning to the United States, his writings and addresses began to show a strong similarity to passages in the letter and sometimes made open reference to it. In 1905, he published a short article in a Boston religious magazine called *The Sacred Heart Review*, emphasizing the need for a foreign mission seminary in America. He reproduced the entire conclusion of Vaughan's letter which confronted the American hierarchy with these words:

Would it not be possible to give expression to some determination on the part of the Catholics of America, to participate to the full in the sufferings & martyrdoms, the triumphs & conquests of the Church's Apostolate throughout the world . . .?[13]

A second reference was clearly made in a paper that Walsh delivered at the Second Conference of the Catholic Missionary Union in Washington, D.C., in 1904. He repeated verbatim the challenge given in 1889 by the English cardinal to the entire American Catholic Church: "And now my Lord Cardinal [Gibbons] . . . has not the time come for the American Church to take its share in the great foreign missionary work of the Church?"[14]

He also quoted Vaughan's warning that the American Church would be less blessed in its second century of existence if it did not send missionaries abroad. Using Vaughan's own words, he dismissed the argument that too much still needed to be done at home to consider undertaking mission work abroad: "It never has formed a solid reason against the diffusion of apostolic zeal, since the Apostles spread themselves over the world leaving their own country unconverted."[15] As Walsh said in his address, Vaughan "struck the keynote" which slowly awakened the American Church to the need to face its missionary responsibilities abroad by establishing a foreign mission seminary.

A Stimulus for Foreign Missions—The Society for the Propagation of the Faith in the United States

Until the early 1900s, the American Catholic Church showed little awareness of a need to participate in world missions. Classified as a mission Church under the authority of Propaganda Fide until 1908, the Church in the United States focused on home missions. These missions encompassed not only Indians and Blacks, but also immigrants and poor dioceses of the South and West with only a few Catholics scattered over a vast territory. Under these circumstances, recalled James A. Walsh, the topic of foreign missions was rarely mentioned:

> Priests came out of the seminary, Brothers and Sisters finished their novitiates without any knowledge of the missions. People never thought of it. We were canonically under Propaganda [Fide] which meant that we were looked upon by Rome as a foreign mission, and even Rome did not expect much from us in the support of foreign missions.[16]

Over the years, the Church in the United States had indeed been on the receiving end of the generosity of European Catholics, especially through funds provided by the Society for the Propagation of the Faith. This Society was started in Lyon, France, in 1822 by French Catholics to raise funds for the work of Bishop Louis W. Dubourg of the diocese of New Orleans. Two-thirds of the first collection was sent to the United States, and for the next ten years the Church in the United States received 42 percent of the Society's total allocations. In 1833 the United States sent its first gift of six dollars to the Society. During the 70 years which followed, American Catholics contributed about $1,283,000, representing only one-fifth of the amount which they had received from the Society in France.

The Church of the United States was slow to organize repayment—at least materially—of its debt to the universal Church. At their first two plenary councils held in Baltimore in 1852 and 1866, U.S. bishops encouraged the establishment of a Society branch in each diocese but with few results. At the Third Plenary Council held in 1884, they passed a similar decree but also ordered each diocese to pay an annual Lenten collection—half of which was to be given to the "Negro and Indian missions" in the country and half to the Society for the Propagation of the Faith—until a satisfactory organization of the Society had been reached.

This appeal brought a substantial increase in the contribution of the United States which grew from $17,500 in 1885 to $53,000 in 1888. The effort, however, was not sustained because no one had been made responsible for further organization of the Society. By 1895 the United States' contribution to the Society had dwindled to no more than $36,500.[17]

While visiting friends in the summer of 1896, James Cardinal Gibbons renewed contact with an old acquaintance, Sulpician Father Gabriel André, who had served many years on the faculties of St. Mary's Seminary in Baltimore and St. John's Seminary in Brighton, Massachusetts. André spoke to him of the project nearest his heart—the establishment in America of a well-organized Society for the Propagation of the Faith. When Gibbons heard André's proposal for an American branch of the Society, he strongly encouraged the idea. His approval led to acceptance of the proposal by the Central Council of the Society in Paris and finally its ratification in October 1897 by the Assembly of the American Archbishops. The Assembly also appointed a national director to help diocesan directors organize the Society throughout the country and recruit members who would help foreign missions with funds and prayers.[18]

The Boston branch grew quickly under the leadership of Father Joseph V. Tracy, appointed as archdiocesan director in 1898 by Archbishop John J. Williams. Under Tracy's management, Boston became the largest U.S. contributor, ranking eighth in the world's list of dioceses contributing to the Propagation of the Faith.[19]

When James A. Walsh took over from Tracy in 1903, he realized that however substantial the sum collected by Boston, it still amounted to less than five cents per Catholic per year. He was even more dismayed to find out that the 12 million American Catholics who gave millions to charitable works and other local and national needs did not contribute even $100,000 or one cent per capita to foreign missions.

Walsh was convinced that the lack of support in the United States for the worldwide work of the Church was not a sign of selfishness, but rather a sign of ignorance. He thought that if Catholics in the United States knew more about the needs of foreign missions, they would respond generously. Missionary education, in turn, would result in better financial backing and also generate vocations. Walsh saw a distinct need to sensitize his fellow Catholics to the breadth of the Lord's command to preach the Gospel to every creature:

> The hope of our foreign missions lies in a more widely diffused knowledge of them. The hearts of our own priests and people are sympathetic and need only to have this sublime cause presented with sufficient force and frequency to secure the necessary cooperation, and to give the missions their proper place in our religious activities.[20]

Walsh launched a well-planned campaign of missionary education. He developed an extensive correspondence with missioners all over the world and by 1910 had exchanged letters with 275 of them. He channeled their information and requests into several hundred letters a year which he sent to pastors in Boston and to benefactors and members of the Society for the Propagation of the Faith.

Walsh also went wherever invited to talk on the missions. Besides addressing congregations at Sunday masses, he frequently gave lectures in churches and halls, school auditoriums, convents, and missionary conferences. He even went to jails to speak with prisoners. Years later, reflecting on this period of his life, Walsh confided to Mother Mary Joseph that for long periods of time he had not slept in the same bed on two successive nights.[21]

To make his talks more lively, Walsh often showed photographs or used a stereopticon to project slides and always included bits and pieces of recent mission news. For example, while preaching in a Boston church in early 1904, he mentioned that he had recently learned that 25 newly ordained priests of the Société des Missions Africaines (S.M.A.) remained stranded in their seminary in Europe for lack of funds to pay their passage to West Africa. At the end of mass, Walsh received two gifts of $200, enough to pay the travel expenses of two of these priests.[22]

Walsh knew from experience that he could reach a much larger audience with the printed word. As a seminarian, he had helped edit a "Mission Notes" column in the parish weekly of the Sacred Heart Church in Cambridge. Because of its quality, *The Sacred Heart Review* circulated far beyond the parish into the entire archdiocese and even across to the Pacific Coast.

As archdiocesan director of the Society for the Propagation of the Faith, Walsh launched an active propaganda campaign of articles and books on the subject of Catholic missions. He resumed his page in *The Sacred Heart Review* and introduced a weekly column in the archdiocesan Catholic newspaper, *The Boston Pilot*. He also sent occasional contributions to local magazines such as *Donahoe's Magazine* and *Working Boys' Magazine*, targeting not only Catholic periodicals but also newspapers with a larger audience such as the *Boston Evening Transcript*.

On the national scene, he pushed for more interesting publications on the theme of foreign missions. In his address to the Second Conference of the Catholic Missionary Union in 1904, he lamented the lack of accounts of mission work in Catholic papers and magazines and urged participants to publish more. He took the initiative himself by publishing an article on "The Society for the Propagation of the Faith in the Archdiocese of Boston" in the January 1904 issue of *The Ecclesiastical Review*. In 1905 he obtained an old translation of the life of Théophane Vénard, the French missioner who had died in 1861 in Tongking as a martyr. He revised it, added annotations and photographs, and published it under the title *A Modern Martyr, Theophane Venard*, selling 3,000 copies in the first year. This modest success prompted him to edit a collection of letters from French martyrs which he entitled *Thoughts from Modern Martyrs*.[23]

Walsh's efforts were successful—at least financially. In 1905 the donation of Boston Catholics to the Society for the Propagation of the Faith reached well above five cents per capita. With a total contribution of $41,239.47, the Boston archdiocese had become the world's second largest contributor, surpassed only by Lyon in France.[24] Yet James A. Walsh was far from satisfied by the overall response of the United States, still giving less than one cent per Catholic. He blamed the poor results on the scarcity of interesting publications on the foreign missions.

The Catholic Foreign Mission Bureau and the Founding of the Maryknoll Fathers and Brothers

Walsh's appeals to the religious and secular press for regular articles on mission work remained largely unanswered through the early 1900s. He had even written an open letter to the editor and the readers in the April 1904 issue of *The Ecclesiastical Review*, asking for the magazine to devote a page to the missions with an occasional longer article with photographs if possible. In 1906, at the suggestion of a Dominican friend, he wrote a thought-provoking article for the Dominican yearbook entitled "An Apology for Foreign Missions" in which he again expressed his dismay at the lack of missionary literature.

> A few days ago I took up the catalogue of a Catholic book concern. Works on history and dogma, books of instruction, devotion and controversy were generously tabulated. So, too, were numerous lists of fiction; —tales for the young and old, by authors, some celebrated, more tolerated, others struggling for a name in the galaxy of Catholic writers. I searched carefully through 4,000 titles and discovered on the subject of Foreign Missions— four—two of them published more than a quarter of a century ago.
>
> How can we know unless we be taught? With few books written in English on the subject, with practically no live periodical to represent the cause, with a scarcity of articles in our various magazines, with hardly an allusion in many Catholic weeklies, we cannot wonder that our people, and even some of our good priests, have not realized the need.[25]

Having achieved little success to date with the press, Walsh began to make plans to publish a mission periodical himself. Prior to 1907, the only world-embracing mission periodicals in the United States were the *Annals of the Propagation of the Faith* and the *Annals of the Holy Childhood*, official bi-monthly editions of the French magazines which were distributed to members of the Society for the Propagation of the Faith and the Society of the Holy Childhood. Walsh felt these American editions were uninteresting: their drab appearance, lack of editorials, absence of photographs and awkward translations "could hardly be expected to arouse and hold American Catholic readers."[26]

During his visits throughout the archdiocese, Walsh often saw piles of unopened *Annals* stacked in dusty corners of parishes. He finally wrote to the head office of the Society for the Propagation of the Faith in Paris saying candidly that the *Annals* failed to match the quality of literature to which American readers were accustomed.

> I regret to say there is nothing of the personal element in [the *Annals*]. The woodcuts which you sent from France are ridiculous to American readers. Something should be done to spread attractive literature well illustrated, all over the country, and until this is done, the work will not expand much more widely than it has up to the present time.[27]

At the same time, Walsh talked to Monsignor Joseph Freri, the national director of the Society for the Propagation of the Faith, about the possibility of supplementing the *Annals* with an illustrated magazine with a wider circulation. It is almost certain that Walsh had in mind something similar to *Les Missions Catholiques*, an illustrated French weekly published by the Society for the Propagation of the Faith in France, or *Illustrated*

Catholic Missions, an English monthly started in 1901 by Bishop Vaughan. The similarities in format and presentation between these two magazines and the first issue of *The Field Afar* were striking.

When Walsh received no definite answer from Paris and Freri told him that there was practically no chance of securing the necessary material and photographs from the general office in France, Walsh decided to launch an organization to produce more appealing mission propaganda. Long before *Life* magazine made the term popular, Walsh was a great believer in photo-journalism. He was convinced that the correspondence and collection of photographs he received from English-speaking missioners would make excellent material for an interesting magazine to supplement the *Annals* and prepare the ground for an American foreign mission society.

With the permission of Archbishop Williams, Walsh met on October 4, 1906, with three other priests who shared his thoughts on promoting the cause of foreign missions. Father James F. Stanton and Father John I. Lane belonged to the Boston archdiocese; Father Joseph Bruneau, a Sulpician, taught at St. John's Seminary in Brighton. Together they established a Catholic Foreign Mission Bureau whose purpose was to organize "a literary propaganda with a view to deepen and widen the missionary spirit in the United States, having for its ultimate end the establishment of a Foreign Mission Seminary."[28]

The Bureau made definite plans for publications which included books, pamphlets, pictures, newspaper articles and a periodical. Within a few months, the Bureau published the story of Father William Judge, *An American Jesuit Missionary in Alaska,* which it advertised as "a most interesting account of the work of Rev. William H. Judge, S.J."[29] At the same time, photogravures of French missionary martyrs such as Théophane Vénard, Just de Brétenières and Henri Dorie were made available. By March 1907, ten inexpensive pamphlets on missionary topics were also ready for distribution.[30]

From the beginning, however, the four priests decided that their main tool of missionary promotion would be a bi-monthly review priced at 50 cents a year. The first issue of the new magazine called *The Field Afar* came out on January 1, 1907. A statement printed under the title identified the scope of the magazine: "Devoted to the Interests of Catholic Missions."[31] As for the purpose, it was stated by James A. Walsh in the opening editorial: "*The Field Afar* aims to deepen and widen in its readers the missionary spirit, . . . [it] will strive to make known conditions and opportunities existing in the foreign missions."[32]

The Field Afar had a definite American accent designed to appeal to American tastes, which distinguished it from most other missionary publications. With a large picture on its front cover, the issue contained half-tone photographs on most of its 16 pages. Following in the steps of the British *Illustrated Catholic Missions*, the first issue carried more stories about English-speaking missioners than the *Annals of the Propagation of the Faith* would normally carry in one year. Moreover, since the magazine emanated from Boston, some materials were chosen to emphasize the link of the archdiocese with the world. The story of Father James Feeney, missionary in Puerto Rico, was Boston news because he had previously been a priest at the Redemptorist Church in Roxbury. Similarly, it was Boston news to tell of the work of Father Rale among the Abenaki Indians in the eighteenth century, under the caption "Early New England."

The appearance of *The Field Afar* was greeted with favorable comments from the Boston press. The *Boston Evening Transcript* of January 12, 1907, praised "the attractive makeup," "the skillful editing," and "the interesting accounts" of the new mission magazine. The response of Catholics in the Boston archdiocese was also positive. Subscriptions immediately began to pour in and circulation rapidly approached 5,000.[33]

Meanwhile Monsignor Freri changed his mind about supplementing the *Annals*; in January 1907, he launched an illustrated magazine called *Catholic Missions*. However, because of the great vacuum in Catholic mission periodicals, *Catholic Missions* and *The Field Afar* did not really compete. The new periodical of the Society for the Propagation of the Faith aimed at a national audience while *The Field Afar* claimed to be a diocesan magazine written mainly but not exclusively for New England readers. The two magazines also differed in the refinement of their goals. *Catholic Missions* aimed broadly at promoting interest in Catholic foreign missions while *The Field Afar* repeatedly stressed the urgent need for a generous harvest of American Catholic missioners.[34]

In his first editorial in *The Field Afar*, Walsh referred to a recent newspaper article in the Boston press describing the departure of seven Protestant missioners to India. He stopped short of asking for the immediate opening of a Catholic foreign mission seminary and novitiate:

> The seven missionaries represent a small detachment of the great army which Protestants in this country have at work today in foreign mission fields. Would that we Catholics of the United States could point to a similar force of men and women, self-exiled for the spread of the *true* faith! . . . The time has surely come when we Catholics should enter upon our task among people who are ours by the inheritance of Jesus Christ.[35]

The time had indeed come. Several international religious orders and congregations, including the Franciscans, Jesuits, Brothers of Mary, Society of the Divine Word, and Congregation of the Holy Cross, were also speculating about an American apostolate in the foreign missions.

In addition to religious bodies, individual priests here and there had also been praying for the realization of an American seminary for secular priests heading for the foreign missions. Father Thomas F. Price was such a priest. When Walsh and Price met at the Eucharistic Congress in Montreal in September 1910, they decided to unite forces and to move swiftly.

By the end of April 1911, they had secured the approval of the American hierarchy to begin a seminary. On June 19, two months later, they arrived in Rome to obtain "all the necessary authorization and direction" from Propaganda Fide, the Church organ controlling the work of evangelization in mission countries. They handed a letter of petition to Girolamo Maria Cardinal Gotti, head of the Congregation, which enumerated clearly what they intended to do:

1. They wanted to establish a society for the conversion of non-Christians. This was to be brought about both by the preaching of the Gospel and the education of native priests in mission countries.

2. The Society was to be made up of secular priests[36] and be directly subject to Propaganda Fide in all that concerns the missions,

3. The form of government would be a superior general and council, chosen from among the members of the Society.

4. Walsh and Price would seek support among Catholics of the United States.

5. They would open a seminary to train foreign missionaries.

6. "The Society will accept any mission assigned to it by the Holy See, but a preference is expressed for the missions in China".

7. The Society would seek financial support from Propaganda Fide.

8. The center for the Society would be located within 50 miles of New York City.

On June 29, they received the good news from Cardinal Gotti that they were formally authorized to begin their work by purchasing a property for a seminary and appealing for students.[37] They named their new organization the Catholic Foreign Mission Society of America: Catholic, to distinguish it from Protestant mission groups; Foreign, to define its purpose; of America, because it had received the full sanction of the American hierarchy, and because the term would distinguish it from European groups and let people in mission lands know that American Catholics were interested in them.[38] Although their initial intention was to form only a society of secular priests for the missions, within a few years after their return from Rome, Walsh and Price also decided to include auxiliary Brothers.

The familiar name of "Maryknoll" by which the Society and the Congregation are commonly known was coined by founders Walsh and Price. A few years earlier, Father Walsh had vacationed in a beautiful resort in New Hampshire called "The Knolls." This designation was combined with

Fig. 1. September 1918: first departure picture (standing from left): Francis Ford, Bernard Meyer; (seated) Thomas Price, James A. Walsh, James E. Walsh. Maryknoll Photo Library.

Father Price's profound devotion for Our Lady, and "Maryknoll" became the name of the large farm on Sunset Hill in Ossining that they purchased to launch their missionary enterprise.

The Field Afar became the official organ of the new Society and its seminary whose goals it had promoted since 1907: to send missioners to the foreign missions and to arouse American Catholics to a deeper appreciation of their missionary duty. A year later, on September 21, 1912, the first group of seminarians and three aspirant Brothers went on retreat to begin their first year of preparation as candidates for the foreign missions. When the first group of Maryknoll missioners left for China in September 1918, the Society had just passed the 100 mark with 16 priests, 10 Brothers, and 75 seminarians.[39]

The Founding of the Maryknoll Sisters

When Mary Josephine Rogers left Father James A. Walsh's office in Boston in December 1906, she took along letters and articles to translate from French into English for future use in *The Field Afar*. For the following two years, she became the nameless translator behind many contributions by French missioners. Walsh was also pleased with her program of mission classes at Smith College; in October 1907 and in February 1908, he presented her syllabus in *The Field Afar* as a model and incentive for other study groups.

In the fall of 1908, Miss Rogers took a teaching position in Boston to devote her spare time to Father Walsh's work. He showed his great appreciation for her help in a dedication he wrote in a bound copy of the first year's issues of *The Field Afar* which he offered her that December: "To my co-worker with deep appreciation of her faithful service."[40]

As Walsh became more involved with Father Price in persuading the American bishops to adopt their proposal for a foreign mission seminary, he entrusted more and more responsibility for the magazine to Miss Rogers and Nora Shea, his secretary. He still wrote editorials and oversaw the selection of articles for *The Field Afar*, but left most of the preparation and publication work to the two women. When Price and Walsh journeyed to Rome in the summer of 1911 to seek papal approval for the new seminary, Miss Rogers and Miss Shea managed the publication entirely by themselves. It was their privilege to put out the first two issues announcing the creation of the Catholic Foreign Mission Society of America and the establishment of a foreign mission seminary.[41]

Following this announcement, letters requesting further information soon piled up on the editor's desk. Many inquiries came from young women asking Walsh if he intended to form a community of foreign mission nuns as well. Walsh did not give a definite yes, but replied in the December 1911 issue of *The Field Afar* that he had been advised "to provide in some way the invaluable aid of Catholic women" and that, therefore, "women willing to offer their lives for the cause of foreign missions" should write to him. Within the next two months, he received 20 such applications.[42]

By the fall of 1912, when Walsh opened the foreign mission seminary on newly acquired property in Ossining, Miss Rogers headed a group of seven "secretaries" who had decided to offer their lives for foreign mission work. James A. Walsh, however, preferred to call them his "Maries of Maryknoll," because, like Mary, their role was to help in the background to prepare other Christs to be sent on mission.[43] On October 15, the Feast of St. Teresa of Avila, the women arrived from Hawthorne, New York, which had served temporarily as *The Field Afar* headquarters and their home. They settled on the Maryknoll hilltop in a large old Dutch colonial house that Walsh christened St. Teresa's Lodge in remembrance of that special day. They soon became known as the Teresians.[44]

The first floor of their living quarters became the new office of *The Field Afar*. Mary Dwyer was the bookkeeper and handled the multigraph machine. Next to her, Sarah Sullivan operated an old addressograph. In the middle of the noise of the machines, Mary Louise Wholean and Mary Josephine Rogers sat among their manuscripts translating, composing, and editing. Nora Shea was Walsh's personal secretary and Margaret Shea went where help was most needed. Upstairs, Anna Towle put her talents as a seamstress to full use. Often Miss Rogers also doubled up as cook and housekeeper for both communities of men and women.

The clerical work at *The Field Afar* and the growing number of house-hold tasks for the seminary were the immediate means by which the Teresians cooperated with Father Walsh to further foreign mission work. The magazine helped attract candidates for the Maryknoll family and to finance its growth and activities. Through their clerical work, the Teresians' role was to maintain *The Field Afar*, which Walsh called "Maryknoll's lifeline." Through their household chores, they kept expenses to the minimum.[45]

These "stay-at-home" missioners found their perfect model in St. Teresa of Avila. On the feast day of their patroness, Father Walsh reminded them "that it was not without reason" that they were called "Teresians." He emphasized that they shared a great desire to go to the foreign missions but, like St. Teresa, they were not yet called to that work. Therefore, like her whose combined life of activity and prayer "won more souls than did St. Francis Xavier by actual ministry," they should contribute their services and prayers "for the advancement of the Seminary."[46]

As they settled into a daily schedule of spiritual exercises and common work for the cause of foreign missions, these laywomen realized that to assure their survival and growth as a group of American women mission-

Fig. 2. October 1912, the seven "secretaries" at St. Teresa's Lodge: (standing from left) Mary Dwyer, Nora Shea, Margaret Shea; (seated) Mary Louise Wholean, Anna Towle, Mary Josephine Rogers, Sara Sullivan. Maryknoll Sisters Archives.

ers, they should find a place within the established structure of the Catholic Church. According to a letter of Miss Rogers in January 1916, religious life seemed to be the answer:

> Our desire is to be so organized that with St. Teresa as our model and patron we may devote all our energies of body and soul to the spread of the foreign mission spirit in this country and to the support of the seminary here. Even our longing to go into the mission field is subservient to this great need.[47]

The Teresians' drive toward religious life met with many setbacks, delays, and prejudices which took seven and a half years to overcome. Among these was the prevalent opinion in European ecclesiastical circles that only a few young American men and certainly no women could endure the hardships of mission life. Such a situation did not attract vocations and many young women who were unsure of the future of the Teresians joined other congregations or preferred to wait. Finally approval from Rome came and on February 14, 1920, Archbishop Hayes of New York canonically directed the Teresians into the religious congregation of the Foreign Mission Sisters of St. Dominic. Official recognition by the Church signaled the beginning of a rapid growth for the new congregation which was familiarly known as the Maryknoll Sisters. Within two years, their ranks swelled from 42 to 139.[48]

The Maryknoll Sisters immediately began to fulfill their mission vocation by taking up two residences on the West Coast to work among the Japanese and by sending a group of six Sisters to China the following year. Yet for many years they continued to carry on the legacy of their Teresian days by performing most of the housekeeping tasks at the major seminary and the preparatory seminary in Scranton, Pennsylvania. They did the cooking, canning, cleaning, laundry, sewing, shopping, and every form of secretarial work. Only in the mid–1940s did the Sisters begin to curtail these services for the Fathers. The hiring of a new printer who also handled the mailing gave Mother Mary Joseph an opportunity to withdraw the Sisters from routine tasks at the magazine. Over the next 20 years, the Maryknoll Sisters gradually ceased performing most other household work for the Society.

The Making of a Maryknoller

Within 40 years after its founding, the name of Maryknoll was well known in most spheres of American society, evoking an image of an American Catholic missioner converting non-Christian people in a distant land, most likely China. To become a missioner, a young man or woman underwent training at the headquarters in Ossining. This specialized formation produced Maryknoll missioners whose training went one step beyond that of diocesan priests, Brothers, or Sisters.

At first glance, nothing in the formation of the Maryknollers departed noticeably from what was taking place in other Catholic formation centers, both in the United States and in Europe. The entrance requirements, the course of studies, the years of seminary and novitiate training, the routine of daily life—all were within the norm. Nonetheless, despite a lack of visible differences, Maryknoll was unique. The uniqueness of life on the Knoll was its atmosphere of mission; all activities were illuminated by the strong spotlight of preparation for mission life.

Admission

Standard qualifications required for admission into a seminary or a novitiate included proper age, intention to embrace the life of a priest—Brother or Sister—good health, intelligence and common sense, piety, and zeal. At Maryknoll, these requirements all had a strong rationale in the context of foreign missions. Candidates should be able to finish their formation before they reached thirty-five in order to maximize their chance of a successful adaptation on the missions. Their intention to join should be signified by a special love for foreign missions and a willingness to die as a martyr if necessary. Candidates should be in good health to face the harsh conditions of mission life and they should have the mental ability not only to complete their courses at the Knoll but also to learn a foreign language on the missions. A closeness to God and a desire to save people were also essential qualities for a good missioner.

To these requirements, Maryknoll added one rarely found elsewhere— candidates were expected to display a sense of humor by not taking themselves too seriously and by showing a willingness to work cheerfully in whatever capacity and place they would be assigned.[49]

The Curriculum

The formation program followed by the seminarians was not specifically mission-oriented. The seminary curriculum included two years of Thomist philosophy and four years of training in dogmatic and moral theology, with courses in canon law, Church history, and Gregorian chant. (In 1932, a special year of spiritual training called "novitiate" was introduced prior to the theological studies.)

Formation for the sisterhood and brotherhood as well as for the priesthood satisfied standard requirements rather than prepared future religious for the missions. Sisters and Brothers in formation followed some courses in religious doctrine, Church history and Gregorian chant, but none of these regular courses was taught from a mission-oriented perspective. For future priests, the course in canon law was perhaps the class with the most direct application to mission life; seminarians had to learn the rules and exceptions pertaining to mission territories and the special privileges applying to missioners.

The regret most commonly expressed by old China hands about their years of training at Maryknoll was the lack of academic preparation for the Orient. There were no courses to prepare future Maryknollers to understand the culture, the history, the geography, or the religious and political climates of the countries where they were to work. The excuse often used in the early years was that since neither of the superiors, James A. Walsh nor Mother Mary Joseph, had lived in the missions, they could not teach these courses. However, the real reason perhaps lay in the assignment policy adopted from the beginning; young Maryknollers were assigned to a specific mission territory only upon completion of their training at the Knoll. Until the late 1940s, this policy still prevented development of an area studies program.[50]

Prior to 1930, the only mission-oriented requirements of the seminary were that all seminarians had to learn some Chinese characters and some basic first aid. After 1930, thanks mainly to the effort of theologians like Fathers Pierre Charles in Louvain and Joseph Schmidlin in Münster, the Catholic Church awakened to the importance of mission studies. Although mission studies as such failed to appear in Maryknoll's curriculum, attempts were made to provide future missioners with a better knowledge of Maryknoll's own history and with more background on the missions.

In the mid–1930s, Father Joseph Ryan, a former missioner in the Wuchow territory of China, was assigned to teach mission history at the Maryknoll seminary. In later years, Sisters with mission experience in the Orient, such as Sisters Alma Erhard, Celine Marie Werner, and Mary Liguori Quinlan were assigned to teach the same course to the novices. In retrospect, however, many China missioners felt these courses had little impact on their preparation. From the point of view of mission, the classes failed to analyze why missioners had successes and failures in the past. From a historical point of view, they were narrowly confined to the history of mission societies and conveyed little information on the history and culture of China.[51]

Even by the late 1940s, there were still no courses at Maryknoll aimed at providing the Fathers, Brothers, and Sisters with a solid knowledge of the Orient or offering theological reflection on the evangelization problems of that region. However, the lack of mission courses and specific area studies in the curriculum was balanced by other characteristics which provided a climate conducive to the development of a missionary vocation.

Manual Labor

On Sunset Hill, manual labor was a way of life and, at the same time, a preparation for the missions. In the early days of Maryknoll, money was scarce and the community had to become as self-sufficient as possible. There were buildings to repair, walls to paint, wood to cut, water to pump, meals to prepare, and animals to tend. Seminarians and Brother-candidates did most of the heavy work, but the Teresians provided two of the most essential services: they did the household chores and staffed *The Field Afar* office. Their work not only ensured that all Maryknollers remained well-fed with clean and mended clothes, but it also brought in financial contributions through the magazine.[52] James A. Walsh readily acknowledged how indispensable the Teresians were to Maryknoll's survival and subsequent growth:

> I can say with all truth that their zealous and intelligent labor [in *The Field Afar* office] is practically indispensable in our work, which depends for its revenue ... upon constant circularizing [of] papers, books and letters [among] the Catholic faithful throughout the country.[53]

As early as 1922, Mother Mary Joseph looked back at the origins of the Maryknoll Sisters and saw their readiness to do whatever work was necessary for the cause of the foreign missions as one of the important characteristics which helped to shape the young congregation.

> The work began with three Massachusetts women. Today we are 136, representing many industries and professions ... training our Sisters as best as we can to meet the needs of teaching, nursing, industrial arts, pharmacy, sewing, domestic work in all its branches, and the all important and very extensive work connected with the office [of *The Field Afar*].[54]

As the two mission organizations gained a sounder financial footing, the Sisters gradually withdrew from routine tasks at the seminary to concentrate their efforts directly on the missions. However, they maintained a close relationship with the Maryknoll Fathers and Brothers which extended beyond the Knoll to their work in the mission territories. They no longer worked in the kitchens, but were in charge of the evangelization of women and children. As time went by and the notion of teamwork gained acceptance, the relationships among Fathers, Brothers. and Sisters became more like those of partners. By the time their first constitutions were approved in 1931, it was clear that the Maryknoll Sisters no longer worked for the Maryknoll Fathers and Brothers. However, although they could work by themselves or with any other missionary group, joint ventures with Maryknoll Fathers and Brothers still remained their ideal.

The Maryknoll Brothers' relationship with the Fathers was very similar to that of the Sisters. As indicated by their early name of Auxiliary Brothers, their spiritual training emphasized that they were to help the Fathers achieve the conversion of non-Christians by the work of their hands. Prior to joining Maryknoll, most Brothers had worked for several years and they readily put to use their skills as bookkeepers, nurses, carpenters, painters, electricians or farmers. During manual labor hours, they supervised small teams of seminarians and taught them the rudiments of their trade.

Because of the burden of their academic training, the seminarians spent the smallest amount of time on manual labor. Before or after breakfast, a 20-minute period called "morning duties" was usually set aside to perform various household tasks such as sweeping and dusting to keep the seminary building in good order. With the exception of Sundays, the seminarians were also required to perform one to one-and-a-half hours of manual work each day. During this time, they were assigned more extensive tasks in painting, electrical wiring, wood chopping, ground clearing, and gardening, and some even learned the basics of animal husbandry. This custom contrasted with most seminaries in the United States whose schedules did not include household tasks or manual labor.[55]

At Maryknoll such duties became a feature of the schedule not only because they reduced operational costs, but also because the founders viewed them as a necessary element of the missionary formation. Manual work was considered to be practical training for the future missionary priest which also contributed to his character and spiritual training. They kept him humble and close to the common people; at the same time, they made him more resourceful and better equipped to face the unforeseen circumstances and the emergencies of mission life. After a few months at the Knoll, James A. Walsh described this major difference between Maryknoll and other seminaries:

> [At Maryknoll] special emphasis is laid on missionary spirit, and [manual] duties are imposed which are designed to test the humility and hardihood of the students. . . . These duties have been carried out not in the camp-life spirit which accepts them merrily as recreative and passing, but seriously and naturally, as part of the training of a soldier of Christ.[55]

Thirty-five years later, the official *Maryknoll Spiritual Directory* published by Maryknoll's second superior general, James E. Walsh, emphasized the same two points:

Manual labor gives the future missioner intimate knowledge of the laborious life of the humble people whom he will evangelize. Understanding is the first quality of leadership. . . . Few things can inure [the missioner] to the humble lot of his flock as personal labor can. . . . It is a splendid means of preparing the aspirant apostles to meet the conditions of life he will find in the missions, where he will often have to be architect and builder, foreman and laborer, in order to construct, maintain and operate the material facilities of his mission parish.[56]

Reminiscing on their own seminary years, many veteran missioners of China, like Father Thomas Brack, identified manual labor as a characteristic which set Maryknoll apart from other seminaries and provided an irreplaceable part of their formation:

Manual labor was one of the great levelers . . . and a wonderful training of character. . . which later led to our being able to accept and handle responsibility and persevere in work.[57]

A Mission-Oriented Atmosphere

Manual work was only one of many ways used to prepare Maryknollers physically, mentally, and spiritually for their life on the missions. Outside of the curriculum, there was practically nothing which did not bring the idea of mission to mind; the whole "atmosphere" of Maryknoll was mission-oriented. There was practically no resident or visitor who did not speak of mission and it was in this climate that the seminarians, the Brother-candidates and Sister-novices matured into Maryknollers.

The most unusual feature of this informal training was the reading at mealtimes of the diaries of Maryknollers on mission. These accounts were not personal diaries but logs in which missioners entered on a daily or weekly basis what happened in their mission stations. The narratives recounted the missioners' whole range of charitable works to reach the Chinese people, such as orphanages and dispensaries. They described long trips to remote villages, fights against "pagan beliefs," and catechumenate work. They also told of many ordeals such as encounters with bandits and the ravages of war and famine.

These diaries projected an overall impression of deep spirituality put into action. Their love of God led the missioners to China to sacrifice their lives for the salvation of the people. The fact that diary accounts occasionally ended in awkward sermonettes seemed to indicate, however, that some veteran Maryknollers purposely inflated the spiritual content of their accounts to edify their younger brothers and sisters. Other readings used to supplement the diaries were books on the lives of missioners like Théophane Vénard and Francis Xavier. They reinforced the desire of the listeners to join other Maryknollers in the company of heroic and saintly predecessors.

From his early days at the Knoll, James A. Walsh never missed an opportunity to invite visiting missioners of other societies to speak to the young religious and seminarians. Later, as Maryknollers themselves began to return for furloughs, sick leave, or temporary assignments in the United States, the sharing of mission experiences became a regular feature of formation. Half-hour conferences given before dinner at the seminary and at the convent were also supplemented by many informal talks and conversation and spiritual counseling. The enthusiasm displayed by missioners, their great dedication, and their longing to go back were moving testimonies which reinforced a desire to serve in the same manner.[58]

Among the old China hands, Father Anthony Cotta was a master of this technique. A former Vincentian priest, Cotta was a veteran of mission work in Madagascar and in China. His role and his stand on the side of the Chinese against the disparaging and seemingly anti-Chinese behavior of foreign missioners had led to his expulsion from China by his fellow missioners. Together with Father Vincent Lebbe, another Vincentian, he had been instrumental in Pope Benedict XV's publication of the 1919 Apostolic Letter, *Maximum Illud*, which stressed the need for well-trained native priests and well-trained missioners who "forget their own country."

After joining Maryknoll in 1924, Cotta was appointed to the faculty of the major seminary, but without specific official responsibilities. His role was like leavening in dough. He constantly mingled with the seminarians or spent recreation periods with the Sister-novices, informally sharing with them his love for the Chinese and his hope for a Chinese indigenous Church—the driving force of his life. Father Daniel Ohmann remembers an evening at the seminary in 1949 when a short talk by Father Cotta during a 45-minute evening recreation period expanded into a three and a half hour story of his life, captivating the attention of 200 seminarians.

Father Cotta's spiritual counseling was sought by many. He became the spiritual director and confessor of James Anthony Walsh and of many seminarians and Sisters. As such, his influence was profound. Perhaps there is no better description of Father Cotta's impact on the Maryknoll spirit than this statement of an eighty-two-year-old veteran of the China mission: "He gave us all the view that 'this is the kind of missioner I must be. I mean doing everything for the Chinese and trying to do as much as you can to make a church over there.'"[59]

The Maryknoll Spirit

The personal influences of Maryknoll's first two superior generals, James A. Walsh and James E. Walsh, and Maryknoll's first mother general, Mother Mary Joseph, contributed to making Maryknoll a unique place, constantly "feeding [students] with a mission spirit and a mission zeal."[60] They were the ones who shaped that "something special and different" about Maryknoll which is known as the Maryknoll spirit.

Father James A. Walsh was undoubtedly the person who forged its mold. Until his death in April 1936, he closely supervised the formation of seminarians and Brothers and gave them weekly spiritual lectures. He also gave regular Sunday conferences and occasional addresses to the Sisters and the novices. He infused his listeners with his admiration and devotion for the French missionary martyr Théophane Vénard. It was not just by coincidence that the first Maryknoll Junior Seminary in Pennsylvania was called the Venard. Théophane Vénard was presented as the model of the Maryknoll missioner prepared to go "the whole way" for Christ. According to Father Robert Sheridan who entered Maryknoll in 1921, this martyrdom mystique was one of the most pervasive characteristics of the formation given by James A. Walsh: "We were filled with this . . . great spirit of self-sacrifice, and we were going to go to China and never come back. That was all in the air we breathed in the beginning of Maryknoll."[61]

But James A. Walsh was also a realist who wanted his missioners to be prepared for the realities of the missions. He was quick to mention that as "picturesque and strikingly impressive . . . the thought of a man or a woman laying down his [or her] life for Christ" might be, the testimony that Maryknollers were asked to give was rarely "the actual shedding of [their] blood," but rather "an opportunity to stand and wear [themselves] out for Christ," even until the last breath, like four of their predecessors who died in China, Father Thomas Price in 1919, Father Anthony Hodgins in 1922, Sister Mary Gertrude Moore in 1923, and Father Daniel McShane in 1927.[62]

In July 1928, Walsh presented his thoughts on the subject at a Sunday conference for the Sisters on the occasion of the Feast of the Precious Blood:

> Very few of us will actually shed blood for Christ, but there is none of us who will not have the opportunity to thin out his blood for Christ. . . . The spiritual sufferings and moral trials we may have to endure are by far the most difficult. There is also the difficulty in physical discomforts. There is great trial to be endured through the first long years of heat which is very weakening. After that it becomes less burdensome because the blood thins

and adapts itself to the climate. This thinning of the blood for Christ is expressive and symbolic of the desire to go to the limit.[63]

In 1936 toward the end of his life, James A. Walsh described what he considered to be the most important considerations for the guidance of future Maryknollers. This 54-page document revolved around a single sentence borrowed from Jesus: "Primum regnum Dei, Seek first the Kingdom of God!" (Matthew 6:33). Walsh used these words of Jesus to his followers as a motto and as a legacy to the Maryknoll family because, in his view, they best expressed "the purpose of Maryknoll":

> Our privileged task is to find Christ enthroned in our own hearts, and then make Him known to others. Our search within and our efforts without will be successful in the measure of our motive. We are to seek Christ for the life of our own souls and for the souls of our fellow-men. . . . Our riches are the riches of Faith. These, with the love of God, a spirit of sacrifice and earnest prayer, will attract souls, though we lack in material help what we think is needful. PRIMUM REGNUM DEI! — We can only do our best with what we have and leave the result to God. . . .
>
>   May "PRIMUM REGNUM DEI!" be our motto and to it may we add the consoling words that have always appeared in our magazine, *Maryknoll— The Field Afar:*—"To those who love God, all things work together for good!"[64]

According to the founder, this loving trust in God was the source of the spirit of Maryknoll:

> There is a spirit which is one of the striking features of Maryknoll—a spirit which I like to call a joyous restraint, and a peace born of a common desire to sacrifice all for God. . . . Its summation is *Charity*—the love of God and the love of neighbor for God.[65]

In 1936 Bishop James E. Walsh succeeded James A. Walsh as superior general. He had almost 20 years of experience in South China and a spirituality deeply rooted in practicality. His classic essay, *Description of a Missioner*, described what a Maryknoller should be: not merely an average missioner, but a good one; and being a good one means becoming a saint. On the path to sainthood, a missioner must arm himself or herself with many virtues and live a life in which apostolic zeal and prayer work together:

> So he will do his best, praying not in the quiet of his chapel, but treading

forest paths and poking into farmhouses and hobnobbing in market places, where the zeal of his vocation should eternally take him in an unceasing quest for souls. His own soul is saved only by saving others.[66]

James E. Walsh's commitment to train accomplished foreign missioners led him to write a treatise on preparation for the mission apostolate and the development of a spiritual life adapted to the missions. *Maryknoll Spiritual Directory*, published in 1947, expanded his previous *Description of a Missioner*. He presented the 20 virtues and qualities he considered most essential to a good missioner: accessibility, adaptability, affability, charity, confidence, courage, hardness, humility, initiative, frankness, loyalty, manliness, objectivity, patience, perseverance, prudence, responsibility, restraint, sacrifice, and zeal. By way of introduction, he wrote:

> Maryknoll students are preparing to be missioners, and there is nothing more important in that preparation than a good beginning in the virtues essential to a successful mission work. The seminary is not simply a house of prayer and study; it is also a laboratory where soul-strengthening and mind-sharpening activities are utilized for the formation of the missionary character.[67]

By this time several Maryknollers had already died violent deaths. The murder of Father Gerard Donovan by Manchurian bandits in 1938 gave Maryknoll its first missioner-martyr. Commenting in 1939 on Donovan's death, Walsh said: "Maryknoll is complete, and America is apostolic."[68]

Walsh stressed that preparation for this ultimate charity was part of Maryknoll's legacy:

> "Go the whole way" and "Give all for Christ" are the two little slogans the founders of Maryknoll were fond of emphasizing. They knew that down through the ages the apostolate of Christ had always demanded this sacrificial charity. So they made it part of their teaching. . . . In short, they knew that Maryknoll would have martyrs, and because neither they nor anybody else knew who the martyrs would be, they thought that all with the same vocation ought to equip and strengthen themselves in the same degree.[69]

While superior general, James E. Walsh often wrote about the Maryknoll spirit. In 1942, he characterized it as a bond of "brotherly interest and family forbearance . . . created by the common pursuit of a soul-stirring aim." He viewed this spirit as "a special cachet" imparted by God to Maryknoll as "a partial and special application of a larger and deeper spirit called the spirit of the Gospel":

> Filled with the spirit of the Gospel, [Maryknollers] will seek success where it
> truly lies, in any and every feasible human effort that is animated by the
> supernatural principle of utilizing and subordinating everything to the king-
> dom of God and the welfare of souls. . . . Animated with the Maryknoll spirit,
> they will love the brotherhood, bearing one another's burdens and forbear-
> ing with one another's weaknesses . . . and set about the work God gave
> them to do.[70]

Writing for the seminarians in 1947, he encapsulated the Maryknoll
spirit in a saying very similar to one of his predecessor ten years earlier:
"That spirit is charity, and if there is any other spirit, Maryknoll does not
want it and could not conceivably profit by it."[71]

Mother Mary Joseph's position of leadership from 1912 to 1946 spanned
the service of both James A. and James E. Walsh. She experienced the
emergence of the Maryknoll spirit and the problems involved with its
preservation and transmission. She spoke about that spirit more than any
other Maryknoller and it was a recurring theme in her correspondence.[72]

She stressed that this spirit had been forged by Maryknoll pioneers. It
was displayed in their "love and tenderness" for one another and in their
lightheartedness toward the physical sufferings and spiritual triumphs.
They lived by this spirit naturally, without knowing how distinctive it
made them. Yet visitors began to mention how their joy and attention to
each other resembled the apostolic spirit of the early Church and truly
reflected the love of Christ.[73]

The rapid growth of the Maryknoll Sisters brought great satisfaction to
Mother Mary Joseph, but it also worried her that the congregation might
lose that spirit by becoming too institutionalized:

> As a community gets larger, it becomes a real problem to maintain that unity
> of spirit and family feeling. . . . No matter how large we may become, we
> want each Maryknoll Sister to know and love her other Sisters.[74]

She kept alert to the smallest outside criticism which might point to a loss
of that spirit. She exhorted the older Sisters to be responsible for transmitting the spirit to the younger ones:

> We are getting a rather unenviable reputation of being uncooperative and
> lacking in the joyousness and sweetness that used to mark our Sisters. We
> don't want that to happen. It is for us to perpetuate the Maryknoll spirit . . .
> in which we grew up and in which we developed.[75]

The Maryknoll spirit, however, was more than just a family feeling.
Mother Mary Joseph called it "this special gift of God to us," and empha-

sized its nature as a "foreign mission spirit" which moved Maryknollers "to reach out for souls," "to seek those lost sheep of the fold and bring them home."[76] "This is the foundation of the Maryknoll Spirit—to be so attractive in yourself; to have such a magnetic power about you that you will attract souls to you."[77]

In 1929 she began to use one of her favorite quotations: "As one lamp lights another nor grows less, so nobleness enkindleth nobleness." These lines from the poem "Yussouf" by American writer James Russell Lowell, illustrated her understanding of the Maryknoll spirit:

> The meaning of these words is clear. We know that if we take a lighted candle and enkindle another with it, the light of the first does not lessen, although it has given of its light to the second. So it is with us, as we give good example. Kindness begets kindness, charity begets charity, and the first act does not grow less because of its begetting. . . . Our spirit as individual Maryknoll Sisters, and the very spirit of our whole congregation, depends largely on the use we make of the abiding truth of these words.[78]

Mother Mary Joseph stressed that, contrary to most other religious groups which modeled their Sisters according to a fixed pattern, the Maryknoll Sisters retained their individuality in order to better reach out to people:

> We have tried from the beginning to cultivate a spirit which is extremely difficult, that is the retention of our individuality, correcting, of course, what is wrong in it, and supernaturalizing it. . . . It is not too hard to settle down to a particular type which you would wish your Sisters to resemble, marking out certain observances, certain postures, certain poses for them to follow . . . but our work in its very nature is absolutely opposed to that. We are seeking souls. . . . For this, we need all our individuality, all our generosity, all our graciousness and sweetness and simplicity, all our powers of gentle persuasiveness, in fact, all the things which the good God has given to us. Each one of us in our own work, with our own particular attractiveness is to be used by God as a particular tool for a particular work in saving particular souls. That explains our spirit. It is an attempt to keep our individuality using and finding what is good and beautiful in it and supernaturalizing this, and then using it . . . to promote God's honor and glory and to accomplish His will.[79]

Mother Mary Joseph often reminded her community of the qualities that revealed the presence of that spirit in the Maryknoll Sisters:

> I would have her distinguished by Christ-like charity, a limpid simplicity of

soul, heroic generosity, selflessness, unfailing loyalty, prudent zeal, gracious courtesy, an adaptable disposition, solid piety—and the saving grace of a sense of humor.[80]

From these characteristics, Mother Mary Joseph identified generosity and adaptability as the two qualities most necessary to be a good missionary Sister:

> There can be no Maryknoll Sister, nor missionary Sister worthy of the name, who is not heroically generous, generous to the very last inch of her being— generous in the giving of her time, her talents, generous in her thoughts, generous in every possible phase of religious life. . . . There is another trait which you should develop and that is adaptability—that power of creating anywhere we may be sent the feeling of "fitting in". . . . You must train yourself to go up or down, in or out with this person or that, in any work whatsoever, and to accept these changes readily, easily and quickly.[81]

Generosity and adaptability helped the Sister with her daily work and prepared her for the eventuality of greater ordeals or even martyrdom. "We may be called upon to serve Christ as He served us, even to the giving of our lives; we may be given the opportunity to do for Him what He has done for us."[82]

Conclusion

When Maryknoll came into existence in 1911, it reflected not only the dream of a few individuals, but the will of the American Catholic hierarchy and the aspirations of many priests and lay people across the United States. The founders' dreams of seeing Catholic America face its foreign mission responsibility brought them together. The encouragement of supporters inside and outside the United States gave them incentive to pursue their idea of forming a group of men and women dedicated to the foreign missions. Funds and vocations from American Catholics supported their efforts. Vatican approval of the Catholic Foreign Mission Society of America in June 1911 and of the Foreign Mission Sisters of St. Dominic in February 1920 meant they could forge ahead with the full support of the highest authorities in the Catholic Church.

The combination of the talents and efforts of Maryknoll's three founders gave it strength during its formative years. James A. Walsh assumed the overall leadership and organization. Thomas F. Price contributed his previous experience in establishing a seminary and doing missionary work. Mother Mary Joseph supervised the women's side and provided all the behind-the-scenes services essential to the smooth operation of Maryknoll, from an efficient *Field Afar* office to the ordinary household tasks of cooking, cleaning, and mending.

On the missions, the goals of Maryknoll were to convert non-Christians and to build a native Church. Yet apart from incidentals such as a first-aid course and daily manual labor, nothing in the curriculum or schedule differentiated formation at the Knoll from that of any other seminary or religious novitiate in the United States. Maryknollers learned to become good priests, Brothers, or Sisters with only superficial academic preparation for China and its people. Similarly, they did not receive much training on how to convert non-Christians or how to train native priests and Sisters.

Following the traditional practice of most Western missionary societies working in China, Maryknoll did not begin any in-depth missionary training of its young missioners until their first assignment on the missions. They learned the practical trade of being a missioner at the side of more experienced missioners through observation and through trial and error.

The lack of a mission studies course in the formation program during the first two decades or so of Maryknoll's existence should not be a surprise. When Maryknoll was founded in 1911, this field of studies had barely begun to receive the attention of Catholic theologians in Europe. Over the next 25 years, mission studies gradually gained acceptance in the Catholic Church under the name of missiology. By then, Maryknoll had made several attempts to offer such a course but none went much beyond a survey of mission history. No one on the faculty was trained to keep abreast of rapid developments in missiology. During the period of active involvement in China, therefore, Maryknoll never developed a mission-oriented curriculum or even a good mission studies course at the Knoll.

Contrasting with the limited academic preparation of Maryknollers for a missionary career was the depth and excellence of their spiritual training which left them well-suited to embrace such a life. Readings from the lives of missionary martyrs, the diaries of Maryknollers already in the mission fields and the stories and the spiritual counseling of returned missioners such as Father Cotta instilled in Maryknollers images to inspire and examples to emulate. They gave meaning to sayings and quotations like "Go the whole way," "Seek first the Kingdom of God," and "As one lamp lights another nor grows less, So nobleness enkindles nobleness."

Their spiritual training toward the priesthood, brotherhood, and sisterhood always stressed the missionary value of the virtues and qualities they should cultivate. They had to possess the quality of personal witness—"attractiveness," Mother Mary Joseph used to say—which would draw non-Christians to them. They were not just supposed to become a good priest, Brother, or Sister; above all, they were to become good missioners. This ambiance at the Knoll and the training associated with it imparted to Maryknollers a special character called the Maryknoll spirit. This spirit inspired them to use their personal talents, the resources at their disposal, and the best known methods of approach and adaptation—without any consideration for their own life—for the sole purpose of making the Christian God known to non-Christians in foreign lands.

This foreign mission zeal per se was not unique to Maryknoll and was shared by many other Catholic mission groups from Europe. In the United States, however, Maryknoll was the only American group entirely dedicated to work in the foreign missions. In other societies and congregations, this purpose was often diluted by other goals and commitments. Maryknollers rightly labeled what differentiated them from other American groups—a spirit: it was a spiritual and mental attitude which sustained them in their missionary goals.

As subsequent chapters will show, this disposition led Maryknollers to become innovators and pioneers in new ways of evangelization. These breakthroughs seemed to occur only after the missioners developed a deep sense of identity with the Chinese people and were able to analyze—to a certain degree at least—the challenges facing the Catholic Church in China from a Chinese point of view. Yet at other times, because of the lack of solid knowledge about China and of theological reflection on mission work, the missioners were misguided. Narrow-minded zeal sometimes led Maryknollers to misunderstand the Chinese and to misrepresent them in the United States and also to err in some of their methods of evangelization.

2

Maryknoll in the Chinese Environment

The Catholic Church Prior to the Arrival of Maryknoll

In search of spices and Christians, the first Portuguese traders arrived in Canton in 1514 and established a settlement in Macao two years later. Catholic missioners soon followed. Francis Xavier, faithful companion of Ignatius Loyola, the founder of the Jesuit order, had visions of entering China. But he died in 1552 on the island of Sancian off the coast of Kwangtung, only a few miles away from Yeungkong.

Thirty years later another zealous Jesuit, Matteo Ricci, and his two companions, Michele Ruggieri and Francisco Pasio, were the first Catholic missioners to receive authorization from the Chinese governor-general of Kwangtung to settle in the province. In 1594 Ricci started toward Peking where he had decided to settle. He moved first to Nanch'ang, then Nanking, and finally reached Peking in 1601.[1] The success of Ricci and the Jesuits who joined him at the Imperial Court facilitated the eventual entry of missioners into China. When the Ming dynasty was toppled in 1644 and was replaced by the Ch'ing dynasty, Ricci's successors such as Adam Schall, S.J., and Ferdinand Verbiest, S.J., won the confidence of the first Manchu emperors.

During the subsequent years in Kwangtung, Catholicism flourished under the Jesuits as well as under the Franciscans, the Augustinians and the French Fathers of the Société des Missions Etrangères de Paris (M.E.P.). Many of the Catholic families Maryknollers found in South China were able to trace their entrance into the Catholic Church back to the late seventeenth or early eighteenth centuries.[2]

By 1704 the province had 40,000 Catholics. Two decades later, however, the worsening of the Rites controversy[3] and the ascendancy of the Yung-cheng Emperor, a ruler suspicious of the missioners' motives, resulted in a ban on the Catholic religion throughout China. Churches were confiscated, converts were ordered to renounce their faith, and missioners, with the exception of a few Jesuits employed at the Peking court, were expelled.[4]

In the century following the emperor's prohibition on Christianity, foreign missioners secretly entered China through the port of Canton, but very little is known about their activities in Kwangtung province. Most of the missionary work seems to have been carried on by Portuguese Jesuits who had entered China prior to the prohibition and went into hiding or delayed their departure on the pretext of illness. The suppression of the Society of Jesus by Rome in 1773, however, prevented younger companions from joining them. Before the end of the eighteenth century, all the former Jesuits had either left the province or died.[5]

Occasionally the bishop of Macao received deputations from Catholics in Kwangtung asking for new missioners. From 1800 on, Chinese priests who were natives of the province were sent to visit the Catholic communities once or twice a year. Because of the constant menace of persecution, their work mainly consisted of trying to keep the faith of the remaining Catholics alive. Efforts to seek new converts were practically nonexistent. The Catholic communities in large cities died out or emigrated to secluded villages in the countryside. Some Catholic settlements served even into the nineteenth century as retirement places for aging priests who preferred to die among the native Catholics.[6]

In May 1848 Pope Pius IX assigned the evangelization of the provinces of Kwangtung and Kwangsi to the M.E.P. Fathers. The French missioners met with many difficulties upon their arrival. The Opium War of 1839-1842 had increased hatred and distrust of the French and the British. A series of treaties between 1844 and 1860 granted foreign missioners the right to reenter China and placed them and their converts under the protection of France. During the remainder of the century, the Catholic Church relied on the French civil and military representatives to obtain compensation for real as well as alleged wrongdoings. Hard feelings arose when missioners, eager for converts, accepted into the Church unsavory characters who had no religious convictions but wanted to stay beyond the reach of Chinese law. The M.E.P. missioners in Kwangtung were no exception to this practice.[7]

Because France had waged three wars against China—in 1839, 1856, and 1883—Chinese at all levels of society became suspicious of the real motives of the missioners. Missioners were increasingly looked upon as agents of the imperialistic ambitions of all the foreign powers who joined France and Great Britain in carving out spheres of influence in China. The Boxer uprising of 1900 was the culmination of these antiforeign feelings which were directed against the most conspicuous foreigners in the interior—the missioners—and their converts. An estimated 32,000 Chinese Christians (Catholics and Protestants) and 200 foreign missioners died during the riots.[8]

Following these incidents, the French Protectorate gradually weakened. In 1902, Italy assumed the representation of Italian missioners. The movement gained momentum when, after the French Separation Act of 1905 which severed diplomatic relations between Paris and the Vatican, the French legation in Peking announced that it would no longer handle cases involving non-French missioners. For its part, in 1908 the Chinese government formally revoked the rank and privileges granted to missioners which allowed them to interfere in Chinese civil affairs.[9]

The Vatican also began to take steps to circumvent France's position as official protector of Catholic missions. In 1918 because of France's protest, a first attempt to establish diplomatic relations between the Vatican and the new Republic of China ended in failure. Rome then took a different approach, attempting to put more distance between the Catholic Church in China and the foreign powers, France in particular. In November 1919, Pope Benedict XV issued the encyclical letter *Maximum Illud* which advocated the establishment of a native clergy and hierarchy in mission countries. In August 1922 Bishop Celso Costantini was appointed the Vatican's first apostolic delegate to China. Although not officially a member of the diplomatic corps, Costantini was the *de facto* religious representative of Rome who supervised the entire Catholic Church in China.[10]

In spite of the difficulties alluded to, the reopening of China to missioners signaled a great expansion of Protestant and Catholic activity in China and a rapid growth in Church membership. In 1848 the M.E.P. missioners found only 8,500 Catholics out of 40,000 left in Kwangtung. The French priests concentrated most of their efforts on the countryside. Accompanied by Chinese catechists, they constantly criss-crossed the province and built a network of small churches, subdividing the large civil districts into smaller mission stations. As a result, the Catholic population in Kwangtung had reached 65,000 by 1918, but the French priests lacked the personnel to sustain such growth. Because of the war in Europe, most of the younger missioners had been drafted into the French army, and those left in Kwangtung could not nurture the Catholics and push on with the work of evangelization at the same time. This situation led Bishop Jean-Baptiste Budes de Guébriant to detach two sections from his vicariate in December 1917 and entrust one to the Italian Salesians and the other to the Maryknoll Fathers and Brothers. Obtaining the territory had been a long and arduous task for Maryknoll.[11]

The Search for a Mission Territory in China

As director of the Society for the Propagation of the Faith in Boston and editor of *The Field Afar*, Father James A. Walsh had developed lasting ties with missioners in China.[12] Walsh sent them money in the form of donations or mass intentions, and they provided him with letters and photographs, which he published. This exchange of letters resulted in several friendships and a great accumulation of knowledge about the mission needs of China.

When Fathers Walsh and Price discussed their plan for beginning a foreign mission seminary, they both agreed that China was the land where their missioners "should be most needed."[13] In Rome in June 1911, they expressed their preference for China to Cardinal Gotti who, as head of Propaganda Fide, had the responsibility to organize the Church's worldwide missionary work.

By that time, however, most of China had already been divided into prefectures and vicariates apostolic entrusted to a dozen missionary organizations. Based on the principle of the so-called *jus commissionis* (or right of entrustment) of Propaganda Fide, once an organization had been given a mission territory to evangelize, no other group could come in to help or to take over part of that territory without the express invitation of that organization. Therefore the task of Walsh and Price was to find a prelate in China willing to yield some of his assigned territory.

At first there appeared to be no problem. Following Rome's approval of Maryknoll as The Catholic Foreign Mission Society of America, James A. Walsh received notes of congratulations from around the world. Among several letters from the Far East were two enthusiastic messages that Walsh interpreted as open invitations to work in China.[14] Bishop Albert Faveau, C.M., vicar apostolic of Western Chekiang, anticipated the day when Maryknollers would work "side by side" with the clergy of his vicariate. Bishop Jean-Marie Mérel, M.E.P., prefect apostolic of Canton, a long-time correspondent of Walsh, wrote with enthusiasm:

> . . . very soon we shall see American priests starting from Maryknoll . . . bring light to those who are sitting in the darkness. . . . America and American people are very popular here . . . let your priests come, then, and sow and reap.[15]

In the ensuing years, letters from the Far East kept coming to Walsh, suggesting courteously that his men might be needed almost anywhere, but with no specific recommendations. The only significant offer came in 1914 from Bishop Jean-Baptiste Budes de Guébriant, M.E.P., vicar apostolic of Kientchang in Szechuan, suggesting his own vicariate as a possible field for the American missionaries, an offer which was repeated three years later when he was assigned to Canton as vicar apostolic.[16]

By the fall of 1915, although only four priests were enrolled in the Maryknoll Society, Fathers Walsh and Price looked with confidence to the growing number of Maryknoll candidates: at the Knoll there were 18 seminarians, two auxiliary Brothers, and 12 Teresians; at the Venard, a preparatory seminary opened two years earlier in Scranton, Pennsylvania, 18 younger students were also studying to become missioners. Walsh and Price felt that Maryknoll would start to produce a steady contingent of missioners within a few years and that the time had come to get a definite commitment of territory from a prelate in China.[17]

Upon the suggestion of Father M. Kennelly, S.J., a missioner friend in Shanghai, Walsh wrote the following letter to a group of vicars and prefects apostolic, who were mostly along the coastal area of China:

October 30, 1915
Rt. Rev. and dear Bishop:

We are considering the serious question of a field for our priests, a few of whom will doubtless be ready for the missions within the next two years.

We are organized for missions to the heathen, and have expressed to Propaganda our preference for China as our first mission.

Our plan is:

1. to find a bishop who wishes, or would be willing, to divide his vicariate;
2. to arrange with him, through Propaganda, for the future division;
3. to send our young priests to labor under this bishop (in that section to be later cut off) until such time as we have enough priests to form a separate vicariate, and the proper one to be their spiritual chief.

We write to ask you (1) if you approve this plan or would suggest another; (2) what considerations, e.g. American prestige, Protestant centres, need of English, relationship with Chinese in this country, etc. should influence us, as an American Society, in the selection of a field, among several offers.

Asking your kind consideration of this letter, I am,

Your servant in Christ,

James Anthony Walsh[18]

Most bishops responded as Walsh expected: he should look for a mission on the coast of China in an area where he could counter the influence of the American and English Protestants.[19] They refrained, however, from issuing a definite invitation; none offered his own territory. A few even hinted that perhaps Maryknoll should look somewhere other than China. Bishop Paul Dumond, C.M., of Tientsin answered that he did not think that the English language was an asset for working in China. Bishop Prosper Paris, S.J., of Nanking expressed the opinion that American missioners by disposition would be more successful in rapidly modernizing Japan than in a China entrenched in its backward customs. Walsh did not appreciate this remark.[20]

No official response came from Canton because Bishop Mérel had resigned in the spring of the previous year and the vicariate was in the hands of an administrator, pending nomination of a new bishop. During his one-year assignment as administrator, Father Antoine Fourquet, M.E.P., indirectly contacted Father Walsh through Sister Mary Angeline Donovan, his former secretary in Boston who now worked with the Canadian Sisters of the Immaculate Conception in Canton. Fourquet listed the five civil districts of Sunning, Hoiping, Sunwui, Yanping, and Yeungkong as strong likelihoods for a mission field for Maryknoll.[21] When Bishop Adolphe Rayssac, M.E.P., of Swatow succeeded Fourquet as administrator, he too wrote to Walsh indirectly through a mutual friend, Father Gavan Duffy, M.E.P., a missioner in India. His suggestion was that Maryknoll should be given Kwangsi province so that M.E.P. missioners could regroup in Kwangtung province and bolster their forces there.[22]

By the fall of 1917, Maryknoll had grown to a total of 12 priests, 59 seminarians and preparatory students, 13 Brothers and 22 Teresians. James A. Walsh decided to go on a mission-finding tour of the Far East and asked the readers of *The Field Afar* to pray for the important matter of the future field of action of Maryknoll.[23] On September 3, he left on his first trip to the Orient declaring a total abandonment to the will of God:

> I do not know just what will be the result of my journey—I simply have this confidence and I do not believe that it is presumptuous, that God is going to bring me to the right place in view of our future work.[24]

The trip took James A. Walsh to Japan, Korea, and then China, where he visited the vicariates apostolic of Mukden, Tientsin, Peking, Chengtingfu, Hankow, Nanking, Ningpo, and Hangchow. At each stop he was courteously received and could see for himself the need for missioners. Since 1910 the flow of new missioners from France had been reduced to almost nothing, first by antireligious laws, and then by the outbreak of war.

None of the vicars apostolic whom he visited, however, mentioned the possibility of turning over a portion of his mission territory. By the time Walsh reached Hong Kong in mid-December he was beginning to worry although he knew he still had not met two of his best friends and allies in China, Father Léon Robert, M.E.P., and Bishop de Guébriant.

Father Robert was a long-time supporter of Maryknoll. In 1912 he had cheered at the news of the opening of the seminary and mentioned the province of Kwangtung as a possible field of action. As the procurator of the Société des Missions Etrangères de Paris in Shanghai and later in Hong Kong, he had great influence. A frequent correspondent of James A. Walsh, he had urged him to visit the Far East in September to avoid bad weather and even provided him with a detailed travel plan. He also assured him that he was doing his best to have the M.E.P. bishops of Kwangtung and Kwangsi present a proposition because they could not possibly administer such extensive territories in South China.[25]

After reviewing the letters of Rayssac, Fourquet, and Robert, Walsh knew that his best chance to find a mission along the coastal area of China was in the "southeast section of China."[26] When the news of the appointment of Bishop de Guébriant as head of the vicariate of Canton was announced in April 1916, Walsh probably sensed that Kwangtung was to become that area in South China to which he would send his first missioners. He immediately wrote a letter of congratulations to this "friend of Maryknoll." In his reply of October 23, 1916, de Guébriant reiterated his conviction of the importance of Maryknoll for the future of the missionary Church. He hinted that, not yet having taken possession of his vicariate, he could not do much for the present but that he would help Maryknoll by his "advice or even otherwise" when the occasion would arise.[27] A few days later, a letter from Father Robert reported that there was an opportunity for Maryknoll in South China but that Walsh should not say a word about it to anybody.[28]

Father Robert and Bishop de Guébriant kept their promises. On February 3, 1917, the bishop, on his way to Canton, met with Robert in Hong Kong and both seemed to agree to grant Maryknoll a mission field in the Canton vicariate. Father Robert informed Walsh unofficially of the good news but remained purposely vague, hinting that de Guébriant would make the official offer when Walsh traveled to China:

> Bishop de Guébriant arrived yesterday and we had a long conversation on your work and on your future visit to the Far East. I am certain you will have every reason to be satisfied . . . should you have one hundred missioners to send to the Far East it would be easy to find place and occupations for them.[29]

From that date on, as he later confirmed, Walsh knew he had found a place: "Before leaving the U.S., I received, through several sources, a strong intimation that if we so desired, and Rome would approve, we should be welcome to a section of the vicariate of Canton."[30]

On the morning of December 17, 1917, Father Robert met Father Walsh at the dock in Hong Kong and took him to meet Bishop de Guébriant who happened to be in the city for business. To Walsh's great surprise, after more than three months of polite talks but no concrete offer, the bishop came right to the point: "I had hardly met Bishop de Guébriant before I realized that Maryknoll's first mission in the Orient had been found, and in a few minutes my eyes were on the map of China, riveted to a point marked YEUNGKONG."[31] Arrangements were made to meet in Canton to finalize the agreement. Walsh recalled with emotion the event of Christmas Day:

> . . . after a short prayer to the Holy Spirit we signed the agreement by which
> . . . The Catholic Foreign Mission Society of America should be entrusted
> with its first mission, that of Yeungkong and Loting in the province of
> Kwangtung . . . it was the Christ Child's gift to our young Society.[32]

A copy of the contract was sent to Rome for approval and a cablegram brought the good news to Maryknoll: "Field found!"

Less than a year later, on September 8, 1918, the first group of Maryknollers left for Yeungkong. Father Thomas Price, co-founder, led three young priests, James E. Walsh, Francis X. Ford, and Bernard F. Meyer. Father Price, who was already fifty-eight, died of a bad case of appendicitis during the first year in South China. The three other Maryknollers, however, went on to become heads of new mission areas entrusted to Maryknoll and to exert profound influences on the development of the apostolate of the Society and the congregation in China.

The Five Maryknoll Mission Territories

When the first four Maryknollers arrived in South China, they walked into an incredibly complex political-military situation. Its main elements were the long-standing rivalry between Kwangtung and Kwangsi provinces, the major feud between the warlord Ch'en Chiung-ming and Sun Yat-sen, minor feuds involving small warlords, and the challenge of the National Revolutionary Government of the Republic of China in Canton to the weak and incompetent leadership of the official government in Peking.

Moreover, Maryknoll's first mission field was far from attractive: it consisted of two civil districts which were not even connected—one on the coast west of Canton and one in the interior along the West River. The territory was mostly rural with no large cities, and English was of little practical use. Dispersed among a population of one million Chinese, 680 Catholics lived in very small communities.

James A. Walsh was well aware of this less-than-encouraging situation, but he faced it with the same faith he had shown so many times: " . . . the more I thought of it the more I felt convinced that the priests of Maryknoll would be stimulated rather than discouraged by the prospect. The future is in God's hands."[33]

James A. Walsh's confidence was not misplaced. Three months after his return to Ossining on April 18, 1918, additional territories were given to Maryknoll which connected the two original districts. Within the next few

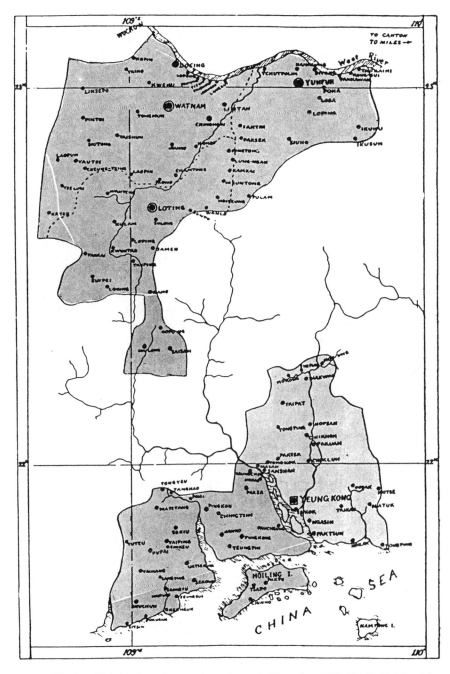

Map 1. The first Maryknoll territory as agreed upon in December 1917. *The Field Afar*, July 1918, p. 105.

years the territory grew until, on March 10, 1924, it became the prefecture apostolic of Kongmoon, which included ten districts, covering 15,445 square miles.[34] Three years later on February 1, 1927, Kongmoon was designated a vicariate apostolic under James E. Walsh, who was ordained bishop on Sancian Island on May 22, 1927. He administered the vicariate until 1936 when he was elected superior general of the Maryknoll Fathers and Brothers following the death of James A. Walsh in 1936. James E. Walsh was replaced as bishop of Kongmoon by another Maryknoller, Adolph J. Paschang.

Kongmoon

The 10 civil districts forming the vicariate had the shape of the letter U, its south arm resting on the South China Sea (Map 2). The tip of that arm pointed east and was separated from both the Macao diocese and the vicariate of Canton by the West River. The bishop's residence at Pakkai was on the outskirts of the city of Kongmoon where the West River opened up toward the sea into a huge delta. Looking west, the base of the U faced the peninsula of Luichow and the island of Hainan. The other arm of the U faced the province of Kwangsi and the Wuchow mission. That arm extended to the West River where it bordered again on the Macao diocese which also filled the entire inner curve of the U.

Located west of the Canton delta where the three main waterways of Kwangtung converge (the West, the North, and the East Rivers), the Kongmoon vicariate was not easily accessible. Despite its long coastline, the hilly nature of the terrain made it difficult to reach most of the interior. The city of Kongmoon was finally chosen over Yeungkong as mission headquarters because its location on the West River made it a better center for communications. Provided there were no pirates, a river network linked Kongmoon with the large cities of Canton and Macao in the east and Wuchow and Kweilin in the north. Even the most remote district of Loting could be reached faster by the West River and a tributary rather than from the coast by hiking through Kochow (Maoming) and Sunyi. As for the coastal cities, they could normally be reached by scheduled boats.

Wuchow and Kweilin

In November 1920 at the invitation of Bishop Maurice F. Ducoeur, M.E.P., vicar apostolic of Kwangsi, Maryknollers took up residence in the river port city of Wuchow, nicknamed by the French missioners the "city of no conversions." Slowly the territory entrusted to the Maryknollers increased, and in 1925 the Wuchow mission was separated from the vicariate of Kwangsi and added to Kongmoon prefecture. Father Bernard F. Meyer, one of the first four Maryknollers in China, was appointed superior of this new territory. On June 30, 1930, the Wuchow mission became independent and was raised into a prefecture on December 10, 1934, with Meyer as prefect apostolic. The territory covered almost 13,185 square miles. On July 20, 1939, Wuchow became a vicariate apostolic. Rome, concerned by reports of Monsignor Meyer's failing health and unwarranted use of authority, chose to appoint as bishop a Maryknoller from outside the territory, Frederick A. Donaghy, the vicar delegate of the vicariate of Kaying.

On January 10, 1933, the Kweilin territory of 12,500 square miles in the vicariate of Nanning was annexed to the Maryknoll territory of Wuchow. Five years later, however, on February 9, 1938, Kweilin was established as a prefecture apostolic under the direction of another Maryknoller, Monsignor John Romaniello.

The vicariate of Wuchow occupied 14 civil districts, and the prefecture of Kweilin occupied 16.[35] Together the two mission territories covered the eastern half of Kwangsi province, while the vicariate of Nanning occupied the western half. The city of Kweilin was connected to Wuchow by a left-bank tributary of the West River, the Kweichiang. At this junction the West River was a half-mile wide, making Wuchow one of the largest inland ports of China. Although great variations in river level between summer and winter made navigation difficult at times, Canton, Kongmoon, Hong Kong, and Macao were easily reached by sampan or motorboat.

Kaying

In October 1925 Bishop Adolphe Rayssac of Swatow entrusted to Maryknoll the mission of Kaying (also known as Moyan or Hakkaland), a territory of some 8,400 square miles in mountainous northeastern Kwangtung. Father Francis X. Ford, the pastor of Yeungkong, was sent as the first superior. The territory became a prefecture apostolic on April 28, 1929, and a vicariate on June 18, 1935, with Ford as bishop. Composed of nine civil districts, the vicariate was bordered in the south by the vicariate of Swatow and in the west, by that of Canton, both in Kwangtung province. In the east across the Fukien border, the Maryknollers' neighbors were the German Dominicans of the prefecture apostolic of Tingchow, and in the north across the Kiangsi border, the American Vincentians of the vicariate of Kanchow.[36] As in the other three Maryknoll territories in South China, the waterways offered the best means of communication with the outside world, mainly through the Mei River to the city port of Swatow or the East River to Canton.

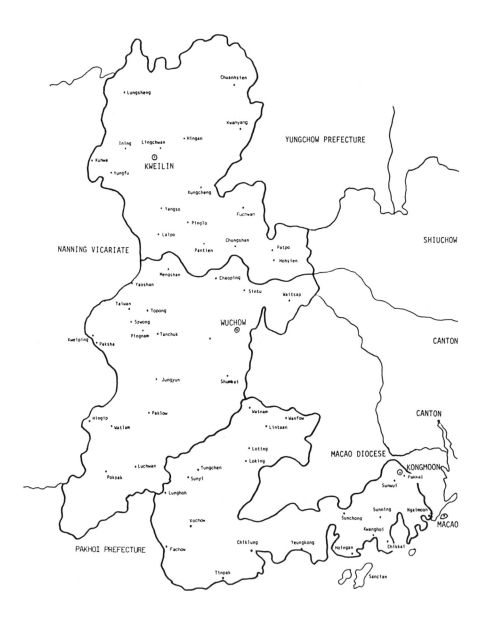

Map 2. Maryknoll Territories in South China (1941)

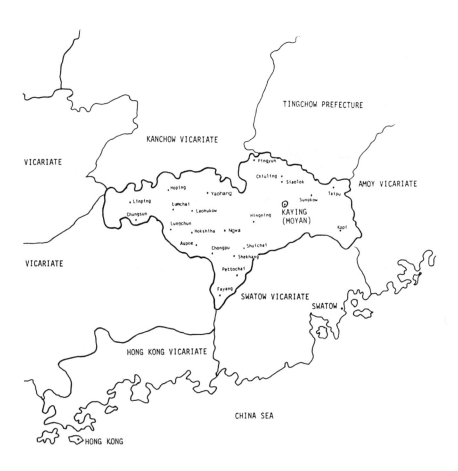

Map 3. Maryknoll Territory in Manchuria (1941)

Fushun

In the fall of 1925 Maryknoll also answered a plea for help from Bishop Jean-Marie Blois, M.E.P., of the vicariate of Mukden. Although the proposed mission of Fushun was located in Manchuria, thousands of miles away from other Maryknoll territories in China, the Society finally decided to accept the offer because the new territory bordered the established Maryknoll mission of Peng Yang in Korea. Father Raymond A. Lane, then Maryknoll procurator in Hong Kong, was chosen as the first superior of the new mission of Fushun which covered 21 districts with an area of 37,500 square miles.[37] On February 4, 1932 Fushun became a prefecture apostolic and eight years later on February 13, 1940 was raised to the rank of a vicariate apostolic.

The vicariate had a very elongated shape, stretching in a southwest-northeast direction from the Dairen peninsula along the Korea Bay and the Korean border until it met the prefecture apostolic of Yenki in the east. In the west, Fushun shared most of its border with the vicariate apostolic of Mukden, except in the most northeastern part where it bordered the vicariate of Kirin. Besides the coal-mining center of Fushun, the vicariate also included two other major cities, the port of Dairen and the border town of Antung. A good railroad system linked Fushun with Mukden, Peking, and Dairen, and ensured easy communications with the rest of China and the outside world.

After April 11, 1946, with the formal establishment of a regular ecclesiastical hierarchy in China by the Vatican, the four vicariates of Kongmoon, Wuchow, Kaying, and Fushun were converted into dioceses, while Kweilin remained a prefecture apostolic.[38]

The Organization of the Mission Work

Understandably, Maryknollers were guided in their first steps as missioners by the veteran M.E.P. priests from whom they inherited their territories. After a period of adaptation under the supervision of an older missioner, each Maryknoll priest was sent on his own to a parish which was generally composed of a central station and several outstations. The central station was located in a marketplace, usually a large village or a small town. It housed the rectory, the church, the dispensary, and perhaps a convent, a church-run school, an orphanage, and an old-age home. Outstations—often called "Christianities" according to the usage of the French missioners—were smaller places with Catholics or catechumens which were visited regularly by the priest and his catechists.

As Father James McLaughlin pointed out, the parishes created by the French Fathers, such as his in Chongpu, were very large:

Chongpu was like the center of a wheel. We went out into the different areas to different homes. We used to joke that the French priests got up early in the morning, said Mass, and walked all day until they couldn't walk any more. Then they laid down for a couple of hours and got up and walked a couple of more hours. . . . Some of these mission centers were 40 miles out.[39]

Once a station had a convent, Maryknoll Sisters came to share in the work. They arrived in Yeungkong as early as November 1922 and in time settled in all five Maryknoll territories: Manchuria in 1930, Kaying in 1933, Wuchow in 1935, and Kweilin in 1938.

As a rule, the priests retained the overall responsibility for parish work but delegated everything which dealt with the apostolate of women to the Sisters. In each Maryknoll territory, the Sisters were entrusted with training female catechists and opening novitiates for training native Sisters. In general, Maryknoll Brothers worked under the direction of the head of the territory. Brothers skilled in nursing, carpentry, or masonry were sent to help in the parishes. Others remained at mission headquarters as secretaries and bookkeepers.

Mission Work in Non-Maryknoll Territories

Although most Maryknoll missioners worked within the limits of a Maryknoll territory, some received special assignments in non-Maryknoll missions. Owing to either the particular nature or the location of the assignment, the work of these Maryknollers—except for Bishop James E. Walsh and the Maryknoll Sisters in Shanghai—falls outside the framework of this study. Yet it seems important to give an overview of Maryknoll work in non-Maryknoll territories of China because sometimes these Maryknollers worked later in a Maryknoll territory or were recruited for their special assignment from a Maryknoll territory; in addition, their work was tangentially important for other Maryknollers in China.

Work of the Maryknoll Sisters in Hong Kong

When the Maryknoll Sisters arrived in Hong Kong in 1921, they had no intention to work there. They planned only to establish a center house to serve as a procure* and a place of preparation for the Maryknoll Sisters

---

*This word, borrowed from the French, is a term commonly used by Catholic missionary societies. It refers to a house or office in some convenient location to which missioners can look for service in procuring needed supplies, exchanging checks, and so forth. A procure also serves, when large enough, as a hostel for passing missioners.

going to join the missions in China. No provision had been made by the headquarters in Ossining to send subsidies to the Sisters, with the understanding that the Sisters would be supported by the head of the Maryknoll mission in which they would work. Openings in the Maryknoll missions were still limited, however, and Sister Mary Paul McKenna, the Sisters' superior in China, had to find an immediate source of revenue for her Sisters in Hong Kong.

Considering education "one of their primary mission efforts," the Sisters started a kindergarten and an industrial school producing vestments. The vestment department was launched both as an educational and a commercial enterprise in late 1924 in the garage of their convent on the Kowloon peninsula. Under the direction of a Chinese Maryknoll Sister, Sister Maria Teresa Yeung, the little factory became a major source of income and enabled the Sisters to build their first school in Hong Kong. Light-weight cassocks and embroidered liturgical vestments were sold in the United States where they brought a good price. The workers were mostly poor, unskilled Chinese girls who were trained by Sister Maria Teresa. They received a salary and were given shelter in the Chinese quarters of the convent. Over the years, Sister Maria Teresa's presence among these girls led to many conversions and to approximately 20 religious vocations.[40]

In early 1925, the Maryknoll Sisters opened a small kindergarten in the community room of their convent and taught classes in English. As years went by, new grades were added, expanding the curriculum to primary and high school levels and necessitating a move into a larger permanent building. The school kept the name of Maryknoll Convent School, growing from its humble origin with a student body of 12 Portuguese children into a prestigious school of several hundred girls belonging to at least 12 nationalities.[41]

In January 1927, the Sisters opened Holy Spirit School on the island of Hong Kong catering more specifically to Chinese girls of well-to-do families who desired an Anglo-Chinese education. Chinese teachers conducted classes in Chinese in the morning, and the Sisters taught English in the afternoon. By 1930, the curriculum ranged from kindergarten to university entrance courses.[42]

Mercy Hospital in Shanghai

The Maryknoll Sisters also worked independently of the Maryknoll Fathers in Shanghai, serving as nurses at Mercy Hospital from 1935 to 1938. Joseph Lo Pa-hong, a successful businessman and the head of the Catholic Action in Shanghai, had asked them to help with one of his philanthropic enterprises, the first hospital for the mentally ill in China. While the

Brothers of Charity of Trier operated the men's section, Maryknoll Sisters were in charge of the women's section. The fame of the hospital spread so rapidly that by the end of 1936 the patient population totaled 170. Unfortunately, the murder of Mr. Lo on December 30, 1937, left the financial support of Mercy Hospital in the hands of the still young Maryknoll Congregation. They finally had to withdraw from the hospital on November 1, 1938, and hand over responsibility to the Franciscan Sisters of Luxemburg.[43]

Independent Work of the Maryknoll Fathers

A few Maryknoll Fathers received assignments not connected with any of the five Maryknoll mission territories in China. Father Frederick C. Dietz, one of the first two pioneers in Wuchow City and pro-vicar of the Kongmoon vicariate, was assigned to Peking in late 1932 as a member of China's Catholic Synodal Commission on Schools, Books, and Press. This was created after the First Plenary Council of China held in Shanghai in 1924 and was placed directly under the papal delegate. Its role was to promote "intellectual and moral reconstruction in China" as well as "to coordinate and unify the work of the missions for the sake of mutual assistance and greater fruitfulness." It published manuals for Catholic Action among youth and adults, supervised the preparation of textbooks for Catholic schools and other educational institutions, and encouraged the distribution of books and pamphlets suitable for Catholic readers. It also directed the *Digest of the Synodal Commission*, a monthly review which treated ecclesiastical questions both from a theoretical and a practical point of view in order to inform missioners of what was being done in China for the diffusion of the faith.

While in Peking, Dietz emphasized the role of the Commission as a news-information office. In 1935, he created the *Lumen News Service* to provide Church-related news for the religious and secular press of China and the Far East. In the fall of 1937 he was assigned as Maryknoll's representative in Rome and was replaced in his functions in Peking by Maryknoll Father William A. Kaschmitter.[44]

From November 1938 to January 1941, Father Robert Cairns was loaned by Bishop Adolph Paschang of Kongmoon to Bishop Antoine Fourquet of Canton to help with refugee work. At the same time, Cairns served on the Executive Committee and the Refugee Committee of the local bureau of the Red Cross, "buying food, inspecting food kitchens, and aiding in medical works."[45]

In April 1946, when Rome formally established the Catholic hierarchy in China, one of the first steps of the newly established hierarchy was to increase the staff of the Synodal Commission on Schools, Books, and Press to generate studies of problems common to all China and the formulation and coordination of plans of action. This enlarged commission was renamed the Catholic Central Bureau of China.

In 1948, shortly after finishing his ten-year term as superior general of the Maryknoll Fathers and Brothers, Bishop James E. Walsh accepted the post of executive secretary of the Catholic Central Bureau of China in Shanghai. He chose to remain at his post even after the Communist takeover of the city. Arrested in 1958, he was the last missioner expelled from China, on July 20, 1970.[46]

Prior to the appointment of Bishop James E. Walsh, other Maryknollers had already filled important posts within the Central Bureau. During the summer of 1946, Father Paul Duchesne of the diocese of Kongmoon was assigned to Canton to head the South China office of the Catholic Welfare Committee of China (C.W.C.C.), one of the 10 departments of the Central Bureau. Assisted by another Maryknoller, Father Francis O'Neill, Father Duchesne was in charge of the distribution in 13 dioceses of the relief goods obtained from a variety of sources such as the United Nations Relief and Rehabilitation Administration (U.N.R.R.A.), United Service to China, the Canadian Committee, British United Aid to China, the New Zealand Overseas Relief Organization, the United States Economic Cooperation Administration (E.C.A.), and, of course, the War Relief Services of the National Catholic Welfare Conference of the United States.[47]

After World War II three other Maryknollers were assigned to Canton. Fathers George Putnam and Joseph Hahn were assigned to the Protestant-run Lingnam University in the Honam section of the city. Hahn taught engineering, while Putnam conducted courses in sociology. They received permission to erect a residence on the campus to serve as a chapel for Catholic students and a meeting place for social gatherings.[48] Such ecumenical collaboration was rare in 1947.

About the same time, the bishop of Canton invited Monsignor Bernard Meyer, previously in Wuchow and Kweilin, to open a parish in the crowded Honam section. In 1948, Meyer rented a three-story building on a main street in Honam. He opened a free dispensary on the ground floor to take care of the sick and to break down prejudice and interest people in the Church. After the Communists took over Canton in November 1949, Catholic Welfare's storage room of Fathers Duchesne and O'Neill was sealed, and any further welfare work was prohibited. They went to live with Father Meyer and his assistant, Father James T. Manning. In July 1950, Meyer became ill and left for treatment in Hong Kong.[49]

Early the following year, the Communists first told Hahn and Putnam and then told Duchesne and O'Neill to leave. From Canton, Duchesne moved to Hong Kong, where he also assumed the direction of Catholic Welfare. The many projects conducted by Maryknollers to help refugees in that city would make a most interesting story.[50]

The Physical Environment

From the first day of their arrival in China, Maryknollers found a physical environment which had an impact on their bodies, their lives, and the effectiveness of their work. For many missioners, working in this environment over a period of time would undoubtedly affect the remainder of their lives.

The Climate of South China

The monsoon rhythm was clearly the basic cause of seasonal variations over most of China, with warm moist inflowing winds in summer and cold dry outflowing winds in winter. The Maryknoll territories all reflected the same seasonal distribution of precipitation, with a maximum in the summer and a minimum in the winter. In South China, a further cause of rainfall between July and November was typhoons, which moved in a north-northwesterly direction with winds of over 100 miles per hour and torrential rains, sometimes over 20 inches in 24 hours. The typhoons brought yearly havoc to the coastal area of the Kongmoon vicariate, often followed by floods, which resulted in the drowning of people and ruined crops. In July 1922, Father Ford described how he was taken by surprise by a typhoon during a mission trip out of Yeungkong:

> Now in my fourth year here we have another typhoon and the very house which had been blown down before (July 1919) and rebuilt into our old folks' home toppled down again. . . . Where fields of grain had been drying yesterday was now a lake or rather a river, the streets of the town [of Chiklung] were canals and I saw a raft of wooden shoes from the boots shop across the way float down the street. . . . In five days the water subsided enough to allow our return to Yeungkong but had I been pilot the boat would have fared ill for all the landmarks were changed. Formerly we docked a quarter mile from shore and poled our way in by sampan. Now we gaily sailed into town and up to a nearby hill. Then what had been a pleasant walk was done in boats. I recognized the roof of a roadside inn. We rowed among the branches of banyan trees, over graves and walls in a beeline instead of walking the winding paths of last week.
>
> As we neared Yeungkong the effects were worse. The river was higher and stronger and whole villages were submerged. Shops had fallen in and the dwellers had taken to boats piled high with furniture and pigs. We rowed up the narrow Main Street until the jam of sampans made further progress impossible. . . . The jammed sampans made a pontoon bridge and we skipped

from one to the other to shallow water and home.

The damage in the villages is not yet fully known. One village nearby had 100 killed by the falling houses. Unfortunately the typhoon struck at midnight and the sleeping villages were unable to escape. In Yeungkong city, the deaths were more by drowning than by falling roofs as the waterfront was lined with flimsy dwellings which were washed away. The typhoon came at a bad time. Rice has been rising in price just before the harvest and this crop was eagerly expected to increase the supply. Most of the rice had been cut and stacked, ready to be threshed. But the five-day flood wrought havoc with the harvest.[51]

Fortunately, however, the typhoons rapidly lost their strength as they penetrated inland and they had little impact on the territories of Wuchow, Kweilin and Kaying. But the prolonged summer monsoon rains plagued these areas with innumerable floods. Kaying city, for example, was flooded twice in the summer of 1937:

> August 18: A cloudburst made the river overflow, flooding part of the downtown district. Forty were killed in towns upstream. . . .
> October 5-6: Heavy rains all day. The river is swollen, flooding shops along the riverfront . . . soon overflowing. Water was waist-deep in the Sisters' house (Rosary Convent) and soon after five feet deep. Sampans came sailing up to our front door. . . . Everybody is on the second floor and the attic of the building.[52]

With the Tropic of Cancer passing just north of Canton, the four Maryknoll territories of South China belonged to the tropical or subtropical zone with low temperatures in the mid–50s around Kongmoon or mid–40s around Kweilin; high temperatures could easily climb into the 90s. There were three clearly marked seasons. From mid-October to mid-January was a delightful time with clear skies and warm and dry weather:

> Kweilin weather in October and November rivals that of California. Ordinarily it's a gay season. Crops are being or have already been harvested. . . . There is plenty of time to bask in the almost uninterrupted sunshine of this balmiest of seasons and enjoy a good night's sleep.[53]

Some years, however, cold weather came earlier, taking everybody by surprise:

> Sunday, November 26: Father Time got off schedule . . . and so Old Man Wind gave us a piece of his mind. We Chongpu people were then caught unaware and so we had to scurry for protection beneath extra clothing as a means of defense against the cold. . . . The small baskets with their char-

coal burners ablaze were much in evidence. The men carried them under their long-sams [gowns] . . . even the altar boys had their basket fires close by their robes.[54]

The coldest period was from mid-January to mid-March, around the time of Chinese New Year, when missioners experienced damp, dull weather with outbursts of northerly wind:

> January and February have been notable for cold and rain. The first three months of the year in South China can compete with any place in the world for complete discomfort and disagreeableness. The cold penetrates every bone in your body and makes life perfectly miserable without allowing you the satisfaction of freezing to death.[55]

At night temperatures dropped sometimes into the 40s, making houses with no heating facilities very uncomfortable. In some higher elevations of Kwangsi and the Kaying territory, sudden frosts in late December and early January were not infrequent.[56]

Then followed a long wet enervating summer when both temperatures and relative humidity were high. From the little town of Pingnam upriver from Wuchow, Father Thomas Kiernan wrote in July 1930:

> The heat in this northern realm of the torrid zone at this time of the year stays pretty much between 92 and 98 in the shade, and no one knows how high the mercury goes in the sun because our thermometers don't go that high. Added to the heat is the intense humidity. We have no way of measuring this but my guess is that the air is just about at the saturation point. We go for days at a time with no breeze and no break in the intensity of the heat and humidity. One just sweats and sweats. Can't sleep and food gets on one's nerves. The ground bakes and reflects the sun and heat in one's face—to the point of suffocation. . . . Besides the usual helmet for head protection from the sun we carried an umbrella. . . . A breeze came up but it was like one from the Sahara. It just burned and stifled.[57]

Except for the rich alluvial plain around Kongmoon and a few other patches of level ground along the rivers, most of the Maryknoll territories of South China resembled "the waves of the sea for it is all hills."[58] Thanks, however, to a generally good combination of temperature and rainfall, most of South China enjoyed a growing season of twelve months. Rice was by far the most important crop. Nearly all the rice was grown in freshwater paddies with double crops. A first harvest was taken from late June in Kongmoon to mid-July in Kaying, and a second between mid-October and mid-November. Most families had their own vegetable garden of greens. In good years, depending on the soil and the area, farmers could usually plant a cash crop of vegetables, winter peas, soybeans, or roots such as taro between the November harvest and the spring planting. In the colder parts of the Kaying and Kweilin territories, the first harvest of rice was replaced by winter wheat. Next to rice, peanuts and sweet potatoes were the most important crops, growing in the hills and in sandy areas where rice paddies could not be built or irrigation was difficult. Although the climate favored its cultivation, corn was not widely planted because it competed with the rice growing season rather than complementing it. Missioners tried to avoid harvest times for their mission trips or catechumenates because farmers were too busy gathering food for the coming months to go to church. The entry in the October 1946 diary of Pingnam station read: "Not many people in for the catechumenate for at this time of the year the people pull their peanuts which are planted in the spring. It is a hard, dusty, dirty job, in which all the family helps out."[59]

Tropical fruits such as citrus fruits, papaya, banana, persimmon, lichee, and longan were readily available in most areas but did not seem to be extensively cultivated. In some parts of the Wuchow and Kweilin territories, the land was so difficult to till that taro, not rice, was the main staple of the people. Chickens and pigs roamed the streets of villages and supplemented people's diets. Saltwater and fresh water fish were widely available and commonly eaten with rice and vegetables.[60]

The amount of precipitation played an important role, especially during the most active growing season of March through December. Too much rain could make the difference between a good and a bad harvest, or a good and a poor planting:

> These people are the poorest of the poor . . . . This summer after they had planted their second crop of rice the West River rose above its banks and their village and fields were under several feet of water for over a week, killing out the rice plants. That meant the loss of about half their second crop and the seed. They replanted of course but it was so late in the season that the yield will be small.[61]

A prolonged dry spell, too, could bring famine, especially if the previous harvest had been small. In Kwangsi, missioners recalled the terrible effect of two droughts almost 20 years apart in the same area:

> December 1928: The rice crop is almost a total failure from lack of rain, and starvation stares thousands in the face. . . . February 1929: The famine grows worse. . . . April 1929: A short distance up the river people are tearing

down their houses to sell the bricks, and giving away or selling their children.

April 1946: April began with a continuation of the longest dry spell in this area in twenty years. In the past eight months there has been rain only five or six times. . . . The grounds remain hard and untilled still. The corn crop is three weeks behind planting time, and if this weather continues much longer the rice planting will be a month to five weeks behind schedule. . . . The charity funds which I am distributing are barely scratching the surface in bringing relief to so many in dire need.[62]

The Climate of Manchuria

The seasonal distribution of rainfall typical of the monsoon rhythm was also clearly marked in the Maryknoll territory of Fushun in Manchuria where the heaviest rains fell in July and August, bringing yearly flooding along rivers and streams. But more characteristic of the area was the wide range of temperatures. Clear winter skies and strong bitterly cold winds from Siberia regularly produced low temperatures of 40 degrees below zero in Fushun where there were five months with average temperatures below freezing. In mid-November 1940, Father Michael Henry, pastor of Linkiang, mentioned how difficult it was to remain warm in the church while hearing confessions:

> We are now down to 18 degrees above zero. . . . We shall keep falling to zero and below. How far below? . . . The confessional can be moved so I gave instructions to have it moved to a position where both confessor and penitents may have the benefit of the one stove in that section [of the church].[63]

In this bitter cold, even chicken coops had to be heated to keep the poultry from freezing to death.

Throughout the whole vicariate summer was short but hot and humid, with temperatures in the high 80s and low 90s. The July 30, 1931, entry in the Chakow diary reads: "It has been raining practically every day for the past two weeks. The heat is intense. With no sun these days, the thermometer keeps between 85 and 90. The nights are nearly as bad as the days."[64] Only a few places like Dairen, for instance, enjoyed less extreme temperatures because of the maritime influence.

The mostly mountainous terrain added to the ruggedness of the climate to make the growing season short. Only one crop a year could be secured. The two principal crops were sorghum and soybeans, with millet also widely grown. Wheat, corn, and head cabbages were found in the valleys. Opium used to be a popular cash crop in Manchuria; although officially forbidden, the government would at times permit farmers to grow as much as they wished if they agreed to pay a heavy tax.[65]

Vermin and Disease

In South China, vermin proliferated, thriving on high levels of temperature and humidity, and mold grew overnight. Concerning vermin, the Yeungkong Chronicle of 1919 notes rather humorously:

> [South China] is a good place in which to meditate on how quickly the works of man crumble into dust. This fact is sometimes brought rather forcibly to one's attention by the falling in of his roof, the destruction of his favorite books or his clothes. . . . Woe is you on the day that you think of looking for something in that trunk full of old books and clothing for you will probably find it a mass of chewed up rubbish. If you don't know what did it, just dig down into it and you will see the albino rascals scurrying to cover. I refer to the so-called "white ants". . . . There is also a worm similar to the one found in hard woods in America that works the same destruction here.[66]

Next to white ants, rats were the most destructive pests, chewing up clothing and books. Domestic cats were a rare sight in the countryside as they tended to be used as a source of food. A few Maryknollers were able to secure cats, which proved to be reluctant to chase after the rodents. In 1934, for instance, the rectory on Sancian Island was so badly infested that the rats chewed all the buttons off Father Robert Cairns' cassock during the night and carried them away, leaving large holes behind. To avoid any embarrassment during a visit of Bishop James E. Walsh, Cairns locked the bishop's clothes in a safe place, only to find the next morning that the rats had eaten a hole in the sheet on the bishop's bed. These rodents were largely responsible for the constant resurgence of cholera in South China.[67]

In the hot weather, cockroaches were a common pest. With such high humidity, cases of prickly heat were common, and so were diarrhea and rheumatism. Mosquitoes and all kinds of biting insects thrived. Malaria and other diseases were rampant. In the infirmary records of Yeungkong for August 1921 was mention of "Father Hodgins' colic belt full of stickers" and of a "bed ready to pick itself up and walk with bedbugs."[68] It is easy to imagine how the Sisters suffered from the heat under the constricting bonnet of their habit, or worse, how painful it must have been when bedbugs got inside it.[69]

Only the cool nights in October and November brought a seasonal end to both cockroaches and biting insects until the coming of the warm days of the following spring. But even if there was a respite from vermin, mold seemed ready at any time to destroy people's food and possessions. In May

1921, the Fathers in Yeungkong noted:

> Some kind heart sent a box of candy and the mold was at it first. . . . The sun peeps out and invites out the camera; the films are stuck to the protective covering and the roll is stuck to the box and whiskers have gathered in and outside, even on the lenses. Why do our books look so pale and our clothes seem a hundred years old? . . . We smell friend mold in the bed, in Mass vestments, in every room. . . . Wipe off the moldy growth, or cut it away from eatables, and not only is there a stain but the foe is back again as soon as you turn your back.[70]

Maryknollers were not demoralized, however, and were able to joke about the situation:

> Our optimists who praise the daily rains in the name of the rice fields remark how keeping after the mold insures against inaction in a hot climate, and what a spiritual lesson is taught by the perseverance of the fungi against the trials we furnish.[71]

The situation in Manchuria was not better. The long winter months made the "bug season" shorter, but few missioners viewed the coming of the punishing cold as a relief. Moreover, with the return of summer the insects were back, perhaps even more abusive than in the south because of the briefness of the warm season:

> Flea, fly, bed-bug or mosquito—which takes the blue ribbon? Each has its defenders among missioners for the honor of being man's most annoying insect animal. . . . After experience with all, we might be tempted to describe the fleas as the most elusive, the fly most obtrusive, the bedbug most voracious and the mosquito most pugnacious.[72]

With so many vermin around and very little preventive medicine or vaccinations available, epidemics of cholera, malaria, and typhoid occurred almost as often as in the south.[73]

In such a context, travels were often a difficult enterprise, especially for women missioners. In some parts of the Maryknoll territory of Fushun, trains were available and made communications between Fushun city and Dairen fast and easy; yet for the most part, mule carts were the most common means of transportation to manage both the deep mud of spring and summer and the frozen surface of winter months. In the south, Maryknollers moved around mostly on foot or by bus, bicycle, or boat.

Sister Mary Paul McKenna recalled the inconvenience of traveling on waterways in the 1920s:

> When on a junk, you slept on the deck. The food was canned beef, beans or rice. There was a common toilet which was nothing but a hole in the deck. You dipped dirty water from the river to wash yourself. . . . There was very little privacy.[74]

The first groups of Maryknollers who went to China to fulfill their goals of evangelizing the Chinese people and building the Chinese Church confronted such an environment. Although modernization made substantial headway during the 1930s and 1940s, internecine wars as well as World War II prevented progress from reaching deep into the countryside where most Maryknollers worked.

PART II

The Evangelization of the Non-Christians

The Priority of the Rural Apostolate

"Go forth and make disciples of all nations" (Mt. 28:19). This mandate of Christ to his apostles appears to be not only the source of activity for the Catholic Church, but also the cornerstone of its identity. It exists to evangelize—to be a messenger of the good news of Jesus Christ to the whole world.[1] At the core of the message is the proclamation that in Jesus Christ, the Son of God made man who died and rose from the dead, salvation is offered to all as a gift of God's grace and mercy. The Church continues Christ's presence and salvific mission in the world. It serves as a visible sign—a sacrament of God's reconciliation with all people. Its presence in the world bears witness to a renewed humanity in which everyone is called by God to share the kingdom.[2]

Within this overall task, the specific work of missioners, traditionally called the "first evangelization," has been defined as the introduction of the faith among peoples who do not yet know Christ, and the foundation of native Churches. Maryknoll was formed precisely to provide this sort of frontier outreach in the Church's commitment to evangelization. The first rule approved by Rome for the Maryknoll Fathers and Brothers and the first constitutions of the Maryknoll Sisters both described one of their main objectives as "the conversion of pagans in heathen lands."[3]

The use of words such as "pagan" and "heathen" should not be seen as judgmental or demeaning descriptions of non-Christians, but rather as a reflection of the prevailing understanding of the mission of the Church, almost until the time of Vatican II. "The Church conceived itself as a kind of sacred vessel or receptacle possessed of saving resources not available, or at least readily available, beyond its visible circumference."[4] Its mission was to extend its unique riches to all people, including the pagans, subjected by the universality of original sin to the servitude of Satan and therefore liable to eternal damnation.[5]

In 1919 as Maryknollers embarked on their second year of missionary work in China, Pope Benedict XV, in his apostolic letter *Maximum Illud* stressed as the particular vocation of missioners the salvation of "the numberless heathen still sitting in the shadows of death" waiting to be saved from their "sad fate."[6] At the same time, Joseph Schmidlin, a respected professor of mission science at the University of Münster, published the first systematic treatise on Catholic missiology. It immediately became the standard textbook used for the apostolic formation of future missioners. Schmidlin emphasized that the goal of Catholic missioners was the "spreading of Christianity" among the "pagans" whose individual salvation was considered dependent upon knowledge of Jesus Christ, interior conversion, and enrollment in the Catholic Church through baptism.[7]

In such a context, the "spreading of Christianity" was generally understood in quantitative terms. The annual report filed by each mission territory with Propaganda Fide in Rome was no more than a statistical sheet which reported progress in terms of numbers of conversions. Even the quality of these conversions and of Christian life was transcribed quantitatively in numbers of confessions and communions. A report showing a steady increase in the reception of the three basic sacraments, baptism, confession, and communion, was a sure sign of a successful mission.

In 1918, the main thrust of Catholic evangelization in China was aimed at the uneducated farmers in the countryside. For the preceding 150 years, from the late sixteenth century to the mid-eighteenth century, the missionary approach to China had been more balanced. One group of missioners had concentrated on the masses in the rural areas, and a smaller group, mostly Jesuits, had worked in the cities, attempting to Christianize the society from the top down, by converting the "literati" or scholarly elite on whom rested the duty to preserve and foster the Chinese socio-political way of life as well as the spiritual tradition known as Confucianism.

In 1742 when Pope Benedict XIV's bull condemned the Chinese Rites and required all missioners in China to take an oath against the Rites, the Jesuit experiment came to an end. By identifying Confucian public ceremonies as idolatrous and superstitious, the Church antagonized the Chinese elite who, because of their rank or office, had to perform or at least attend these ceremonies. The ban on Christianity and the persecutions which followed drove most missioners out of China. The few who remained or who were able to enter China hid in remote Catholic villages in the countryside. In most cities, Catholic communities did not escape the scrutiny of the Chinese authorities; they either died out or moved to the countryside.

In the mid-nineteenth century, the reopening of China to Christianity under the guns of Western nations rekindled the hatred of the Chinese officials and elite. Forced to bow down to the technical and military superiority of the West, they resented the cultural arrogance and encroachment displayed by its missioners.

At the same time, however, since most of the old Chinese Catholics lived in villages, the Catholic Church naturally focused its apostolic work on the countryside to the detriment of the cities. The ideal Catholic missioner in China was not the intellectual whose Western academic training and polished knowledge of Chinese classics attracted the educated city dwellers, but rather the frontier type who mixed with the buffalo herders and farmers of China. The Church considered city dwellers to be too engrossed in their work to find the leisure, the energy, and the reflection necessary to consider conversion. In addition, because the city met most of the needs of its inhabitants in matters of livelihood, protection, education, and health, it was not viewed as a favorable milieu for conversions. Wuchow, for instance, had been nicknamed the "City of No Conversions." In contrast, the Chinese village was considered a better environment for a successful apostolate by the Catholic missioners, who could assist in helping with the basic needs of the people.

As a result, when the modernization of the early 1900s brought about the collapse of Confucianism and intellectuals sought ways to reconcile these changes with their proud past, most Catholic missioners lived in rural areas and had little experience in dealing with educated Chinese. Progressively, however, some missioners realized that if the Catholic Church were to have a lasting impact on China, it would also have to reach the educated circles in the large cities who were directly involved in molding the new thought and life of the country.

In Shanghai the Jesuits responded to the strong demand for Western education and opened Aurora University in 1903. In 1911 Father Vincent Lebbe opened the first Catholic public lecture hall in Tientsin. Most of the lecture topics were directly concerned with the Catholic faith but, nonetheless, the hall was packed with listeners from the non-Christian elite. The success of the venture led Lebbe to open half a dozen other halls in the city and initiated a movement of Catholic lectures throughout China. In 1915, Lebbe launched *Yi Shih-pao* (*The Social Welfare*), the first Catholic daily newspaper. Within three months it had become the Chinese newspaper with the largest circulation in north China, widely appreciated by intellectuals for the accuracy of its news and its independent outlook.[8]

Despite the increased interest of some missionary circles in the Chinese elite, by the time Maryknollers arrived in China the bulk of the foreign missioners still insisted that the hope of the Church in China was in converting the countryside where four-fifths of the population lived. This certainly was the impression of Fathers James E. Walsh and Bernard Meyer from their first meeting with the French Fathers in Canton in November 1918:

> Regarding the Chinese and the mission, [Father Alfred Fabre] the director of the seminary said that conversions are almost impossible in the cities. The people there have left their gods of stone and wood to serve Mammon and Venus. The people in the villages are more simple-minded and accept the faith much more readily. So Christ foretold and so it has always been.[9]

During the following months, the veteran M.E.P. Father Auguste Gauthier took the first Maryknoll band to Yeungkong where he too advocated a mission apostolate directed primarily at the country people.[10] The example set by Gauthier and the rural nature of western Kwangtung province oriented Maryknollers toward the evangelization of the villages. As a result, the Maryknoll apostolate in the cities developed slowly and always remained secondary to the rural apostolate.[11]

To convert as many Chinese as possible, Maryknollers first followed and then further developed the mission methods of their French mentors. The methods fell into two broad categories. The direct apostolate, also called direct evangelization, emphasized the spiritual approach—to go out to the non-Christians and preach salvation in Jesus Christ through conversion and entrance in the Church. The second method emphasized a more practical approach: it stressed the establishment of medical, educational, and charitable institutions which, by their display of Christian charity and love, would attract non-Christians and ultimately result in their conversion.

3

The Direct Apostolate

Emphasis on Local Catechists

The French Missioners' Legacy

> It may be stimulating to vision the apostolic missioner in patched cassock
> with cross upraised, pouring forth a stirring call to the enraptured crowd to
> seek salvation, or hunting in hovels and at the water's edge for abandoned
> babies. But if such be the life of a missioner, I have not seen it.[1]

This remark of Father Francis Ford in April 1921 is revealing of the
transformation of the pioneer band of Maryknollers during their first two
years in China. Under the guidance of Father Auguste Gauthier, they shed
their poetic view of the heroic missionary life for a more realistic assessment of the work ahead.

At first glance, Gauthier seemed to fit the romantic image of an apostolic missioner. Early Maryknoll correspondence described his repeated
tours of the countryside. A soul-seeker, he believed that the chief goal of
the missionary apostolate was to convert the non-Christian Chinese, and
he insisted that missioners should concentrate on works directly related to
this end. He advised Maryknollers against starting institutions such as
hospitals, schools of higher learning, or orphanages, pointing out that
these should develop later as a natural expression of a responsible Christian community.[2]

For Gauthier, the missioner's vocation was to go out to meet non-
Christians and to preach to them. "In journeyings often," the motto
chosen when he became a bishop in 1921, appropriately reflected his apostolic zeal and his lifestyle.[3] During the first two and a half years Maryknoll
was in China, he became "the elder brother" to a dozen priests whom he
took along on his trips to familiarize them with the techniques of reaching
the Chinese people of the countryside. At the same time, these trips were

an occasion for Gauthier to show his American friends that without a well-trained corps of catechists, their apostolic zeal alone would never result in a significant program of conversions: their personal, direct contacts with the Chinese were too few and too restricted.[4]

Most of the existing Catholic communities in Kwangtung owed their existence and continuity to itinerant catechists trained under the French missionaries. Bishop John Wu of Hong Kong, for instance, remembers the strong influence of his paternal grandmother when he was a young boy in the Hakka village of Pettochai. She used to tell him how she received the gift of faith many years earlier through the teaching of catechist Muk Lam. When, once in many months, he visited, the whole village crowded around to listen. Not only did his grandmother captivate young Wu with many of these same stories, but she also showed him their direct application to life:

> When I went to the seminary, I recognized all these stories in the Bible, the parable of the son who went astray and came back, the story of Job, etc. When my aunt's husband and son died, she cried her eyes out. Then my grandmother told her the story of Job. It was not strange that my grandmother knew the story; however, she was able to apply it and use it to comfort my aunt.[5]

Maryknollers quickly discovered that they were ill-suited to live in a physical environment which weakened their bodies and undermined their energy—a subtropical climate with poor food, spartan conditions and lack of medical care. The human environment was equally trying because the Chinese people were often suspicious of foreigners, and their language, culture and customs were impossible to master in a brief period of time.[6] Gauthier reminded Maryknollers that the best way to overcome these handicaps and to significantly increase the rate of conversions was to train and support a well-organized and widely spread group of catechists. In fact, from the first day he briefed the newcomers prior to their departure for Yeungkong, Gauthier's central theme emphasized catechists. He urged Maryknollers to concentrate their energies and funds on a catechist program so they could instill their apostolic zeal in native Catholic men and women in a relatively short period of time and greatly increase their contacts with the people.[7]

World War I was coming to an end at the time of Maryknoll's arrival in China, and it was blamed for the lack of increase in foreign missionaries. In 1918, there were at most 1,600 priests, 1,000 Sisters, and 200 Brothers, all foreigners, with probably less than half engaged in the direct apostolate. In fact, in several mission areas, including the Maryknoll territory in the vicariate of Canton, the number of personnel involved in this apostolate had actually diminished despite an increase in the number of Chinese priests and Sisters. As a result the number of conversions in China leveled off to just under 100,000 a year. At that rate, said an article in *Missions de Chine et du Japon*, it could take 4,000 years to convert the 400 million Chinese.[8]

In search of a solution, missioners all over China took a fresh look at the old institution of catechists. Maryknollers seriously considered Gauthier's advice. Barely four months after their arrival in China, Father Thomas Price, the leader of the pioneer group, identified the training of catechists as the number one task in a letter to Father James A. Walsh, the Maryknoll superior in Ossining:

> You ask what institutions I am planning. I think that the putting out of catechists, handling them and training them, should be our chief work at the present time. The institutions will come gradually as they are needed; there is no pressing need now. . . . I should like to see at work by next year as many catechists as we can afford.[9]

Plans for a Catechist School

Among the three priests accompanying Price, Father Bernard Meyer rapidly emerged as his closest collaborator in the preparation of catechists well grounded in the faith. Meyer's first step was to analyze the situation: with only 15 or 16 catechists at their disposal, it was impossible for the four American priests to reach two million people in a territory of 5,000 square miles. It was equally impossible to nurture the faith of the 1,200 Catholics who lived in small communities separated by great distances and who, for the most part, had not seen a priest for at least the past four years.[10]

Meyer then worked out a plan of action and presented it to Price in March 1919. He proposed to hire as catechists local Catholics who had successfully attended a four- to six-week training course in doctrine, skills, and techniques. In addition, he planned to call the catechists together annually for a month-long improvement course and to review their work plans.[11]

After Price's death in September 1919, Meyer assumed the responsibility to develop the program. Quoting from one of the last letters received from his elder, he implied that Price was still in charge and had departed to heaven only to increase their chances of success: "The matter of catechists is life and death to our work and to the souls committed to us. . . . We must supply them. I will move heaven and earth to get catechists and make them efficient."[12]

During the first year Meyer, Francis X. Ford, and James E. Walsh could do nothing to launch the program because they did not know the language well enough to preach in church, much less to instruct catechists. They took up residence in former M.E.P. parishes at Yeungkong, Tungchen, Tungon, Loting, and Kochow to concentrate on language study. They relied on the few catechists already in these stations to familiarize them with the local situation and to contact and inform the Catholics of their new pastor and their newly reopened church.

As Maryknollers became more fluent, they discovered a wide discrepancy in the training of their catechists. Some were so poorly instructed that, like the two catechists in Tungchen, they did not know how to make a proper confession.[13] Others, however, like Cato Cheung, John Lye, Mary Low, and Clara Yip in Kochow, were able, zealous men and women with engaging personalities. Most outstanding was the head catechist at Kochow, Epiphanius Yip. Maryknoll diaries and letters constantly praised this catechist who, as a young man, had opened up the area under the French Fathers. Fairly well educated and well connected, he gained for the Church the friendship and the respect of city officials and notables. In Father Francis Connors' opinion, he was the priceless co-worker every missioner wished to have by his side.

> When you are new at the game and a tyro at the language, and have a large mission and school to look after, and the country is upset, and fighting is near, and bandits on all sides . . . then is a "Piffy" [Epiphanius] like a jewel set in a royal crown.[14]

"Super catechist Yip" died in 1936 at the age of forty-nine, worn out by tuberculosis. The doctor had promised him a longer life if he curbed his nonstop activities; but after 34 years, serving the Church had become a lifelong habit.

Meanwhile in parishes like Kochow and Yeungkong, Maryknollers used a few good Catholics as catechists; in other areas, where the level of doctrinal knowledge was inadequate, they borrowed trained catechists from Canton. By September 1920, with 40 catechists, Maryknollers had more than doubled the number of catechists they found at their arrival.

The addition of a well-trained catechist often produced immediate results. In Tungchen, for instance, where Meyer lamented his lack of progress, the presence of a catechist triggered a surprising comeback of fallen-away Catholics and a movement of conversion. Between February and September 1920, the Catholic community of Tungchen grew from 50 to 230 members. Capitalizing on his success, Meyer concentrated on finding new catechists and training them. In March 1921, he held a two-week retreat-training course for his catechists, who had grown in a year and a half from a two-man unit to a team of seven men and one woman.[15]

In November 1921, the Maryknollers in China decided to support

Meyer's plan to open a catechist school and appointed him director. His long-term plan was to open a permanent school on the model of those run by the Vincentian, Steyl, and Scheut Fathers in North China, where catechists received training over a period of seven to 12 months. At the same time, however, Meyer realized that, out of many attempts, especially in South China where no missioner had ever succeeded in running a catechist school for more than a year, these schools represented a few successes.[16]

Burdened with the responsibility of a parish and with no replacement in sight, Meyer scaled down his project to a one-month course which he offered for the first time in Kochow in 1922. By 1923 the course was well established as a requisite summer exercise for all men and women catechists.[17] Together with Epiphanius Yip, his co-director, and Lady Wong, a well-trained catechist from Canton, Meyer taught four classes daily. The first lecture was on dogma and focused on the explanation of the catechism. The second on ethics dealt mainly with the Ten Commandments and the sacraments. The third topic was a study of the Gospel to help the catechists illustrate their preaching and their catechetical classes. The fourth aimed at explaining the meaning of the daily prayers and the Sunday mass. Beside these lectures, male catechists had to attend preaching sessions during which they took turns preparing and delivering a 15-minute sermon on an assigned topic. At the end of the course, an examination was given (fig. 1) and the catechists were ranked according to their grades. A higher grade usually meant an increase in responsibility and in salary. A head catechist was someone with good overall qualifications who received good grades over a period of two or three years. After 1923, theoretically, no salaried catechist could be hired who had not taken at least one summer course and passed the examination.[18] The thoroughness of catechetical training apparently had results; after a few years, Maryknollers observed signs of deeper personal faith among the catechists and of an increased earnestness in their work.[19]

The success of Meyer's summer training course stimulated inquiries from other mission societies. In 1923 the Salesians of the neighboring territory of Shiuchow opened their own summer school for catechists modeled on the Maryknoll school at Kochow.[20] Meanwhile Maryknollers pursued the idea of opening a year-round catechist school with a training program of one to two years. From Pingnam, the center for the new Wuchow mission, Fathers George Wiseman and John Murray proudly announced the opening of a "real catechist school" in October 1923. Four candidates received intensive training from a seminarian loaned by Bishop Ducoeur of Nanning. Although the experiment proved successful, it was discontinued after six months when the seminarian was recalled to complete his final preparation for ordination.[21] For several years, the idea of a year-round school remained an elusive goal. The rapid expansion of Maryknoll in China from three districts to large sections of Kwangtung, Kwangsi, and Manchuria created a chronic shortage of personnel which prevented qualified missioners like Meyer from being released to direct a school.

I

1. What do you know about God's nature? (Most Chinese conceive of Him as a sort of super-man.)
2. Are devils the souls of dead men? (as many Chinese think)
3. Has man three souls? (as is commonly thought by the Chinese)
4. What is original sin?
5. What were the effects of original sin?
6. What do you mean by the Incarnation?
7. As God did Christ have father or mother?
8. As Man did Christ have father or mother?
9. Mary is called "ever virgin." How do you explain this since she is the mother of Christ?
10. Why is the Catholic Church called universal?
11. What is the difference between sanctifying and actual grace?

II

1. How often may the various Sacraments be received?
2. What is the use of the Sacraments?
3. What are the rules for the ministration of Baptism by a layman?
4. Whom should catechists take care to baptize? (On account of the distances in China catechists baptize the children of Catholics in the absence of the priest as well as those of pagans in danger of death, and adult catechumens who are in danger of death.)
5. Must daughters of Christians be baptized? (There is a tendency to neglect it in some places because the scattered condition of the Christians makes it very difficult to find Christian husbands for them later.)
6. Must catechumens keep the commandments and precepts of the Church?
7. At what age must a person make his first confession?
8. Do parents commit grievous sin if they do not see to it that their children go to confession? (This duty is not always realized.)
9. What are perfect and imperfect contrition?
10. If one's purpose of amendment is sincere what must it include?
11. What is meant by restitution in matters of the seventh and eighth commandments?

Fig. 1. Questions for Written Exams, Catechist Short Course, with comments by Meyer (FARC, Box—Meyer, Training of Catechists, Kochow, June 15–July 15, 1924)

Financial Support for the Catechists

Each new Maryknoll territory needed large sums of money to get started, and much of the burden fell on Maryknoll Fathers and Brothers' headquarters. The Society for the Propagation of the Faith in Rome did not seem to realize that American missioners were in need of money. Their first allocation in 1923 for the Maryknoll missions was no more than the token amount of $1,250.[22]

Maryknoll headquarters at this time was financially very hard pressed. At the end of 1922, Maryknoll owed banks some $245,000 in secured and unsecured loans contracted mainly for the purchase of their seminary properties in Ossining and Scranton, and the subsequent construction and furnishing costs. The following year, James A. Walsh was able to send a total of $82,160 to his missioners in South China and Korea (a newly opened Maryknoll territory); however, Meyer had estimated the building costs in the near future for Maryknoll in South China alone at over half a million dollars. Naturally priorities had to be set. Building a catechist school at an approximate cost of $5,000 was deemed less urgent as long as some training program could be implemented during the summer in empty school buildings. As a result, Maryknollers in China were forced to manage with insufficiently trained catechists, to hire fewer catechists, and to let some go for lack of money.[23]

In 1920 Maryknoll headquarters provided salaries of the equivalent of US$15 a month for only 30 of the 40 catechists employed in the Yeungkong-Loting territory. The missioners had to provide their own funds for the remaining 10 salaries. Nine years later, Maryknollers were in charge of four territories but could not afford to employ more than 116 catechists because the headquarters sent salaries for only 50 of them.[24] Even though Maryknoll assumed the financial support of its missioners, the allotments were not sufficient for pastors and curates to save enough money to pay for additional catechists. Following the first General Chapter of the Maryknoll Fathers and Brothers in 1929, missioners in South China received an annual allowance of $350 for living expenses (viatique), $150 for personal needs, and $150 for travel within their mission territory. Life in a missionary parish with its recurring expenses for food, fuel, light, water, laundry, servants, stationery, altar wine, candles, and necessary trips and visits absorbed most of the allowance for room, board, and travel. Whatever was left from the personal allowance after ordinary expenses such as clothing, magazine subscriptions, tobacco, and the yearly vacation to Hong Kong was usually spent on charities for the poor and the sick. Therefore, although the balance left from the annual allowance could be used by a priest to supplement mission work of his choice, such as the catechist program, in reality he rarely had any money left.[25]

Naturally, criticism arose from missioners in China concerning the large amounts of money spent in the United States at Maryknoll. Father Robert Sheridan recalled strong words exchanged in 1926 between the superior general visiting in Hong Kong and some Maryknollers who wanted more funds for their mission work. Father James A. Walsh was obviously hurt and cut short the debate by warning them not to "suck dry the breasts of Mother Knoll."[26] Similarly, in 1927 and 1928, Meyer complained bitterly about the continuous curtailment of funds for catechists and warned James A. Walsh several times that, if prolonged, it could jeopardize the Church's growth in Maryknoll territories: "I have already mentioned how the number of catechists has decreased resulting in a difference between 370 adult baptisms in 1924 and only 187 in 1927 in the Kongmoon mission."[27]

The following year James E. Walsh, the vicar apostolic of Kongmoon, reported sadly to the superior general that the funds received from Maryknoll for the period of July 1928 to July 1929 for catechist salaries had reached an all-time low of $3,000 against a budget which called for $15,000.[28] Fortunately for James A. Walsh, the second half of 1929 brought a definite improvement in Maryknoll finances because after almost nine years of construction, the main body of the major seminary on Sunset Hill was completed. Therefore, more funds became available for the China missions. At the same time, allocations increased sharply from pontifical institutions such as the Societies for the Propagation of the Faith, the Holy Childhood, and the Work of St. Peter the Apostle. By the mid–1930s, each Maryknoll mission territory could plan on approximately $30,000 per year from Rome.[29] Yet there were some lean years such as 1935, when James E. Walsh had a budget deficit of $15,300. If the Maryknoll center had not sent $10,000 in emergency aid, he would have been forced to close the institutional work of his vicariate and to dismiss most of the 100 catechists.[30]

Throughout the years of the Depression, Maryknoll headquarters faced intermittent difficulties which several times forced them to reduce or suspend the missioners' viatique. Yet as Francis Ford and James E. Walsh explained, the missionary work and building program of each mission territory were never severely affected for a long period of time because most of the operational costs were met by funds from Rome and the unrelenting generosity of American Catholics for specific mission needs. In his budget report of 1933, Ford pointed out that, with the exception of viatiques, Maryknoll had provided for less than 30 percent of his operating budget. The rest had come mainly from Rome, private gifts, and, to a very small extent, from contributions from Chinese Catholics.[31]

This combination of factors explained the definite turnaround in the catechist program. In the Kongmoon vicariate, the number of catechists, which had dwindled from 90 to 66 between 1925 and 1929, suddenly increased to 86 in 1930 and then grew steadily to reach a high of 135 in 1939.

More funds became available not only for hiring more catechists but also for implementing Father Meyer's plan for year-round catechist schools. The summer school established by Meyer in Kochow became Maryknoll's first year-round catechist school and was opened in February 1929 under the direction of veteran catechist Yip. Within the next three years, permanent catechist schools, three of which were founded by Meyer, were opened in each Maryknoll territory under the direction of a native priest, Sister, or catechist. In mid-October 1931, he put Father Ley, a Chinese priest from Canton, in charge of catechist training in Pingnam. The first class of students had not yet graduated when the Kweilin area was added to Wuchow. Meyer immediately planned the opening of another school for this Mandarin-speaking area. Following his ordination in May 1933, Father Thomas Tao, the first native priest of the Wuchow-Kweilin region, became the director of the new school in Laipo.[32]

In the Wuchow territory, the men's section of the school at Pingnam was a model. No candidate was admitted without at least four to six years of schooling (the highest level of formal education available in the countryside at that time) and a letter of recommendation from his pastor. Catechists were usually recruited from the most promising catechumens or from among old Catholic families. The position itself was attractive to rural Chinese, offering a monthly salary of $15 and the status of a "teacher." After signing a contract binding him to serve the Church, he normally underwent a two-year course embracing "Christian doctrine, Scripture, apologetics with open forum and discussion, Church history, liturgy, homiletics, chant and ceremonies, Catholic Action, teaching methods and duties of catechists, Chinese literature, arithmetic, geography and history."[33] Graduates worked first as primary school teachers or assistant catechists. If they fulfilled their duties with zeal, displayed signs of deepening spiritual life, attended the annual summer course, and scored well on periodic examinations, after two or three years they would be given more responsibility and receive a raise.[34] A well-trained experienced catechist was invaluable to a missioner, especially a novice to China. One new arrival recalled being told by his superiors:

> "We'll send [Father] Sprinkle there because the catechist in Watlam is the finest catechist that ever existed on the face of South China. He can do everything that has to be done. . . ." He was an old experienced catechist, not a young man. Whatever he told me to do, we did.[35]

The Need for Women Catechists

Maryknollers found that the separation of sexes rigidly observed in the Chinese countryside prevented priests and male catechists from instructing women and had resulted in a predominantly male Catholic population. One of the early decisions made by the American missioners, therefore, was to avoid baptizing only men. Experience showed that this practice rarely led to the conversion of whole families or villages because non-Catholic wives continued to maintain traditional practices in the homes and controlled the children. Although Maryknollers wanted to concentrate on baptizing families and villages as units, they were hampered by a lack of women catechists. Diaries contain numerous laments about delaying baptisms of men converts until one of the few women catechists was available to instruct their wives and children.[36] A letter by Meyer reprinted in the December 1932 issue of *The Field Afar* forcefully presented the need for women catechists.

> I do not hesitate to estimate that the number of Catholics in this part of China would at least today be no less than double if the baptism of the wife had always been secured at the same time as that as her husband. When this is not the case, the little ones grow up under the influence of their pagan mother and after the father's death the family is once [again] wholly pagan. For the instruction of the women, catechists of their own sex are necessary. The most successful of these women catechists go into the homes and sit beside the mothers as they make shoes, mend clothes or pull flax for thread and twine. While lending a helping hand, they unfold the beauties of the faith and teach them the catechism and prayers, a few words at a time.[37]

In view of the need for more female catechists, it is surprising to find that, of the five catechist schools, only the one in Pingnam originally had a women's section. Fushun never developed a training program for female catechists, and the others rarely went beyond offering an annual summer program or individual coaching by the Maryknoll Sisters.[38] The difficulty faced by the mission heads was to find a woman with enough education, spiritual depth, and experience to direct the women's section of a year-round catechist school. A female director was necessary not only because of the segregation of sexes, but also to direct a program specifically geared to evangelizing the female population.

Since its introduction in China in the late seventeenth century by M.E.P. missioners, the institution of Catholic Virgins had provided the bulk of the female catechists. These women were bound only by a private vow of chastity and instead of living in a community like most religious Sisters, they usually stayed with their relatives, working among the closely knit entourage of the village and those nearby. Most Maryknollers, like Father James McDermott, pastor of Toishan, were most appreciative of the work of these female helpers:

> She touches all phases of human as well as spiritual understanding. She acts as the Ladies' Auxiliary, the Altar Society, the Ladies' Charity, the Bureau of Social Service and the Travellers' Aid Society. Were it not for [her] help, the missioner would find himself severely handicapped.[39]

By and large, however, the virgins were too few in number to instruct the growing number of catechumens and too uneducated to direct a catechist school. In fact, by the early 1920s they had become an aging group with practically no new recruits. Missioners preferred to direct young females considering a life of serving the Church toward the more structured institutions of the emerging native religious congregations. For the most part, these congregations failed, however, to take over the tasks of the virgins because their constitutions prevented Sisters from living in isolated villages without sacraments or the protection of convent walls.

Once again, Father Meyer was first with a solution. He laid the foundations for a native sisterhood whose members would be catechists and eventually take over the training of female catechists. In his plan, religious catechists would coordinate the work from the parish and help the priest to complete instruction prior to baptism and confirmation, while lay catechists would be the roving wing of the female apostolate in remote villages.

In 1931 Bishop Fourquet of Canton loaned Meyer a veteran Chinese priest of 20 years' experience as well as two experienced native Sisters to enable the new permanent catechist school at Pingnam to include both female and male sections. In September 1935, Maryknoll Sisters arrived in Wuchow and, under the supervision of Sister Moira Riehl, assumed the direction of the women's catechist school.[40]

Since country girls received very little schooling prior to the mid–1930s, most women candidates spent the first six to twelve months practicing reading and writing. The catechetical training *per se* lasted one year. Unlike men catechists who had to learn to preach and instruct large audiences, women catechists were taught to make use of daily contacts and conversations to instill the rudiments of faith in the female population. They also became skilled teachers who could explain the catechism and the prayers to small groups of uneducated girls and women who could commit them to memory. Upon completion of the course, they were usually assigned to a parish and worked in designated outstations. They came back to the parish on a monthly basis to discuss plans and programs with the local missioner, to go to confession, to attend mass, and also to receive their salaries.[41]

Within a few years, the combination of year-round catechist schools and the summer enrichment program provided Meyer with an impressive group of well-trained, faithful catechists. In 1933 he had only 25 men and 15 women for the combined territory of Wuchow and Kweilin. Three years later, graduates from his two catechist schools had swelled the ranks to 65 men and 34 women, while the Catholic population had more than doubled from 2,565 to 5,891.[42]

The Wuchow Method

The Legacy of Bernard Meyer

When Father Meyer arrived in Wuchow in early 1927, there were only 322 Catholics in the whole territory. Five years later he received a message from Propaganda Fide congratulating him for reporting five times as many. In fact, this rapid growth was only the prelude to an even more impressive expansion. In the next nine years, there was an average increase of 900 Catholics per year. Although the last four years of World War II brought this boom to a standstill, the increase resumed with renewed vigor in late 1946 and averaged more than 2,000 new Catholics a year. In 1950 when the Communists brought Church activities to a halt, the Catholic population in Wuchow had reached a total of 19,871. Behind this success stood Meyer's emphasis on catechists and village catechumenates.

For Meyer, catechists were the indispensable key to a successful program of evangelization in the Chinese context. Their role was crucial at all three stages of Christian development: conversion, instruction, and nurture.

In areas with few Catholics, the catechists were traveling salesmen for the Church who brought in candidates, known as catechumens, desiring religious instruction. Catechists were also teachers who shared the life of the catechumens and prepared them for baptism. Finally catechists were the ones who followed the new Catholics, continuously building their faith.[43] These various roles of the catechists are well reflected in the statistics of Table 1. As a result of the sharp increase in well-trained catechists following the establishment of the Pingnam catechist school in 1931, more catechumens were enrolled, instructed, examined, and baptized.

After 1940, Maryknoll's mission activities were curtailed owing to the chaos of the Japanese bombings and offensives in Kwangsi as well as the difficulties of securing funds from outside of China. The catechist program was severely affected by the repeated closures of the school and the laying-off of catechists. Between 1941 and 1946, the number of catechists fell from 116 to 20, almost halting the number of catechumens enrolled and baptized. It is impossible, however, to assess how much of the decline in conversions resulted from the war and how much was owing to the reduction in the number of catechists. More revealing was the effect of the lack of catechists on the Catholic population. After taking into account numerical changes which occurred because of Catholic refugees pouring in and out of the territory, it is clear that in some years the Catholic population in the Wuchow vicariate, deprived of the support of catechists, dropped as new Catholic communities apostasized en masse. After the war, when the

Table 1

Catechists and the Conversion Movement in the Wuchow Territory (Annual June Reports)

Year	Catechists	Enrolled catechumens[a]	Baptisms[h]	Catholics leaving church	Catholic population
1927	9	550	42	—[c]	322
1928	11	702	17	—	365
1929	16	800	304	—	721
1930	—	—	—	—	—
1931	28	1,335	475	—	1,448
1932	—	1,225	315	—	1,689
1933[d]	40	3,063	384	5	2,565
1934[d]	—	4,907	814	—	3,306
1935[d]	78	2,196	1,114	0	4,601
1936[d]	99	3,132	1,245	71	5,891
1937[d]	—	1,918	944	—	7,045
1938	99	1,585	1,226	—	7,493
1939	103	1,644	1,028	0	8,588
1940	116	979	1,069	0	9,745
1941	79	753	592	0	10,344
1942	50	385	703	955	10,169
1943	34	156	157	31	11,922
1944	27	162	138	146	12,072
1945	—	—	—	—	—
1946	20	56	49	238	11,422
1947	66	7,953	963	—	12,122
1948	176	7,323	2,235	—	14,414
1949	248	4,588	2,380	—	16,805
1950	188	3,811	2,034	1	19,871

Source: FARC, 38-07, Wuchow Reports, 1927-1950. Annuaire des missions catholiques de Chine, 1934-1940.

[a]Refers to the number of catechumens who, at the end of the year, were still under instruction or waiting for the opening of a catechumenate.

[b]Refers only to adult Chinese who converted from a non-Christian belief.

[c]No data available.

[d]Statistics are for the combined territories of Wuchow and Kweilin.

number of catechists soared to new heights, the conversion movement accelerated and no additional apostasies were reported.

The Village Catechumenate

In 1929 Father Meyer launched a program in the Wuchow territory which he labeled "village catechumenates." His idea was to make religious in-

struction available to large numbers of village people in their own surroundings. This method contrasted with the more traditional one of bringing catechumens to the missioners' residence for a four- to five-week
intensive course.

Although Meyer acknowledged that his plan removed catechumens
from the missioners' close supervision and the daily exposure to the religious life of an established parish, he thought that these shortcomings
were a small price to pay for much greater advantages. In the village
catechumenate, he explained, the people acquired their habits of daily
prayer, Sunday observance, and Christian life in general within their own
familiar environment. Moreover, they were able to attend classes in larger
numbers than was possible when the catechumenate was held at the
parish. Larger Catholic communities were formed and the missioner was
relieved of the burden of maintaining on his compound separate catechumenate buildings for men and women. Finally, a definite pattern emerged
which showed that village catchumenates were preferable to parish catechumenates because they caught the attention of people miles away from
the mission residence. Father Mark Tennien recalled how, in his parish:

> The news that Blue Cloud Village was joining some religion people had
> never heard about got bruited around. The village roadside stand run by
> Uncle Wong, a devout convert, was Radio City. Gossipy old women in faded
> blue [pants] stopped for a bowl of rice gruel and gobbled up the news to carry
> along. Curious farmers on their way to market sat a while under the straw
> roof and pulled at their long bamboo pipes, asking Uncle Wong about the
> new religion. Road peddlers posed and sat on their heels sipping a cup of tea
> while they pried news loose to carry around on their round of villages. As the
> months of study went on, wandering crowds dropped in for a "look-see" [at
> the catechumenate]. There were government officials, village heads, and
> high school students. There were farmer boys, shopkeepers and idlers. This
> was spontaneous spreading of the Good News. . . .[44]

Interested villages formally signified their desire for religious instruction by addressing a signed petition to the missioner. Once their request
was acknowledged, people were officially enrolled as catechumens and
entered a period of six to twelve months' probation. Tennien was convinced that the period of probation, useful as a time of preparation, could
not be extended for too long.

> If the interest is high, and the people are readied and clamouring for instruc-
> tion, it may be fatal to let the right moment pass. We have all learned in
> sorrow that grace is sometimes passing and not returning.[45]

This waiting period was often necessary because petitions for instruction outnumbered the availability of catechists. Moreover, it allowed the missioner to send an experienced catechist to appraise the sincerity of those asking for instruction, to provide them an overview of Church doctrine and to give them an opportunity to call off the catechumenate without losing face.

During these visits, explained Tennien, the catechist spent much time refuting rumors against the Church and building up a desire for religious instruction.

> Those who are against us follow on our heels, telling [the new catechumens] that the Catholic Church would gouge out their eyes at death to make medicine. Our enemies whisper that the Church is using the doctrine as a wedge to take away the land from the people who join the Church. The Church is disrespectful, they say. It cuts away the religion of their ancestors to whom they have bowed to from time unknown. . . . The false stories must be debated away, the fears must be calmed, the doubts must be solved, the questions must be answered, and the hunger for the [Catholic] religion must be whetted. When built up properly the people come begging and clamoring for their instruction.[46]

Under Meyer's plan, the probation period was the first of three consecutive steps to transform large numbers of converts into strong Catholic communities and avoid later indifference and apostasy. Next came the catechumenate course under the direction of experienced catechists. The final step was a careful follow-up over several months after baptism.[47]

Father Tennien was one of the early Maryknollers who implemented the village catechumenate with Meyer. He was able, by the late 1940s, to refine it into a technique which led to amazing numbers of conversions in his parish of Shumkai. Above all, Tennien stressed the importance of at least one outstanding catechist per station. In his case, he had Ue Chi Cheung, familiarly called Big Six. A man endowed with a pleasant personality, good speaking ability, and some sense of business, Ue used his own knowledge of Chinese medicine and the rudiments of Western medicine learned from Tennien to make contacts among the Chinese in the countryside. Tennien remembered one of his catechist's biggest successes in the early 1930s.

> He hired a small shop in the market town six miles from Wuchow, hanging out his sign as a native doctor. Loquacious Big Six soon had crowds waiting for treatment, and at the same time listening to his chats about the Catholic Church. In a few months, he had a class ready to study in preparation for baptism. In addition, Big Six roved around the countryside,

visiting patients and interesting [more] people in the Catholic Church. He loved his busy days spent curing the sick and opening up places for the study of the doctrine.[48]

In late fall of 1946, when Tennien was given the task of opening new stations in Paklow and Shumkai, two county seats some 70 miles apart, he left Ue in Shumkai while he settled in Paklow. While Tennien's efforts brought only a few inquiries for the Church, his catechist's medical work and gentle persuasion generated much interest. Within a few months, Ue gathered over one thousand signatures in the village of Blue Cloud, some five miles from Shumkai. In March 1947 a catechumenate opened at Blue Cloud, and its success was the beginning of a tremendous conversion movement which, over the next three years, brought the number of Catholics in the Shumkai area from zero to 2,871.

To handle such large numbers of catechumens at one time, Tennien further refined Meyer's original technique. He believed that evangelization methods should be updated "in an age of streamlining and mass production." He impressed upon his catechists that in "going out for souls, they are to fish with a net, not with a hook and line."[49] Consequently, no petition with less than 200 signatures was accepted. Catechumenates lasted four months and as many as possible were held in a year to keep up with the demands from villages.

In order not to interfere with the people's daily work, religious instruction took place in the evening after people had finished work in the fields, and had their baths and supper. Classes were held every evening for two hours. The candidates over seven years of age were divided into groups of 35 to 50, and every three groups formed a unit under the supervision of an experienced catechist.[50] Meeting with each group separately, the catechist gave them a half-hour explanation of the doctrine, devotions, and prayers included in the lesson. He or she also kept the attendance records and administered examinations.

After the catechist's daily explanation, leaders in each group would take over and teach the fundamentals of the catechism and the prayers. These instructors, male and female, had been selected during the probation period and given a special training course of one month to prepare them to assist in teaching catechism. They received baptism together with the other members of their group at the end of the catechumenate and the best among them were selected for the catechist school.

Tennien called the end of the first month of instruction "D-Day" or "Decision Day." On that day catechumens signified their decision to carry on toward baptism by throwing all signs of non-Christian beliefs out of their homes.

We started out in procession. At each convert's house, we stopped before the door. The catechumens started to chant the Come, Holy Ghost, the Our Father and the Creed while I read the prayers for the blessing of Catholic homes. The catechists and the people of the house undertook the spiritual housecleaning. Good luck papers were torn down, pictures of the god of fertility were scraped off doors, joss stick racks and bowls were hurled down. Then they led me through the rooms to sprinkle them with holy water. Simple country folk feared the devil's harm to their livestock so next they ushered me to the shed. Wading through the manure, I gave generous aspersion of "chase-devil water" over the water buffalo or a yellow cow that lay there unconcernedly, or pigs that scrambled into the corners with frightened grunts.[51]

By the end of that first month, attrition and refusal to cast out the traditional religious beliefs usually reduced the number of catechumens by one-third. The next three months were devoted to the study of the catechism in preparation for the reception of the sacraments of baptism, confession, and communion. At the end of the course, the missioner and the catechists reviewed each file to determine if the candidates fulfilled three requirements: real faith, solid religious instruction, and the prospect of living a Christian life. The selection process was rigorous, and usually only half of the catechumens were called to receive the sacraments. All those whose attendance had been poor or who had not scored well for their age bracket were rejected with their children and told they needed further study if they wanted to be considered. Eliminated also were those who had indulged in non-Christian practices during the past three months. Girls engaged to non-Catholics—even if they displayed a strong faith—could not be baptized either, because the bishop refused to give dispensations for Catholic girls to marry non-Catholics. Similarly, in areas where there were too few Catholics, Tennien refused to baptize girls over fourteen because of the high probability of their marriage to non-Catholics.

Consequently, only about one-third of the people who began a village catechumenate were baptized at the end of the four months. Even by counting those who were delayed and required an extra month or two of instruction, the number rarely came to one-half of those who started. However, Tennien was not dismayed by these statistics; he considered them a credit to the commitment of those who persevered.

Only one-third, or one-half at best, are baptized. This is not surprising under

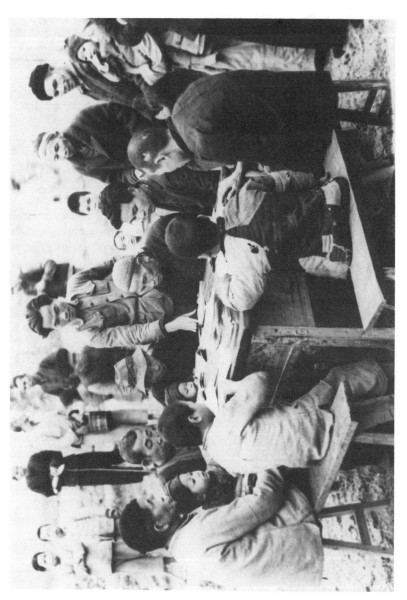

Fig. 2. A graduate of Monsignor Meyer's catechist school leading a village catechumenate for men and boys in Wuchow. Maryknoll Photo Library.

Fig. 3. Decision Day in the parish of Shumkai in Wuchow in 1949. Father Mark Tennien removing joss sticks and "superstitions" from homes of catechumens preparing for baptism. Maryknoll Photo Library.

the circumstances. The grind is every evening for four months and after a hard day's work in the field. These people are for the most part unlettered, and almost half of them have to learn to read as they learn the catechism. If the weather is cold or rainy or the walk is far to where the group studies and prays, it is easy to start skipping and then drop out. Unless the catechist is exceptional and has a personality that sparkles, the sing-song study is tiresome and dry, and the evening is dull. And so, the course is a severe test, and only a person of character or one who grasps the faith prematurely will stick it through.[52]

For the Maryknoll missioners, the baptizing of so many candidates at the same time was both exhausting and exhilarating. Tennien's vivid description of the 235 baptisms he administered in a 24-hour period at Blue Cloud Village is a masterpiece which needs to be appreciated in its entirety.

On the evening of June 28, I started the ceremony and baptized some 30 [candidates]. Next morning after the mass, I started again and baptized until noon. The cook brought a pot of boiling water for me to add sugar and coffee grounds. Stirring a few minutes, I had a bracing pot of black coffee to drink, then went at the task again. It meant racing against a deadline if all the candidates ready were to receive the sacrament on the Saints Peter and Paul day. The native Sisters and catechists got the people in line and prompted their answers. They also handed me the blessed salt, the holy oils, and wiping cotton, unbuttoned the jacket or lifted the pigtails for the anointing. Again at the proper time they handed me the pitcher of baptismal water and the receiving bowl, then one in the back of the line went along bending each head for the pouring. All this quickened the task. Without lifting my eyes from reading the ritual, my hand reached out for the salt, the holy oils, the white veil cloth or the candle. Came 5 o'clock and we stopped for evening rice and a spell from the all-day standing. Smoking a cigarette I watched the shadows stretch grotesquely across Blue Cloud Valley while the sun slowly tucked itself in for the night behind a huge dark blue mountain. But my day's work was not yet done. I was baptizing them a group at a time. Two groups were still left. We started on the first group by the twilight, then a catechist held the lantern to shine on the ritual while I read. The clock had reached 10:30 when we finished with number 235 and I saw the moon's soft light painting Blue Cloud Valley in silver. That night Blue Cloud was consecrated to the Immaculate Heart of Mary.[53]

During his first 10 years in Kwangtung and Kwangsi, Meyer encountered many Catholics who had been converted under French missioners and had since fallen away or turned into "lukewarm" believers. In his opinion, this sad situation resulted not so much from any lack of faith on the part of the converts nor from speedy or superfluous instruction by the

French missioners, but rather from the absence of a system to sustain the Catholic faith and practices of the new converts. Therefore, Meyer established a program of ongoing formation for the new Catholics which spanned an entire year, from the catechumenate through confirmation. The topics of the two-month course held in the villages covered not only confirmation, but the three remaining sacraments, ordination, marriage, and unction for the sick and dying.

Meyer's system provided for a careful nurturing of faith, the building up of solid Christian habits, and the smooth integration of the new Catholics into the religious life of the parish. Sister Dorothy Rubner recalled regular visits of priests and Sisters to converts in the parish of Szwong:

> We constantly visited in the villages and created reasons for them to come to church by having special religious ceremonies, special remembrances, special feast days; or just encouraging them and showing them that their family would be blessed and that they would prosper if they gave up that time in order to come to church, and they did find that that happened. . . . We spent our days with the people, either in the catechumenate or in the villages, visiting the families, bringing the records up to date or searching out the children who needed instruction, seeing if there were any people who had family problems and needed help, somebody sick who needed visiting, somebody who died in the family or needed consoling, or funeral arrangements to be made, helping or participating in weddings or baptisms. Our daily life was completely absorbed in the people with whom we were working. . . .[54]

From the beginning, each new Catholic village was grouped with other nearby villages to form a regional unit with a central chapel where the missioner went to say Sunday mass at regular intervals. In addition to these frequent contacts with Catholics of neighboring villages, there were also large meetings of all parishioners at the compound for the four feasts of Christmas, Easter, Pentecost, and Assumption.

Special attention to the village and its individuals also continued after confirmation. All regional units were supervised by an experienced catechist who visited each village frequently. He or she also accompanied the missioner, who spent a day or two in the villages of the unit in the fall, winter, and spring.

These periods of instruction in the sacraments and the essentials of Christian life also provided training and experience for catechists. After the original catechumenate, the experienced catechists moved on to another village and one or two catechists stayed behind with any available Sisters to establish a solid Christian life in the village. At the same time, the group leaders from the catechumenate were sent back to the parish for advanced training. If successful, they were promoted to the rank of assistant catechist and returned to their villages to complete the training of

Fig. 4. Father Mark Tennien baptizing converts in 1948 in Wuchow, assisted by a Chinese Sister. Maryknoll Photo Library.

those catechumens whose baptisms had been delayed. After completing additional summer courses, the best assistant catechists were, in turn, promoted to the rank of regular fulltime catechist. Others were used as "flying catechists"; they traveled to outstations during the weekend to preside at Sunday services, but were free to pursue their own affairs during the rest of the week. Meyer's well-thought-out plan, which was further refined by Father Tennien, provided a continual source of catechists and nurtured the lives of the Catholics as well.[55]

The Kaying Method

The Legacy of Francis Ford

At the time Father Meyer launched his method of evangelization in the Wuchow territory, his classmate, Father Francis Ford was unfolding a different plan to reach the non-Christians in the Kaying territory. While the Wuchow method put most of the responsibility for direct evangelization and instruction of converts on the shoulders of catechists, Ford's method tended to place more of the burden on the missioners themselves. Instead of keeping teams of two or three priests in large parishes serving distant outstations, Ford preferred to send his men to small parishes where they would have a chance to live closer to the people: "Our general policy is to build up a strong Christianity *near* the church for Sunday mass."[56] When the parish grew to the point that some converts lived a day or more away from the church, Ford always looked for an opportunity to make the nucleus of a new parish. Through this process, the seven original parishes of the Kaying territory had grown to 23 by 1941.

Equally innovative was the position in mission work Ford gave to the Maryknoll Sisters. Normally confined to live in the shadow of their convent at the parish center, Sisters had been usually assigned to institutional work such as schools, orphanages, hospitals, and dispensaries. Under Ford, they were able to leave the sanctuary of their convents for the first time, travel "two by two" like the early apostles, and make direct contact with the Chinese in the most remote outposts of a parish.[57]

Although Ford emphasized reaching out to contact the people, he positioned the catechumenate at the parish center under the direct teaching of Maryknoll priests and Sisters rather than in the outstations. Ford involved his missioners in all phases of the conversion process and required that most mission efforts and funds be spent on direct evangelization. He strongly denounced the mission custom in China of initiating charitable works and continuing to support them. In outlining the mission work policy in his territory, he stressed "the primacy of evangelical work over school projects or asylums or even more intensive parochial activities" as his "norm."[58] To this end, he avoided building institutions and concentrated on establishing the Church as a community of believers with the hope that the community would in turn help itself and provide for its own needs.

Since there could be no Christian communities without converts, Ford identified "direct evangelization [as] the missioner's work *par excellence.*" In his talks to Maryknoll men he constantly reminded them that their vocation was to be:

> ... primarily a *vox et praeterea nihil,*—a voice in the wilderness, a messenger of God, an apostle with a commission. ... A man who simply administers the sacraments and superintends the temporalities of a mission has not qualified as a missioner. A missioner is something active; he *conveys* a message *to* men; his activity pertains to the essence of his career.[59]

To the Maryknoll Sisters, Ford gave similar directives reminding them that to qualify as missioners, they should become experts at making contacts:

> A "contact" Sister is expansive, expressive, exhilarating and exhibitive; in common language, a person large-hearted, ready-tongued, easily pleased and not dismayed by crowds. ... As contact visitor to pagan women, she literally penetrates into the inner courts where superstition has its firmest foothold; she attacks the enemy at his strongest fortress and until this has fallen, it is vain to hope for a solid Catholic family.[60]

The methods originated by Ford and Meyer are similar in their approach to the evangelization of male Chinese. The priest and his catechist formed a team: one, the leader; the other, his "auxiliary" lay missioner. Ford defined the catechist essentially as the "contact man" with non-Catholics, but would not tolerate his reduction to a simple doorman. He required that this "lay helper in the apostolate" spend "a definite number of hours [daily] in active contact work." The catechist opened the way for the Chinese to be approached by the priest.[61]

At the same time Ford cautioned his missioners not to delegate to the catechist what should be done *ex officio* by the pastor, especially in their dealings with Chinese Catholics.

> A pastor should never be second fiddle to a catechist. How often is the priest

content to busy himself in the sacristy while the catechist is outside explaining the doctrine to the people? To a pagan onlooker which of the two would appear to be the head man—the one in the sacristy or the one at the altar rail?[62]

The Maryknoll Sisters and the Female Catechists

Ford's approach to the evangelization of female Chinese proved to be most innovative. In selecting Maryknoll Sisters to spearhead this apostolate, the head of the Kaying territory tried something without precedent in the mission history of the Catholic Church. Together with the Sisters, he refined what became known as the Kaying method. It was not only highly successful in converting women, but it also revolutionized the role of religious women in the work of evangelization.

When the first group of Sisters disembarked at Yeungkong in 1922, Ford had nothing more in mind than putting them in charge of what had traditionally been the responsibility of Sisters all over China: a school, an orphanage, a house for a few old folks and blind girls, and some dispensary work. However something happened which he had not anticipated. The Sisters' arrival aroused much more interest among the local population than the presence of the male missioners. A year later, on the occasion of Mother Mary Joseph's first visit to China, he described the special attraction of the Sisters for women and children and alluded for the first time to the important role religious women could fill in apostolic work.

> Mother Mary Joseph saw China from the inside of the kitchens. The interior of the family quarters and smiled her way into the hearts of the womenfolk. She saw family life as we cannot see it. . . . I always thought it was the foreign face and clothes that frightened children, but I look and dress more Chinese than the Reverend Mother did, and yet they ran to her and lost their bashfulness. Her whole trip emphasized the hold our Sisters will have on Chinese women and the utter need of such influence to gain these women's hearts.[63]

When Ford shared his views with Mother Mary Joseph, he discovered that she too envisioned a life of apostolic work for her Sisters. Her approval opened the way for the Maryknoll Sisters' direct apostolate in China. As a start, Ford tried to reduce the institutional responsibilities of the Sisters in Yeungkong and encouraged them to multiply their neighborhood contacts among women. Finally in March 1924, Ford started "something new in China" by taking Sisters Mary Rose Leifels and Mary Lawrence Foley on an extended mission trip,

> I have asked Mother Mary Joseph for permission to take two of the Sisters
> on trips into the country villages. Mother said this kind of work is what she
> had visioned the Sisters as doing here in China. Although it may seem a bit
> novel, it is surely necessary, and I can see the time when the Sisters will take
> charge of the womenfolk just as we do the men and boys. Then—we shall
> simply jump along in conversions.[64]

For a whole week the two Sisters and their female catechist, Rosa,
accompanied Ford and his assistant, Father Maurice Gleason. The Sisters'
house diary described them proudly as "'our missioners,' the first [Mary-
knoll] Sisters to make a trip to the interior for the sole purpose of doing
missionary work."[65]

In each outstation, while the Fathers administered the sacraments and
met with the men, the Sisters spent their time with the women: they
visited in their homes, mingled with them during Rosa's daily instruction,
and stayed for chats before and after the evening prayers. In their report,
the two Sisters described themselves as two "happy missioners" who
experienced a week of sleeping on Chinese beds, eating Chinese food, and
speaking the Chinese language, and concluded that "we were somewhat
tired, very dirty but happy for the privilege of this mission visit. We had
missed Sunday mass this morning but that too is included in mission
experiences."[66]

The excitement of Sisters Mary Rose and Mary Lawrence was soon
shared by the other Sisters in Yeungkong. This first mission trip was
followed by many other distant visitations during which Ford gave his
attention to the men and boys and the Sisters organized the care of the
women and children.

The recall of the Sisters to the safety of Hong Kong following the
antiforeign incidents of June 1925 in Canton and the assignment of Ford to
Kaying in the fall of the same year put an end to the experiment. If
Yeungkong served as the cradle of the direct apostolate for the Maryknoll
Sisters, it was within the boundaries of this new territory that Ford's
plans for the Sisters reached fruition. However, unsettled conditions in
Kaying, difficulties regarding church buildings and property, and a scarcity of financial resources and personnel forced him to postpone his plan for
nine years. Finally in 1934 he invited the Maryknoll Sisters to Hakkaland
for the exclusive purpose of evangelizing the women. His request received
the full approval of the Maryknoll Sisters' leadership. Sister Mary Paul
McKenna, the China superior, saw it as a better opportunity for the
Sisters to realize their missionary vocation:

> Monsignor Ford invites us to the Kaying mission as missioners—not only as

Sisters for this or that work. Other openings such as the orphanage at Loting or the school at Yeungkong set up a definite line rather than a wide-open door for mission activity. Having the broader outline, more on the basis of the [Maryknoll] men will give us the broader viewpoint which will make us *more truly missioners*—foreign missioners to a pagan people.[67]

Mother Mary Joseph gave Ford all the Sisters he requested.

I am anxious to give you the full number of Sisters you desire; for, this particular phase of work has always been dearest to my heart. I believe it is our essential missionary work, along with the training of native Sisters.[68]

The nature of the apostolate Ford had in mind for the Sisters was radically different. Their purpose was not to supervise asylums, hospitals, or schools; they should not perform medical or charity work, or engage in any educational project. Their sole aim was "direct evangelization," leading women to embrace Catholicism, instructing them for baptism, and watching over them during their first years as new Catholics. This contact with non-Christians, catechumens, and new Catholics sometimes entailed indirect works of charity, but more as an opening for direct evangelization than as an end in itself.

This new approach responded to the deepest aspirations of the young Maryknoll Sisters. In 1935 when 14 Sisters were assigned to China, Sister Louise Kroeger remembers how excited she was to be among the four sent to Kaying. Upon hearing the news, she said, "We jumped and screamed and shouted because Bishop Ford's mission was always our ambition, especially among the young Sisters. . . . I just never felt that there should be such happiness."[69] In the home novitiate at the Knoll, Mother Mary Joseph was constantly showered with requests to be assigned to the Kaying mission. In 1936 she wrote to Ford, "The Sisters are most enthusiastic over their work in Kaying and the ones at home are all clamouring to be assigned to what seems to be the ideal life for one who is called to missionary work."[70]

The future of the Kaying method of direct evangelization by the Sisters remained uncertain, however, because it was only an experiment the Holy See could discontinue at any time. Finally, in March 1939, Cardinal Pietro Fumasoni-Biondi, the prefect of the Sacred Congregation for the Propagation of the Faith, wrote a letter to Mother Mary Joseph, telling her of Rome's approval.

I wish you to know that I believe your greatest accomplishments lie before you through your direct cooperation in the conversion of non-Christian souls. I am aware of the courage and devotion which many Maryknoll Sisters have displayed in the work of conversion, particularly in the vicariate of Kaying, where they have gone from house to house among the people and they have proven valuable helpers to the Fathers in reaching the non-Christians. Let us hope that this work may grow and that God may bless it with abundant fruit.[71]

When Ford learned of the letter, he jubilantly told his missioners:

Roma locuta est. Rome considers the greatest accomplishments of the Sisters will result, not from institutional work, but from direct cooperation in reaching non-Christians. This spontaneous approbation on the part of Rome has resolved whatever misgivings I may have had on the experiment. Rome has gone out of its way to orientate the work of the Maryknoll Sisters, differentiating it from work hitherto considered the province of Sisters of older congregations. In short, Rome sets its approval on our thesis that foreign women can be missioners, just as foreign men can; or rather, it can be interpreted even more strongly as affirming that our Sisters should be direct missioners.[72]

Ford's innovative approach to the apostolate of Chinese women and children would not have been possible without the Sisters' complete cooperation and helpful suggestions. Sister Rosalia Kettl, one of the pioneer Sisters in the Kaying territory, played a major role in shaping some of Ford's ideas and in training newcomers for this type of apostolate. After 13 years of experience in Kaying, she was chosen in 1946 to introduce what had become known as the Kaying method in the territories of Wuchow and Kweilin.[73]

The Kaying technique was a multi-faceted type of direct apostolic work which involved: (a) making friendly contacts with Chinese women until they spontaneously asked about the Sisters' Catholic beliefs; (b) instructing women who were interested in pursuing the topic of Catholic faith; (c) visiting and providing follow-up instruction for newly baptized Catholics including courses toward confirmation and marriage; (d) visiting old Catholics, faithful as well as lapsed or lax Catholics; (e) conducting Sunday school classes; and (f) training catechists through class and field work.[74]

The distinctive feature of the Sisters' method of apostolate was that instead of residing in a large convent, they were sent two by two to live in a Chinese house which often was also used as the women's catechumenate. They were to visit and mingle with the women. Their small convents were not meant to provide an enclosure but to serve as a rallying point for old and new Catholics, non-Christians, and catechumens. Sister Madeline Sophie Karlon recalled the experience of living in a Chinese village, never far away from the constant pressure of the people:

If we were sitting at our window, the lady next door would come and talk to us through the window. Or the lady on the other side of the place would come and talk to us while we were eating our meal. By degrees we would get the people to understand not to bother us too much during a meal . . . but to come into the *tong* [parlor] and sit down and talk with us there.[75]

With two Sisters to a convent, the work was divided so that they took turns between staying at the station and going on overnight or extended trips. At the station the Sister visited the Chinese people nearby, gave religious instruction to catechumens, converts, and children, and organized community activities for the women in the parish.

The convent diary in Pettochai during the first six months of 1939 is representative of the many facets of the Sisters' work at the parish center:

January 2: Sister Luella went to Liouc Hong today to visit Song Ma in order to instruct her in preparation for first Holy Communion.

January 11: Sister Joseph Marian to Song Ha Ts'ai to visit Liao A Gni. This little girl has just been sold to a family living in the village. We hope to have her come to the catechism classes.

January 12: Sister Luella to Tch'ac Tchou T'ong, one of the near villages to visit some of the new Catholics there.

January 30: Visited P'ac Mou Ha today. Everyone in the village has planted opium. Sister spent all her time there explaining the Church's stand in the matter.

March 6: Four little girls arrived at the convent today, the first of a number we are going to teach for a period of three weeks in preparation for their first Holy Communion.

March 9: Five Catholics from four *poulou* [circa 15 miles] came in for a visit with us. . . . We enjoyed the news of their home happenings.

March 14: Sister Luella with about 25 women and children walked to Pan Kang, a village about 2 *poulou* from here to the funeral of an old lady recently baptized.

April 1: Sodality Sunday for the women.

April 9: Easter Sunday and we were busy welcoming Catholics from distant stations.

April 13–15: We got a crowd of people ready for confirmation.

May 6: We registered women who intend to come to our catechumenate which will open on the 10th.

June 7: We started teaching confession today, and the next few days will be busy ones on the sacraments, and getting the catechumens ready for baptism and first Holy Communion [on the 16th].

June 10: 47 little girls stayed three nights at the mission. They were called in for a special meeting to encourage a large sodality enrollment. While here, they heard doctrine talks, studied more prayers and enjoyed their meals and playtimes together.[76]

The work of the Sister going to more distant villages was equally varied. Sister Mary Paulita Hoffman recalled how visits were planned in her parish of Hingning.

We had a real good system. Father would say "I am going on visitation to this village and then this one and that one, etc." So the two Sisters would divide and one would go one time and the other would stay home. The Sister would always go first [before the priest]. She was something like John the Baptist—the forerunner who went ahead. We would notify the village of our coming the Sunday before. Upon arriving, the Sister and her catechist-companion would visit some homes to have everybody notified. That night at the meeting place we would give a doctrine renewal review of whatever liturgical season it was. It always ended up with a discussion of problems which had come up, what was the news, etc. [since the last visit]. That would go on until about 11 o'clock. Then after night prayers we would go to bed. The next day we would go out house-to-house visiting. We took notes of the very sick who needed the last sacraments, the girls who were going to be married, the babies who should be baptized. People would tell us that so-and-so was really interested in the doctrine. They would take us to visit these women. We would try to give them some information and to set up a time for later visits. Then on the second day that we had been there, Father would come in with a man catechist. We would give him all the information we had gotten by sitting around at night and around the kitchen stoves during the day. Father would have mass and stay to give people the sacraments and act upon our report while we went on to the next place.[77]

Sister Madeline Sophie Karlon recalled many incidents which made the Sisters' trips memorable. There was gracious hospitality even among the non-Catholic, including an old couple happy to give her the bedroom of their daughter-in-law who had gone home to her girlhood village. Alas, the inviting Chinese bed was also host to bedbugs. Karlon had a sleepless night, but being young of heart, she had a good laugh about this hapless adventure.

Another time the catechist, thinking that Sister Madeline Sophie would find the long day's walk tiring, hired a sedan chair to carry her. Sister recalled with amusement that the two porters had barely gone a mile and a half when they complained about her weight and refused to go further. She gladly finished the journey on foot. On other occasions, women offered to carry her on their backs over streams. Once her cook actually tried it but the two of them laughed so much as they forded the river that Sister almost fell in the water.

In a village where she was preparing children for confession and communion, she was awakened the first night by a loud crunching noise. She then remembered that the lady of the house had told her that the huge buffalo she had eyed warily the previous evening liked midnight snacks. As the noise grew louder and louder, she also recalled that her room served as storage for sweet potatoes. As she let out a series of shrieks, the lady chased out a small baby buffalo that had wandered in.

The Maryknoll Sisters recalled these stories so clearly because they often shared them with the village women to have a good laugh, break down barriers,and establish a friendly rapport.[78]

Their participation in the direct apostolate challenged the traditional chapel-oriented and community-structured prayer life of religious Sisters. In Kaying, the Sisters found that during the days and weeks of long isolation, often without sacraments, they needed a different kind of spirituality. Under these circumstances, Sister Rosalia Kettl and her companions regarded as particularly appropriate Mother Mary Joseph's decision to adopt the reading of the Divine Office[79] as the official prayer of the Sisters.

> I went to Kaying in 1933 and in 1936 we adopted the Divine Office. Mother's idea was that because so many of us would be alone many times, have nobody to pray with and perhaps not even have mass, we would have at least the "Prayer of the Church," the Divine Office, and therefore feel united with the universal Church.[80]

Meanwhile, Mother Mary Joseph prepared recruits in the novitiate at Maryknoll for a life that she foresaw as a delicate balance of contemplative prayer and mission activity. She liked to remind them that Maryknoll Sisters had been known first as Teresians because they aimed at following in the footsteps of the greatest woman mystic and "roving nun" of all times, St. Teresa of Avila:

> We soon learned that a missioner must be a contemplative in action. Faithfulness to times of prayer and trying to be constantly mindful of God's presence in our hearts were the foundation of this missionary life we had

chosen to follow, a life so busy that we often wondered how we could live at once a life of prayer and a life of extreme activity. St. Teresa obtained that gift for us, I truly believe, and so laid the foundation for our . . . life which combines perfectly the ways of prayer and activity.[81]

In Kaying this way of life was put to the test. Under the guidance of Ford and Sister Mary Imelda Sheridan, the Kaying superior, the Maryknoll Sisters developed a unique spirituality which, recalled Sister Thérèse (Marcelline) Grondin, they in turn passed on to the newly formed community of native Sisters.

[In Kaying] none of our "little houses" of those days—not even the formation center—had a chapel. I was taught and taught others accordingly that we should carry "our cloister" wherever we went, much as a snail carries its shell wherever it lives or moves about. We were to be living houses of prayer, so to speak, on the streets, over the mountain passes, wherever our work took us, inside or outside. We visited with God, not in the chapel, but as we sat alone in the garden or on the buses or on the back of bicycles. This was my introduction to incarnational prayer.[82]

Every time Ford addressed the Sisters, he emphasized the link between contemplative prayer and mission activity by reminding them of their role as contact persons. He stressed that he had invited them to Kaying primarily to "visit pagan homes." Ford said, "Sisters, I want you to go out to the villages. I know you're going to miss Mass, but your presence there is going to mean much more than what you give up in regard to the Mass for those people."[83]

Among the many stories of such visits, perhaps none is more telling than Sister Rosalia Kettl's account of one of her first attempts as a young Sister still struggling with the language.

We didn't know how to enter the homes because we didn't know anybody. Bishop Ford said we should go out at least once a day even if just to walk up and down, so we started. One day I was out walking and not knowing what to do, when I saw some beautiful flowers over a wall. They were kind of little lanterns [on a tree] so I thought I would go in and tell the family that their flowers were beautiful. But I really didn't know how to say that because I didn't know the language very well. I walked in and pointing to the tree, I said something. I don't remember what it was but, oh, they were just thrilled. They thought that I wanted to plant a tree! They went to the back of the house, dug up one of the smaller trees and gave it to me. In the meantime all kinds of people came around and we just sat but I couldn't say very much. Anyhow, I went home with the tree. We planted it and in our idealism we said that if that tree grew, that meant that our mission work would flourish.

Every day we watered the tree and every day we watched it and every day it grew and grew. So we were very happy missioners because we knew our work would flourish. I used to go back to that particular village because I had made some kind of an impression. After about a year's time, I invited some of the women to come and see us. I gave them a date and I said we were going to start talks about God and maybe they would like to learn something about this new religion. Nine of those people came. We started out with this little catechumenate and not one left! So the tree blossomed and they became quite an influential village in the faith, bringing in their neighbors. They were the first fruits of our apostolate there.[84]

Catechumenates in Kaying

Ford favored the center catechumenate or instruction at the parish compound for the religious instruction of groups of catechumens, rather than Meyer's method of village catechumenates. He saw at least four advantages to conducting instruction at the parish rather than in the catechumens' villages: (a) by bringing together people of different clans, the center catechumenate broke down the barriers of clannishness and was a practical application of the word "Catholic"; (b) it eased the integration of catechumens into the parish congregation by putting them in touch with Catholics who came regularly to church; (c) it facilitated the division of catechumens into several age groups and made teaching more effective; (d) above all, the catechumens experienced the link between the lessons they memorized, the omnipresence of God, and corporate liturgical worship as expressed in the mass. As Ford put it,

> The center catechumenate is not merely a school of doctrine where religious instruction is taught apart from worship, but a sort of vestibule to the Church where our people are prepared to meet God and learn what to say to Him, and what to think of Him.[85]

As a rule these six-week catechumenates took place twice a year, in the spring and in the fall after the rice was planted. The opening dates were always announced well ahead of time so that Catholics could urge their non-Catholic friends and relatives to register. Men and boys gathered under the pastor's direction in a building next to the rectory, while women, girls and small children studied with a Sister next to the convent. The catechumenates varied in size from as few as a dozen people to as many as fifty in each section. The priest and the Sister led most of the instruction, while men and women catechists helped as needed, especially with memorization drills.

One of the drawbacks of the parish catechumenate was that when candidates lived too far away to walk each day, their room and board was an expense of the parish. The cost amounted to about US$2.50 per person for the entire course. Catechumens usually contributed some firewood, peanut oil, vegetables, and other edibles from their gardens, but few among them could remain away from their secular jobs for such a long period of time and still pay for their sustenance.

The practice of feeding and housing catechumens during the period of instruction at the station was prevalent in China. If it was not handled properly, however, it produced "rice Christians," people who joined the Church for its material advantages. In Kaying, Ford guarded against rice Christians by submitting candidates to careful screening and serious instruction, and by refusing to prolong material support beyond the catechumenate period. Reflecting on her 13 years of direct apostolate in Kaying, Sister Frances Murphy said that she knew of many catechumens given rice to alleviate the burden caused on their family by their six-week absence. She also saw some of them leave before baptism, but she claims she never met a rice Christian.[86]

A contrasting account was given by Mrs. Cheuk Yee-Chiu, a convert, who recalled that in some parishes the missioner's charity often resulted in questionable Catholics:

> When the missionaries ran doctrine classes, they also provided people with meals and lodging to attract them. Some people were greedy and some were not. Some were genuinely looking for the good and some were not. Some stopped going to church after they were baptized. They were a different kind of Catholic.[87]

Another convert, Peter Chum of Kweilin, acknowledged the sometimes materialistic motivations of catechumens, but saw positive results as well:

> According to my knowledge, people became Christians in order to gain something. For example, the four sumptuous feasts of the year, the chance of educating their children. . . . They got to know God after they were baptized. Then they would not care for those small gains and they would become [true] faithful.[88]

Although the center catechumenate was ideal in Ford's opinion, it was not always feasible. War conditions often endangered large groups congregating in the parish compound, and lack of funds sometimes made it impossible to feed the catechumens. Ford encouraged the Sisters to carry on with private instruction in homes or at the convent or to have a less intensive course which met only two or three times a week.

Experiments in village catechumenates were also conducted. In the late 1930s, Father Maynard Murphy, the pastor of Big Dipper Village (Pettochai), was already conducting center and village catechumenates and encouraged Sisters Luella Veile, Joseph Marian Mahoney, and Clara (Albert) Venneman to do the same for women.[89] Ford, however, was still reluctant to put village catechumenates on a par with center catechumenates because they "dissociated doctrine from corporate liturgical worship, of which nothing can take the place."[90]

The crisis of World War II finally forced him to accept village catechumenates as a valuable alternative. This decision further enhanced the missionary character of the Maryknoll Sisters and the newly established Chinese Congregation of Sister-Catechists of Our Lady and gained for them the full respect and admiration of their male counterparts.[91] The American women religious did what the missionary community at large thought no foreign Sister could do: remain with a catechist companion in a remote village for as long as three weeks without sacraments. During this time, boarding in the homes of the people, with very little privacy, the Sisters experienced the meaning of being poor.

Not even the Chinese Sisters, who were used to these living conditions, were expected to be able to endure the spiritual desert of the village catechumenate. Yet, these Sisters also successfully endured conditions which wore down the strongest nerves and most sanguine of temperaments. There were very few cases of nervous breakdowns among the Sisters in Kaying; on the contrary, most seemed to come back from the villages as spiritually invigorated as if they had been on a long retreat. Sister Jean Theophane Steinbauer could not remember how many village catechumenates she conducted, but one stood out in her memory:

> I remember crossing a very high and narrow bridge constructed of two narrow planks without any kind of railing on the sides. Many a time I thought I was going to fall off and stopped to get my balance, trying not to look at the water but to see the plank so that I would step on the plank and not on the air! A woman companion carried my equipment in baskets suspended from her shoulders. She cooked for me and also helped to teach prayers and catechism as well as to visit the people in their homes. The women in that village all day long went to the mountains to collect a fern-like leaf that they had to dry out and use [as fuel] for their cooking. At noontime, I would go and visit them in their smoked-up kitchens. I would joke with them and then remind them of classes. [In the early afternoon] they would come over where I was staying and I would teach them. . . . After, they would return to the mountains to cut more kindling. During the evening meal, I would visit again the women in their kitchen. After supper, about 100 of them would come for another class. During the breaks we had a lot of fun together. At the end of the six weeks, 70 women were baptized and many had their marriages blessed.[92]

Sister Mary Paulita Hoffman recalled not only the classes but how each day used to be a continuous drill session in the fields:

> Because not many women went to school, everything had to be learned by rote. So I sat out with them in the fields, digging sweet potatoes . . . or picking the peanuts off the stalks, shouting [the questions and answers of the catechism]. I would say, "Why are you in this world?" and they would repeat "Why are you in this world?" and I continued, "We are in this world to worship God and to save our souls," and they again repeated after me. And that's the way we did it. It just went on and on, but that got *stuck into their minds*. They memorized it and they *knew* what it meant.[93]

When the native Sisters became ready for apostolic work in 1942, Ford sent them to the west of his vicariate, while he kept the Maryknoll Sisters in the eastern part. In the west, the Sister-Catechists of Our Lady found people in an even more primitive stage of development, but these native Sisters lived up to their name of being apostles of the Word of God and handmaidens of Our Lady. They carried on their work in the direct apostolate with a dedication which was greatly admired by the bishop and the Maryknoll Sisters who had trained them. In her book, *Sisters Carry the Gospel*, Sister Thérèse Grondin, their novice mistress, sounded like a proud mother when she quoted from a letter she had received from one of them, Sister Catherine Mary Lee.

> Yesterday [at the end of a two-month village catechumenate] we brought into the church 35 people—28 of whom are to receive baptism and 7 of whom will make their first confession and their first communion. We thank God for blessing the village we worked in, and for bringing our instruction there to fruition.[94]

With the exception of a few Sisters assigned to the native novitiate, Ford sent pairs of Sisters, American or Chinese, to his parishes where they engaged exclusively in the direct apostolate of women according to a plan they worked out with the pastors. This arrangement, combined with the dedication and the missionary success of the Sisters, led to a good working relationship with the Fathers, many of whom in the beginning had serious reservations about the experiment. Father Allan Dennis of Kaying once said: "Sometimes the Sisters got in our hair, but they were very good too. Some of us said, 'You can't get along with them. You can't get along without them.'"[95]

Yet in 1981, when asked who was the Maryknoll missioner he admired most, Father Dennis Slattery, a veteran of Kaying, said:

Fig. 5. Sister Magdalena Urlacher visiting with a village woman at work in Kaying. Maryknoll Sisters Archives.

As a group, I admire the Maryknoll Sisters. I admire any Sister who could live the way they lived, take what they took. They had a great influence on the women because in China women didn't have much of a place. The Sisters were women like the Chinese women and they had time for them. They came, admired the babies and expressed sympathy for the hard work the peasants had to do. The Sisters had a very special place in our missionary life. We would have been much less successful without them. I was delighted to have a couple of them in parishes I had.[96]

The two-Sister convents were not a threat to the pastor's leadership and authority because they routinely informed him of all their activities. Although the autocratic structure of the traditional parish organization was maintained, the approach to the work became more that of a team. Indeed, while the priest continued to assume the overall direction and to personally manage the apostolate among the male population, the Sisters took charge of the evangelization of women. The success and the entrepreneurship of the Sisters gave more weight to their opinions and suggestions, and their example proved to be a stimulus for better work among the men of the parish. By 1942, they had become more than auxiliaries. They were shepherdesses of the womenfolk who, by virtue of their appointment by the bishop, had been called, together with the pastor of the parish, to "lead the elect sheep to the pasture of the Good Shepherd."[97]

Wuchow and Kaying Methods Merge

Kaying

The two methods of direct apostolate emphasized by Bishop Ford on the one hand and Monsignor Meyer on the other were not mutually exclusive. In the Maryknoll missions, an exchange of views and personnel among territories resulted in many variations and combinations of these two methods. For example, although the Kaying method had the reputation of being innovative, the Kaying missioners adopted equally effective techniques designed by Meyer in Wuchow. In addition to making greater use of village catechumenates, Maryknollers in Kaying also experimented with Meyer's idea of a training school for female catechists. In 1940, Sister Mary Imelda Sheridan opened a catechist school for women of the vicariate. A year or so later, Ford decided to recruit lay catechists from among candidates of the Sister-Catechists of Our Lady who had withdrawn from the novitiate, another idea of Meyer.[98]

Wuchow

In 1939, when Bishop Frederick Donaghy was assigned from Kaying to Wuchow to replace Bernard Meyer as head of the territory, he expanded the Wuchow method by drawing on his Kaying experience with the Maryknoll Sisters. At the end of World War II, he arranged to have Sister Rosalia Kettl, a colleague from Kaying, assigned to his new vicariate to head a group of Maryknoll Sisters devoted exclusively to direct evangelization. Previously, Meyer had confined the Maryknoll Sisters to training native Sisters and female catechists, an important but limited role in the direct apostolate of women. Donaghy's plan allowed the Maryknoll Sisters to continue in their former capacity but also to become personally involved in the direct apostolate. Between 1946 and 1948, seven Maryknoll Sisters were assigned to Wuchow to learn the direct evangelization technique from Sister Rosalia Kettl. One of these young Sisters, Agnes Cazale, remembers:

> [Under Meyer] the main work of the Maryknoll Sisters was the novitiate work. After the war, Sister Rosalia came to Wuchow because she had had experience in pastoral work in Kaying. Having two Sisters go to different places to do catechumenate work, that's why she was sent, and she really taught us.[99]

Sister Rose Bernadette Gallagher summarized the mission program they were told to fulfill: "Going two by two into the villages, staying for sometimes two weeks, a month, to instruct women of an entire village and then bringing them to the point of baptism—that was our primary work."[100]

Together with the 10 professed native Sisters of the Congregation of the Sacred Heart of Wuchow, the Maryknoll Sisters were already anticipating a time in the near future when they would have two-Sister teams in each parish of the vicariate. The Communist interruption of all missionary activities shattered their hopes of growth for the Church. Sister Dorothy Rubner recalled:

> Direct evangelization was the most successful program. In some areas, the priests brought into the Church large numbers of villages through this method. But because the Communists came in 1949, we didn't have enough time to get to that point.[101]

Kweilin

The last territory given to Maryknoll benefited from experience in both

Wuchow and Kaying. In the countryside, Monsignor John Romaniello, the new prefect apostolic, implemented a form of catechumenate identical to the one conceived by Meyer for Wuchow's villages. For towns and cities like Kweilin city, however, he recommended a form of catechumenate which borrowed features from both the Wuchow and Kaying methods: catechumens studied in the evening and returned home afterward (as in Wuchow); classes began on a given date and were limited to 40 catechumens placed under the direct supervision of a priest and a Sister (as in Kaying).[102]

In 1940, Sisters Barbara (Rose Victor) Mersinger and Cornelia Collins arrived in Kweilin to begin the direct apostolate. During their novitiate at the Knoll, they had already studied the method developed by Ford and the Kaying Sisters. Benefiting from the years of trial and error in Kaying and Wuchow, they developed their own version of the direct apostolate, including a three-Sister convent in which each Sister developed her particular specialty. "In Laipo," said Sister Cornelia Collins, "we were three. Sister Dominic took care of the clinic, Sister Miriam Carmel taught in the novitiate and I did catechumenate work."[103]

In Kweilin, not all Sisters worked full time in direct evangelization, but none was excused from visiting in Chinese homes for at least a few hours each day. Sister Antonia Maria Guerrieri, a medical doctor in Kweilin city, explained how well medical work and the direct apostolate worked together. The addition of a Sister-nurse to each convent brought a new dimension to their small convents:

> We all three visited, there was no staying at home. I had my clinic in the morning and in the afternoon, I would go see patients who could not come to the clinic. Then when they were better, I would turn them over to Sister Barbara Rose and Sister Gabriel Marie who would continue dropping in to see how they were doing. So gradually we would have a catechumenate opening up.[104]

The Maryknoll Sisters in Kweilin also gave priority to the village catechumenate approach over the center catechumenate, mainly to avoid the danger of creating "rice Christians." Sister Cornelia Collins explained:

> Catechumens gain nothing material from attending the catechumenate classes. We didn't give out anything. When they studied at the centers and were given their meals, they would be "rice Christians." To get two meals a day, that would be quite an incentive! But I went out to the homes to teach. I remember one time I went to a village and lived there for two or three months while conducting a catechumenate.[105]

Like their counterparts in Kaying, the Chinese Catechist-Sisters of the Blessed Virgin in Kweilin primarily did direct evangelization. They lived in small convents of two or three Sisters and went out daily to visit people. At the end of World War II in the parish of Laipo alone, the native Sisters had 30 villages on their visiting list. Included was the hamlet of Sister Joan Ling, a Chinese Sister who later joined Maryknoll. She remembered most clearly the patience of the two native Sisters who came on weekly visits before her family was baptized. "They just came to see what we had been doing. They sat around and had to be very patient. If you showed interest, they would tell you a little bit more. If you didn't, they would stop."[106]

After half a year of contacts in a village, the Sisters sent catechists to live there and teach the people. Sister Agnes Chau (who also joined Maryknoll at a later date) described the procedure followed in the parish of Laipo.

> Usually after half a year, we made arrangements to send the catechists there to preach. Almost every month we went to the village to see what people were doing and to examine them. Often we would live there for a week or two before they were baptized. In this way we could observe them.[107]

As in Kaying, the Maryknoll Fathers and Sisters in Kweilin developed a team approach to direct evangelization. The Sisters, however, learned to refrain from mentioning that "in Kaying, they do this or that" to avoid eliciting resentment from the Fathers. They also realized that since the pastor made all the decisions in the end, they had to use some psychology to carry out their suggestions. The tactic, said Sister Barbara, was to present the idea—for instance, the need for a women's sodality—as a suggestion that would almost certainly be rejected by the pastor. A few months later the priest would resurrect the proposal, and the Sister would then welcome it as a great idea and implement it.[108]

Fushun

In the Fushun territory, Bishop Raymond Lane employed 33 Maryknoll Sisters in 1940. About one-third were assigned to the Maryknoll High School Academy in Dairen, the Chinese novitiate, or the liturgical vestment workshop in Fushun city. The other Sisters were attached to parishes in or near the big centers of Dairen, Fushun, Antung, and Tunghwa. Their assignments were to work in dispensaries, visit Chinese homes, and teach in catechumenates at the parish compound.

From the beginning, Lane made it clear that parish Sisters in his territory should "be one with the people." He did not allow them to have a chapel in their convent, but asked them to participate with the parish community in all religious services. In addition to their parish work, each Sister was assigned a village or a part of the city which she was expected to visit for a full day each week to make the Church known. Because of widespread banditry in Manchuria, the Sisters never received permission to stay overnight in the countryside.[109]

As in other Maryknoll territories, the Sisters had a special appeal for the women and found a way to their hearts. The Fathers were proud of these "wonderful Sisters," and they wholeheartedly attributed most of the credit for conversions to their efforts. In Fushun, an expression coined by Father Thomas Quirk became very popular among Maryknollers: "The Sisters make the converts and the priests baptize them." Years later Bishop Edward McGurkin remarked:

> There is a lot of truth in that [Quirk's comment]. The Sisters would go to the families and would really get to know them. The contacts were made through the Sisters and through the catechists who worked for the Fathers.[110]

Kongmoon

Strangely enough, it was in Kongmoon, Maryknoll's first mission, that the Maryknoll Sisters were least involved in the direct apostolate. While they trained the native Sisters at the Pakkai novitiate to work in the direct apostolate, they themselves worked almost exclusively in institutions such as orphanages and clinics. Sister Ann Carol Brielmaier, who worked in both the Wuchow and the Kongmoon vicariates, acknowledged:

> In Yeungkong the Sisters worked in the clinic and had an orphanage for abandoned baby girls. They did some direct evangelization but they did it from the center. They didn't go out and live among the people. I think perhaps it was just not their charisma or not their direction. . . . In Loting, they also seemed most concerned about their orphanage.[111]

However, interviews from other Sisters who spent their whole career in Kongmoon leave the impression that many Sisters felt themselves prisoners of institutional work. Assigned to orphanages and clinics, they all looked forward to more involvement in parish-oriented activities such as women's catechumenates, visiting prisoners and the destitute, and making Saturday afternoon calls to remind Catholics of their Sunday obligations.[112] Some Sisters recalled, above all, the opportunity to go on mission trips as the spiritual highlight of their life in China. Sister Candida Maria Basto summarized 13 years of experience in the Kongmoon vicariate, describing the feelings shared by the Maryknoll Sisters in Kongmoon:

> If I were to start all over in China, I would like to be more with the people. We had a nice house and we didn't do much visiting. On my own, I did ask to go to the villages and stay in the outposts, and those visits were for me a great feat, a life-saver. Though we had a large orphanage and we were needed there, we could have also put women in charge. But to be among the people in their homes, stay with them and get into their work and problems, I would have liked to do that.[113]

The Lay Apostolate

The Rise of Chinese Catholic Action

To identify direct evangelization only as the conversion of non-Christians through the apostolic zeal of priests, Sisters, and catechists would be a misrepresentation of the methods used by Maryknollers. The ultimate aim of these methods was to have the Chinese converts become apostles to their own people. Therefore, Maryknollers viewed their missionary role in China as two-fold: the first step was to make converts and baptize well-defined social units such as a family, clan, or village, rather than individuals with no group support. Equally important was the second step of organizing the new Catholics into faithful parishes which would radiate Christian life into the surrounding villages and towns. Maryknollers were convinced that the Church would expand by leaps and bounds only when each lay Catholic brought in several converts a year. Such apostolic zeal would also generate the priests, Sisters, and catechists necessary to instruct the growing number of catechumens and animate the spiritual life of newborn parishes.[114]

At least during the first 20 years in China, however, there was a large discrepancy between this grand scheme for an apostolic laity and the actual achievements. Most Maryknollers failed to train their parishioners to be apostles to their own people. In most cases, mission work was reduced to "making Catholics" who practiced their faith. A study of catechetical methods shows that catechumens received instruction which overemphasized the doctrinal aspects of Catholicism to the detriment of the apostolic spirit. Converts and the faithful were mostly concerned with saving their own souls. As Dr. David Tse, who lived in several Maryknoll parishes of Kwangtung and Kwangsi provinces, recalled, "We knew that every Catholic should go to church, and it would be terrible if you missed it."[115]

Christian life in established parishes was somewhat reminiscent of traditional rural Europe:

> There was a bell to assemble the Catholics to recite the Angelus, morning and evening prayers. The sound of the bell could reach as far as five to six miles. Upon hearing the bell, Catholics working in the fields would recite the Angelus, and on Sunday would come to hear Mass.[116]

In contrast to its old European counterpart, however, the Chinese Catholic village was an island in a sea of different beliefs. The Chinese parish was protective, providing its members with the routine and peer support necessary to remain faithful to the commandments of God and the Church's regulations. It was more a self-centered community than the hub of apostolic activity that Maryknollers had hoped to create. Mission work was the responsibility of a special team composed of the priest, a few Sisters, and paid catechists. The priest was often so busy caring for the Catholics that he had little time to visit the non-Christians. As for the Sisters and catechists, they spent as much time in the catechumenates as they did seeking new recruits.

Ironically, the expansion of the Church into new areas was mainly owing to untrained lay Catholics and even catechumens. People noticed that their Catholic relatives and friends were less prone to misbehavior and weaknesses such as fighting, gambling, stealing, or opium smoking. When they asked for an explanation, they were invariably introduced to Catholicism and to the catechists, the Sisters, or the priest. "I could meet a few people myself," said Father Van den Bogaard, "but it was their own [Catholic] people and friends in the villages who really got them started learning more about religion. Then it was up to the catechists to take over and begin to teach them."[117]

Meanwhile, with the encouragement of Rome, the idea of an organized lay apostolate, called Catholic Action, gained momentum in the Church. Following in the footsteps of Pius X, the first pope to issue an entire encyclical on the subject of Catholic Action, Pope Pius XI, an ardent promoter of the lay apostolate, dispelled the prevailing opinion that apostolic work was a privilege of the clergy and insisted it should be the responsibility of every Catholic.[118] In China the Catholic hierarchy officially approved a constitution for Chinese Catholic Action in 1918. A few years later when the bishops met for their first plenary council in Shanghai in 1924, they agreed to support the pope's view that "inducing of Christians to convert their own people" was one of the main objectives of evangelization.[119]

Throughout China the missioners gradually organized Catholics into

Catholic Action units called sodalities, with the specific goal of being apostles to their own people. Until the late 1930s, however, with few exceptions, Catholic Action failed to have an impact on the non-Christian society. This failure was mainly owing to the nature of the Catholic Action groups whose constitutions made little provision for the apostolic or spiritual formation of members. Sodalities often were little more than monthly meetings where Catholics listened to speeches and passed resolutions which were rarely carried out.[120]

In the Maryknoll territories, most missioners did not feel the need for lay apostolic groups until late in the 1930s. The realization that most conversions came from personal contacts with lay Catholics, combined with reflection on the writings of the popes, slowly revealed the need for organized involvement of the laity. Yet even as late as 1938, some Maryknollers, including missioners in the Kaying vicariate, were not convinced that Catholic Action was a good idea; Bishop Ford had to order them to open sodalities in their parishes.[121]

By the 1940s, some Maryknoll parishes had extensive Catholic Action programs. All kinds of sodalities came into being: for married and unmarried people, for different age groups, for different purposes ranging from the direct apostolate to works of mercy such as visiting the poor. After their first communion, children were organized into the Knights of the Blessed Sacrament to instill in them the desire of becoming apostles among their peers. Sodalities for women, in the opinion of Sister Rosalia Kettl, turned Catholic women into co-workers with the Sisters. "Our initial perspective was trying to make women the apostles of their own people. Sodalities helped a great deal in Christianizing the homes of the people and bringing them all into the life of the Church."[122]

Pioneers like Ford and Meyer urged other Maryknollers to take great care of the spiritual and apostolic training of the Catholics. They emphasized that monthly meetings should contain the three ingredients of prayer, instruction, and meaningful progress reports. Once again Meyer made some important contributions to the Church in China. In 1941, he published the first manual in Chinese for the instruction of Chinese missioners and Catholics in the best methods of conducting Catholic Action. The manual explained the origin and purpose of Catholic Action, gave the text of the constitution, and devoted a section to various activities to be pursued by local groups. At the same time, he published a series of materials to use in Catholic Action study clubs to increase the members' knowledge of their religion and their apostolic zeal. The series consisted of three sets of 30 units each, including Catholic doctrine, Christian morality, and Christian life.[123]

A Maryknoll Pioneer of the Lay Apostolate

In Fushun, Father Sylvio Gilbert's innovative use of sodalities transformed amorphous Catholic parishes into vibrant apostolic communities. In the fall of 1929, barely two years after his arrival in Manchuria, he was assigned to his first parish in Antung, a cosmopolitan city on the Yalu River across from Korea. Within a few months, he started several sodalities to interest his lukewarm Catholic flock in the activities of the parish. He told them, "This parish is yours, not mine."[124] He found activities for everyone. When he noticed that the Koreans liked to sing, he started a choir sodality. The Japanese* were much better off financially, so he organized the Japanese women into a Tabernacle Sodality which took care of the linens and decorations in the church; for the Japanese men, he launched a St. Vincent de Paul Society which visited the poor in the parish.[125]

Antung was his training ground. After a year, Gilbert was moved to Tunghwa where he served for more than 10 years. His contagious energy and spirituality turned the parish into a showcase of the lay apostolate. Although some Maryknollers were described by their Chinese Catholics as shy, passive, and difficult-to-reach persons hidden behind the walls of their compounds, Gilbert was not. Edward McGurkin, his curate, described him as the opposite of a desk man; when you ran into him, he was always on his way out to meet people. In 1935, Monsignor Raymond Lane, the head of the territory, said there was something "radioactive" about Gilbert, whom he called "the energizer."[126]

Gilbert's mission formula was simple: to make converts, one should organize a lay apostolate. He organized sodalities according to their professions: teachers, workers, merchants, peasants. His visits and instruction infused an apostolic spirit in them; their task was to propagate the faith among their relatives and friends. They were also asked to be living proof of the charity of Christ. On the big feasts, Catholics residing in Tunghwa city were asked to give overnight lodging to those from the outstations. When poverty became a serious problem in the parish in the summer of 1935, each Christian was asked to bring a bowl of corn or rice on Sunday to be distributed in town later by the St. Vincent de Paul Society.[127]

As a stimulus, Gilbert erected a large bulletin board in the church vestibule where he posted the names of the best "convert-getters." Apostolic training started as soon as candidates were accepted as catechumens. In outstations, they were supposed to signify their desire to become

---

*After defeating Russia in 1905, Japan took over the Russian leasehold of the Kwantung Peninsula and tsarist railway and economic rights in Manchuria. Thus began a long and intensive process of Japanese colonization in Manchuria.

Catholics by paying for the rent, fuel, and food of the catechists who came to instruct them. Moreover, they had to prove their sincerity by actively recruiting new catechumens from among their neighbors. Gilbert asked the three native Sisters who worked with him in Tunghwa to follow the same methods with women.

Gilbert's methods quickly brought good results: the number of catechumens rose from 40 during his first year in Tunghwa to some 600 at the end of his third year. At the annual clerical meeting in November 1934, Lane, the prefect apostolic, asked him to describe his methods to fellow Maryknollers.

In addition to energy and enthusiasm, Gilbert also brought prudence to his mission work. He felt that "wishy-washy preparation was not enough." Rather than boasting of quick progress, he kept candidates under instruction for as long as three years if necessary before baptizing them.[128]

When he served temporarily in the parish of Chaoyangchen in 1938, he came to the conclusion that the Catholics' lack of apostolic spirit came from their ignorance of the faith. "They had been baptized without knowing [well] their religion. It didn't mean much to them. So I got them together and said, 'In two weeks we will have a catechetical contest.'"[129] For two weeks, assisted by two catechists, he had morning sessions for the women and evening sessions for the men. He reported:

> In the end we had amazing results. Many of the women brought their pagan friends around. And the men the same way. They would be around the church hall and point and tell them all about the church. They began to understand what it was all about."[130]

Impressed by the results, Lane decided to expand the experiment to the whole vicariate. The following year, he announced that the third Sunday of Lent, 1939, would be a Christian Doctrine Sunday, with a contest in each parish to determine the best trained Catholics. In Tunghwa, Gilbert "by far got the best results."[131] Building on his experience in Chaoyangchen, Gilbert launched a whole month of intensive visiting of Catholics and reviewing the catechism. The Catholic Action groups helped the catechists make the round of visits and prepare the mission grounds for the celebration. The day was superbly organized and began with a morning mass at which Father Gilbert emphasized the theme of the necessity of a lay apostolate. While the contestants were divided into groups of men, women, boys, and girls and quizzed, catechists presented skits to prevent monotony and ease the tension. At one time, for example,

The Christians were entertained by two of the catechists who conducted a dialogue on Actual Grace and Sanctifying Grace. Mr. Pai introduced himself as a farmer who had just strolled in from [a neighboring village] and heard something about the Church but could not grasp many of its teachings. Mr. Hsieh answered his questions. Of course the dialogue was prepared beforehand. The people followed it with deep interest. They got several laughs out of the "stranger's" questions and his frequent interruptions; but at the same time learned a good bit from the catechist's lucid explanations.[132]

The pastor held the final hour of the elimination contest:

He did his best to stick the [remaining] 16 contestants, asking questions on grace, faith, the six days of creation, etc. But after an hour, they were still standing. It was decided to reward the grownups with a crucifix and the boys and girls with books.[133]

At the end of the day, members of the parish returned to the church for a concluding ceremony, and Gilbert reemphasized the importance of the Catholics' work as apostles.

Because of Gilbert's concern for quality rather than quantity, the Tunghwa parish roster grew slowly from some 235 in 1932 to 549 in 1938. He was convinced that apostolically successful Catholics were those with both faith and a solid knowledge of their religion. A slow beginning would later give way to a geometric progression of impressive proportions.

By December 1938, Gilbert had finally built up the nucleus for an expansion among the 80,000 non-Christians of the Tunghwa district. He inaugurated one-year plans, beginning and ending on the Feast of the Immaculate Conception. Catholics of the parish were divided into 10 groups according to where they lived. Within each group, each Catholic family was entrusted with the instruction of a catechumen family and assigned a number of non-Christian homes to visit. On the following Feast of the Immaculate Conception, results were tallied and posted, prizes were awarded to those families and groups who secured the most converts, and another cycle began. The parish roster showed a definite improvement: the Catholic population expanded from 557 in 1939 to 712 in 1940 and 858 in 1941.[134] The results also showed in the form of a deeper commitment among the Catholics; groups of Catholic Action sprung up among the young men and women. Following the arrest of the American missioners by the Japanese in December 1941, the Catholics of Tunghwa were on their own for all practical purposes—with their faith and their firmly based Catholic practices.

The Legion of Mary

After World War II, sodalities thrived in all the Maryknoll territories in

South China. They molded the Catholics into units which provided spiritual support, enrichment for the members, and a team-like approach to the lay apostolate. In 1947, the papal nuncio in China, Archbishop Antonio Riberi, urged all the bishops to adopt the Legion of Mary as a form of Catholic Action to strengthen the lay apostolate in view of the Communist threat. Established in Dublin in 1921, this association of lay Catholics had been organized on the model of the army of ancient Rome to battle in the spiritual "warfare waged by the Church against the world and its evil power."[135] From Ireland it had spread throughout Europe and into the United States with great success.

In China, the Maryknoll bishops' response to the nuncio's request was not unanimous. Although they all recognized the Legion of Mary as an excellent form of Catholic Action, some thought its rigid structure prevented its adaptation to the Chinese context. Indeed, compared to the ordinary sodalities, which were loosely regulated groups, the Legion of Mary allowed no variations from its rules and practices. Bishop Ford, in particular, thought that some regulations were unnecessary for his Kaying Catholics, such as regular and punctual attendance at weekly meetings, performance of weekly work obligations, written logs of work cases and accomplishments, and daily recitation of certain prayers. Therefore, to the disappointment of some Maryknoll Sisters, he never permitted the establishment of the Legion of Mary in his vicariate.[136]

By contrast, Maryknollers in the Kweilin territory encouraged the formation of Legion of Mary units called *praesidia* to reinforce the existing sodalities and strengthen the lay apostolate. Many Maryknoll Fathers and Sisters as well as the native Catechist-Sisters of the Blessed Virgin became involved as spiritual directors of *praesidia*. As in other regions of China, the Communists in Kweilin singled out the Legion of Mary as a spy organization financed by the American government and disguised under the cloak of a religion. A small book prepared by the Communists, *Reactionary Technique of the Catholic Church: The Legion of Mary*, alerted the Chinese people to the dangers of the Legion: "The Legion of Mary is a secret political organization by which the imperialists use the church to hide their greatest efforts to overthrow the people."[137]

Several Maryknollers vividly recalled the strong faith of their legionnaires. Father Edwin McCabe told of a young girl taken to the police station on charges of supporting a subversive organization. He heard her declare:

> No, the Legion of Mary is not subversive, and I will not sign any statement against it because it's a spiritual organization. It is an organization that would give glory to any country, that the citizens of any country would be so zealous and so interested that they would sacrifice themselves for the service of others![138]

In his book *Calvary in China*, Father Robert Greene also quoted some of the legionnaires in his parish of Tungan who continued meeting in spite of Communist disapproval. There was Tong Ta Sao, the leader of the women's *praesidium* who would "carry out her assignments with contagious joy and tireless energy." All the Catholics saw Lin Tse Pei, the seventy-year-old president of the men's *praesidium* as the "perfect legionnaire." This gentle-mannered Catholic, grandfather of Maryknoll Sister Joan Ling, was one of the first Kweilin Catholics to be arrested and suffer in jail as a leader of the Legion of Mary.[139]

In their interviews, all Maryknollers expressed the strong conviction that, in spite of the missioners' many mistakes, the Chinese Catholics had the faith and the religious training necessary to survive on their own under Communist oppression. Beginning in 1949, churches throughout China were systematically closed by the Communists; over 20 years later, only two churches remained open, both were in Peking and were attended primarily by foreigners. Yet, in 1979, with the change in policy which guaranteed religious freedom, churches began to reopen. Five years later, Western observers were amazed to find approximately 800 Catholic churches open with a Catholic population of approximately three million faithful. They had kept the promise that Sister Theresa, a native Sister of Tungan, made to Father Greene: "We are not afraid, Father. We will never deny our Lord. They can kill us but we will be loyal [to the Church]."[140]

Conclusion

Maryknollers' commitment to take the Gospel directly to the Chinese people was undeniable. The realization that they could not achieve this goal by themselves led them to promote the role of catechists as apostles and religious teachers of their own people. The first step was to ensure that catechists had a sound knowledge of the doctrine, personal faith, and apostolic zeal. Meyer saw a possible solution in the results of catechist schools and summer programs developed by some missionary congregations in north China. Borrowing the idea, he put it at the center of an all-inclusive mission program with Chinese catechists as the key people. His program was widely followed in all the Maryknoll territories. It also caught the attention of the entire missionary community in China when it was described in the June 1937 issue of the *Digest of the Synodal Commission* under the title of "Launch Out into the Deep."

In an attempt to describe what catechists were, James E. Walsh wrote a vibrant tribute to those well-trained zealous persons whom he called "the real St. Pauls of modern mission work":

[The catechist] is the man who smiled his way into the strange village, braved the first opposition if not persecution, made friends, smoothed difficulties, calmed fears, explained away prejudices, weeded out the old superstitions, insinuated the new hopes. It was he who cured the sick, comforted the sorrowful, counseled the doubtful, took the accumulated troubles of the entire village on his obliging shoulders. . . . His were the constant visits in burning sun and pelting rain and the perils of robbers . . . his were the thousand and one other perplexities of the inevitable sowing in tears.

He is the same man who spent his days in the incessant hobnobbing, and his nights in the interminable discussing that were needed to bring diffident souls to the point of accepting the pearl of great price. And he is also the man who will yet devote many tedious hours to teaching them the doctrine, catching them early in the morning before dawn, waylaying them as they come home from the fields in the evening, explaining, exhorting, encouraging, repeating, until by hook or by crook he has instilled in them the knowledge of their new found Faith that is required for Baptism.[141]

Yet Meyer's program had some potentially dangerous flaws. Some Maryknoll priests became overreliant on their catechists. A missioner with poor language skills or a propensity to be shy or lazy could let the catechists run his parish while he remained anchored in boredom behind the walls of his compound. In such a situation, his grasp of the language remained weak, and his occasional contacts with the people were superficial. He went out only to dispense the sacraments and to make the biannual visits to Catholics living in outstations.

Another flaw of the catechist system was its reliance on a large number of paid catechists, which made the apostolate dependent on finances. For example, when funds from outside China became almost impossible to secure between 1941 and 1946, Maryknollers in South China had no alternative but to dismiss most of their catechists. Wuchow lost 96 catechists out of a total of 116; in Kaying, the number dropped from 99 to 31; in Kongmoon, the total fell from 135 to 33.

As a result, the conversion movement almost stopped. The number of catechumens, previously in the thousands, dropped to a few hundred. The steady growth of the number of Catholics in Maryknoll territories came to a standstill between 1941 and 1946 and even decreased in Kongmoon and Wuchow. Kweilin had appeared to be a showcase of growth during the adversity of war with one of the fastest growing Catholic populations in China. Between 1938 and 1943, it more than tripled, from 1,066 to 3,514. However, with the Japanese drive of 1944, apostolic work came to a stop. Statistics for 1947 showed the Catholic population of the Kweilin territory to be 3,603, a gain of less than 100 in four years.

Maryknollers in China had been so engrossed with the development of an efficient catechist program that they had delayed launching Catholic Action groups, a broader form of organized lay apostolate. When the war hit the Maryknoll territories in South China, the sodalities were too few in number and too new to be effective in the unsettled environment. After the war, however, the rehiring of catechists and the strong emphasis on Catholic Action groups resulted in a sharp increase in the Catholic population. Between 1946 and 1950, the number of Catholics grew from 19,1086 to 22,819 in Kaying; from 11,422 to 19,871 in Wuchow; and from 3,603 to 8,539 in Kweilin. Only in the vicariate of Kongmoon, where the emphasis was still more on institutional works, did the Catholic population fail to grow; it remained stable with 8,500 faithful.[142]

During that period, these four Maryknoll territories together registered the highest percentage of conversions in China. This success, publicized in the *China Missionary Bulletin*, was mainly attributed to Maryknoll's methods of training catechists and of supporting the direct apostolate.[143] Maryknollers in China tried to generate an all-out effort to establish a laity eager to evangelize their own people. Complaining in 1949 that in too many parts of China the priests, catechists, and a few Sisters were the only missioners, Bernard Meyer wrote a long article in the *China Missionary Bulletin* on "The Lay Vocation," in which he said:

> The laity are called to be active missioners on their own level. With a well-organized lay apostolate, instead of the slow growth by arithmetical progression, as at present, the Church would grow by geometric progression because lay apostles beget more lay apostles.[144]

The Communist takeover did not permit much further development of the laity. Yet the groups in place proved to be strong. As Maryknoll priests' movements became more and more restricted in 1949 and 1950, the vitality of the Catholic Action did not abate, with record enrollments in catechumenates. Reflecting on this phenomenon, Meyer echoed the feelings of many veteran Maryknollers when he wrote that the chief regret of his 32 years in China was that it took him so long to appreciate "the natural place of the laity in the mission of the Church."[145] Having learned his lesson, he consecrated the rest of his life to the spiritual and apostolic training of lay people.

An interesting facet of Maryknoll's involvement in the direct apostolate was its impact on the role of women—both religious and lay— in the Church. Until the arrival of the Maryknoll Sisters in China, the direct apostolate, considered inappropriate for women religious, was primarily reserved for the priests and their male catechists. The Sisters' place was in institutions such as schools, orphanages, hospitals, and dispensaries. If they were involved in catechetical work, it was always on or near church premises.

Given the opportunity to become involved in the direct apostolate by Bishop Ford, the Maryknoll Sisters dispelled the objections which kept religious women from serving as missionaries. They proved, for example, that women could endure as many physical hardships as men, that they could handle dangerous situations as well, and that they could adapt their religious rules and schedules to fit an apostolic life outside convent walls.

The traditional organization of the mission was altered. The Sisters were no longer auxiliaries, but full participants. The priest still assumed the overall direction of the parish but the approach to the work, including the direct apostolate, was more that of a team. The Sisters were in charge of the women and children while priests concentrated on the apostolate among men. The Sisters were able to accomplish things which no male missioner had been able to do: mingle with the women in their own environment, speak their "kitchen" language, talk from a woman's point of view, and gear their instructions to the concrete daily life of Chinese peasant women.

As a result, the Chinese Catholic Church in Maryknoll territories began to change. Its membership, which had been prominently male, became more balanced; more children were baptized with their mothers and continued to receive religious education in Sunday school and during the summer vacation. Women converts joined the budding Catholic Action groups and became actively involved in the apostolate with other women. In some parishes, said Sister Rita Marie Regan, newly converted women gave a day each week to take the Sisters into the homes of non-Catholic friends.[146]

The Maryknoll Sisters imparted this same zeal for the direct apostolate to the native sisterhoods they were training, to be described in Chapter 5 on "Indigenization." Some of these Chinese sisterhoods focused primarily on direct contact with non-Christians and on catechumenates. They became the first of a new breed of women religious who would follow the same path in the 1950s and 1960s.

Because the lifestyle and apostolate of the Maryknoll Sisters in China established a new pattern of Catholic apostolic work, it not only affected communities of Chinese Sisters, but also had repercussions on the role of women religious in the Church. Out of their convents, on the roads, mixing with the Chinese people, the Maryknoll Sisters provided a new model of mission activity for Sisters and contributed to modernization in the Catholic Church. Other women's religious orders—many of which were not primarily aiming at foreign mission—adopted methods of direct apostolate similar to those of the Maryknoll Sisters. In 1957 Léon-Joseph Cardinal Suenens of Belgium wrote to Sister Thérèse Grondin that, inspired by the

Maryknoll Sisters, he had just launched an experiment in Europe involving 40 convents of Sisters and 20 houses of Brothers who were stressing direct evangelization by apostolic teams. He further extolled the value of this program in his book *L'Eglise en état de mission.*[147]

In 1967, at an international meeting in Rome of superiors general of missionary organizations, Gregorio Petro Cardinal Agagianian, prefect of the Sacred Congregation for the Propagation of the Faith, stressing the primacy of evangelization and the direct participation by religious women in evangelizing, singled out the "itinerant evangelical penetration" of the two-Sister convent system in Kaying and the type of mobile missionary apostolate as a model to emulate.[148] The small experiment started in 1934 by Francis Ford and a few Maryknoll Sisters had led to an important change in the role of women in the apostolic mission of the Church.

4

Corporal Works of Mercy

Expressing God's Concern for the Poor and the Afflicted

Our priorities were One and all else flowed from that priority which was expansion of the Church through conversion, through baptism. The mandate of Christ to His apostles was just as clear to us: just go and baptize and preach. To us, that meant creating the opportunity or seizing whatever opportunity might arise to enable us to get closer to the people to execute that mandate. Hence corporal works of mercy were logical . . . to get to be known and recognized by them as one willing and able to help.[1]

This assessment of the rationale for Maryknollers' involvement in medical, educational, charitable, and social activities by Father Peter Reilly was based on a commonly accepted pre-Vatican II mission strategy: Preaching the Gospel was the paramount method for making conversions and for expanding the Church. Corporal works of mercy opened doors and caught people's attention. Bishop James E. Walsh described this technique in detail in his *Mission Manual of the Vicariate of Kongmoon:*

Missioners who convert pagans in any numbers know that the way to do so is to find some human, and usually more or less material, need that is pressing upon them, and when found, to proceed to find some way to relieve it. . . . Any sincere attempt to help the people in any of their little needs will usually be appreciated and may indeed result in conversions. . . . From the very beginning, the missioner must make his motives plain to the people, explaining and repeating and harping upon the fact that his chief object is not so much to help their bodies as to save their souls.[2]

Yet to reduce these corporal works of mercy to a simple strategy is misleading. The approach was founded on the belief that service and the exercise of charity were the essence of Christianity and that they exerted a magnetic attraction on nonbelievers to investigate the motivating force behind such works. Describing the crowds of refugees who passed through his parish of Chikkai in 1938 and 1939, Father Donat Chatigny said, "I was doing the best I could to treat them well, to prove to them that the Church was out to help the poor and the afflicted and that we didn't force anyone to enter the Church."[3] These concrete expressions of Christian charity projected the Gospel's message that concern for other people, especially those in direst need, was the true mark of someone's love for God and a path to salvation:

> When the son of man shall come in His majesty. . . . He will say to those on His right hand: "Come blessed of my Father, take possession of the Kingdom prepared for you . . . for I was hungry and you gave me to eat; I was thirsty and you gave me to drink; I was a stranger and you took me in; sick and you visited me; I was in prison and you came to me." (Matt. 25:31–36)

The foundling homes, orphan asylums, dispensaries, hospitals, homes for the aged, leprosaria, cooperatives, relief distribution centers, and schools scattered throughout the mission world were proof of the missioners' drive to alleviate the physical, social, and educational handicaps of people around them. As Sister Herman Joseph Stitz, who served three and a half years in the Shanghai Mercy Hospital for the mentally ill as a medical technician, recalled, "Serving these unfortunate people had been accepted as an opportunity for the practice of pure charity as a demonstration of the love of God with little hope of personal satisfaction or consolation."[4]

Two different approaches emerged as Maryknoll worked to serve the people of China. The vicariate of Kongmoon used the more traditional approach where the mission organization began, directed, and financed service and medical institutions. The vicariates of Kaying and Wuchow followed another approach in which missioners encouraged or inspired the foundation of social and medical institutions by the Chinese themselves.

Maryknoll's Medical Mission

Maryknoll's commitment to medical mission work began very early. A few months after the formal opening of the Seminary on September 21, 1912, Dr. Paluel J. Flagg, a young physician on the staff of St. Vincent's Hospital in New York City, joined the faculty to give weekly lectures on medical practices and health care under primitive conditions.[5] He also arranged for seminarians to receive practical training during the summer in Catholic hospitals in New York to learn as much as they could about first aid, injections, and the treatment of common diseases. Over the years, Dr. Flagg was able to enlist the help of other doctors such as Dr. C. C. Sweet, Dr. Edwin H. Huntington of Ossining, and Dr. Frederick Gould of New York City to teach a weekly course at the Seminary. In 1922 and 1923, for example, the plan of instruction provided for 30 lectures on anatomy, physiology, and first aid, 22 lectures on the essentials of medicine, 20 lectures on tropical medicine, and five lectures on laboratory techniques. Meanwhile, some Maryknoll novices went to the Ossining Hospital prior to their assignment to receive some exposure to "bedside nursing and surgery or laboratory techniques" under the supervision of Dr. Sweet.[6]

In addition to providing Maryknollers with medical knowledge to take better care of their own health and to relieve the sufferings of the Chinese, Dr. Flagg also became a strong proponent of the need for Catholic medical missions. When somebody asked him to give the reasons for the necessity of the medical missions, he replied:

> Because a billion human beings know nothing of medicine, surgery, hygiene or sanitation; because hundreds of thousands of your fellow creatures not only die, but live long lives of suffering from preventable and curable diseases; because here is an opportunity to practice medical charity which can not pauperize the profession or foster in the recipients a spirit of evasion of just fees; because medical missions are Catholic in their burden, and their charity is and always has been extended to all.[7]

As early as 1914, he began "the doctor's column" in *The Field Afar* and spread his ideas by writing articles in the major Catholic newspapers and the *Journal of the American Medical Association*. He urged sponsors from the medical profession to donate equipment and medicine for the missions. He even asked for financial support for those who volunteered to serve. Although he would have liked to join Maryknoll as a missionary doctor/priest, Flagg was convinced by Father James A. Walsh that it was not meant to be. As a recent widower, his responsibility was to his infant daughter, Virginia. Moreover, added Walsh, his role in establishing a medical movement in the United States was perhaps more important than entering the priesthood:

> Your first duty is of course to your soul. After this comes the child for whom you must toil. . . . Perhaps God wishes to use you as one of the lay priests who

like Ozanam and many of his followers are doing so much good in this old world."[8]

Walsh was right on all accounts. Flagg remained a layman; however, his dedication to medical mission work had a strong influence on his daughter. When she joined the Maryknoll Sisters in 1930, the doctor was delighted to see her fulfill the missionary vocation he had not been able to answer. Meanwhile, the organization known as the Catholic Medical Mission Board grew by leaps and bounds. By the time Dr. Flagg died in 1970, it was sending more than 2 million pounds of medical supplies a year to some 3,000 medical missions staffed by over 100 religious orders in 57 countries.[9]

The beginnings, however, had been difficult. In spite of all his efforts, Flagg was not able to solicit much response from Catholic medical professionals. However, when Maryknoll acquired territory in China and reports started to appear in *The Field Afar* and various newspapers and magazines, these stories by American missioners of the successes of dispensaries and their appeal for more medicines and for well-trained nurses and physicians gave life to Dr. Flagg's medical mission movement. Donations for medical supplies and gifts of drugs, medical textbooks, and equipment increased considerably. Meanwhile, the first two registered nurses applied to Maryknoll. They sailed for China in September 1922, and news of their welcome by the people not only reinforced Maryknoll's commitment to the medical apostolate but also evoked a strong positive response from the American Catholic population.

When Sister Mary Gertrude Moore arrived in Yeungkong in October 1922, she fixed up a temporary dispensary on the ground floor of the rectory. Her total devotion to the sick earned her the title of "Sister Doctor." By the time she died of typhoid fever ten months later, she had treated over 6,000 patients affected by worms, blood poisoning, skin disease, and eye afflictions and made daily calls to the homes of those too ill to visit her. In such a short period, although she had not been able to learn the local dialect, her laughing eyes, smiling face, and skillful care of the sick won her the love and respect of the population. Her only regret was that the language barrier prevented her from telling people about her faith: "We long to talk to these people. When a pagan picks up your crucifix and asks questions, you long to tell him the wonderful story."[10]

The reputation of Brother John Dorsey, the other nurse, as "the doctor who cures" was well known throughout western Kwangtung. Yet in the beginning his medical expertise had not been welcomed by the Chinese. The real turning point occurred in the spring of 1923 when smallpox and then bubonic plague hit the town to Tungchen. Dorsey spent his time vaccinating and treating the population, dispensing medicine, and visiting those who could not go to his miniscule dispensary. When the danger of these epidemics subsided, he noted in a letter to James A. Walsh:

> A shopkeeper whom I visited every day has asked Father Dietz for books explaining the doctrine. The changed attitude of the townspeople in our favor is very noticeable and I think it safe to ascribe the new feeling to the good done in our dispensary. People who formerly never looked at me now treat me with respect. Dispensaries seem to be the only way of winning the people's good will over here.[11]

From then on, he became known as "the man from Heaven with the big heart."

James A. Walsh and Mother Mary Joseph visited South China in 1921 and 1923, respectively, and came back fully committed to the development of Maryknoll's medical mission. Upon his return, Walsh asked Dr. Flagg to strengthen the medical training of the Brothers and seminarians, declaring that in the Maryknoll territory "the time [was] now ripe to seriously consider dispensaries, small hospitals, and the personal assistance of physicians."[12]

Similarly, the trip reinforced Mother Mary Joseph's conviction that Maryknoll missions needed qualified Sisters to staff the growing number of dispensaries and future hospitals. As early as 1919, she had started to send young professed Sisters to complete nursing school or receive specialized medical training. At the same time, the letters of Brother John and Sister Gertrude published in *The Field Afar* and the news of Sister Gertrude's death inspired more young nurses to enter the Maryknoll congregation.[13]

Except in the vicariate of Kaying where Ford basically opposed the involvement of his missioners in medical work, clinics and dispensaries were considered to be the best method to come in contact with the people and become their friends. Consequently, most Maryknoll mission parishes had a small medical facility. As reflected in the following remarks of Father Robert Cairns, Maryknoll Fathers usually expected the Sisters to run the clinic:

> The Sisters are free to take over the kitchen any time they wish though I urge them not to do so in order to have time for visiting the people and running the dispensary which is their main reason for being here. They didn't come to Sancian to be cooks."[14]

Since there were often no nurses available, many Maryknollers were called upon to do the best they could with their limited medical knowledge. Those who knew very little confined themselves to administering aspirin, quinine, worm medicine (santonin was commonly used), and cough syrup; they also cleaned cuts and boils and taught basic hygiene.[15] As Father Paul Duchesne said:

> We were far from being professional but yet we saved a lot of lives, when you could do it with just two grains of santonin. I remember one time when Father Krumpleman went on a mission trip 50 miles up the road and the barber of the town said to him, "My son has gone crazy, he is only 15 years old. We have got him tied up." So he gave the kid one grain of santonin with one grain of calomel which was a purgative. In three or four days the child was all cured. Of course the father was delighted and the story went around the village and the neighborhood, and the promotion of that accidental cure was worth hundreds of hours of preaching.[16]

The Sisters also caused many similar "miraculous cures" which caused people to ask about the Catholic religion. Sister Cornelia Collins, for instance, became famous for having brought back to life a man who people thought had died:

> One day there was a group of people waiting at the clinic door when all of a sudden I heard a thump. A man had passed out. Everybody screamed and ran including my helper. . . . I got some spirits of ammonia and held it under the man's nose and poured some down his throat. And he came to. When the people came back to the clinic, a woman said, "He was dead and she brought him back to life!" So my reputation spread.[17]

The quick reaction of the Chinese to the most ordinary Western medicine also astounded Maryknollers. Sister Angela Marie Coveny, a nurse in Tunghwa, remembered how she had used two aspirins to cure a lady who had been suffering from headaches for the last five years.[18]

Maryknollers with more medical experience tackled more serious cases: they inoculated people against cholera, gave tetanus shots, performed minor surgery, did all kinds of suturing, mended broken bones, worked on frozen hands and feet, cured people afflicted with asthma, tuberculosis, malaria, and eye diseases, and extracted teeth.[19] As Sister-nurse Monica Marie Boyle said, "Where I was, there was no doctor. Many times I had to do things because there was no other [medical] professional to do it."[20]

Like Sister Gertrude and Brother John in the early years, Maryknollers did not confine their medical help to the dispensaries. They went out to visit the sick, taking their medical bags with them to outstations. In Kaying, only this kind of medical work was sanctioned by Ford because it fit his scheme of direct evangelization. During an epidemic of diphtheria in a Kaying village, Sister-nurse Ignatia McNally stayed with the people for several days, injecting penicillin every three hours until the sick were out of danger.[21]

Maryknollers shared their medical knowledge and often trained Chinese help to take care of the dispensaries. Father Mark Tennien taught Big Six, the zealous catechist of Blue Cloud County, how to use Western medicine to cure ordinary cases. In Loting, Sister Monica Marie Boyle taught several women how to run small clinics in their villages. They treated minor ailments, administered tetanus shots to prevent lockjaw in newborn babies, and campaigned against superstitious beliefs which led to the abandoning of babies.[22]

Although missioners dispensed medical service without discrimination to everyone who needed help, they also used it to introduce the tenets of the Catholic Church. In the dispensaries, a catechist usually talked about Church doctrine while patients were waiting, and missioners always instructed the very sick and dying. People who benefited from the missioners' medical care or witnessed their dedication did not necessarily convert; however, they developed a profound respect and admiration for the missioners. Even bandits came in for treatment and, in return, allowed them to travel in areas where no one else dared to venture.[23]

Because Maryknollers administered treatment free of charge or for only a nominal fee, the Chinese people soon realized that they were not working to make money. The love and kindness of missioners who had come from so far to help apparently without expecting anything in return stimulated wonder and interest in the Catholic Church. Paraphrasing the words of many of her patients, Sister Ignatia McNally recalled their saying:

> This Catholic Church must be really something. Look at these priests—they go out on sick calls. And here is this Sister-nurse who came all the way over from America, looks after us every morning, and charges us only 10 cents. And she goes out to look after the sick in their homes. And if some patients come to the clinic one day and Sister finds out they are too sick to come back, she goes to their home.[24]

Ultimately, said Sister Rita Clare Comber, many people would ask, "Why did you come?" and we would tell them, "Because I wanted to help people know the God I love."[25] If the people showed interest in knowing more, they were enrolled in a catechumenate class in the village or in their own parish.

The medical work of Maryknollers in their clinics and their visits to the sick were indeed the cause of many conversions. Several converts rated clinics as one of Maryknoll's best contributions to the Chinese people.

They considered the medical care provided by Maryknollers as their most effective tool for attracting people to the Catholic Church: "It put them in touch with the population, it filled an urgent need, and displayed the meaning of Christian charity."[26]

Maryknoll Orphanages

Background

In countries caught in the turmoil of war, children are often the first to suffer. In China, tens of thousands of orphans were caught in the vicious circle of war, epidemics, and famine with few public institutions to help them. The abandonment of children was no more prevalent a practice in China as a whole than it was in America or in Europe; however, in some areas and cities and in the overpopulated coastal areas of western Kwangtung, in particular, families lived in such dire poverty that they could not feed any more mouths.

Baby girls were less desirable because they had to be fed by their natural family with no prospect of a profitable return in later years when they would leave their natural parents to live with their husbands' families. Indeed, the custom of marrying between the ages of twelve and fifteen caused only their in-laws to benefit from the labor of their adult life. Boys, on the contrary, remained at home even after marriage and contributed to the betterment of their extended family.

To make matters worse, many people in South China believed that if baby girls born in certain months or on certain festivals were kept in the house, they would bring illness or even death to their father or eldest brother. Superstitions took many forms, but all protected the male offspring. Some people believed that if a girl was killed, the next child would be a boy; others added that if a mother gave birth to four girls in a row, it proved that she was possessed by a devil and the only means of driving the invader out of the mother was to get rid of the newborn girl.[27] Babies to be abandoned were usually discarded immediately after birth to ease the grief of the mother.

The major cause of infant mortality, however, was unsanitary care at birth. In the Yeungkong area, for instance, the umbilical cord was tied with a piece of rice straw or a bit of hemp, then cut with a broken piece of a dish and dressed with the ashes of old rags. According to Sister Richard Wenzel, most of the children received at the Yeungkong nursery until 1944 were dying from lockjaw. Commenting on the infant death rate, she said:

No wonder that more than half of the children born in China never live more than a few hours. Another twenty percent of the girl babies born [in Yeung-kong] are either suffocated to death by putting them in a crock and covering the children with ashes or dirt, or by wrapping the child so tightly in rags that it is not able to breathe or cry, thus slowly extinguishing the baby's life. We visited pagan temples where we found abandoned infants tucked away in dark places and left to die.[28]

When the Catholic missioners reentered China in the 1860s, zeal and concern for individual souls led them to choose abandoned babies as one of their most important works. If the infants died, baptism ensured them eternal life; if they survived, the orphanage offered a chance for a Christian life. By 1948, 102 of the 147 ecclesiastical territories in China had at least one orphanage. It should be pointed out, however, that the name "orphanage" given to these institutions by the missioners was really a misnomer since the infants were abandoned rather than actually orphaned. Their parents were usually alive and sometimes even stepped forward to reveal their identity.

The Yeungkong and Loting Orphanages

A few days after their arrival in Yeungkong, the first group of Maryknoll priests was able to gauge the gravity of the problem in their area:

> Today as our priests were coming down the river, the boy pointed to an object that a dog had in the water some distance away and said that it was the body of a child that had been floating in the water. Father Gauthier remarked that such a sight was not at all infrequent![29]

The town had an orphanage but it did not accept infants or sick children. Father Francis Ford, the first pastor of Yeungkong, found himself compelled to do something for the abandoned babies and opened an orphanage in early 1920. Father Daniel McShane opened another in Loting by the end of the year. To encourage the people to bring abandoned babies to the orphanage, Maryknollers adopted the custom of the French missioners in Canton who paid a few cents for each one. During some months they baptized several infants each day. Most of these were so sick or weak that they died within a few hours. The hope of the Fathers, however, was to keep as many as possible alive and to use the orphanage to win over the people.

But, as Ford soon found out, running an orphanage required skills. the Maryknoll Fathers had no experience in handling infants; they did not know what amount of condensed milk to give at each feeding or how many feedings there should be in a day. Since neither the first-aid manual nor the local people had answers to their questions, the Fathers realized that the sooner they could get Maryknoll Sisters to help, the better chance of survival the infants would have. Accordingly, James E. Walsh, the superior of the Maryknoll mission in China at that time, wrote to the Sisters telling them to plan for their work on the missions by undergoing nurse's training. At the same time, he singled out orphanages as their first responsibility.[30]

When five Sisters arrived in Yeungkong in November 1922, Ford gave them a warm welcome. A few weeks later he was glad to report to his superior in New York that their presence was a great improvement:

> Take the orphanage, for example. We ourselves knew little about baby rations and less about preparing them. The seminary course, except for the tract on Infant Baptism, never touched on babies at all and our home training gave us no practice in handling them . . . Since the Sisters have taken charge, the babies cry whenever they are hungry. In my time, they gave up crying in disgust as it brought no results but exercise and that only made them more hungry. Then perhaps for the first time in their lives, they have been washed in warm water and dusted with talcum powder.[31]

Moreover, continued Ford, the work of the Sisters exerted a positive influence on the female segment of the population that normally had little contact with male missioners"

> Our old affair was a step better than the pagan public orphanage so you may imagine how the Sisters' spotless place has taken the feminine world by storm. The pagan women gather in front of the orphanage and whisper and exclaim over its cleanliness. The mere sight of a Sister carrying the tiny infants to the chapel for baptism will draw these pagan women for they see love expressed in every nook and corner of the orphanage.[32]

Following the examples of other religious congregations, Maryknoll adopted the practice of using foster nurses for healthy infants. These ladies, called "out" or "wet" nurses if they nursed the babies, received a monthly salary of US$1.00 for raising the girls in their own homes. Every week or 10 days they brought them back to the orphanage for a checkup. Before placing each baby, the Sisters pricked either the back of the ear or the space between the big toe and the next toe with a needle dipped in indelible ink. The tiny tatoo identified each infant during examinations. The Sisters found this system necessary after they discovered that some of their babies had been deposited in the town orphanage or that the foster mothers had been bribed to exchange a sick or dying child for a healthy Maryknoll baby.[33]

When the girls reached the age of two or three, they became residents of the orphanage and attended the school run by the Sisters. A house for blind or crippled girls and a small old folks home which housed seven elderly ladies was attached to the Yeungkong nursery and orphanage. These older women, with no relatives to support them, were able to earn some money by helping the Sisters in the orphanage and in the blind girls' home. Ford had a great love for these elderly people whom he called his "best ad in Yeungkong":

> The Chinese with their ingrained respect of old age can see the need of an old folks home and appreciate it. . . . [Moreover] old women the world over are famous for their love of gossip. They trot from one end of the town to the other and talk Catholic Church and what [we] are doing; in this way, they are as good as six catechists and a ton of printed matter. Of course people may not pay much attention to the idle prattle of the old women, but they are hearing about us and the constant hearing tends to break down prejudices, fear of foreigners and their doctrine.[34]

In his annual report of June 1923, seven months after the arrival of the Sisters, Ford used figures to back up his praise for the Sisters:

> The Sisters' presence reformed our orphanage and nursery and grandmothers' home into thriving institutions. We had the happiness of baptizing over 350 dying babies in our nursery. The orphanage sheltered about 30 blind and lame girls; and 10 homeless boys found a refuge with us.[35]

The success of the Sisters in Yeungkong prompted the sending of four more Sisters to Loting to take care of Father McShane's growing orphanage. When they arrived in September 1924, they found 55 orphans and blind girls waiting for them. Because of widespread anti-foreign demonstrations, Bishop James E. Walsh decided to recall all the Sisters to the safety of Hong Kong in July 1925. The Yeungkong Sisters were not able to return until September 1930. The Loting Sisters went back in March 1926 but had to withdraw several times in the first part of 1927.

During one of their absences in May, a baby with smallpox was brought to the pastor. It was the 2,483rd dying infant baptized by McShane since his arrival at Loting in 1920. Some days later he himself began to experience the symptoms of the disease. When the Sisters returned in early June, Father McShane had already died from smallpox. Two months later, Bishop Walsh became alarmed by a new round of antiforeign manifestations and ordered the Sisters back to Hong Kong. As on previous occasions, the Sisters expected to return quickly to Loting, but this exile lasted for five years.[36]

During that period, the Fathers kept the orphanages open for the most part. They entrusted the charge of the babies, the children, the blind, and the old ladies to Catholic ladies and "virgins" who had been trained by the Sisters.[37] With the return of the Sisters, the orphanages expanded. Within one year, the number of Loting orphans grew from 60 to 90. By 1938 the orphanage cared for as many as 124 orphaned and blind girls between the age of a few days and sixteen years. In Yeungkong, the Sisters had 45 orphans, 23 blind girls, and 10 elderly women.[38]

The Sisters taught the blind and the crippled to be as self-supporting as possible. Because Yeungkong was a fishing town, the girls made nets. They also wove bamboo baskets which they sold by size at US$.50 to $.86. Later they went into the trade of towel weaving. In Loting the older orphans made Chinese-style slippers that the Sisters sold in the United States.[39]

Healthy orphans received a primary school education from the Sisters and were taught how to sew and to cook both foreign and Chinese food. When they reached the age of fifteen or sixteen, they were much sought after as wives. In Yeungkong and Loting, however, only Catholic boys were considered, and the Sisters never forced an orphan to marry. When a young man came to ask for a girl's hand, they were always introduced to each other. After the meeting, the girl would let the Sisters know how she felt. In several instances, in fact, a young lady did refuse to marry her suitor because he was just a country boy or had no education. It seems that life in the orphanage had considerably raised the expectations of some of these girls who had no desire to share the harsh life of a small farmer. However, if the girl liked the boy, preparation for the wedding would begin. During the two or three month interval, the Sisters took on the role of parents and prepared a wedding trousseau, dress, and veil. If the girl had any known relatives, she could invite as many as she chose to the celebration. On August 4, 1937, when the second oldest child in the Loting orphanage married at the age of sixteen, not only her non-Christian mother but around 200 of her non-Christian relatives attended the wedding mass.[40]

Not all girls at the orphanage married; some joined the newly-founded native Sisters of the Immaculate Heart, and others were placed outside to learn a trade. By 1950, eight of the former orphans from Loting worked as nurses in hospitals in Canton and Toishan.[41] Of course not all the girls who left the orphanage as young adults adapted well to life in South China. Some had become too used to the artificially sheltered life of the orphanage. Commenting on those children who "did not know how to behave [socially]," Sister Candida Maria Basto said that her only regret was that they were "too much shut off from the outside world."[42]

Problems with the Orphanages

Despite all their efforts, the Sisters did not totally overcome the local superstitions against baby girls. The monthly figures for baptized babies fluctuated widely, with highs on the third, fifth, and ninth months of the Chinese year which local customs regarded as inauspicious for girls. Statistics also showed that before the Sino-Japanese War spread to South China, the Sisters baptized an average of 450 babies a year in Yeungkong which had a population of some 30,000 people. In Loting, with a population of about 20,000, the Sisters baptized 1,000 babies a year. Because of infection from unsanitary conditions at birth, neglect, and exposure, most children who reached the orphanage were at the point of death.

As the war encroached on Yeungkong and Loting and left many homeless, the Sisters found even more children at their door. In 1940 the Sisters in Yeungkong baptized 731 babies; in Loting, they baptized an average of 2,500 a year between 1937 and 1942. By 1944 China had some two million war orphans in need of care. Sister Richard Wenzel wrote from Loting, "Tiny infants were brought to us in increasing number each month. We receive an average 400 to 500 children [each month] from one to fifteen years old—dying of rickets, dysentery and smallpox."[43]

Altogether, Maryknollers were not able to save more than three to six percent of all the abandoned children brought to their doors. These statistics—as appalling as they seem—are not out of line with other Catholic orphanages. In 1935 the 365 Catholic orphanages in China received and baptized 299,000 infants, while they maintained a total enrollment of 28,900 orphans who represented the survivors of several years. Nonreligious institutions did not fare better. In his report for the years 1948 through 1951, the chief medical officer of the United Nations Relief and Rehabilitation Administration (U.N.R.R.A.) in Canton wrote:

> The hardest thing to bear was the indescribable sights seen daily in the children's ward. The mortality rate of these children picked up in the street where they had been discarded when the mothers despaired of being able to cure them was over 90%. TB, meningitis, and tetanus were prevalent in the new babies. Mortality rate [for the TB children] was almost 100%.[44]

The Sisters' diaries often related their struggle to keep the little ones alive. The sadness to see them die was soothed only by the consolation of having opened to them the "door of paradise."[45]

The turmoil of war and the ravages of epidemics often hindered the Sisters' efforts. Yeungkong was especially hard hit. In December 1934 the orphanage stopped receiving new children for almost one year because of

144

Fig. 1. Father Joseph Lavin and Sister Mary Francis baptizing a group of abandoned babies in Loting 1935. The infants are being held by older orphans. Source: Maryknoll Sisters Archives.

lack of funds. In August 1937 it closed again for four months because of an outbreak of cholera in the nursery. As the Japanese air raids increased in February 1943, some of the orphans and blind girls were moved to a safer place further inland. Finally, in June 1944 the Yeungkong orphanage closed for two years while the Sisters took refuge in Loting.[46]

In both Loting and Yeungkong, however, the most difficult task for the Sisters was breaking down local prejudice against orphanages and against the Catholic religion. While the Sisters saw their work as a service that benefited the people and witnessed to Christian charity, they soon realized that many Chinese thought they had other motives. The Chinese had always been intrigued by the Catholic Church's interest in the dead. Since the time of Matteo Ricci, missioners had been accused of gouging out the eyes of the dead to use for medicine. When Catholic orphanages came into being, the old slanders were often used again. Three months after their arrival in Loting in 1924, the Maryknoll Sisters found themselves at the center of such accusations:

> A group of about ten women and children came to see the convent and the catechumenate. After looking carefully, they asked the catechist's mother where the Sisters put the bones of the babies they killed. . . . We hear there is much more unpleasant talk about us. It is the old story—that we are using the bodies of the babies for medicine. They say that we strike the babies on the foreheads and their eyes drop out and these we make into medicine.[47]

Soon after, they were horrified to hear rumors that they were not only killing the babies but eating their flesh. Posters often appeared near the city gates or on the orphanage walls describing these same accusations. Believing the stories, some mothers even went to the orphanage to attempt to poison their babies, thinking they would be better off dead than with the Sisters. The people also objected to the orphanage undertaker passing in front of their houses daily with so many dead bodies.[48]

The city magistrate often played an important role in supporting either the Sisters or their accusers. For example, a poster was hung on the south gate of the city of Loting in February 1927, charging that foreigners were removing the eyes of Chinese babies and using them to make medicine. The city magistrate counteracted by issuing a proclamation stating that the charges against the Sisters were false. He also explained that the orphanage was a charitable institution where children not wanted by their parents were fed, clothed, and raised by the Sisters. Finally he warned against posting slanderous notices and promised severe punishment for their authors.[49]

A few years later, Maryknollers in Yeungkong encountered a much less accomodating city magistrate. Since it was widely believed that the Sisters removed the eyes and hearts of the babies to make medicine, he decided that no infants could be buried without prior examination by a city official. Strongly negative coverage in the local press prompted the pastor of Yeungkong, Father Maurice Feeney, to stop receiving dying infants for a period of six months.[50]

With the passage of time, however, the populations of Yeungkong and Loting became more and more appreciative of the Sisters' work. They came to realize that the same Sisters taking care of the sick at the dispensaries could not be killing babies. They saw that the orphanage was not a "death house" but a place for the living. Babies whose health had been restored grew into children and paraded through the streets in joyous bands on the way to the park. Young girls learned housekeeping and received primary schooling. The lame and the blind could stay as long as they wanted and earned a living by performing a trade they had learned from the Sisters.

Although most babies and children brought to the orphanage had been abandoned and had no traceable parents, there were some who had been voluntarily placed in the orphanage by their parents. In these cases, the Sisters insisted that the parents sign a release paper which stated that the child had been given to the orphanage. Once a child had been baptized, the only way her parents could regain custody was to become Catholic themselves. If the child was six or older and not in immediate danger of death at the time she was given to the orphanage, the Sisters usually delayed baptism for several months, suspecting that she was already betrothed and that the parents, accordingly, had no right to give her away.[51]

Since the Sisters were in constant need of wet nurses, the natural mother sometimes offered to breast-feed her own child for a small fee. At first the Sisters turned down such arrangements because they feared the children would not be returned and thus not raised as Catholics. Eventually, however, they changed their minds because they felt that the infants had a better chance to gain strength if fed and cared for by their own mothers. Before giving the child to her natural mother, however, they always made sure that it was understood that the child belonged to the orphanage and would be returned.[52]

The arrangement usually worked well. The mothers became attached to their infants but, at the same time, returned them after a year or two to the orphanage where they were provided with clothing, food, and a good education. The mothers and other relatives came to visit and took them home for big Chinese festivals—the Dragon Boat, the Mid-Autumn and the New Year.[53]

In the mid-1920s, however, several instances of friction between the parents and the Sisters created pockets of resentment which lasted for

B. Document to be signed by those who present a foundling to the orphanage.

A. Document to be signed by the parents whose children are adopted by an orphanage.

堂 顧 某
作 將 縣
主 此 某
不 孩 村
與 送 立
送 於 送
之 仁 嬰
人 慈 孩
相 堂 字
干 永 據
恐 遠 人
口 收 某
無 養 茲
憑 日 因
立 後 在
字 長 路
存 大 或
照 出 街
嫁 一
等 女
事 嬰
全 無
由 人
仁 照
慈 管

中 立
保 字
人 人
某 某

中 華 民 國 年 月 日

DOCUMENTUM SUB-
SCRIBENDUM

A PARENTIBUS QUORUM
INFANTES ADOPTANTUR IN
ORPHANOTROPHIIS

S. INFANTIÆ

恐 出 某 日 某
口 嫁 年 維 縣
無 等 某 眼 某
憑 事 月 顧 村
立 全 某 將 立
字 由 日 觀 送
存 仁 送 生 嬰
據 慈 於 女 孩
堂 仁 孩 字
作 慈 年 據
主 堂 幾 人
不 永 歲 某
與 遠 零 茲
送 收 幾 因
孩 養 個 家
之 日 月 道
家 後 或 貧
相 養 生 寒
干 大 於 虔

中 立
保 字
人 人
某 某

中 華 民 國 年 月 日

TRANSLATIONS

B. Document signed at ____ village of ____ county

_____, who has found an abandoned infant girl, agrees to let her be adopted by an orphanage. The orphanage will assume responsibility of raising the girl and see to her marriage, etc. upon her coming of age. The undersigned shall not interfere under any circumstance.

This document, properly signed, shall be the solemn proof of mutual consent.

Signed _____
Witness _____

A. Document signed at ____ village of ____ county

_____ because of poverty and hardship agrees to let his own daughter, aged __ years __ months, or born on __ day __ month of __ year, be adopted by an orphanage. The orphanage will assume the responsibility of raising the girl and see to her marriage, etc. upon her coming of age. The family shall not interfere under any circumstance.

This document, properly signed, shall be the solemn proof of mutual consent.

Signed _____
Witness _____

Fig. 2. Orphanage Documents. Source: Bishop James E. Walsh, *Mission Manual of the Vicariate of Kongmoon* (Hong Kong: Nazareth Press, 1937), p. 222.

many years. When the Loting Sisters were recalled to Hong Kong in July 1925, they left the orphanage in the hands of two capable women, Mary Chan and Shi I Koo. To be able to carry on with their task, Miss Chan and Mrs. Shi asked the parents and the former wet nurses of the 15 older children—all between the ages of three and five—to take them back temporarily, with pay. They made them sign an agreement to return the children upon the Sisters' return.

When the Sisters came back to Loting ten months later, they found some parents reluctant to give back their daughters. Conditioned by the then prevalent Catholic theology of salvation, the Sisters and their pastor, Daniel McShane, considered themselves responsible for removing these baptized children from the influence of their non-Catholic mothers. They wrote: "With us it is a question of souls and we are doing all in our power to find the little ones who have been baptized."[54] In the process, however, they undoubtedly dismissed too easily the genuine love of the non-Christian mothers for their daughters. The Sisters wrote in their diary:

> Some of the parents refuse to give back our "old" babies. We doubt if it be because of their love for them, but rather because they can get a good sum of money for them now [by selling them]. . . . Some harsh measures will have to be used before we get the little ones back.[55]

Sister Maureen Au, who later joined the Sisters of the Immaculate Heart of Kongmoon, was one of these babies. She was very sick when she was brought to the orphanage. Her Buddhist parents had tried many types of medicine with no success and had finally concluded that their daughter could not be saved by Chinese doctors. Maureen Au was baptized in the orphanage by the Sisters who cured her and then entrusted her to her mother for a few years. She recalled that her parents told her how they wanted to keep her, but finally returned her to the orphanage when the Sisters threatened to take them to court.[56]

Within a month after their return, the Sisters retrieved most of the children; four families, however, still refused. Finally, in late August, the Sisters took their grievance to the assistant magistrate of the town, whom they had befriended, and they filed written charges with the chief of police.

The parents were given a few days to return the girls to the orphanage or face imprisonment. One family escaped prosecution by claiming that the child had died during the Sisters' absence. They succeeded by hiding her in a bandit-controlled village; ten years later the Sisters were still attempting to get her back. The mothers of the three other girls begged the Sisters to let them keep their children for a few more years, but the Sisters were adamant in asserting their rights over the children: "We refuse as we feel perfectly able to take care of [the girls] and besides want them out of their pagan surroundings as soon as possible."[57]

The families then resorted to the stratagem of bringing in substitute children. The Sisters knew that these poor people had paid as much as 80 dollars in local currency (US$20) for a substitute. Yet the Sisters were so preoccupied with the "Christian souls" of these girls that they refused the substitutes. As a result, two mothers and one father were thrown in jail until the right child was produced. The families had no recourse. By September 7, Clothilde, age six, Octavie, age four and Christine, age five, were back in the orphanage. Eventually, however, time smoothed away most of the hard feelings. Ten years later, Clothilde's mother and many of her non-Christian relatives were filling up the front benches of the Loting church to see her happily married.[58]

Communist Accusations

By the time the Communists came to Loting and Yeungkong in 1949, earlier grudges against the Maryknoll orphanages were practically nonexistent. At first, the Sisters received praise for their work and were told to carry on. They continued to receive abandoned children, but, as a precaution, sent most of the older children home if their parents were still living. In Yeungkong they also stopped receiving old women.

By late 1950, however, the Communists began to use the orphanages to discredit and incriminate the Maryknollers. The first signs that the Maryknollers had fallen into disfavor appeared on November 12, 1950, when the mission compound in Yeungkong was put under guard. Both the rectory and the convent were searched for hidden radios and arms. In the next days, while the compound was meticulously combed, Maryknollers were confined to their rooms. When no incriminating evidence was found, they were set free but were so closely watched that they preferred to stay inside. Sisters Beatrice Meyer and Mary Dolorosa Oberle, the two Sisters in Yeungkong, renewed their efforts to place most of the remaining children in homes, except for 25 blind and crippled girls. Following the official freeze of all foreign assets and the compulsory registration of all foreign property in December, they applied for exit permits. On March 15, 1951, two weeks after they were forced out of their convents and housed together with their pastor in the blind girls' home, the Sisters were given their exit permits. Two days later they crossed the border at Hong Kong without having been formally charged with any wrongdoing.[59]

Father Aloysius Rechsteiner, pastor of Yeungkong, remained in the home for the blind for another nine months. The Communists tried to charge him with mismanagement of the orphanage but were unable to elicit accusations from the Yeungkong people. The blind and crippled orphans refused to accuse Father Rechsteiner of causing the death of infants who had been brought to the orphanage. At first, the Communists used persuasion by bringing the orphans gifts of sweets and fruit; when this did not work, they tried threats but to no avail. The orphans kept telling them, "Good. If he is guilty we will go and die with him."[60]

In December 1951, the Communists formally took over the orphanage and moved Rechsteiner to a separate house.[61] On this occasion, they published a long article in the local newspaper and in *Wen Hui Pao* of Hong Kong on the conditions in the Yeungkong Catholic orphanage. The accusations were very similar to those published earlier in the year by the Communist press against other Catholic orphanages, especially the one in Canton run by the Canadian Sisters of the Immaculate Conception. the article in *Wen Hui Pao* described the Maryknoll Sisters in Yeungkong as "corrupt and depraved nuns who were utterly indifferent to the fate of the infants and children in their charge." It further implied that they were lucky to have escaped Chinese justice before the extent of their crimes was uncovered. Sister Mary Dolorosa Oberle was specifically referred to as the head of this "slaughterhouse" where more than 40,000 babies were killed. A caricature similar to the one which had been previously used against a Canadian Sister depicted Sister Mary Dolorosa receiving a healthy well-fed infant in one hand while discarding the emaciated body of another one down a trapdoor hiding the remains of all those she had previously killed.[62]

After December 1951, the Communists spent seven months trying to build a case against Father Rechsteiner. The local population knew the facts and missioners too well to believe the far-fetched accusations in the newspapers. The Communists submitted the blind and lame girls to a series of threats, bribes, and indoctrination classes but somehow these girls stood firm in their refusal to accuse Rechsteiner. Soon word leaked into Hong Kong that the Communists were calling Yeungkong the "worst orphanage in China and the orphans the most obstinate." Finally, realizing that they would never be able to build a case against Rechsteiner, the Communists expelled him in July 1952.[63]

In Loting, Maryknollers began to encounter serious difficulties in mid-January 1951 with frequent inspections of the mission compounds, sometimes in the middle of the night. Following the February 27 and 28 publication of articles in the Canton *Nanfang Ribao* and the Hong Kong *Ta Kung Pao* and *Wen Hui Pao* denouncing the incompetence and the neglect of the Canadian Sisters at the Catholic orphanage in Canton, the police in Loting started to question the five Maryknollers (two priests and three Sisters) about how many babies had been received and how many had survived. On

Fig. 3. The caricature above of Sister Mary Dolorosa Oberle which appeared in a Yeungkong newspaper charged that the "orphanage [in Yeungkong] is a veritable slaughterhouse for infants and children." Similar caricatures were used against the Canadian Sisters of the Immaculate Conception in Canton. Source: SARC, Box—War Years, File 2, Drawer 3, Iron Curtain Diaries and Accounts, Sister Mary Dolorosa Oberle, "Memories of Yeungkong."

March 17, Father Robert Kennelly, the pastor, was arrested and charged with wrongdoings which were almost verbatim the same accusations brought against the Canadian Sisters in Canton: that he had let most of the orphans die due to lack of food and neglect; and that he was also a trained spy raising orphans to become spies.

Meanwhile, a large antiforeign parade circulated through the streets of Loting, branding Kennelly as a murderer who used babies' eyes and brains to make medicine. The local newspaper published a series of accusations against Kennelly and Sister Monica Marie Boyle, the nurse in charge of the orphanage. Among other charges, they were said to have killed a girl by giving her the wrong medicine and to have extorted money from people who wanted to retrieve their babies from the orphanage.

Within the next few weeks, the three Sisters, Colombiere Bradley, Monica Marie Boyle, and Candida Maria Basto, and the curate of Loting,

Father John Graser, were also taken in for questioning and then arrested. The Maryknollers stayed in prison until late June while the Communists tried to instigate a public trial against them. They soon realized that they could not build their case solely on charges of killing babies because no one came forward to accuse the missioners. The local population was not aroused by the Communist propaganda. The Communists then fell back on minor charges: that the two Sisters were found to be in possession of unregistered American money, and that American guns and ammunition and anti-Communist literature were retrieved on the Fathers' property. But even these were not sufficient to inculpate the missioners: the amount of money was insignificant; the guns and most of the ammunition were so rusty that they were useless; and only two "reactionary" books were found. The Communists finally abandoned the idea of a trial. At the end of June 1952, the five missioners were taken to Communist headquarters in Shuihing where they were deported on the basis of four charges: killing 4,000 babies, possession of guns and ammunition, possession of unregistered American money and possession of reactionary and anti-Communist literature.

It was only after the Loting missioners had left that the Communists had gathered enough confidence to try them—*in absentia*. Kennelly was found guilty and sentenced to two years imprisonment, and the story was officially reported by the Communist News Agency.[64]

The Hospital in Toishan

The Pioneer Work of Dr. Blaber

In March 1922, Dr. Flagg's column in *The Field Afar* was renamed "Maryknoll Medical Activities" and included letters from Maryknoll missioners in China waiting for a doctor to come and open a Catholic hospital. In late 1922 there was no government-run hospital for the 2.8 million people living in the Maryknoll territory of South China. Two small Protestant hospitals in Yeungkong and Loting totaled only 50 beds. Although Maryknoll received generous gifts for its medical missions, Dr. Flagg and Father James A. Walsh were unsuccessful for many years in their appeal to young lay doctors to join Maryknollers in South China for "a few years of a lonely life with very few distractions."[65]

Finally, in early 1930, a young doctor from Brooklyn pledged five years of his life to Maryknoll. By September, Harry Blaber was at work in the station of Tungon in the vicariate of Kongmoon with a salary of US$100 per month. His accomplishments in China tell the success story of a man with the ability and ingenuity to make the most of what was at hand. In the first six months, he turned a makeshift dispensary into a field hospital where he treated 9,250 cases without charge. He partitioned the small house into a consultation room, clinic surgery ward for six inpatients, pharmacy, and laboratory. His laboratory was ingenious. He made a sterilizer from an old trunk, insulating the inner compartment with old newspapers, woolen rags, chicken feathers, and other poor heat conductors. A pipe channeled steam into the compartment from a big Chinese kettle with a lid soldered above and a charcoal fire below.[66] Blaber also trained a staff of native nurses with the idea of later sending them to run dispensaries in other stations, freeing the priests for preaching and doctrinal instruction. "The doctor is truly a Godsend," remarked the pastor, Father Otto Rauschenbach. "Since his arrival, inquiries about the doctrine have been on the increase. The prospects look so good that I have started a little catechism class after Sunday mass for those seeking information."[67]

After two years, Dr. Blaber opened Sacred Heart Hospital in Toishan, the largest city in the Kongmoon vicariate. The mission consisted of a two-story cruciform building 25 by 70 feet, originally intended for a church and living quarters for the priests. Blaber converted it; the ground level became a hospital, and a second floor was partitioned into a small chapel and a few rooms for the priest and the parish activities. The beginnings were very humble. Blaber used to say that he started with only "a bottle of Mercurochrome, a bottle of iodine and a roll of bandages." He turned this one room of vacant space into an efficient hospital that he called his "dollhouse." To those who wondered how he was able to fit a laboratory, a pharmacy, an examination room, a ward with 30 beds and an operating room into such a small space, he said, "You can't imagine the size of my examination room. If I turned around quickly, I poke the patient in the stomach. It's tiny but efficient."[68] He cared for about 13,000 patients a year, half of them suffering from tuberculosis. Eighty percent of his work was charity.

> Those who can pay us, give 20 cents Cantonese. This is just 7 cents here [US]. Most can't pay at all but they get the same treatment as others. After all, we are not in the business for money. If we were, I would have taken in my shingle the day I landed.[69]

With the arrival in 1934 of a nurse, Brother Gregory Brennock, and two young doctors, Louis Chan, a graduate of Canton Medical School, and Artemio Bagalawis, a graduate of the University of St. Thomas in Manila, Blaber extended his service to dispensaries in neighboring towns and villages. In 1936, using an old car, the doctors took turns making weekly visits to six clinics scattered over a 20-mile radius from Toishan.

Blaber seems to have been the first to develop the idea of wrapping medicines in colored papers printed with information on the Catholic Church. The bright paper and a natural curiosity to understand the writing led many patients to examine the wrappers. Later Monsignor Meyer and other Maryknollers borrowed the idea and also reported increased inquiries about Christianity.[70]

Blaber also improved the training of his native staff by opening a formal training school for male nurses. The curriculum, including practical training in the hospital and courses taught by the three doctors, was comparable to that of a nursing school in the United States.[71] In addition to the hospital, Blaber wanted to build a sanitorium for tuberculosis patients, who accounted for 50 percent of his caseload. Unfortunately, he was never able to fulfill this dream.

When his contract with Maryknoll expired in late 1935, Blaber went back to New York to marry his fiancée, Constance White, a nurse. Together they pledged to serve Maryknoll for life and she accompanied him to Sacred Heart Hospital in Toishan. However, it soon became evident that Mrs. Blaber could not endure the climate of South China. The bombing of Toishan by the Japanese in September 1937 further contributed to the deterioration of her health. Before the end of the year, the doctor, his wife, and their baby girl sailed back to the United States.[70]

Because Dr. Bagalawis was fully occupied with the newly opened leper colony in Ngaimoon, Dr. Chan took charge of the Toishan Hospital. When he contracted typhoid three years later and returned to Canton for treatment, the hospital was left without a doctor. During the summer of 1941, Father Francis O'Neill, the pastor of Toishan, was forced to close the facilities because the Japanese blockade of Hong Kong made the procurement of medical supplies very hazardous. He converted the hospital into a refugee center.

When a unit of the British Army Aid Group headed by Captain Surgeon Raymond Lee came to the city in 1943, O'Neill welcomed them with open arms as they brought not only rice and money but a large stock of medicine. Sacred Heart Hospital was reopened to serve the poor exclusively and it was "easier for a camel to pass through the eye of a needle than for a rich man to enter it." The four nurses assisting Doctor Lee were native Sisters. When surgery was needed O'Neill served as anesthetist. However, when the Japanese advanced toward the city in June 1944, the British moved out and O'Neill himself joined the ranks of refugees.[73]

Sister Dominic Marie Turner Takes Over

After the war, the bishop of Kongmoon, Adolph Paschang, reopened the Toishan hospital with a group of native Sisters in charge until he was able to assemble a professional medical staff. In April 1947, Maryknoll Sister

Dominic Marie Turner, a nurse, became the administrator and Sister Maria Corazon Jaramillo, the doctor. Dr. Bagalawis joined the hospital staff as surgeon in July 1948. Together they reopened the nursing school to provide the native Sisters of Kongmoon with the medical and hospital management skills necessary for them to one day take over the hospital.

During the war, most of the furnishings and equipment had disappeared. Through gifts, mostly from U.N.R.R.A., the United States Economic Cooperation Administration (E.C.A.), and the Canton branch of the Catholic Welfare Committee of China (C.W.C.C.), the Sisters refurbished the hospital with beds, matresses, blankets, mosquito nets, sheets, pillows, and towels. These organizations also supplied an operating room, laboratory equipment, infra-red and violet-ray lamps, and an electric generator. The Sisters were even promised an X-ray machine and an ambulance, but had to leave the hospital before they were shipped. They also received large quantities of medicine, "much more than we could use over a space of ten years," said Sister Dominic Marie.[74]

Between May 1947 and August 1949, the Sisters took care of 200 to 300 people a month in the outpatient clinic. Three days a week were reserved for the poor people of the city, which meant that at least half of the outpatients were treated without charge. In January 1948, the Sisters started weekly visits to surrounding villages to take care of patients who would not come to the hospital. They became increasingly concerned with the deteriorating situation in and around Toishan and the growing number of destitute people. For Christmas 1948 they collected enough funds from well-to-do families to organize a dinner for 1,571 of the poor. The following spring, they applied to C.W.C.C. and E.C.A. in Canton for supplies to open a soup kitchen. As a start they received 10,000 pounds of oatmeal and the same amount of soybeans. The food line grew from a couple of hundred people to about 5,000 daily by the time the Communists took over the city in late October 1949.[75]

As none of the 20 available beds was left empty for long, Bishop Paschang sought a way to expand the hospital. In September 1949 a four-story building one block away was rented to serve as the new Sacred Heart Hospital. With the old building kept for contagious cases, the new hospital reached a capacity of 60 beds. The Sisters treated at least two-thirds of the patients without charge. In the new building, the Sisters also opened a weekly afternoon free clinic for babies and taught mothers how to take better care of their infants. They usually saw 10 to 15 children per session. Meanwhile the number of poor people treated without charge in the out patient clinic increased to more than 200 a month.[76]

For the first six months after the arrival of the Communists to "liberate" Toishan, the hospital seemed to have the favor of the new authorities. The Sisters received courteous visits from officials who praised its cleanliness, the quality of medical work performed, and the invaluable service rendered to the people by the free clinic and the soup kitchen. Then in April a series of ordeals began which continued for almost three years for Sister Dominic Marie.

At first the Communists treated the hospital as a place of business and expected Sister Dominic Marie to buy war bonds and pay taxes. She refused, emphasizing that the hospital was a charitable institution where, since "liberation," over 75 percent of the patients had been treated without charge. To prove her point, she decided that all outpatients would be treated without charge as of January 1951, and in August she extended the policy to all hospital services.

In March and August 1951, respectively, Dr. Bagalawis and Sister Magdalena Urlacher were allowed to leave the hospital and China. In early December when Sisters Corazon and Dominic Marie received the order from their superior in Hong Kong to apply for exit visas, they stopped accepting patients in the hospital but continued the daily free clinic. They continued to treat over 2,000 people monthly until the last day of February 1952 when they were imprisoned in the hospital together with Father John Toomey, the pastor of Toishan, and a small group of Chinese Sisters.

The hospital's medical supplies and apparatus were transferred to the government hospital and most of the Sisters' personal belongings were confiscated. Toomey and the Sisters were accused of spying; the building was searched for transmitter sets, arms, and special mirrors to signal planes. The septic tank of the hospital was left uncovered to show the fate of the remains of the thousands of babies allegedly killed by the Sisters and flushed down the toilet. Because she was considered the leader of the group, Sister Dominic Marie had to endure many more humiliations than the others: she was slapped, spat upon, and yelled at; she was kept standing in the sun for long hours and was subjected to lengthy interrogation sessions. Yet she never admitted to any crimes. Twice the authorities tried to bring the trio to a public trial but failed to build a strong enough case. Finally in June 1952, Sister Corazon and Father Toomey were expelled and a little later the Chinese Sisters were ordered back to their native villages. Sister Dominic Marie, however, remained imprisoned in the hospital to await punishment for the crimes she had allegedly committed.

The ensuing months took their toll on Sister Dominic Marie. A public exhibit recounting all her supposed crimes was held under her window. From there she could also see the public trials held on the parade grounds, listen to accusations blared over the loudspeakers, and hear the accused being shot. These scenes affected her and it became increasingly difficult for her to sleep. Her daily food was reduced to half a bowl of cooked rice with two spoonfuls of green vegetables and a cup of coffee in the morning. One night her guards tried to force open her door and made it appear as if they intended to rape her. The next morning, the two women officials who came to visit her each day found the Sister unconcious. After this incident Sister Dominic Marie's health, which had until then remained relatively good, deteriorated rapidly. She experienced frequent dizzy spells, her sight began to fail, and she was unable to retain food. A local doctor was called in and diagnosed her condition as due to malnutrition and cancer. At the end of October she was finally sent to Canton for treatment. After three months, she regained some of the 67 pounds she had lost in Toishan and was then given her exit permit. She reached Hong Kong on January 14, 1953.[77]

The Shanghai Mercy Hospital

When she passed through Shanghai in October 1923, Mother Mary Joseph had been the guest of Lo Pa-hong, a well-known philanthropist and an earnest Catholic committed to helping the destitute of his country. They toured the large St. Joseph's Hospice he had opened in 1912. Run by the Sisters of Charity of St. Vincent de Paul, it cared for more than 3,000 patients. Mother Mary Joseph was very impressed by the care provided in all the departments, except the one for the mentally ill. She was taken aback to see that most of the mental patients were chained to keep them from running away or hurting themselves. She was even more surprised to learn that it was the best that could be done under the circumstances because China had no modern facilities for the treatment of nervous diseases.

When Lo Pa-hong approached her a decade later to staff the women's section of China's first modern hospital for the mentally ill, she readily agreed. The first group of Sisters selected for the task included five nurses, a laboratory technician, and an occupational therapist. Sister Roma Schleininger, who had training in mental illnesses, and previous experience with deranged patients, went as supervisor of the women's section. She was also in charge of the Chinese nurses and nurse aides. The only Sister with no medical training was the bursar, Sister Joan Miriam Beauvais.[78]

At the same time, six Brothers of Charity of Trier who were trained as psychiatric workers arrived from Germany. The medical director, an Austrian psychiatrist, Dr. Fanny Halpern, was assisted by an international staff of seven doctors. The hospital was administered by Chinese personnel directly responsible to Mr. Lo.

The Shanghai Mercy Hospital for Nervous Diseases opened on July 6, 1935. It was located in Pei-ch'iao, a suburb ten miles outside of the city. The patients were housed in eight pavilions, four each for the female and the male sections. Pavilions One and Two were for paying patients who could afford private or semiprivate accommodations. Pavilion Three was the free ward, and Pavilion Four with padded cells was reserved for the most disturbed or troublesome patients. In a few months, the number of in-patients grew from 56 to as many as 300. Two years after it opened, the hospital had already treated 508 free patients, for a total of 935.[79]

Although Mr. Lo built the hospital with the latest facilities and equipment, including hydro-therapy and electro-therapy, his ideas were not always practical. He was so firmly convinced that mentally ill patients would respond positively if put in beautiful buildings with pleasant surroundings that he refused, at first, to heed the demands of the medical staff for safety and protective devices. The doors had no locks, and windows had no gratings. When the first 56 patients arrived in mid-July, the Brothers and Sisters found it very difficult to keep watch over them. With few personnel on duty at night, pandemonium broke loose: patients wandered up and down the corridors, climbed on window ledges, and jumped out into the garden. The second night, a woman managed to escape and was found two days later drowned in a nearby ditch. The incident was reported in the *Shanghai Foreign Press* as a sign of carelessness. Mr. Lo agreed to install locks on pavilion doors and protective bars on verandas, glass doors, and windows, afraid that more incidents would ruin the reputation of his new hospital.[80] Sister Virginia Marie Lynn, the superior of the group, recalled:

> The following months were spent in an attempt to establish some kind of order. Each day there were patients who broke out into new and sometimes startling phases of activity. The most overactive and unstable cases were placed in hydro-therapy baths. Packs for some, medication for others were the order of the day. All patients needed individual care and study. Names and family histories were obtained when possible; symptoms recorded and laboratory examinations made for each patient.[81]

The Sisters learned the need for constant vigilance not only with the most disturbed patients but also with others who experienced occasional violent fits and hurt themselves and others. Showing a scar on her arm, Sister Herman Joseph Stitz recalled that patients in Pavilion Four were called the "man-eaters" because they thought nothing of taking a bite out of whoever approached them. The diary for August 30, 1936, mentioned humorously that most Sisters were so badly bitten that their favorite pastime was to compare who had the biggest scars. The latest incident had involved Sister Espiritu Venneman who, while putting a patient to bed, was thrown on the floor and then bitten in the knee exposing the bone. The same vigilance was needed on the men's side. A few days before Christmas

1937, a patient in the occupational therapy room suddenly went on a rampage and stabbed a Brother and his attendant before taking his own life.[82]

In spite of these incidents, the compound gradually became an effective psychiatric hospital with records of almost every type of mental illness, often compounded by medical problems such as malnutrition, tuberculosis, epilepsy, and Parkinson's disease. After comparing Mercy with a hospital she visited on Ward Island in New York in 1942, Sister Herman Joseph concluded that Shanghai's was an improvement. She was especially proud of the laboratory where she used guinea pigs, rabbits, and sheep to prepare the media necessary to run all her tests. "We did a very thorough check-up on each patient. Each had a blood count, urine analysis, a stool examination, Wasserman test for syphillis, and sugar chemistry test; some were even tested for tuberculosis."[83] After two years of operation, the hospital was on a very good footing: eight doctors, nine Sisters, and 11 Brothers supervised a nursing staff of 40 Chinese nurses and 90 male and female attendants, with a total of about 400 patients.

The bombing of Shanghai by the Japanese on August 13, 1937, signaled the beginning of a different experience for the Sisters. Within a few days the sounds of war grew closer and most of the Chinese help and all but one doctor left. Pei-ch'iao, the site of the hospital, was an important junction which controlled the road from Shanghai to Nanking. While the Chinese dug in all around the hospital to stop the invasion, Japanese planes bombarded the area for three months. Towns were destroyed, railways cut open, roads strafed, and the power plant blown up. Yet while most of the medical institutions of the Shanghai area were hit, Mercy Hospital was spared.[84] The three different flags floating over it probably confused the Japanese flyers, but the Sister diarist preferred to attribute their safety to God's protection.

> September 11: Six bombs dropped in the fields near the hospital. We account for the protection which has been ours not to the swastika raised above the Brothers' building, not to Old Glory unfurled above our house, not even to the Red Cross flag which floats from our church spire, but to the prayers offered for our safety.[85]

In early November it was clear that the Chinese defense of Shanghai was being crushed and that the front line would soon reach the hospital. By the time Mr. Lo decided to move the patients and staff to the protection of the French Concession, the roads were no longer passable. Shanghai fell on November 9. Due to the explosion of a major electric power house, the hospital was left without electricity or water which added to the Sisters' and Brothers' sense of isolation. And yet, as witnessed by the entry in the house diary for that day, the Sisters maintained their spirit and a healthy sense of humor.

> You would smile if you saw how we went to bed tonight—fully dressed with our passports, a candle, matches, a bottle of holy water and a clean handkerchief in our pockets. Sister [Antoinette] gave us each some money so that in case we get separated, we could get along.[86]

Finally in the early hours of November 12 the hospital found itself in the middle of the "Battle of the Crossroads." The Japanese arrived in Pei-ch'iao from two directions, and some element of the Chinese army entrenched next to the hospital offered a strong resistance in an effort to deny them the road to Nanking.

> Our day began at 2:30 a.m. when it seemed war started right at our back door. All the Sisters and nurses went on the floors so that in case the fighting came closer we would all be with the patients. We could hear the shouts of Chinese soldiers "Shah! Shah!" Which means "kill, kill," the crying of the women and children and the snarling of dogs.[87]

Hearing the fierceness of the fight, one Brother said, "Sister, we will never see the dawn."[88] Yet when the machine guns finally stopped firing four hours later, no one in the hospital was hurt. The Japanese had won the battle. After a few days they allowed the Brothers and Sisters to go out and look for wounded Chinese soldiers and to bury the dead. Sister Herman Joseph remembered the stench which filled the countryside. In a week's time they recovered 600 bodies and buried them in the trenches dug a few months earlier.[89]

In order to avoid reprisal bombing by the Japanese, the hospital had not admitted wounded Chinese soldiers before the Battle of the Crossroads, but had given them first-aid treatment in a little house outside the main gate. After the military takeover, however, the Japanese authorities granted permission to admit wounded soldiers. Their number grew to as many as 50 and added to the hospital's food burden at a time when Mr. Lo, who had been financially ruined, told the Brothers and Sisters not to expect money or supplies from him for months to come.

Since the beginning of the Japanese bombing in August, refugees sought shelter and food at the hospital. When people noticed that the buildings were never hit, they arrived in even greater numbers. Sister Herman Joseph, who was put in charge of the Chinese kitchen, remembered that by the end of October they were already feeding 1,200 refugees and that their number grew to 3,000 before they started to return home at the end of December. Procuring the 900 pounds of rice necessary each day to give three meals to the 300 mental patients and two meals to the refugees looked like an impossible task. Yet when they seemed to be down to the last grain, something would happen and they managed to continue feeding everyone. One sister wrote:

> We were hungry but God sent us food in many ways, like that one time when sampans going to Shanghai to sell rice found that the Japanese army had advanced so far up that they gave their rice to us for the patients.[91]

By the end of December 1937, the fighting had moved out of the area. The Japanese occupation of Shanghai restored order, and the situation began to improve. Mr. Lo was again confident he could gather funds to operate the hospital. That Christmas was a very happy celebration at the hospital: the church bells, silenced since August, rang; there were small gifts and a party for the patients, the wounded soldiers, the nurses and attendants who had returned. The best celebration, however, was reserved for the refugees' children—each received a stocking stuffed with small gifts from a Brother dressed up as St. Nicholas.

Five days later, however, the Catholic population of Shanghai was stunned by the news of the assassination of Mr. Lo. The Japanese had approached him to chair a civic organization to restructure the destroyed power and light plant. Mr. Lo had been warned by some Chinese that if he accepted, he would be viewed as a collaborator. On the other hand, he knew that if he refused, millions of Chinese would remain without electricity and water. After much reflection and prayer, Mr. Lo decided that charity and the relief of the people of Shanghai were more important than his reputation or his life. The morning after he signified his acceptance to the Japanese, he was shot.

The death of Lo jeopardized all the institutions he had sponsored. A Committee for the Organization and Continuation of the Works of Mr. Lo Pa-hong was formed to try to keep these institutions afloat. Bishop Auguste Haouisée of Shanghai was chairman and Francis Lo, a son of the deceased, executive secretary. In early 1938, the operating expenses of Mercy Hospital alone amounted to US$5,000 a month. The French Municipal Council and the International Settlement, which had contributed to its support in return for a free allotment of 50 beds, temporarily assumed most of the costs. They made it clear to the bishop, however, that they would withdraw their donations entirely unless he found foreign management and additional sources of revenue, and endeavored to make the hospital more profitable.

When the bishop approached the Maryknoll Sisters to see if they would consider assuming full responsibility for the hospital, they thoroughly reviewed its financial situation. Besides operating expenses, the hospital needed US$70,000 for repairs and owed US$15,000 in interest on loans of over a quarter of a million dollars. The Maryknoll Sisters, themselves, faced with serious financial difficulties from the long years of the Depression in the United States, told the bishop they could provide trained personnel but not finance the hospital. Since the bishop had made it clear that unless he could find a community to assume total responsibility for the institution, he would close it down, the Maryknoll Sisters signified their intention to withdraw. They left on November 1, 1938, and were replaced by the Franciscan Sisters of Mercy from Luxemburg.[92] In 1949, the communist authorities took over the direction of Mercy Hospital, which still provides care for the mentally ill.

Leper Colony

Upon their arrival in South China, Maryknollers quickly realized that leprosy was a major illness in that part of the world. Because of the fear of leprosy, lepers were banished from their homes and towns and forced to seek shelter in the countryside where no one else would live, often in old cemeteries and marshes. Missioners seemed to be the only people interested in caring for them. At Sheklung near Canton, two M.E.P. priests, three Canadian Sisters of the Immaculate Conception, and one native Sister ran a leper colony for 700 patients. Maryknollers visited Sheklung several times and expressed admiration for its accomplishments.

In the Kongmoon territory, they encountered their first leper village on cemetery land north of Yeungkong. They were impressed by the charity of Dr. W. H. Dobson, the Presbyterian minister of Yeungkong Hospital, who went once a week to administer modern treatment to 50 lepers and gave them materials and money for better living quarters. In Loting they met another American Presbyterian minister, Dr. Ellsworth Dickson, who had no difficulty finding personnel to staff his hospital but could find no one willing to work in the leper asylum he had started outside the town.[93]

Bishop James E. Walsh, receiving reports of more and more of these leper villages, decided that Maryknoll should establish a leper colony. He waited patiently, however, until he could assign personnel full time to the care of the lepers and, in the meantime, he asked his missioners to survey the conditions of the lepers in their parishes.

In late 1932, he assigned Father Joseph Sweeney to make an extensive survey of the care and treatment of leprosy in modern facilities. This study tour took Sweeney not only to American leprosaria in Louisiana and the Hawaiian Islands but also to China and in particular to many groups of leprous beggars who lived outside towns in the Maryknoll vicariate of Kongmoon. He was appalled to find that in all of China with an estimated two million lepers, there were only 12 leprosaria, mostly Catholic-run, with a total of 2,000 patients. He was most impressed by the care given to 700 lepers at the St. Joseph Asylum in Sheklung. He visited Dr. Dobson in Yeungkong and saw that he had neither the time nor the funds to do more for the lepers. Sweeney talked to Dr. Blaber, the Maryknoll lay-physician, who estimated the number of lepers at 2,000 in the prefecture of Tungon alone. He saw in Blaber the "ideal foundation to build the [Maryknoll] medical work of leprosy."[94]

In October 1933, although he had no money at hand for the work, James E. Walsh appointed Sweeney to head the leper work in Kongmoon and assigned Father Francis Connors to assist him. As a start, they went to a group of 20 leprous beggars who lived in a cluster of huts on the grounds of an abandoned Taoist shrine near the city of Toishan. Dr Blaber had already started weekly treatment of these lepers and had gained their confidence. According to Sweeney and Connors, the place was:

> Worse to sight and smell than any pig sty. . . . Here were vermin-infested human beings who slept on the bottom of Mother Earth at night or sat by day bloating and decaying in the sunshine. Dirt was their chief characteristic; only despair made them as human. . . . We dug a well for them and built new houses while using the old ones for fuel. Bathrooms, dispensary, new clothes and wholesome diet were provided. The poor wretches heartily cooperated. . . . The place became a little park and the lepers turned out to be God's own children.[95]

Although this was the time of the Depression, a leper fund had accrued over the years at the Maryknoll Center, and the superior general quickly released the money for the new enterprise. In response to periodic articles in *The Field Afar* and other appeals describing Maryknoll's work among lepers, American Catholics kept the fund well supplied. In addition, Sweeney received money directly from a successful fund-raising drive launched during a visit to America.

Owing to the new injection of money and the arrival of a Brother-nurse, Walsh extended the leper work to other hamlets in Kongmoon. At Sheung Yeung near the parish of Chiklung, Father George Bauer provided food, medication, and other necessities to some 30 lepers. The nurse, Brother Gregory Brennock, took charge of Toishan while Sweeney and Connors moved north to the hilly burial grounds of Sunwui. They found 48 lepers dwelling in homes made of old coffin boards, eking out a miserable existence by planting tiny vegetable patches in hollows too wet for graves. Rats infested the place and at night gnawed on the feet of the bed-ridden lepers, who had lost all feelings in their extremities due to the disease.

Establishment of the Sunwui Colony

The Fathers cleaned and disinfected the site and poisoned the rats. They burned all the coffin-board hovels, the beds, and the grimy mats that covered them. Some able-bodied artisans among the lepers gladly helped them erect temporary bamboo homes covered with woven palm leaves. Later the Fathers received enough money from the United States to put up sturdier buildings with mud bricks and cement floors. Paths were cleared and bordered with hedges; flowerbeds were laid out; orchards of banana, papaya, and orange trees were planted.[96] The two Maryknollers also provided daily medical treatment. Dr. Blaber and Dr. Bagalawis took turns giving up their Sundays as days of rest to go out from Toishan to treat the more serious cases and plan the medical work for the rest of the week.

Within a few months, the regional grapevine carried news of these "red-haired devils"—a Chinese term for Caucasians—who restored life and hope to the lepers in the graveyards of Sunwui. By September 1934, 157 lepers had already come to the cemetery. At the end of the first year, Maryknollers were caring for 218 patients in Toishan, Sheung Yeung, and Sunwui. These settlements were intended to be temporary until more permanent quarters could be built.

In January 1934, Maryknoll received some 300 acres of uninhabited land for that purpose from the Chinese government. The land, located at Ngai-moon at the mouth of the Kongmoon river, overlooked the South China Sea about 30 miles from Sunwui. Maryknollers saw an auspicious coincidence in an old Chinese legend which claimed that China's first leper had appeared precisely in that location. According to the legend, when the Manchus followed the remnant of the Ming forces, the Chinese emperor and his entourage were drowned after losing a battle on that spot. The legend said that a woodcutter who found the corpse of the empress on the shore and did not show proper respect became China's first leper. From him, the disease spread to many others.

Maryknoll's hopes of quickly erecting the new colony were hampered by unforeseen difficulties. Because of changes in the government and opposition from a powerful local clan, construction was delayed for three and a half years.[97] Meanwhile, Maryknollers had regrouped their lepers in Sunwui, where Sweeney had started a well-run leprosarium. During his study year in 1933, he had visited the world's largest leper asylum at

Culion in the Philippines. He had arranged with the Culion laboratories to send monthly supplies of drugs used in the treatment of leprosy such as Ethyl Esters of Hydnocarpus Oil. He also equipped the Sunwui colony with a modern laboratory and kept a file of each patient's medical history and treatment.

In 1935, as Dr. Blaber prepared to return to the United States, Sweeney enlisted the services of a retired British Army surgeon and former member of the Medical Bureau at Lourdes (France), Dr. John J. Sherry. In that same year, Perry Burgess, president of the American Leprosy Foundation, visited Sunwui. He was so impressed by what the Maryknollers had accomplished in such a short period of time that he gave them high praise in an address to the joint session of the Medical Section of the American Association for the Advancement of Science and the American Academy of Tropical Medicine in St. Louis:

> I have visited leprosaria in which were as many as 1,000 men, women and children stricken by this disease, not a single one of them receiving medical attention of any sort. On the other hand, I visited one place in South China [Sunwui] where . . . I found a clinician and a bacteriologist with modest but adequate laboratory equipment, and examinations were being made and treatment given with care and intelligence.[98]

Later, he dedicated a eulogistic chapter in his published memoirs to Father Sweeney and his work at the leprosarium:

> What Big Joe Sweeney could do with half a chance would make the world sit up and take notice. What he did with practically nothing was incredible. The most impressive thing to me was the fact that these patients were getting excellent medical care. He had built a clinic and a laboratory of palms . . . but it served its purpose. Routine laboratory tests were made and every effort put forth to give those who were ill improved treatment. I have visited leprosaria where the homes and hospitals were of the finest, but no where have I seen a group of patients more contented than those whom I visited that day.[99]

The stories of these lepers were very poignant. There was Lo Mo, an old mother who had been a handsome and rich woman for 40 years, mother of two boys and a girl. After discovering she had leprosy, she had been hiding in the graveyard for the past 18 years. Once she had returned to her former village and sat begging by the roadside, watching her old servants, her husband, and her sons go by without recognizing her. Before she could see her daughter and her newly born granddaughter, she was driven out of town.

Fig. 4. A child lived with his leper parents in this house made of coffin boards, located in an old burial ground littered with broken urns. Maryknoll Photo Library.

Fig. 5. Maryknoll's two lay doctors, Artemio Bagalawis and Harry Blaber, in the leper colony of Sunwui ir 1934. Maryknoll Photo Library.

Then there was Ah Chai, the eight-year-old leper girl who was brought in by the police a few months after Sweeney arrived in Sunwui. For three and a half years, she patiently took care of the bed-ridden lepers, smiling all day long. Something special about her touched the hearts of everyone she approached. When she died of leukemia, every cripple who could move attended her funeral, calling her a saint.

A far different type was a fellow nicknamed "Joe Gangrene" by Sweeney.

> He was brought to us suffering not only from leprosy but also from severe malaria and infections of both feet, crawling with maggots. Later he contracted meningitis. But his mental state was worse than his physical. . . . He had the foulest tongue we have ever heard here. Several times a day when giving treatments or dressing his sores, we would say a few words on the essentials of religion which he invariably received with jeers. Anyway we tried gently to continue instruction though he seemed utterly hopeless. Then suddenly, the day before his death, he became peaceful and begged for baptism. . . . All our other leper charges who have died received baptism but Joe Gangrene gave us happier memories than all the rest.[100]

Establishment of the Ngaimoon Colony

During the summer of 1937 construction started at Ngaimoon, but difficulties still had to be overcome. On September 2, 1937, the colony of Sunwui, which had been leveled by a typhoon the previous summer, was hit again and its palm-leaf mat-sheds blown away. The winds which reached a velocity of 164 miles per hour also flattened some of the half-erected structures of the new leprosarium. The damage was so extensive that the inauguration had to be postponed until the following summer.[101]

When the 300 lepers disembarked from the two junks which had brought them downriver from Sunwui, they were overjoyed at the sight of the Gate of Heaven (Tinmoon), Sweeney's name for the new leprosarium. Ngaimoon had no dismal burial mounds but a majestic view of the delta and of mountains soaring toward the blue skies. The grounds were beautifully planted with azaleas, hibiscus, papaya, and peach and apricot trees brought down from Sunwui. Comfortable cots were lined up in each house which held eight men or women. The typhoon-proof buildings had strong brick walls, concrete floors, and roofs set under ridges of mortar. The windows and doors were screened to keep out disease-bearing insects. Brother Albert Staubli, the architect and builder, was proudest of the chapel, a spacious building lightened with pink and golden panes set in by the leper artisans. Behind the chapel was a modern dispensary, better equipped than the one in Sunwui. A hospital for the bedridden and the very sick was not yet completed so Staubli converted the wings of his chapel into temporary wards.

Sweeney was assisted by Father Joseph Farnen, and Dr. Bagalawis was in charge of the medical treatment. Father Connors was on furlough, and Dr. Sherry had returned to England with failing health.[102] When Sweeney moved the lepers to Ngaimoon, he thought they would be safe from the dangers of war. During their last year in Sunwui, Maryknollers had spent many hours hiding with the lepers in the cemetery hollows as the Japanese bombers pounded the area. In March 1939, after the fall of Canton, the Japanese advanced into Kongmoon and Sunwui but left the coastal area of Ngaimoon relatively undisturbed. The Chinese people within a distance of 20 miles began to visit Ngaimoon in search of medical aid because Dr. Bagalawis was the only skilled physician left in the region. A dispensary for nonleper patients was set up in one wing of the chapel. Because some nonlepers needed hospitalization, a mat-shed hospital was built along the river; its capacity gradually increased to 70 beds.

Meanwhile the number of lepers also grew. In April 1941, the Hong Kong government asked permission to send its lepers to the Gate of Heaven because the fighting around Canton prevented sending them to Sheklung. Sweeney agreed and 196 men and women patients arrived by sea from Hong Kong. This new contingent brought the number of lepers at the asylum to nearly 450. Including the nonleper patients at the hospital, the colony had a population of well over 500 people. Sweeney looked forward to the day when the Gate of Heaven could care for 1,000 patients and operate several outstations as well.

The arrival of the Hong Kong lepers coincided with the end of the relatively peaceful days in Ngaimoon. In March 1941 the Japanese stepped up the bombing and shelling of the area around the Ngaimoon peninsula because it had become a guerilla stronghold. Refugees poured into the Gate of Heaven for temporary help and shelter. The Fathers set up a soup kitchen which soon fed as many as 1,000 people a day. The mat-shed hospital gradually became a field hospital for Chinese soldiers and guerrillas.

On June 3, 1941, in order to strengthen their grip around Hong Kong and facilitate communication by sea, the Japanese occupied a fort directly across the river from the colony, just 400 to 600 yards away. Although the wounded soldiers had already been evacuated from the hospital, the Japanese deliberately shot at it apparently to show that they were informed of activities at the leprosarium. From that day on, life at the Gate of Heaven became increasingly difficult. The Japanese across the river used the leprosarium for target practice over the next four years. While the refugees could move to safer places, the lepers lived in constant fear of being shot. In the beginning Sweeney used to joke that freshly dug shell holes

Fig. 6. Brother Albert Staubli's chapel constructed at the leper colony at Ngaimoon in 1937. Maryknoll Photo Library.

were perfect for planting new trees, but soon the specter of hunger compelled him to go to Hong Kong to find food and medicine. On his return trip in September 1941, his boat loaded with supplies was sunk by a Japanese vessel and he barely escaped.

At the leprosarium, the lepers grew weaker and more susceptible to disease, and the death rate climbed. By June 1944 the patient population had dwindled to 81. Without the support of the local population, the entire colony would have probably been wiped out. The same people who had strongly opposed construction of the leprosarium had grown to appreciate the work of Maryknollers. They supplied rice to the lepers although they themselves were hard pressed for food. In the spring of 1944, Sweeney, who normally weighed about 220, was down to 150 pounds with signs of failing health. When he left for the United States for much needed rest, Father John Joyce of Sancian Island took his place, working with Father Farnen.[103]

After Joyce's arrival, the Japanese occupied the districts surrounding the colony, leaving only the mountains to the west as an avenue of escape. The Fathers took to the hills several times when the Japanese came too close. On March 24, 1945, the Japanese finally crossed the river and stormed the Gate of Heaven. The two Fathers barely escaped and were saved by Chinese guerrillas. Some of the female help were not so lucky and were caught and raped by the pursuing Japanese. The Japanese chased out the lepers, killing those who could not move. They fumigated the houses and used them as barracks.

Meanwhile Joyce and Farnen searched for the refugee lepers and gathered them into small settlements of palm-leaf shacks in the hills. "The work has been set back 13 years," wrote Joyce. "We are beginning all over again!"[104] The lepers led a pitful life. No village received them and they had to endure the terrible heat and rain of the monsoon season. The guerrillas, however, helped to keep them alive by providing several tons of rice. Joyce had gone to Yeungkong to get funds to buy food when the Japanese moved again. The Fathers were cut off from their patients and, in spite of repeated attempts, Joyce was unable to get funds through. Many of the lepers starved to death or died of exposure. Only a few succeeded in crossing the Japanese lines and were rescued by Maryknollers.

When Joyce reentered the Gate of Heaven in October 1945, only 15 of the original 450 lepers accompanied him. The place had been badly ransacked. Two of the 18 houses had been burned down; every building had lost its furniture, windows, and doors. The Albert Memorial Chapel had been used as a barn and was a foot deep in manure.[105]

The following March, Joseph Sweeney went back to the Gate of Heaven and relieved Joyce. Sweeney immediately began to restore the colony. While making an inventory of building materials available in the region, he remarked wryly: "There is a shortage of everything but lepers."[106] Under his leadership, the chapel was repaired, the dispensary refurbished, the other buildings renovated, and the gardens replanted. He converted the unused leprosarium jail into a chicken coop.

The Gate of Heaven soon provided asylum to about 500 lepers. Before and during the Japanese war, Sweeney had become a sort of local hero. After the war, his renewed charity and knowledge of leprosy won the hearts of the few "hold-outs." When Father Carroll Quinn, his new assistant, arrived in 1949, he was surprised to see what Sweeney had accomplished:

> The work he had done had been nothing but extraordinary. . . . The colony was an expression of Christian charity and also a center of evangelization. He was far ahead of his time. Everyone he touched became interested in the Church even though converts were hard to come by. He was setting the stage for a big push when everything fell apart.[107]

The new trouble Quinn referred to was the approach of the Communists. While fighting raged in the hills around the colony, Sweeney continued his even-handed charity. In the outpatient clinic he treated all comers, often as many as 5,000 a month. He rebuilt the mat-shed hospital for serious nonleprous cases. Under its roof, he often kept Nationalist and Communist soldiers in different rooms.

When the Communists came to Ngaimoon in 1950, they allowed Sweeney and his assistant to continue active direction. The first signs of hardening came in May 1951, when the Communists entrusted the administration to the Chinese doctor, a Dr. Chang, and downgraded the two priests to the role of "medical assistants." Luckily, the doctor was a good friend of Sweeney's. During the day Sweeney and Quinn continued to give medical and spiritual attention to the lepers. At night, they were kept in a small cubbyhole which had served as a sacristy for the church. The Communists gave them an allowance of 200,000 Chinese dollars a month which amounted to about US$.03 a day. They lived very frugally for over two and a half years, with sometimes nothing more than a little tea and a hard-boiled egg.

Meanwhile, the Communists tried to bring charges against Sweeney. They confiscated his outpatient records and tried to find people on the lists who would accuse the Fathers of maltreatment. Not even one person turned against Sweeney. The Communists were also dismayed by the Christian convictions of the lepers and their loyalty toward the Fathers. Each time they attempted to convert the church into a meeting hall for political indoctrination, the lepers staunchly refused. The church remained exclusively a church until the Fathers left; Sunday after Sunday,

95 percent of the leper population continued to attend mass.

The two priests refused to request exit permits, and the Communists did not dare to expel them outright for fear of trouble from the 500 lepers. Finally, in August 1953, the police took the priests to their district headquarters for what seemed to be another routine investigation. Somehow, one leper sensed that the Maryknollers would not return and told Sweeney as he was leaving, "Don't worry about us. Just keep on saying mass." The two priests were taken to Canton and told they were being deported. On August 10, 1953, they crossed the border at Hong Kong. Sweeney's devotion to lepers did not end there, however; in 1955, he began work among the lepers of Korea and continued until his death in 1966.[108]

Relief Work

During the Sino-Japanese conflict, the Maryknoll territories of South China suffered not only the direct blows of the war but also experienced its terrible side effects. Difficulties in obtaining money and supplies combined with a large influx of refugees from wartorn areas resulted in starvation and epidemics. The work of Maryknollers to relieve the suffering of the Chinese people in Kaying, Kongmoon, Wuchow, and Kweilin did much to reveal the compassionate side of the Catholic Church. Relief work took the edge off the suspicion and hatred of foreign missioners previously felt by many Chinese.

When the Japanese started shelling and bombing the coastal area of Kwangtung in September 1937, Maryknollers began to feed and shelter the homeless. After the fall of Canton in October 1938, Maryknoll mission stations provided overnight housing for fleeing refugees.[109] In May 1939, two months after the Japanese occupation of the city of Kongmoon, such large numbers of refugees stopped at the compound in Pakkai to ask for sanctuary that people were sheltered in the bishop's house, the seminary, and the convent. A large mat-shed was erected to accommodate the growing number of the destitute.[110] After the first bombing of Wuchow city in July, a crowd of 500 people in need of help had lined up at the mission gate by 9 o'clock in the morning although distribution of food was not scheduled until six hours later.[111]

The uprooting of people, the continual disruption of planting and harvests, and the destruction caused by bombing resulted in a scarcity of food and skyrocketing prices. Father John Tierney noted that in Sunwui near Kongmoon city the price of rice jumped during the month of April 1940 from $38 to $100 a picul in Chinese currency. Following the collapse of the local economy, Maryknollers often became the main providers of food for refugees and hungry residents.[112]

The Soup Kitchens of Kongmoon

In 1939 the Sisters opened a soup kitchen in Pakkai, where each morning they fed six ounces of rice each to approximately 200 people. As the months went by, the line grew longer and supplies became more difficult to secure and more expensive to buy. In May 1940 the number of people fed on a single day reached 1,000, and the Sisters had to cut the ration of rice to two ounces for adults and one ounce for children. Nonetheless, people arrived in greater numbers. Even after they started to charge ten cents a bowl for rice, the Sisters were still unable to buy enough rice for all. When the number of people began to exceed rice supplies, a system of tickets was devised. Rice was given to ticket bearers; others, instead of being turned away disgruntled, were given a ticket for food for the next day. Using this system, the Sisters were able to provide some relief to between 800 and 1,200 people each day. During the month of October 1941, they served 27,000 meals to refugees.[113]

Other missions experienced the same long lines waiting for rice. In 1939 at Sunwui, Father Francis O'Neill fed 600 people per day; by 1943, he was feeding 1,500 people per day. While refugees were usually fed cooked rice, local people were often given dry rice to take home to cook, saving the missioners the expense of fuel and allowing them to buy more rice for distribution.[114]

As Western relief began to reach China, missioners were often asked to help with administration. Money and grain provided by the Red Cross, the American Advisory Committee of China Relief, and the International Relief Committee supplied food lines, replenished the dispensaries' medicine cabinet, and paid for clothing for the needy. Often, however, the relief came too late or in quantities too small to quell famine. In 1942, Sister Mary Francis Davis described the gruesome scene of human flesh being sold on the streets of Loting, and there were several other reports by Maryknollers of cannibalism.[115] In 1943 Father O'Neill, a popular figure in Sunwui and Toishan, was chairman of a relief committee which supervised 25 soup kitchens and seven orphanages. Yet, owing to the failure of both the spring and fall crops, O'Neill could not procure enough rice to feed the long lines of the destitute. In Toishan that year, 5,200 people starved. [116]

Forty miles away in Hoingan, "Iron Man" Joseph Lavin and John Joyce on Sancian Island operated what they called the "Sancian Rice Ferry." Between 1939 and 1941, when the Japanese refused to let the Sancian natives sail to the mainland to buy supplies, Lavin and Joyce brought tons of rice from Hoingan to the island despite a Japanese threat to sink their boat.

With the crop failures of 1943, famine spread through Hoingan. Lavin was chosen as the famine relief representative; for three years he directed the weekly dispensing of a ton of rice, which was made into gruel to fill thousands of rice bowls. Cholera and smallpox followed in the footsteps of starvation, and Lavin made many trips to the hospital in Toishan to secure serum and vaccines for his dispensary.[117]

Just north of Hoingan and Toishan in the city of Sunwui, signs of famine appeared as early as 1940. Father John Tierney's mission was nearly stormed by a crowd of hungry people.

> When 1,300 had passed through and gotten their rice, I decided to go as far as possible to help the others outside. Before long the stronger were trampling the weaker under foot; old women and children as well as the weak were in imminent danger of death, so we called off the distribution. . . . It was a most unpleasant task for one could find they were either just swollen from beri-beri, or skin and bone.[118]

With the Stranded Refugees in Kweilin

For many years Kweilin was the westward terminus for thousands of refugees fleeing the Japanese advance. Between 1937 and 1944 the population of the city swelled from a normal size of 80,000 to almost half a million. Maryknollers worked in government-built camps to provide assistance and relief to the most needy. To help the sick, Sister Antonia Maria Guerrieri ran a free dispensary. To help the destitute buy their daily food, Monsignor John Romaniello and several Maryknoll Fathers residing in the city distributed refugee funds provided by the British Army Aid Group and the American Advisory Committee. When the central mission station was reduced to a pile of rubble after a Japanese air raid, Romaniello moved to a houseboat on the waterfront and continued his assistance to the refugees.[119]

The Japanese drive southward along the Hankow-Canton railroad line in 1944 brought havoc to the Kweilin territory. In Kweilin and Chuanhsien cities, trains, roads, and boats were jammed with people trying to move further west to Kweichow province. During the evacuation period from June to September, Maryknollers, helped by catechists and native Sisters, made daily visits to the train stations to care for the sick, baptize the dying, and give financial assistance to the most needy. Medicines were in short supply, and malaria and dysentery claimed many victims among the evacuees.[120]

In the summer of 1944, Fathers Leo Walter and Robert Greene and Monsignor Romaniello volunteered to follow the evacuees to a place on the railroad line near the Kwangsi-Kweichow border called Chinch'engchiang, Gold City River (see map p. 368). Although the tracks continued, the bridge across the river had been destroyed. Trainloads of passengers arrived one after the other. Frightened migrants with no other destination filled the station and lived in hundreds of empty freight cars along the sidings. With thousands of refugees arriving daily, Gold City River became "a madhouse of confusion, a place of filth and squalor, suffering and death."[121] Everywhere people were dying of hunger, exposure, and exhaustion. Cholera was rampant. With no provision for sanitation, a terrible stench engulfed the city.

In the midst of this chaos, the three Maryknollers secured food, medicine, and vaccines from the American Advisory Committee in Chungking and also received a generous grant—$1 million in local currency—from the "Lord Mayor of London's Refugee Fund," which was administered by R. 0. Hall, the Anglican bishop of Hong Kong, himself a refugee in Kweiyang. Hundreds of sheds were constructed and several dispensaries and soup kitchens were set up. By fall, however, it became obvious to Romaniello that the refugees were condemned to certain death unless they could be evacuated before the Japanese stormed the city. Several days before, many refugees had been killed when a bomb exploded on several boxcars loaded with ammunition. Romaniello finally obtained help from American GIs at a nearby U.S. army camp who moved hundreds of thousands of refugees in army trucks to Kweiyang, the capital of Kweichow. Once in Kweiyang, refugees were able to find other means of transportation to less dangerous areas. In Kweiyang the three priests joined a group of Maryknoll Sisters working in a Catholic hospital with the wounded and the refugees. Within a few weeks, however, they were forced to retreat further west to Kungming. [122]

The Relief Committee of Moyan

During the summer of 1943, Bishop Ford applied for aid to the International Relief Committee to cope with growing famine conditions in the Kaying territory. His inquiry led to the formation of a Moyan (Kaying) Branch of the Kwangtung International Relief Committee. Ford was appointed chairman of the local group, which included a representative of the mayor, a Baptist missioner, a doctor of the Basel Lutheran Society, and Maryknoll Father John Donovan. Maryknoll Sister Joan Marie Ryan served as secretary and bookkeeper.

The committee supervised three distribution centers in Kaying city and nine in other towns of Ford's vicariate. Maryknoll Fathers and Sisters ran eight of them, the Lutherans ran three, and the Baptists, one. In August 1945, Bishop Ford reported that after 22 months of operation, his committee had administered $8 million (close to US$150,000) in relief with a cost of only .019 on the dollar for administrative salaries and wages for cooks and helpers. They had distributed about two million meals of rice gruel (congee) and helped in defraying costs of clothing, medicine, and travel. Sister

Joan Marie devised a clever accounting system that was adopted by other relief committees throughout the province. The bishop noted with satisfaction that although relief work had no direct bearing on missionary activities, it earned the good will of the community as well as the refugees.[123]

Post-1945 Relief Work

At the end of the war, most of China was in a pitiful state. According to an U.N.R.R.A. report, some 84 million Chinese or 20 percent of the total population needed relief in the form of 8.7 million tons of food, 840,000 tons of clothing, and 12 million temporary shelters.[124] In Kwangtung and Kwangsi, the local economy was so weakened that it could not sustain the population without outside help. Too few buffalo remained to plow all the fields and, more than ever, a bad crop meant starvation for hundreds of thousands of people. In some areas of Kweilin and Kaying, the great influx of refugees added to the local population made conditions even more precarious.

To help refugees returning to north and central China or the big coastal cities of Swatow, Canton, and Hong Kong after the war, Maryknollers organized shelters and soup kitchens in mission compounds which were located along the main roads or close to railroad stations or wharves.[125] As soon as they received fresh supplies, Maryknollers also continued their distribution of emergency relief to the local population, mostly in the form of food, clothing, and medicine provided by various relief agencies as well as by friends from the United States.

Meanwhile, after the capitulation of 1945, the situation had turned from bad to worse for the estimated one and a half million Japanese civilians and military living in Manchuria. They came in large numbers to repatriation centers established in the major cities. In Fushun city, more than 40,000 destitute Japanese refugees arrived in the center in dire need of food and medical care. According to Maryknollers' reports, more than two-thirds were wiped out by typhus, dysentery, and typhoid fever. Faced with a general lack of concern for the Japanese, the native Sisters of the Sacred Heart of Jesus of Fushun volunteered to work in the center giving help to the refugees. Although three of them contracted typhus, the Sisters continued their mission of mercy and Christian charity, taking care of orphans, distributing food, and comforting the dying.[126]

In 1946, the apostolic delegate, Archbishop Mario Zanin, promoted the creation of the Catholic Welfare Committee of China (C.W.C.C.) in order to coordinate and assure a more equitable distribution of the welfare and relief efforts of the Catholic Church in China, including Manchuria. Within a few months, C.W.C.C. was entrusted with large amounts of supplies from many relief agencies which had become alarmed by growing reports

Fig. 7. A typical crowd waiting for food relief in postwar China. This group in Shanghai was estimated at over 10,000 daily. Maryknoll Photo Library.

of graft, misappropriations, and blackmarketing by corrupt officials. The creation of regional offices, such as the one in Canton headed by Maryknoll Father Paul Duchesne, further ensured that regional allocations were based on specific needs.[127]

Foundling Association and Boys Town in Chuanhsien

One city which had endured great hardship during the last few months of the war was Chuanhsien in the northern section of the prefecture apostolic of Kweilin. When Father Edwin McCabe returned in October 1945, he found most buildings reduced to shells or rubble. Famine was widespread: 20,000 people out of a population of 400,000 had died; infants were left at the door of the mission compound; orphans roamed the streets with no place to go. When relief supplies began to arrive, McCabe not only started distributing supplies to some 400 people per day, but also immediately organized a Foundling Association for the Abandoned Babies. Instead of opening an orphanage, he encouraged families to adopt the infants and supplied them with milk powder and clothing donated by the relief agencies. Four years later, Father Lloyd Glass reported that the Foundling Association had been "an unqualified success with almost no burden on the Chuanhsien mission." Out of 60 rescued infants, 40 had survived and only four of the foster families still needed some material assistance.[128]

Once the Foundling Association was well established, McCabe turned to the problem of orphans, since many of those in the food lines were beggars between the ages of nine and fourteen whose parents had been killed during the war. In early 1947, he entrusted the realization of his project to Father Glass, the new pastor of Chuanhsien. Glass succeeded in shaming the local government into donating a large building with five surrounding acres of land and opened what came to be known as Boys Town in April 1947. The China National Relief and Rehabilitation Agency (C.N.R.R.A.), U.N.R.R.A., and the American Advisory Committee supplied blankets, quilts, mosquito nets, clothing, rice, and flour. Glass also received strong financial support from American servicemen whom he had befriended in Kweilin during the war, as well as from people in his home state of Iowa.

When the boys arrived, they were thoroughly cleaned and received a medical checkup. Their old rags were burned and they received clean shirts and pants made of flour bags. Glass used part of the land for a large garden where the boys grew green vegetables, tomatoes, and sweet potatoes. Glass hired five teachers to give the boys schooling through the eighth grade and elementary industrial training. By 1949, 480 boys had already been adopted or been trained to be self-sufficient, and 110 were

Fig. 8. Two beggar boys from Chuanhsien invited to join Boys Town. Maryknoll Photo Library.

still completing their education.[129]

The citizens of Chuanhsien noticed the difference in their city. The streets were emptied of beggar boys, and children were receiving an education and job training. In 1949 Glass was glad to report that the non-Christian population had begun to contribute regularly to the support of Boys Town.[130]

Cooperatives

As necessary as relief work was, Maryknollers always considered it as a temporary and extraordinary measure to be discontinued as soon as the people could support themselves. Even before the Sino-Japanese War, the development of self-sufficiency had been their goal. Since their arrival, Maryknollers had been involved in several projects meant to improve the standard of living of the Chinese around them and to make the Catholics less dependent on the Church.

Happy Life and Death Societies

When they arrived in South China, Maryknollers found that M.E.P. missioners had established an organization called the Happy Life and Death Society in the larger stations. Its role was to make the parish as self-supporting as possible, and capital for the society came from initiation fees collected from the Christians in the station when the society began. The French Fathers usually invested these funds by purchasing rice fields which were then rented out for 10 to 20 percent of the value of the year's crops. The rent compared favorably with the 50 to 70 percent demanded by local landlords in the 1920s and 1930s and the 200 to 300 percent charged in the late 1940s. This income was used to defray the costs of food and other amenities provided to Christians for the annual gatherings of Easter, Pentecost, Assumption, and Christmas. The money also ensured that deceased members would have two masses said for them each year. At the end of each year, remaining funds and initiation fees of new members were used to buy more rice fields.[131]

Maryknollers soon discovered, however, that this system had its share of difficulties. Although the interest charged by the society was much less than that charged by the landlords, renters sometimes refused to pay. Maryknollers were also uncomfortable with the role of the Church as a rich landowner. Therefore when a new Happy Life and Death Society was formed in a recently opened mission station, the American missioners often sought means other than buying land to invest fees and profits.

In 1939, Father John Smith, pastor of Chiklung in the Kongmoon vicariate, described the investment procedures followed by most Maryknollers:

> Up to last year the mission was feeding the Christians when they came in to the mission for the four major feasts. Last year we organized a "Happy Death Society" to take care of this expense. Membership at present totals over 90, and our original capital is $200. . . . In December right after the second crop of rice has been harvested, we buy rice, and in May sell it when it is expensive. We did this last year and made a profit of $68. Then in June buy soya beans, and sell them sometime in November when they are expensive. At present our capital is in soya beans, and if sold now would realize a profit of about $100. Our Feast Day expenses for the first year are about $50, so this means our capital has increased about $100.[132]

In most instances, these societies helped to reinforce a sense of community among the Catholics who soon managed the transactions themselves with the mission providing only storage. The system brought such good returns in some stations like Chiklung that the Catholics decided also to provide for the expenses of the customary funeral banquet for members.[133]

When inflation pushed prices high in the late 1940s, Maryknollers in stations with no Happy Life and Death Society had difficulty paying the expenses of the four big feasts. Father Russell Sprinkle, the pastor of Pingnam in the Wuchow vicariate, reported that without counting the cost of wood and kindling, he had spent US$350 to feed the 400 people who came to attend the celebration of Easter in 1947 but had received only US$4.50 in the collection basket and US$76 in fees for the meal.[134]

The Development of Agricultural Cooperatives

The success of the Happy Life and Death Societies encouraged Maryknollers to search for other ways to help people help themselves. In the 1930s and 1940s, for example, using funds from the American Advisory Committee, Maryknollers in Kweilin and Wuchow initiated several small irrigation projects. The most impressive one was established in Chuanhsien by Father Wenceslaus Knotek after the Japanese left. Under his direction a lake was constructed which supplied water to 1,200 acres of rice fields, reducing the danger of seasonal flooding and serving as a community fishpond for three villages.[135]

Meanwhile, in September 1935 as part of its effort to build up a strong self-reliant national economy, the Chinese Nationalist Government enacted a law which encouraged and facilitated the establishment of "mutual aid societies" or cooperatives under the supervision of the Ministry of Industry. Experts like W. K. Campbell of the League of Nations went to Nanking to give advice. Training schools were established for personnel who were sent to each province to organize the cooperatives in the rural areas.[136]

It is not clear if Maryknollers' incentives to develop cooperatives came from the measures taken by the Chinese government or if they had arrived at the same conclusion on their own. The fact remains that from the late 1930s on Maryknollers launched a great variety of small cooperatives. In addition, they always welcomed the arrival of the representative of the Chinese Industrial Cooperatives in their area and gave him a hand. In 1940 and 1941, for instance, the Kochow diary mentioned several times the efforts of Mr. Herman and Mr. Wong, the local government representatives sent to establish soap, rice milling, knitting, leather, and soybean milk cooperatives in the villages around Fachow and Kochow.[137]

Since Maryknollers worked mainly in rural communities, they often established a rice bank at the core of their cooperative system. A rice bank was usually started by a small group of Catholic farming families with a little capital of US$50 to $100 provided by the parish priest. The money was used to buy rice after the second harvest in November when its price was lowest. The rice was stored until March or April when prices were high and peasants had consumed most of their harvest yet needed seed for the new planting. Seed rice was then loaned to the Catholic peasants and the surplus sold at market value. At harvest time, the cooperative members returned the loan plus 10, 20, or even 30 percent interest. Interest was usually paid in kind. The loan itself was repaid either in rice from the new crop or in cash at the original price of the previous fall. The rice banks usually prospered and were able to augment the amount of rice to be loaned. In Fachow, Father Paul Duchesne reported that the holdings of the rice bank grew from 10 to 150 bushels within three to four years. Once the cooperative was well established, new members could be added, until a maximum of 50 families was reached.[138]

Father Lloyd Glass, who borrowed his model of cooperatives from a neighboring M.E.P. missioner, tells how his system operated in Chuanhsien until the arrival of the Communists:

> The missioner secures the money necessary to buy 5,000 lbs. of rice. The members elect their own leaders, 3 in number, to supervise the whole affair, both distribution and collection. Whereas the loan sharks charge a minimum of 300 percent, the cooperatives charge 30 percent. . . . In May each family [of the cooperative] borrows 100 lbs. and after the August harvest returns 130 lbs. to be stored in the cooperative granary at the central mission. The following year the same family may borrow in May 130 lbs. and in August repay 169 lbs. and the third year they may borrow 169 lbs. and return 219.7 lbs. This is the three-year plan. At the end of the third year, the missioner withdraws the original 5,000 lbs. to be used in starting other cooperatives and more than 5,000 lbs. remained in the cooperative to start the process over again by the local families themselves.[139]

Father John Smith in Chiklung was undoubtedly one of the most enterprising Maryknollers. By 1940 he had not only established thriving rice, pig, and cow cooperatives, but had also launched a profitable fertilizer cooperative which shipped bags of cow bones from Kongchowwan at a much lower cost than in Chiklung. The cooperative was able to sell bags from its first shipment to members at a savings of over $10 per bag in local currency. Forty-seven remaining bags were sold at the local market price for a profit of $500. The following year, Smith was contemplating use of an organic fertilizer developed by an American company with an office in Hong Kong. Experiments with the new fertilizer in some of the Chiklung

Catholics' fields yielded five times more than before. Unfortunately, Father Smith never was able to bring his fertilizer cooperative to its potential because the Japanese occupation of Kongchowwan and the blockade of Hong Kong cut off outside supplies.[140]

Home Industries

Any cash profit realized by the rice banks was often used to start home industries based on the same cooperative pattern. Among the most commonly initiated were pig and cow banks, cotton spinning and weaving industries, and soap factories. Most of these cooperatives were useful to the rural economy; they provided work for the unemployed and gave farming families extra income. The idea itself was simple, and profits from the rice banks served as the initial investment. In spring, for example, when piglets were cheap, the cooperative would buy a few. The families were given a young sow to raise. After the first litter was born, they kept a small sow and returned the mature sow and the rest of the litter, which were then loaned to other farmers. The families given a young male were charged a small fee which was repaid a few months later when they sold the fattened pig at a profit.

The cow banks operated in a similar fashion. Cows were loaned to the farmers who took care of them for life. Each time a calf was born, however, the farmer gave it to the cooperative, which loaned it to another family. Since a good cow gave birth almost every year and the first calf matured by the fourth year, the herd owned by the cooperative grew steadily.[141]

In the Wuchow vicariate, Maryknollers set up several cotton spinning cooperatives using the profits of the rice banks. The cooperative bought the machines and provided a teacher. Each student paid a share of the teacher's salary and gradually reimbursed the cost of a machine until he or she became independent. Sometimes the cooperative also helped to market the thread by financing a store in the local market place. The same procedure was followed in the weaving and soap manufacturing cooperatives started by Father James McCormick at Siaoloc in the Kaying vicariate.[142]

Not all the cooperatives and home industries begun by Maryknollers necessarily derived their existence from a rice bank. In 1943 Father Edwin McCabe, secretary-treasurer of the local American Advisory Committee, authorized the funding of a cooperative for the making of cloth shoes in order to help people support themselves and avoid the rice lines and the dole system. He described the system:

> Families where there were members able to do this work received materials purchased by the committee. Upon completion of the shoes, the local market

price was paid to the maker. When enough pairs were completed, they were taken to the nearest large city and sold at a profit. The money from the sale was returned to a fund for the purchasing of new materials. This fund was increased by the committee as the need grew.[143]

In Kweilin city prior to the Japanese takeover of 1944, Father Robert Greene pursued the same idea of providing people with work. He also organized some primitive cooperatives such as the ABC cigarette cooperative which enabled members to earn enough cash to buy their daily food.[144]

In 1939, Father John Joyce established a kind of boat credit union on Sancian Island. The mission advanced US$100 to a group of fishermen to buy a boat and a net. From the proceeds of their catch, they repaid the loan as well as a small amount of interest. When the credit union had recouped its US$100, it reloaned it to another group for the purchase of another boat, and so on.[145]

Social Work as a Missionary Task

When the war finally ended in 1945, Bishop Francis Ford was a strong proponent for substituting other types of secular training for the usual first aid course given at the seminary in the Knoll. He asked that newcomers to the missions be knowledgeable either in social service methods, economics, industrial problems, or youth services. From the requests he had received during the previous few years, he felt such expertise would be an asset to any missioner in his vicariate:

> For example, we have been asked by the local government to run two industrial schools which I had to turn down as our priests are not equipped to undertake such work; we had requests to design a middle school, a magistrate's office, two bridges; our advice was sought in laying out a public park and playground; we have headed a committee on an irrigation project, and were asked to head another of the same sort; numerous requests have been made to start musical bands or orchestras and had we such, it would be in prominent demand on hundreds of occasions; besides very many requests on information about starting ice factories, electrical plants, waterworks from Chamber of Commerce men or the like; we also helped organize the fire brigade with modern equipment. I mention these at random as actual past requests, merely to show the trend of the times in which our priests could take an intelligent part if equipped.[146]

Obviously, the course of events in China and the increasing involvement of missioners in relief work and cooperatives were gradually changing the perception of many Maryknollers, including Ford, concerning their missionary task. Social work was viewed less and less as a way to gain converts but, increasingly, as an urgent priority in witnessing the love of Christ and helping the Chinese people achieve a better standard of living.

Maryknoll Schools

The Catholic Church's emphasis on educational work as a tool of evangelization and contact with the Chinese people was not a recent development. Since instruction to the first vicars apostolic in 1659, many documents from Rome periodically reiterated the importance of schools in the missions. In China, the regional synods of the late nineteenth and early twentieth centuries all gave instructions on the establishment and conduct of primary schools, high schools, and even colleges.[147] Yet it took some time for the bulk of the Catholic missioners to modernize their approach to education. They were challenged by the influence of the Protestant mission-school system, by reforms in China's educational system, and by the abolition of the old system of civil service examinations in 1905. The First Plenary Council of China held in Shanghai in 1924 identified education as a major priority of the Catholic Church in China.

Emphasis on Elementary Schools

Maryknollers arriving in China took their American experience with them. To protect the faith of its predominantly immigrant minority, leaders of the Catholic Church in the United States had recommended that each parish have an elementary school. Perceiving the success of the American experience and noting several similarities with the Chinese context, Maryknollers immediately emphasized the establishment of elementary schools in each mission parish. In 1922 Father Francis Ford wrote:

> The parochial school in America is the backbone of the Church. Without it, non-Catholic influences would weaken the faith of the growing generation. In China, the situation is yet more serious. Our boys and girls are in the midst of a pagan atmosphere and so few in number as to be otherwise inevitably weaned away from the practice of the highest standard of morality required of Christians. But our Catholic schools in China are not only safeguards against pagan corruption, but positive nurseries of manly virtues and refined habits. So much so that pagan parents are anxious to send their children to our schools and conversions both of parents and pupils result. More important, Catholic schools are our only source of vocations without which it is hard to vision the conversion of China.[148]

As defined by Ford, Maryknoll's educational goals fit perfectly into its broader goals of converting the people and building a strong Chinese Church. Moreover, the schools were to produce the lay leaders, the clergy, and the sisterhoods that would replace Maryknollers and develop a self-sufficient Chinese Church. Until 1950, many Maryknollers were assigned to some type of educational work in each of the five Maryknoll territories.

Because 99 percent of the Catholics and catechumens in their territories belonged to the uneducated peasant class, Maryknollers emphasized elementary education. Two months after their arrival in Yeungkong in December 1918, they opened their first school with an enrollment of 20 boys and girls. In his diary, Father Bernard Meyer described how the missioners hoped to establish small schools in each village to raise the instruction level in the countryside and, at the same time, to Christianize the people.

> We are making an attempt to establish what we shall dignify with the name of "schools" in every village in which we can get together enough children. They will learn the catechism and prayers and how to read and write Chinese, with perhaps some arithmetic. . . . The Chinese are anxious for education but in many of these villages they have been too poor to rent a building and hire a teacher. So we give them some assistance and thereby get Christian instruction into the course. Of course, this is only a poor beginning: but as we grow we shall try to train better teachers who can teach other branches and gradually bring these village schools up to at least the standard now obtained in the government schools in the cities.[149]

As Maryknollers spread their sphere of influence, they opened elementary schools for boys and girls in most of their parishes. With the arrival of the Maryknoll Sisters, separate schools for girls and kindergartens were opened in Yeungkong, Loting, and Fushun. These schools were opened to both Catholics and non-Catholics and varied in size from 20 to over 100 students. With an enrollment of 135 boys and 40 girls in 1925, the Catholic primary school of Hoingan was the largest Maryknoll school. Non-Catholics were charged full tuition, while Catholics paid a reduced fee. However, as income from tuition was far less than the expenses of the school and the teachers' salaries, Maryknollers relied heavily on the generosity of American Catholics.

Located in different regions of South China and Manchuria, the Maryknoll schools were not of equal quality. In the outstations, the missioners often helped finance a rudimentary village school by sending a catechist who also served as the teacher. This man or woman instructed adult catechumens in the evenings and taught the children to read during the day. The catechism often became their principal textbook. The most promising boys and girls were then selected to attend a more advanced program at the parish center's school. Knowing that children often could not attend classes because of the distance, schools at the parish centers usually provided sleeping accommodations.

The beneficial influence of a Catholic school was described by Father Adolph Paschang, the head of Kochow's Sacred Heart School, Maryknoll's most outstanding school in the Kongmoon vicariate:

> A well-conducted school is a good advertising medium for the Church and helps to gain the good will of respectable people who might be opposed to the school but cannot ignore it. The school changes the Catholic Church from a place of mystery on some side street to a lively participant in the daily life of the town. Not many of the students may become Catholics, but they will certainly have a better knowledge of the Church, and be less suspicious of its leaders and members.[150]

Impact of the Antireligious Movement

The eleventh Conference of the World's Student Christian Federation which met in Peking in 1922 aroused the hostility of some Western-trained Chinese intellectuals and led to the creation of a Student Antireligious Movement. Branch organizations sprang up all over China and contributed to the resurgence of anti-Christian and antiforeign sentiments. Teachers and students of government schools accused the mission schools of denationalizing their students, and prominent Chinese educators demanded more stringent policies toward the Christian schools. In 1924 the *China Press* and the *China Weekly Review* gave prominent editorial space to the China Education Conference held in Kaifeng. Its participants passed resolutions denouncing the denationalizing character of mission schools and urged that the government take measures to curb them.

This growing antagonism led the warlord government in Peking and the Nationalist Government in Canton to issue almost identical sets of new regulations concerning the registration and the daily operation of private and Christian schools. In South China, only "registered schools" were recognized by the government and allowed to issue diplomas. All existing mission schools had until April 1928 to file their registration application. They were inspected by the provincial and local authorities and had to adopt textbooks and curricula prescribed by the provincial government. The introduction of "religious propaganda" was strictly forbidden. Students could not be required to attend classes in religion or participate in religious exercises, and in 1929 any religious teaching in school buildings was prohibited. In Manchuria, similar measures were imposed by the Peking government and later continued by the puppet government of Manchukuo.*[151]

In practice, these measures had little impact on the small village schools run by Maryknoll missioners. Recurrent political disturbances and the lack of government funds and trained teachers prevented their implementation. On the whole, the missioners were able to continue to use teacher-catechists to teach children the basic three "Rs" as well as the catechism. Most of these schools were open to Catholic children under the name of *ching t'ang,* or prayer school. Father Bernard Meyer wrote in his annual report of July 1929 for the Maryknoll territory in Kwangsi:

> In the villages, the policy has been continued of giving a small subsidy to groups of poor Catholics who desire to open elementary schools. The government does not permit religious instruction to be given during school hours . . . so night classes in Christian doctrine are held elsewhere by the [Catholic] teacher.[152]

Registered Schools and Hostels

In larger villages and towns with existing government schools, the missioners had to register their schools or close them. However, in view of the antireligious attitude displayed in many government-operated schools, Maryknollers felt it important to offer Catholic children a place where they would not be forced to submit to the "corrupt ideas" of the government schools. They also realized that without diplomas their Catholic students would not be admitted to higher schools. Missioners needed "recognized elementary schools" to train the Catholic teachers of the future and to form lay leaders. Until it was specifically forbidden in 1929, religious courses were added to the curriculum and taught to all children. After 1929, missioners had to schedule religious instruction in different buildings after school hours.

In August 1923, Sacred Heart in Kochow became the first registered Maryknoll grade school. After only two years of government recognition, the school had 105 boys and was already among the best in the county. At a competitive examination held for the 40 registered grade schools of the area in June 1925, Sacred Heart students gathered an impressive collection of first, second, and third prizes in English and Chinese languages, ethics, history, and Chinese classics. One student earned the highest average grade of all the participants.[153]

---

*Manchukuo was the name given to the Japanese-controlled state formed in Manchuria in 1932.

In time the Catholic elementary schools in Yeungkong and Hoingan were also registered. Government regulations were followed and students and teachers participated in all government sponsored civic and social efforts. The Sisters' diary of Yeungkong is particularly rich in recounting the variety of these extracurricular activities: meetings to propagate the New Life Movement; night classes for women; cleanliness, fly-catching, and anti-opium campaigns; arbor days; and clothing drives and other collections for the war effort.[154]

When Father Bernard Meyer took charge of the Wuchow territory in 1926, he felt that in view of the prevalent antiforeign feelings and the small number of Catholics to be served, there was no need to open new schools. Instead, in 1928, he opened a hostel for 10 Catholic boys from the countryside who attended primary schools in the town of Pingnam. A priest supervised their study and provided them with religious instruction. Father Bernard Meyer wrote:

> So the hostel fills a real want in providing for the discipline and religious instruction of our boys who come to the city to pursue their education. Care is taken to correct the misinformation about the Church that is frequently handed out to them under the guise of learning. . . . We hope to gradually form a corps of Catholic elite who can hold their own in the community, besides providing a source from which to draw material for catechists.[155]

In 1929, Father Francis Ford reported that 10 of his 11 schools in Kaying were up to government standards and followed the curriculum of higher elementary schools. The school in Chongpu, for example, started in 1927 as a small boarding school for 40 students; by 1942, the school enrolled 120 boys and girls from the surrounding countryside who were attracted by the status of the school, which taught the government curriculum. Father John Driscoll, the pastor, recalled that 85 percent of the students were non-Catholics.[156]

In larger localities, however, Ford opted for hostels. In 1927, barely two years after he arrived, he opened the first dormitory for Catholic boys attending high school in Kaying city. That same year he also sent eight young men to the Catholic University in Peking and the Jesuit Normal School in Shanghai to be trained as teachers for a future Catholic school. By 1934 the Kaying vicariate sponsored four high school dormitories for students attending government schools in the larger towns and, in 1936, the Maryknoll Sisters opened Rosary Hall, a hostel for girls attending the government middle school in Kaying city. Although these small hostels accommodated no more than 30 students each, they enabled Maryknollers to come in contact with students and teachers at the government schools.[157]

（六）．籌備完竣後呈請某某縣長文稿

為呈請事現率

某某主教命令由某某處天主堂內設立某某級學校俟茲校成立與

貴國教育聯絡一禮辦理等由業經遵照籌備經費建築校舍用具粗備一竪籌備完竣理合遵照

貴國部章就近呈請備案並加委校長某某除呈復

某主教備案外相應咨請

貴縣長查照准予備案、及加委校長某某並蔣委任狀送過俾得進行招生開學實級公誼此咨

某縣長某某姓

某某國教士彙學校籌辦員某某縣

TRANSLATION

Application submitted to the Magistrate of ____ County upon completion of preparatory work.

This is in reference to a school of ____ grade level, established at ____ Catholic Church following the instruction of Bishop ____ so that this school will be an integral part of your country's educational system. Now as funds for school building and furnishing have been raised, and preparatory work carried out according to regulations of your country, this is to apply for official accreditation and appointment of principal nominee ____.
In addition to notice sent to Bishop ____, this application requests your honor to confer official accreditation and appoint to principal nominee ____. Upon receiving the letter of appointment, the school shall be able to recruit students and begin instruction. All that is done for the good of the public.
The application is submitted to ____, Magistrate of ____ County.

Missionary of ____
Nationality and school preparation
board member

Fig. 9. Formula of Petition Asking Approval of School and Principal. Source: Bishop James E. Walsh, *Mission Manual of the Vicariate of Kongmoon*, p. 221.

The Fathers and Sisters felt that their role in the hostels was to provide an atmosphere of quiet study and to enhance the development of the "natural and supernatural virtues" of their students. The Sisters, in particular, felt they had an important role to play in guiding middle school-age girls.

> The middle school girl in Hakka China was a pioneer in a new field: she lived a life that her elders had never lived; there were no traditions to guide her; she was a puzzle to her mother and the older women of the village. . . . As a member of a new movement among Chinese girls, the middle school student needs understanding and direction. Therein lay our apostolate.[158]

Maryknollers provided a variety of enrichment classes, from English conversation to etiquette and choral singing. Religious instruction was offered, but attendance was voluntary. Maryknollers also encouraged recreational activities in the form of parties and plays which were often jointly sponsored in Kaying by the boys and girls' hostels.

During World War II, the Fathers and Sisters cooperated in the creation of a musical production called "Cinderella Goes to a Christmas Ball." The performance was held in one of the city's theaters to raise funds for the national war effort. Several Sisters mentioned with amusement that while Bishop Ford taught the boys the German style of waltzing, Sister Joan Marie Ryan taught the girls the American style. "When they got together," said Sister Mary (Mary Augusta) Hock, "for a while there was pandemonium, but the girls adjusted, and it was the German waltz that Cinderella and the prince and their friends danced." Sister Mary Hock and several of the students who participated in the play remembered the impression it made in Kaying:

> After the first gasp of the audience at seeing the boys with arms around the girls whirling around in their lovely clothes, all was well. These were war years and Kaying had refugees from families from Hong Kong and Singapore who were familiar with modern music and dance. I think the Bishop wanted our people in Kaying city to realize that dancing was fun and relaxation and beautiful and not a sinful pastime.[159]

In the Fushun territory, Maryknollers also sought recognition of their schools by complying with government regulations and permitting inspection by government officials. Elementary schools in Fushun-Honan, Chakow, Erhpatan, Tunghwa, Hsinpin, Linkiang, and Shanchengtze all received government recognition. The rapid growth of schools, however, created heavy financial burdens for some parishes. The enrollment in Sacred Heart School at Shanchengtze grew to 130 in 1934 and passed the

200 mark toward the end of the decade. The school used one of two large rooms in the parish church, but when the parish church had to be enlarged in 1940 to accommodate its growing congregation, more than two-thirds of the students were let go.[160]

In 1940, the Nationalist government's relaxation of its policy against the teaching of religion in registered schools eased some of the strain on Christian schools in nonoccupied Japanese territories. Soon, however, the turmoil of war engulfed most of the country, often disrupting teaching and closing schools. In Manchuria, the Maryknoll schools were closed by the Japanese. In South China, with the exception of the Kaying territory, which remained on the periphery of the conflict, many Maryknoll schools and hostels were bombed and ransacked. The first few years after the war, Maryknollers' educational activities were mostly confined to rebuilding and refurbishing the damaged buildings. They had barely recovered when the Communist takeover of schools terminated the educational work of all missionary groups in China.

The Maryknoll Academy in Dairen

Although there were two Maryknoll high schools in Hong Kong, Dairen was the only city in China where Maryknollers established a high school. When Sisters Mary Eunice Tolan, Mary Gemma Shea, Mary Angelica O'Leary, Juliana Bedier, and Mary Coronata Sheehan arrived in Dairen in March 1930, they expected to do mission work among the Japanese and Chinese people and perhaps tutor English on the side to earn some income. They had barely settled down, however, when women of the foreign community begged them to open a school to teach English to their children. Father Leo Tibesar, the pastor of the Japanese parish in Dairen where the Sisters resided, favored the idea. He knew that the authorities had recently revoked a permit previously given to the White Russian Committee to operate their own school for Russian children. The White Russians were anxious to find a school for their children, and Tibesar felt they would welcome foreign Sisters as teachers.

In February 1931, to get a better sense of the desire for a school for foreign children, the Sisters put a notice in the local newspaper inviting the community to their convent for a discussion. That afternoon the Sisters' parlor overflowed with foreigners anxious to see an English-language school started. However, the Sisters lacked the money to post the $50,000 bond (local currency) necessary to obtain the permit to open a "school." Following the advice of Mr. Ijiri, a Japanese convert, they circumvented the difficulty by calling their new educational institution an "academy." In actuality, the academy functioned as a school, but technically, it was exempt from the school permit requirements. The Sisters' received their "academy" permit without delay.

In April, Sister Peter Duggan, a principal of St. Francis Xavier School for Japanese in Los Angeles for eight years, was assigned as principal. Later, two other Sisters, Anne (Famula) Clements and Ellen Mary Murphy, along with Sister Mary Coronata, completed the teaching staff. On September 28, 1931, the new school opened its door under the name of Maryknoll Academy. [161]

The school started with an enrollment of 41 boys and girls who represented a wide array of linguistic and racial groups: three-fifths of the children were Russian, the others were American, British, Yugoslavian, Polish, Armenian, and Chinese. The Sisters were challenged to transform the multi-lingual group of children ranging in age from five to fourteen years into an efficient smooth-running English-speaking school. After a few months of experimentation, the Sisters divided the students into three groups according to their level of comprehension of English and their native tongue. In May 1934, the Sisters used the Achievement and Intelligence Test from Columbia University to place each child. The Academy absorbed the parish kindergarten and became a fully integrated educational system, with kindergarten through the twelfth grade by September 1936. Its enrollment included 128 children of 15 different nationalities. English was taught to the youngest children when they entered school and Japanese instruction began in the second grade. The training was thorough: high school graduates could read and write hiragana, the traditional Japanese written language, and in later grades, the students learned Russian or German from lay teachers. In 1937, three more Sisters were assigned to teach at the Academy to cope with the growing number of children.

The general course of study followed the American pattern, with some minor adaptations. Grades one through eight used the curriculum of the California school system. In December 1936, the four-year high school was officially affiliated with the Catholic University of America in Washington, D.C., and the first senior class graduated the following June. The Sisters could not have been prouder of their graduates: five of the first seven graduates received 100 percent in mathematics on examinations from Washington. [162]

From the beginning the school was mainly supported by tuition fees of 10 yen per month—about US$3.50 in 1932. Many of the children enrolled at the Academy came from families in the diplomatic corps or in business and paid full tuition. Students from families with smaller incomes, however, paid only half tuition. The Sisters also accepted free of charge the children of several stateless White Russians who, for the most part, were poor refugees. Figures for 1931 showed that of the total enrollment of 41, only 22 students paid full tuition. The remaining 19 received reduced or free tuition or were given private scholarships. By 1936, 33 students were exempt from full tuition.

In the spring of 1936, the city authorities showed their appreciation of the Sisters' educational work by voting a yearly subsidy of 500 yen (about US$175) to the Academy. The Sisters' income was supplemented by revenues from tutoring in English and music, a summer school, cooking classes, and the salary of one Sister who taught English twice a week at the Dairen Japanese Girls High School.[163]

The Sisters always stressed that the Academy was a Christian school. One of their requirements was that all students received religious instruction. These classes, they insisted, aimed at providing students with a good moral foundation; however, no one was forced to attend services or to follow the practices of the Catholic religion, and there were few conversions at school. In April 1937 Sister Peter acknowledged that the school had been directly responsible for only nine baptisms and the return of nine fallen-away Catholics to the sacraments.

The influence of the Academy, however, was much more pervasive than indicated by the number of conversions. The natural admiration of students for their teachers, the religious nature of the Sisters, and the quality of teaching in the compulsory religion course combined to leave a lasting impression on many of the students. In May 1936 the Sisters felt flattered to learn that one of their young Soviet students had been taken out of the Academy and sent back to Moscow after his parents concluded that he had been too greatly influenced by the Sisters. The Sisters felt, as a result, that they had one more friend in Moscow—along with the many consuls' wives and secretaries that they had taught privately over four years.

Parents who did not agree with the school policy had no recourse but to withdraw their children. When a Jewish rabbi complained that his children were marked absent when they did not go to school on Jewish holidays, one of the Sisters said bluntly, "We are not here to teach them as Jews or Germans or Russians; this is a Christian school.[164]

In September 1936, when the secretary of the Soviet Consulate went to enroll Felix, the son of the new consul, and suggested that Soviet children be allowed to play outside during religious instruction classes, the Sisters refused to compromise: "If they come to our school, they have to take whatever we teach in school!" Since the Academy offered the only cosmopolitan education in Dairen and the only alternative was a boarding school in Mukden, the Soviets kept their children in the Academy.[165]

A sign of the Sisters' long-lasting influence on the students is correspondence maintained over the years with their former students, many of whom became Catholics as adults. Almost every year, students in the junior and senior classes expressed their desire to be baptized and waited patiently for their parents' consent. The profound influence of the Sisters

on their students was described in a farewell poem given to them by a
Jewish girl graduate of the class of 1941.

> "Parting is such sweet sorrow" is quite untrue
> For me it is as gall to part from you.
> My yearning heart has often said to me
> "True happiness is only found upon the Sacred Tree."
> And haunting fears beset me then, and I was afraid,
> I turned to you, and seeing your courage, I prayed.
>
> Many have words to make them outshine the rest
> But yours have been example—the example of the blest,
> For when I saw your smiles instead of tears
> And through all of your hard and agonizing years,
> I sought for One Who lavished such abundant love
> To help along His servants: I turned to God above.
>
> And does God hide from those who seek and yearn?
> I know the answer, though 'twas hard to learn.
>
> It was hard to learn that suffering was bliss
> But who was it that proved the truth of this?
> It was you and God's unbounded grace
> That taught me this, and now the world I'll face
> With greater courage, because I'll think of you
> Who gave up all to teach that Christ was true.[166]

When this girl told her father of her desire to become Catholic, he was
irate. He wanted to take her and her two sisters out of the Academy and at
first threatened to go to the American consul to accuse the Sisters of
perverting his children's minds. After further discussion with the Sisters,
he calmed down but still held them partly responsible for his oldest
daughter's attitude. He told them, "Maybe you don't teach the Catholic
religion in school as such, but the children are in an atmosphere of prayer
all day long. Every place they turn they see the Sisters." He finally
decided to keep his children in the Academy, but refused to give his
consent for his oldest daughter to become a Catholic until she investigated
several other religions.[167]

Through their students, the Sisters also reached deep into the foreign
community which comprised close to 1,800 people in 1948. They were very
familiar with the families of their Catholic students whose native languages were as varied as Italian, French, Spanish, German, Croatian,
Czech, Polish, and Armenian. Whenever a foreign priest visited the city,
the Sisters, through their students, contacted all Catholic foreigners
speaking that language and arranged for confession and mass.[168]

Little incidents, however, betrayed the fact that the Sisters could not escape the intransigent attitude of the Church as the true guardian of God's revelation. Each spring from May 8 to 10, Dairen held its highest festival of the year to honor what the Sisters believed was the local deity, Dairen Jinja. In fact, Jinja was the Japanese name for the Shinto shrine and the celebration was not to honor any particular god but to commemorate the anniversary of the shrine. The fervor of the people and the beauty of the procession never seemed to touch the Sisters, who were taught to see only paganism in such rituals. The richness of the Catholic Church's celebrations during May supplied them with a spiritual tool to fight back. In 1933 when the Jinja festivities coincided with the feast of the Sacred Heart, the Sisters spent the days "reciting the Act of Consecration to the Sacred Heart in reparation for the ignorance and idolatry of these poor people." In 1938, when it coincided with the Feast of the Blessed Sacrament, the Sister-diarist stated that the pagan custom of carrying shrines through the streets had its roots in Nagasaki where the Catholics used to have a public procession of the Blessed Sacrament amidst songs of faithful devotion.[169]

Some of the Sisters seemed to derive a certain satisfaction from having non-Catholic children complete religious acts which went against their parents' beliefs or convictions. At the end of May, the crowning of the statue of the Blessed Virgin was turned into a school ceremony. Girls who had displayed the best conduct and the best efforts during the year were rewarded with the honor of bringing the crown to Mary. The May 30, 1941, diary noted:

> The shrine was beautiful. The ceremony was very touching when you thought that most of those present were Jews with some pagans and Mohammedans. Many of them were they to be struck at that moment, would have had baptism of desire in their hearts. Josephine Fronskevich, one of the few Catholics in the school, read the Act of Consecration. Toshiko Kodama, a Japanese, who only waits for her parents' permission to be baptized, crowned. Lucien Beerbrayer, a Soviet, and Rita Rimshaw were candle-bearers. Vindari Melvani, an Indian child, a Hindu, carried the crown.[170]

At other times, the Sisters used subterfuge to teach the students Catholic prayers, like the time they taught them to sing the Latin Ave Maria. "It's amusing," wrote the diarist, "to see those [Jews] who would never say a Hail Mary aloud singing the Ave Maria with all their hearts.[171] In June 1937, the Sister who taught first-graders was delighted with the fact that she sent home Felix, the son of the Soviet consul, with a medal of the Sacred Heart pinned under his clothing.

In April 1939, the first clouds of difficulty appeared. The Soviet Consulate succeeded in pressuring the Japanese authorities into letting it start its own Russian school. The following September all the Russian students in the Academy had to register in the new school. After much complaint from the Russian Jews in Dairen, however, 40 Jewish children were allowed to stay with the Sisters. A few Soviet students entering the senior class were also permitted to complete their high school at the Academy. In June 1939, the school's graduation ceremony was shunned by the mayor.[172]

Except for the absence of Soviet citizens, however, the school continued to be well attended by children of the foreign community until a few days after the attack on Pearl Harbor. On December 12, 1941, the six American Sisters teaching at the Academy—Rose Benigna Hanan, Mary Luke Logue, Rachel Jackson, Virginia (Stella Marie) Flagg, Mary Corita Herrgen, and Xavier Marie Shalvey—were interned with the other Maryknollers in Dairen. Sister Sabina Nakamura, a Japanese citizen, was the only one not arrested. The authorities told her to make plans to resume school as soon as possible for some 50 foreign children, mostly White Russians, Armenians, and Arabs, for whom they were no other facilities.

In January 1942, she reopened the Academy with the help of Sister Maria Talitha Yamagishi who was reassigned from Korea to Dairen. The Japanese teacher, Furuya San, and two former graduates, Helen Kozlenko and Joseph Lerner, formed the rest of the staff. In April, Sister Marie Elise Baumann, who held a German passport, came from Fushun to join the group. Maryknoll Sisters Rose Ann Nakata, a Japanese, and Margaret Kim, a Korean, came from Japan to help in 1943. Father Wilhelm Schifer, a German Jesuit, was also allowed to stay at the Academy. None of these five Sisters had English as her mother tongue; nor had any one of them been trained as a teacher. Yet they carried on valiantly and provided the students with an education they could not otherwise have received. The course of study was directed by Sister Marie Elise who had graduated from the American School in Manila and gone to college in the United States. Sister Sabina kept smooth relations with the Japanese authorities and Sister Margaret Kim, whose knowledge of English was minimal, did most of the housekeeping.[173] Throughout the war, the enrollment of the Academy increased, reaching an all-time high of 170 students shortly after the Japanese surrender of August 15, 1945. During those years, the Sisters lived in complete isolation from the Maryknoll center in the United States.

Victory Day, however, brought a new ordeal for the Sisters, who found themselves at the mercy of the Soviet soldiers, described by Sister Marie Elise on September 13, 1945:

> The biggest strain and the most disagreeable and dangerous time has been

during these past few weeks since the Russian army has come in. We tried to help the people who came running to us for protection though we were not safe ourselves. Placing all our trust in the Sacred Heart and the Blessed Mother, we had the people sleep in our convent, while we took turns on watch, day and night. . . . Many of the incidents were so terrible that I cannot write about them. . . . Bishop Lane wrote an official notice that we are under his jurisdiction. Thus, the Japanese Sisters are safer, and as for me, this move will save my life. The hatred of the Germans is so great that at first the [Russian] soldiers were allowed to do as they pleased with them.[174]

The graduation held on June 29, 1946, proved to be the last at the Academy. During the summer the Soviets opened a Russian school in the Academy building and told the former staff to move out. The following September the Sisters attempted to carry on with the school but had to close the Academy in early 1947 because of the lack of facilities and increasing difficulties with the Soviet and Chinese authorities. In September 1947 the five Sisters obtained exit visas; Sister Marie Elise went to the Philippines and the four other Sisters left for Japan. The accomplishments of these five Sisters were described by Bishop Lane who had resided with them at the Japanese parish since Victory Day.

If there is anything approaching the heroic in these parts, it is the conduct of our Maryknoll Sisters here in Dairen during recent years. . . . The school is the result of their perseverance in the face of the great physical and mental suffering, disease and lack of food. The enrollment has reached almost 200 and twice that number would gladly attend if there were enough Sisters to teach them.[175]

Conclusion

The scope and impact of Maryknoll's involvement in corporal works of mercy during its 35 years in China are surprising—considering that Maryknoll had not yet celebrated its fiftieth birthday. The large sums of money the missioners were able to channel to China directly from the United States were a tribute both to the ingenuity of Maryknollers and to the generosity and mission spirit of American Catholics.

The most striking feature of Maryknoll's work was that the missioners focused on major needs in the community, giving priority to the poor and the defenseless. By distributing free medication and sponsoring vaccination programs, the Catholic dispensaries provided better medical care in the countryside. The hospital in Toishan eased the shortage of hospital beds for seriously ill patients in the Kongmoon vicariate, and the orphanages tried to counter local aberrations caused by poverty and customs which were unfair to female babies. The leper colony and Shanghai Mercy Hospital treated as human beings people who lived as outcasts because the Chinese misunderstood the nature of their diseases. The mission schools gave the first rudiments of literacy to villagers who otherwise would never have had that opportunity. Hostels allowed poor Catholic students from the villages to pursue higher studies. Cooperatives protected villagers from loan sharks, brought economic stability to some localities, and helped others launch new business ventures.

A second important characteristic of Maryknoll's medical, educational, and social works was that they contributed to the modernization of rural China by introducing some ideas from the West which had already been accepted in the big cities, including such basic practices as hygiene. Maryknollers, however, had been cautioned about "Westernizing" China, and during their seminary and novitiate years, they had been taught to appreciate and respect Chinese culture and tradition. The corporal works of mercy begun by Maryknoll did not aim indiscriminately at creating a replica of the United States in China. Rather Maryknollers hoped the Chinese would incorporate what they saw as the best of Western civilization—including the Catholic Church—into their own set of cultural values.

A third characteristic of the corporal works of mercy was their effort to counter China's traditional attitudes toward females and give a new status and role to Chinese women. The orphanages gave testimony to the equal value of female life. The education received by girls in Catholic schools put them on a par with their male counterparts; the grades they obtained proved that they could perform intellectually as well as boys. The participation of the Maryknoll Sisters came at a crucial time; as young women in China were on the threshold of a type of life new to most Chinese women, the Maryknoll Sisters served not only as their guides but as their models. To some, the Sisters offered the model of the educated woman or the teacher, to others the model of the celibate woman fully engaged in the service of the community.

The corporal works of mercy also played an important role in stimulating Catholic laity in both the United States and China to participate more actively in the Church. Compared to their more enterprising Protestant brothers and sisters, the American Catholics did not fully awaken to their worldwide responsibility until the first decade of this century. When they steadily began to increase funds and supplies to support the foreign mission apostolate, a few among them also began to consider the possibility of a missionary vocation. Dr. Paluel Flagg—although he never left the United States—became the pioneer of the Maryknoll Lay Mission Program which was formally launched in 1975. Long before the program actually existed, Dr. Harry Blaber and Dr. Artemio Bagalawis had been the first lay medical missioners sent by Maryknoll to witness Christian charity.

In the Chinese missions, Maryknollers let the Chinese people take charge of the social, educational, and medical works whenever possible. Villagers ran the cooperatives; Chinese nurses were trained and local doctors hired; students were sent to universities to prepare to take over dispensaries, hospitals, and schools as soon as possible.

Maryknollers did make their share of mistakes: for example, refusal to return children in the orphanage to their non-Catholic parents and occasional manipulation of non-Catholic children in schools. The all-pervasive preoccupation of Catholic teaching of that time—salvation in the Church through baptism—sometimes blurred the missioners' message of Christian charity. These mistakes seem to have been mostly the results of inexperienced or zealous individuals who tried to abide by a rigid interpretation of the Church's teachings.

As Maryknollers gained a deeper understanding of the reality of China and its values—and to a certain extent were transformed in the process—they often averted many of their earlier blunders. In general, Maryknollers were relatively successful in creating friendly contacts with the population. These contacts often led to questions and inquiries about the Catholic faith and the motives which brought missioners to China to heal and to teach. No statistics show the number of conversions directly ascribed to the missioners' works of mercy, but it is certain that without them many Chinese would have never had contact with the Catholic Church.

As a result of their frequent involvement with the sick, the poor, and the rejected, some Maryknollers' views on the corporal works of mercy evolved beyond what they had been taught during formation at the seminary or novitiate. Corporal works of mercy, they felt, should be more than a manifestation of Christian charity or a device to attract converts. These works should also be more than temporary measures to alleviate misery and suffering or a means of promoting the Church through the establishment of schools and hospitals. Reflection on their experience in helping people caused many Maryknollers to realize that relief work had little value if it was not accompanied by plans to provide the people with means of improving their living conditions through medical, educational, and social works. Gradually the commonly accepted view in the Catholic Church today emerged, namely that the intrinsic value of corporal works of mercy is to prepare the coming of the Kingdom of God by collaborating with all people of good will, Christians and non-Christians alike, for the building of a world that is more just and fosters full human development.

PART III

The Building of the Native Church

Tensions Surrounding the Emergence of the Chinese Church

The first rule of the Catholic Foreign Mission Society of America approved by the Vatican in 1915 called for the Society "to form at the earliest opportunity a native clergy as the most efficacious means of perpetuating its work of conversion." It specified that the Society should strive to give its mission territories "the form and constitution of regularly established dioceses." The Maryknoll Sisters were convinced as well of the importance of native sisterhoods; their first constitutions called for cooperation with the work of the Fathers and Brothers. In 1931, the Sisters' constitutions were made even more explicit by identifying "the training of native sisterhoods" as a major duty of the Maryknoll Sisters.[1]

Through the years of formation at the seminary and in the novitiate, this idea of establishing a native Church became deeply rooted in every Maryknoller. When asked about the goals of Maryknoll, most old China hands responded in a strikingly similar fashion: Maryknoll's overall purpose was to spread the Gospel among non-Christian Chinese, but a special emphasis was given to building an indigenous Church by training native priests, Sisters, and catechists, by stimulating the laity to apostolic action, and by founding Christian institutions. Upon completion of the task missioners would move on to other areas and start over.

This goal was not original. In the Catholic Church, recruitment and training of young Chinese for priesthood and sisterhood had been traditionally recognized as the first step toward building a local Church. After all, the Maryknoll Fathers borrowed most of their first set of rules from the M.E.P., a missionary group 250 years old. Moreover, the new climate created in China by the Treaty of Nanking in 1842 and other treaties shortly after provided opportunities for religious activities besides evangelization. Seminaries were established in most mission territories, and the number of Chinese priests swelled from about 130 in 1842 to 320 in 1886 and to 942 in 1918 when the first Maryknollers arrived. These remarkable figures reflect great credit on the Western missioners who brought about such results in less than 80 years.[2]

Given exceptional opportunities to work in hospitals, dispensaries, orphanages—and in schools after the abolition of the traditional Chinese educational system in 1905—religious congregations of Sisters began to send groups to China. The French Sisters of Charity were the first to arrive in 1848 and were followed by 12 other groups prior to the arrival of the Maryknoll Sisters in 1920. Organized religious life became available to Chinese women. Many joined foreign sisterhoods while others entered newly established native congregations under the supervision of foreign congregations. By the turn of the century, 10 Chinese sisterhoods had been founded.[3]

The successful building of a native Church, however, was threatened by major impediments. To some extent, missioners had yielded to the colonial mindset which considered Westerners as the only fully developed people. Members of other races, insofar as they became Westernized, might share this wisdom and goodness. Because of their natural inferiority and lack of leadership ability, they needed supervision by Westerners for a very long time, perhaps forever. Chinese priests and Sisters were considered to be "auxiliaries" and were entrusted—under close supervision—with the instruction of the Christians and the care of the sick and the orphaned. This attitude was reinforced by the Catholic tradition of equating the leadership of the Church with male ministry in the persons of the pope, the bishops, and the priests. Male European missioners were in control and could not imagine that the Chinese Church could manage without their direction for a long time to come.[4]

By training native Sisters to be submissive and to undertake works of mercy and education as in Europe, Western Sisters helped promote the establishment of a form of native Church which ensured the control of the male missioners over all segments of the Chinese Christian population. This situation, instead of fostering a Chinese Church strongly rooted in its own culture and free to express its own originality, tended to create a subservient Western-like Chinese Church.

With the turn of the century, however, some missioners were becoming critical of the reliance of the Church in China on the protection of foreign powers. They realized that the growth of Chinese nationalism was inexorable and that a time would come when everything foreign, including the Church, could be swept away, perhaps in a more drastic way than during the Boxer uprising. On the contrary, a *truly Chinese Church* would be a force to invigorate a new China. Fathers Vincent Lebbe and Anthony Cotta, two Vincentians, were the most outspoken members of a movement telling Westerners and Chinese as well that as long as European missioners stayed in control there would not be a true Chinese Church; only under Chinese leadership would the Church become Chinese and prosper. Their message, provocative at times, met opposition from the missionary community as a whole, but eventually was carried to the Holy See itself.

Other people were less vocal but no less effective in proposing a native Chinese Church to Rome. Bishop Jean-Baptiste Budes de Guébriant was one of them. In 1915 in his first quinquennial report to Rome as vicar apostolic of Kientchang in Szechuan, he deplored that the Catholic Church in China still relied on the protectorate of foreign nations such as France. He pointed out that by jealously guarding mission territories for themselves, Western religious societies were in fact working against the establishment of a Chinese Church. He called for seminaries stressing not only religious formation but also the cultural education of Chinese priests in order to counteract the prevalent notion of a poorly educated subaltern clergy.[5]

Transferred to Kwangtung in 1916, de Guébriant moved to implement his ideas. He subdivided his huge vicariate and called upon Maryknollers and Salesians for help. The first Maryknoll priests arrived in December 1918 and found they had the full support of the bishop in fostering their idea of a native Church. Within a year, Rome also took a clear stand in the apostolic letter *Maximum Illud*, which favored the "decolonizing" of the leadership of native Churches and warned missioners that methods aimed at giving native priests "a raw and unfinished preparation . . . for the sole purpose of assisting in subordinate ministry. . . [were] lame and faulty."[6] The encyclical also made it clear that "wherever there exists a native clergy adequate in numbers and in training, and worthy of its vocation, there the missionary work must be considered brought to a happy close, there the Church is founded."[7] For Maryknollers the words of Rome confirmed their mission and encouraged them to devote their energy to the establishment of a full-fledged native Chinese Church.

5

The Indigenization of the Clergy and Sisterhoods

The Training of Native Priests

Establishment of Seminaries

Kongmoon. From the early days of Maryknoll in China, Father Francis Ford was the driving force behind the establishment of seminaries. In 1921, while pastor of Yeungkong, he and his fellow Maryknollers of Tung-chen and Kochow began to teach Latin to some boys they viewed as possible candidates for the priesthood. Two years later, Ford decided to start a formal program by grouping promising candidates in his rectory: 11 boys arrived and became the nucleus of the seminary.[1] In 1924 he wrote in his activity report:

> . . . the preparatory seminary is without doubt the strongest effect of the year's work, for the future Chinese priests will be the backbone of the Church in China. The seminary is really our motive for coming to China—to found a native Church—and the vocations so far presented to us argue well for the strength of the Catholicity in our section of China in years to come.[2]

In the ensuing years, the seminary moved twice in search of better facilities. Finally, the Little Flower Preparatory Seminary was opened at Pakkai in October 1926, next to the cathedral and the bishop's house. By 1931, the building had become too small, and the seminary moved into a new structure in the same compound originally intended as a novitiate for a native sisterhood. The Sisters inherited the old building. The Little Flower Seminary sent its first graduates to the regional major seminary in Hong Kong in the fall of 1933 and remained opened until 1950, except when closed by the Japanese between 1942 and 1945.[3]

Kaying. Meanwhile Father Ford had been transferred to eastern Kwangtung in 1925 to direct the new Maryknoll mission territory of Kaying. He found 10 young Hakka boys ready to study for the priesthood. Rather than send them to the minor seminary in the neighboring vicariate of Swatow where they would have confronted a different language, he transformed his rectory of five rooms into a seminary. A few months later he had 13 boys and by the next fall, 21, which forced him to look for a more permanent solution. He undertook the construction of the St. Joseph Minor Seminary, which was to remain open until 1950.[4]

Wuchow-Kweilin. Father Bernard Meyer was another pioneer in seminary work. In 1921, as pastor of Tungchen in the Kongmoon vicariate, he had recruited several boys and sent them to Father Ford in Yeungkong. However, when he arrived in Wuchow in 1927, statistics showed only 300 Catholics for the entire territory. His first task, therefore, was to build up Catholic communities from which vocations could spring. By 1931 his efforts started to bear fruit: the number of Catholics had passed the 1,000 mark and he had recruited a first group of 15 boys whom he sent to join the seminarians of the Kongmoon vicariate at the Little Flower Seminary in Pakkai.

In 1933, with the addition of the Mandarin-speaking territory of Kweilin to his prefecture, Meyer also fostered the recruitment of Mandarin-speaking seminarians from that region. His second group of 14 seminarians included two boys from Kweilin who later became priests.

Soon it became evident that the Kongmoon seminary would not be able to accommodate all the seminarians from Wuchow, Kongmoon, and Kweilin. Therefore in 1934 Meyer opened the Holy Family Minor Seminary of Tanchuk in Wuchow.[5] After Kweilin was raised to a prefecture apostolic in 1938, Maryknollers started a preseminary in Laipo to teach primary school subjects and screen students, who then went on to Tanchuk for their secondary school studies with seminarians from Wuchow.[6]

Fushun. After one year of training with the M.E.P. in Mukden, Father Raymond Lane led the first group of Maryknollers to the mission territory of Fushun in March 1927. In the fall of 1928 he opened a probatorium (primary-level program) in a small room and finished the school year with 25 students, with four more advanced students being trained at the minor seminary in Mukden. Three years later St. Francis of Assisi Junior Seminary was opened in the Chinese section of Fushun city. The first graduation exercises took place on January 28, 1940, with seven students. The seminary had barely celebrated its tenth anniversary at this location when the Maryknollers were interned by the Japanese following Pearl Harbor. Consequently the seminary had to close its doors and the 21 seminarians were sent to the seminary of Mukden.[7]

Curriculum and Training

Following the abolition of the system of civil servant examinations in 1905, China had adopted a new educational system based on that of Japan, which in turn had been adapted from the United States system. Primary education was divided into a compulsory lower school (*ch'u teng*) of four years for children from six to nine years of age and a higher school (*kao teng*) for children from ten to eleven years of age. Secondary education was divided into two stages of three years, known as junior middle school and senior middle school. After graduation, college and university education was available upon passing an entrance examination.[8]

Until 1937 many Maryknollers, confused by the Chinese terminology, often made mistakes reporting the equivalence between the Chinese and the American systems of education. They overestimated the Chinese system by equating *kao teng* to two years of high school, or sometimes by equating the Chinese middle school to four years of high school plus two years of college.[9] Maryknoll's seminaries usually combined the last two or three years of primary school and six years of secondary school. Probatoriums enrolled students at the primary school level and minor seminaries—also known as junior seminaries or preparatory seminaries—at the secondary school level.

From 1936 to its closure in 1941, the seminary in Fushun operated under the educational system of the puppet state of Manchukuo which did not differ substantially from the one adopted in China. The curriculum in Fushun, however, was more advanced and already included two years of college in the humanities.[10]

At the primary level, the course of studies in the seminaries was, according to Father Dennis Slattery of Kaying, no different from that of an ordinary grade school, but included in addition "the study of Latin, Plain Chant, Religion, Scripture, Public Speaking, and Manual Labor."[11] Father Raymond Quinn explained that at the secondary level the seminary curriculum was patterned as closely as possible along the curriculum of a standard Chinese middle school:

> The full middle school course in Chinese literature is given. Every class has at least one hour of Latin every school day. . . .
>
> In countless middle schools such sciences as Higher Mathematics, Physics, Chemistry, Geology, and Anthropology are taught. The native priest must be able to meet on an equal footing the graduates who have a knowledge of these subjects. At present the Kaying seminary offers Algebra, Geometry, Trigonometry, and one science, Physics. Later it is hoped to expand the scientific department when the proper equipment can be ob-

tained. In Kongmoon Seminary, Chemistry and Biology are given in addition to the above. Ecclesiastical, world and Chinese history have an important place. There are advanced classes in Catechism, and Plain Chant, the music of the Church which the students like very much. They all seem imbued with a natural love of music; on holidays they often gather of their own accord to sing hymns or patriotic Chinese anthems.

Civics and Geography are taught in the lower classes. The last three years have several periods of English a week. Almost all Chinese students realize the value of English as the most widely diffused modern language and are eager to learn it. Then too, the information offered a reader of English in the fields of every art and science is often unobtainable in Oriental languages.[12]

Most of the secular curriculum was entrusted to lay teachers who taught in Chinese. At the secondary level, however, most seminaries had difficulty maintaining academic standards because missioners could not always afford to pay the most qualified teachers. Often a young priest with only a rudimentary knowledge of Chinese was first assigned to teach at the seminary. Father Quinn explained the American rationale:

> [The newly arrived priest] can give almost all his time to the language preparation . . . his students are acquainted with his mentality and probable vocabulary, because they have been taught by others of his colleagues. His gropings are not unfamiliar to them. As a result they are quick to grasp his meaning when other Chinese might be completely at a loss.[13]

The truth, however, is that such young priests "had difficulty in expressing themselves" and that many seminarians "did not really understand" and were often convinced that the medium of teaching was Latin. Nonetheless a few Maryknoll priests were assigned to the seminary long enough to become proficient at teaching English as well as scientific subjects, such as physics and mathematics, which required only a limited, though technical vocabulary.[14]

Although finances remained a constant problem, Maryknollers eventually developed a system of sponsorship in the United States for Chinese seminarians. By 1927, for instance, Father Ford had already found sponsors for all but four of his 20 seminarians. The sponsor's fee of $100 a year per student provided sufficient funds to hire competent teachers as well.[15] In 1933, for example, Bishop Lane hired Mr. Ambrose Hsü, a graduate of Holy Cross College in the United States, to head the faculty of the Fushun seminary. Mr. Hsü helped train inexperienced teachers, planned courses, and developed a method of evaluating each course to determine the progress of the seminarians. Within a few years the seminary became a fully accredited high school.[16]

Ford also hired the best teachers he could afford and paid special attention to the education of the seminarians, sending his most promising students to Rome for theology and graduate work. As a result, St. Joseph School became known not only as one of the best minor seminaries in South China but also as an outstanding high school.[17]

The course of studies in seminaries was also influenced by the regulations of canon law and instructions from Propaganda Fide, which required, among other things, the study of Latin. From the fifth year of primary school on, Latin was taught one hour each day and considered the most important subject. A Chinese priest was expected not only to sight read Latin but also to carry on a conversation. Latin was deemed necessary for three main reasons: it was the official language of the Church used for Mass and the sacraments, and in all papal documents; it was the medium of teaching in the regional major seminaries of China; and it was the only language common to all priests in China, native and foreign.[18]

Although seminary courses were generally taught in Chinese and often with relatively low academic standards, Latin was the exception. As one Maryknoller said, "the seminary course of study was short on Chinese classics and long on Latin."[19] In an attempt to catch up on Latin, students often neglected other subjects, which occasionally led to their dismissal: "Fachow's one Pakkai seminarian is not returning. He has a fine character recommendation from Father Paulhus but he has fallen behind his class in studies."[20] It is no surprise therefore to hear former seminarians report, "If a student's Latin was good, he would have no difficulties in his studies. Otherwise he would be left behind since Latin was the core of the studies."[21] Failure to keep up with Latin was indeed the most common cause of dismissal. Few of the older students who joined at the age of sixteen or seventeen seemed to have been able to pass the Latin hurdle.[22]

As a final preparation for the major seminary in Hong Kong, some courses were intentionally taught in Latin during the last year of high school, such as the Introduction to Logic offered by Father Cyril Hirst in the late 1940s. Latin was also used outside the classroom but the emphasis varied from time to time and from seminary to seminary. Maryknoll priests often encouraged conversational Latin by requiring its use during specified periods such as manual labor and certain mealtimes in the refectory, and for notices on bulletin boards.[23] Most seniors graduated with a good grasp of the language as witnessed by this remark of Father Francis Donnelly of Kaying following a visit to the seminary by the Maryknoll superior general: "Father General gave a short talk, speaking in Latin. When questioned later most of the older boys seemed to have understood everything that was said and could quote Father's words at some length."[24]

The horarium of the Kongmoon seminary for the year 1927 shown in

Table 1

Kongmoon Seminary Horarium

5:45	Rising
6:15	Meditation
6:30	Mass and thanksgiving; morning prayers during Mass (a Chinese custom)
7:30	Class
8:30	Breakfast and recreation
9:30–10:20	Class
10:30–11:20	Class
11:30–12:20	Class
12:30	Angelus, collation, recreation
1:30–2:20	Class
2:30–3:20	Class
3:30–4:00	Gymnastics
4:00	Dinner, recreation or manual labor, gardening
6:15	Spiritual reading
6:30–8:15	Study
8:20	Night prayers, Rosary
9:00	Lights out

Saturday afternoon, free from 12:20 to 6:15. Sunday free from 7:50 a.m. to 6:15 p.m. with Missa Cantata at 9:00 and Benediction at 4:00. Also Benediction at 4:00 on all Thursdays, feasts of our Lord, our Lady, or the Apostles. Source: FARC, 9–05, Letter from Father Anthony Paulhus, February 12, 1927.

Table 1 is a good example of a seminarian's schedule in China.

Although manual labor figured in the curriculum of Chinese middle schools, it was rarely enforced because of the deeply ingrained tradition in China that scholars do not work. Maryknoll seminaries, in that sense, differed sharply from governmental schools and other private schools. Seminarians were responsible for keeping the building clean and for washing and mending their own clothes. They also grew their own vegetables and raised farm animals.

If the seminarians appeared to do all of this willingly, they remembered, however, how humiliating other manual assignments were, such as tidying the Fathers' bathrooms: "We felt very indignant. Why did we have to clean the toilet for them? Why did we have to clean the place after they shaved?"[25]

One of the American innovations was an emphasis on sports and recreation as a way of developing sportsmanship, leadership, and the ability to cope with both success and failure. Joint participation of the Maryknoll priests and the Chinese seminarians in recreation was part of the spirit which set the Maryknoll seminaries apart from those run by European priests. It was not without boasting that the Maryknoll rector of the Wuchow seminary, who had both Maryknoll priests and Irish Jesuits on his faculty during World War II, remarked:

> We [Maryknollers] were definitely much closer to the seminarians and they were getting the spirit of priesthood from us. . . . The Jesuit Fathers would attend class and then go up to their rooms to correct papers and prepare for the next class, but they were never really in with the seminarians so they could be an influence on them.[26]

To develop and strengthen the call to priesthood, all the activities of the seminaries revolved around daily prayers and spiritual exercises, supplemented by weekly confessions and bimonthly recollections. Father Quinn explained this most important characteristic:

> The primary aim of the seminary is to develop the spiritual life of the student. The day starts with morning prayers for the community, meditation which lasts for twenty minutes, and Mass. In the forenoon time is set aside for the particular examination of conscience. Each student reads some portion of Holy Scripture in private just before the Angelus. After the evening recreation comes spiritual reading in common and fifteen minutes' adoration of the Blessed Sacrament. Before the last study period at night the Rosary is said. The end of the day is marked by night prayers. In addition one Sunday in every two months is set aside as Recollection Day, when the students make a retreat.[27]

The seminary was a shelter protecting the young students "from scandals and evil influences." The daily communion, meditation, prayer, and religious instruction encouraged the spiritual growth of the seminarians by keeping "before their eyes the example of Christ and the saints." The horarium ensured "the formation of habits of regularity, punctuality, and exactness."[28]

Maryknollers found, however, that their limited knowledge of Chinese and their Western background hampered their ability to nourish and motivate the religious and spiritual growth of the seminarians. Bishop John Wu of Hong Kong, who studied in the Kaying seminary, explained: "The priest, because he was a foreigner, had difficulties in expressing himself. He found it difficult when he really had to explain to us. . . . Mainly he used his style of life to lead us."[29]

Fig. 1. Chinese seminarians playing volleyball in Wuchow in the early 1950s. Maryknoll Photo Library.

From the beginning, Chinese priests from neighboring vicariates were sought to preach retreats to the seminarians. As the years went on, the trend was definitely toward entrusting spiritual formation to Chinese priests. It was felt that a Chinese priest would be more effective as a spiritual director of seminarians than a Maryknoller because he was a more meaningful role model and had no language handicap. Bishop John Wu remembered very well Father Paul Tsong, his spiritual director in Kaying, as the one who really "taught us the doctrine."[30]

Recruitment and Perseverance

Because of Maryknoll's strong emphasis on work in rural areas, most of the candidates to the seminaries came from villages of farmers and fishermen. The Chinese custom of early betrothal, especially in Kwangtung and Kwangsi, eliminated many possible candidates from the better educated and wealthier families. By the time boys reached ten or twelve years of age, many were already engaged. Since such engagements were not easily broken, Maryknollers made very few attempts to interfere with such arrangements. As a result, the majority of the seminarians came from poor families who could not afford a bride for their young sons.[31]

Parents were usually pleased that a small child, still of little use around the farm, would receive free room, board, and education, especially since most schools in the countryside offered only four years of compulsory lower primary education. At the age of fifteen or sixteen, however, the same parents often put pressure on their son to withdraw from the seminary because he was needed at home. It sometimes "meant to the family all the difference between poverty and comparative comfort in the later years." For all practical purposes, a son-priest was as useless as a daughter: "For when a girl marries, she goes to the home of her husband and becomes a member of his family. Once [a son] is ordained priest . . . he is lost as completely as ever a daughter could be."[32]

Well aware of another Chinese custom which compelled firstborn sons to marry and carry on the family line, Maryknoll Fathers also avoided their recruitment. An exception was made for boys who belonged to "old Christian families." In Kaying, four candidates who reached the priesthood belonged to that category: Bishop John Wu and Fathers Paul Tsong and Anthony Tsoc were firstborn sons, and Father John Tse, an only child.[33]

A survey of interviews with Chinese priests shows that well-established Catholic surroundings were necessary to produce lasting vocations. Most of the candidates who became priests belonged to families who had been Catholic prior to the arrival of Maryknoll. Many came from Catholic villages with a reputation for fostering vocations, like Siaoloc, known as the little Rome of the Kaying vicariate, or Chakow in Fushun, which produced six priests surnamed Pai out of the 20 priests from the vicariate.[34]

The great majority of the Catholic families in Maryknoll territories, however, were new to the faith and did not really understand the difference between a seminary and a regular school. Father Francis Donnelly wrote from his small rural parish in Kaying:

> It is hard to make most of them understand just what the probatorium and seminary mean. Even after a long explanation they persist in thinking of them as ordinary schools and a good chance to get a free education. The idea that boys are studying in preparation for the priesthood is not always . . . clear.[35]

Maryknoll priests, aware of that fact, intentionally kept the requirements to enter the probatorium very simple: "any boy of good character and reputation," preferably between the ages of ten and thirteen, "whose parents are practicing Catholics" would be admitted with the recommendation of his pastor. Study at the probatorium was intended to make the candidates realize what the priesthood actually meant. At the same time, it allowed Maryknoll to assess if the candidates were physically and intellectually fit to become priests.[36]

This Maryknoll policy explains the attrition rate of 80 percent during the two years of the probatorium prior to entering secondary school. For instance, Bishop Wu started the probatorium with a group of more than 40 students. After a few months, many had already been sent home, and by the time he entered the minor seminary, only 10 were left. When Peter Chum entered the two-year probatorium of the Kweilin prefecture in 1941, there were 100 students in the school. By the time he moved to the Wuchow minor seminary two years later, only 10 were left in his class.[37]

Maryknollers felt that if the boys spent even a few years in the seminary, this experience would strengthen their faith and prepare them to assume Catholic leadership in their villages and communities. Indeed, this proved to be true over the years as many village leaders, catechists, and seminary teachers were former seminarians.

Because of the heavy "weeding" during the years of probatorium, seminaries built by Maryknoll were rarely overcrowded. In June 1937, before the Japanese presence became too disruptive in China and Manchuria, Fushun had 46 seminarians in the primary and secondary levels; Kaying had 34; Kongmoon, however, had reached a critical point with a total of 81 at the seminary at Pakkai.

It seems that some priests in that vicariate had been too zealous in sending candidates to the probatorium. The situation prompted the bishop to send his clergy a list of 10 guidelines concerning prospective candidates.

The reason given for the more stringent policy was very practical: "Since our seminary is fairly well filled, it is time to be more selective in accepting applicants."[38] This measure, combined with the flight north of students from the occupied city of Pakkai, produced a sharp decline in enrollment. Only 64 seminarians remained at the end of the school year of 1938–39, and only 49 were left prior to the closing of the seminary by the Japanese in 1941.[39]

During the years of secondary schooling, the rate of perseverance among seminarians failed to improve substantially. Bishop Wu was the only one of his class to become a priest; similarly Father Simeon To became the only priest in a group of 16 from his village of Pantien in Kweilin.[40]

During these years, many students felt obliged to withdraw because of filial piety. They went home to work on the farm or to take a job as a civil servant or a teacher. Some candidates were also asked to leave because of poor health. Dismissal for disciplinary reasons was rare. But, as previously explained, the great majority of those sent back home were dismissed because of academic difficulties, mostly in learning Latin.[41]

Difficulties after Pearl Harbor

From 1936 on, disturbances caused by the thrust of Japanese troops into parts of China hindered academic progress in most seminaries. Under-staffed faculties struggled to maintain classes, and many courses had to be skipped or were inadequately taught.[42] In 1941, with the bombing of Pearl Harbor and the entrance of the United States into the war, the Maryknoll seminaries in Japanese-occupied territories were not allowed to continue: Fushun and Kongmoon were closed and Wuchow and Kweilin were constantly relocating.

Fushun. When the St. Francis of Assisi Junior Seminary opened in Fushun in 1931, the vicariate had five Chinese priests. Ten years later when the seminary closed, the five priests remained but the seminarians moved to seminaries in Mukden and in Hsinking in the vicariate of Kirin. In 1946, when the Communists occupied Manchuria, the seminarians moved on to Peking or Hong Kong. Nonetheless, when the seminary closed in 1941, 15 of the 52 seminarians in Fushun persevered and were ordained between 1945 and 1952; however, only nine returned to their native diocese. Today only two of these nine priests, Fathers Pius Chin and Paul Tsui, are still alive. In 1980, when the church property of Fushun-Honan* was returned to the Catholics, they were put in charge. They have lived there since, providing mass and sacraments to the Catholic community of the city. They are assisted by a somewhat younger fifty-seven-year-

---

*A river divided the city into two sections, Fushun-Honan and Fushun-Hopei.

old priest, Peter Chao, who was ordained in 1983 by the Chinese bishop of Kirin, who now has jurisdiction over most of the former diocese of Fushun.[43]

Kongmoon. In late 1941, the Japanese also closed the minor seminary of Pakkai in Kongmoon. The vicariate had only three Chinese priests, but 12 seminarians were studying theology and philosophy in the Hong Kong major seminary. In the following years, eight became priests. Since the Japanese insisted that all students at Pakkai be sent home, the Maryknollers chose 10 of their 49 middle-schoolers and secretly sent them to further their training at the Wuchow seminary. Four of them, Fathers Peter Ma, Thomas Tam, Anthony Chan, and Phillip So, persevered and were ordained in Hong Kong in 1954, but did not return to Kongmoon. Of the 11 Chinese priests left in the Kongmoon diocese after 1949, only three, Fathers Linus Wong, Paul Liu, and Thomas Ma, were still alive in the spring of 1987. In 1981, the Kongmoon city parish house was returned to Fathers Liu and Wong, who settled there with a group of five Chinese Sisters. In August 1986, the nearby former cathedral of Pakkai was finally reopened and entrusted to the care of the two priests. Meanwhile the church of Wanfow was also returned to the Catholic Church and entrusted to Father Ma.[44] As of 1987, five seminarians from the former Kongmoon diocese area were studying at the major regional seminary in Wuch'ang, and a few young men were receiving preliminary training in Pakkai.

Wuchow-Kweilin. With only a handful of Catholics to supply candidates, the formation of a native clergy had a slow start in both territories of Wuchow and Kweilin. In 1933, a year before the opening of Maryknoll's seminary at Tanchuk, Thomas Tao, trained by the M.E.P. had been ordained but he was not the type of priest the Maryknoll missioners wanted to produce for China:

> He is a nice lad, but the usual product of the old type of mission training. Judgment, comprehension and initiative seem to have been beaten out of him in the process of training. Besides his education is woefully lacking in his native literature, history and any kind of sciences.[45]

For 15 years, Father Tao remained the only local native priest until Benedict Choi and Mark Tsang were finally ordained in 1948. They were the only priests trained by Maryknoll in Wuchow and Kweilin prior to the fall of Wuchow to the Communists.

These grim statistics, however, hide the true story of the Wuchow seminary. The mere existence of this seminary between 1942 and 1945 was a tribute to Maryknoll's commitment to building a native Church. Bishop Frederick Donaghy, the head of the vicariate, told Father Albert Fedders, the rector, that they

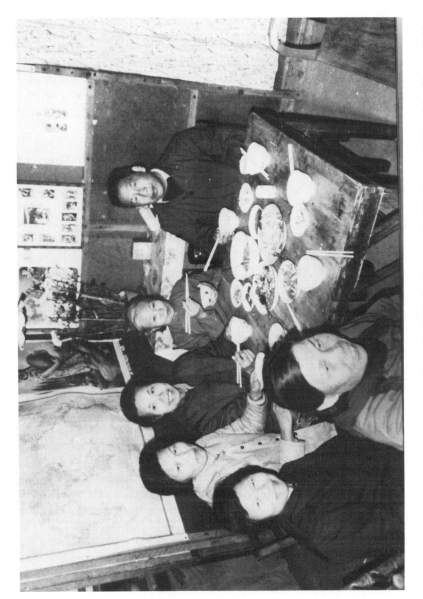

Fig. 2. Some of the Kongmoon Sisters with Father Paul Liu in Kongmoon in 1981. Source: Father John Cioppa, M.M.

... would keep the seminary going as long as they could and as well as they could no matter what happened ... even if it meant going around with a tin cup from door to door to beg for money in order to keep these boys in training for the priesthood.[46]

Between 1942 and 1945, the school became a type of regional seminary, hosting a small group of seminarians from Kongmoon and also training seminarians from Wuchow and Kweilin. For two years they also gave asylum to 10 Jesuit scholastics and three Irish Jesuit priests who had fled Hong Kong. These Jesuits helped the students who had finished high school get started in their studies of philosophy.

The saga of these four years of survival could fill an entire book. In 1943, when the seminary in Tanchuk became unsafe because of the constant Japanese bombing of the American air base behind the seminary, the students moved to Paksha, some 80 miles upriver near Kweiping. They settled into the building of a former M.E.P. minor seminary. A year after, in September 1944, the Japanese made a drive up the river and came within 20 miles of Paksha. Because of this new menace, the Jesuit priests and scholastics withdrew to Kunming, and Father Fedders, the rector, sent home the seminarians from the area. He then led the other 20 away from the river into the hills with the intention of staying at the large mission compound of Taiwan. He found this unsafe as well because the Japanese were only nine miles away "as the crow flies." The group kept moving and took a 20-mile-long steep and rocky path to Topong, a little adobe-walled mission hidden in the mountains, where they stayed until the end of the war.

From Paksha they had carried not only books, clothing, and bedding, but also brought along 10 small pigs, 47 ducks, two guinea pigs, a dog, and four puppies. The situation remained precarious in Topong. People in the mountain passes watched for approaching Japanese patrols. As soon as an alert was given, Maryknollers and seminarians would grab prepared emergency bags, run to higher ground and hide for two or three days at a time. Despite these disruptions, classes were kept as regular as possible. Life in the mountains was very spartan, with no electricity or running water. The provisions and money brought along from Tanchuk rapidly diminished as all contact with the outside had been severed. The diet became more and more similar to that of the poorest people: first meat was suppressed, then rice too became out of reach and was replaced by sweet potatoes. There were about 80 mouths to feed: 10 Maryknoll priests, two brothers, seven Maryknoll Sisters, 20 seminarians, three novices and two aspirants, one lay professor with his wife and seven children, several catechists, and hired hands of various other missions with their families.

Father Fedders had completely run out of funds and was wondering what to do next when on Friday the 13th, October 1944, money literally dropped from the sky. Another Maryknoll priest, Father Arthur Dempsey, had traveled 200 miles of mountain trails and white waters to the American base of Liuchow where he took up a collection among American servicemen. The generous donation, tightly wrapped in a bamboo basket, was then placed in the bomb slot of a plane and dropped over the Topong mission—to the amazement of villagers, who thought it was a miracle. The basket contained enough money to take care of everyone in the compound until the end of the war.[47]

After August 1945, the seminary moved to Pingnam because the building in Tanchuk had been heavily damaged. Maryknollers in the vicariate again began to recruit candidates, and enrollment at the seminary gradually increased. In September 1948, Father Frederick Becka, professor at the seminary, reported an all-time high of 36 seminarians. Relative tranquility, however, barely lasted five years. When the Communists arrived in Pingnam in December 1950, they requisitioned the seminary building for a jail. Once more the seminarians were on the move, and they returned to Tanchuk.

In June 1951 the Communists notified the rector, Father Joseph Laai, that following the summer recess the seminary would become a "national" seminary abiding by the three principles of "self-rule, self-support, and self-propagation." As a consequence, the teaching staff was reduced from four to two: Father Becka was barred from teaching because he was a foreigner, and one of the two lay professors was dismissed for lack of funds. By September, the seminarians had already planted a garden and built several rabbit cages and a pen for their three pigs in an effort to become self-supporting. Nonetheless, the Communists closed the building so that the boys could return home to take part in the government-supervised redistribution of the fields.[48] Of the 20 seminarians who had found refuge in Topong in late 1944, 10 were ordained in Hong Kong between 1952 and 1956, three for the diocese of Wuchow, three for Kweilin, along with the four from Kongmoon previously mentioned, but none returned to his native diocese.

After all Maryknollers had left Kwangsi province in 1952, the Kweilin prefecture was left with no native priests and the Wuchow diocese with only three. Father Tao died, and Father Tsang has not been heard of since he was sentenced to forced labor in 1951. Father Choi was released after 20 years in prison in December 1979; as of 1987, however, his former parish in Wuchow city has not yet been officially reopened for public worship.[49]

Kaying. Because the Japanese never occupied the mountain area of eastern Kwangtung, the Kaying vicariate operated rather normally throughout the war. In his report of June 1942, Bishop Francis Ford mentioned that courses had been added to the curriculum of St. Joseph Minor Seminary in Kaying so that seminarians who should have entered the major regional seminary in Hong Kong could continue their formation:

> Our three graduates from the local seminary could not go to Hong Kong, so we opened a philosophy course here under Father Hilbert, whose special studies in the various Chinese systems of Mencius, Confucius and others, enable him to adapt the course to our nationals more thoroughly even than is done in the course offered at the Regional Seminary.[50]

After the war, graduates from Kaying resumed their philosophy and theology in Hong Kong while St. Joseph's continued to offer courses. In 1948 Bishop Ford appointed a Chinese rector, Father Paul Tsong, to head an all-Chinese faculty of competent priests and lay persons.

When the Communists occupied Kaying in April 1949, they required that the seminary become a regular high school. In October, St. Joseph's Middle School opened with 69 students, of whom 45 were seminarians. A year and a half later, the seminarians were ordered home to take part in land reform, and the seminary never reopened. One of the students, however, persevered in his goal of becoming a priest, even though he had to serve 15 years of forced labor for his religious convictions. In 1982, Peter Jong was admitted to the recently opened regional seminary at She Shan near Shanghai where he was ordained in December 1986.

In assessing the successes and failures of Maryknollers in training a Chinese clergy, consideration should be given to the fact that it took from 14 to 20 years to train a priest. In Kaying, for instance, between 1926 and 1940, six Chinese, all of them seminarians at the time of Maryknoll's arrival, became priests. In 1941, the first student sent by a Maryknoller to the Kaying seminary, Paul Lam, was ordained, and he was followed by 10 more in less than a decade: one in 1942, four in 1943, and five in 1948. After the Communist occupation of Kaying in April 1949, Ford chose Father Lam as his vicar general. Between 1952 and 1958, eight more Hakka priests were ordained in Hong Kong but did not return to their native diocese.

If circumstances had not stopped the trend, it seems practically certain that the Kaying vicariate would have had more than 30 Chinese priests by the late 1950s or the early 1960s, and would have been more than ready for a native bishop. Of the 17 native priests in the Kaying diocese in 1949, five are still alive. So far, the church in Siaoloc, officially reopened in 1983, is the only church available for public worship; it is the residence of Father Paul Lam, the vicar general. In Hingning, Kukong, and Meihsien (Kaying) city, Fathers Peter Liao, Paul Leong, Anthony Chung, and John Wong have transformed small quarters into temporary chapels.[51]

The Training of Native Sisters

Since the late eighteenth century, the institution of the Virgins had played a great role in the life of the Church in China. Usually called "*chuchiati*" or "live-at-home" because they remained unmarried in their native villages, these women acted as catechists; cared for the orphans, the aged and the sick; kept the sanctuary and church linens in good condition; and served the missioner in the varied activities of the mission station. For all practical purposes, these women were native Sisters although their institution was never canonically defined.

With the arrival of foreign Sisters and the development of native communities in the late nineteenth century, the Virgins slowly became redundant as religious congregations offered Chinese women a well-defined place within the structure of the Church. When the Maryknoll Fathers arrived, they still found some of the Virgins in their missions and praised their services; however, they never envisaged perpetuating that institution, but rather thought religious congregations would train women for religious life.

The Establishment of Novitiates

Kongmoon. Prior to the opening of the pre-novitiate of the Sisters of the Immaculate Heart of Kongmoon, the native congregation of the Sisters of the Immaculate Conception of Canton was the only outlet for female vocations from Kongmoon. In 1921 Father James E. Walsh was instrumental in making it possible for Mary Chan, his first convert from Kochow, to enter this community. By 1924 there were four more candidates from the Hoingan parish studying in Canton, despite the fact that admission was "quite difficult as applications far outnumbered the accommodations."[52] It seemed natural to the Maryknoll Fathers that the Maryknoll Sisters establish a novitiate to train native vocations within their own territory.

In 1923 the Maryknoll Sisters started to look into the possibility of admitting Chinese postulants into their ranks. Sister Mary Paul McKenna, superior of the Maryknoll Sisters in China, gathered information from other congregations, such as the Little Sisters of the Poor, which had already taken such a step. When asked his opinion, Father Walsh suggested training Chinese girls for a native sisterhood as another possibility. "Our great present need is catechists and for that work it would appear to me that a native sisterhood of catechists such as they have at Canton would prove more practical." This idea had been prevalent among the Maryknoll Fathers since 1921.[53]

Both ideas finally matured. Sister Maria Teresa Yeung was the first Chinese from Hong Kong who entered the Maryknoll Sisters in 1927.

Better known as "Tessie," she helped launch the Sisters' industrial department in Hong Kong, a very successful venture in self-support. A few months before, in December 1926, James E. Walsh, then prefect apostolic of Kongmoon, brought Chiu Uelaia of Hoingan, the first applicant from his prefecture to a native sisterhood, to the Maryknoll Sisters in Hong Kong. She was soon followed by nine others who were placed under the guidance of Sister Mary Imelda Sheridan, who was replaced in 1928 by Sister Mary Patricia Coughlin. Sister Mary Patricia labored for over 20 years in the formation of the first native sisterhood founded by Maryknoll.

In September 1928, formal classes for grades one through four were organized because most of these girls had never been to school and did not even know how to write their names.

> Sister Mary Bernadette taught the doctrine and a teacher came in daily for the other school subjects. Classes were from 9 to 1 followed by a short remission period. They went to chapel, then for the Angelus and the Rosary. In the afternoon up until 4, they were taught sewing, cutting, and making their own clothes, and also embroidery. Each day from 4 to 5 was spent in the gardens, planting, weeding, etc. At this time was begun reading at morning rice. Also regular spiritual reading for 15 minutes daily in common. After evening rice and the remission period, they prepared their school work for the next day. This was followed by common recreation and then night prayers. At Easter of 1929 they began saying Vespers and Compline in choir in Chinese daily. They loved it very much.[54]

Meanwhile a permanent building was erected in the Kongmoon territory in Pakkai, next to the cathedral, the mission seminary, and the bishop's residence. On December 8, 1931, the novitiate for the Sisters of the Immaculate Heart of Kongmoon opened with the arrival from Hong Kong of Sisters Mary Patricia Coughlin and Mary Rose Leifels and six candidates. Five of them were received as novices on October 3, 1933. Permission from Rome to open the novitiate was not received, however, until February 9, 1934. The first profession of the first group was reported on February 11, 1936, in order to satisfy the two years of formation required by the Kongmoon Sisters' constitutions.[55]

By the fall of 1937, war had descended on Kongmoon, with the almost daily appearance of Japanese bombers in the sky. When the Japanese occupied Kongmoon on March 29, 1939, the Maryknoll Sisters stayed on duty and continued to train candidates for the novitiate. Following Pearl Harbor, the Maryknoll Sisters were expelled and the novitiate was closed. The 24 native Sisters, novices, postulants, and candidates, accompanied by Father Linus Wong and three seminarians, moved inland toward Loting in nonoccupied territory in three separate groups. The trip was long and dangerous. One group of seven Sisters fell prey to bandits who mercilessly robbed and raped them. Eventually able to rejoin the two other groups, all 24 reached Loting on December 23, and Sister Mary Francis Davis assumed the formation of the postulants and the novices. Late in 1943 she became ill and passed that responsibility to Sister Eucharista Coupe. In spite of the precarious situation and several temporary moves to other locations such as Loking and Kap Shui, their training was uninterrupted, and several native Sisters were professed. In 1945, 20 professed Sisters from Kongmoon worked in nonoccupied territories.[56]

In December 1945, Sisters Mary Patricia Coughlin and Beatrice Meyer, the sister of Father Bernard Meyer, returned to Pakkai to resume training at the novitiate. By February, the community had started to grow again, adding nine novices to its ranks. At the last ceremony of profession on August 15, 1949, the congregation counted 28 professed, two novices, and 11 aspirants.[57]

In 1951, after the Communists moved in, Adolph Paschang, the bishop of Kongmoon, closed the novitiate and ordered all the native Sisters and novices to remove their habits and return home. He gave some money to each one to help her while looking for employment. Some professed Sisters, however, were able to continue living with Maryknollers at Yeungkong and at the Toishan hospital for another year or so, until they too were sent home by the Communists. Prior to 1958, 15 native Sisters managed to emigrate to Hong Kong where they became a firmly established, growing, and self-supporting community governed by their own mother general. As of 1987, the 13 others who remained behind have returned from prisons, factories, hospitals, and other jobs and are leaders of Catholic parishes in villages of the Kongmoon-Pakkai area. Five of them have received permission from the local authorities to live again as a community of Sisters and have begun receiving new recruits.[58]

Wuchow. Father Meyer sent his first Chinese candidate for sisterhood to study with the Maryknoll Sisters in Hong Kong in 1928. As soon as Wuchow became an independent mission, he nurtured the idea of founding a congregation of Wuchow Sisters. In February 1931, he started a one-year pre-novitiate in Pingnam under the care of two native Sisters of the Immaculate Conception of Canton. He felt that a year of formation in the Wuchow territory would give the girls a sense of belonging to the prefecture. After their first year of formation he entrusted the candidates to the Maryknoll Sisters in charge of the novitiate of the Immaculate Heart Sisters of Kongmoon. Of the 11 girls he sent to study at Pakkai in 1932 and 1933, four persevered to become the first professed Sisters of the Congregation of the Sisters of Charity of the Sacred Heart of Wuchow.

In September 1935, Maryknoll Sisters Mary Gonzaga Rizzardi and Moira Riehl took over the pre-novitiate of Pingnam, which had an enrollment of 38 students from the Kweilin and Wuchow areas, ranging from ten to twenty years of age. With the return of the aspirants studying in Pakkai, a postulancy was started on August 8, 1936, but word of canonical erection was not received until July 1, 1937. On January 6, 1940, in the pro-cathedral of Tanchuk, four novices became the first professed Sisters of the new congregation. Nine years later on July 3, 1949, in the same church, these four Sisters made their final vows.[59]

The war with Japan caused many worries to Sister Moira, who assumed the responsibility of the novitiate after the departure of Sister Mary Gonzaga in 1937. After Pingnam was bombed on October 23, 1939, air raid alarms became an almost daily occurrence. Each time, the girls ran to the river bank and boarded three rented sampans which took them downriver to safety. In December the novitiate was moved to Tanchuk, thought to be safer. But a year later, because of the proximity of an American airbase, the situation in Tanchuk became even more dangerous, so the novitiate moved back to Pingnam. In 1942 the bishop halted recruitment for the pre-novitiate because he was short of funds and allowed only enrolled students to continue. To reduce expenses the students planted sweet potatoes and vegetables, raised pigs, chickens, and ducks, and agreed to eat two daily meals of rice gruel and only one of rice. Despite the war, the young congregation continued to grow, and by 1943 seven professed Sisters and two novices were responsible for three two-Sister convents at Tanchuk, Pingnam, and Taiwan.[60]

By June 1944, however, the situation had deteriorated to the point that the Maryknoll Sisters were evacuated. The small convents were closed and the students, as well as several professed Chinese Sisters, took refuge with the seminarians in the mountain village of Topong. This proved to be a very trying time for the community, which feared disbandment. Several times they fled farther up into the mountains and even put on civilian clothes as disguises. Finally, in September 1945, the Pingnam novitiate was reopened. The following January it was decided to move to Ue Fa T'ong on the outskirts of Wuchow City to allow the girls in the pre-novitiate to attend middle school.[61]

At the last report on July 1, 1950, the native Sisters included 10 professed Sisters and six novices. In addition, eight aspirants were studying at one of the city's high schools. In December 1950, with the arrest of Bishop Donaghy, Father Justin Kennedy, and Maryknoll Sister Superior Rosalia Kettl, the Communists' harassment of the missioners and the Catholics increased. At the novitiate, however, two more native Sisters were professed in 1951 before all Maryknollers left the diocese.

Meanwhile, the Maryknoll Sisters had prepared the Chinese Sisters to be self-sufficient. Some Chinese Sisters took paying jobs outside the convent; others went to work at a small towel-weaving factory set up especially for the native Sisters by Bishop Donaghy. The Communists allowed the

Chinese Sisters to live together but not without pressuring them to marry. Sister Paul, their superior, became a special target of intimidating measures. She was often summoned to the police station and reminded that she could be jailed again as she had been on trumped-up charges in 1951 for having ill-treated an orphan. In 1957, a frightened Sister Paul finally broke under pressue, left the convent, and married. Since none of the other professed Sisters was willing to take her place, the community had to disperse. Contact with the Sisters has been lost, and there has been no recent sign of the revival of the community.[62]

Kweilin. After the Chinese New Year in February 1937, Monsignor Meyer implemented his plan to develop a second sisterhood by sending eight Mandarin-speaking girls of the Kweilin territory to a new novitiate in Laipo. Their training was put in the hands of three native Sisters of the Holy Family from Nanning who had already been working in the Kweilin territory before the French M.E.P. turned it over to Maryknoll.

In the meantime, Kweilin became a prefecture apostolic under Monsignor Romaniello. By February 1939, the group had grown to 18, and four of them were getting ready to enter their postulancy. Monsignor Romaniello then requested three Maryknoll Sisters, Mary Gonzaga Rizzardi, Dominic (St. Dominic) Kelly, and Agnes (Gabriel Marie) Devlin, to take over the direction of the novitiate and help in the parish of Laipo. The superior, Sister Mary Gonzaga, was a somewhat familiar figure because the candidates had studied under her earlier in Pingnam.[63]

The congregation was officially recognized on March 2, 1939. Six months later, on the Feast of the Holy Name of Mary, the first postulancy for the native congregation of the Sister Catechists of the Blessed Virgin Mary began with the reception of four candidates. These four girls persevered and were professed on May 31, 1942. They were joined by three more the following year.[64]

In September 1941, Sister Miriam Carmel Lechthaler, assisted by Sister Cornelia Collins, took over the direction of the novitiate and prenovitiate with responsibility to keep them open in spite of constant bombing. When the Maryknoll Sisters were evacuated in September 1944, the students were dismissed and the postulants were sent to Wuchow with the professed Sisters. When the Maryknoll Sisters returned a year later, they found the novitiate and all the church buildings in ruins, but the native Sisters were already there to greet them. The novitiate reopened on October 15, 1945, with three novices and nine students under the direction of Sister Barbara Mersinger assisted by Sister Agnes Devlin. In the following five years, seven of these young women were professed, bringing the total to 14.[65]

Between September and December 1950, most Maryknollers were asked to leave, the native Sisters were sent home, and the novitiate was closed. Monsignor Romaniello dispensed the professed Sisters of their vows; however, three of them, Sisters Agnes Chau, Joan Ling, and Rose Chin, were in Macao for studies and subsequently joined the Maryknoll Sisters.[66]

Kaying. Just as Bishop Ford was convinced that the Kaying Church had no permanent future if he did not prepare a native clergy to take over the duties of his Maryknoll priests, so was he convinced that for a successful apostolate among women and children, Chinese Sisters were essential. From the moment he started to build his seminary in 1927, he also planned the formation of a native sisterhood under the leadership of Maryknoll Sisters. At that time, however, early Communist agitation in the area deterred him from inviting foreign Sisters to Kaying. He decided instead to send his prospective candidates to Hong Kong for training, where they joined candidates from the Kongmoon vicariate. A first contingent of 14 arrived in October 1930. The Maryknoll Sisters' house in Kowloon proved too small with the addition of the Kaying recruits so they moved to Hong Kong Island at the end of December to occupy the third floor of the Maryknoll Holy Spirit School. There, under the direction of Sisters Mary Dolores Cruise and Anthony Marie Unitas, the group became known as the Hakka Apostolic School.

In October 1933, with peace restored in the Kaying area, Bishop Ford recalled his candidates to Siaoloc to continue their primary school studies. Accompanying them were Sisters Mary Dolores Cruise, Anthony Marie Unitas, Joan Miriam Beauvais, and Rosalia Kettl, the first four Maryknoll Sisters to set foot in Hakka territory.[67]

After the Chinese New Year in February 1935, the school moved to Rosary Convent in Kaying city to allow some of the students to start secondary studies at one of the city's public middle schools. It was around that time that Sister Mary Dolores broke her hip while partaking recreation with the Chinese aspirants. In 1936 she returned to the United States for treatment and was replaced as novice mistress by Sister Thérèse Grondin, who continued to direct the novitiate for some 15 years until her arrest and imprisonment by the Communists in December 1950.

On February 11, 1938, after completing three years of lower middle school, the first group of six candidates entered the postulancy of the Sister Catechists of Our Lady of Kaying. Bishop Ford called that day the foundation day of the new congregation. This first group of six was professed in August 1940.[68]

The Japanese threat was less disruptive in Kaying than in the three other Maryknoll territories of South China. Nonetheless, when an invasion seemed to be imminent in October 1938, the entire novitiate group was moved to the village of Tungshek in the shadow of high mountains. The middle school education of the students was put in the hands of hired lay teachers. During the novitiate the Sister Catechists began their field-work, going out by twos into the neighboring markets and villages.[69]

As more native Sisters graduated from the novitiate, the Maryknoll Sisters sought to expand their mission work. At their suggestion, Bishop Ford agreed to leave the students during the summer of 1942 in Tungshek under the direction of Sister Mary Hock and to move the professed Sister Catechists and the novitiate to the west of the vicariate where no Sisters—Chinese or foreign—had yet penetrated.

The place chosen for the new novitiate was called Laohukow, "a beautiful spot in the Hakka hills . . . a little over 100 miles from Kaying City." Sister Thérèse recalled this new beginning:

> In order to get [there], having no money for fare, we walked the mountains roads over a period of four days from Tungshek. We pioneered the really glorious way—improvising our own cupboards out of milk boxes, bookcases out of odds and ends of boards, lighting from tallow and camphor oil, bath-tubs in the form of wooden pails; we acted as masons, carpenters, gardeners and nurses. With no glass on many of the windows we simply moved the scanty furniture to the middle of the room and let the rain pour in. . . . Providence watched over our larder; Providence also was head nurse. We bought very few medicines yet always had what we needed. Health was exceptionally good.[70]

In March 1942, this village became not only the training center for the postulants and novices, but also the headquarters for the new congregation where the Chinese Sisters returned for recollections, seasonal brush-ups on catechetical doctrine and methodology, as well as for discussions of apostolic work in the vicariate. After the war, the Tungshek pre-novitiate moved back to Kaying city to allow the aspirants to receive a proper secondary education before admittance to the novitiate in Laohukow. In March 1950, there were 15 professed Catechist Sisters, no novices, six postulants, and fifteen aspirants. The professed Sisters were responsible for evangelization in seven centers.[71]

In December 1950, aspirants in Kaying were sent home. On March 7, 1951, after the arrest of most Maryknollers, the Communists closed the novitiate of Laohukow and used the building to expand the local primary school. A few months later, the professed Sisters who worked in the mission stations were sent back to their native villages where they still live today. One of them, however, Sister Catherine Mary Lee, succeeded in reaching Hong Kong and in 1957 entered the Maryknoll Sisters' community.[72]

Among the native congregations started by Maryknoll, the community of the Sister Catechists of Our Lady is the only one which never reached the stage of canonical erection but remained in an experimental stage.

This delay was owing partly to the length of their educational training and partly to Rome's cautious attitude toward a group of Sisters whose aim was so unique among religious congregations of women: "the Christianization of souls . . . by the chief and almost exclusive message of direct evangelization."[73]

Fushun. Prior to the arrival of the first Maryknoll Sisters at the central mission of Honan in Fushun city, the Maryknoll Fathers had been recruiting young girls showing an interest in becoming Sisters. The consensus was to start a native congregation for Fushun rather than to send the girls to the community of Chinese and Manchu Sisters founded by Bishop Jean-Marie Blois of Mukden.

In 1930, while awaiting the arrival of Maryknoll Sisters, the Fathers arranged to have a group of these girls stay at the parish of Ehrpatan where they were under the direction of a native Virgin called Bibiana. Bibiana was a *"chuchiati,"* a live-at-home Virgin. Her village of Ehrpatan was an entirely Catholic settlement. In 1900 when she was seventeen years old, the village was raided by the Boxers. She saw her mother, who could not flee fast enough because of her bound feet, confess her faith and perish under the sword. Profoundly impressed by the death of her mother, whom she considered a saint, she decided to dedicate her life to the service of the Church by becoming a Virgin.

Over the years, she took care of the orphans, the aged, and the sick; taught catechism; directed the school for girls; settled disputes; suggested matrimonial matches; and helped keep parish records straight. To train their first candidates, the Maryknoll Fathers naturally turned to this pillar of faith, who by her daily life was a witness to the many tasks native Sisters could fulfill in the Fushun territory. Bibiana also had a keen perception of the need for a native Church: "As long as the priests and Sisters are foreigners, the Catholic Church will be considered foreign. To remedy this, we need Chinese priests and many, many Chinese Sisters."[74]

On December 17, 1931, Bibiana brought eight candidates to Fushun-Honan and turned their formation over to the four Maryknoll Sisters who had arrived two months earlier: Sisters Gloria Wagner, Veronica Marie Carney, Mary De Lellis McKenna, and Mary Eunice Tolan. For nine years, the candidates underwent a period of probation. Since they had little or no schooling, they first completed six years of primary education. At the same time, they assisted the Maryknoll Sisters in the parish clinic and catechumenate. They also accompanied them to visit Catholics in the city and the surrounding villages.[75] On September 8, 1939, the first six postulants were officially admitted into the native congregation of the Sisters of the Sacred Heart of Jesus of Fushun.

With the permission of Rome, Bishop Lane canonically erected the new congregation on March 19, 1940, the day the first six postulants received the white veil of novices. The outbreak of the war with Japan in December 1941 brought the internment of all American priests and Sisters, and the end of the Honan novitiate. At that time there were 12 novices, six postulants, and 19 aspirants. The aspirants, with the exception of five, were sent home. Those remaining joined the novices and the postulants of another Chinese congregation in Mukden to finish their training under the care of Bishop Blois. By February 11, 1943, all but one of the novices and postulants had been professed.[76]

After profession during Easter week in April 1942, three of the native Sisters returned to the center in Fushun-Honan and obtained authorization from the authorities to carry on instruction and to visit homes but not to hold public gatherings. Other native Sisters soon followed and assumed the same responsibilities in Fushun-Hopei. By the time the American Maryknoll Sisters were repatriated in 1942 and 1943, the native Sisters had taken charge of the work in the two parishes. In 1945 after V-J Day, the Chinese Sisters, who had returned to the Fushun center, experienced severe difficulties with the occupation of Fushun by Russian soldiers. One of them, Sister Mary Rose Lu, became permanently crippled when she jumped from a second-story window and was trampled by two soldiers.

By the end of the year, in addition to taking over parish work in Fushun, the native Sisters also took charge of the orphanage and school in the Chinese parish in Dairen. When the novitiate in Fushun-Honan was reopened after the war, the aspirants returned; the program was placed under the direction of the native Sisters with the guidance of Father Edward McGurkin. Nine new novices received their habits on March 19, 1946. The native community totaled 16 professed, nine novices, and 18 aspirants.[77]

In December 1947, Father Joseph McCormack arranged for the community to assume the direction of "Star of the Sea," a small hospital and dispensary in Peking. In 1949 they elected their own mother general, Sister Mary Herman Ting. Their number kept growing and reached 29 in 1952. In 1956 the Sisters moved back to Fushun and continued to do mostly hospital work. They were disbanded in 1968 during the Cultural Revolution, and several were sent to work on a farm. In 1980, the Fushun-Honan property was returned to the Catholic Church, and some Sisters went back to live in the convent. In 1984, they received a formal authorization from the government to operate again as a religous community. Twelve Sisters have since gathered together and in June 1986 reopened the novitiate by receiving five aspirants.[78]

Curriculum and Training

Pre-novitiate. The training of the native Sisters was divided into pre-

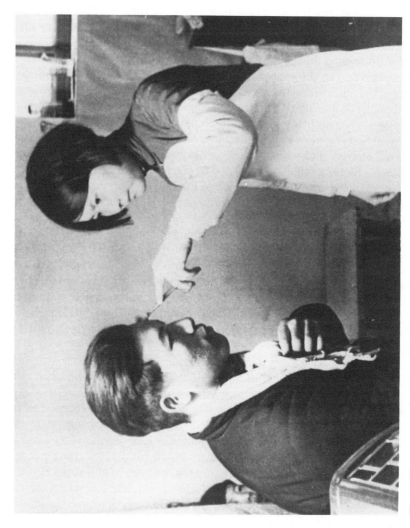

Fig. 3. Dispensary work was part of the training for girls preparing for the Chinese sisterhood in Fushun. Maryknoll Photo Library.

novitiate, postulancy, novitiate, and post-novitiate. The members of the pre-novitiate were known by various names, including "student," "candidate," or "aspirant." Most of the recruiting was done by the Maryknoll Fathers, especially in the early years before the Maryknoll Sisters were involved in the direct apostolate; the Fathers usually "hand-picked good girls from families that were old Christians."[79] Some Catholic villages were famous for the vocations they produced, like the parishes of Hoingan in Kongmoon, Pantien in Kweilin, or the villages of Erhpatan and Chakow in Fushun. Good health, intelligence, industry, docility, a good character and disposition, and piety were qualifications for entrance.[80]

The Chinese custom of early betrothal, which forced the Maryknoll Fathers to choose prospective candidates for the priesthood at the tender age of ten or twelve, also led them to recruit future native Sisters from among very young girls.

> As a general rule no girl whose parents have engaged her to marriage [before their conversion] can be accepted [to the novitiate]. . . . Even for families that have been Catholic for generations it is impossible not to be affected by their surroundings. So, Catholic girls aspiring to the religious life are taken young into the preparatory school for native nuns.[81]

Occasionally, however, when the candidate seemed an unusually good prospect for the convent, Maryknoll Fathers intervened and broke the wedding engagement by reimbursing the family of the groom-to-be the money (plus interest) given in earnest to the family of the girl.[82]

The great majority of these girls came from small villages and had received even less formal schooling than their male counterparts. Prior to being officially admitted to the novitiate as postulants, the candidates had to undergo an extensive period of schooling during which they also learned the rudiments of religious life. Since many had no schooling, the pre-novitiate often started with Primary 1.

In the beginning, Maryknollers were not all convinced of the necessity for well-educated Sisters. The amount of education required to be admitted to the postulancy was only four to six years of primary school. Only admission to the Kaying Sisters required the completion of three years of secondary school.[83]

Secondary education was indeed the main reason behind the move of the Kaying novitiate from Siaoloc to Kaying city in February 1935. By the fall of 1936, 14 candidates were already studying in the city's government-run secondary school. By comparison, Kongmoon had only two professed Sisters attending secondary school. As a rule, the Maryknoll Sisters in charge of the Kongmoon, Wuchow, and Kweilin communities sent for secondary studies only those professed native Sisters whom they judged to be intellectually inclined. Most of them were sent to middle schools run by the Franciscan Missionaries of Mary in Macao or Shiuhing. Sister Joseph Lam, one of the first candidates to the Kongmoon Sisters, complained bitterly that during her nine years of training in Hong Kong and Kongmoon from the late 1920s to the late 1930s, she was forced to repeat primary schooling and denied access to higher education.[84]

By 1942 most aspirants were required to complete Chinese middle school prior to entering the postulancy. On the whole, however, the level of education remained higher among the Kaying Sisters. In 1948 when most of these Sisters had their secondary school diploma, diplomas were still rare among Sisters of the other communities.[85]

Expenses for the formation of prospective Sisters, from the aspirants' school through the novitiate, were paid almost entirely by the vicariate or prefecture. In 1946 the cost of education alone per student amounted to $8,000 in local currency, about US$150 per year.[86] Schooling through the third year of secondary school was usually carried on with the help of native teachers, preferably female. In Kongmoon, however, the first native Sisters who graduated from the Franciscan Missionaries of Mary Middle School were assigned to teach the aspirants, and lay teachers were eliminated. Additional classes were taught by Maryknoll Sisters. For example, in Kongmoon, Sister Chanel Xavier taught enrichment classes in catechism, music, physical drill, drawing, and organ. Sister Ann Carol Brielmaier taught Gregorian chant and sewing. House chores and gardening were also part of the daily routine. For their spiritual formation, the aspirants' horarium included morning prayers, mass, noon prayers, the Rosary, visit to the Blessed Sacrament, spiritual reading, evening prayers, Stations of the Cross every Friday, Benediction when possible, weekly confessions, and monthly recollection days.[87]

In February 1935, Kaying became the first Maryknoll vicariate to send aspirants to attend government middle schools. In late 1938 when the Japanese advanced, the aspirants were moved to the mountain village of Tungshek; however, their education was resumed immediately after the war. During the fall of 1943, five aspirants from the Kweilin sisterhood started to attend the public high school of Laipo. In February 1946, the Wuchow novitiate moved to the outskirts of Wuchow city to allow its aspirants to attend a better government middle school.[88]

In 1947 Sister Thérèse Grondin of Kaying explained the reasons for such a departure from the usual mission procedures:

> 1. Capable lay female teachers are almost impossible to find. Men teachers find it difficult to teach small groups of girls, especially girls planning to become Sisters. Native Sisters could be assigned but then the need for them in parishes cannot be met.

2. From a financial point of view, sending girls to government school is often less expensive: no teacher salary to pay, no pre-novitiate building to maintain. The aspirants live in a hostel for girl students run by the Maryknoll Sisters.

3. The city government school broadens the "village outlook" of the aspirants and offers a wider range of educational programs and more extra-curricular opportunities. By being a much larger and diversified community than a pre-novitiate, a city school gives the aspirants more opportunities for learning the art of living with others.

4. The pre-novitiate does not equip aspirants with a state diploma.[89]

At the same time, the religious and special vocational development of the aspirants was not neglected. In Kaying the aspirants boarded at Rosary Hall, a hostel run by the Maryknoll Sisters, while they studied catechism as well as Old and New Testament history. They were given lessons in "good form, character building, received girl guidance, and were assigned selected readings." They were also introduced to Latin and Gregorian chant and encouraged to become as fluent as possible in English. As part of their apostolic training, they were required to be actively involved in the local parish choir and sodalities.[90]

Postulancy and novitiate. The postulancy marked their official admission into the congregation. Provisions were made in the constitutions for a dowry, but most of the time this clause was waived by the bishop. The postulant was required only to bring some personal clothing and belongings. The six-month postulancy was considered a time of probation to acquaint the postulants with the obligations of religious life and the nature and responsibilities of the Sisters in their community.[91]

Upon completion, the postulant was received as a novice Sister and given the habit of her congregation. The novitiate lasted for two additional years. The first year, called canonical, was entirely devoted to spiritual formation and study of the constitutions, rules, and directory of the community. The second year was similar but also included catechetical training and offered opportunities for short mission trips and part-time work in dispensaries and orphanages.

During this two-year period, Scripture and religion courses were considered as major subjects to ensure the native Sisters of a solid spiritual and catechetical training. The courses consisted of advanced catechism, Church history, apologetics, liturgy, and New Testament studies. Pedagogical subjects were also included in their training: principles of education, mission work and catechetical methods, methods of teaching singing, and recreational training. Familiarity with Latin was required for Sisters whose work might call for consulting parish records, reading the liturgical calendar, or preparing a sung mass. Miscellaneous courses covered a wide variety of subjects such as English, sociology, character-building, religious etiquette, foreign table manners, chironomy, first aid, arts and crafts, stars and constellations, typing and organ playing.[92]

The readings in Chinese listed in Table 2, which were assigned for the two-year novitiate in Kaying during the year 1942–43, give a good overall idea of the comprehensive training the Maryknoll Sisters intended to give the native Sisters. Classes and studies generally occupied only half the day. The rest was devoted to charges and manual work. One of the goals was to turn "native Sisters into jacks-of-all-trades: able to use with equal dexterity either needle and thread, hoe or spade, hammer or trowel, washing tub, sewing machine, or frying skillet."[93] With some differences from one community to another, the native Sisters did their own cleaning, washing, ironing, and sewing; they made their own habits, they sewed their own cloth shoes; they embroidered Chinese clothes, church vestments, and linens; they baked altar breads and melted beeswax to make candles; they painted and arranged their own living quarters; they spent long hours in the garden growing their own vegetables and flowers and planting trees; and they did their own cooking.[94]

These activities were certainly devised to make novitiates as self-supporting as possible, but most of all they were intended to develop in each Sister the ability to improvise and to work under less than propitious conditions. In fact, more than once in times of crisis the native Sisters proved their ability to support themselves and to get financial help from the population. In the summer of 1942, for example, when the novitiate moved into a dilapidated building at Laohukow, the vicariate was in financial difficulty because the war prevented the arrival of outside funds. The Chinese novices took it upon themselves to collect $130,000 in local money and other gifts in the form of household equipment and staple foods from the population.[95] In Wuchow in the mid–1940s, Sister Moira Riehl initiated a different approach to manual work. After an initial period of performing various manual tasks, the Sister candidates were trained for responsibility by being put in charge of one kind of work such as kitchen tasks, laundry or gardening.[96]

The horarium of the postulants and novices differed only slightly from that of the aspirants. Meditation before mass and the study of the Little Office of the Blessed Virgin Mary were introduced during postulancy. During the novitiate the Chapter of Faults was added. At this weekly spiritual exercise—meant to develop humility and docility—each Sister accused herself of her faults against the constitutions or the rules in front of the assembled community.[97]

Post-novitiate. Upon completion of the novitiate, the Sisters professed the three simple vows of chastity, poverty and obedience which they renewed annually or triennually for a period of 9 to ten years, after which they took their perpetual vows. The Kaying Sisters, however, because they were still in an experimental stage, did not take the three simple vows but only a vow of chastity, which was considered to be private. They were bound by their rules, however, to practice poverty, and furthermore, they made a solemn promise of obedience on the day of their reception as novices.[98]

In the post-novitiate years, the native Sisters lived in small convents in the larger mission stations. They went back regularly to the novitiate for retreats and conferences. Before the war, the Wuchow Sisters went back to the novitiate in Pingnam the afternoon of every first Thursday and stayed through Saturday morning for a recollection, a conference on a mission-related question, and an interview with Sister Moira Riehl. In the same way, the native Sisters of Kaying used to return to Laohukow every two months for a day or two of recollection and reunion to refresh themselves spiritually, review mission methods and current events, exchange ideas, and discuss developments and possible improvements.

Soon, however, the dangers of war and its aftermath of destroyed roads and disrupted public transit systems made it impossible to have such frequent meetings. Moreover, the native Sisters were being assigned to parishes farther and farther away from the novitiate. Meetings were limited to two or three longer ones a year, with one or two follow-up visits by the Maryknoll novice mistress or the local superior. In Kweilin in September 1949, Sister Barbara Mersinger probably sensing that the fall of Kweilin would bring restrictions on travel, started to mail the native Sisters a bulletin which provided thoughts for spiritual reflection.[99]

Since the five Chinese congregations of Kongmoon, Wuchow, Kweilin, Kaying, and Fushun were founded by Maryknoll Fathers and trained by Maryknoll Sisters, differences from one novitiate to another were small, and the best accomplishments and ideas of one were quickly shared and used by the others. The constitutions of the Kongmoon Sisters, for instance, were written by Bishop James E. Walsh and patterned after the Maryknoll Sisters' constitutions. In turn the Kongmoon constitutions were also adopted by the Wuchow Sisters and served as a model for the constitutions of the Kweilin Sisters. They also served as guidelines for the Kaying Sisters whose constitutions were not yet completed.[100]

The Hakka community, in spite of its formative stage, set the pace for the others in the field of education and training of the native Sisters. Bishop Ford's idea of "direct evangelization" as the main goal of the native Sisters was also adopted with some modifications by the other communities—Fushun first, followed by Wuchow and Kweilin and even Kongmoon to a certain extent.[101]

On the other hand, after a meeting of the Maryknoll novice mistresses

Table 2

Chinese Books and Pamphlets Used in Laohukow Novitiate, 1942–1943

Required Reading of Class Texts

Studies in Spiritual and Religious Life
Treatise of the Seven Victories, D. Panteja, S.J.
Golden Arrow to Kill Pride, Dom Sans
Honor Thyself, Dom Glorieux
God Within Us, P. Plus, S.J.
The Christian Life, Dom Sullerot
Christ, Our Leader, Dom Glorieux
Catechism of Three Vows, Cotel
Autobiography of St. Therese
Spirit of St. Therese

Scripture
O.T. Brief History, N. Chen, S.J.
N.T. Brief History, N. Chen, S.J.
Gospels and Epistles (New Testament)

Doctrine
Shanghai Catechism in Four Volumes

Liturgy
Daily Missal
Explanation of the Mass, J. Mao, S.J.
Cantus Gregoriani Methodus

Apologetics
De Veris et Falsis Compendium, Tohang, S.J.
Proof of Holy Religion, Mark Chai
Some Problems in Religion, Mark Chai
Re: The 8 Errors of Roman Church, Mark Chai
The Four Marks of the True Church, Answers to the Protestants, P. Wong

Church History
Church History, V. Suen, S.J.
Church History in China (Magazine Reprint)
Church History in Kaying Vicariate

Pedagogy
Catechumenate Course, Sr. Anna Mary
First Communion Course, Sr. Rosalia

Languages
Alphabetum Latinum

ABC Linguae Latinae, Weig & Mittler, SVD
The New Method Catholic Readers, Primer and Readers 1–6, Michael West
Shanghai Catechism in English

Assigned Readings for Background or Round-Table Discussions

Ethics and Psychology
Ethics, A. Vagnond, S.J.
The Soul of Man and Future Life
A Summary of Natural Law, L. Li, S.J.
Compendium of Psychology, J. Aleni, S.J.
Rudiments of Psychology, J. Zi, S.J.

Social Studies
Manual of Sociology, J. Zi, S.J.
Manual of Economics, J. Zi, S.J.
History of Works of Mercy, G. Neyron, S.J.
Refutation of Evolution, L. Li
True Notion of the State, J. Siu, S.J.
Dr. Sun's Attitude Towards Christianity
I Was a Communist, A. B. Liverov
Philosophy of Communism and Its Application, Sheen-Chai
Socialism, J. Siu, S.J.
Sovietism, J. Wang, S.J.
Summary of Enc. on Communism, Pius XI
The Church on the Social Question
Catholic Action Manual, Mgr. Haouisée, S.J.
The Church and Womankind, J. Zi, S.J.
Questions on Womankind, J. Zi, S.J.
Encyclical on Chaste Marriage, Pius XI
Dignity of Motherhood, P.Sommer
Shall I Be a Priest, W. Doyle, S.J.
Shall I Be a Nun, E. Chaw
On Sodalities: 17 vols. on Knights of Blessed Sacrament
Frequent Communion, L. Li, S.J.

Principles of Education
Encyclical on Christian Education, Pius XI
Catechism on Education Encyclical
Principles of Education, J. Siu, S.J.
Family Education, F. Sen, S.J.

Courses in Religion (Get familiar with)
Our Holy Religion, I, II, B. Meyer, M.M.
My First Holy Communion, L. Morrow, C.S.
Catholic Doctrine Course: Through Grades and Middle School
Method of Teaching the Shanghai Catechism, Mgr. Haouisée, S.J.

Table 2 (continued)

Extra-Curricular/Cultural

Organ (for those who have aptitude)
Melodeon Playing, P. Singenberger

Nature Appreciation and Star Study
Girl Scout Manual

Aesthetics
The Sudden Rose,[a] Blanche M. Kelly

Arts and Crafts
Chinese Songs and Hymns

(Source: SARC, Box—Novitiate, Kaying, File 2)
[a]This is the only book in the entire list that was not written or translated in Chinese.

---

of China which took place in Pakkai in 1947, Sister Thérèse Grondin became convinced that the spiritual formation of her novices at Laohukow was lagging behind and should be revised. Her chief concern was that perhaps Laohukow rushed the novices too quickly into outlying mission work without enough nurturing of their spiritual habits through the daily mass, a regular horarium, and prayer in common.[102]

Recruitment and Perseverance

The pre-novitiate years were used by the Maryknoll Sisters as the main period to eliminate unsuitable candidates. Dismissal came mostly for unruly behavior and poor health.[103] The disturbances of the war years, of course, also took a big toll. Some girls simply got tired of waiting so long to become professed or discovered that a life of celibacy was not for them. Generally, half of the candidates dropped out or were dismissed before entering the postulancy. Of the nine girls sent to Hong Kong in 1927 and 1928 as the nucleus of the future native Sisters of Kongmoon, six were received as postulants and five persevered through the novitiate to become professed.[104] Of the 11 girls studying at the Fushun-Honan center in early 1932, six persevered to become the first group of postulants of the new congregation of the Sisters of the Sacred Heart in 1939. In Wuchow, seven girls were selected between August 1936 and July 1937 to become the first group of postulants, but only four were officially admitted to the postulancy.[105]

These figures, however, refer only to early groups of native Sisters because data showing enrollment of candidates is incomplete. The sisterhood in Kaying, however, where it is possible to consider enrollment over a period of 10 years, shows the same perseverance rate of about 50 percent from candidacy to postulancy. From 1930 to 1940, there were 32 candidates for the Sister Catechists of Our Lady of Kaying, of whom 15 became postulants.[106]

As shown by Table 3, from postulancy on, the rate of perseverance of native Sisters trained by Maryknoll Sisters improved markedly for most of the five native communities, from a high of almost 89 percent for Fushun to a low of 60 percent for Wuchow.

Relationships with the Native Clergy and Sisterhoods

Maryknollers always took pride that relationships with their Chinese counterparts, priests, and Sisters were exemplary, marked by a deep sense of equality:

> The Chinese priests were considered equal to ourselves and they were always good company and a swell bunch of persons. Whenever any of them visited my place, they certainly stayed in my rectory and ate at my table.[107]

The Maryknoll Fathers, in particular, were quick to point out that this all-American liberal attitude distinguished them from their old world brothers:

> I have seen in Kunming the Chinese priests on one side of the room and on the other side, the Italian Salesians. They didn't talk to each other during the meals, because the Chinese ate Chinese and the Italians ate Italian. . . . That was [in 1944] after 12 years [I had been] in China. That kind of shocked us, the way they were treating their Chinese priests because our Chinese priests were right in with us.[108]

Similar remarks are common and seem to betray a certain American chauvinism which, in turn, raises a question of whether Maryknoll's pursuit of indigenization was more successful than the efforts of other missionary groups.

The brunt of Maryknoll Fathers' criticisms of other missioners was directed against the French. Interestingly enough, these French were rarely missionaries with whom they had contact, but always those of faraway areas like Nanking, Shanghai, or Peking where the Church was well established and seemed to prosper. In fact, early Maryknollers had nothing but praise and admiration for the French M.E.P. who guided their first steps as missioners on the Chinese soil. Even the subsequent generations of Maryknoll priests who seldom met French missioners acknowl-

Table 3

Numbers of Native Sisters in Novitiates

Fushun Sisters (1939–1947)

Group	Postulants	Novices	Professed
1	6 (9/39)	6 (3/40)	5 (2/42)
2	6 (8/40)	6 (3/41)	6 (3/42)
3	6 (8/41)	6 (2/42)	6 (2/43)
Total	18	18	16[a](88.8%)

Wuchow Sisters (1937–1950)

	Postulants	Novices	Professed
1	4 (2/37)	4 (1/38)	4 (1/40)
2	4 (7/38)	4 (1/39)	1 (1/41)
3	2 (1940)	2 (1/41)	2 (1/43)
4	2 (1942)	2 (1/43)	1 (1/45)
5	2 (1943)	2 (1/44)	1 (7/46)
6	1 (1944)	1 (7/46)	
7	1 (1/46)	1 (7/46)	1 (7/48)
8	4 (12/48)	4 (7/49)	2 (3/51)
Total	20	20	12 (60%)

Kweilin Sisters (1939–1950)

	Postulants	Novices	Professed
1	4 (9/39)	4 (3/40)	4 (5/42)
2	3 (10/40)	3 (3/41)	3 (5/43)
3	3 (10/43)	2 (5/44)	2 (9/46)

4	7 (10/47)	6 (5/48)	5 (5/50)
Total	17	15	14 (82.4%)

Kaying Sisters (1938–1950)

1	6 (2/38)	6 (9/38)	6 (1940)[b]
2	3 (1939)	3 (9/39)	1 (1941)
3	6 (1942)	6 (11/42)	5 (11/44)
4	5 (9/47)	5 (4/48)	4 (3/50)
Total	20	20	15 (75%)

Kongmoon Sisters (1931–1949)

1	6 (1931)	5 (10/33)	5 (2/36)
2	3 (8/37)	3 (2/38)	3 (2/40)
4	5 (8/40)	5 (2/41)	4 (9/43)
7	4 (1945)	3 (8/47)	
8[c]	5 (2/46)	5 (8/48)	
Total	14	22	17[d](77.3%)

Source: **Fushun**: SARC, 55, Folders 9–11. Sister Mary Eunice Tolan, "Manchuria, Book 3," p. 90. **Wuchow**: SARC, 51, Folders 3–4, 6–10, 12; 50, Folders 1–4, –08. TC46, Rose Lam, pp. 13–15. **Kweilin**: SARC, 52, Folders 1–6, 8–10, 12. Box–Novitiate, Kweilin, Kweilin Convent House Files. **Kaying**: SARC, 42, Folders 2–3; 43–11; 47, Folders 3–4. **Kongmoon**: SARC, 40, Folders 1–2, 5, 8–9, 11–14; 49–16. TC23, Sister Maureen Au, pp. 5–6. *The Field Afar*, November 1942, p. 41.
[a]One professed Sister left before 1947.
[b]One professed Sister left in 1946.
[c]In 1949, there had been 8 groups of Kongmoon Sisters, for a total of 28 Sisters; records, however, are too incomplete to account for each group.
[d]Three professed Sisters left before 1949.

edged that during occasional visits they were always treated with hospitality and courtesy. Thus Maryknollers' opinions of French attitudes toward the Chinese clergy were usually based on hearsay or written accounts. The reality is that isolated French missioners, as well as Maryknoll priests, often turned into staunch individualists with whom it would have been hard to live anyway, without regard to race or nationality.

Maryknollers' criticisms, however, were directed at the French not so much as individuals but as a group who, imbued with a sense of superiority, had become reluctant to pass on the leadership to a budding Chinese Church. This again raises the question of Maryknoll's own attitude toward the young Chinese Church within its own territories, especially after World War II. Maryknoll's aim was to move on to other areas once the local Church had become strong enough to govern itself. Were Maryknollers true to their goals or did they end up much the same as those they criticized? Much of the answer lies in the story of their relationships with the Chinese clergy.

The Maryknoll Fathers and the Chinese Priests and Seminarians

During their first few years in China before the Yeungkong-Kongmoon territory was officially detached from the vicariate of Canton in 1924 and became a prefecture apostolic, the handful of Maryknoll priests had opportunities to meet Chinese priests from neighboring parishes. The contacts were invariably friendly. Maryknollers appreciated these "most likeable, extremely affable" neighbors for their "quiet, obliging services" and advice, their "practical knowledge of the territory," and their "judgment in settling affairs."[109]

By 1924, however, these Chinese priests had been reassigned to other parishes in the vicariate of Canton, leaving the new prefecture apostolic of Kongmoon without Chinese priests. Because of the long years of formation required for ordination, it was a decade before Kongmoon had its first native priest, Simon Lei of Hoingan, and not until 1941 that two more were added. The two other territories of Wuchow and Kweilin found themselves in exactly the same situation. Father Thomas Tao, who had studied under the French M.E.P., was ordained for Wuchow in 1933. The two Chinese priests trained by Maryknoll, Benedict Choi and Mark Tsang, were not ordained until 1948. As for Kweilin, erected as a prefecture only in 1938, its first priest, Stephen Liang, was ordained in 1954 in Hong Kong and could not go back to his native place.

Kaying and Fushun, with a larger Catholic population from the start, were more fortunate. By 1933, Kaying already had five native priests, working mainly in the city of Kaying and not in daily contact with Maryknollers except for Monsignor Ford. In Fushun, the first Maryknoll priests arriving in 1926 found a handful of experienced native priests who were their seniors in the priesthood. Fushun became the only Maryknoll territory where Chinese pastors could be found who had Maryknoll assistants: "Father [Antoine] Pan and Father Martin Pai were both pastors when we came and we served under both. . . . They were our seniors; we were youngsters."[110]

After Pearl Harbor, during the three and a half years Maryknoll priests were absent from Fushun, five native priests were ordained for the Maryknoll vicariate by the bishop of Mukden. Together with the five older priests, they ran the territory. After the war, Bishop Lane and later Father Joseph McCormack reassumed the leadership, but the Chinese priests were in the majority and were doing most of the work. The Maryknoll priests, who never numbered more than five at a time, worked closely with them until December 1947 when they were once again driven out, this time by the Communists.

In Kongmoon and Wuchow, when young Chinese began to be ordained, they were usually entrusted as curates to a Maryknoll pastor for a period of six months to one year. The reverse situation seems to have never occurred. Maryknoll priests freshly out of language training were always assigned to a Maryknoll pastor. When one of them volunteered in 1926 to work under one of the six newly consecrated Chinese bishops, the Maryknoll leadership did not grant permission.[111] The Maryknoll Fathers' objective was to leave when the native clergy was formed rather than to serve under it.

From the beginning, Ford adopted an unwritten policy of not assigning a Chinese priest as curate to a Maryknoll pastor. The Chinese priests, if qualified, were given positions of responsibility in the seminary and the city of Kaying; those appointed as curates in the countryside were always put under a Chinese pastor. Bishop Ford seemed to have realized that a key to true indigenization was to let the Chinese take charge and to reduce any outside interference by Maryknollers as much as possible. In the transitional stage, the best way to maintain harmonious relationships was to keep responsibilities and places of work for foreign and Chinese priests separate.

A fraternal spirit of unity and cooperation was renewed at the clergy's annual meetings and kept alive in the interim by visits between priests of the two groups. Maryknollers and Chinese could see each other at work, exchange ideas and, at the same time, avoid the frictions and confrontations brought about by a combination of daily contacts and cultural differences.[112]

In accordance with Maryknoll's ultimate goals to turn territories over to the native clergy, Chinese priests were given more and more responsibilities as the years went by. More seminary positions were filled by Chinese priests. The Kaying seminary reached the point where it was entirely run and staffed by Chinese priests and lay people. Native priests were also generally put in charge of parishes with large Catholic communities, while Maryknoll priests were assigned to areas where mission work was still plentiful. Certainly Maryknollers recognized this as part of their vocation and did not complain. At times, however, they would have liked more encouragement and support from their bishop in recognition of the difficulty of their task. Some missioners in Kaying, for instance, remarked almost with a touch of jealousy that Bishop Ford had become so totally pro-Chinese that he seemed oblivious to the feelings of his fellow missioners.

As pointed out, not all Maryknoll territories progressed at the same speed toward the goal of indigenization. But by the late 1940s, through a combination of good planning, increasing native vocations, and favorable circumstances, the dioceses of Kaying and Fushun were almost ready to be placed under the jurisdiction of a Chinese bishop.

When interviewed, Chinese priests who were trained by and worked with Maryknoll showed a very touching appreciation of the work of Maryknoll and individual Maryknollers. They often told how the real motivation for their vocation had been the desire to emulate the Maryknoll spirit in helping people. The relationships between the two groups were those of seminarians and young priests interacting with generally older missioners toward whom they maintained that traditional Chinese sense of deference given to teachers and elders. They were grateful for these men who had supported them materially and spiritually, cared for them, brought them up, and given them the opportunity to become priests.[113]

The two most frequent criticisms raised against Maryknollers resembled those made against most foreign missioners in China, namely, a certain attitude of superiority and a lack of insertion into the Chinese society. However, even when mentioning such flaws and mistakes on the part of Maryknollers, the Chinese priests were always quick to mention that these reflected the character and imperfections of individuals, but not the attitude of the Society as a whole. They all acknowledged—with the most positive statements coming from the Kaying area—that the Society was actively building a native Church.[114] It seems that it is precisely because Maryknoll was deeply aware of these weaknesses inherent in most foreign missioners that it championed the idea of building a native Church. In 1927 Bishop James E. Walsh wrote:

> The work would be incomplete if the Church were always to remain a foreign institution in the eye of the native. . . . The native priest is the best person to show that the Church is as much at home in China as it is in Europe and America.[115]

Strained relationships between some Maryknoll priests and some Chinese priests developed mainly after 1952, particularly in Hong Kong. Hard feelings are especially strong among some Chinese priests from former Maryknoll missions who were ordained in Hong Kong in the early 1950s and could not or would not return to China. The causes of their grievances fall into two categories.

First, Chinese priests complained of unjust and humiliating treatment by some old China hands who, after 1952, were put in charge of parishes in Hong Kong. They blamed these Maryknollers for keeping unnecessarily tight control over their Chinese curates, for not listening to them, and for being unwilling to pass parish responsibilities on to the Chinese priests.[116]

The second cause of hard feelings was the question of finances. Grievances stemmed from an economic chasm separating the missioners and the Chinese. The personal allowance received by Maryknoll priests had always been larger than that of Chinese priests and certainly gave Maryknollers a standard of living well above that of an average Chinese. In Wuchow, for instance, where the Maryknoll priests received a yearly allowance of US$350 for living expenses, Father Simeon To remembered that the Chinese priests in the late 1940s received only US$140. This relatively affluent lifestyle of Maryknollers (although spartan by Western standards) was usually justified on the grounds that to live otherwise would endanger the missioners' health and the efficiency of their work. "Face," as well, required them to adopt that lifestyle.

Like the rest of the Chinese Catholics in rural areas, Chinese priests at first accepted this rationalization. They knew that the missioners' health was indeed at stake. Moreover, they also benefited; Maryknoll supplied them in turn with education and an allowance to maintain a respectable standard of living. By contrast, Chinese priests soon realized that missioners' health was less at stake in Hong Kong and that differences in allowances should have been reduced if not eliminated. They considered it most unjust to receive only US$25 or US$30 as a monthly stipend for the masses they offered when Maryknollers received at least US$40. By not receiving the same income, the Chinese priests felt discriminated against, reduced to some kind of "second-class priests," victims of injustice within the Church. The same missioners who had given them "face" had taken it away.[117]

Although this tension between Chinese priests and Maryknollers was far from prevalent, one wonders how much of it stemmed from the Hong Kong situation, with a limited number of parishes and no other place to go for both Maryknollers and the Chinese priests in exile. How much stemmed from the excessive dependence on Maryknoll of young, homesick Chinese priests who chose to stay under the control of Maryknoll rather than take the bold step of joining a new diocese? How much stemmed from simple personality clashes? How much stemmed from Maryknollers talking about developing a native Church and turning over responsibility to the Chinese but not actually doing it? How much stemmed from Maryknollers' individualism acquired in order to survive in China?

The Maryknoll Sisters and the Chinese
Candidates and Sisters

Contacts between Maryknoll and Chinese Sisters developed in part out of the desire of poor young girls to share some of the quality of life of the foreign Sisters:

> We were all very poor, and life was very simple. But the Maryknoll Sisters seemed to be quite different. They always seemed so composed as if they never had anything to worry [about]. . . . They were very refined and spoke gently. We didn't know much about manners and we sure envied their taste on dresses and their manners. . . . The calmness and the gentleness they possessed affected me most.[118]

Chinese girls were especially envious of the special group admitted to the native novitiate. Their infatuation with the Sisters and the postulants led them to view everything at the novitiate as "nice and special": the prayers and chants surpassed in beauty anything they had heard before; even manual work, although not much different from the tedious tasks performed at home, exerted a mysterious attraction for them.[119]

During the years of postulancy and novitiate, however, the Chinese girls became painfully aware of the reality involved in becoming a Sister under the supervision of an American novice mistress. The rules and constitutions of the native Sisters, adapted from the constitutions of the Maryknoll Sisters or other Western groups, were Western in style and in spirit. Consequently, there were regulations which clashed with Chinese ways and customs, especially those which made the young Sisters lose face or, as they said, "look like first-class criminals" in front of the whole community. The Chapter of Faults and the punishments administered in front of the community humiliated the postulants and novices and caused them to shed many bitter tears, but often failed to teach them the religious spirit of humility.[120]

The Chinese Sisters never blamed the Maryknoll Sisters for their suffering because of the rules. On the contrary, they were thankful to the American Sisters for teaching them "the ways of a religious woman." They felt that even though the foreign Sisters were too strict in administering the punishments prescribed by the rules, they did it out of concern for the native candidates.

During the novitiate, clashes between individual Chinese and Maryknoll Sisters did occur. Again, the worst memories of the Chinese Sisters were related to incidents when the Maryknoll Sisters made them lose face or refused to give them an opportunity to gain more face. One Chinese Sister, for instance, recalled an altercation with a novice mistress who

Fig. 4. A group of young Chinese girls in Laipo, Kweilin, being taught by Sister Agnes Devlin. Maryknoll Sisters Photo Archives.

refused to take her word and almost dismissed her for a hot temper and insubordination. Another Sister is still bitter because her request to study beyond primary school was turned down several times.[121]

Another source of difficulties between the Chinese Sisters and the Maryknoll Sisters seems to have been the relative inexperience of the missioners in conducting novitiates. During their early years at the Motherhouse, practical training for the missions did not emphasize specialization. Like the Fathers, the Maryknoll Sisters were driven by generosity and a deep sense of self-sacrifice. Taught to obey their superiors without question, they relied on the grace of God to guide them and help them fulfill whatever task was assigned. As a result, most novice-mistresses assigned to native novitiates often had no training or even prior experience in that position. Anecdotes and other stories told by the native Sisters indicate that, at times, the Maryknoll Sisters assigned as novice-mistresses were perhaps not the most appropriate choices. Some, however, managed very capably and were held in deep reverence by the native Sisters. One reason usually surfaced as the source of these cherished memories: "Sister understood and respected the Chinese."[122]

Despite the Maryknoll Sisters' goals and efforts to create true native sisterhoods, their first attempt with the Kongmoon Sisters was less than satisfactory. Although the seminarians had limited contact with their families and the outside world during vacations, the Sister candidates used to be strictly cut off from the rest of the world from the time they came to the pre-novitiate at the age of ten or twelve. The training they received was almost entirely Western: they developed Western habits, adopted Western customs, and came to think and behave like Westerners.

Even after profession, the relationship of novice to superior failed to disappear because the Kongmoon Sisters usually remained under the control of the Maryknoll Sisters for post-novitiate training, visitations, and retreats. Moreover, during the long years of training, the Chinese Sisters lost touch with the outside world and were often totally inexperienced in handling ordinary human relationships; a typical example was a Sister who, while in Hong Kong, bought a birthday cake for HK$40 and wrangled with a shopkeeper over one cent of change. Since they never learned how to deal with administration or carry on simple business with the outside world, they continued to be dependent on Maryknollers. However, the disturbances of the war shattered their sheltered way of life and brought the Kongmoon Sisters back to the Chinese reality which existed beyond their convent.[123]

This situation of dependence, however, was responsible for two lingering attitudes, one among the Maryknoll Sisters and one among the native Sisters, which posed a great danger for the future of a native Church. Some native Sisters, not only in Kongmoon but also in Kweilin, became so submissive and so used to Western customs that they concluded that Chinese ways were inferior to Western ways. They also grew to accept as normal, as a matter of fate, that the Maryknoll Sisters were superior and that they themselves should not be treated as equals.[124]

Some Maryknoll Sisters became so used to dealing with the native candidates from such a young age that they never stopped treating them like children. They also assumed that their years of experience in China had given them a true sense of the Chinese way of life and the right to tell the Chinese Sisters what they should wear, eat, and do. In fact, their view of the Chinese was often "stereotyped, stubborn," and not flexible enough.[125] The stern statement, "You Chinese should [do/wear/eat] . . . this and that," led to many bad feelings among the Chinese Sisters:

> They had been to China. They had some experience. They saw what one Chinese ate and decided the same for all other Chinese. . . . They insisted we eat congee and rice in the morning. I said that at home we just took a piece of cake and soybean soup as breakfast. We didn't eat rice. However, they insisted that we must eat rice. We said that we couldn't but they insisted that we were Chinese and so we must eat rice in the morning.[126]

Toward a new type of Chinese Sister. It has already been suggested that not all Maryknollers were blind to the shortcomings in their training of the native Sisters. Over the years, a more liberal approach was gradually adopted and as a result the Chinese Sisters professed after 1940 were a quite different group than those professed earlier. In the Maryknoll territories of South China, Bishop Ford's innovations in formation were implemented and carried further by Sisters Rosalia Kettl and Thérèse Grondin.

Ford was the first Maryknoller to suggest that aspirants not be rushed into religious life. Instead he asked that they first complete their middle school studies in a government middle school. During these years, the girls could weigh the pros and cons of married and unmarried life. By keeping in touch with Chinese society, they learned to manage ordinary human relationships. They gained poise, self-confidence, and a spirit of their own which armed them against becoming second-rate submissive copies of Maryknoll Sisters.

On the surface, the Kaying native Sisters followed two and a half years of postulancy-novitiate training similar to other sisterhoods founded by Maryknoll. But, the fact that they were still in an experimental stage allowed Bishop Ford and the Maryknoll Sisters in charge to bring about changes and improvements much faster than was possible in other congregations with binding constitutions.[127]

Bishop Ford wanted his native Sisters to be like the Maryknoll Sisters, fully engaged in direct evangelization, and even better because they were

Chinese. Consequently, he asked the Maryknoll Sisters to train them for that specific purpose. During their first year of training, the native Sisters studied more than the traditional courses on the obligations of religious life, religion, and apologetics. Courses in psychology, sociology, and economics were added to prepare them to become as self-reliant as possible. A wide range of manual skills were constantly practiced to make the novitiate self-supporting and to develop in each Sister the ability to be resourceful and to work well in any situation.

During the second year of novitiate, emphasis was put on letting the native Sisters develop on their own. They were sent for short periods in twos or threes to outstations without being accompanied by Maryknoll Sisters. Living in two-Sister convents prepared them for their life as professed Sisters; they had to order their lives and their apostolates by themselves, guided by their Chineseness and their religious training. Such training did not give the native Sisters any sense of inferiority. They felt that they and the Maryknoll Sisters were sisters in the same big family, Sisters whose main role was to spread the good news by living among the people.[128]

Proposals for a Chinese Bishop

Prior to 1950 the Maryknoll Fathers were presented with two opportunities to put into practice their policy of supporting a native hierarchy. In 1925 in Kaying and in 1938 in Wuchow, the possibility arose to have Maryknollers work under a Chinese ecclesiastical superior, but the Fathers did not show much eagerness to turn these proposals into reality.

A Chinese Prefect Apostolic for Kaying

In 1922 Bishop Adolphe Rayssac of Swatow in eastern Kwangtung proposed to turn part of his vicariate over to Maryknoll. At that time the original Maryknoll mission of Yeungkong-Loting was about to be enlarged into the Kongmoon prefecture, and part of the Wuchow territory had also been entrusted to Maryknoll. Afraid that his small group of missioners would be overstretched, Father James E. Walsh, the superior in China, thought that Maryknoll "had better to draw in [its] horns a little" and declined the offer.[129]

Two years later, in June 1924, at the First Plenary Council of China in Shanghai, Bishop Rayssac renewed his offer to give Maryknoll the nine Hakka-speaking subprefectures of his vicariate. This time Walsh was amenable to the offer; Maryknoll had grown and he did not have "enough [existing] missions to give all [his] possible pastors a place" in Kongmoon.

The Wuchow territory still needed missioners but it was such a rough place with no Catholics and no church buildings that it required specially hand-picked men "capable of breaking new ground." By comparison, the territory proposed by Bishop Rayssac with 8,000 Catholics and five complete mission compounds was already an area with a solid Catholic presence where even inexperienced Maryknollers could easily be appointed as pastors. Father James A. Walsh, superior general of Maryknoll, gave prompt approval, and Father Francis Ford was chosen as superior of the new mission.[130]

Bishop Rayssac's offer was quickly countered by two proposals coming from other M.E.P. bishops, de Guébriant and Fourquet. The interwoven and overlapping nature of the three proposals is somewhat confusing and was further complicated by delays in mail and differences in language.

In November 1924, Archbishop de Guébriant, the M.E.P. superior general in France, advised James A. Walsh against accepting Bishop Rayssac's offer and, instead, to accept Bishop Blois' proposal of the Fushun territory in Manchuria. Maryknoll agreed promptly to acquire Fushun.[131]

In the meantime, Bishop Antoine Fourquet of Canton came up with the idea to give Maryknoll administration of six of the nine subprefectures in Rayssac's original plan. As for the three others, Fourquet proposed adjoining them to three of his own vicariate to create a Chinese prefecture apostolic. In this new territory, Maryknoll and M.E.P. priests would work together with Chinese priests under a Chinese prefect.[132]

In October 1924, when Bishop Fourquet shared this idea with James E. Walsh, the Kongmoon prefect apostolic answered that he was personally delighted and thought that Father James A. Walsh would probably agree under certain conditions to Maryknoll priests working with a Chinese bishop. Subsequent discussions focused on a determination of the exact size and location of the new Chinese ecclesiastical territory. The idea of Maryknoll taking charge of the six subprefectures was dropped; James A. Walsh was presented only with an undefined proposal for a Chinese prefecture as an alternative to Rayssac's original plan.

For James E. Walsh in Kongmoon, the new offer of a Chinese prefecture was "a noble idea" worth considering. For Fourquet, it was Maryknoll's call to "heroism" and to "adaptation to the *new* conditions of the Church in China."[133] On February 27, 1925, the Maryknoll Superior General and its Council voted to "cooperate in the manner suggested with the efforts to establish a native vicariate."[134]

Fourquet, in his eagerness to have his plan adopted by Maryknoll, had assumed the backing of de Guébriant in Paris and had given both James E. Walsh and James A. Walsh the impression that, in fact, he acted as "agent for the M.E.P. Superior."[135] When a letter from de Guébriant called the project of creating a Chinese prefecture in the backward, land-locked districts of the Swatow vicariate "utopian," James A. Walsh realized that the plan was not de Guébriant's idea. Therefore, he answered de Guébriant in March 1925 that, although Maryknoll had expressed interest in collaborating in an "experiment" of a Chinese prefecture, it was "quite indifferent" as to how the M.E.P. would divide the Swatow territory.[136]

Meanwhile, James E. Walsh also had second thoughts concerning Fourquet's plan and expressed his true opinion to his friend, Father William O'Shea, then vicar general of Maryknoll. In January 1925, he had come to the conclusion that Fourquet's plan could not be judiciously implemented and would lead to a "foredoomed failure." Walsh proposed a list of stringent conditions which he knew Rome would not support. A very prudent person, he preferred, in fact, to abort the project rather than to risk failure. He also knew that by acting in this manner he was giving Bishop Rayssac—"a very determined man"—the opportunity to carry through his original plan which called for "Father Ford going over as future vicar [of Kaying]."[137] As revealing as they may be, James E. Walsh's attitudes and actions served no purpose; the decision to follow Rayssac's plan to divide Swatow had already been made by Archbishop de Guébriant.

For some undetermined reason, de Guébriant appeared to have wanted to keep Maryknoll out of eastern Kwangtung and had therefore directed Maryknoll's attention toward the offer of Bishop Blois in Manchuria. At the same time, he had tried to satisfy Rayssac by asking Fourquet to annex three subprefectures adjoining the Canton vicariate. De Guébriant did not anticipate, however, that Fourquet would not only accept, but also make an additional proposal of his own, which ruined the archbishop's efforts to keep all of Swatow under M.E.P. jurisdiction. De Guébriant was obviously annoyed by Fourquet's move and "utopian" idea. In January 1925, left with no alternative but to support either Rayssac's plan or Fourquet's idea, de Guébriant sided with Rayssac on the grounds that this plan had come first and that the bishop of Swatow and Maryknoll had already reached a preliminary agreement.

De Guébriant's decision was delayed in the mail and took two months to reach Fourquet. In late March, upon receiving the M.E.P. superior's letter, Fourquet immediately withdrew his plan but not without warning de Guébriant of the impending storm that such a decision and other similar ones would have for the Church in China:

> I am afraid that we will have to repent for delaying too much in putting the natives in charge of the ecclesiastic administration. . . .
> I want to draw your attention to storms I see on the horizon. . . . I have forewarned you. The rest is up to you.[138]

James E. Walsh could hardly hide his relief when he learned that Bishop

Rayssac's plan to give the entire Kaying territory to Maryknoll had prevailed. In June he was instructed by the Maryknoll General Council to send Father Ford as superior to Kaying.[139]

A Chinese Bishop for Wuchow

In 1926, just one year later, Rome announced the appointment of six Chinese bishops, the first since Lo Wenzao, the only other bishop, was consecrated in 1685. James E. Walsh received the news with great excitement and went to Hong Kong to greet the new appointees on their way to Rome for consecration. To James A. Walsh and readers of *The Field Afar*, he described the appointment as a step forward of great significance, "one of those milestones like the coming of St. Francis Xavier and the preaching of Father Ricci, that will mark prominently and permanently the history of the Church in China."[140] He even confided half-jokingly to a friend, Father John Considine, that if he had seven million dollars, he would give one million to each of them and keep one million for himself.[141]

James E. Walsh was again showing ample verbal support for the native Chinese hierarchy. A second chance to prove it in practice was offered two years after he became superior general on April 4, 1936, following the death of James A. Walsh. In early 1938, Rome decided to raise the Wuchow prefecture to the status of a vicariate. The head of that territory, the vicar apostolic, would be a bishop.

The result of a *terna* or consultative ballot sent by Maryknoll headquarters to each Maryknoll priest in Wuchow showed that Monsignor Meyer, the incumbent prefect, had not received a strong enough majority to be recommended to Rome as vicar apostolic. In the report he hand-delivered to Cardinal Fumasoni-Biondi, the prefect of the Congregation of Propaganda Fide, in May 1938, James E. Walsh outlined the reasons for the missioners' dissatisfaction with Meyer.

Although Meyer was indeed "one of the most successful foreign missionaries in China, a man of unbounded apostolic zeal, and a master of the native language," there was some question about his capability for administration: "He has a penchant for making endless rules about minutiae and changing them endlessly . . . [and] for accepting the words of the Chinese catechists in preference to that of the missionaries." Another factor was a nervous breakdown Meyer suffered in 1932 which required a year of recuperation and left a question mark about his health.[142]

For these reasons the Maryknoll Council suggested that the time had come for Maryknoll to realize "its long cherished ambition" to turn one of its territories over to a Chinese vicar apostolic. This appointment would give Monsignor Meyer the satisfaction of fulfilling his missionary ideal. His career would be "the story of a gifted priest who squandered and spent himself in building a mission by his personal efforts and then stepped aside to give the fruits of his work to a native superior."[143]

Propaganda Fide liked James E. Walsh's suggestion and sent him to China to find a suitable Chinese priest to become vicar of Wuchow. Fumasoni-Biondi suggested, however, that it would be best if the native priest had been trained by Maryknoll and cautioned against selecting a Chinese who would be a mere puppet.[144]

In Wuchow James E. Walsh met with an unfavorable reaction from the Maryknoll priests to the appointment of a native vicar:

> Ten priests said that while they readily espoused the idea in principle and were a priori disposed to give a Chinese superior their full cooperation, they [also] felt it would not work in practice in the present condition of Wuchow.

Only one priest felt that there was a fair chance of practical success if the right man were chosen.[145]

The Wuchow Maryknollers thought that the two best Maryknoll-trained candidates, Mark Tsai of Kaying and Simon Lei of Kongmoon, were too young. Objections were also voiced about non-Maryknoll trained candidates from neighboring vicariates: Fathers Aloysius Ma of Hong Kong, John Wong of Swatow, Dominic Yim of Macao, and three Jesuits of Shiuhing.[146]

Rather discouraged, James E. Walsh left Wuchow to visit other missions in north China, feeling that all probabilities were against the General Council's original plan to select a Chinese bishop. Upon leaving, however, he asked the Wuchow priests "to reflect and to report their reflections" to him in the fall.[147]

Father James Drought, as a spokesman of the Council, urged Bishop Walsh to stick to the plan: "Granted a native priest of normal ability and admirable character, our choice should favor him over one of our own missioners who might have extraordinary ability and extraordinary character." Moreover, Drought stressed that Maryknoll, looking to the future, "should expressly favor the replacement of our present Maryknoll vicars by natives. If all our missioners realize that this is the policy, they would inevitably train the native priests with additional care and concern."[148]

While in the north, Walsh continued his quest for a Chinese vicar and had a long interview with Archbishop Mario Zanin, the apostolic delegate, to discuss the candidates. Bishop Paul Yü Pin, a national figure, was even mentioned as a possibility. Upon returning to Wuchow in November, Walsh discovered that Maryknollers considered the question of a native bishop for Wuchow closed. "Who closed it?" he asked. "Certainly not I since I took great pain to say the exact opposite. . . . I could discover no more [except that] somebody wanted to believe the case was closed."[149]

Nonetheless Walsh took a new survey of the question which showed that seven Maryknoll priests, including Meyer, were against and only two were in favor; five missioners, mostly newly arrived, remained neutral, saying that they lacked experience to render a judicious opinion.

At the same time, Walsh became aware that the tensions in the mission territories ran deeper than he had previously thought. He wrote to the General Council that the prevalent feelings among Catholics in Wuchow were that some of the priests had voted against Meyer because too often he sided with the catechists rather than the missioners. Given these circumstances, Walsh felt that the alternative of choosing a bishop from among the existing Maryknoll clergy in Wuchow was also out of the question.[150]

Bishop Walsh then considered the advice of Monsignor Romaniello in Kweilin and Bishop Ford in Kaying. Both had adverse reactions to the plan to have a Chinese bishop. Ford was particularly opposed to the idea of having any of his Chinese priests considered for the position and instead recommended Father Antonius Liu, superior of the minor seminary in the neighboring vicariate of Swatow.[151]

When this last suggestion reached Bishop James E. Walsh in late March 1939, it was too late to revive the search for a native bishop for Wuchow. The superior general of Maryknoll, overwhelmed by the opposition, had given up the idea. In concluding his visitation report to the General Council, he listed as insurmountable handicaps many of the traditional reasons of European missioners to keep the native priests in subordinate positions, such as the Chinese lack of discrimination, their mistrust of foreigners, and their "sensitiveness."[152]

The opposition had taken its toll on Walsh and finally outweighed the sound advice of his General Council. Once he had made up his mind, Walsh had no difficulties expounding the defects he saw in each candidate to his Council, Archbishop Zanin and Cardinal Fumasoni-Biondi. Even Bishop Yü Pin was passed over because Walsh rightly felt that rustic Wuchow was too inappropriate a field for a man who was called to do greater work for the Church in a larger sphere. The superior general then conducted a new consultative vote, and Father Frederick Donaghy of the vicariate of Kaying emerged as a strong first choice of the clergy in Wuchow.[153]

Rome understood that the year-long battle for a Chinese vicariate in Wuchow had been lost. On July 21, 1939, the Congregation of the Propaganda Fide cabled Maryknoll: "Wuchow vicariate, Donaghy vicar."[154] By regarding a Chinese vicar for Wuchow as "too big a chance to take," as Bishop Walsh said in his December report to the General Council, Maryknoll had lost a second opportunity to participate in the movement to establish a native hierarchy in China.[155]

Conclusion

The Society and the Congregation of Maryknoll were both created to foster native clergy and sisterhoods, and their constitutions were constant reminders of that priority.

The commitment of Maryknollers to developing a native Church in China is undeniable. In each territory seminaries were always one of the first institutions initiated. Except for the Yeungkong-Loting experience of the early 1920s, the first group of Maryknoll Sisters always went to establish a novitiate and train native Sisters.

Maryknoll's experiment in indigenization went through three overlapping phases of development. During the first phase, Maryknoll rectors and novice mistresses, with only one or two exceptions, had little or no prior training or experience. Consequently, they organized mission seminaries and novitiates along the lines of the only other seminaries and novitiates they knew—the ones they had previously attended in the United States. The daily routine and training in these institutions allowed for only superficial and minimal accommodations to China and its culture; in contrast, they forced upon native seminarians and novices a Western culture and way of life. Maryknoll's attitude was somewhat contradictory. On the one hand, Maryknollers in the countryside were to be as Chinese as possible; on the other hand, training in the mission seminaries and novitiates tended to Westernize their Chinese recruits.

As Maryknollers gained experience and understanding of the Chinese, they began to break away from the traditional methods of seminary and novitiate training, developing a new approach. In this second phase, Maryknollers brought a new dimension to the missionary community. They were not just forming native priests and Sisters; they were training Chinese replacements who would perform better than Westerners and who would take over as soon as possible. The curriculum was coordinated with that of the public schools, the spiritual formation was solid, and there was a definite trend to have Chinese supervise formation of their own priests.

This attitude of aiming for first-rate Chinese priests and nuns, and of treating them on an equal footing, led to the third stage, the actual passing of leadership to native priests and Sisters. This stage had barely begun when it was cut short by the ousting of foreign missioners. Only a few Chinese priests and Sisters were left to fend for themselves. The fact that most of these priests and Sisters in Maryknoll territories persevered despite long years of isolation and persecution is a tribute to the training they received from Maryknoll.

It seems, however, that even without the Communist victory, several hurdles stood in the way of a smooth transfer of command from Maryknollers to their Chinese counterparts. Although deeply in love with China and committed to the goal of their Society and Congregation, Maryknollers were products of their time and had some deeply ingrained racial prejudices about the Chinese. They readily cited inclinations to personal jealousy, poor executive ability, lack of discrimination, and oversensitivity as some of the most inherent Chinese defects, and as good reasons to delay or deny them command of the Church.[156]

Maryknollers were also proud to be Americans to the point that they tended to be biased and viewed themselves in a better light than their European counterparts. To every defect pinned on the "traditional" missioner, they attributed the opposite quality to themselves: Europeans were distant; Maryknollers mingled with farmers in the countryside and shared all their time with seminarians or novices. Europeans were class-conscious; Maryknollers did not make distinctions between themselves and Chinese priests or nuns. Europeans were reluctant to relinquish their authority; Maryknollers were ready to pass the command to the Chinese at the first opportunity. This chauvinistic attitude was self-defeating, blinding them to their shortcomings and limiting their contributions to the development of a Chinese Church.

Moreover, twice Maryknoll had backed down from taking the ultimate step toward indigenization—entrusting the overall administration of a territory to a Chinese bishop. The decisions may have been considered wise and prudent because conditions were certainly less than satisfactory. One cannot, however, refrain from contrasting these decisions with the bold and risk-taking attitude that Maryknoll displayed in other situations. Did Maryknoll not accept large territories with just a few priests and Sisters at hand? Did Maryknoll not start seminaries, novitiates, dispensaries, and orphanages with priests and Sisters who lacked experience? Were not Maryknoll's first two vicars apostolic, James E. Walsh and Francis Ford, young and inexperienced? One wonders, therefore, if Maryknoll did not partly fail to answer its call to promote a native Church by being too prudent or, to put it another way, by lacking confidence both in the Chinese and in God's grace. These questions remain; they challenge Maryknoll to look deeply into itself and constantly to review its relationship with God and with others.

In the five Maryknoll territories, the vicariate of Kaying showed the best record on indigenization. Kaying's achievements can be attributed to several causes, including the existence of well-established Catholic villages to provide vocations and a locale, relatively untouched by the war, which did not disrupt religious training. Yet the key explanation lies in the personal mission vision of its leader, Bishop Francis Ford, who emphasized the establishment of the Church rather than the conversion of individual souls.

> The object of mission work is not primarily to convert pagans, it is to establish the Catholic Church in pagan lands. The purpose is to preach the Gospel and to build up as complete an organization as possible, which will itself later continue with better success the work of converting the native population.[157]

To carry out this objective, Ford needed well-trained Chinese priests and Sisters who belonged to Hakka society. To reach the female population, Ford enlisted the help of outstanding Maryknoll Sisters, such as Rosalia Kettl and Thérèse Grondin, who totally espoused his ideas and put them to work.

Together they aimed to bring the Church to China, but without the methods, the "civilization," and the control of the Western Church. It was mentioned above that the innovative methods of Bishop Ford and the Maryknoll Sisters in Kaying were gradually introduced in other Maryknoll territories. The comments of Bishop Frederick Donaghy at a meeting with the Maryknoll Sisters of his diocese in August 1949 are a testimony to the depth of Maryknoll's vision for a native Chinese Church:

> In considering Chinese priests and Sisters, we must have vision: they will be the custodians of the Catholic Faith. . . . It is not for us . . . to strip them of their Chinese customs and graft on them a foreign culture alien to their way of life and thought. It is hardly for us to set ourselves up as judges of their way of doing things when it differs from ours—rather it is for us to adapt our minds to their way of thinking when it involves no principle and in thus doing preserve for them intact that heritage of Chinese thought which is their own treasure. It is hardly for us to set them far above their people by raising their standards of living so that village work and normal Chinese existence will be difficult for them. If in our training of them we do this, we have defeated our own purpose.[158]

In this climate, it is possible to imagine a scenario in which the Maryknoll leadership of each Maryknoll territory would have stepped down rapidly as the native leadership rose. This scenario, however, required a certain amount of risk-taking because it had to be rooted in trust and confidence. After twice backing down, was Maryknoll actually ready to take the step in 1950?

6

Adaptation and Accommodation

The training of native priests and Sisters is only one phase of the building of a native Church. To survive and become indigenous, that Church has to speak a language, present a message, and teach practices which will touch the hearts and minds of the people. Here, too, missioners are called upon to play a major role. Ideally, the more they identify themselves with a people and the better they understand their culture, the more effective will be their evangelization efforts. Consequently, they strive to lay the foundation of a native Church which will develop a personality of its own rather than replicate a Western Church.

When Maryknollers arrived in China, they stepped into a complex situation. In the eyes of many Chinese, Christianity was part and parcel of Western imperialism, imposed on China through religious protectorates, unjust treaties, and gunboat diplomacy. With such a handicap, the task of building an indigenous Chinese Church was an arduous enterprise.

After the apostolic letter *Maximum Illud* of November 1919, few in the Roman Catholic missionary community objected to the notion of the gradual rise of a Chinese-led local Church. The question was what kind. Two trends were at work, one which tried to accommodate the Church to China and the other one which tried to accommodate China to the Church. The first tendency attempted to immerse the Church into the Chinese culture and context; the second tendency aimed at creating a Chinese Church which was as Roman as possible. From hindsight, it is easy to condemn the second tendency for being tarnished by cultural imperialism and to hail the first tendency as leading to a genuine self-expressing indigenous Church; in practice, however, these two trends were generally not perceived as opposites. They appeared rather as two different facets of the same goal of building the Church in China. As a result, the policies, attitudes, and actions of many missioners from the highest echelon to the lowest were often ambivalent.

Was Maryknoll ambivalent? In theory, the Society and the Congregation both stressed the building of a self-governing Chinese Church as one of their highest priorities. Did the lifestyle of Maryknollers, their handling of the language, the message they conveyed, and the Christian practices they encouraged tend to reinforce, alleviate, or eradicate the foreign character of the Catholic Church in China?

Life-style of Maryknollers: Degrees of Personal Adjustment

The personal adjustment of the missioners to their Chinese surroundings played a major role in the way the Chinese perceived the Church. Often a missioner's adaptation to his surroundings served as a catalyst enabling him or her to evangelize and to foster Christian practices in forms which Chinese did not resent as foreign.

Father Peter Reilly recalled:

> The first step was to get to know the people, understand them, sympathize with them, win them over to your side through respect. Hence, revealing one's true inner self was absolutely necessary for it was to that that they responded. If they could come to realize that you were good and kind and honest and sincere, then you had an excellent chance at converting them.[1]

James E. Walsh and Adjustment

From the beginning of the Society and the Congregation, letters, reports and conferences of Maryknoll leaders frequently mentioned the importance of personal adjustment to a new country and environment. This idea, however, was usually presented in passing and rarely given more than a few lines. In 1937, Bishop James E. Walsh's publication of *Mission Manual of the Vicariate of Kongmoon* provided the first detailed analysis of the problem of adjusting to China. During that same year, he was elected superior general of the Society and remained in that position for 10 years.

This combination of events allowed Bishop Walsh to firmly plant his views of missionary adjustment in the hearts of Maryknoll seminarians. These views, in fact, have so deeply permeated the Society and the Congregation that they have become part of their spiritual heritage.

The section of the Manual entitled "Personal Plan of the Missioner" is significant because it describes in detail the adjustments a missioner should make on arriving in China:

As a fish out of water, so the missioner must regain an environment in which he can function normally. . . . The problem is one of adjustment, and an adjustment implies a change somewhere, somehow. . . . China will not change; at least, not immediately and completely as a mere matter of accommodation to the missioner and in order to make him feel at home. . . . Therefore it is the man, the missioner, I myself and no other, who must do violence to myself in order to change and to conform to what I find in my new country, rather than to expect that country with its 400 million people to conform itself to me.[2]

"Goodwill, intelligent effort" and, most of all, "patience" were necessary to pursue the lengthy process of adjustment. Together, these qualities served to shape and refine the proper tools for a successful adjustment: familiarity with the language, and knowledge of Chinese customs and the philosophy that underlay them. Walsh pointed out several pitfalls which were often "hard on nerves and cruel to vanity" and could abort the metamorphosis. First, there was the problem of filling up a life which had been stripped of its usual activities:

[The missioner] is a stranger in a strange land suddenly bereft of any power to see, to understand, to judge, to act. . . . He can by conscious effort replace his lost activities by other equally pleasant and profitable ones, until he finds himself living a perfectly full and normal life in his new surroundings. . . . Or, on the other hand, he can drift along aimlessly and allow his life to be filled up gradually with the triviality that creeps in to compensate for the loss of normal activities.[3]

Another danger was to assume an attitude of contemptuous superiority toward a puzzling culture and unfamiliar people:

Experience shows that with the average man, not to know a custom is usually to belittle its force, if not even to regard it with some contempt. . . . Likewise in dealing with the people, the less he knows about them, the less esteem he will have for them . . . because his inability to know his surroundings creates in him the impression that he is merely sojourning in an outlandish place among outlandish people where nothing matters.[4]

The third danger, and the greatest of all, according to James E. Walsh, was to become satisfied with a limited understanding of China.

With a little study [the missioner] will pick up a modicum of language. . . . He observes the doings around him in a general and rather vague way, notes a few of the more important customs, remarks some of the striking peculiarities. He sees a little, hears a little, reads a little, reflects a little. But only a little. He misses half of what goes on around him and he often misunderstands the other half. . . . He is still a foreigner in China.[5]

On the contrary, the totally adjusted missioner "has ceased to be an American and has become Chinese."[6] During this lengthy metamorphosis, he or she has made China the center of his or her life and activities. How closely did individual Maryknollers come to such complete transformations? Did they avoid the pitfalls pointed out to them by Bishop Walsh? Although there are as many shades and nuances of adjustment as there are Maryknollers, enough common attitudes and behaviors also exist to account for the great similarities among individual Maryknollers.

Clothing

Prior to taking charge of a Chinese mission territory, Maryknoll priests were obliged to follow the ecclesiastical rules of their French hosts. At the time when most vicars apostolic allowed their missioners to wear a long Chinese gown, the M.E.P. bishops in Kwangtung, Kwangsi, and Manchuria still required the wearing of a black or white cassock except for traveling. For instance, Bishop Blois of Mukden took great pain to remind Maryknollers that:

> In the vicariate of Mukden the compulsory ecclesiastical habit (*habit ecclesiasticus*) is the cassock, "vestis talaris, secundum legitimas consuetudines, et Ordinarii praescripta." This rule is such that if the priests in the vicariate were to adopt another outfit, even the American clergyman suit, they would be severely punished.[7]

When James E. Walsh became head of the new prefecture apostolic of Kongmoon in 1924, he gave his priests permission to dress in a long Chinese gown. Most Maryknollers preferred to wear the Chinese gown over a Chinese shirt and trousers, not only because they thought it was more meaningful in the Chinese context, but also because it was more comfortable than the cassock; besides, the gown had no buttons to be chewed off and carried away by the rats.[8]

During World War II, many Maryknoll priests in South China picked up the habit of dressing in GI tans. Some even continued to do so after the war was over. Military dress was convenient but it may have given the wrong impression about who Maryknollers were and what ultimate goal they were pursuing in China.[9]

The Maryknoll Sisters, like other religious congregations of women, were bound by their constitutions to wear their regular habit. Except for

Fig. 1. An acculturated Maryknoller—Father Robert Cairns with his catechist and family in Fachow, 1924. Maryknoll Photo Library.

the substitution during summer of a lighter white habit for the usual gray habit, no other changes were permitted to alleviate the intense heat and humidity of South China. Winter was more bearable because Sisters could always add layers of clothing, like the long, padded Chinese gown they wore under their habit in Manchuria.[10]

When the Sisters traveled, the inappropriateness of their habits became evident. They had to walk and ride bicycles for long distances under the blazing sun and dust or in downpours and mud. Trips by junks or steamers were hardly a relief; passengers had to bear the brunt of the elements on deck or opt for hot, airless little cabins. In any case, the Sisters' clothes, often soaked with rain or perspiration, were a health hazard. To make matters worse, the ubiquitous bedbugs sometimes crawled into the habits and the Sisters had no recourse but to stoically endure the bites and the itching.[11]

Diet

The diet of the missioners also gave a clue to their degree of accommodation. On the whole, Maryknollers followed the rule of eating Chinese food in the company of the Chinese and eating Western-style when by themselves. Most of them replenished their supply of powdered milk and coffee, granulated white sugar, wheat flour, and canned or dried food in the big ports of Hong Kong, Swatow, or Dairen. They rarely did their own cooking, but rather hired Chinese cooks who could cook Western food or else taught them how to do so. Since Chinese stoves were not designed for baking, several rectories and convents had a Western stove. This appliance allowed Maryknollers to enjoy bread, cakes, and pastries.[12]

Father Thomas Kiernan's account of meals at the parish of Pingnam in South China shows no real attempt to include local fare. Chinese ingredients are introduced only as substitutes for unavailable Western ingredients.

> Our meals were quite simple, they were basically Western meals. For breakfast we would have steamed rice as cereal and of course powdered milk or evaporated milk. You could buy brown sugar out in the market but we usually got white granulated sugar on our trip to Hong Kong every year. Then we would have fried eggs or boiled eggs or poached eggs and a piece of pork. You wouldn't have any bacon or ham unless you were affluent enough to import it from Hong Kong which we didn't do. For lunch you would have rice again instead of potatoes or you could have noodles, and then again pork, usually roasted or perhaps baked or maybe even boiled. And about the same thing for the supper meal. Some of our cooks could make beautiful bread and good pies with canned apples or dried apples. From the powdered milk and eggs and so forth they would make custards. If

you cared for dessert, you had it.[13]

Sister Philomena Chan, a Precious Blood Sister, who worked in the Loting orphanage as a teenager, recalled that in the mid–1930s the Maryknoll Sisters in Loting ate Chinese food only once a week, on Thursdays. On that day, she was always invited to have dinner with the Sisters.[14]

These eating habits, even in the privacy of a rectory or convent, were not unnoticed by the people and often prevented missioners from being accepted by the Chinese. The people saw the cook buy meat for almost every meal, they talked with him, and they learned about the food served at the table of Maryknollers. Except for meat, which they certainly would have liked to eat more often, the Chinese, especially in the countryside, were not attracted to Maryknollers' eating habits. Regarding these habits as a sign of their differences, the Chinese said, "They were foreigners and it was natural for them to eat in a different style."[15]

Father John Yeung mentioned that in his native prefecture of Kweilin, the use of rare food items such as milk, coffee and bread, however, convinced most rural people that the missioners were like rich Chinese or perhaps even better off:

> From the point of view of many people, the lives of the priests were first-class. They were like the rich, even better than the rich Chinese. . . . If the people got in touch with the priests, they would find that they didn't have the food of the priests. The village people didn't eat those things. They ate rice, congee, sweet potatoes, taro. . . . But the priests, they had bread to eat. The bread was made by the cook. There was no shop to sell bread. Even if you wanted to eat bread, there was no one to bake it for you. You couldn't buy it even if you had money. As for milk, coffee, only Westerners had these things. In the countryside, Chinese didn't have these things, hence in their eyes they would feel that missioners had a higher standard of living.[16]

By contrast, when they visited outstations, Maryknoll Fathers and Sisters shared the meals of their Chinese hosts and often brought along a supply of rice to help defray expenses. They seemed to have eaten almost everything. Most Maryknollers did take a real liking to Chinese food. Sometimes accommodation was easy: the noodles and dumplings of Manchuria differed only slightly from the noodles and ravioli found in America. Sometimes it took a while to develop a taste for a particular type of food, such as the favorite salted vegetables and pork of the Hakka people.

It was difficult, however, to completely shake off some Western dietary taboos; dog meat, for instance, remained repulsive to the great majority of Maryknollers. Monsignor Bernard Meyer was viewed by missioners and Chinese alike as the Maryknoller who adjusted the most thoroughly to the

Chinese ways of eating. Father Thomas Lau of Wuchow recalled that Meyer "was like the common folk. For example, when the foreigners ate chicken, they would not eat the internal organs. He would. He also ate the head and the feet."[17]

Such a complete adaptation to Chinese ways of eating was, in fact, not favored by Maryknoll superiors, who recommended missioners to maintain "a fairly decent diet."[18] They felt, quite realistically, that most Maryknollers would not be mentally and physically able to live totally on a Chinese diet because of their American upbringing. Thus, the superiors never officially discouraged the habit developed by Maryknollers of eating American-style in their private dining room and Chinese-style in the company of Chinese.

The adjustment was supposed to be progressive, each missioner finding and accepting his or her own limit. Bishop Ford, for instance, always found it difficult to eat rice. He was delighted to have bread instead. From personal experience, he knew that a good cook often made the difference between a disgruntled missioner and a happy one, especially when feuds and wars interrupted supplies of canned food from the port cities.

> I think the crux of our living over here is training your cook. The man who was used to depend on the can opener usually was satisfied with a mediocre cook, and without canned goods his meals became wretched. Up here importing canned goods was such a nuisance that we trained our cooks fairly well with local stuff. Ten years ago [1933] I imported a Hong Kong cook who trained about a dozen of the local boys, others were trained by the [Maryknoll] Sisters, so that we really were not at a loss for desserts, bread, or home-made soups and that makes the difference in a pinch.[19]

Only a few Maryknollers were able to follow Father Meyer's example in their diet. According to Sister Irene Fogarty's experience in the Kaying vicariate, most Maryknollers who broke down or burned out were zealous missioners who tried to live and eat exactly as the Chinese did.

> [Our] motives were good. . . . We wanted to be poorer. We had very little but we wanted to give up everything but it was not always possible and it was a hard balance between good common sense and the desire to be as poor as possible.[20]

Arriving at this healthy balance was one of the conditions of a successful and lasting adjustment to China.

Language

In recent decades, modern teaching methods have elevated knowledge of spoken and written Chinese from the exotic or erudite to the possible for ambitious students. This was not yet the case when the first groups of Fathers, Brothers, and Sisters crossed the Pacific Ocean in the late 1910s and early 1920s. They had little or no formal linguistic preparation, and their inability to understand the Chinese language was the most immediate and formidable problem confronting them.

They quickly perceived that familiarity with the language was one of the keys to personal adjustment and success as missioners. They also found out that this view had been defended by Rome for quite some time, and that Propaganda had given two specific instructions on language. According to the first instruction in 1774, new missioners were supposed to demonstrate some proficiency in the language six months after their arrival. According to a subsequent instruction in 1883, heads of mission territories in China were urged to open schools for the language training of missioners. It is not surprising therefore that someone like Father Thomas Kiernan who joined Maryknoll in 1921 would vividly remember letters from the early groups of Maryknollers stressing over and over the necessity of mastering the Chinese language.[21]

The Fathers' and Brothers' First Experiments

Early Maryknollers usually spent the first two years learning the language. During that period the young priests were assigned as curates to senior priests who hired tutors to give them daily private lessons. The first year was a period of full-time language study, while the second year was a transition, mixing study with practical applications in pastoral and missionary work. However, as Father William Downs of Kaying remarked, there were often more stations to fill than priests to man them; consequently many newcomers were almost immediately sent alone to a parish, not only to study but also to care for the pastoral needs of the people.[22]

These arrangements proved to be less than ideal for acquiring a solid knowledge of the language. Good teachers were often difficult to secure in the countryside. Busy pastors were often reluctant to supervise their curates' studies. Some newly arrived priests, burning with mission zeal, became involved in pastoral and missionary work without sufficient language training. Others, conscious of their limited knowledge of the language, would shy away, rely too much on the catechists, and never achieve the fluency developed by daily contact with the people.

Finding a suitable textbook was also a problem. A variety of primers were available for the study of Cantonese, but none was entirely satisfying to Maryknollers. Therefore, in 1927, Father Meyer prepared the first official Maryknoll textbook for students of Cantonese by adapting and romanizing a now obscure book of a certain Wisner.[23]

When Fathers Francis Ford and James Drought were transferred to

Kaying in 1925, they met an even greater obstacle. Chinese in the area spoke Hakka, a dialect quite different from both Cantonese and Mandarin. The only book at their disposal was a small dictionary composed by Charles Rey, an M.E.P. Father of the Swatow vicariate. During his one-year stay in the Hakka territory, Father Drought, with the help of Father John Wong, a Chinese priest of Swatow, wrote a 300-page course entitled *Introduction to Hakka*. Until 1948 the book remained the standard Hakka course for Maryknoll priests.

In 1926, Monsignor James E. Walsh designed a five-year course consisting of three years of study in a language school, interspersed with two one-year periods of half-study, half-practical training in a parish. This ambitious program was never fully implemented. The language training was scaled down to a nine-month intensive program at a language school, followed by one year of part-time practical training and part-time study with a private teacher. Standard reference books on Chinese customs, such as *Village Life in China* and *Chinese Characteristics* by Arthur H. Smith, were required readings.

The Language Schools of South China for Maryknoll Priests and Brothers

The first Maryknoll Chinese-language school was opened in Pakkai in Kongmoon in late 1927 under the direction of Father Frederick Dietz, who was recognized by the Chinese themselves as an excellent speaker of Cantonese. The course lasted nine months and included two daily sessions with Father Dietz, one on language and one on Chinese culture and customs, and two sessions of oral drill and reading with Chinese professors.[24] In the fall of 1928, Dietz went to Pingnam to help Bernard Meyer start a language school for the Wuchow territory. Dietz then began to expand the Wisner-Meyer language book, adding annotations, a commentary, and a series of translation exercises.[25]

With the departure of Father Drought to the Philippines in 1926, no one in Kaying was qualified to open a language school until late 1931, when Father William Downs was made director of a new Hakka language school in Siaoloc.[26] In 1935 the Maryknoll Fathers decided to merge the three language schools at Pakkai, Pingnam, and Siaoloc into one school under the direction of Father Thomas O'Melia at the Maryknoll Stanley House in Hong Kong. At first, only Cantonese and Hakka were taught; Mandarin was added in 1939. The course was spread over four years. Upon arriving in China, generally in September, the new missioners spent their first year at Stanley learning the language. Their daily schedule included two hours of private study, two hours of private class with a Chinese teacher, and two hours of common class by O'Melia assisted by Chinese teachers.

O'Melia used a series of lessons he had been working on since 1931. Finally published in 1938 as a textbook entitled *First-Year Cantonese*, the course was divided into four parts: sentence structure, simple readings, familiar conversations, and random idioms. The lessons followed a grammatical progression which reflected Father O'Melia's impeccable knowledge of both American and Chinese idioms. The last months of the first year were usually devoted to study of the *Children's Catechism*, a series of 87 simple questions and answers, and the vocabulary used for the sacrament of penance. To introduce his students to the writing of characters, Father O'Melia published a small handbook entitled *Teaching Chinese Script to Foreigners*.

Following this period of intensive study, the missioners went to their territories, but were still supposed to devote a few hours each day to language study through the end of their fourth year in China. Moreover, they were supposed to go back to Hong Kong during the first six months of their third year and the last six months of their fourth year to take a course in preaching and in newspaper and classical readings. These last two stages proved to be almost impossible to implement. Once a missioner joined his vicariate or prefecture, he was faced with so many urgent tasks that he could not be released for further study in Hong Kong. Refining his knowledge of both the spoken and the written language was left up to the individual.[27]

Father O'Melia's *First-Year Cantonese* was an excellent primer aimed at giving a solid foundation in spoken Cantonese and in written Chinese rather than at rushing the student through the memorization of Christian vocabulary. Together with *The Student's Cantonese-English Dictionary*, first published in 1935 by Monsignor Meyer and Brother Francis Wempe, it gained recognition as one of the best tools for learning Cantonese. In 1940, the Hong Kong government formally notified O'Melia that his book had been adopted as the official textbook for all government offices whose duties required a knowledge of the Cantonese dialect. In addition, O'Melia was invited to sit on the Government Board of Examiners to review the Chinese qualifications of civil servants. His textbook remained in use by Maryknollers for more than 30 years.[28]

To extend the benefits of O'Melia's primer to all students, the Maryknoll Fathers' General Council encouraged production of a Hakka and a Mandarin version. Father Downs and Francis X. Keelan of Kweilin were sent to Hong Kong to help O'Melia with his teaching and to adapt his textbook. The fall of Hong Kong to the Japanese in December 1941 ended the Stanley language school experiment and delayed the publication of *Beginning Hakka*, by Father Downs, and *Spoken Chinese—First Year*, by Father Keelan until after the war.[29]

In 1946, Maryknollers were again assigned to China, but the Stanley school remained closed. There had never been many candidates for the second and third years of study, and the Maryknoll Fathers agreed that Hong Kong provided too Western an environment. A Cantonese school for both the Wuchow and Kongmoon vicariates was opened in Pingnam under Father Patrick Donnelly. Father Keelan took charge of the Mandarin school in Kweilin city, and a Chinese teacher, Mr. Yap, ran the Hakka school in Siaoloc. The courses lasted nine months after which the missioners were expected to continue a program of individual study varying from two to four years.[30]

The Language Program of Fushun for Priests and Brothers

The Maryknoll territory of Fushun in Manchuria was too remote and too different to share in the language school program of the territories in South China. In Manchuria the variety of nationalities, Chinese, Japanese, and Korean, presented an enormous linguistic challenge. Maryknollers going to Manchuria were usually assigned to a particular nationality and mastered that language first. Of the 42 Fathers and Brothers assigned to the Fushun territory between 1925 and 1941, 35 started by learning Mandarin. Before 1933, they combined private lessons from hired tutors, catechists, or seminarians with contact with the people and the help of an experienced pastor, often a Chinese himself.[31]

The period of intensive study lasted from nine to ten months, usually at the Fushun center. The primer entitled *An Introduction to Mandarin* was borrowed from the Protestant College of Chinese Studies in Peking. It was a small book written entirely in Chinese characters by the English Baptist missionary, Reverend John Sutherland Whiteright. In order to hear confession in Chinese, the priests studied the *Confession Phrase Book*, a simple question and answer method which took about two months to master.

In 1933, Monsignor Raymond Lane asked Ambrose Hsü, a graduate of Holy Cross College in the United States, to design a language program for the study of Mandarin. Borrowing from the Franciscan, the Scheut, and the Jesuit language schools in Peking, he gradually developed a three-year course in Chinese which was adapted to the special idioms of Manchuria as well as to Catholic mission work.

It was not until the fall of 1935 that the language school opened. Located at the Fushun center, it soon moved to Antung, next to the Korean border. After nine months of formal language training, the missioners were assigned to a particular parish but were required to study Hsü's course for two additional years.[32]

No attempt was made to develop a language school in Fushun for the study of Japanese and Korean. Of the six Maryknoll priests who were assigned to work primarily among the Japanese of Manchuria, three studied Japanese in Tokyo before going to Manchuria, and the three others, as well as Father John Coffey, the only priest assigned to learn Korean, studied with private tutors. Among the 42 Maryknollers in Manchuria, only a few attempted to learn more than one language. Monsignor Lane felt, as head of the Fushun territory, that he should be able to address all his Christians; besides Mandarin, he also spoke some Japanese and Korean.[33]

The Sisters' Approaches to Language Study

In learning the Chinese language, the Maryknoll Sisters initially benefited from the experience of the Maryknoll Fathers. The Sisters had first considered Canton as the site for their headquarters in China. Vivid recollections by the Maryknoll Fathers of their own frustrations and early difficulties, however, caused them to advise the Sisters against Canton. Father James E. Walsh suggested that the Sisters go instead to Hong Kong, a place where English was spoken. There they could gradually adjust to climate and culture, learn Chinese, and gain experience in such mundane yet important matters as how to shop for supplies. When Sister Mary Paul McKenna arrived in Hong Kong in 1921 with the first group of Sisters, Father Robert Cairns, the procurator for the Maryknoll Fathers, arranged for them to have a Chinese teacher. The Sisters soon found it more appropriate to have a female teacher, and they spent the first year in "days of concentrated application to language study."[34] They were avid readers of books on Chinese culture and customs such as *Village Life in China* by Smith. Every week they arranged mission and orientation conferences by Maryknoll Fathers in Hong Kong. These meetings formed a regular first-year pattern for each new group of Sisters assigned to China.

Some Sisters, however, were denied the opportunity for language study. Knowledge of the local language was not deemed necessary for those Sisters assigned to teach at the Maryknoll Convent School and the Holy Spirit School in Hong Kong or the Maryknoll Academy of Dairen in Manchuria. These Sisters began teaching almost immediately and had no time for language study.[35] Any fluency was acquired strictly on an individual basis. Sister Virginia Flagg, who taught in Dairen, confirmed that:

> When we taught in the school we had no time to take language study. . . . I never had a chance to study the language. I picked up a little Mandarin from my friends and then a Japanese lady used to teach me once a week. It was not much.[36]

The Sisters assigned to the Shanghai Mercy Hospital were not much better off: "I arrived there on the 18th of October," said Sister Agnes Regina Rafferty, "and on the 19th, I was in uniform in the hospital! I didn't know any Chinese." Eventually it was arranged for the Sisters at the hospital to receive one hour of private tutoring a day in the Shanghai dialect to facilitate conversations with the nurses and patients.[37]

Sisters not assigned to teaching positions or to the Shanghai hospital were supposed to spend regular time in language study. At first they stayed at the convent, learning the local dialect from a language teacher. Emphasis was on the spoken language, and the vocabulary learned was that of the local inhabitants concerning religion, crops, weather, the family, and homemaking. Readings in English about Chinese culture and customs were also an integral part of the language training. Sister Mary Paul McKenna set up a central library in Hong Kong to provide the Sisters in South China with books on almost any Chinese topic. After they gained some knowledge of the religious vocabulary, they were assigned to a specific job, usually at the parish catechumenate, dispensary, orphanage, or novitiate.[38] Sister Teresa (Claudia) Hollfelder remembered her arrival in Yeungkong with Sister Mary Dolorosa Oberle in early 1931:

> After about a week, the Mandarin's daughter came to teach us Cantonese. We studied individually for about one hour each morning, then studied the rest of the morning. In the afternoon we were supposed to practice what we had learned in the morning. For instance, I tried to use Chinese in the sacristy [sic] and the other Sister tried hers on the cook. We also had a home for blind children and one for old folks. We used to go over to talk with them and practice our Chinese. We studied that way for about ten months.[39]

Help in learning Chinese was sought not only in books and teachers, but also through prayers. In 1923, when Sancian Island was included in the Maryknoll territory in South China, Sister Marie (Mary Magdalen) Doelger conceived the idea of a pilgrimage to the site of Francis Xavier's death for the purpose of begging the saint's help in learning the Chinese language. A group of Maryknoll Fathers and Sisters joined together in that pilgrimage to present "their plea to God through the intercession of St. Francis Xavier that more souls might be reached through greater facility in the language of the people of their adopted land."[40]

The Language Schools of the Sisters
in South China

The first language school for Maryknoll Sisters assigned to South China opened at Tungshek in Kaying prefecture in 1934 with the arrival of a group of Sisters selected to work in the direct apostolate. Sister Mary Imelda Sheridan, the youngest member of the original 1921 group of Sisters, had 13 years of experience with the Chinese in Hong Kong. She was fluent in Cantonese and had a good knowledge of Chinese characters. With this background, she did not find the transition to Hakka too difficult. Because Monsignor Ford had never found time to learn to speak Hakka well himself, he was determined to provide the Sisters with a definite plan of study of the language, history, traditions, mores, and mentality of the Chinese people and especially of the Hakka women. In planning the program, Ford and Sister Mary Imelda utilized all the guides and methods devised by other Maryknollers and designed a five-year Hakka program.

The first year the Sisters did nothing but study the language with the help of language teachers who did not speak English. Ford insisted that the students' task was to learn to speak, read, and write Hakka. "We had to study five hours a day which became tedious after a while but there was always the history of the Chinese people or the history of the Catholic Church in China to change off to."[41]

Following this year, the Sisters received their assignments to a mission station to help an experienced Sister. They were still required to study two hours a day, one hour with a teacher and one hour alone. A system of study slips ensured that they kept track of how many hours they studied as well as interruptions in study time, the cause of the interruptions, and the made-up study time. Six months of the third year were devoted to a tertianship, or period of spiritual renewal, as well as further concentrated study at the language school. Another interval of mission work was followed by a second tertianship, which completed the five-year cycle of training. The Sisters could graduate only if they had passed all the courses, otherwise they had to continue their study.[42]

This program taught the Sisters to read and write Chinese and to adapt their spoken Hakka to various levels of the society, making it possible for them to do Scripture reading and to explain the catechism. It gave them some acquaintance with primary and secondary school textbooks, and provided an introduction to Chinese classical literature and to the intricate study of Chinese character writing and newspaper reading.

In the beginning, Father Drought's language book, *Introduction to Hakka*, was used as the basic text. To familiarize themselves with the vocabulary used in direct evangelization and catechumenates, they studied the religious course, *Jesus and I*, published by Bishop Auguste Haouisée of Shanghai; the large charts and posters accompanying the text appealed to the rural people. But it was Sister Anna Mary Moss who enabled the Sisters to preach the doctrine in the *t'u t'am*, the "earth" language. Between 1935 and 1940, with the help of a Chinese catechist, she wrote a series of 24 booklets in the colloquial language. Through simple stories taken from local life, these booklets presented everything a person needed to know for baptism. The series became an important element of the study program at the language school.[43]

A second language school opened in Hong Kong in 1938 for Sisters assigned to the three other Maryknoll territories in South China. Both Mandarin and Cantonese were taught under the direction of Father O'Melia following the same methods he used at the Fathers' language school.[44] Occupation by the Japanese in December 1941 brought this experiment to an end. When new Sisters arrived again in 1946, those assigned to Hong Kong usually studied for one year with a private tutor. Those assigned to Kongmoon and Wuchow were sent for one year to the Wuchow native novitiate, where Sister Rosalia Kettl designed a five-year program closely modeled on the one of Kaying.

After studying O'Melia's *First-Year Cantonese* extensively for one year with a private teacher, the Sisters in South China were assigned to a specific mission work; nonetheless, they were expected to complete the program successfully, no matter how long it took. To graduate, the Sisters had to study the equivalent of six grades of Chinese primary school and had to be able to speak, read, and write Chinese. None of the young Sisters was able to complete her language study before the Communists arrived in Wuchow and Kongmoon. Seven years after she began in Wuchow in 1947, Sister Mary Louise Martin became the first Sister to complete the entire five-year program. She recalled with humor that in order to graduate she had to be excused for 80 hours of study that her record slips showed she had missed.[45]

The Sisters' Language Program in Fushun

In 1929 the first five Maryknoll Sisters arrived in the Fushun mission territory and settled in the city of Dairen. Sister Mary Gemma Shea and Sister Juliana Bedier were assigned to the Japanese parish with Father Leo Tibesar. Sister Mary Gemma had previously worked in the Japanese mission in Seattle and had studied Japanese for one year in Tokyo. She found private tutors to teach herself and Sister Juliana. Since there were more Maryknoll Sisters assigned to work with the Chinese than with the Japanese, there was no attempt to set up a formal study course for the few Sisters assigned to Japanese parishes; instead they received their language training from lay tutors. Meanwhile Sister Mary Eunice Tolan, the Sister superior in Manchuria, hired Mandarin-speaking tutors to teach Chinese to her and Sisters Mary Angelica O'Leary and Mary Coronata Sheehan. They used Reverend Whiteright's textbook.[46]

In the fall of 1933 the Maryknoll Sisters' Mandarin language school opened at the center house in Fushun city, using the same course as the

Fathers. Sister Mary Angelica O'Leary played an important role at the language school by assisting the teacher, Mr. Hsü, with instruction and with translating his course into English. After one year of intensive study, the Sisters were assigned to work in parishes or at the native novitiate, but they were still supposed to study two to four hours a day until they completed the program.[47]

Familiarity of Maryknollers with the Language

When Sister Rita Clare Comber stated that "language study was both the most difficult and the most rewarding," she spoke for most missioners.[48] Language was a difficult obstacle to overcome. Maryknollers, in general, studied hard and became fairly competent in the spoken language, but sometimes only a slight variation in accent or dialect made it impossible to understand the people. "In Yeungkong, for example," explained Father James Smith, "the people spoke a different dialect than the Cantonese I had studied. So much so that in the beginning I couldn't understand a word they said."[49]

The more Maryknollers were in contact with the people, the more fluent they became. For instance, the Sisters involved in the direct apostolate spoke better Chinese than those working in orphanages or dispensaries. Recalling her experience in the small rural parish of Szwong in Wuchow, Sister Mary (John Karen) Diggins said: "We had nobody, but nobody who spoke English. . . . The fact that we had complete daily dealings with the Chinese, that's what forced us to learn."[50]

Similarly, priests who continued to rely on their catechists as intermediaries even after their first year or two in China seem to have never mastered the language. Sister Mary Diggins humorously remembered a near tragic event which illustrates some Maryknollers' limited knowledge of Chinese. One day during the distribution of communion, the cloth on the altar caught fire. The people were trying to tell the priest and he "was so ignorant of Chinese that he didn't know what they were talking about. . . . He kept smiling sweetly at them but he didn't know that his whole background was just blazing away!"[51]

Maryknollers who could communicate well with the people were the ones who most regretted their inadequacies in the language; they would have liked a better foundation with good books and good teachers. Those who never learned Chinese well seemed to have accepted that limitation as a fact of life, resigned to be marginal people in China for the rest of their lives. According to the testimonies of Chinese Catholics, few Maryknollers could carry on a conversation with officials or intellectuals. The American Catholic missioners' vocabulary was geared to the local people, and their reading and writing ability were limited.[52]

With the development of language schools, Maryknoll had certainly made a beginning in providing its missioners with a solid foundation in speaking, writing, and reading Chinese. Too much, however, seemed to have been left up to the individual after his or her initial nine months at the language school. Inertia, as well as too much apostolic zeal, often prevented Maryknollers from gaining any more than limited skills in the spoken local dialect. Sister Joan Ling of Kweilin remarked:

> [Rural] people did not use very difficult language. They only discussed simple things about their life. . . . I remember the Bishop preaching when he came to give Confirmation. "Your faith has to be as solid as the mountain." He used a lot of gestures to describe the mountain so that we understood. We all accepted it was the foreigner speaking Chinese. We would not expect too much.[53]

The five-year program adopted by the Sisters in Kaying and Wuchow with its system of checks, reviews, and refresher courses was closest to an ideal course. It deepened and broadened the language of the missioners as they became closer to the Chinese people and grew more attuned to their way of life.

Chinese were usually polite with the missioners. The less familiar they were with Maryknollers, the more they congratulated them on their mastery of the language. Missioners knew enough of their inadequacies not to take such compliments seriously. When they encountered a sure sign that they had crossed the language barrier and could pass as Chinese, it always brought them great joy even in the most frightful circumstances. No better compliment could have been given to Father Maynard Murphy than that of a robber who almost took his life. "He said in Hakka to the robber, 'I am from America.' That robber didn't believe him because he was wearing the Chinese long gown and speaking Hakka."[54]

In another instance, Father Murphy went to the post office and asked for the parish mail. The postmaster was busy at the time, facing away from the priest. Murphy's accent was so good that he was mistaken for one of the catechists and told rather rudely: "We're busy and we have not gotten around to setting your mail aside yet. When we get ready, we'll give it to you." The postmaster then turned around and, seeing Father Murphy, apologized profusely; but the priest smiled broadly and insisted that no offense had been taken.[55]

When Maryknollers worked with individual tutors, their progress was often hindered by the reluctance of their Chinese teachers to point out errors openly for fear that the foreigner would "lose face." Language schools helped to alleviate the problem in many ways. On the one hand, classes in culture helped Maryknollers to interpret nonverbal communications and to appreciate the value of Chinese courtesy and politeness; on the other hand, Chinese teachers were specifically trained to point out mistakes as frankly as possible.

Closeness to People

Armed with their often imperfect knowledge of the language, Maryknollers opened the doors of their rectories and convents, reached into the villages, and grew closer to the Chinese. This assertion is often repeated in the interviews with Maryknollers:

> You really lived with the people; you were with them constantly. . . . You were just part of the people; part of their lives. . . . [When I was expelled by the Communists] it was the first time anybody cried over me except for my own family.[56]

Even the Chinese interviewed stressed this closeness to the people as typical of Maryknollers at that time. Sister Joan Ling recalled Father Joseph Regan in particular as being one with the Chinese Catholics; she added with a touch of melancholy, "The priests were able to do so in those days. Our priests today cannot."[57]

Out of this life-sharing, the fiery zeal for souls of many young missioners matured into a personal identification with the Chinese people.

> All of us, we loved the people and that came through regardless of personalities. When the Chinese people had trouble, we had troubles. When they needed us, we were there. . . . We laughed together and we did things together [with them]. As much as we could, we lived just as they did.[58]

With sadness in their voices, Maryknollers expelled from China told how the country had become their home. Father Sylvio Gilbert said:

> I loved the Chinese to the nth degree. I was so relaxed with them—this was my home. I felt I could do anything with them. They allowed me to get to them because they knew I was with them one hundred percent.[59]

However imperfect in speech or manner the missionary priests and Sisters might have been, however different their lifestyle appeared to the Chinese, this closeness to the people and display of love and understanding were the decisive factors which gained them acceptance. Michael Tsa remembered how Brother Anthony Boyd, in spite of his broken Chinese, had gained the friendship of many students of the Kaying Tung San Public

Middle School by sharing in their activities.[60]

Father Peter Reilly described how the adjustment of missioners was a long process of shedding their own Western culture and accepting all facets of Chinese culture.

> *Culture*, this word cannot be minimized. A missioner was rejected or accepted on his score of adjustment. Language, accepting *their* way of doing things, eating, speaking, arguing, discussing. Even the place where one slept was part of the culture that had or should be accepted. I note this because often one was forced to sleep with the communal pee-ary in the corner. Often people visited it at night and stirred up the contents, thus causing a most sickening odor, for the small barrel was not removed until filled and then used for fertilizer. . . .
>
> Much of our time was spent in villages, visiting Catholic homes, celebrating Mass, conferring the sacraments. One got the feeling of being very close to the people, to the land and quite removed from Western ideas and practices. One either had to adjust to the culture, become part of it or it became part of him, or else he would remain stagnant in the mission, passing his time in despair or waste. It did happen.
>
> There was a special thrill in missionary trips. . . . One ate what they did and as they did. Boat trips were practices in communal living and for me, it was thrilling. A learning process for invariably the twenty-odd passengers asked questions about the U.S., the Church, about Protestantism and the celibate life. It reminded me of the early apostles going about preaching the Gospel. It was one of the most convincing acts of the missionary vocation which made it so different from the ordinary parochial priest or priestly administrator. . . .
>
> My day-to-day life in China, my close association and life amongst a strictly Chinese culture and environment opened my eyes to the natural good and natural virtue of the Chinese race. . . . It took years to learn and it took years to be fully accepted to the extent that one felt a union with the people in thought and sensitivities and feeling and ideas.[61]

As the missioners came to identify more fully with the Chinese, they grew to respect the differences between themselves and the Chinese. They came to realize that they would never be able "to reach the core of Chinese thinking" and that only a Chinese Church could do so.[62] The Chinese fully agreed. In the words of a Chinese Sister, "No matter how much they understood, they would not completely understand."[63]

The degree of adjustment varied from one missioner to another; a small minority failed to adjust. Some Maryknollers disliked life in China and left after only a few months. Among those who stayed, a few turned into chronic complainers, a few took refuge in hobbies, a few indulged in drinking. Maryknollers who did not show personal interest in the lives of the people or who avoided involvement with the people on an individual basis were never accepted and remained isolated and lonely.[64]

Perhaps a remark of Sister Mary Gemma Shea best summarizes the fundamental personal attitude necessary for a successful integration in another culture. "I have only one degree—an M.A.—but it only means 'master of adjustment.' Ever since I came to Maryknoll, I had to adjust, adjust, adjust, but I never minded it."[65]

Adaptation of the Message

Architecture

As the Chinese people grew to know Maryknollers, they formed a positive or negative opinion of the Catholic Church by observing the lifestyle of the missioners, their mastery of the language, and their understanding of the culture. Yet often the first contact the Chinese had with Christianity was with its buildings. Was Maryknoll aware of the message conveyed by its convents, rectories, and churches? Did Maryknollers try to develop a form of Christian architecture which would appeal to the Chinese?

The Chinese appearance of Maryknoll's first construction in 1919, the major seminary on Sunset Hill in New York, is most significant. From the beginning, the Maryknoll leadership realized that architecture was a way to address people: the Chinese roof and lines were intended to tell Americans about the Church's concern and care for Oriental people. In the same way, Maryknollers sent to China viewed architecture as a means of telling the Chinese that the Catholic Church belonged to them. As early as 1920, responding to a letter of Father James E. Walsh who was making long-range building plans, Father James A. Walsh noted with enthusiasm, "I am particularly pleased that there will be a pronounced Chinese touch of architecture. . . . Let the arrangements of the building be European, but for architectural points of view, Chinese as far as possible."[66]

In April 1923, when James E. Walsh was about to embark on his construction program, the apostolic delegate, Archbishop Celso Costantini, confirmed the Church's commitment to foster Chinese Christian architecture. In a letter addressed to Walsh and to Father Edward J. Galvin, superior of the Columban Fathers in China, Costantini urged American and Irish missioners to support the pope in his drive to develop native Christian art and architecture. He pointed to the Roman and Gothic churches erected in China as strange forms not understood by the people because they were not an expression of their artistic and cultural patrimony. Most of all, for many Chinese they were a visible symbol that the Catholic religion was "a foreign importation." To root the Church in China required not only that the missioners become as Chi-

Fig. 2. The Maryknoll seminary in Ossining, New York. Maryknoll Photo Library.

nese as possible, but also that religious buildings take on a Chinese appearance.[67]

Chapels and churches built by Maryknoll in South China. The delegate's instructions were taken "as a command."[68] Maryknollers immediately tackled the problem of adapting Chinese architecture to church building. In September 1924 Father Robert Cairns, the pastor of Fachow in southwest Kwangtung, was busy setting up a temporary chapel. He specifically mentioned how he had followed Costantini's instructions:

When we came to building the new altar, I called a committee of prominent

Chinese and had them design it. Now we have a finished altar in many colors, including purple, gold, yellow and brown, bronze and cerise. To our fair eyes, the many hues are not pleasing, but to the almond eyes of the Chinese, the glare of color is gorgeous. We are here to convert them so our ideas must be kept in the background.[69]

From the beginning, Brother Albert Staubli was the person who was most effective in fostering Chinese architecture. Although not an architect by profession, the Swiss-born Brother was a talented sculptor and an accomplished builder with a deep appreciation for Chinese culture. His first work of substance was to restore the church at Sunchong which had fallen prey to bad weather and white ants. The new roof, altar, and interior decoration gave the chapel a Chinese appearance.

The one-storey chapel is distinctively Chinese in architecture with its curved roof cornices, and new tiles gleaming in the sun. . . . [Inside] wooden signs hanging between windows and doors tell in Chinese characters of the Trinity, of Christ, and of his Blessed Mother. The two large pentagonal lamps at either side of the main altar are Chinese and the sanctuary lamp, also. . . . The large Chinese banner hanging above the sanctuary proclaims to the world that God is here. . . . The main altar is the jewel of the entire building. It is supported by four pillars, and the back is solid teakwood. Upon the altar itself, at the rear, are three canopies, covered by Chinese roofs, and the alternating strips of white tea wood and the darker teak, with the upward curves at every corner, makes these canopies peculiarly Chinese, and different from anything you have ever seen before. Under the large canopy at the centre is the hand-carved tabernacle, upon which stands a bronze crucifix, mounted upon light-colored tea wood. Under the side canopies are two hanging signs of light colors, with the Chinese characters carved, and painted red. The three canopies blend into an artistic whole, and taper toward the centre, which has a series of Chinese roofs, at the apex of which is a cross.[70]

According to James E. Walsh, the main problem encountered by Brother Albert was in decorating the chapel:

No Chinese mason or artist can do anything but dragons, bats, and the other superstitious things he has been taught. You should see the angel our man drew! We will have to take some Christians and teach them to draw Chinese angels.[71]

Brother Albert's first efforts received "the delegate's hearty commendation" when Costantini stopped in Kongmoon in 1927 on his return from Rome where he had attended the consecration of the six Chinese bishops. Encouraged by this sign of approval, Staubli continued to build chapels,

Figs. 3 and 4. The altar in the Sunchong Chapel designed by Brother Albert Staubli. 1926. Maryknoll Photo Library.

convents, and other church buildings in the Kongmoon and Wuchow territories. Not all new buildings, however, blended into the Chinese landscape or had shapes which appealed to the Chinese. Father Francis MacRae remembered the chapel he built in the village of Taiwan in the mountains west of Wuchow:

> [It was] nothing like the Chinese of the countryside had ever seen. The spire was very high and the people were afraid that it was going to bring down the disapproval of the devil on them. . . . Father Meyer had the plans drawn up and I don't think it blended with the surroundings . . . , it was just a big, flat building, no lines or anything like that. . . .[72]

Father MacRae pointed out that the main reason for avoiding Chinese architecture in these difficult-to-reach parts of China was to keep down costs and to minimize the impression that the missioners had plenty of money. Building with baked bricks rather than mud bricks provided a lasting structure and gave much face to the Church; he added, though, that fancy sloping roofs with colored tiles would have sealed the reputation of the Church as a "rich enterprise."[73]

The real difficulty, however, was not so much with small chapels. As Father Francis Ford noted, they generally blended well with the local surroundings because the French missioners had given free rein to local Chinese builders.

> At Yeungkong, and it is true everywhere, most of our village chapels are Chinese in style, simply because they were built for small congregations by local masons and the line of least resistance, if for no other reason, would naturally impel us to let the native mason plan his own way. But larger churches are a different problem.[74]

The real difficulty, Ford added, was adapting Chinese temple architecture to the needs of larger Christian congregations.

> There is no difficulty with roof or sanctuary. It is the nave which is lacking; in temples, an enclosed unroofed court is substituted. For a Catholic congregation, this must be roofed but that would exclude light and air and rob the building of a characteristic feature. Much of Chinese worship is done out of doors at roadside shrines and pagodas on the hills, so Chinese temples with the open courtyards have preserved much of the freedom of outdoor worship.[75]

Because of the rural setting and the small percentage of Christians in the population, Maryknoll did not have to contemplate building many large churches. Even the churches which served as cathedrals in the Kongmoon and Wuchow vicariates and in the Kweilin prefecture were small, with low lines and a Chinese exterior which blended with the surroundings. The Chinese cathedral in Pakkai and the church in Loting, both built by Brother Albert, were among the more successful adaptations of Chinese temple architecture to church buildings. The entrance was placed on the short axis of the building so that on approaching, one saw the sweep of the roof rather than a built-up facade.

In 1940 Bishop Ford began to plan a cathedral for Kaying that expressed Chinese artistic taste. Earlier, he had decided to move from a rented makeshift chapel to a real church only when the Catholics themselves had contributed sufficient funds to build it. When the time finally came, Ford carefully weighed every detail with the help of his Chinese friend and architect, K. S. Kit. The church was not to tower over the city. Built on a long stretch of the river, it was to be seen by anyone traveling by boat. All the material would be local: sand, lime, and clay for the structure; granite for the altar; trees for the pews; baked tiles for the roof. As far as possible, the cathedral would be built by local Christian workers and artisans.

Ford also wanted to erect a recognizable landmark for his Chinese Catholic community. Since Chinese architectural principles did not permit a steeple on the church, Ford built a seven-tiered pagoda next to it and crowned it with a cross. He had a plan for each story; one would house a water storage tank, another would contain a generator, and the highest level would receive the cathedral bell. This pagoda was perhaps the bishop's stroke of genius in adaptation. Architecturally, he had erected a structure liked by the Chinese and regarded as an essential element of the landscape. Practically, he had established a highly visible Christian landmark, comparable to a steeple. How Chinese the cathedral would have been remains an unanswered question because the building was never completed; however, the pagoda still overlooks Meihsien City (Kaying).[76]

Chapels and churches in the Fushun territory. In 1926 in faraway Manchuria, Father Raymond Lane began to plan the building of church compounds, one in Dairen for the Japanese community, and the second in Fushun as a center for the future vicariate. His first idea was to build in Oriental style. For that purpose he entrusted the design of the buildings to Joseph Oka, a Japanese Catholic, chief architect for the South Manchurian Railways, and president of its Technical College. Contrary to Lane's expectations, Oka drew plans which showed only a slight Oriental touch. When Father James A. Walsh and Mother Mary Joseph reviewed the drawings in New York, they were equally dismayed by "the idea of erecting a purely Gothic church in what should be an Oriental background."[77]

Fig. 5. The Kongmoon cathedral in Pakkai opened on June 29, 1929. Maryknoll Photo Library.

Fig. 6. The Loting church opened on Pentecost Sunday, 1928. Maryknoll Photo Library.

The plans were sent back to Fushun and were redrawn, but, curiously enough, the Japanese officials in charge of building permits rejected most changes suggesting Oriental architecture. Lane, who wanted to build, had no alternative but to comply. Of the buildings eventually erected in Fushun city, only the cathedral was allowed to assume a Chinese look. Nonetheless, the central house, which had minimal Oriental

Fig. 7. Bishop Ford's pagoda in Kaying, designed to serve as a power house and water tank as well as a landmark. Maryknoll Photo Library.

touches, was commended in *The Field Afar* in 1932:

> The Central House erected by Fr. Lane won him a niche in the Manchu hall of fame. . . . The architect, Mr. Oka . . . most successfully combined utility, comfort and fireproof construction with a graceful and striking Oriental design. . . .[78]

The Star of the Sea church in Dairen was given such a Gothic appearance that in the photograph on page 291 the two men dressed in long Chinese gowns are the only clue that the church bordered the streets of Dairen and not a North American or European city.[79] This time there was definitely nothing Oriental in the design that *The Field Afar* could praise, so the church was simply described as "pleasing to the eye and 'devotional.'"[80]

Mr. Oka told Maryknollers in Manchuria that building in an Oriental style was not necessarily always the best way. In many cities of China and Japan, educated people who had come to appreciate Western art and architecture were probably more impressed with a beautiful Western-style church than with a pale imitation of a Chinese temple. This was true, Oka argued, in the case of the Japanese community in Dairen:

> The Buddhists in Dairen have just built a one million dollar temple. In erecting our inexpensive church in Oriental style, we place ourselves in competition with them and we may be laughed out of town. My plans will be in Tudor Gothic style which the Japanese have not seen before and will find very interesting.[81]

Father Leo Tibesar, pastor of the Dairen Star of the Sea parish recalled that indeed Mr. Oka was right. Japanese were attracted to the church which became the home of "one of the best parishes of Japanese Catholics in the world."[82]

Other edifices erected by Maryknoll. For buildings other than churches and chapels, Maryknollers' attempts to combine Western convenience and facilities with Oriental architecture had uneven results. Most edifices ended up as square or rectangular structures of two or three stories, completely devoid of the grace of Oriental architecture. In an article for the May 1927 issue of *The Field Afar*, Father Philip Taggart made fun of the attempts of missioners to imitate Oriental art by constructing:

> ... serviceable monstrosities best described as a cross between a Chinese-temple and a railroad station. ... Up to the present the least the foreigners have been able to do is to erect foreign buildings with a little Chinese headgear on top.[83]

The Kongmoon seminary building pictured on page 292, which later became the home of the native novitiate, certainly fit that description. And yet, next to it, a large gate in the wall surrounding the property was unmistakably Oriental. By contrast, the Kaying seminary was perhaps one of the best attempts by a Maryknoller to adapt Chinese architecture. The Kaying seminary was built to resemble the Venard Preparatory Seminary of Maryknoll at Clarks Summit, Pennsylvania. The resemblance between the two buildings shown on pages 293 and 294 is unmistakable, if we take into consideration that the chapel of the Venard was not erected until

290

Fig. 8. The Fushun cathedral opened December 3, 1932. Maryknoll Photo Library.

Fig. 9. The Fushun center house opened in spring 1928. Maryknoll Photo Library.

Fig. 10. The Star of the Sea Parish church in Dairen, Manchuria, opened on June 24, 1928. Maryknoll Photo Library.

Fig. 11. The Kongmoon seminary opened in September 1926, with a view of the gate and the wall surrounding the Pakkai mission center. Maryknoll Photo Library.

1930. The differences are also striking. The Venard is massive, towering over the countryside. The Kaying seminary has a distinctly airy look—its first floor arcades extend beyond the building into a cool, quiet covered gallery. This gallery supports a large balcony which surrounds the second floor, creating a feeling of light and spaciousness. To keep the building from dominating the landscape, the entire third floor was eliminated and the tower shortened.

The styles of the towers of the Venard and Kaying are also strikingly different. That of the Venard resembles a medieval belfry while the Kaying tower has the look of a Chinese garden pavilion. In 1929 Ford looked at his attempt at Chinese architecture and wrote with satisfaction:

> The building is still in the rough ... but it seems to fit into the bamboo background; and viewed at a distance with the Hakka hills behind it, its mottled colors melt into the scene. It is a greenish brown in color and will darken more with the climate.[84]

When Monsignor Bernard Meyer opened his seminary in Tanchuk in 1934, he opted for a structure which was similar to Ford's building.

Other buildings, such as the Loting orphanage, had a definite Chinese

Fig. 12. The Kaying seminary in 1929. Maryknoll Photo Library.

Fig. 13. The Venard Apostolic School in Clarks Summit, Pennsylvania in 1966. Maryknoll Photo Library.

style, but perhaps the most appealing example of Chinese architecture built by Maryknollers was the rectory of Tungon in the vicariate of Kongmoon. Father Otto Rauschenbach's graceful edifice was set against a breathtaking background of rugged peaks called the Marbled Mountains.

Throughout China, many cities, large villages, and big estates were protected by tall walls which allowed outsiders to enter only through a few well-guarded gates. Government offices and private homes of important civil servants, well-to-do landowners, and merchants also enjoyed the protection and seclusion of their own walls and gates. In the countryside the main purpose of this type of structure was to defend the inhabitants against attacks of bandit groups, rival clans, or robbers. Most villages, however, could not afford a system of walls and gates, and villagers lived in unprotected mud-brick houses.

Mission compounds, on the contrary, including those of Maryknoll, were usually walled. Since only rich landowners and government officials could afford the privacy and luxury of such structures, the non-Christian population assumed the Catholic Church was rich. Father Simeon To described the impressions of people in his little village of Pantien in Kweilin prefecture:

Fig. 14. The Tungon rectory opened in 1930. Maryknoll Photo Library.

> The Church had a very big surrounding area and surrounding walls. Inside there were several houses: the priests' residence, the church, and others. From outside, it looked like a garden with trees called Nine Mile Fragrance planted all along the path. So from the point of view of many people, the life of the priests was first class. They were like the rich.[85]

In times of danger, the population appreciated the protection of the mission compound; but in ordinary times, the villagers were suspicious and not inclined to enter. Walls were capped with broken glass, and gates were securely locked at night. Some compounds even had ferocious-looking German shepherds that chased passers-by and sometimes bit them. Dogs and walls were not a welcoming sight and may have increased the sense of loneliness which afflicted many missioners.[86]

The Spoken and Written Word

Following the printing of the first catechism in Chinese by Jesuit Father Michele Ruggieri in 1584, missioners and Chinese priests published many other materials on the tenets and practices of Catholic doctrine. The First Plenary Council of China in 1924 unanimously passed a resolution to adopt a single nationwide Chinese catechism to replace the over one hundred types of catechisms already in circulation.[87] Acting on the resolution, the apostolic delegate Costantini appointed a special commission in 1928 to write the official catechism. The traditional series of questions and answers was published in 1934 under the simple title of *Catechism* (*Yao-li wen-ta*). Out of 377 questions in the standard edition, 87 were taken to form a simpler version for children and illiterate adults (*Chien-yen yao-li*). Each catechism was divided into four sections: Tenets of the Catholic Faith, Commandments, Grace and the Sacraments, and Prayer Life and Religious Celebrations. To facilitate memorization, every answer was concise and factual. For example, the first three questions-and-answers were as follows:

1. Why are you in this world?
   —We are in this world to worship God and to save our souls.
2. Do you believe in God?
   —I believe in God.
3. Who is God?
   —God is the creator and true Lord of heaven and earth, of the angels, of men, and of all things.[88]

How much the candidates really knew and understood depended largely on the quality of the explanations given by missioners and catechists.

Although it is impossible today to examine the oral presentation of Mary-knollers, the materials they used show instances of significant adaptations of the Christian message to the Chinese people.

Bishop Walsh's catechism in colloquial Cantonese. The official catechism was written in vernacular Mandarin, the official daily language of the Chinese. Everybody with a few years of schooling could read and understand it. However, for those people who did not speak Mandarin, the sentence structure and the words of the catechism pronounced in their dialect were often odd or even incomprehensible. Bishop James E. Walsh was aware of the problem for Cantonese-speaking people who used sentence patterns different from those found in modern Mandarin. He concentrated his efforts on adapting the simplified version of the official catechism to the colloquial Cantonese spoken widely in the Kongmoon vicariate. His Cantonese catechism, entitled *Uêt-ŭe kaán-in iù-lei*, was published in 1937.[89]

Monsignor Meyer's catechetical approach. Meanwhile in Wuchow, Monsignor Meyer had already sought a catechism which his catechumens could understand. In one of his bi-monthly circulars addressed to his clergy in 1930, Meyer had strongly advised against buying catechisms and prayer manuals from the Catholic publishing houses in Shanghai or Peking because the books were written in a language which was difficult for the Cantonese-speaking farmers of Kwangsi to understand. On the contrary, he had recommended as more "suitable" some of the catechetical materials printed by the M.E.P. in Hong Kong or Nanning.[90]

Still not entirely satisfied with the M.E.P. publications, Meyer, with the help of Father Mark Tennien, started to develop his own catechetical materials. By December 1930, they had published, in colloquial Cantonese with romanization, two books of apologetics, a book of sermons, a guide to preaching, and a book of Old Testament Stories. In preparation were a book of New Testament Stories and the Gospels for Sundays and holidays. A simplified catechism for the use of children and converts in Wuchow prefecture was published in August 1931, but unfortunately no copy has been preserved.[91]

Like most catechisms printed in China, Meyer's 1931 catechism had no illustrations. To enhance instruction, missioners occasionally used large posters printed in Europe because catechisms in general were dull little study books. Prior to 1928, the only illustrated catechism seems to have been the *Yao-li hsiang-chieh* published by a Chinese priest, Father Peter Tcheng of the vicariate of Paotingfu. It was a translation of the text with black and white reproductions of 70 illustrations from a French catechism published by *La Bonne Presse* in Paris. Neither the text nor the pictures made any reference to the Chinese way of life or cultural heritage.[92]

In late 1928, a Scheut missioner, Father Leo Van Dyk, designed the first

298

Fig. 15. Outdoor catechism class in Shumkai, Wuchow, 1948. The posters used by both catechists belong to the Van Dyk series. The poster against the wall appears in the next illustration. Maryknoll Photo Library.

Chinese catechism with color illustrations, *Wen-ta hsiang-chieh*. The 40 illustrations, also available in 30x22 inch posters, were widely used as teaching aids. The characters in the pictures looked somewhat stiff, but each illustration as a whole was pleasing to the eye and depicted the Catholic religion as part of the Chinese way of life. For the first time, most posters showed representations of Chinese people in their daily activities and of Chinese Catholics at worship. Even in the few illustrations which depicted scenes and characters from the Old and New Testaments, Van Dyk managed to create a Chinese flavor by setting the foreign landscape and people against a background of delicate Chinese decorations.[92]

Using Van Dyk's materials, Meyer was impressed by the success of this use of illustrations not only with children but also with adults. He conceived the idea of combining the effectiveness of drawings with some recently developed teaching techniques he had been testing.[94] His publication of an illustrated catechetical series entitled *Our Holy Religion (Ngŏh-moŏn-tik Shing-kaaù)* was a giant step in adapting the Catholic Church to China.

The first course in Meyer's series appeared in 1937 and was intended for children in lower grade school. It was comprised of a student study book and a teacher's manual. The purpose of the pictures in this catechism was to remind children of the explanations given during class as well as to illustrate some of the stories told by the missioner or catechist. Pictures were drawn in such a way that they could be colored with crayons at the end of the lesson.[95]

In this first edition of his children's catechism, Meyer closely followed Van Dyk's model. Scenes from the Old and New Testaments represented traditional Western people and backgrounds. Scenes from daily life represented Chinese people and scenery, but the attempt was inept and the drawings more Western than Chinese in style. All priests were depicted as foreigners.

The second edition in 1939 brought a drastic change. Every detail was Chinese, from the landscape and the buildings to the people themselves. In a marked contrast with the first edition and Van Dyk's posters, God the Father, his surrounding angels, Jesus, Mary, the Apostles, and the priests had all taken on a Chinese appearance. In a short history of the Church added to the second edition, individuals such as the Emperor Constantine, Saint Jerome, and Copernicus were also sinicized.

By comparison, other catechisms developed by missioners before World War II did not show a similar effort at adaptation. For instance, the pictures in the illustrated version of a new Chinese catechism published by the Salesians of Hong Kong in 1939 were, on the whole, no different from those found some decades earlier in the catechisms of France and Italy. Most of the illustrations were black and white reprints of European reli-

Fig. 16. An illustration from Van Dyk's catechism (1928) of the Church's teaching on the Third Commandment. (Translation of top line: Obligations on Sundays and holy days for the worship of God. Bottom line: Listen to the Doctrine, read spiritual books, pray, meditate, and do other things beneficial for your soul or the soul of other people.)

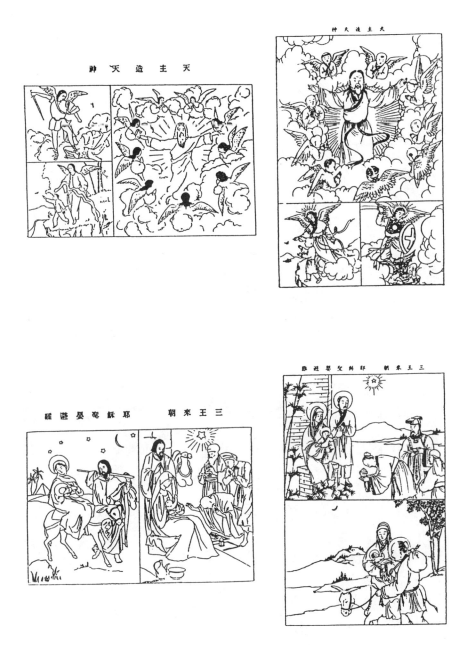

Fig. 17. Drawings of the angels and the nativity from Meyer's *Our Holy Religion*, 1937 and 1939 editions. Note the Chinese imagery of the later edition (right).

婚配宜領聖體

Fig. 18. Illustrations of the nativity and a wedding mass in *Illustrated Catechism* (*Iù leî mân taàp*), first published by the Salesian Fathers in Hong Kong in 1939; the 1951 edition still included the same illustrations.

gious paintings or posters. In rare drawings of daily life, the characters were Chinese but transported into primarily non-Chinese settings.[96]

Meyer's catechism prepared children to receive the sacraments of baptism, reconciliation, the Eucharist and, if necessary, the sacrament of the sick. Meyer used what he called the "St. Francis Xavier method" of instruction, which he explained to his clergy in these terms:

> Perhaps in reading that St. Francis Xavier was followed by the children of the villages as he walked along ringing a little bell, we imagine that he was a kind of Pied Piper who had the power of hypnotizing them. Not at all. But he made his instruction classes most interesting, told stories, set the prayers and catechism to simple airs which the children sang everywhere, and gave little prizes for excellence.[97]

In Meyer's catechism, each lesson began with several questions to direct the attention of the children to a particular topic. A story, usually taken from the Bible, was then told to illustrate the subject. Following a brief explanation of the story, the catechist asked questions to make sure the children had understood the main points. The theme of the lesson was recapitulated in the traditional Chinese way, using eight rhymed verses of three characters each that the children chanted together until they had memorized them. The verses were followed by one question and answer which summarized the whole lesson. At the close, some practical applications of the lesson were elicited from the children and a short prayer was said together. As an example, the catechist would start the first lesson of the catechism, The Creation, by asking the children: Who made their clothes? What material were these clothes made of? Was any person able to create the flax and the cotton which made up the fabric of their clothing? The answer to the last question led to the story of the creation as recounted in the Bible. The catechist then asked questions to make sure that the children understood the story: In the beginning did sky and earth exist? What did God create on the first day, the second day, etc.? The chanted verses followed.

起 初 時　　有 天 主·　造 天 地　　俾 我 住

In the beginning - there was God - Who created Heaven & earth - for us to be

不 勞 力　　料 不 用　　命 令 出　　即 成 功

Without effort - out of nothing - [God] gave an order - and it was done

Fig. 19. Illustrations of Copernicus and St. Jerome from Meyer's Catechism of 1939.

The question-and-answer to be memorized from the official catechism was: "Who is God? God is the creator and true Lord of heaven and earth, of angels, of men, and of all things." The practical application to remember was that God lived in the church and you should go often to worship him. The concluding prayer was "Lord, I believe in you with all my heart. I beg you to increase my faith."[98]

After the lesson, the children were given small prizes of holy pictures, medals, candy, or small amounts of money as a reward for their attendance and diligence. Although Meyer was certainly not the first missioner to use rhymes, the format of his lessons combining a variety of activities seems to have been unique in China at the time.[99]

In 1938, Meyer published two additional courses which were based on the official catechism. Course 2 was intended for ordinary catechumens and students in school. Like the children's catechism, it was comprised of an illustrated study book accompanied by a teacher's manual. Course 3 was intended for people who studied privately. It combined in one book the illustrated study text of Course 2 and a detailed explanation of each lesson.[100]

Meyer's Courses 2 and 3 followed the same "inductive or psychological" approach as that found in the children's catechism. By opening each lesson with a story, he avoided a mere intellectual learning of the catechism and aimed instead at reaching people's hearts. At the same time, the story made the lesson more interesting and helped retention. Like the Shanghai catechism, Meyer's catechism had some of the less important questions marked for omission by the less literate.[101]

Meyer's catechism presented the Catholic faith as a chronological narrative, unfolding the history of salvation from the creation through the main characters and themes of the Old and New Testament to the Catholic Church of the twentieth century. Meyer repositioned the questions of the Shanghai catechism according to this chronological order; as a result, his section on the expansion of the Catholic Church had a sense of continuity and universality absent in the official catechism. Christianity was shown spreading from the Holy Land to the Roman Empire and later to India, China, the Americas, and Africa, each time generating its own clergy. The text, combined with the Chinese style of the drawings, reflected Meyer's aim to try to:

> Remove from Christianity the stigma so widely attached to it in China of being a 'foreign religion.' Hence in addition to arguments showing that it is a universal religion, the missioner should . . . carefully avoid everything that smacks of imposing or advocating Westernization.[102]

Sister Anna Mary Moss' catechetical approach. Prior to the development of the official catechism, Bishop Ford's problems in Kaying were similar to those of Walsh and Meyer. When Ford was assigned to Kaying in 1925, the area was still under the jurisdiction of the bishop of Swatow. The catechism in use—with only minor variations—was the same one used in the vicariates of Hong Kong and Canton. Printed in vernacular Mandarin, it could be read in most dialects of these vicariates by people with some schooling.[103] As already mentioned, however, Mandarin was often unintelligible to uneducated people who spoke a local dialect and could not rely on the written word to grasp the meaning. To circumvent the difficulties, M.E.P. Father Charles Rey had published an *Explication du Catéchisme* in romanized Hakka dialect.[104] Romanization had to be used because many Hakka words and colloquialisms did not exist in Mandarin. Through Rey's pioneer efforts, Ford became conscious of the necessity to reexplain the doctrine in the Hakkas' daily language, the *t'u t'am*, or "earth language." He felt use of the earth language was a priority, especially in the countryside where women with fewer educational opportunities were, in his opinion, the key to the conversion of the Chinese family.

When the Maryknoll Sisters arrived, Ford entrusted them with translating into colloquial Hakka catechetical teaching materials, as well as the daily prayers and mass prayers which were written in very literary Chinese. When the Sisters taught the Hail Mary, it was not sufficient to have the women memorize it in Hakka (*Von-fouc Ma-li-a*); each word had to be explained in the colloquial language.[105]

During catechism classes, the Sisters used a variety of large posters, such as the *Jesus and I* or the Van Dyk series. Sister Rosalia Kettl recognized that in the early years when there were not many women catechists in Kaying, these charts did more to teach the people than the Sisters' explanations in broken Hakka. "[These posters] were very popular and useful to us in explaining the different parts of the catechism. Actually, I think it was through the pictures that the people learned, not our language."[106]

Bishop Ford, well aware of his own inability to speak with the rural people, insisted that the Sisters become fluent in the colloquial language. Sister Mary Paulita Hoffman recalled that Ford used the example of the kitchen to tell them they had to mix with the women and speak their language:

> We are never going to get to these people until we get into their kitchens. The women really have the feel of the sentiment of the children. They instill knowledge into those children—into their hearts. We won't know them until we get into the kitchen. . . . You have to use their examples, you have to use their language, you have to take the concepts of the doctrine and put it into their words. You Sisters have to do it. You are the only ones [who could go into their kitchens].[107]

When the official catechism came out in 1934, Ford readily adopted it as the official text of his vicariate to be memorized by all catechumens. At the same time, he asked Sister Anna Mary Moss, who had had experience in the United States as a catechist, to develop materials in the colloquial language which would parallel the official catechism and to illustrate them with examples from the peoples' daily lives.

With the help of Sister Rosalia and a native catechist, Sister Anna Mary wrote a series of 24 booklets in colloquial Hakka entitled *Preaching the Catholic Doctrine in Plain Language*. Basically the catechetical materials were teacher's handbooks which allowed the Sister or woman catechist to explain the 24 lessons in simple spoken Hakka. The series met with such success among the women in rural Kaying that Sister Rosalia adapted it into Cantonese and Taiwanese after World War II and even recorded it on tape. Each Sister assigned to catechetical work was required to master the series, which continued to be used in Hong Kong and Taiwan through the late 1950s.

Each booklet was a self-contained unit of several teaching sessions which ended with a drill session of the appropriate questions and answers from the official catechism. The doctrine was interspersed with stories and examples to make the lesson as concrete as possible. A Sister in the Kaying vicariate, Sister Mary Paulita Hoffman, recalled:

> The stories in it talked about little Mary and Number Three Girl who went down to the river to wash their clothes; about Number Six Granny who came to water her buffalo. She [Moss] put these stories right into the context of countryside people, and not, you know, he's riding his bicycle down the street. . . .[108]

Even the stories about Jesus or the parables had local settings. Examples of hatred and love, harshness and kindness, jealousy and unselfishness were also put into the context of daily dealings, such as the relationships between a daughter-in-law and a mother-in-law.

The next part consisted of a series of questions to see if the people had understood the applications of the lesson to their daily lives. For instance, questions related to the First Commandment to worship only the one true God asked if Catholics were permitted to believe in dreams, geomancy, fortune-telling, or to consult the eight traditional Chinese diagrams.

The booklets usually contained stories from the lives of saints for use in evening sessions to reinforce what had been said earlier in the day. The section on the supreme commandment to love God and neighbor was illustrated by the examples of St. Martin of Tours who, while still a catechumen, gave half of his coat to a poor man in rags; or St. Francis of Assisi who first ignored a beggar asking for help, but then turned around and gave his whole purse away. The story of St. Dorothy who died on the rack rather than give up her chastity or bow to idols was used to teach the first and sixth commandments and the importance of avoiding sin at all costs.[109]

Sister Mary Paulita Hoffman, who knew Anna Mary Moss well, gave her work much credit: "It was not fancy language but it's [what] people understood. That's why they made such good Catholics."[110]

Adaptation of Christian Practices

The process of accommodating the message, even at its best, was vitiated, however, by the missiology of the time which allowed hardly any departure from a narrow Western understanding of the Catholic faith. Membership in the Church through baptism was considered the surest means to salvation; therefore, baptism had to be made available to as many people as possible. Catechumens had to believe in God, accept Jesus as the only savior, and reject the devil. Moreover, to show their good faith, they had to renounce many beliefs and practices of their native culture as evil and follow instead the practices presented by the missioners.

Missioners were trained to propagate this understanding of Christianity. However, as they grew to understand Chinese culture better, they became less prone to condemn it and more inclined to preserve it. By the second decade of the twentieth century—despite this change of attitude—the mission enterprise was still based on thought patterns reflecting Western philosophy and theology.

Although couched in Chinese language and adorned with some local cultural features, the Catholic message failed to be readily accepted in China because it ran counter to some of the most cherished values of the Chinese. To become Catholics, people had to renounce important practices of their cultural heritage. To what extent did Maryknollers in China understand that Christianity had to be sustained by practices anchored in the people's cultural heritage in order to lose its foreign stigma and gain a strong foothold? In the long run, their emphasis on the development of native clergy and sisterhoods proved their conviction that Chinese priests and Sisters would best know how to make the Church at home in China. In the meanwhile, however, what kind of Christian practices did Maryknollers try to develop or to prevent?

Until the mid-twentieth century, the repeated condemnation by Rome of the Chinese Rites between 1645 and 1742 had been a major impediment to the acceptance of the Catholic Church in China. In the bull *Ex Quo Singulari* of July 11, 1742, Pope Benedict XIV specifically forbade Chinese Catholics to participate in any way in ancestral and Confucian rituals and ceremonies. All missioners assigned to China were required under oath to "carry out without any evasion" the mandate of the bull.[111]

The pope sought to dispel any fear that observance of the bull would hinder the progress of the Church. He reminded missioners that conversions came from divine grace which would not be lacking if they fearlessly preached the Catholic message in its purity and were prepared to shed their blood for it. He certainly did not realize how embedded the rites he had condemned were in the social life of China. Meanwhile, as an answer to Rome's condemnation of the Chinese Rites, the Chinese emperors banned missionaries and the practice of the Christian religion. Another 100 years passed before China, under duress from the West, again permitted the practice of Christianity.

By the time the first Maryknollers arrived, China was undergoing profound changes which made condemnation of the Confucian rites obsolete. The apparatus which assured the continuance of the Confucian cult had disappeared: the Ch'ing dynasty had collapsed, the traditional civil service examinations based on the Confucian classics had been abolished, and the bureaucracy had been dismantled. With the exception of Manchuria (Manchukuo), which restored the official Confucian ceremonies in 1932, Confucianism had lost the appearance of a state cult. It remained a philosophy which emphasized the cultivation of the ancient virtues of propriety, proper conduct, honesty, and integrity.[112]

If Confucianism had lost much of its social influence, ceremonies to honor the ancestors still occupied a central role in the traditional family system. The influence of Western culture and individualistic thinking had not yet reached into the countryside. The term "cult" summarized the judgment of the Catholic Church on these Chinese ceremonies: only God should be worshiped; all other forms of adoration should be rejected as blasphemous and superstitious. Ceremonies in ancestral temples, at home and at graves, which followed a religious ritual were forbidden, and the traditional ancestral tablets had to be destroyed as false idols.

Because the West had long separated religious and nonreligious rituals, Rome failed to understand that in China the same ritual could be religious or nonreligious according to its context or location. In China, a genuflection or a prostration in front of gods were signs of worship; in front of the dead and the ancestral tablets, they became signs of remembrance and family continuity; in front of a living person, they were signs of respect or filial piety. The burning of incense also had different meanings: in front of gods, it was a form of prayer; in front of the tablets, it became a form of filial piety; in the house, it was a way to keep away mosquitoes or to perfume the air.

There is no doubt, however, that in the minds of many Chinese the rituals they performed to Confucius and to the deceased were at least tinged with superstition, but then, by comparison, Christians in the West were also superstitious. Father Thomas Kiernan remembered that in Kwangsi:

> [He] never saw any superstition which was any worse than some of our own. Some of the more educated Chinese used to laugh and say "you don't like us to put food on the graves of our ancestors at the Spring Festival for the dead, but yet you put flowers on the graves of your relatives. Now when do they come up to smell the flowers? So don't expect our ancestors to come up and eat the food. We do it as an idea of sharing. They have shared their life with us and we want to show our continuous gratitude to what we have received from our ancestors."[113]

Most Maryknollers applied Rome's condemnation diligently but without pressuring people. Their eagerness in ridding the catechumens' homes of "idols of old fellows that looked like pirates and had whiskers" contrasted with their patience in having the ancestral tablets removed.[114] Catechumens were usually asked to formally signify their belief in God by renouncing all forms of superstition after studying the First Commandment. The catechist or Sister visited their house to take down and burn statues, images, or pasted prayers linked to Buddhism or local deities, and to replace them with a cross and a holy picture. Since most Chinese peasants were poor, there were not many visible signs of superstition to remove. The main items which ended up in the bonfire were the ancestral tablets and the joss stick bowl. If people refused to comply, Maryknollers usually displayed understanding. Catechists were instructed not to force the issue but simply to inform the catechumens that when they felt ready to take down their tablets, they would be welcomed to baptism.[115]

Besides being forbidden to perform traditional rituals in their homes, the Chinese Catholics were also cut off from many social activities in their villages or towns, like public festivals in honor of Confucius and the deceased. Even in times of grief, such as the death of their parents, Catholics were not allowed to display their filial devotion in the most natural way, by kneeling at the coffin and saying a prayer. The practice was forbidden because it could be interpreted by onlookers as a sign of superstition.

Father Thomas Kiernan recalled a personal story which vividly captured the incongruity of the Church's condemnation of the Chinese Rites.

> The first funeral I went to was out in Bell Village. I got there, immediately blessed the place, knelt down and said a couple of prayers for the dead man. After the funeral, Father Meyer, our superior, told me that the catechist had reported I performed a superstition at the funeral by kneeling beside the man's coffin and saying a prayer. He laughed at me and said "Well, you are excommunicated."[116]

Within the limits set by the bull, the vicars apostolic had some discretionary powers to decide if superstition was or was not involved in particular cases. In the 1920s and 1930s as missioners deepened their understanding of Confucian values and Chinese culture and customs, their intransigence diminished. Father Edward Mueth recalled a man who had been refused baptism several times because he used to carry a "superstitious" offering to the grave of his parents at their request. When presented with the case, Bishop James E. Walsh told Mueth to baptize him: "He is not performing a superstition, he is performing his filial duty."[117]

Father Sylvio Gilbert related another case in Manchuria when one of his parishioners, the Japanese vice-consul of Antung, asked that his deceased daughter be cremated after the wake at the church. When consulted, Bishop Blois of Mukden, who was aware of Japanese customs, responded to Gilbert, "Fermez les yeux, laissez faire."[118]

In the mid–1930s when the governments of Japan, Manchukuo, and China clarified that the Confucian ceremonies were only a civil tribute to a great philosopher, Rome considered changing its position. Changes occurred first in Manchukuo and in Japan, in part to ease the tensions between the Catholic Church and the governments of these countries. In 1935 and 1936, Propaganda recognized that Catholics in Manchukuo and Japan could partake in official Confucian rites because these were civil and not religious ceremonies; also permitted were inclinations of the head and other signs of civil respect in the presence of the dead or before their pictures or even a tablet inscribed simply with the name of the deceased. Finally, by the instruction *Plane Compertum Est* of December 8, 1939, Cardinal Pietro Fumasoni-Biondi, head of Propaganda, extended these permissions to China and abrogated the oath against the Chinese Rites.[119]

These measures simplified the task of all missioners and allowed Catholics again to partake in most aspects of Chinese social life. In cases where the civil or religious character of an act remained doubtful, the missioners usually let the Catholics decide what line of conduct to follow. For example, Sister Catherine Mary Lee remembered that her family was the only Catholic family of the Lee clan in her village. At the New Year gathering of the clan, her father and mother refrained from bringing chickens because traditionally they were first offered to the dead in the ancestral temple. Instead they brought wine, which all drank at the banquet.[120]

After 1939, Maryknollers also felt freer to adjust Church regulations to Chinese customs. A Maryknoll Father once went to a remote village of the Kaying vicariate for a funeral mass. Since there was no chapel, he decided to celebrate mass in the main hall of the house. For convenience he had a temporary altar set against the wall opposite the door, but the family refused to have the head of the deceased face the altar as the Church's rules demanded. They objected that it was against Chinese customs because people in the village believed that turning the body around would bring more deaths to the household. Understanding their reasons, the priest did not insist and instead moved the altar to the door so that the head of the deceased faced both the exit and the altar.[121]

The Maryknoll Sisters also recalled that for funerals they followed the Chinese traditional customs of kneeling down, lighting firecrackers, and returning from the burial grounds by a different path; the only ritual they absolutely refrained from was burning joss sticks.[122] If converts threw away the joss stick bowl and formally signified that they did not believe that the spirits of the dead inhabited the tablets, Maryknollers generally did not insist on their removal.[123]

Missioners tried to cultivate the Chinese taste for ceremonies by orchestrating the major Catholic celebrations and special occasions to create the atmosphere of the local popular festivals. Days of obligation were widely advertised, plays were given, and a high Mass was celebrated with great pomp, followed by a banquet. Moreover, since the Chinese were fond of processions, missioners held many, making them as visual and magnificent as possible.[124]

In his parish of Shumkai in the Wuchow vicariate, Father Mark Tennien even turned private ceremonies into big social events, such as the renunciation of all forms of superstitions by catechumens. A day was advertised as "Decision Day." Father Tennien, dressed in cassock and stole, led a procession of catechists and villagers to the house of the converts, chanting the Come, Holy Spirit, the Our Father, and the Creed. Then a "spiritual house-cleaning" took place while he read aloud the prayers for the blessing of Catholic homes and "gave everything a generous aspersion of holy water."[125]

Nonetheless, the Roman Catholic ceremonies were generally no match for their equivalents in the Chinese culture. The Chinese rituals surrounding marriage and death, for instance, were very elaborate, and by comparison the Christians rites seemed a poor replacement: a few prayers in Latin and a few words by the priest or catechist. "To the people," said Sister Agnes Chau, "it seemed all too simplistic, it seemed that the Catholic priest had done nothing."[126]

Even after the instruction *Plane Compertum Est* in 1939, Maryknollers, like many other missioners in China, did not seem to know how to insert Christian practices within the context familiar to the Chinese. They did not want to introduce Western customs, yet the Roman Catholicism they preached was colored by these customs.[127] Reflecting on that period in China, Sister Rose Bernadette Gallagher aptly expressed how little meaning most Christian practices had for the Chinese.

We did not understand that keeping the Friday fast was not their form of penance because they were too poor to have meat, and fish was their delight. So to impose fish as a fast was simply not in touch with their likes or their culture.[128]

It is not clear to what extent Maryknollers were aware of these inconsistencies at the time. The Sino-Japanese War drifted into World War II and made a shambles of the already weakened traditional Chinese order. Nothing was left on which to graft Christianity. Feeding and giving shelter to refugees became the priority for most Maryknollers. In this context of crisis, many Chinese, looking for relief and in need of restructuring their lives around a new order, saw the Church as an answer and sought baptism. After the war, conversions soared to new levels. Where there had been only a handful of converts each year, Maryknollers now had hundreds and thousands. In June 1947, Father Mark Tennien had 1,100 people ready for baptism in two large villages of his parish, with another 3,000 signed up for instruction.[129] Under these circumstances, most Maryknollers, absorbed in their day-to-day work, did not have time to think about adapting Catholic practices. Those who did usually felt helpless because the leaders of the Church at that time lacked flexibility. As Sister Rose Bernadette Gallagher said, "There could be no deviation to our presentation [of Catholicism]."[130]

The only hope was in forming native priests and Sisters who would strive for a Chinese Catholicism rooted in practices meaningful to their people. Catholicism allowed to grow from the inside would take on Chinese features and sinicize the Catholic rituals and practices.

Conclusion

A remark made by Francis Ford in 1923 was typical of the American attitude toward China at that time: "I will honestly confess that before I came here I didn't know that China was civilized. School books, I think, still class her among the 'semi-civilized nations.'"[131] Maryknollers assigned to China understood, of course, that they would have to learn the language, get used to the food, endure rough living accommodations, and follow local customs. They conceived of these adjustments, however, only as a means to reach and convert the Chinese people; they were not perceived as steps toward an immersion of the Catholic Church into the Chinese context.

When Maryknollers arrived in China, their eyes opened on an unanticipated world. They discovered a rich civilization and fell in love with it:

> I dare say we shall not respect her civilization long before we begin to admire and wonder at it and some might take a step further and propose for

adoption the good points of a civilization that has endured so long.[132]

This discovery gave focus to the work of Maryknoll in China: baptism should introduce Chinese people to a Church they recognized as their own, and the native Church should rise from the "good points" embedded in the Chinese civilization.

In the United States, Maryknoll seminarians and novices were formed with a deep respect for other cultures. The *Maryknoll Spiritual Directory* published a set of directives to be followed; included was the long-forgotten instruction of the Sacred Congregation of Propaganda Fide to the first M.E.P. vicars apostolic in 1659:

> [Missioners should be persons who] can accommodate themselves to the character and customs of others . . . becoming all things to all men with the Apostles. . . . Do not attempt for any reason whatever to persuade the people to change their rites, customs and manners, provided they are not openly contrary to religion and good morals. For what could be more absurd than to drag France or Spain or Italy or some other part of Europe into China? Not these things should you import, but the Faith; which neither rejects nor offends the rites and customs of any nation except they be evil, but rather desires them to be preserved safe and sound. . . .
>
> There is nothing more likely to cause enmity and dislike than the changing of national customs, especially in the case of those which men have inherited from their fathers; and particularly if in place of the abrogated practices you substitute the customs of your nation. Therefore never compare the habits of those people with the ways of Europeans, but rather accustom your own selves to their ways with all diligence.[133]

Arriving in China, Maryknollers found a totally different environment and culture. Their insertion into this culture was often facilitated by examples and advice of their elders in the same mission territory. As time went on, the Maryknoll heads of mission territories frequently cautioned their missioners against "Westernizing" China, and also reminded them to put in practice the respect and appreciation for China learned during the seminary and novitiate days:

> [The missioner] misses half of what goes on around him, and he often misunderstands the other half. . . . His success as a man and a missioner will largely depend upon the extent to which he can absorb China. He must learn China, know China, embrace China, love China, live China; in a word, fill up his life with China.[134] (Bishop James E. Walsh)
>
> [The missioner] should make his people feel that he is working for them and their interests, even fighting for them if need be. . . . Every effort should be

made to remove from Christianity the stigma so widely attached to it in China of being a "foreign religion." He should not introduce western customs, such as the Christmas tree, nor make the mistake of condemning Chinese medicine, or the native way of doing things, as in farming, carpentry and the like.[135] (Monsignor Bernard Meyer)

It is hardly for us to set ourselves up as judges to their [i.e., Chinese] way of doing things when it differs from ours. Rather it is for us to adapt our minds to their way of thinking . . . and in thus doing preserve for them intact that heritage of Chinese thought which is their own treasure.[136] (Bishop Frederick Donaghy)

Allowance for racial traits is a cardinal principle in our intercourse with others. . . . We are in China to become all things to all men and that means much accommodating of our own preference to Chinese customs. It also means viewing things from the people's viewpoint which is acquired only by putting ourselves in their place mentally.[137] (Bishop Francis Ford)

Sister Thérèse Grondin stressed the importance of the talks given regularly by Bishop Ford to the Sisters of Kaying.

He helped us to change our values, like, being Americans, we liked cleanliness and were afraid of ants and bugs. He would tell us: "Dirt is not sinful." So, if a house is dirty, it doesn't matter. It is the people that are the ones that count. He also said: "A perfect lady is unmoved. If a lady is sitting at the table and a cockroach runs across, instead of running off, or gesturing with her arms in excitement, the perfect lady is unmoved."[138]

At a deeper level, Sister Jean Theophane Steinbauer remembered how the bishop helped them to see the good side of customs seemingly unfair to women.

The Hakka women did most of the heavy manual labor in the fields. We thought that terrible and that something should be done about it. . . . When we told him of our feelings, Bishop Ford told us that the women benefitted by working in the fields. They were healthier. The men, on the other hand, who did babysitting, reading, etc. in the dark, windowless rooms, had a lot of T.B. In this way, Bishop Ford helped [us] to see the advantages of customs we did not approve of because of our different background.[139]

Most Maryknollers did their best to adjust to the Chinese environment. Over a relatively short period of some 30 years, their achievements in the fields of architecture, religious education, and language were remarkable. These results not only made the Church in China less foreign at a local level, they also were a service and a contribution to the Chinese society at large.

The personal adjustment of Maryknollers varied greatly from one individual to another. Some, like Father Robert Cairns, seemed by nature to adapt easily to almost any situation. In his diary for June 27, 1924, he noted that the day before he "had supper in Chinese, went to confession in French, prayed in Latin, sang in Scotch, and slept in 'American.'"[140] However, most Maryknollers found they had limitations in enduring the climate, adjusting to the conditions, or absorbing the culture. In a letter printed in the February 1927 issue of *The Ecclesiastical Review*, Francis Ford admitted with a touch of humor that he could not relinquish some Western eating habits. By comparison, the neighboring missioner he visited did much better.

> I found my host away. . . . I landed in after suppertime and said to the cook: "Please, don't prepare anything much: just a cup of coffee and some bread will do, but first give me a warm drink." He stood on one leg and then on the other and finally apologized: "Father has no wine and we have been out of coffee for the past two months and we never have bread!" For the moment I was nonplussed; the wine I could forgo. . . . I could do without a tablecloth and rather like chopsticks, but I haven't yet got to the stage where coffee and bread are not part of my meal.[141]

Despite their constant efforts to adapt their lifestyle and the Catholic message and practices to the Chinese context, Maryknollers realized at a very early stage that they would always fall short of the mark because they were not themselves Chinese. Francis Ford perhaps best described these feelings in the same narrative of his visit to a neighboring missioner:

> I went to his room. . . . I smiled as I sat down in the most comfortable of the chairs. Here was a room that the poorest at home would consider unfurnished, yet it represented all the missioner's possessions. And I smiled still more broadly when I realized that not a Chinese in the neighborhood but would have considered it very well furnished and I thought of the phrase, "He emptied Himself," and of St. Paul's quote, "All things to all men." Here was a man faithfully trying to become Chinese of the Chinese and yet in some degree living much better than the best of his flock. He had a room to himself and privacy and neatness and windows for light and air.[142]

Maryknollers knew that because they were foreigners they would never totally understand the Chinese culture. For that reason, they stressed the formation of native Sisters and priests who could take on the responsibility of leading a self-expressing Chinese Church firmly rooted in the culture of the country. In the pursuit of that task, they made mistakes because they could not entirely escape their own Western culture. Only a few, though, could be suspected of not having tried hard enough. Maryknoll can therefore share the pride of one of the China veterans who, reflecting on the years spent in China, proclaimed:

> I have never felt guilty because I believe that at that moment of history we were trying to follow the insights that we had, and we were products of our training, of where the Church was in her own understanding, and Maryknoll's understanding of herself. . . . We can *only* operate out of the insights we have at this moment. That was true *then*, that is true *now* . . . because hopefully we are continuing to grow in understanding and knowledge of ourselves, of the world, of people. So if we are all growing, there *has* to be a progression of insights, of knowledge, of wisdom.[143]

7

Maryknoll and Politics

When Maryknollers first stepped on Chinese soil, they found themselves swept up in China's turmoil. Willingly or not, they often became implicated in events with political repercussions. They lived through successive conflicts: the wars during the 1920s between Kwangtung and Kwangsi provinces, followed by the Japanese invasion, and the civil war of the 1940s. They witnessed the rise and fall of Chiang Kai-shek and the spread of communism. They acted as peace emissaries between rival armies, they gave asylum to refugees, they withstood outbursts of nationalism, and they suffered at the hands of the Japanese and the Communists.

Their behavior under these circumstances contributed to crystallizing a certain image of the Church in the minds of the Chinese. If the attitudes of Maryknollers toward the culture and traditions of China were an indication of their success or failure to establish a genuine native Church, their political involvement also played an important role in the acceptance or the refusal of the Church by the Chinese.

Attitude toward the Local Wars of South China, 1920–1930

When Maryknollers arrived in China in late 1918, the parliamentary republic that Sun Yat-sen had envisioned had already turned into a parody. China was torn by civil wars among warlords, and the government in Peking was no more than one of the competing parties. In South China, Kwangtung and Kwangsi provinces were controlled by strong man Lu Jung-t'ing, a former bandit who had risen to the position of commander-in-chief of Kwangsi province. Sun Yat-sen had reached one of the low ebbs of his career. Ousted from Canton by Lu, he had lost his power base and taken refuge in Shanghai. Still fired by his dream to reunify China under a strong democratic government, he wrote his "Outline of National Reconstruction" and planned the recovery of Canton. His opportunity came during the summer of 1920 when Cantonese commanders rebelled against Lu, and Ch'en Chiung-ming of Fukien allied with Sun to invade Kwangtung. This campaign began 10 years of fighting and changed many alliances among the warlords of Kwangsi and Kwangtung.[1]

Maryknollers were convinced that they should stay out of politics. When called into "consultation" by the various warring parties, they followed the American consul's request not to mix in local politics, and to provide only "safe, sane, and conservative advice."[2] In fact, one of the few criticisms they raised against the French M.E.P. priests was that they meddled in local politics and relied heavily on the power of the French government. In no time, however, the American missioners also found themselves in the thick of the Chinese struggle for power.

Overview of the Decade

During these years of confusion and constant fighting, the Maryknoll Fathers' diaries and letters often described the events from first-hand experience. Because, during the first decade, the Sisters spent only a short time in China—32 months in Yeungkong and 10 in Loting—their diaries offer less information and reflection on the political situation.[3]

The Maryknoll Fathers' and Sisters' combined accounts follow the course of events in South China in some detail and offer a unique perspective. In late 1920 they were witnesses to the withdrawal of the Kwangsi forces from Kwangtung. Father William O'Shea described in detail the surrender of Kochow to the Kwangtung army; Father Frederick Dietz recounted the pursuit of Kwangsi troops by Cantonese troops into Kwangsi province.[4]

Sun Yat-sen returned to Canton and established a republican government on April 1, 1921, to oppose the warlord government in Peking. That same month, Lu Jung-t'ing counterattacked into Kwangtung. Many villages, towns, and cities, including Kochow, changed hands a second time. This drive, however, turned into a fiasco as Ch'en Chiung-ming and Sun mounted a counteroffensive. In late June 1921, Dietz described the fall of Wuchow. A few days later, O'Shea told of the quick exit of some of Lu's forces from Kochow, and in December, Father George Wiseman reported the further advance of the Kwangtung army along the West River into Pingnam, Tanchuk, and Konghau.[5] By the end of 1921, all major centers in Kwangsi were under the control of the Kwangtung forces and Sun was planning to launch the Northern Expedition from Kweilin to reunify China.

Ch'en, however, disagreed with Sun, turned against him, and in June 1922, succeeded in driving him out of Canton.[6] Meanwhile, Sun had lost faith in Western intentions to help him restore China's territorial integrity and political independence. He decided to welcome Soviet advisors and allowed Chinese Communists into his Nationalist (Kuomintang) Party. From then on, missionary records labeled Sun's troops as "Reds."

From 1923 through the end of 1925, the two provinces were in a state of internal turmoil: in Kwangsi, Lu's supremacy eroded and militarists battled each other; in Kwangtung, Sun quickly recovered Canton but, until his death in March 1925, continued to fight against Ch'en for control of the rest of the province.[7]

By June 1925, Kwangsi was unified again under three new leaders: Li Tsung-jen, Huang Shao-hsiung, and Pai Ch'ung-hsi. The core of what came to be known as the Kwangsi Clique, they allied themselves with the newly formed Nationalist government at Canton under the presidency of Wang Ching-wei. With their help, the Nationalist forces defeated Ch'en Chiungming.[8] On March 15, 1926, all opposition had been suppressed and the two provinces adopted an official act of unification. Four months later, Chiang Kai-shek was named commander-in-chief of the National Revolutionary Army and resumed the Northern Expedition to complete the reunification of all China. Li Tsung-jen and Pai Ch'ung-hsi joined him in the campaign, while Huang Shao-hsiung stayed in Kwangsi as governor.[9]

In April 1927, a victorious Chiang banned the Communists and chose Nanking as the capital of the Nationalist government. From then on, the missioners stopped referring to the forces of the Nationalist government as "Reds"; they reserved the term for Communist elements like those who took control of Canton and established the Canton Commune in December 1927.[10]

By 1929, the alliance between the Kwangsi Clique and Chiang Kai-shek had badly deteriorated. The Clique, which had extended its control over Kwangtung, Hunan, and Hupei, was pushed back to Kwangsi, and Chiang branded its leaders traitors and bandits. Outraged, the Clique regrouped and in April launched a drive down the West River toward Canton. At first the attack was so successful that the city was threatened, but soon the Kwangsi forces were thrown back. On June 6, Wuchow was occupied by Chiang's forces. Li, Huang, and Pai went into hiding in Hong Kong.[11]

Meanwhile, the Nanking government had replaced Huang Shao-hsiung as governor of Kwangsi with Yü Tso-po. Yü, who was close to the Communist Party, was planning a Red uprising in Wuchow. In October, troops technically in allegiance to Nanking uncovered the plot and deposed the governor; however, these troops actually allowed Li, Pai, and Huang to regain control of the province.[12] The following year, in their pursuit of Yü, they crushed the two soviets which had recently been established west of

Nanning in the Right River valley at Pose and on the Left River at Lungchow.[13] At the same time, the Kwangsi Clique, reinforced by other elements opposed to Chiang Kai-shek, tried to regain control of Kwangtung. As before, success was short-lived. In late 1929 and in the summer of 1930, they were beaten back in disarray into Kwangsi. This last crushing defeat marked the end of the Kwangsi Clique's dream to establish themselves as overlords of several provinces.[14]

Maryknollers as Political Figures

Although they generally avoided taking sides in the wars which ravaged South China, Maryknollers found it difficult to remain bystanders. Their assessment of the situation, their concern for the suffering of the people, and the privilege of extraterritoriality which they enjoyed turned the missioners in the rural communities into important political figures.

Assessment of the situation. In addition to detailed narratives of the battles which took place around them, the Fathers' and Brothers' diaries and letters often provided a kind of "who's who," with expressed opinions of political and military figures. They accused Huang Shao-hsiung, the governor of Kwangsi, of practicing graft and of issuing paper money while running away with all the silver coins he had amassed.[15] Neither did Sun Yat-sen and his troops receive high marks. In the battle between Ch'en and Sun for the control of Kwangtung, Maryknollers favored Ch'en. Francis Ford wrote:

> If Ch'en wins out and joins with Woo Pei Fu [in Peking], it will be a closer and stronger approach to a united China than has been possible for several years. If Sun is victorious, affairs will return to the *status quo ante* [of civil war].[16]

Among Maryknollers, James E. Walsh, the China mission superior, was the most outspoken in voicing his dislike of Sun. In early August 1922, he wrote:

> Sun Yat-sen appears to have reached the end of his rope. All the foreigners in South China with the exception of the American Protestant missioners will be heartily glad to see his end. His action and his public statements have revealed him as a self-seeker, pure and simple. He seems willing to subject his innocent countrymen to any sort of trouble and suffering in order to gain his own personal ends. He is out for glory at any price. . . . With the elimination of Sun, we will all breathe more freely. General Ch'en and his crowd appear much more stable and conservative and under their regime we would hope for a return to settled conditions.[17]

It is not surprising, therefore, that Maryknollers in Yeungkong celebrated

Sun's defeat a few weeks later by inviting to dinner the victorious briga-
dier general of Ch'en's forces, together with the newly appointed civil and
military prefects of the region.[18]

When Sun joined with the Communists in the fall of 1923, he confirmed
Maryknollers' negative opinions of him. Father Phillip Taggart reported
that "the Maan Kwan, Sun Yat-sen's Citizens Army," was living up to its
bad reputation of being "an undisciplined band of thieves."[19] By contrast,
the same missioner raved about the well-behaved soldiers of one of Ch'en
detachments under the leadership of a Catholic commander. Father Bernard Meyer best expressed the basic fear of most Catholic missioners
when he stated that "Bolshevistic" Sun was organizing Red forces as fast
as possible with Soviet aid.[20]

In early 1925 just before Sun's death, Fathers Thomas O'Melia and
Meyer were glad to report that Sun was losing the support of the international community and that Canton would soon be back in Ch'en's hands.
O'Melia added with much scorn, "Sun Yat-sen is considered by some
Westerners as China's George Washington. He may be, but he is not my
idea of George Washington. Ch'en seems to be a better soldier and ruler."[21] Even after Sun's death, Maryknollers remained negative and, like
Taggart, accused him of selling out to the Soviet Union: "For almost a year
before his death, Sun Yat-sen had the Soviet emblem flying before his
headquarters in Canton."[22]

When Chiang Kai-shek first emerged as a possible leader of a unified
China, Maryknollers were not sure if he was "a great deal better than the
ordinary warlord." Nonetheless they hoped he would succeed because
they saw in him the strong man who could keep communism in check.[23]

Advantages and disadvantages of extraterritoriality. Since the Convention of Peking signed in 1860, missioners in China, their goods and
property and, to some extent, their Chinese employees and converts
enjoyed the protection of extraterritorial privileges. They were immune
from Chinese authority and could appeal for the protection of foreign
gunboats.

During the 1920s in particular, Catholic missions became refuges for
people seeking protection from the ruthlessness of soldiers. The American
flag was hoisted at the gate, the words "Catholic Church" were posted on
the walls and sometimes even painted in large characters on the roof.[24] In
mid-January 1923, the Maryknoll Sisters, who had been in Yeungkong only
two months (Sisters Marie Doelger, Mary Francis Davis, Mary Rose Leifels, Mary Lawrence Foley, Mary Barbara Froehlich, and Mary Gertrude
Moore), experienced their first war scare. Following the advice of their
pastor, Francis Ford, they bought extra supplies, flew a large American
flag on their building, dimmed their lights, and remained on the first floor
of their convent, because they would have made good targets on the

second and third floors. Meanwhile, the Fathers posted signs on the walls surrounding the mission compound stating that it was American property. Ford even managed to have proclamations signed by the three generals who stalked the city, stating that the mission compound was foreign property and off-limits to their men.

In the weeks that followed, the Sisters displayed the American flag so frequently because of constant fighting that on the Fourth of July they refrained from flying it, afraid that people in the city would think it signalled an impending battle and seek shelter at the mission.[25] Throughout the fighting, the Sisters had complete confidence in the protection of the American flag. One of them wrote: "It [is] as if Uncle Sam is back of us."[26]

During these trying times, Maryknollers tried to give sanctuary to as many people as possible. In June 1921, Dietz wrote from Wuchow city, "We gladly admitted whoever wanted to come. The place was crowded with men, women, children, chickens, dogs, baggages, boxes, and household furniture, and we had indeed as much privacy as goldfish."[27] Through their hospitality, Maryknollers broke down prejudices and gained friends among a population who had formerly chosen to ignore them or "look at the clouds" when they passed. They had no illusion that gratitude would prompt numerous conversions but, as Dietz said, "The ice had been broken," and a few non-Christians became catechumens.[28]

Merchants and people of some wealth often presumed on their alleged close relationships with missioners to ask protection for themselves, their families, and possessions. In January 1923, the Sisters at Yeungkong, agreed to hide the wife of the local official in their attic.[29] Maryknollers felt they were being used; nonetheless, they let the rich benefit from their protection on the grounds that they had to "keep in well" with these people as their good or ill will meant much to the success of their work.[30] Maryknollers did deny refuge to military personnel bearing arms unless they gave up their arms and acted as civilians.[31]

In several instances, the missioners, as neutral third parties, were asked to serve as peace emissaries between belligerent forces. A most colorful case took place in June and July of 1921 in Kochow. The previous December the city had fallen to the Kwangtung troops but was now on the verge of recapture by a Kwangsi army. William O'Shea recounted how the defending general begged Bernard Meyer, George Wiseman, and him to meet with the Kwangsi commanders and arrange the best terms for Kochow to change hands without violence. Dressed in a cassock and carrying a small 15x20-inch American flag, Meyer jumped down from the town wall, braved sniper fire, and reached the Kwangsi camp. A three-hour cease-fire was arranged to enable the Kwangtung troops to leave the city. Upon returning, Meyer found that the Kwangtung general had changed his mind and would not evacuate.

When the Kwangsi troops resumed shelling the city with four-inch shells, the Kwangtung general and his staff, followed by his soldiers, burst into the church compound to ask for asylum. While Meyer and Wiseman proceeded to disarm them, O'Shea stood at the main gate waving a French flag to catch the attention of the oncoming Kwangsi troops and to signal them to stop firing. However, the Fathers could not prevent the Kwangsi soldiers from climbing over the walls and looting. The surrendering troops were stripped of all their clothes, the school rooms and the lodgings of the catechists were ransacked, and O'Shea's horse was stolen. Meyer went again to parley with the Kwangsi generals and complained about these "violations" of the privilege of extraterritoriality. By midnight he succeeded in clearing the compound of all troops. Meanwhile, the Kwangsi soldiers had been looking for the Kwangtung general. They suspected he was hiding in the Fathers' house but did not dare to force their way in as Meyer and Wiseman stood bravely in front of the door. In fact, the Fathers had given refuge only to women catechists and had refused the safety of their house to the general on the grounds that it would have been "violating the spirit of extraterritoriality to admit combatants to the right of sanctuary."

The next day, the Kwangtung general came out of hiding from a room overlooked by the soldiers and joined the Fathers to pay a visit to the victorious Kwangsi commanders, who happened to be his old friends. O'Shea's horse was returned and the Fathers were praised by both sides for the important part they played in stopping the bloodshed.

Two weeks later, the situation was reversed again and the Kwangsi troops were besieged by an incoming Kwangtung army. This time the compound served as a refuge for the Kwangsi soldiers, who were properly disarmed. When peace was restored, the previously defeated Kwangtung general and two other generals entertained the Fathers and, as an expression of their gratitude, proposed to draw up a petition requesting President Sun Yat-sen to bestow decorations on the three Americans. The Fathers declined the honor and instead requested restitution for the damages sustained by the catechists and the people of two nearby villages. In recounting the events, however, O'Shea lamented that in all probability the request would not be satisfied without consular intervention, which was not sought by Maryknoll except in matters of life and death. In the end, Yip, the ever resourceful chief catechist of Kochow, managed to benefit from the whole episode by receiving the face-giving title of "Mandarin" from the Kwangtung general.[32]

Although the missioners considered themselves "ministers of the Prince of Peace," misunderstandings sometimes occurred which compromised their neutrality. In the case just mentioned, for example, the Kwangsi generals could have promptly stopped the looting of the church compound, but did nothing for several hours because they suspected the Fathers were on the side of the Kwangtung troops and had hidden the general.

The Fathers knew from experience that the American flag on the compound gate did not always keep away looting soldiers. They also felt that in such unsettled times the carrying of arms was necessary for their safety. In December 1920 in Kochow, Fathers Joseph Donovan and George Wiseman each had a .45 caliber automatic, while O'Shea displayed a small .25 caliber pistol. As if this was not enough, one day O'Shea, accompanied by catechist Yip, took a long walk into the countryside on a mysterious errand and returned with a Mauser carbine and 200 rounds of ammunition. During the siege of Wuchow in 1921, the Maryknoll Father posted at the mission gate displayed a Colt .45.[33]

At times Maryknollers recalled with envy occasions when the French missioners had successfully armed and organized their Christians for self-defense. Of course, said James E. Walsh, Maryknollers knew the Church of China had rightfully abandoned this practice and that as missioners they should take what comes and turn the other cheek. Nonetheless, their hearts ached at the suffering and the constant fighting imposed on the people.[34]

Although they regarded the soldiers as mercenaries and former bandits, Maryknollers never refused help to the wounded. In 1924, for instance, Brother John Dorsey's medical expertise saved so many men that grateful soldiers came to Tungchen to offer him a banner which read, "Brother John has a great heart for the soldiers and the people."[35] His fame spread throughout western Kwangtung. Nicknamed the "Doctor Who Cures," he was called to Kochow when the military commander-in-chief fell sick. After the commander was restored to health, he was showered with gifts. A year later, Brother John performed a similar feat by curing a general who had been poisoned.[36]

These occasional cures of wounded or sick soldiers did not mean that Maryknollers had turned their backs on the civilian population. They were deeply distressed to see the havoc troops raised in the countryside: people slain or wounded without much reason, houses ransacked, crops destroyed, villages burned down.[37] The missioners welcomed refugees into their compounds. They provided first-aid to countless wounded civilians in their dispensaries, and they led relief parties to provide food and comfort to devastated areas. In the Pingnam diary of January 1922, Wiseman wrote:

> January 5: As soon as the report of the burning of Konghau [by Cantonese troops] reached Pingnam, the merchants started a relief committee. Within three hours, $400 was collected and handed over to us as custodians. They

asked us to go to Konghau as the head of the relief expedition.

January 7: Off for Konghau in a sampan. To prevent being fired upon, we had the Stars and Stripes flying and also a Red Cross banner. Six of the Chinese walked in order to visit the towns not on the riverfront and give out tickets for rice which we were bringing up for relief. It is impossible to describe the ruins, sufferings, and misery which those soldier-bandits of a so-called modern government left in their wake.[38]

In contrast to their refusal to accept honors from the military, Maryknollers enjoyed the gratitude of civilians. In the same January diary, Wiseman, who had narrated how the Fathers saved the lives of many civilians, wrote:

The mission was "bombarded" by the mayor and merchants of Pingnam and they presented us with a large banner as a token of gratitude for what we did. They must have had intuition that our food supply was almost nil as they brought along chicken, eggs, cakes and other eatables. General Poon offered us $100 to help us in our work but we refused it.[39]

The local newspaper even printed a public note to the Fathers thanking them for their protection during the conflict.[40]

Impact on the Rural Population

Prior to May 1925, Maryknollers noticed the apathy of the rural people toward political issues and the almost total absence of nationalism and patriotism. The Chinese Republic was an empty shell. The political figures were mostly self-seeking warlords bent on destroying one another. Only after 1927 did Chiang Kai-shek emerge in the missioners' opinion as a leader with the ability to unify China. The military—from the soldiers to their generals—were mercenaries who had little idea of why they were fighting. Whole detachments changed allegiance for better pay or, following a defeat, joined forces with the victors.

Especially in the countryside, civilians did not seem too concerned with what kind of government they had "so long as they enjoyed peace and had plenty of rice."[41] When fighting broke out, however, they suffered most from extortion, forced coolie work, rape, looting, and destruction of property. Witnessing such horrors motivated Maryknollers to assume political roles. Like their fellow French missioners of Kwangtung and Kwangsi, they claimed the privilege of extraterritoriality to offer sanctuary to civilians, and to threaten whoever tried to enter by force with foreign reprisals. They also realized that their prestige and respect as foreign nationals could avert fighting, stop looting, and facilitate the distribution of relief supplies. They knew the crowd which gathered at their doors sought foreign protection and not anything even vaguely resembling the medieval European Christian right of asylum.

Maryknollers did not expect many conversions to result. People began the catechumenate course out of gratitude but rapidly dropped out because of lack of real interest.[42] Although few conversions resulted, Maryknollers considered political involvement necessary for two reasons: on a short-term basis, it enabled them to demonstrate Christian charity by providing refugees with food, shelter, and medicine; on a long-term basis, it enabled them to work to restore peace so that planned mission work could resume.[43]

During this period of local wars, the Fathers developed the habit of writing home about the political situation in their area. They continued to do so through World War II and during the Communist takeover of China. If intercepted, their comments and remarks could have easily brought reprisals, but the Fathers did not seem to realize that their activities could be interpreted as spying. The seizure of so-called compromising correspondence and documents was a scheme later used by the Communists to accuse missioners of being imperialist spies.

Attitude toward Chinese Nationalism, 1925–1932

1925, an Eventful Year

In February 1922, the Nine-Power Treaty, signed at the end of the Washington Conference, agreed in principle to China's territorial integrity and political independence; it even had provisions for phasing out the existing privileges of the foreign powers in China. However, since the Treaty was based on good will with no enforcement power, nothing happened. Many humiliating signs reminded students and many Chinese city dwellers of China's semicolonial status, including foreign concessions up and down the China coast and far up the rivers; foreigners in high posts in the Chinese Maritime Customs, the Salt Revenue, and the Postal Service; gunboats flying foreign flags; and railways owned and managed by foreigners.

Fueled by anger and frustration, national consciousness was on the rise. The time was ripe for an incident of major proportions, fueled by the antiforeign sentiments which contributed to the Boxer uprising of 1900, and the nationalist feelings which led to the May Fourth Movement of 1919. In May 1925, following a strike protesting low wages at a

Japanese cotton-weaving mill in Shanghai and the arrest of a number of Chinese workers on charges of disturbing peace and order, 3,000 city students staged a demonstration in support of the workers. At this point, a British police lieutenant in the British concession ordered his men to open fire. Several dozen Chinese were wounded, 11 were killed, and about 50 were jailed.

This "May 30th Atrocious Incident" rekindled antiforeign sentiments all over China and provoked a chain reaction of protests and boycotts by students, workers, and merchants in the cities. On June 23, 1925, 20,000 marchers demonstrated in Canton. Before the day ended, 52 Chinese lay dead, and 117 were wounded by the British and French soldiers protecting the foreign settlement on Shameen. The Canton incident triggered a general strike in Hong Kong and Canton against all foreign goods and personnel, as well as many demonstrations throughout the province of Kwangtung.[44]

On June 29, Father Robert Cairns witnessed a demonstration in Kochow when students borrowed drums and trumpets from the Maryknoll Sacred Heart School to orchestrate a parade. Similarly, Maryknollers in Loting reported an antiforeign schoolboy parade led by a detachment of heavily armed troops with the Red flag as their standard.[45] On June 30 in Yeungkong, the Sisters' diary also reported that the Christians urged the Sisters to leave as soon as possible, following a parade during which antiforeign slogans were shouted at the mission.[46] Father James Drought noted:

> The growing political agitation was filtering into the city and handbills were distributed urging that foreigners be expelled and beaten. The local students held mass meetings, the guilds organized a parade in which the Maryknoll school children participated with the pastor's consent. It looks as if, given a little time, Yeungkong might become a dangerous place to hang one's foreign hat in.[47]

In Wuchow, a circular was distributed informing the public of the massacres of Chinese people in Shanghai, Tsingtao, and Canton. It also accused Americans of having forcefully taken over a hill overlooking Wuchow, referring to the unpopular acquisition of the hill in question by one of the four Protestant denominations in the city. The people of Wuchow were forewarned that "China will shortly be absorbed by foreigners." The circular also announced a forthcoming demonstration and a boycott of British and Japanese goods. The document was signed by the "Propaganda Bureau of the Executives for the Nationalist party in Wuchow." The eight slogans proposed for the demonstration mirrored the roots of Chinese discontent with foreigners, calling for the overthrow of imperialism and the abolition of foreign concessions, extraterritorial rights, and unequal treaties.[48]

Fearing that growing antiforeignism might lead to another Boxer uprising, foreign consuls advised their nationals to leave the interior. The American consul in Canton, Douglas Jenkins, sent confidential notices asking all American women and children in Kwangtung and Kwangsi to depart immediately for Hong Kong or other safe places. By coincidence, most Maryknollers were already assembled in Hong Kong for their annual retreat.

At the news of the Canton incident, James E. Walsh, the Maryknoll superior in China, decided to follow the advice of the consul and of Bishop Fourquet, and recalled the Maryknoll Sisters to Hong Kong. As prefect apostolic of Kongmoon, his order could not be disobeyed. In early July, Walsh sent more urgent telegrams to all remaining Maryknoll personnel to "clear out *quam primum* [as soon as possible]" or, if they could not get out, he would send a relief party.[49] The Fathers and Sisters in Loting left unharmed, but those in Yeungkong could not be reached because the telegraph was down. Concerned for their safety, Walsh secured the services of the Hong Kong governor's yacht and a few days later, the U.S. gunboat *Simpson* escorted the four Fathers and three Sisters stranded in Yeungkong back to Hong Kong. By July 15, all Maryknollers, except five men who had opted to stay, had made their way back to Hong Kong under the protection of British and American gunboats.[50]

Walsh ordered the withdrawal of Maryknoll personnel because he felt nothing would be gained by keeping them in China. He blamed the Russians and corrupt Chinese politicians for using the foreigner as a "red herring to draw across the trail." He told James A. Walsh that since the nature of the unrest was political and not antireligious, he saw no reason why he should endanger the lives of his missioners. By preventing them from becoming focal points of antiforeignism, he protected the missioners and their work from falling prey to the anger of the demonstrators.[51] The Sisters completely shared his views. On closing the Loting convent diary in July 1925, the narrator summed up the Sisters' attitude toward their mission work and reasons for leaving in these terms:

> Here the Loting diary stops for a while. A very short while we trust until in God's time we are told we can return to the interior to our beloved mission and our charges. As has been very truly said, we are willing to lay down our lives for our faith but no one cares to be killed simply because she is a foreigner.[52]

James E. Walsh soon realized that he had made an error in judgment and within three months reassigned all his men to their missions. Their withdrawal had caused much embarrassment to Maryknoll in China, in Rome, and in the United States. In China and in Rome, some French priests criticized Maryknoll missioners for prematurely leaving their missions. In the United States, James A. Walsh kept the affair as secret as possible to avoid explaining what could have appeared as a sign of weakness or cowardice.[53]

Fortunately the well-publicized story of the capture and release by bandits of Fathers Otto Rauschenbach and Thomas O'Melia from their mission on Sancian Island helped to smother rising criticism. The superior general called this event providential:

> Yesterday I received the cable about the captivity of Fathers O'Melia and Rauschenbach and also news of their release. The Associated Press has, I believe, spread this news well through the country as we were called up from Baltimore. It has been a very good thing—a providential happening I believe—as insinuations were beginning to come in the form of inquiries as to the whereabouts of our missioners, and why they were obliged to leave their flocks.[54]

As local wars continued and more missioners, including James E. Walsh himself, fell prey to bandits, he used extra caution in sending the Sisters back to their two missions in Yeungkong and Loting. In November 1925, an attempt by the Maryknoll Sisters to return to Yeungkong ended in catastrophe when pirates detained them a few days, robbing them of supplies, money, and personal belongings. Returning to Hong Kong, they were not allowed to reopen the Yeungkong convent until 1930.[55]

The Loting convent reopened in March 1926 and remained open until early April 1927. At that time, a new upsurge of antiforeign feeling caused the Sisters to flee and then return to Loting several times. When they left in August 1927 under Bishop Walsh's orders, they did not return until 1932.[56]

Although James E. Walsh wrote that criticism by his French colleagues did not bother him, he certainly learned a lesson from these events. Never again would he recall Maryknoll priests and Brothers under his jurisdiction because of danger. When the time came for him to make a personal choice in 1952, he elected to stay at his post in Shanghai and face imprisonment. When he was finally released in June 1970, he was the last foreign missioner to leave Chinese soil.

In 1925 all Maryknollers reporting on the unrest in China agreed that the Soviet Union was operating behind the scenes and had placed agents in almost every camp, especially among newsmen, educators, and students.[57] The missioners' interpretation of events, however, varied widely. In a biting manner, Bishop Walsh labeled strikers and students as "the

most irresponsible and generally idiotic elements in China," easily manip-
ulated by Communist demagogues. He thought that a new Chinese war
would probably defuse the situation by giving the demonstrators "something else to think about."[58]

Father John Toomey probably came closest to understanding the reasons behind the unrest in Kwangtung. As foreign nationals of countries
suspected of giving financial help to Ch'en Chiung-ming, missioners were
naturally included in the opposition to the Nationalist government in
Canton. The purpose of the demonstrations was not to attack religion but
to raise support for the Canton government.[59]

Even prior to the June demonstration in Canton, Father Taggart had
written a long article for *The Field Afar* on "The Present Anti-Christian
Movement in China" in which he was sympathetic to the Chinese desire
"to run their country to suit themselves." At the same time he was critical
of the false solicitude of other nations toward China: "It is so easy to
assume the white man's burden, especially when the territory in question
has trade advantages."[60] However, he deplored the alliance made with the
Soviet Union by Sun Yat-sen prior to his death which had given Chinese
nationalist aspirations an anti-Christian coloration: "Christianity has
been branded as a by-product of imperialism and something that is hurtful
to China."[61]

As for the immediate cause of the demonstrations against Christianity,
he blamed it on the Protestants. He referred to the meeting and statements of the World Students' Christian Federation held in Peking in 1922
which irked nationalistic Chinese students and led to the formation of a
countergroup called the Student Antireligious Movement. In all the
major cities of China, this movement led retaliatory measures against
religions labeled as superstitious, unscientific, and unprogressive, and
specifically against Christianity because of its foreign and imperialist
stigma.

Taggart also accused the Protestants of irritating the Chinese through
other forms of excessive zeal such as interfering with the legitimate use of
wine and tobacco which were about the only indulgence known by the
ordinary farmer and rarely used in excess. The Protestants' zealous drive
against opium, said Taggart, fell into a similar pitfall. It antagonized many
Chinese officials and the opium commissioner:

> Opium is a curse but after all it was the foreigner who introduced the curse
> and it is the foreigner who still keeps the country supplied with the bulk of
> this drug. I wonder how the Southern Baptists or northern Presbyterians
> would feel if a crowd of Chinese flocked to America and started to enforce
> the laws of the United States over the heads of the duly appointed officials of
> that country.[62]

Finally, Taggart pointed to the Protestant practice of anglicizing names as one of the reasons that Christianity denationalized its followers:

> When you read of native Protestant ministers calling themselves Lincoln Tang, Robert E. Lee, Wilson Tsu, Gladstone Wong, and Donald Fay, you are tempted to believe there is something to the accusation after all.[63]

Francis Ford concurred that the unrest was mainly political. He agreed with Taggart that the current unrest had been going on for at least the past 10 years and that it was part of China's effort to get back her independence. He mentioned that the boycott of 1925 was the most effective weapon the Chinese had used because all foreigners in China, be they missioners, educators, doctors, or salesmen, could not operate without Chinese help.[64] He thought, however, that the Chinese still lacked the motivation and leadership to succeed. He compared them to "schoolboys who impulsively smash the school desks and then simply wait for the teacher to return and punish them."[65] He added that if the countries who were party to the Nine-Power Treaty showed some justice to China at their meeting of December 1925, even without restoring her full rights, disturbances would die out.[66]

Among all the causes of antiforeign demonstrations, Ford also singled out the Protestants and their system of education: "The students are the backbone of the antiforeign movements and the Protestants schools are prime movers due to the 'liberty' of views and 'self-expression' encouraged by the faculty."[67]

Ford was one of the more moderate Maryknollers in his assessment of the political situation. He urged Maryknoll to use much caution. He mentioned that although most demonstrations seemed to be fueled by Communist agitators, he did not think that the Nationalist government in Canton was necessarily "Bolshevik" or a bad alternative for China. He pointed out, for instance, that in Kaying the "so-called Reds" of the Canton army dislodged the non-Bolshevik forces of Ch'en Chiung-ming and received an open-armed welcome from the population.[68] He added that he was pleasantly surprised because:

> They [the "Reds"] have conducted themselves as well as any American soldiers would: they paid for what they use, have not quartered themselves on the people, collect only the usual taxes, and showed no animosity to me in the street.[69]

Other Maryknollers without similar experiences had little respect for the Canton government. They tended to side with James E. Walsh, hoping that foreign nations would tire of these "ridiculous tactics" and give the Nationalists a "spanking."[70] They favored the government in Peking and Ch'en Chiung-ming, who claimed allegiance to that government. Even though they never praised the behavior of either army, they always described the Canton forces as the worst of the lot.

Since only the Soviet Union was willing to help the Nationalist government in Canton while the other major Western nations still recognized Peking, it came as no surprise that the Cantonese troops agitated against foreigners. In the rural areas and small towns, missioners were the only foreigners around to shoulder the brunt of these demonstrations. The threatening shouts were not so much against members of a foreign religion as against citizens of a foreign country which was suspected of financing a rival faction. For example, the series of antiforeign demonstrations which occurred in Loting between June and November 1925 were sparked by allegations that Great Britain was giving financial help to Ch'en Chiung-ming to fight Sun's army. Intolerance toward Maryknollers in the town grew until they too were included among the "honorary members" of the enemies of China.[71] If the crowds had known that some missioners personally favored Ch'en Chiung-ming's forces over the Nationalist troops, they certainly would have resorted to physical violence.

Although individual Maryknollers became sensitive to Chinese nationalistic aspirations, the Maryknoll leadership was less desirous of seeing changes take place: James E. Walsh, an advocate of foreign protection of missioners, was still convinced that less than one percent of the Chinese wanted foreigners to give up the concessions and extraterritoriality.[72] When a meeting of the signatories of the Nine-Power Treaty was scheduled for Peking in December 1925, James A. Walsh proposed that the National Catholic Welfare Conference of America send a representative who could lobby to preserve the American missioners' interests. Ford was selected and sent with instructions from the N.C.W.C. to get in touch with as many representatives of the foreign powers as possible. He was given a letter which spelled out the rights and privileges acquired by missioners through treaties, money payments, or gifts, to which the central government at Peking should agree.[73]

The Maryknoll Leadership Awakens to Chinese Nationalistic Aspirations

Upon returning to their missions in October 1925, Maryknollers in Kwangtung and Kwangsi witnessed periodic demonstrations stirred up by the success of the Northern Expedition and by an intensive campaign of propaganda from the Nationalist government for the "Revolution of China and of the World." Missioners blamed Bolshevik agitators for coaxing children away from schools and leading them in parades of protest. Acting as cheerleaders, the revolutionaries made the children yell slogans: "Down with the capitalists!" "Boycott the foreign goods!" "Down with greedy officials!" or "Down with militarism!"[74]

Occasionally demonstrations were specifically anti-Christian. In 1926 diaries and correspondence from Fachow, Pingnam, Kochow, Yeungkong, and Siaoloc all reported student parades in front of the Catholic church, the pasting of posters on the gate and walls of the compound, and the distribution of accusatory handbills. Paraders usually confined themselves to shouting slogans such as "Down with the Catholic Church!" Missioners in Siaoloc reported the only case of extensive destruction of church property. Interestingly enough, that demonstration was fomented not by Bolshevik revolutionaries but by a renegade Catholic.[75]

As 1927 began, newspapers reported anti-Christian demonstrations in Canton, Fuchow, and Kanchow, and antiforeign manifestations in Hankow and Nanking. In Kwangtung province, antagonism against Catholic personnel and property increased noticeably until it erupted in a serious incident in Fachow.[76]

In March 1927, according to the report from the pastor, Father Charles Walker, soldiers from a Nationalist regiment recently stationed in Fachow washed their coats in the river and hung them on a line in the church property. Walker sent a Chinese hired hand to tell them to take their uniforms somewhere else. This request angered the soldiers who, upon leaving, wrote a few defamatory remarks on the walls of the compound. Two days later, the soldiers returned, armed with rifles and bayonets. They smashed all the pieces of broken glass encrusted on top of the mission wall, entered the compound, and headed for the church. While George Bauer, the curate, tried to delay them, Walker and a helper set out to find the city magistrate. A few bayonet jabs kept them from going further while other soldiers finally broke the chapel door and began smashing windows and statues and tearing up liturgical vestments. Fearing for their lives, the two priests fled on foot to Kochow. The next day some Christians reported to them that during their absence looters had broken into the priests' residence and walked away with all its contents. To prevent further destruction, the local magistrate posted a guard of local militia.[77]

The report filed by the magistrate of Fachow with the Chinese Ministry of Foreign Affairs of the Nationalist Revolutionary Government in Kwangtung differed, not only in minor details but on the major cause of the incident. While the Fathers accused the soldiers, the magistrate blamed one of the priests' hired hands. According to his source, the Chinese servant had not only told the soldiers to leave but had thrown one of their coats in the mud. As the owner of the coat tried to argue that he saw no harm in drying his clothes in front of the church, he was rebuked by a volley of stones and hit on the head. The incident was witnessed by townspeople who sympathized with the wounded soldier. As the news spread, an angry mob converged on the mission and ransacked it before the magistrate could intervene and dispatch local troops and the police.[78]

It seems that neither of the reports was entirely accurate. The magistrate's communication avoided blaming the soldiers of the Nationalist Revolutionary regiment recently garrisoned at Fachow, although Walker's detailed account left no doubt that they ransacked the church and that civilian looters followed suit. It appears that the magistrate did not want to antagonize a military force far superior to his local police. Walker also seems to have hidden some of the facts. The Maryknoll Archives contain three accounts of the incident by Maryknollers. In the two narratives written by Walker, it appears that he told the soldiers to take their coats off the church property. In the third account, written by James E. Walsh and published in *The Field Afar* in February 1928, it is acknowledged that Walker ordered his servant to tell the soldiers to leave. No ensuing fight is mentioned, however.[79]

When Walker learned of the magistrate's report accusing one of his servants of stoning a soldier, he dismissed it as a lie, saying that neither of his two teenage hired hands was daring enough to attack the military.[80] It seems probable, however, that the man working for the Fathers felt he had the authority to act roughly with the unarmed soldiers. As they left, uttering unflattering words, the servant may have answered with a volley of stones and hit one of the soldiers. If Walker had been aware that these soldiers belonged to the same regiment which, for two years, had forcibly occupied the rectory of Father Pierre Baldit, his M.E.P. neighbor at Mui-luk, he might have been more cautious.[81]

As soon as he learned of the Fachow incident, Douglas Jenkins, the American consul at Canton, proposed sending a gunboat to evacuate Walker and Bauer. James E. Walsh refused the offer because the trouble had already subsided; however, he asked the consul's assistance in filing a formal complaint. He also suggested some steps to obtain "a rectification of the affair" which might prevent a recurrence: (a) a public statement by the civil magistrate of Fachow guaranteeing protection to Americans in his district; (b) an indemnity of 3,000 Cantonese dollars for losses sustained; (c) apprehension of the culprits; and (d) transfer of the detachment of soldiers.[82]

In deciding the case, the acting Chinese foreign minister at Canton concurred with the Fachow magistrate's version of the events and refused to take any precise action. However, he gave instructions to the local troops, police, and the military garrison to search for lost articles and the culprits. He also issued a general proclamation aimed at preventing the recurrence of such an incident.[83]

When the Maryknoll superior general first learned of the Fachow incident, he decided not to publish it in *The Field Afar*. James A. Walsh feared that the American public, already sensitive to the unstable situation in China, might stop contributing money for missions in that country if they learned that the fruit of their donations was destroyed or stolen.[84] The incident was finally reported in *The Field Afar* in February 1928, almost one year after it took place, cleverly rewritten by James E. Walsh as the story of a promising mission field:

> "Unless the grain of wheat falling into the ground die, itself remaineth alone. But it if die, it bringeth forth much fruit." Opposition is not a reason to abandon a work but rather an indication that something good lies at the end for those who have the faith and courage to push on. Fachow is accordingly encouraged by the privilege it has had of suffering for the faith.[85]

After the minister of foreign affairs refused to act, James E. Walsh sent the dossier of the Fachow affair to James A. Walsh, suggesting that the superior general seek the aid of the U.S. State Department. He hoped that a strong protest by the State Department to the Chinese Foreign Ministry would prevent similar incidents in the future.[86]

The superior general felt that the less business Maryknoll had with the American government, the better; however, he did not want to give a categorical "no" to the bishop of Kongmoon. Writing to James E. Walsh in September 1927, James A. Walsh finally found a solution by referring to a letter of the apostolic delegate Costantini to all the bishops of China in which the archbishop asked, in the understanding of James A. Walsh, that all claims for compensation go through his office. The letter actually urged missioners to remain with their congregations in time of danger and to stay away from anything that savored of politics.[87] The superior general commented further:

> Personally, I am pleased to see that we are getting away from contact with American home government officials. When I talked with the consul at Shanghai on the occasion of my first visit to China, he expressed his delight at the advent of American priests, believing it would add to the prestige of the American government. I told him quite plainly that we were not coming for that purpose, although we loved our country and would be pleased if our presence reacted favorably in any way on our country. He saw the point of view, but remarked on the tremendous value of the French missionary influence as affecting France. The mind of Rome seems very clear in these days as to the attitude we should take and with China awakening, I presume that all along the line there will be less and less tendency to turn to consuls.[88]

This time James E. Walsh understood that James A. Walsh wanted the matter closed. "In regard to the Fachow affair, we can now dismiss the pressing of the claim for our compensation. The matter is not of great importance."[89] As a matter of fact, when James E. Walsh wrote this letter in late October 1927, the situation for foreigners in China had improved substantially, and most demonstrations had stopped. Since April, the Bolsheviks had gradually been ousted from the Nationalist government and had gone into hiding.

In December 1926, prior to the Fachow incident, Bernard Meyer had already expressed a view, later proved correct by future events:

> I am becoming convinced that any appeal to the consul whether in case of brigandage or of insult and injury by the soldiery will only serve to add fuel to the flame. In the past, the protection of the various powers may have had its use; but today I feel that we are going to have to give it up whether we will [sic] or not. I am sure that new confidence in our non-connection with imperialistic schemes is not going to be established without suffering and inconvenience if not martyrdom. We have no argument that will have weight with those opposed to us except to stay at our posts, come what may, without attempting to use the customary means of obtaining redress.[90]

The superior general agreed. He questioned whether a Chinese in America who had been robbed by bandits could appeal to his consul to request compensation from the American government in a similar manner. He closed his reflection by adding, "I certainly hope the time will come when we can get along without anything more than formal and occasional intercourse with the consuls."[91]

While the rumor circulated among Maryknollers in China that the Fachow incident might have been caused by a "breakdown" on the part of either Walker or Bauer, no proof exists.[92] Later that year, however, a second incident occurred in Yeungkong which left no doubt as to the responsibility of the Maryknoller involved. Father William Fletcher, while taking a stroll with a fellow priest, became upset with a student who deliberately passed between the two priests instead of stepping aside. In anger, Fletcher hit him on the foot with his cane. A similar incident had taken place a few months earlier and Fletcher had been reprimanded. If the first blow of the cane did not result in major difficulties for the Catholic Church in Yeungkong, the second almost destroyed the compound.

The second incident happened a few days before Sun Yat-sen's birthday, while students were preparing for a mass meeting and a parade. On the eve of the parade, the incident was described in the local Nationalist party newspaper under the caption, "Foreigner Strikes Student Disdainfully." By the next day, hostility toward foreigners ran high in the city. At the mass meeting, the incident was portrayed as an insult to the entire student body by imperialists. The parade turned into a violent demonstration against the Catholic mission. Students, joined by members of various guilds, would have stormed the compound if local military officials had not intervened by posting a guard around the property. Receiving news of the incident, the American consul in Canton sent the *S.S. Ashville* with a detachment of Marines to rescue Fletcher and the two other priests at Yeungkong. By that time, however, the riot had already been quickly quelled by local Chinese military officials.[93]

James E. Walsh was outraged at Fletcher's repeated mistake and thought the missioner was hopelessly stupid and obstinate. "It is a disgrace to the [Maryknoll] Mission that one of its members should have no better sense than stir up a storm like this by a piece of childish petulancy."[94] He was convinced that if the Fletcher episode had occurred six months earlier when the extremists were in ascendancy, blood would have been shed. He wrote to James A. Walsh, strongly advising against sending similar individuals to China because their inability to handle crisis situations endangered the Catholic Church. A few months later, Fletcher was reassigned to the Philippines.[95]

Maryknoll Reactions to Chinese Nationalism

During the mid–1920s, the shouts of demonstrators alerted many missioners to China's awakening nationalism. Like other foreigners, many Maryknollers became sensitive to some of the injustice hidden in the unequal treaties. Maryknollers in both New York and China read books like *What's Wrong with China?*, by Rodney Gilbert, and *What's Right with China*, by O. D. Rasmussen, which discussed some of the key issues.[96] The explanations in *What's Wrong with China* appealed primarily to foreign businessmen in the big port cities. In *What's Right with China*, published shortly after as a rebuttal, Rasmussen explained the difficulties of the young republic and how Sun Yat-sen failed to get the support of foreign countries who willingly left China underdeveloped for their own advantage.[97]

Maryknollers knew that China's troubles were owing in part to Western imperialistic interference, but they never publicly condemned these activities. Instead, they favored preserving extraterritoriality although they themselves preferred not to resort to it. Even by 1929, Maryknollers' opinions had not changed too much. Thomas Kiernan, for instance, reacted strongly to an editorial in *Commonwealth* calling for the abolition of extraterritoriality:

> The average Westerner can hardly conceive how utterly unable the Chinese are to administer justice. Instead of abolishing extrality [sic], the foreign

powers would render a great boon to the Chinese people themselves if they were to make them, too, the protégés of the system. Granted, there are and have been abuses, but there is nothing else which can possibly be substituted, less than international policing of China.[98]

By claiming that their sole purpose was to preach religion, they sought to avoid taking sides. The gap was wide, however, between their intentions and their actions. Upset by China's inability to follow a single leader and by the venting of her frustrations on foreigners, Maryknollers favored a strong reprimand by Western nations to restore law and order. Many missioners hurried to request American protection when disturbances came close to mission doors. Even after Maryknoll's leadership decided to shun foreign help, nervous consuls still sent gunboats to rescue missioners along with other foreign nationals. Moreover, the Chinese would not let Maryknollers stay out of politics. Because missioners were foreign nationals, the Chinese used them, according to the circumstances and their need, as protective buffers against the enemy, as peace emissaries, or even as pawns to be exchanged.

Inadvertently, Maryknollers' behavior often fueled accusations that they were agents of Western imperialists. They owned rice fields, handled large sums of money, bought large properties, lived behind big walls, and ate foreign food; they traveled regularly to Hong Kong and held meetings with other foreigners several times a year; they wrote to the American consul in Hong Kong and sent coded telegrams to Maryknoll headquarters; they kept an extensive correspondence with the United States and wrote house diaries in which they gave information concerning locations of villages, crops, weather, troop movements, and discussed the latest developments in Chinese politics.

They also failed to realize that their associations with foreign businessmen and the crews of foreign gunboats could be interpreted as signs of their imperialist connections. These encounters, although rare, occurred in the course of trips to and from Hong Kong. However, in the open port of Wuchow, these contacts were frequent. The sight of Maryknoll missioners being wined and dined by foreign soldiers and merchants, and the visits back and forth between Maryknoll priests and the crews of American, French, and British gunboats in the port reinforced wrong impressions of missionary intentions.[99]

Maryknollers did not really understand, however, that their lifestyle, their use and support of extraterritoriality, as well as some of their religious practices often smacked of foreignism. Instead of totally embracing the aspirations for a China free from Western interference, they griped about the "Redness" of Chinese nationalism and preferred to maintain close contacts with Western interests. They believed that antiforeign demonstrations were staged by Communist agitators and did not represent the sentiment of the Chinese people who, in their opinion, welcomed foreigners and liked to borrow their ideas and improvements.[100]

The purge of the Communists in Shanghai in April 1927, and the subsequent ousting of all Communists from the Nationalist Party and government dealt a serious blow to the Bolshevik movement. In Kwangtung and Kwangsi provinces, after the failure of a Communist coup at Canton and the fall of the two Kwangsi soviets, anyone suspected of being Communist was shot or put in jail. Antiforeign sentiments did not disappear altogether, but the Catholic Church ceased to be a target for demonstrations except when, as in the Fachow and Yeungkong incidents, the missioners' actions gave substance to the people's discontent.

This turning of the Chinese national government from "Red" to "White" coincided with the results of earlier efforts of the Holy See to respond positively to Chinese nationalism. Both the apostolic letter *Maximum Illud* of 1919, and the encyclical letter *Rerum Ecclesiae* of 1926, were written with China in mind—condemning imperialistic attitudes among missioners and confirming the rights of the "natives" to govern their own Church. Pope Pius XI addressed a second letter, *Ad Ipsis Pontificatus Primordiis*, to the missionary bishops of China to make sure they understood that Rome's message had referred primarily to the situation in China. He objected vehemently to missioners who used the Church to foster the schemes and interests of their native countries. As a gesture toward the Chinese people, the pope also urged missioners to respect lawful authority, both civil and religious, and encouraged patriotism within responsible limits.[101] In October 1926, to emphasize his statements, the pope personally consecrated six Chinese bishops with jurisdiction over vicariates and prefectures in China.

Meanwhile Chiang Kai-shek completed the unification of China. After the fall of the Peking warlord government in June 1928 and the solidification of the Nanking Government, Western nations hesitated to give recognition to Nanking. The pope was the first to react positively to the news that China was at peace and unified after many years of internal struggle. His message on August 1, 1928, to "the great and most noble people of China" expressed hope for universal recognition of their legitimate aspirations; rejoiced at the end of civil war; acknowledged the greatness of China's history and culture, reminding them of the obligation to respect and obey legitimate authority; and conveyed his blessing.[102]

This gesture by the pope was well received by the Nationalist government, which began a series of overtures to the Catholic Church. In January 1929, Chiang Kai-shek held an official reception for the papal representative, Archbishop Costantini. Although the government prohibited the teaching of religion in schools, it made repeated endorsements in support of religious freedom. Meanwhile, with Rome urging missioners to respect civil authorities, and the Nationalist government casting off its Communist ties, missioners in China began to revise their opinion of the Nationalists. They stopped labeling Sun Yat-sen a villain and endorsed the teaching of his Three People's Principles—the dogma of the Nationalist party—in schools. These changes allowed the development of a strong relationship between the Nationalist government and the Catholic Church.[103]

Maryknollers in South China welcomed the return to quieter times and the ousting of the Bolsheviks. They rejoiced at the opportunity to resume or, in many instances, to start a systematic mission program. Local wars had been bothersome, but missioners had been more fearful of the possible negative impact of anti-Christian and antiforeign demonstrations on future mission work. In 1925, Taggart wrote in the Tungchen Chronicle:

> The Chinese farmer is always threatened by trouble and if entering the Church adds to this trouble, none but the more courageous will think of entering, and unfortunately, the "more courageous" are not produced in bountiful crops.[104]

Taggart's comment was certainly correct, although he failed to realize that a large segment of the population had turned its back on Christianity precisely because it was foreign rather than because it was a source of "trouble." Maryknollers had unknowingly contributed to clothing the nascent Chinese Church in foreign garb. Much of the next two decades was spent trying to remove it.

Under the strong leadership of Rome, most of the missioners in China embraced the Nationalist government's programs. Maryknoll schools put up pictures of Sun Yat-sen, taught patriotism, and used the San Min Chu I (Three People's Principles) as a textbook.[105] When the magistrates of Yeungkong sponsored a speech and essay contest for lower school children in February 1937 to promulgate the Nationalists' New Life Movement, the Sisters entered their school girls in the competition. The next day, they accompanied the children to plant trees along the main road in celebration of Arbor Day. The Sisters even participated in national clean-up campaigns such as "The Fly Catching Program" of 1937 and reported having met their civic obligations.[106]

More than anything else, the Japanese invasion caused many missioners to ally themselves with the Chinese people's drive for national development and liberation. During the ensuing years, this change of attitude alleviated some suspicion on the part of the Chinese and helped the Church shed some of its foreign appearance. Yet by 1949, the stigma of foreignism was still present; in addition, the Church had strongly backed the Nationalist government and was now accused by the Communists of having sold out to the Western nations in order to exploit the Chinese people. The Communists found plenty of proof—real and fabricated—to condemn the Church for Western conspiracy and foreign allegiance. Much of the suffering endured by the Chinese Church since 1949 occurred in the process of proving her allegiance to China.

Involvement during the Japanese Invasion, 1931–1945

On the evening of September 18, 1931, a bomb exploded on the South Manchuria Railway track outside of Mukden. Planned by the Japanese Kwantung Army command in charge of protecting the leased territory of Port Arthur and Dairen and the South Manchuria Railway zone, this incident started Japan on the road of militarism, conquest and, ultimately, defeat.

From the occupation of Manchuria to the aggression against the rest of China and the final widening of the conflict into World War II, Maryknoll missioners in China were often at the center of the action. Their behavior in the face of Japanese encroachment had a strong impact on the budding local Churches. It also helped many non-Christian Chinese form an opinion of the Catholic Church based on facts rather than on rumors or hearsay.

Maryknoll Policy in Manchuria

In five months, the Japanese army overran the three Manchurian provinces of Heilungkiang, Kirin, and Liaoning. To legitimize the aggression, the Japanese created the puppet state of Manchukuo in March 1932 with the last Ch'ing emperor, Puyi, as head of government. In Manchuria, the tense situation created by guerrilla activities and increasing Japanese control formed a backdrop for Maryknoll's activities until the end of World War II. To cope with the growing suspicion of the Japanese-backed Manchurian government, Raymond Lane led his missioners on a road of strict political neutrality. His purpose was to safeguard his missioners' presence in Manchuria and to establish clearly that their work "was primarily and solely religious," directed toward Chinese, Japanese, and Koreans alike.[107]

The bandit scare of the late twenties and early thirties. When Maryknollers entered the Fushun mission territory in February 1927, Dairen and the tip of the Liaotung peninsula contrasted sharply with the rest of the territory. Since the Japanese victory over Russia in 1904, Dairen, together with the South Manchuria Railway, was part of an area leased to the Japanese. Under Japanese control, the city had become a prosperous model of law and order for the rest of the Manchurian territory, which was ridden with bandits. Banditry, a traditional part of life in Manchuria, periodically increased in late summer and early fall when fields of tall ripening sorghum offered opportunities for ambush and quick hiding.

Encounters with bandits on the road and at the missions were taken for granted and viewed almost as normal. Initially the missioners believed their religious status and foreign nationality would protect them. In fact, the first report of robbery of a Maryknoller was not filed until June 1931, four years after their arrival in Fushun.[108] However, Maryknollers wished for a more peaceful environment and safer travel conditions in which to pursue mission work and appreciated efforts made by both Chinese and Japanese soldiers to curtail banditry and robbery.

In October 1930, at the mission center in Fushun city, Brother Benedict Barry praised the cooperation between Japanese and Chinese police authorities in several successful roundups of bandits. "We are more fortunate than our confrères down south. The police here seem to be on the alert." A year later Father Albert Murphy also commented that, thanks to the good work of the Chinese and Japanese police, he had quickly recovered most of the items stolen from his church in Antung.[109]

In addition to the bandits who were often called "Red Beards" by the people, the mountains in the eastern districts of the territory were home to the Big Sword Society (*Ta Tao Hui*). An offshoot of the Boxers, the Big Sword Society had been originally formed as a defense against banditry. Following the economic collapse of Manchuria under the leadership of warlord Chang Tso-lin, the Society had led a peasant uprising in 1927 and 1928 but was later defeated by Chang's army. Outlawed and officially branded as bandits, groups of the Society continued to fight the government.

Maryknollers tended to be wary of Big Sword members because of their Boxer connections. In 1932 Thomas Quirk reported how he found his little town practically deserted after a short absence because:

> . . . the famous Big Sword Society had frightened these superstitious people almost out of their wits by the rumors connected with them. They openly profess devil worship, abstain from meat perpetually, fight only with enormous swords, and aim to terrorize their opponents with such myths as invulnerability and impassibility. However they have respected the church buildings everywhere but we are wondering how long they will continue this policy.[110]

These groups of outlaws were fiercely opposed to the Japanese presence. After Chang Tso-lin was assassinated by Japanese officers, his son, Chang Hsüeh-liang, organized local resistance to Japanese control. The bombing of September 1931 and the proclamation of Manchukuo in March 1932 accelerated the formation of a National Salvation Army of regular soldiers reinforced by units of bandits and Big Sword Society members.[111] They soon controlled most of the countryside in the eastern mission districts of Tunghwa, Hsinpin and Erhpatan.

Through the spring of 1932, Maryknollers were unharmed as officials of the new government and the guerrilla leaders both sought to cultivate the friendship of the United States. The police then occasionally insisted on providing a travel escort. In other circumstances the local resistance let them pass unharmed through roadside ambush points. When questioned about their views of the conflict, Maryknollers always refused to take sides, maintaining that politics was the affair of politicians and not of priests.[112]

In May 1932 the Kuantung Army, reinforced by units of the new Manchukuo Army, launched a major counteroffensive in the eastern districts. The countryside turned into a battleground. With villages continually changing hands, Maryknollers found themselves in the midst of major battles.[113] The Japanese used artillery and airplanes to shell and bomb the opposition and destroyed several villages in these districts, including Catholic compounds. By June 1932, the mission in Linkiang lay in ruin; a few months later several 52-pound bombs fell in and about the compound at Erhpatan. Luckily, a bomb that landed in front of the priest's house did not explode.[114]

The Japanese distributed tracts aimed at the foreign residents of the eastern districts. Handed out and dropped from planes, these flyers explained in English and in Chinese that the present campaign was aimed at suppressing insurgents and Big Sword Society followers who disturbed peace and order. Accordingly, foreigners were urged to seek refuge outside the district if possible. If unable to leave, they were asked to inform Japanese and Manchukuo authorities and to display signs clearly visible from the air and the ground.[115]

Except for very short periods of time, Maryknollers stayed at their posts and did whatever they could to protect the local population. When they left, it was to escort their Christians to safety or because not much remained to protect. Thomas Quirk, for instance, went to Fushun for protection when he realized that most of his parishioners had already fled the village. He added philosophically that he thought the mud house which served as his combination church/rectory was in danger of collapse anyway and not worth protecting. [116]

During the fighting and shelling, mission compounds flew the American flag, which guaranteed only limited protection from bombing and looting. Civilians recognized the flag and sometimes as many as 500 a day sought asylum. To maintain their strict neutrality, Maryknollers refused shelter to soldiers. However, wounded—soldiers and civilians alike—were treated without consideration of allegiance or uniform.[117]

When the Japanese campaign was launched in May 1932, Lane took the precaution of regrouping his missioners in units of two or three. Travel became particularly hazardous, and missioners did not venture on the road except when absolutely necessary.[118] In October 1932, Lane spent a few days of anguish when John Comber, on his way from Hsinpin to Fushun to fill his new assignment as procurator, was reportedly killed in an exchange of fire between Japanese troops and guerrilla elements. Before Lane could confirm or deny the report, eager reporters had already sent the story to the United States where it received prominent coverage. The report proved to be partly false, however; although an American had been shot, he was not John Comber but a Presbyterian minister in Hsinpin.[119]

Not surprisingly, Maryknollers welcomed every piece of news signaling the end of the bandit scare. In September 1932, when the front pages of newspapers in Dairen boasted that the new puppet government had been recognized by Western nations, the Maryknoll Sisters were quite enthusiastic:

> The bells on the newsboys' backs made us wonder what the bandits were doing now. [However] it was not bandit news but the glad tidings that the new Manchurian government had been recognized by the world.[120]

However, the news proved far from true: the United States refused to recognize the new regime. Lane took extra precautions to inform the Japanese authorities that his missioners worked for the Church and not for the United States.

> I visited the Chief of Police, the Head of the Mining Administration who is likewise the civil head for the city of Fushun and I called later on the Chief Military man. . . . I emphasized the fact on all of them that we were here to save souls and to propagate the Faith among the different races in Manchuria, but they should not expect us to say one word on the political situation.[121]

Japanese suspicion on the rise, 1931–1933. From 1931 to 1933, while Maryknollers in the countryside were caught in open warfare between the Kwantung Army and anti-Japanese forces, Maryknollers in the cities fell under increasing surveillance and had to be extremely cautious to avoid becoming tools of Japanese propaganda.

The first Japanese attempt to use Maryknollers for their own purposes came just a few days prior to the Mukden incident. On September 15, 1931,

the first page of the *Peking Times* and the *Tientsin Times* carried a
release by the Japanese Rengo News Service of a speech falsely attributed
to Father Joseph McCormack, the senior Maryknoll missioner in Fushun.
In a fabricated article entitled "Direct Action against Banditry," McCormack was reported to have said that:

> Well-informed British, American and French in Manchuria who were in the
> habit of watching Japanese actions with suspicions, partly because of their
> superficial sympathy for China and partly because of China's bold and selfish
> propaganda, seemed to have realized the innocent nature of Japan's ambi-
> tion and learned that in nearly all questions related to Japan, China is
> wrong.[122]

Informed immediately by apostolic delegate Costantini, McCormack
wrote to the editors strongly denying authorship of the article. In a letter
to James A. Walsh, he commented that it was not the first time that the
Rengo News Service had distorted missioners' words and deeds.[123]

The Japanese began to scrutinize missioners' activities. Lane learned
that insinuations were made accusing American missioners of using their
mission network, their control of the native clergy, and their contacts with
the Christians to gather information on Japanese activities for the United
States. He took great care not to write anything which could be misinterpreted by the Japanese. He asked James A. Walsh to exert extreme
caution in printing any article in *The Field Afar* concerning Japan or
Manchuria. Much information, Lane warned, is strictly to inform the
Maryknoll General Council but should never be published. "Due to the
tense situation," he also advised the superior general not to use Knights of
Columbus letterhead for his correspondence. The surplus stationery had
been a gift to Maryknoll. Obviously Lane felt that the prominent headline
of "War Activities" flanked by an American flag could easily be misunderstood and implicate Maryknoll as a spy organization in the service of the
United States.[124]

Lane was careful to avoid any activities which could antagonize the
Japanese. After the bombing of the mission compound at Erhpatan, he
made no claim for repairs and was satisfied with an official apology. At the
same time, he preferred to be accused of noncooperation by the American
consul in Mukden rather than to release information about the Japanese
and risk political embarrassment. He also chose to keep silent on the gory
circumstances surrounding the massacre of 3,000 Chinese by the Japanese
during the siege of Fushun and its surrounding villages in the early spring
of 1932. At one point he learned that an old lady was the only survivor of
another incident in which the Japanese killed 10 Christians. Lane gave
her asylum in his center, advising her not to talk while he turned away
journalists.[125]

KNIGHTS OF COLUMBUS

WAR ACTIVITIES

CAMP_____

Fr. McCormack ___191__

September 10, 1938

Dear FatherJoseph:

Thanks for your letter of August 9.

The news that two missions are closed and two others in danger - particularly of the havoc at Ha-Ma-Ho-is disturbing. However, it is good of you to keep us informed, if only that we may pray more fervently for peace and security in China, especially the detached and distracted section of it where your labors are cast.

It is consoling to know that such trying conditions have actually brought an increase in the number of catechumens. I note that reports from other parts of China show a similar result - that the continual troubles are bringing many closer to the Church. It is true, as you say, that some of these will be like the well, but not favorably, known rice Christians. However, it is not likely that it will all be chaff, thank God!

The arrival of Monsignor Lane and the new missioners is timely, and with the better conditions you hope for with the cutting of the crops, I trust you will be able to recoup most of the losses.

You may be sure of our special interest and prayers during these difficult times.

With best wishes, I am,

Devotedly yours in Christ,

Superior General

wom

Fig. 1. Example of a letter by Father James A. Walsh on Knights of Columbus letterhead which could raise Japanese suspicions. Source: Maryknoll Fathers' Archives, Box 47, Folder 3.

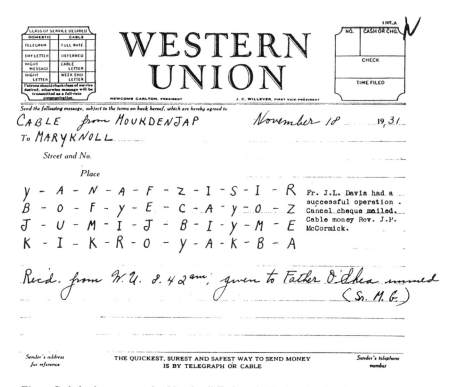

Fig. 2. Coded telegram sent by Maryknoll Fathers in Fushun to Maryknoll Center in New York. The decoded text was typed in upon reception of the cable at the Center. Source: Maryknoll Fathers' Archives, Box 47, Folder 3.

Despite their efforts to maintain a low profile, Maryknollers came under increasing suspicion by the new government. Their mail was routinely opened, they were watched by plainclothes policemen, and their Bentley telegram code of communication with Maryknoll headquarters was under constant scrutiny. Accusations finally surfaced in the press. In October 1932 Lane wrote to Maryknoll headquarters:

> Recently a rather stupid article was printed in one of the newspapers in Mukden, containing a personal attack on me, questioning our methods and our work here. One of the statements was to the effect that I had a private code through which I kept in contact with the American government. Another was to the effect that I had received two million dollars gold which I was to spend in this section for dubious purposes. The whole article was a mass of falsehoods. I immediately sent for Mr. Sato, our best Christian in Dairen, who confronted the editor. This worthy admitted that he had not read the article, and explained that it was merely a mass of rumors. He consented to a retraction, and is willing now to print a series of articles explaining our work.[126]

Subsequently, Lane hosted a group of reporters at the Fushun center to explain Maryknoll's activities. The newsmen then published an article that portrayed the missioners in a more favorable light. "There are some inaccuracies but the article shows good will, and evidently, at least one of them was impressed."[127]

Lane was convinced that the accusations were instigated by suspicious governmental officials and did not reflect the attitude of the people. Always optimistic, he noted that conditions had been steadily improving since the new article on the true nature of the Catholic Church and its activities: "The officials are beginning to realize that our work is primarily and solely religious." [128]

Lane had barely written these words when he became the target of new accusations. The Japanese accused him of providing Edward Hunter, a staff correspondent for the International News Service, with information detrimental to them concerning the Fushun massacre. The journalist attempted to exonerate Lane by going to the Japanese Foreign Office in Tokyo and denying that he had met any Catholic missioner in Fushun. Hunter emphasized that he knew the language well enough to obtain information from the Chinese by himself. Furthermore, he mentioned that he had learned that foreign officials of other countries had gathered similar confidential reports from refugees and businessmen.[129]

Although Lane and Hunter had never actually met, suspicious Japanese intelligence officers had a different impression. A priest had met Hunter at the railroad station. Instead of telling him immediately that an interview with Lane was impossible, the Maryknoller had brought the newsman to the center house for a cup of coffee. It appeared to the Japanese as if information had been relayed to Hunter by the Maryknollers.

Despite all their efforts, American missioners were not able to convince the Japanese and Chinese authorities in Manchuria that Maryknoll was neutral. As citizens of a country which refused to recognize the government of Manchukuo, Maryknollers became the targets of continual accusations. In November 1933 Lane mentioned that in the past 15 months, a dozen such calumnies had sprung up in the local newspapers and even on the radio.[130] On November 21, venomous attacks on the missioners hit the newsstands. Articles carrying titles such as "Catholic Priests Suspected" and "Camouflage in Religion: American Spies in Manchukuo" appeared simultaneously in two Mukden newspapers, *Sheng-ching Shih-pao* and *Hoten Mainichi Shimbun*, and two Dairen newspapers, *Ta-lien Hsin-pao* and *Manshū Nippō*. The following day, these same articles appeared in a Chinese newspaper in Fushun.

These articles accused the American Catholic missioners of being spies who spoke fluent Chinese and some even Japanese. Diversified activities, such as mission outstations, seminaries, old folks' homes and orphanages, gave missioners numerous contacts with the people and opportunities to gather information, which they passed on to the American government. According to these reports, these spying activities had become more frequent since the arrival of 11 new missioners who were all university graduates with expertise not only in theology but also in other disciplines such as economics, medicine, agriculture, and engineering. The articles went on to say that the appointment of Chinese priests, who were graduates of Maryknoll seminaries, into the "branch offices" had made "the deployment of their forces [even] more complete." As a consequence, the Manchukuo and Japanese police kept a close watch on missioners and allegedly discovered among them American soldiers and officers in priests' cassocks.[131]

This time, Lane reacted strongly and enlisted the help of the American consul in Mukden. He sent Brother Benedict to the consul for advice on seeking a retraction. As a result, John Paton Davies, Jr., the American vice-consul, accompanied the Maryknoll representative to the office of the Japanese vice-consul, who promised to do everything in his power to obtain a public retraction.

At the same time, Lane invited a representative of the police department to visit the Fushun mission center, explained the mission work to him, and volunteered to go to the police station if it could be proven that any missioners were spies in the employ of the United States. Otherwise, Lane added, unless the new government forbade the Church to exist in Manchukuo, the police should protect the missioners' reputations as well as their lives.[132] By December 1933 a triumphant Lane wrote to the Maryknoll superior general that he had already secured one retraction and hoped for more.[133] Despite this progress, Maryknollers in the cities remained under constant surveillance by Manchukuo detectives. Policemen went to the rectories almost daily to inquire about the missioners' activities and report back to their Japanese superiors. These visits—which were not unfriendly—became a nuisance and kept the missioners on edge.[134]

Compromised neutrality, 1934–1945. In 1934 the Holy See decided to consider Manchuria as a mission field independent of China and to appoint Bishop Ernest Gaspais as the official "Representative of the Holy See" in the capital of Hsinking. This occasion was interpreted by the Manchukuo government as a sign of political recognition. The bishops of Manchuria, including Maryknoll Bishop Raymond Lane, had indeed persuaded Rome that any continuation of mission work depended on the Church's positive reaction to the new regime. This change of attitude was immediately reflected in Maryknoll diaries. On March 1, 1934, all Catholic churches celebrated the coronation of the Emperor Puyi by flying Manchukuo and papal flags. The Sisters in the Japanese parish of Dairen celebrated by giving a holiday to the children of their school. Puyi apparently showed his appreciation of the Catholic Church by making a substantial donation.[135]

Through the years Maryknollers got deliberately involved in activities that, they thought, would lessen the suspicions of the government. In 1934, for example, Lane sponsored a concert in Fushun. The proceeds of 900 Manchukuo yüan were turned over to the authorities for social welfare in Manchukuo and the relief of victims of a recent typhoon in Japan. In 1935, Father John Murrett willingly agreed to be an examiner of harbor pilots in Dairen to ascertain their knowledge of English.[136] At the request of the authorities, Maryknollers testified in court cases, visited local reformatories and prisons, gave occasional radio broadcasts, and even provided street preachers to give patriotic as well as religious talks.[137] They also cooperated with officials when asked to provide shelter for the homeless at critical times such as the flooding of the Yalu River in 1936 and 1938.[138] As a result of this official cooperation between the Church and the government, open criticism in the news media disappeared, although the "infantile and puerile interference" on the part of local police remained "most annoying."[139]

In 1934, the movement of resistance to the Japanese shifted from open confrontation to guerrilla activities, especially in the mountains and forests of eastern and southeastern Manchuria where Maryknoll had most of its rural missions. to counteract this resurgence of resistance activity, the Kwantung Army began a drastic program of counterinsurgency, and the Japanese implemented special techniques such as issuing residence certificates, organizing a self-defense corps, and creating collective hamlets.

The unfolding of the plan in the area surrounding Linkiang is well described by Father Howard Geselbracht. In late 1934 farmers were forced off their farms into collective hamlets. The goals of the Japanese were to eliminate hiding places and sources of food for the resistance and to strengthen the self-defense capability of the peasants. These measures proved very unpopular because the farmers were reluctant to leave their lands. Farmhouses were burned down, and the government did not assist in their rebuilding. Many local residents went to the church for assistance, putting more and more strain on the vicariate's finances.[140]

Although the collective hamlet program physically separated the guerrillas from the masses, in the end it created anti-Japanese feelings which drove the masses closer to the guerrillas. Guerrilla activities picked up during 1935, and some mission locations like Hsinpin took on "a world war appearance with barbed wire defenses, deep trenches encircling the town, and special barriers at the entrances."[141]

Nonetheless, by the following year the Manchukuo troops gained the upper hand. In the eastern section of the vicariate, from Linkiang in the north to Chakow in the south, the Fathers' diaries recorded the progress of the Japanese and Manchukuo troops.[142] However, the troops of the puppet government were never able to thoroughly implement the relocation program or to crush the resistance movement which lay dormant waiting for an opportunity to resurface. When the Japanese applied pressure to one area, the resistance fighters simply moved and resumed activity in another location.[143] Between 1932 and 1937, in Fushun city, for instance, the Sisters' diaries reported the periodic threat of the Red Beards against Fushun-Hopei, the nonwalled part of the city. Conditions became so precarious in 1932 and 1933 that Bishop Lane ordered the Sisters and the Chinese aspirants back to Fushun-Honan, for three months. Following the kidnapping of Father Gerard Donovan in Hopei in October 1937, Raymond Lane again closed the Hopei convent.[144]

As the Japanese tightened their control, missioners were subjected to all the measures imposed on the population. Mission activities were strongly curtailed, particularly in the eastern areas of the vicariate. Some schools had to be closed, and overnight trips to outstations became almost impossible as missioners were not allowed to stay in unprotected towns at night.[145]

None of the missioners' diaries or letters ever questioned these measures. Maryknollers were careful not to write or say anything which could be misinterpreted by the Japanese and result in their expulsion. Years later, Father Sylvio Gilbert, the pastor of Tunghwa from 1930 to 1941, recalled in an interview that this was done on purpose because Maryknollers knew their correspondence was monitored. Gilbert's interview gives a better understanding of the real attitudes of Maryknollers in the countryside regarding the growing resistance movement. Maryknollers in the predominantly Chinese countryside found themselves on the side of the resistance. "These [so-called] bandits," confessed Gilbert, "were my parishioners. They were my friends."[146] Indeed they had such great respect for him that during the decade he spent in Tunghwa, he never had any bad encounters on the road. He was once told that when he had a blowout bicycling back from a sick call, he was watched at all times and protected by a group of bandits. They would have liked to help him repair his tire but preferred to remain hidden for fear of frightening him since he did not know any of them.[147]

As the Japanese closed in on Tunghwa, Gilbert gave asylum to important figures of the resistance and the former government and stored trunks containing their personal belongings. He also took care of wounded soldiers from the defeated Chinese army. Not surprisingly, the Japanese put him on their blacklist and, after the fall of Tunghwa, prepared to raid his place for evidence. He was warned, however, by a Japanese interpreter who had been his parishioner in Antung a few years before. When Gilbert hurried to burn the contents of the trunks left with him, he realized they were mainly military uniforms and official papers. He also arranged for an old lady from his old folks' home to slip out at night and join her son, a general in the resistance movement. As for two wounded Chinese soldiers still left in the compound, he told the Japanese commanding officer that they were invalids who could no longer carry guns and that he was keeping them out of pure compassion.[148]

From that time to his arrest on Pearl Harbor day, Gilbert was shadowed and subjected to continuous harassment. The police questioned him in the rectory for an hour or two at a time, monitored his church services, and submitted him to continual road checks when traveling:

> If I went on the train, they would always ask me for my passport; if I went through a town, they went through the lining of my coat and my pipe to see if there was any message. When I would get off the train, they would keep me at the gate just to humiliate me as though they wanted me to get out [of the country] without forcing me out.[149]

The diaries and letters conveyed very little of these activities. It was only in the late 1950s that Sister Mary Eunice Tolan, the Sisters' local superior, wrote a history of the Maryknoll Sisters in Manchuria and expressed her real opinion by quoting from a November 1942 issue of *National Geographic*:

> Even people who suffer at the hands of bandits don't talk against them. They are the only ones fighting the people's fight against the Japanese. They loot and kill but often do so to get food and arms to carry on their war against the Japanese army. Many people no longer call them bandits but volunteers.[150]

Totally aware of "the delicate Manchurian situation," Maryknollers preferred to call the resistance fighters "bandits" and to maintain a facade of neutrality. Their goal was to stay in Manchuria by any means rather than to provoke the Japanese and face deportation.

> The Japanese were on occasion very unjust and we didn't like what we saw. We resented it but we couldn't do anything so we just kept minding our Ps and Qs and went about our missionary work.[151]

The only striking exception was when Fathers Sylvio Gilbert and William Kaschmitter chose to accompany to jail six of their Christians who had gotten into a fight with a Japanese policeman. The incident began during a church service when a policeman refused to remove his hat and slapped a catechist. At the police station, the Japanese officer quickly realized the possible repercussions of jailing the missioners under such circumstances. After a "pep talk" to the Christians, who promised never again to hit a policeman, he let everyone go free. Gilbert savored that moment of victory by hiring a droshky to take them back to the mission.

> We came as prisoners. We were going back in triumph. As we went through the main street, the people with their thumbs up were saying "Hurrah! Only the Catholic Church can hit a policeman and get away with it."[152]

As the decade progressed, non-Japanese foreign residents were subjected to an increasing number of measures of control. Checking of resident certificates and questioning by detectives became almost a daily routine. Travel without permits was forbidden, and all travel was finally restricted to three days a month. Nonetheless, most missioners preferred to blame the "bandits" rather than the Japanese for this curtailment of their freedom.[153]

At first, the relocation program and the antibandit drives of the Japanese seriously weakened the resistance movement. With the removal of their bases of support and their sources of food, many bandit units resorted to kidnapping and looting. The increase in bandit-type activities and the growing evidence of Communist backing tended to discredit the resistance movement in the eyes of the missioners.[154] In their vocabulary, the name "Red Beards" became interchangeable with "Red bandits" and "Red guerrillas." Sister Celine Marie Werner recalled that when she and other Sisters went to visit outstations along the mountain path, the thought was never far from her mind that the so-called Red bandits were in that area.[155]

At the same time, Japanese supervision brought law and order to Manchuria. "Even the trains ran on time," commented Father Edward Weis. "With the Chinese you didn't know when they would come."[156] Most Maryknollers who longed for peace to build a stable mission program saw some hope of its realization under Japanese rule—despite the unpleasant conditions. By contrast, the resistance continued to degenerate into outright banditry and spelled a return to chaotic times.

The kidnappings of Fathers Clarence Burns in February 1936 and Gerard Donovan in October 1937 were decisive events which turned Maryknollers away from the bandit-guerrillas and made them more dependent on the Japanese authorities. Burns was detained for nine months and then released; Donovan was strangled four months after his abduction. In both instances, the American priests were first entrapped by bandits and then turned over to uniformed resistance fighters. The group which detained Burns was a unit of the self-defense army, led by Wang Feng-ko, the head of the Big Sword Society. Among all the anti-Japanese groups, Wang's organization offered the stiffest resistance, especially in the Tunghwa region. At the time of Burns' kidnapping, Wang, who had always been hostile to the Communists, had recently allied himself with the anti-Japanese Communist forces.[157]

Burns' account of his captivity offers a glimpse of the organization of the guerrilla movement — its means of sustenance, its strong ties with the local people, and its relationships with other bandit units.[158] In the case of Father Donovan, the details surrounding his capture and death indicate that several Maryknollers knew that he had been detained by a Communist guerrilla unit but preferred not to mention it.[159] In neither case did the captors seem to have intended to hurt the missioners. The demand of a hefty ransom as well as the rash of kidnappings of rich Chinese made it obvious that the bandit-guerillas were in need of money. Maryknollers had finally become targets, explained a Maryknoll Father, because America and Americans spelled gold to the bandits and that was what they were after:

> The Beautiful Country, their name for America, means a land where autos race like ants and the sky is filled with planes and music; where railroads and good roads cobweb the country. A country like this should be willing to pay the ransom asked for one of her sons.[160]

Maryknoll refused to satisfy the bandits' demand. Since the capture of Father Harry Bush in South China in 1935, the Society had adopted the policy of not giving in to ransom demands for fear that they would trigger more kidnappings. In fact, ransom did not appear to be the ultimate reason for kidnapping Burns and Donovan. During his captivity, Burns learned that his captors planned to keep him for three or four years to pressure both the United States and Japan—even if a ransom was paid. After his release, he added, "The bandits captured me for the purpose of precipitating a war between the United States and Japan."[161]

When the bandits were pursued by the Japanese and Manchukuo troops, they were continuously on the move and, given the rough living conditions, the prisoners could not maintain the pace. Decisions had to be made. The softhearted leader of Burns' group set him free. Donovan was not as lucky and was strangled.

Realizing the political repercussions that could result from another kidnapping, Lane withdrew his missioners from areas of special danger: for example, the Fathers moved from Chakow to Chuang Ho, a city defended by the government, and the Sisters in Fushun city returned every evening from Hopei to Honan for better protection.[162]

After 1938, as Japan moved toward a position of hegemony in Asia, Maryknollers experienced additional surveillance and restrictions. In December 1941 all the Maryknoll Fathers and Sisters of American and Canadian nationality were arrested by the Japanese. The American Maryknollers in Dairen—three priests, one Brother, and eleven Sisters—were put under house arrest in the convent of the Japanese parish.[163] In the rest of the vicariate, the priests were sent to an internment camp at the Mukden Foreigners' Club. The Sisters, with the exception of Sisters Miriam Schmitt and Angela Marie Coveny who were also interned, were allowed to stay in their convents at Fushun-Honan and Hopei.[164]

In March 1942, the Japanese authorities asked if Maryknollers wished to be repatriated and were surprised to hear that none wanted to return unless ordered to do so by the bishop. The decision, therefore, rested with Lane, who knew that the general policy of the Church was that pastors should remain with the people. He was equally aware that Mother Mary Joseph had ruled that the Maryknoll Sisters should follow this general policy. After meeting with Bishop Ernest Gaspais, the papal representative, and Father John 0'Donnell, the Maryknoll Society superior in Manchukuo, Lane decided to repatriate half of the Fathers and Sisters from Mukden and Fushun.[165]

In late May 1942, a group of 13 priests and Brothers and nine Sisters left Manchuria by train via Korea and Japan on their way to the United States. In Yokohama they boarded the exchange vessel *Asama Maru* with Maryknollers from Korea and Japan as well as other non-Japanese nationals. In Lourenço Marques, Mozambique, they were among 1,550 American and other nationals exchanged for Japanese citizens; they returned to the United States on the Swedish ship *Gripsholm*.[166]

During the last leg of the trip home, John O'Donnell wrote an 11-page report to the superior general, James E. Walsh. In it, O'Donnell gave an angry account of distressing events on board the *Gripsholm*. One of the passengers, Bishop William O'Shea, the Maryknoll bishop of the vicariate of Pyongyang in Korea, gave permission to American government officials to question the Maryknoll priests about conditions in Japanese-occupied territories. Many priests completed as many as three questionnaires and were told that any information given would be kept confidential. Some were asked, if Society permission were obtained, to serve in special capacities such as interpreters. O'Donnell was particularly incensed at the bishop for overstepping his authority and for not consulting the three Society superiors on board, Fathers Everett Briggs of Japan, James Pardy of Korea, and himself for Manchuria. None of the Society superiors knew what arrangements O'Shea had made with the various officials in charge of the questioning, but he certainly appeared to have breached the neutrality previously followed by Maryknollers in Manchuria.[167]

As most of the internees at the Mukden Foreigners' Club had been repatriated, the Maryknollers who remained at the Club returned to Fushun city. Around that same time, Lane learned that the pope had expressed his desire that missioners should seek repatriation. Consequently the bishop notified the remaining Maryknollers to ask for passage on an exchange ship. The 15 missioners under house arrest in Dairen were the first to receive permission to leave; they were transferred to Shanghai in September 1942 and sailed a year later on the *Teia Maru*.[168] By that time, the 14 Maryknollers who had remained in Fushun city with Bishop Lane were ready for repatriation; they also boarded the *Teia Maru*.[169]

Bishop Lane chose to remain, with Father Edward McGurkin as his companion, to symbolize Maryknoll's desire to be with their people. They were sent to an internment camp in Ssupingkai where they were re-united with Father Armand Jacques, a Canadian Maryknoller who had been there since his arrest on December 1941. The three men stayed in the camp with other Canadian internees until the end of World War II.

In Dairen, three non-American Maryknoll Sisters—two Japanese and one German citizen—also stayed to comply with the Japanese author-ities' request to keep the Maryknoll Academy open. In 1943 they were joined by two more Maryknoll Sisters, a Korean, and a third Japanese. Cut off from communication with their motherhouse in New York and their bishop in Ssupingkai, deprived of funds, and hemmed in by stringent regulations, ration shortages, and other wartime hardships, the five Sisters — Sabina Nakamura, Marie Elise Baumann, Maria Talitha Yamagi-shi, Rose Ann Nakata, and Margaret Kim—taught about 200 students in the Academy until June 29, 1946, when the Soviet Army took over its direction.

At the same time, the Sisters assumed most of the pastoral work in the Japanese parish, visiting Catholics, comforting the sick, conducting cook-ing and embroidery classes, instructing catechumens, and running a kin-dergarten. Together with three native Sisters who were engaged in the same kind of work at the Chinese parish, they assumed the entire respon-sibility for the Catholic community in Dairen. Toward the end of 1942, the bishop of Mukden sent a Chinese priest to the city to resume distribution of the sacraments. More help came in 1943 when an Italian Salesian took charge of the Japanese parish and in 1944 when a German Jesuit was added to the faculty of the Academy.[170]

Sister Sabina, the group superior, played a most important role in maintaining the morale of the Maryknoll Sisters throughout these years. Moreover, she belonged to a Japanese noble family and could deal skillfully with Japanese officials. More than once she defused situations which threatened to get out of hand. Sister Margaret recalled, for example, how the police detained her on suspicion of spying for the Americans when she joined the group in Dairen. With Sister Sabina's intervention, she was freed in less than a day.[171]

After Lane's release from detention, the bishop visited the Sisters in

Dairen in the spring of 1946 and was so moved by what they and the native Sisters had endured during the past four years that he wrote to Maryknoll headquarters:

> If there is anything approaching the heroic in these parts, it is the conduct of our Maryknoll Sisters in Dairen during recent years. An epic poem could be written about their work, their sacrifices, their sufferings and their loyalty. The native Sisters whom they trained likewise share the laurels![172]

Consequences for Maryknoll and the Church in Manchuria

From the day they arrived in Manchuria, Maryknollers chose to remain as politically uninvolved as possible. Lane chose to emphasize the religious purpose of his group of missioners. Their work among all three major nationalities in Manchuria was proof of their nonpolitical involvement. In Dairen, Maryknollers established Chinese and Japanese parishes, and in Fushun and Antung, they had Korean parishes as well.

Maryknollers also tried to show their willingness to be law-abiding foreign residents by complying promptly with the ever increasing regulations. Yet the Japanese were never totally convinced that Maryknollers did not work for the United States government or did not secretly plot with bandits against the new government. For a while the authorities even doubted the story of Donovan's kidnapping and believed he had voluntarily joined the resistance as an advisor.

They had raised the same suspicions about Father Burns. John Paton Davies, Jr., the American vice-consul in Mukden who was dispatched to Tunghwa to officially receive Burns from his Japanese rescuers, recalled: "Not until after the army had 'saved' and thoroughly interrogated Father Burns were the Japanese persuaded that he had indeed been seized against his will and was not a Freedom Fighter." Moreover, Davies commented how everyone in Tunghwa must have been relieved to see him—a representative of the United States—leave as soon as possible:

> The Japanese because they are absurdly suspicious that I would spy on them. The Maryknoll Fathers because it would mean that the [Japanese], under whose sadism they sought to survive, would be a little less edgy and vengeful.[173]

When Japan and the United States went to war, Maryknollers' pledges of neutrality and efforts to please the Japanese did not succeed in preventing their arrest and deportation. Their record of good behavior, however, might explain why they were not maltreated by the Japanese authorities. Nonetheless, in the end the missioners' nationality determined their fate. Of the 63 Maryknollers in Manchuria at the time, only five Sisters who were neither American nor Canadian were allowed to remain and continue their work.

Maryknollers were more successful at convincing the Chinese people that they were neutral, or rather, on their side. In Manchuria, Chinese antiforeignism was directed against the Japanese rather than toward the Western missioners. The Chinese could clearly see that missioners were also subjected to annoyances and restrictions by the Japanese-controlled government. Maryknollers' visits as well as their material and medical help were appreciated. Their good reputation spread as well among bandit groups. Even if the Chinese Christians trusted the missioners enough to discuss politics in front of them on occasion, they did not expect the missioners to take a stand against the Japanese. In fact, they preferred to keep them out of their "secret meetings" altogether because the presence of missioners was bound to attract Japanese suspicions.[174]

The American missioners were certainly not blind to the Chinese resistance movement; yet in order to maximize their chances of not being expelled from Manchuria and to stress the religious priority of their missionary work, they chose to not mingle in politics. Moreover, most of them did not seem convinced that ousting the Japanese would bring better times to Manchuria. Father Edward Manning remarked:

> Apart from those annoyances that I mentioned about the Japanese, they really did not bother us and we saw no occasion to attempt anything. Moreover the people themselves did not seem to be suffering from such great oppression. I don't think they were taxed more than under the warlords and the bandits that followed; to some extent they were even better off. It was a rather quiet time.[175]

Maryknollers in Manchuria made the choice of remaining apolitical and staying as long as they could. From a religious point of view, the results of this decision are difficult to assess. Owing to the uncertainties of the time, Maryknollers were not able to implement a stable program of missionary work to foster conversions. Between 1929 and 1941, the mere doubling in the Chinese Catholic population of the Fushun vicariate from some 4,000 to 8,000 seems to indicate that most of the increase came from the normal growth of Catholic families rather than actual conversions. In many places these families had been Catholic for several generations. They had proven the strength of their faith during the persecution of the Boxer uprising. Maryknoll's real achievements during that period lay in the nurturing of a native clergy and Sisterhood, which indeed could not have begun without their presence.

The Chinese population seemed to look favorably on the American missioners and to appreciate their works of mercy and education. Yet the noncommittal attitude of the same missioners toward Chinese aspirations for a free Manchuria prevented the Catholic Church from having a deep influence on Chinese society. Out of a population of five million Chinese, there were only 8,000 Catholics in 1941. If missioners had taken a stand against Japanese domination and endured jail and expulsion, would they have reached a larger segment of the population? Their silence left Catholics involved in the resistance movement without proper guidance. Communism remained unchallenged as an ideology for the nationalist aspirations of the Chinese in Manchuria. As leaders of the Catholic Church, Maryknollers provided an image of a group which, in order to survive, chose to bow down to the Japanese. Although Maryknollers took good spiritual care of the Catholics and built the foundation for native leadership, they seemed to have missed an opportunity to let the Church identify with Chinese aspirations. Their aloofness to the political situation served to fuel accusations later on that the Catholic Church was working against Chinese interests and that Chinese Catholics were unpatriotic.

Maryknoll Policy in South China

The political attitude of Maryknoll missioners in South China differed substantially from the attitude of those in Manchuria. Until 1936, they showed little concern about Japan's repeated encroachments into China. Their diaries, letters, and reports only mentioned several times in passing the Japanese aggression in Manchuria in 1931, the attack on Shanghai in 1932, and the occupation of the province of Jehol in 1933. These rumors of war came from far away and were overpowered by the local reality of the Nationalists' ruthless hunting down of Communist sympathizers. This attitude reflected the general support by the Catholic Church hierarchy in China for Chiang Kai-shek's campaign of extermination against the Communists and implicitly recognized the Generalissimo's argument that prior to waging a foreign war, it was necessary to achieve internal peace. By 1936, however, popular sentiment in China was mounting for an end to civil war and the turning of guns against the Japanese.

Supporting the war effort against Japan. Following his spectacular kidnapping and release at Sian in December 1936 by Manchurian troops anxious to fight Japanese invaders and not Chinese Communists, Chiang Kai-shek announced that the time had come to prepare the fight against the invaders. The Catholic Church again immediately rallied behind him. In December 1936, the *Kongmoon Bulletin*, the official newsletter of the Kongmoon vicariate, reported a press release from a Cantonese newspaper stating that 7,000 Chinese and foreign Catholics had attended a pontifical mass in Hankow as a public act of thanksgiving for the release of Chiang. Two months later, the *Bulletin* asked all Maryknollers in the vicariate to urge Catholics to contribute to the nation's war effort. Their donation would be the vicariate's contribution toward the payment of two ambulance-airplanes presented to Chiang by the Catholic Action headquarters in Shanghai as a symbol of the Chinese Catholics' patriotism.[176]

When following the Marco Polo Bridge incident of July 1937 the Japanese resumed their aggression against China, Maryknollers did not hesitate to take sides. In August 1937, the *Kongmoon Bulletin* stressed that "Christians should be exhorted to pray for peace and for the welfare of China. Encourage them to contribute funds for the wounded soldiers, food for refugees and similar works of mercy."[177] The importance of taking up a collection for war relief was periodically mentioned in the *Bulletin* with examples to stimulate the generosity of the Catholics. In October, the *Bulletin* singled out the lepers of Sunwui who lived on soupy rice for a week to contribute 75 Chinese dollars of their food allowance to the Catholic Relief Society. The following month, the seminarians in Pakkai emulated the patriotic lepers and saved 130 Chinese dollars which was forwarded to a war relief fund under Catholic auspices.

Throughout China, the Catholic missioners were urged to provide assistance. As early as 1938, Chiang Kai-shek and several newspapers in China praised the manifestations of charity and Chinese patriotism displayed by the Catholic Church. Prayers for peace were incorporated into the daily mass. In Wuchow starting with Chinese New Year of 1938, Monsignor Bernard Meyer instituted a three-day prayer for peace which rotated in each mission of his prefecture for a whole month. This observance was praised by local officials and given coverage in the Wuchow newspapers.[178]

Yet as the Japanese encroached on an ever-expanding portion of China, some foreign bishops and missioners in occupied territories began to waver in their support of the resistance movement and to advocate neutrality. They argued that, for the purpose of evangelization, it did not matter if the government of China was Chinese or Japanese as long as it was not Communist. In March 1939, the papal delegate, Archbishop Mario Zanin, apparently heeded the minority voice when he issued a statement urging all the Catholic bishops of China to restrain their missioners from taking sides in the conflict. Not only were his words immediately seized upon by the Nationalist government, almost provoking a major diplomatic incident between China and the Vatican, but they also caused much embarrassment to most Catholic missions in free China.[179] In fact, contrary to Zanin's wishes, missioners' support of the Chinese cause strengthened. By then, Maryknollers in South China were experiencing Japanese bombing and saw the aftermath of destruction, injuries, hunger, epidemics, and death. As the events drew them closer and closer to the Chinese people, they felt victimized by the Japanese and became involved in the effort to stop the invasion. Forced out of their mission routine, Maryknoll priests, Brothers, and Sisters performed many deeds of courage, sacrifice, and charity, conveying a good impression of the Catholic Church to the non-Christian population.

Staying with the people. One of the best testimonials Maryknollers gave of their dedication to the Chinese of South China was their decision to remain with them through the war years. Instead of yielding to the advice of the American consul-general in Canton to evacuate, Maryknollers chose to stay in their missions.[180] From September 1937, when Japanese shelling and bombing started along the coastal area of Kwangtung, until December 8, 1941, Maryknollers kept all their missions open. They stayed at their posts in spite of all the difficulties. Instead of curtailing their work because of the Japanese invasion, Maryknollers shouldered more responsibility, accepting the administration of Kweilin prefecture and increasing the number of personnel in Kwangtung and Kwangsi. Between 1937 and 1941, the number of Fathers and Brothers expanded from 75 to 97 and the Sisters from 28 to 38.

In November 1937, the first Japanese incursion into the Kongmoon vicariate occurred on Sancian Island. At the time, most Maryknollers of the vicariate were in Hong Kong for their annual retreat and the consecration of Bishop Paschang. However, two Maryknoll Sisters who had just opened a convent in April remained on Sancian with a Chinese priest from Canton who was filling in temporarily for the absent pastor. Suddenly, the Japanese landed and all the inhabitants, including the Chinese priest, went into hiding in the hills, leaving the Sisters alone in their convent. The news spread across the channel to the mainland and reached Father Francis O'Neill of Toishan who had just returned from Hong Kong. O'Neill immediately hired a boat for Sancian where he found the Sisters unharmed. He decided to take them back to Toishan as he did not know if the bishop would let Father Robert Cairns, the pastor of Sancian, return to his post. Both Bishop Paschang and Sister Mary Paul McKenna calmly reassessed the mission work on Sancian. Within a few days, Father Cairns was on his way back to the island; however, the convent experiment was abandoned. Sister Candida Maria Basto was sent to Yeungkong, and Sister Monica Marie Boyle went to Loting.[181]

Before December 8, 1941, Maryknollers used their status as nationals of a neutral nation as often as necessary to continue their missionary work and offer protection to the people who took refuge in their compounds. As in Manchuria, missioners prominently displayed the American flag to identify their status. In January 1939, the Kongmoon diary mentioned that there were more American flags flying over the compound than pennants on an admiral's flagship.[182] However, as the intensity of the bombing increased, the protection of the flag became more and more tenuous, even in inland locations such as Loting in Kwangtung, which was bombed on February 25, 1939, and Pingnam in Kwangsi, which was bombed on October 23, 1939.[183]

A 14-by nine-foot flag flew on the roof of the rectory at Loting during its first bombing. Japanese planes dropped three bombs on the Maryknoll mission compound and strafed it several times with machine gun fire, killing and wounding some 200 people. Although there was no direct hit, the roof of the mission building was severely damaged, and all the windows were blown out. Father Robert Kennelly was wounded in seven places in his left leg by fragments of the first bomb and a machine gun bullet. At the sight of Father Kennelly, Sister Monica Marie Boyle, who had received her baptism of gunfire on Sancian a year before, braved the bombing and ran to the dispensary to get a bottle of peroxide and some cotton. When she realized that she could not stop the flow of blood, she ran back to the dispensary for a tourniquet. The people of Loting treated the Maryknoll Father like a war hero, although there was no doubt in his mind that the real hero was the courageous Sister-nurse.[184]

On March 22, 1941, Father John Joyce's presence on Sancian almost cost him his life. Although the Japanese had given up the idea of occupying the barren and inhospitable island, they regularly landed parties to deactivate any guerrilla or military activities. During a routine search, a rifle was found in the home of one of the Catholics. As the man was dragged off to be punished, he tried to tell the Japanese that the gun was used to protect his fields from thieves, but he could not make himself understood. Afraid that they would kill him, he led them to the mission where Joyce, the curate, was alone. The missioner tried to explain in English, but had little success. One of the Japanese officers became angry at Joyce, probably suspecting him of involvement with the guerrillas. He motioned Joyce to stand against the wall of the church and then, raising the rifle found in the Christian's house, shot at the priest. The bullet missed, but instead of firing again, the officer left to continue the search in another village. His intention seemed to have been to scare Joyce into cooperation. Indeed, a couple of hours later, the commanding officer came to apologize for the rash behavior of his petty officer but, at the same time, asked Joyce to send his catechist to collect all the rifles hidden by the people in the village. Joyce, who had had the scare of his life, refused. Such an event could not but gain the respect and admiration of the Sancian people.[185]

In early September, Father Joseph Sweeney, in charge of the leper colony, the Gate of Heaven near Chikkai, also came close to death. The Japanese blockade of Hong Kong had cut the leper colony off from its supplies of medicine. When malaria and pernicious anemia broke out, Sweeney decided to get the needed supplies in Hong Kong and run the blockade. On the way back at night between Macao and the Gate of Heaven, Sweeney's motorboat came under the crossfire of two Japanese patrol ships. As one of the Japanese boats rammed into it, the priest jumped overboard and swam for six hours before reaching shore. When some of the Chinese who were on the same boat came to the Gate of Heaven to recount the incident, Maryknollers thought that Sweeney had drowned. However to the great joy of the lepers, he appeared at the colony 10 days later in the company of a Chinese fisherman who had given him food and shelter.[186]

In the occupied areas of Kongmoon and Sunwui, the Japanese avoided harming the Americans but kept them under increasing surveillance. Kongmoon fell in March 1939, but the guerrilla movement remained strong in the surrounding countryside. One night in August, a group of guerrillas called at the rectory in Pakkai and forced the Fathers "to contribute all the money they had in their safe." The incident became a pretext for the Japanese to confine the missioners in the occupied coastal area to their compounds. Special permits became necessary to travel within the area or to leave. However, Bishop Paschang did not let the Japanese prevent him from fulfilling his functions as head of the vicariate. He assigned his missioners within the vicariate as if there were no occupation lines. Through persistence, he managed to secure enough passes to continue his confirmation tours and visits of the various missions, although he was well aware that this constant traveling was "a rather risky business."[187]

On December 8, 1941, the day after the Japanese attack on Pearl Harbor, Maryknollers found themselves suddenly classified as enemies of Japan. Those in the Japanese occupied territories of Fushun, Dairen, Hong Kong, and Kongmoon were arrested. The arrest of Robert Cairns, the pastor of Sancian, was undoubtedly one of the most dramatic events of this period. Cairns, who stayed on Sancian with two Chinese Sisters while Joyce was away, was arrested on December 14. The next day the Sisters tried to leave the island but were forced to return to a cove for repairs on their boat when it sprang a leak. On December 16, they saw a Japanese gunboat putting out to sea with Cairns. When the boat returned, the pastor was no longer on board. His pith helmet was later found at sea. Although his fate was never known, local rumors said he was bound in a pig crate and thrown overboard.[188]

In early December 1941, 28 Maryknoll Sisters, 22 Fathers, and five Brothers were in the colony of Hong Kong (which consisted of the island of Hong Kong and the peninsula of Kowloon on the mainland). During the first weeks of the Japanese attack on Hong Kong, the Sisters on the island served as nurses at Queen Mary Hospital while the Sisters on the Kowloon side used their school as a first-aid station even after Kowloon fell to the Japanese. Most of the Fathers and Brothers were at Stanley House, their headquarters on the island. On Christmas Day, they were put under house arrest and for months went through a terrible ordeal at the hands of the Japanese who suspected them of being soldiers in disguise. Finally, in late January and early February, all Maryknollers who were American citizens, 26 men and 23 women, were sent to an internment camp on the grounds of the prison at Stanley where they joined some 2,400 British, 3,000 American, and 42 Dutch prisoners.[189]

Sister Mary Paul McKenna immediately began to negotiate the release of the Sisters. In April, she was set free because of her Irish ancestry, along with three other Sisters. When the opportunity came for repatriation on the exchange ship *Asama Maru* in June 1942, Sister Mary Paul sent 12 Sisters to the United States, including those who were sick, spoke no Chinese, or had not yet been assigned to a mission in Kwangtung or Kwangsi. The remaining Sisters were released in small groups during the summer, except for Sister Eucharista Coupe and Sister Christella Furey, who chose to stay in the camp until January 1943.

From June 1942 to January 1943, Sister Mary Paul continued to arrange the departure of the 16 Sisters still in Hong Kong. Four went to Macao to help at the orphanage or to teach English at St. Rose of Lima College. All the others reentered unoccupied China and worked in missions in Kongmoon, Wuchow, Kweilin, and Kaying. Sister Mary Paul made Kweilin her operational center and in 1944 was one of the last Sisters to leave the city for refuge in Kunming.[190]

At the Stanley camp, the Fathers followed about the same policy as the Sisters. In June 1942, under the leadership of Fathers John Toomey and Bernard Meyer, they repatriated six priests who were sick or due for furlough, and four Brothers. Meanwhile, Sister Mary Paul obtained exit permits for the remaining 16 Maryknoll men in the camp who were released in September. Among them were nine young priests who had arrived in Hong Kong for language study on December 7, 1941. In January 1943, they entered free China under the leadership of veteran missioners Fathers Francis Keelan, John Toomey, John Troesch, and William Downs. Fathers Bernard Meyer and Donald Hessler opted to stay in the camp where they served as chaplains to the remaining 450 Catholic inmates until the Japanese surrender on August 15, 1945.[191]

Meanwhile, at the Kongmoon mission center of Pakkai, Bishop Paschang, Fathers Anthony Paulhus, James Smith, and William North, and Sisters Mary Patricia Coughlin and Beatrice Meyer were put under house arrest on December 8, 1941. A few days later they and four other American and British citizens were escorted to the barrier gate of Macao and released. By May, Fathers North and Smith were already back in the nonoccupied area of the vicariate. Paschang and Paulhus followed suit in October and went to Loting, which became the wartime residence of the bishop. Sisters Mary Patricia and Beatrice stayed in Macao where they operated a home for 300 destitute children.[192]

Following news of the imprisonment of the Maryknoll Fathers, Brothers and Sisters in Japanese-occupied areas, Maryknoll Superior General James E. Walsh stated, after consultation with Mother Mary Joseph, that under the present conditions he saw no possible good coming out of another period of internment and ordered repatriation if possible. He also advised all Maryknoll heads of missions in unoccupied China to move their missioners to other areas if they were in danger of falling into Japanese hands.[193] Most Maryknollers in South China in missions which were not in Japanese controlled areas stayed until 1944; but whenever an alert sounded they took to the hills with the rest of the population. If Japanese parties moved through their area, they temporarily went into hiding until the patrols had gone.

Although larger cities had bomb shelters, casualties were numerous. In 1943 and 1944 Kweilin and Wuchow were practically destroyed under several heavy bombings. On the morning of September 4, 1943, the Maryknoll mission in Wuchow suffered a direct hit. At the time, three Maryknoll priests and three Sisters were in the house along with 40 Christians who had attended morning mass. Everyone had taken refuge in a bomb shelter on the ground floor and in the chapel sanctuary adjacent to it. The front of the three-story building collapsed on the rear of the chapel where Sister Chanel Xavier had been leading school children in the Rosary a few minutes earlier. The only casualty was Father Russell Sprinkle who was watching the Japanese bombers from the third floor of the mission. A few hours later he was retrieved from the rubble, badly hurt but alive.[194]

In the spring of 1944 in an effort to break the back of China, the Japanese launched a major offensive against South China. Bishop Paschang of Kongmoon, Bishop Donaghy of Wuchow, and Sister Mary Paul McKenna, the Sisters' superior in South China, became concerned about the safety of the Maryknoll Sisters and asked them not to stay behind Japanese lines. As the Japanese progressed, the Sisters moved from one convent to another, a few days—sometimes just a few hours—ahead of the Japanese troops. On June 8, 1944, the Yeungkong convent was the first to be abandoned. Missioners, who had shared so many experiences and sufferings with the people during the past eight years of war, found it difficult to leave. Upon receiving orders from the bishop to leave, Sister Richard Wenzel closed the diary with these words:

It was our privilege to have borne the burden of war with our beloved

Chinese people. From 1936 to 1944—eight years of a most cruel war, which had brought airplane attacks, bombs, machine guns, fire, death. Roads, schools, industrial plants, and all methods of travel had been destroyed. The Japanese invasion for seven days in March 1941 brought unbearable sights and tales of robbers, rape and murder, fire and destruction everywhere. Refugees by the thousands driven from their homes, starved and half-naked, traveled aimlessly to an unknown destination. Cholera, malaria, smallpox, beri-beri raged—half-dead bodies being eaten by maggots and dogs. The dead were strewn along the roads—over them swarmed thousands of flies, covering them like a living black blanket. Mud, blood and filth, nursing of the sick souls as well as sick bodies, all the weight of human misery seemed to form a spiritual human comradeship never to be forgotten.[195]

Six Maryknoll Sisters from the Kongmoon vicariate, Colombiere Bradley, Eucharista Coupe, Monica Marie Boyle, Richard Wenzel, Mary Dolorosa Oberle, and Candida Maria Basto settled down to work in Loting, helping in the parish, visiting families in the countryside, caring for 100 girls at the orphanage, and supervising the formation of 20 Chinese Sisters and 12 postulants of the native Congregation of the Immaculate Heart of Mary.

On July 7, however, the Japanese advance forced the Sisters from Loting; their destination was the convent in Pingnam in the Wuchow vicariate. When they arrived, the situation was so precarious that Sister Mary Paul had already moved 18 of the Maryknoll Sisters in Wuchow and Kweilin to Kweiyang in Kweichow province, where some worked as nurses at the local hospital. In September she closed the two convents in Pingnam and Wuchow city and moved the remaining Sisters to Kweilin and then on to Chungking in Szechwan province and finally to Kunming in Yunnan province. There they were joined by the Sisters who had stayed in Kweiyang. By the end of 1944, most of the Sisters in Kunming had been reassigned to the United States; five Sisters were temporarily assigned to two convents of the Italian Loretto Sisters in Calcutta and Simla, India, where they helped in schools until the end of the war. Sister Mary Paul maintained only two skeleton staffs in China. Seven Sisters worked under her in Kunming as secretaries at the American air base or as nurses at the Air Force hospital. Farther north, Sister Moira Riehl headed a group of four Sisters who worked in the Catholic hospital of Chao-t'ung run by the Yugoslavian School Sisters of St. Francis.[196]

Meanwhile, as many Maryknoll Fathers as possible were kept at their posts in Kongmoon, Wuchow, and Kweilin. Their number had already been reduced by illness and by the difficulty of obtaining return visas for men on furlough. During the Japanese drive of 1944, Maryknollers stayed until the last minute. In Kweilin, Monsignor John Romaniello decided to remain as long as possible to aid the refugees. The Japanese had already entered the city when he and two fellow Maryknollers jumped on their bicycles and

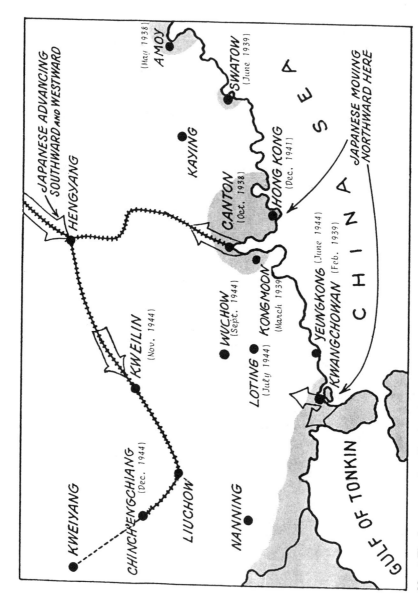

Map 4. The Japanese spring offensive of 1944 into South China. Shaded areas were occupied by Japanese at the start of the offensive. Dates show when cities were occupied. Adapted from *The Field Afar*, April 1944, p. 3, and November 1944, p. 5.

escaped.[197] In the end, all 14 Maryknoll Fathers were driven out of Kwei-lin prefecture.

In Wuchow and Kongmoon, however, Bishops Donaghy and Paschang managed to maintain a presence of a few priests with strong morale. In Wuchow, Donaghy stayed with nine men out of the original 17 present in 1941; he divided them into three groups to cover the main missions of Wuchow, Pingnam, and Jungyun-Watlam.

In Kongmoon, Paschang kept 21 men out of the 32 he had in 1941. These men knew they were encircled and that Maryknoll had waived all offers of evacuation from the American consul or the U.S. Army in Kunming. They were ordered to hide in the hills if necessary and not to surrender to the Japanese.[198] Life became increasingly perilous for these priests. The Japanese took over the leper colony at Ngaimoon in March 1944, chased the lepers away, and killed those who could not move. From then until the end of the war, Fathers John Joyce, Joseph Lavin, Joseph Farnen, and Lawrence Conley ran ahead of the Japanese, setting up temporary stations for the lepers who followed them. They often hid in the hills, finding shelter in camps run by guerrillas or units of the U.S. Office of Strategic Services and the British Army Aid Group.[199]

During a Japanese aid raid on Toishan, Father Frank O'Neill saw a child trapped under a wall across the street from his rectory. He hurried out to free the child and started to run back with the victim in his arms. He had not gone 20 steps when he was knocked down by the concussion of a bomb that dug a crater on the spot where he had rescued the child. This well-publicized act of bravery gave O'Neill much "face." In appreciation, the city presented him with a testimonial banner.[200]

In September 1944, when the Japanese stormed the small town of Watnam, along the West River close to the Wuchow border, Father Otto Rauschenbach took refuge in a hut in the mountains. Whenever the Japanese were not in the vicinity, he went down on market days to visit people and dispense medicine. Paschang recalled how Rauschenbach had turned down a suggestion to move to Loting because "he wanted to stay on the mountain so that he could be in touch with his people." Unintimidated by danger, he felt secure on the mountain near the guerrillas. On his missioner's cross, he had already made notches for the six times he felt God had saved him from imminent death. However, on May 14, 1945, some 12 miles out of Watnam, he was robbed and killed, most likely by bandits.[201]

Most of the 33 Maryknoll priests and Brothers driven out of South China by the Japanese ended up in one of two houses Maryknoll opened in Chungking and Kunming. Missioners due for furlough and a few who had become too emotional or unstable during the war were sent back to the United States. The remaining 19 men found temporary employment in unoccupied China, half of them serving as contract chaplains in the U.S. Army.[202]

The Japanese troops never entered the mountainous region of Kaying, but surrounded it on all sides. Maryknollers in the vicariate found themselves isolated from the rest of the world until the end of the war. They proceeded with their mission work relatively undisturbed; however, from 1938 on, Kaying and other towns were bombed and several Maryknollers narrowly escaped death. One day, for example, Sisters Mary Imelda Sheridan and Rosalia Kettl were caught in an open field under the fire of Japanese planes. They were saved by the quick action of a Chinese companion who, at the risk of her life, broke off branches from nearby bushes to cover them. In November 1940, Sister Mary Imelda had another series of memorable encounters with Japanese planes on a return trip to Kaying from Hong Kong with Sister Clara Venneman and Father Carroll Quinn. Their sampan was strafed, bombs fell around them, and the priest gave the group general absolution twice while under fire. The most terrifying experience was pershaps when a plane chased them along the bank of a river and bullets pierced the sand within inches of the two Sisters who had fallen prostrate in the shallow waters.[203]

At the end of a lengthy tour of the Maryknoll missions in South China ending in Kunming on February 1, 1945, James E. Walsh wrote a long circular to Maryknollers in unoccupied China stressing that the purpose of the two Maryknoll houses in Chungking and Kunming was to help missioners working behind Japanese lines. Since Chungking was the banking center of free China, the Chungking house was to channel money to Maryknoll missions in the Wuchow, Kongmoon, and Kaying vicariates. The house in Kunming, the city which was headquarters of the U.S. Army in free China, was to secure army help in forwarding supplies of medicine, clothing, and food to the missioners. Moreover, both houses were reminded they had to be "on the *qui vive* for opportunities" to maintain contact with the encircled missions. In the closing paragraph, Walsh reminded all Maryknollers that the decision to evacuate a priest, Brother, or Sister from China rested first with the ordinary of each mission territory. Maryknoll Society and Congregation superiors in China, regional or local, could make that decision only if they could not get in touch with the mission head.[204]

During the long years of conflict between China and Japan, Maryknollers in South China displayed much patriotism toward their adopted country and hostility toward the Japanese. While the Maryknoll Sisters usually showed restraint in the use of derogatory vocabulary, the Fathers' diaries abound with unfriendly remarks toward the Japanese military. Typical of these is the comment found in the Kongmoon diary of May 1939: "The little Nipponese are everywhere. The emblem of the Flied Egg is Frying over us, although the same Flag of the Rising Sun reminds us of nothing but a Blood Clot."[205]

In many instances they remained at their posts to suffer with the common people and to carry on with their tasks of giving shelter, food, clothing, and medical help to the refugees. In the process, they earned the friendship and respect of many of the Chinese who witnessed their selfless dedication or benefitted from it.

Relationships with U.S. Armed Forces personnel. In the early years of the conflict between Japan and China, Maryknollers in South China kept a certain distance from the American consul-general at Canton. They did not follow his advice urging American personnel to leave the coastal areas for more secure locations. There seemed to be little effort on his part to gather intelligence from Maryknollers. Maryknoll Fathers' diaries abound with details of Japanese activities in their areas but, prior to 1941, there was infrequent mention of requests for information from the American consulate.

With the entrance of the United States into the war, missioners saw very little of the Japanese but had increasing contacts with U.S. military personnel. The establishment of U.S. Air Force bases in the interior of China began several years of close relationships between the Maryknoll Fathers and American airmen. One of the first contacts came early in the war when Father Russel Sprinkle of Wuchow helped rescue a downed P-40 of General Claire Chennault's Flying Tigers before it was located by Japanese reconnaissance. Thanks to Sprinkle's help and connections, the pilot was soon on his way back to Kweilin with his dismantled plane packed in crates.[206]

Each Maryknoll mission territory of South China reported several instances of American pilots and crew members rescued by Chinese guerrillas and peasants who brought them to the Catholic missions. Maryknollers were delighted to lodge them for a few days before arranging transportation to the nearest American base: "We are happy to be of service to these fine young men and to do our own little bit for Uncle Sam here in this corner of far-off China."[207]

When U.S. Army engineers arrived at Tanchuk in Kwangsi to construct an air base, they lived at the Catholic mission until their own quarters were ready. In Kaying city, another group of engineers stayed in Father John Donovan's rectory for two months while they operated as closely as possible to the Japanese-occupied areas around Swatow and Canton. Years later, reflecting on these contacts, Donovan noted:

> It seemed quite normal and natural for the missioners to treat the soldiers with hospitality: indeed after two years of isolation, the missioners [in Kaying] were delighted to see people recently arrived from the U.S. Certain-

ly there was never a hint [from the Chinese] that the Maryknollers might be suspected of working in any capacity with the U.S. military forces.[208]

Maryknollers in the Wuchow and Kweilin territories began to serve as Sunday chaplains on bases near their own parishes. Contacts created strong ties of mutual respect and friendship between the missioners and the U.S. military personnel. GIs and airmen visited the missioners' homes for meals, and the missioners were frequent visitors at the bases. American planes brought mail and medical supplies for the missions. When the time came to leave their parishes to escape from the Japanese advance, several Maryknollers signed up as contract chaplains and served on bases in free China until the end of the war.[209]

Even in remote parishes, contacts with passing U.S. Army men became more frequent. In 1944 Father John McLoughlin of Tanguen said that "quite a few of them" had passed through his village. Their cigarettes and magazines were appreciated, but most of all their visit was welcomed because "from them we get news of what's happening in the rest of the world."[210] After 1949 these close relationships with American personnel brought suffering to Maryknollers and to the Christians.

Some of the Americans hosted by Maryknollers in their rectories were members of intelligence units. The missioners' knowledge of the language, terrain, and customs provided valuable information. Moreover, because the local people—especially the Christians—trusted them, the missioners were often among the first with information and warnings about Japanese troop movements.

In Kaying, Donovan received several of these units with the approval of Bishop Ford, while the Maryknoll Sisters provided their meals at cost. Under the name of SACO (Sino-American Cooperation Organization), these units grouped U.S. Naval personnel and Chinese Army weather specialists. Under the cover of gathering weather reports, these specially trained soldiers sent scouting parties behind enemy lines and then relayed information through a large generator and transmitter installed on Donovan's compound to U.S. Army bases in western China.[211]

Maryknollers in Kaying did not know that General Tai Li, chief of the secret police in the Nationalist government, was also the head of SACO. During the summer of 1943, he began a program he called "F.B.I. school instruction," which used SACO to train his anti-Communist intelligence-terrorist organization called the "Blue Shirts." When the Nationalist-Communist civil war intensified in 1945, Tai Li was therefore able to put American aid in SACO to active use against the Communists. As Professor John K. Fairbank commented in his memoir, *Chinabound*, "this amounted to a 'premature' initiation of US-anti-Chinese Communist Party activity that the Chinese Communist Party bitterly resented and properly enshrined among the iniquities of American imperialism."[212]

Policy at Maryknoll Headquarters

As the Sino-Japanese war intensified, Maryknoll's leadership in the United States wavered between strict neutrality and support of Chiang Kaishek. This attitude is reflected in *The Field Afar*, Maryknoll's official publication for the American public. With mission territories in Japan as well as in Manchuria and China, articles written at the beginning of the war stayed away from politics, focusing on the response of the local people to Christianity.

Prior to Pearl Harbor Day, for example, articles and letters published on Manchuria deemphasized the difficulties encountered by missioners because of shifts in the political climate. As previously mentioned, Monsignor Lane actually asked the superior general as early as 1933 to excise any portions of articles or letters which might be offensive to the Japanese:

> The situation is quite tense and for the present it is wise to exert extreme care in printing any articles concerning Manchuria and Japan in *The Field Afar*. . . . You would be surprised how words are pulled out, misunderstood, misinterpreted.[213]

Lane's request was closely followed; articles and letters from missioners in Manchuria were carefully edited. Any mention of the mission field as a battleground between Japanese and Chinese troops or guerrillas was eliminated. In fact, a special effort seems to have been made to show the many improvements made in Manchuria by the Japanese. Articles praised the Japanese for improved railways, roads, health facilities and other economic developments. After his visit to Dairen in 1932, James A. Walsh wrote in *The Field Afar*:

> Manchuria, owing to the remarkable developments of Japanese enterprise in that country has been the economic salvation of hundreds of thousands of Chinese, pauperized by conditions prevailing in the provinces south of the Great Wall.[214]

Although by that time missioners were experiencing warfare and hostility in the wake of the Mukden incident, Walsh chose to reflect a positive view of the situation.

The Field Afar also refrained from mentioning any activities of the anti-Japanese resistance, the Chinese Nationalists, or the Communists in

Manchuria. Bandits were consistently equated with ordinary robbers, and the Japanese were praised for curtailing their activities. In his account of Gerard Donovan's death at the hands of bandits, Lane emphasized the part played by the Japanese soldiers who found the body and "did everything possible to honor and respect the remains." He did not express his real feelings that the Japanese had purposely failed in their efforts to intercept the bandits and save the missioner.[215]

Meanwhile, *The Field Afar* kept silent about the Sino-Japanese conflict in the rest of China. During 1939, the war was rarely mentioned and, if it was, only in euphemistic terms without indicating who was fighting or if Maryknoll sided with the Chinese against the Japanese. In February, a small insert in the magazine stressed that "all is well in South China" and that,despite many inconveniences, "reports from the missions have been unfailingly optimistic and encouraging."[216] Only two articles related to the Sino-Japanese war, one in April and one in June. Both provided vignettes of Chinese suffering and missionary works of mercy among refugees, with no mention of Japan or Japanese aggression.[217] Similarly, the diaries of the Fathers written even before Pearl Harbor were carefully edited after their arrival in New York. Every reference to the Sino-Japanese war was given a marginal annotation of "omit," meaning that this particular part should not be released for publication.[218]

In 1940, the Maryknoll Fathers' General Council learned that Father Robert Kennelly had submitted a formal claim for damages from his injuries in the Loting bombing. He had asked the American consul in Canton to forward his claim to the Japanese authorities. As a consequence, the Council ruled that individual Maryknollers were forbidden to submit claims for damages. Maryknoll ordinaries, although free to submit claims if they judged them appropriate, were advised to do so only through the General Council. The reason given was the overall benefit of the whole Society:

> We have missions in Japan, Korea, and Manchoukuo which are under the government of Japan. We must be very careful not to place ourselves in an unfavorable or even awkward position in relation to the Japanese government.[219]

This constant preoccupation with not irritating the Japanese government placed the Maryknoll leadership in a position which, on the whole, did not reflect well on Maryknoll and was labeled by some as a "Munich-like plot to sell out China."[220]

In late 1940, James E. Walsh, superior general of the Maryknoll Fathers and Brothers, was preparing to tour the Maryknoll missions in the Far East when Monsignor Patrick J. Byrne, prefect apostolic of the Maryknoll mission in Kyoto, and the other foreign ordinaries in Japan resigned their posts in favor of native priests. Suspecting that the resignation was prompted by the Japanese government's announcement that all Christian institutions in Japan should be headed by Japanese nationals, Walsh left immediately for Japan to assess what the change meant for Maryknoll. Contrary to the usual practice, he took along his second-in-command, Vicar General James M. Drought. Drought's long-time support of Japan was no secret, and he had previously dealt with Japanese officials.

Long before stepping on Japanese soil, Drought had written a letter in the summer of 1934 to the president of the Foreign Policy Association in New York to complain about what he considered to be repeatedly biased articles against Japan under the Association's imprint. He thought that there was "too much of Big Bad Wolf psychology" in current American commentaries on Japan; he was in favor of a "de facto recognition of Manchukuo" based on historical and political grounds as well as for reasons of expediency.[221] In 1939, when compelled to lodge a protest concerning the Loting incident and the wounding of Kennelly, Drought wrote a surprising letter to the Japanese Embassy in Washington in which his complaint was secondary to his strong words of support:

> I am keenly aware that the peace-loving Japanese people, and their government, have engaged upon active hostilities prompted by the compelling conviction that only the arbitrament of arms could effect a constructive solution of the cultural and economic conflict which has arisen between your people and the Chinese. Being sensitive to the large issues involved, I have consistently tried to represent the Japanese viewpoint to our American people. . . . I like to believe that I have contributed not a little to promoting goodwill and explaining the mutuality of interest between the American and Japanese people.[222]

In late November 1940, Walsh and Drought arrived in Tokyo and stayed in Japan for a month. Over the years, the bishop had relied on his vicar general and had allowed him considerable freedom. Therefore, while Walsh pursued his religious duty of visiting Maryknoll missioners in Japan, Drought was free to engage in meetings with business and government leaders. The vicar general also arranged for his superior to attend some of those meetings to discuss questions of peace in the Far East and Japanese relationships with the United States. The two Maryknollers even met with Foreign Minister Yosuke Matsuoka, who asked them to convey his desire to maintain peace with the United States to President Franklin Delano Roosevelt.

Evidence shows that Walsh was reticent to accept this mission of a "go-between" because he did not believe that "amateur individuals [were] more likely to solve these problems than the responsible officers of government whose speciality this [was]."²²³ Drought, on the contrary, was convinced that Japan badly needed an "intelligible" presentation of her case in America. He was able to persuade Walsh into undertaking the peace mission.

Back in the United States, they met with President Roosevelt and Secretary of State Cordell Hull on January 23, 1941, and told them the unbelievable news that Japan was prepared to make a drastic change in her foreign policy. Japan would nullify her participation in the Axis Pact and recall all military forces from China as soon as the Chinese government maintained order and cooperated with Japan to suppress communism. In return, the United States was expected to provide economic assistance to Japan, and the Western nations were expected to recognize Japan's special interest in East Asia.

Following the January meeting at the White House, Drought took up residence in Washington to assist the Japanese ambassador and other officials in drafting a proposal to reconcile the outstanding differences between Japan and the United States. The document disappointed the secretary of state and his staff, who found no evidence of earlier assurances given by the two Maryknoll priests that Japan intended to divorce herself from the Axis alliance. In addition, Japan's conditions for withdrawal from China were more qualified than the priests' oral message had led them to understand. Japan would only negotiate with a "newly coalesced Chinese government" formed of Chiang Kai-shek's regime and the pro-Japanese regime of Wang Ching-wei in Nanking. If Chiang was not amenable to the idea, the United States government was asked to discontinue its assistance to his regime. Moreover, Japan insisted on maintaining agreements previously signed by Japan and Wang Ching-wei, including the recognition of Manchukuo and the "joint defense against communistic activities." This last demand, in fact, allowed Japan to station troops in China to fight against communism.²²⁴

Although the Japanese proposal was not the peace overture Hull had expected, he did not reject it. He made it clear, however, that no agreement could be reached if Japan was not prepared to abandon her present doctrine of military conquest, to relinquish title to all seized properties and territories, and to forsake the use of force as an instrument of policy.²²⁵ The two countries reached a deadlock, and serious discussion never resumed between the State Department and the Japanese envoys.

Following the sweep of the Japanese Army into Indochina and the freezing of all Japanese assets in the United States by July 1941, the situation between the United States and Japan became very tense. Drought still tried to get negotiations under way in Washington, insisting that Foreign Minister Matsuoka was anxious to complete a peace agreement. Walsh returned to Japan to resume his visitation of Maryknoll missions; again he was pressed into service by American and Japanese embassy officials to act as a liaison between the State Department, and Matsuoka and the Japanese Prime Minister, Prince Konoye. Until mid-October, the bishop spent most of his time in this capacity in and around Tokyo, transmitting coded messages to Drought to be passed on to the State Department. However, since neither side was willing to change its position, nothing substantial came of Walsh's services. All that he was able to bring back to his government was Prince Konoye's message of a "sincere desire for peace." By the time Walsh arrived in Washington on November 15, Japan had changed its Cabinet; Prince Konoye and Matsu-oka were out and the War Party was in power.

Walsh and Drought had been victims of their wishful thinking. They had not realistically assessed the situation in Japan or the opinions of their Japanese interlocutors. They tried to convince the American government that Japan was prepared to abandon her policy of military expansion in favor of peaceful commercial expansion, yet all the facts pointed in the other direction. Walsh and Drought were taken advantage of by Japanese officials who probably wanted peace, but were unsure of the means to achieve it.[226]

Maryknoll headquarters allowed the tone of *The Field Afar* to change substantially toward the war in China only after they received word that most interned Maryknollers were safe and would soon be repatriated. In April 1942, one line mentioned China as "a heroic nation fighting for freedom."[227] However, the June issue of the magazine abruptly turned patriotic, stressing that the United States was now "fighting on two fronts." It drew an idyllic portrait of American military personnel expos-ing their lives to defend "peace, brotherly love and justice to men of all nations." The magazine raved about the "600 sons and daughters of Uncle Sam in China, priests, Brothers, and Sisters, writing a glorious page as they dedicate themselves to China's suffering millions."[228]

The next issue of *The Field Afar* began to develop the theme of Ameri-can missioners rallying patriotic Christian Chinese behind the Christian figure of Chiang Kai-shek for a China free of Japanese intruders.[229] Be-tween 1942 and 1946, at least 10 articles gave quotes and excerpts from speeches and letters of the Generalissimo and his wife in which they praised the Catholic Church for its service, welcomed missioners, and presented them as models of virtue to emulate: "These men are single-hearted, constant, persevering, undaunted by any obstacles, unremitting at their work."[230]

Even Chiang's first name was interpreted by Maryknoll as providen-tial: as "shek" means "rock" in Chinese, they thought that the Generalis-simo was the foundation of modern China.[231] In the December 1944 issue of *The Field Afar*, a prominently displayed picture of Bishop James E. Walsh standing next to Chiang Kai-shek symbolized the strong ties between Maryknoll and the Nationalist government.[232]

This infatuation with the Nationalist leader was not peculiar to Maryknoll, but represented the general mood of the Catholic Church in China at the end of World War II. When the Communist threat materialized, the Church still clung to Chiang as the rock of China and linked her destiny with his.

The Impact of the Sino-Japanese War on Maryknoll Missions

If the Sino-Japanese War left the Maryknoll missions in Manchuria almost undisturbed until December 1941, it severely affected those of South China in Kongmoon, Wuchow, Kweilin and, to a lesser extent, Kaying. Even though Maryknoll headquarters in New York exhorted all missioners to remain politically neutral, those in South China could not escape the reality of the Japanese invasion and not denounce their aggression.

By vocation the missioners were already inclined spiritually and mentally to a life of dedication and sharing with the people. The circumstances of war put this relationship to the test and often brought it to new heights. Missioners and Chinese lived together through many moments, some filled with acts of real courage, some rich in shared emotions. These experiences led to a better understanding of each other.

Ford was able to capture this feeling in an article for *The Field Afar* in 1941. He recalled his fear and the fear of the Chinese around him as everyone scrambled for a hiding place during a surprise air raid. Hampered by his cassock, he described his clumsiness and how he was nearly left behind in the open when the planes arrived. A group of Chinese let him squeeze into a hole for four men which already sheltered 10. When the bombing was over, the mud and dust-covered survivors, including the bishop, started to laugh and tease one another, Ford understood that something unique had happened.

> War has its purifying element—not only that resulting from pain and misery shared with others, but also that from lighter moments shared in common. ... As all scramble for the light and meander home, you feel closer to the people and understand them better.[233]

After Pearl Harbor, Maryknollers, now in danger of arrest, had a chance to display the depths of their commitment to the Chinese. As the Japanese troops advanced, some Maryknollers went underground, re-

Fig. 3. "Bishop Walsh Meets the Generalissimo—Generalissimo Chiang, President of the Chinese Republic, at a recent meeting with Bishop Walsh, Maryknoll's Superior General, showed a keen interest in the work of our missioners. Father Mark Tennien, Bishop Walsh, Generalissimo Chiang, Father James Smith, Mr. Francis Yeh," *Maryknoll—The Field Afar,* December 1944, pp. 24–25.

maining behind in occupied territories. Others with no place to hide shared the life of the Chinese refugees, moving from one mission or convent to another, sometimes only a few hours ahead of the Japanese. The substantial increase in conversions in Maryknoll territories after the war was triggered in part by the support missioners had given to the Chinese cause, and by their compassion in handling relief programs.

At the same time, the war revealed weaknesses in the Chinese Catholic Church. When the missioners left to escape imprisonment by the Japanese, few leaders remained among the Catholics. Only a handful of native priests and professed Sisters were available in the Maryknoll territories. Although their activities were limited by their small number and the circumstances of war, the Chinese priests and Sisters in Manchuria and South China stood firm and managed well without Maryknollers. After the war, the development of a native clergy and sisterhood, which had always been a priority in the Maryknoll territories, received even more attention. Maryknollers wanted the Chinese Church to be better prepared if missioners had to leave a second time; they had no way of knowing at the time that they had scarcely five years to perform the task.

During the war years, the behavior of missioners gave the Catholic Church a patriotic pro-Chinese outlook and wider acceptance among the Chinese. At the same time, however, their behavior laid the groundwork for the many accusations of deception and spying that the Communists would soon raise against the Church and the missioners.

Maryknoll and Chinese Communism, 1925–1960

Early Contacts, 1925–1945

Maryknollers were first exposed to Chinese Communists in the Kaying territory. In July 1928, following abortive coups in Canton and Swatow, the anti-Communist extermination drive of Chiang Kai-shek at the conclusion of the Northern Expedition, and the establishment of the Nationalist government, a large group of Communists, under the leadership of Mao Tse-tung and Chu Teh, entrenched themselves in July 1928 at Juichin in Kiangsi province just across the border from the Kaying vicariate. Organizing the peasants into well-trained guerrilla units, they strengthened their position and initiated an egalitarian revolution, redividing land equally among the peasants.[234]

From their base at Juichin, they made frequent forays into other areas of Kiangsi as well as Fukien and northeastern Kwangtung. Missions of the German Dominicans in Fukien and the American Vincentians in Kiangsi were among the first to be burned and looted by Communist attacks. Signs of trouble for the Kaying missioners appeared in June 1929 in Siaoloc when two Catholic men of the village were seized by Communists and executed as spies sent out from Kaying by the Nationalists.[235]

On October 25, a large Communist contingent crossed the Fukien border and occupied Kaying city for two days. They released prisoners from jail, set fire to the courthouse and city hall, held mass meetings in the streets, and demanded financial contributions from the merchants. They announced their intention to burn the three Christian missions belonging to Maryknoll, the Baptists, and the Basel Lutherans. Before they could carry out their plans, they were ousted by Nationalist soldiers who had followed them from Fukien.

During the next week, the Communists made a second attempt to take the city but finally retreated to Kiangsi. They passed through Siaoloc but left the mission undisturbed. On the other hand, Father Patrick Malone's mission in Shakchin was completely ransacked and looted. During these events, the missioners in Kaying, Siaoloc, and Shakchin quickly fled, although some priests showed a certain uneasiness in leaving their missions. Reports of what had happened to other missioners in South China were alarming: a kidnapped German Dominican priest and a Sister from Fukien were released after a payment of one million dollars in Chinese currency (about US$15,000), and four Lutherans of eastern Kwangtung were held for a ransom of over two million Chinese dollars.[236] Maryknollers were afraid of similar ransom demands. Yet Malone was not sure fleeing was the right solution. He remarked that "the report went about among nearby pagans that Shan Foo (the priest) knew enough to run when the Communists came too close."[237]

For the following two years, sporadic attacks created danger and turmoil around most Maryknoll missions in Kaying not only because the Communists crossed over from Kiangsi and Fukien but also because communism began to spread among the Hakka population. In December 1929, Father William Downs, the pastor of Kaying, wrote that "practically all the people along the river up to Tsia Hang are Communists and they are forcing those who have not already allied themselves to the cause to join up."[238] The uncertainty created by the Communist forays led Ford to postpone the scheduled arrival in Kaying in 1930 of the Maryknoll Sisters until four years later when the Communists left the area and embarked on their Long March.

Meanwhile, the Maryknoll Fathers in Kwangsi were braced for a possible encounter with the Communists after hearing of the capture and torture of some French priests and Canadian Sisters who were their neighbors in the Nanning vicariate. The soviets in Pose and Lungchow in Nanning were short-lived, however, and never posed a threat to Wuchow or Kweilin.[239] Four years later, between September and December 1934, portions of the Communist Long March crossed from Hunan into northern Kwangsi and came very close to Kweilin. The situation was tense when rumors spread that some Maryknoll missions lay in the path of the Communist retreat from the Nationalists. In actuality, the missions were not on the route. Fathers Joseph Reagan and Timothy Daley of Pinglo were the only Maryknollers to catch a glimpse of some Communist soldiers who were being led captive to Kweilin.[240]

During the Sino-Japanese war, the missioners shared the sufferings of refugees and could not remain impervious to the manifestations of patriotism on the part of the Chinese population. Despite some localized wavering and the Zanin incident (see p. 361) in 1939, the Catholic missionary community in China became convinced—especially after the Axis drive for expansion shook most of the world—that the Japanese occupation was another evil and not the solution for ridding China of communism. Chiang Kai-shek appeared as the only figure who could oppose both the Japanese and the Communists.

After the defeat of Japan, the Catholic Church was firmly aligned not only with Chiang Kai-shek, but with the Nationalist cause. Missioners openly advertised and promoted this alliance. Their anti-Communist stand and their infatuation with the Christian general blinded them to the reality of a widely corrupt Nationalist Party unable and unwilling to bring about reform. Although many missioners were aware of the corruption, they accepted it as a shortcoming which could be later remedied and which was preferable to communism:

> Chiang Kai-shek was an honest man, but too many officials under him were no good, and he was helpless. . . . We knew something about communism from what the popes had written and certainly we didn't expect anything good to come from it. If we could have chosen, we would have chosen to stay with the Nationalists and tried to correct their faults.[241]

Reflecting on her political conviction in the late 1940s, Sister Barbara Mersinger summarized the attitude of most Maryknollers at that time: "In my mind, anything that was Communist was bad and anything that was Nationalist was not that bad."[242]

Finally, after 1945 a large portion of the missionary community was too busy to pay much attention to politics. Deeply involved in works of mercy and the distribution of relief and confronted with an unprecedented conversion movement, many Maryknollers did not take time to examine the issues dividing the Communists and the Nationalists. A few, however, dared to look further down the road and saw communism as a possible stumbling block. In his annual report sent shortly after the allied victory of 1945, Bishop Ford noted:

> Socially the year was profitable for the Church as due to our nationality, we became prominent locally and were automatically included in all festivities. . . . On half a dozen occasions, the mayor or generals invited the clergy to banquets of a civic organization, at which the bishop was given the place of honor and where we made friendly connections that had been useful to the Church. . . . Spiritually, we made slight gains after three years of diminishing returns [due to the war]. . . . I confidently predict that with the advent of peace we shall resume our successful work with less effort and with perhaps greater results. Much will depend, of course, on the progress of Communism in this region.[243]

Like most Catholic missioners in China, he failed to realize that the Church leadership's position against communism and its support for the Nationalist government often ran counter to his personal and genuine compassion for the people.

Post-War Communism in Manchuria

Maryknollers who had resumed mission work in Manchuria in August 1945 were unrealistically optimistic about the future. New groups of Sisters and Fathers arrived in early 1947. By June, however, the Communists obviously controlled most of the Fushun vicariate. In the absence of Bishop Lane, elected the new superior general of the Maryknoll Society, Father Joseph McCormack was put in charge and decided to evacuate most Sisters and Fathers to Tientsin. Like many other missioners, he still did not think the situation was desperate and held to every piece of news which could indicate a reversal. In late June, after a Nationalist victory in Ssupingkai, he planned the return of the Maryknollers.[244]

Following the visit to Tientsin and Fushun of General Albert Wedemeyer who had been sent on a fact-finding mission by President Harry S. Truman, Maryknollers were hopeful for American intervention, at least financial, in support of the Nationalists in Manchuria. They believed that although Nationalist corruption was to blame for the present defeat, the party still had enough honest officials to warrant American backing.

> There is certainly much corruption in the Nationalist government here. Many of the leaders are not good; if they would fight against the Communists, they would be put down in short order, but there are some who are 100% O.K. and we should back them.[245]

Wedemeyer's report, however, was not encouraging, and the United States government decided that no amount of aid could alter the situation. By late December 1947, Fushun was about to fall to the Communists, and McCormack decided to move all Maryknollers out of the territory. While he and Father Thomas Quirk stayed behind in Mukden, he evacuated the remaining six Sisters and four priests to Shanghai for reassignment to other Maryknoll territories. He wrote a letter for Maryknoll headquarters explaining his reasons for ordering everybody out.

> Our work is very limited. We have a good number of Chinese priests who can carry on very well for the time being. . . . If the Communists ever broke in on us suddenly, it would compromise the natives to be caught with us. Our presence would even compromise the Catholics and the whole work, for the Communists are death down on America and all it stands for.[246]

A month later McCormack himself sought refuge in Peking and reported the news of the death of Father Maurus Pai, shot in Fushun after a month in prison for being a teacher of "American religion."[247] He also made arrangements for the Chinese seminarians, Sisters, and some priests to join him to study in Peking. He was soon responsible for 31 minor seminarians, six major seminarians, 18 professed Sisters, and 10 postulants from Fushun, plus 18 seminarians and Sisters from the diocese of Ssupingkai. He also corresponded with the Chinese priests in Fushun and provided their funds.[248]

In October 1948, Archbishop Riberi, the Vatican internuncio in China, was still optimistic about the future of the Church in China. When McCormack asked if missioners would ever go back to Manchuria, Riberi's answer was, "Absolutely."[249]

The following month, the Communists threatened Peking; the foreign community fled and McCormack took refuge in Shanghai, where he joined Bishop James E. Walsh. Before leaving, he had made arrangements for the Chinese Sisters to work in a Peking hospital to earn their living. He also continued to provide for the financial support of minor seminarians at the Peking seminary while the major seminarians were sent to Hong Kong. Until his arrest on June 15, 1954, he maintained contact with the native priests and Sisters in Peking and Fushun.[250]

As a result of these activities, the Communists charged Father McCormack with collecting political and economic information in Fushun for the American government. In fact, his correspondence for that period showed no involvement in spy activities but only a concern for keeping the Church in Manchuria alive as a religious organization. Nonetheless, some letters contained abbreviations and veiled terms which, if intercepted, could have easily caused suspicion. Sometimes McCormack also used terminology suggestive of an underground political organization. In 1948, for example, he wrote a story for *The Field Afar* recounting the 500-mile walk of his seminarians from Fushun to Peking. He explained his decision for the move in these terms: "If our Chinese personnel was to be saved from torture and death, it was a matter of transporting it [out of Manchuria]. We decided to set a temporary base in [Peking]." Looking to the future, he concluded the article by saying, "For centuries, Ireland smuggled its seminarians to the Continent for training. So today we are preparing China's priests and Sisters for the Red areas. The time will come when we shall all return."[251] The Communists used the article to prove that McCormack intended to send ordained young men and professed young Sisters back to China as spies. Consequently, he was sentenced to five years in prison and not released until June 14, 1958.

The Communist Takeover of South China

Until late 1948, Maryknollers in South China did not think that the Communists could take over all of China. They still believed that world-wide prayer could stop their advance. When the pope chose the month of May in

1947 and 1948 as a time to hold special services throughout the world for "The Salvation of Russia and Against Communism," Maryknollers in China eagerly responded to the sense of urgency of his appeal. In May 1948, Sister Mary Patricia Coughlin noted that they had even added a special prayer in Pakkai because the Communists had arrived in nearby Hoingan; and Father Michael McKeirnan in Szwong commented on the large crowd at the service.[252]

In directives sent to his clergy on Easter 1948, Bishop Ford of Kaying asked that Sunday, May 2, be a special day of prayer in his diocese in order to coincide with Communist May Day (International Labor Day). He made three recommendations on conducting the service: (a) the ceremony should appear official by inviting local officials and public schools; (b) the ceremony should be conducted in the open air when possible to reach a wide non-Christian audience; and (c) the purpose of the ceremony should be made clear to all, and "it is an opportune time to explain the Church's stand against the enemies of all social order, and the need of relying on God and the practice of social virtues."[253] By "Church's stand," Ford meant the Church's position against communism; it appears that he never considered that Nationalists could have been included in "the enemies of China's social order."

These ceremonies varied widely from place to place, but established a connection in the people's minds between the Catholic Church and the Nationalist government. The Sister diarist for the Holy Child Convent in Tungshek wrote:

> Before the meeting began, Father removed the Blessed Sacrament [from the church] and a screen on which was hung the National flag was placed in front of the altar. After the singing of the Chinese National anthem, Father opened the meeting with a little talk, after which one of the invited guests spoke, and finally our catechist. At the end of his talk, the catechist explained the meaning of the Benediction of the Blessed Sacrament which was to follow.[254]

In Kaying city, the ceremony described by Sister Rita Marie Regan also had political overtones.

> Father Lam, professor at the seminary, delivered a splendid talk on the stand of the Church and communism. Kou Tsoun Men, representative of the Nationalist party here, spoke on the necessity of a clear understanding of the Communist doctrine. Bishop Ford's inspiring talk explained how Catholicism and Communism were opposed.[255]

Yet the Communist advance could not be stopped, and its progress can be easily followed through the diaries. Writing from the native novitiate in Laohukow in May 1947, Sister Thérèse Grondin referred to the Communists only as "bands of thieves who camped out in isolated mountain districts" and preyed on small unprotected towns and villages. By the beginning of spring 1948, she mentioned that the Communists controlled many villages where the native Sisters worked. Another year later, she called all places where Sister catechists were stationed "liberated areas."[256] The vicariate of Kaying fell into Communist hands in the spring of 1949. The three other Maryknoll territories were occupied in turn during the last two months of that year.

Meanwhile, the prevailing attitude in the missionary community was to continue working as usual. At their regional meeting held in Hong Kong in October 1948, the Catholic bishops of South China, in conjunction with Archbishop Riberi, ruled that "Regarding Communism and its imminent spread in our territory, pastors are obligated to remain with their flock." They also exhorted Sisters to stay on because the experience in North China had proven that Sisters could remain safely under the Communist regime.[257]

Maryknollers as a whole were pleased with the bishops' ruling. With the exception of those due for furlough and a few who needed medical attention, they volunteered to stay at their posts. In fact, during their first two years under the Communist regime, Maryknollers assigned to South China—Hong Kong excluded—slightly increased their ranks, from 37 Sisters, three Brothers, and 91 priests in June 1948 to 38 Sisters, two Brothers, and 97 priests in December 1950.[258]

When the Communists finally took over South China, Maryknollers still refused to believe that communism could take hold in China: "It is almost impossible," wrote Father Joseph McGinn, "to vision the Chinese people becoming genuine all-out Communists in the Soviet sense."[259] In the Wuchow diocese, Father William Morrissey and Sister Agnes Virginia Higgins stated that no Maryknollers "believe that communism can take hold of the Chinese. They are too individualistic, too independent, too proud of China as the center of the world for any foreignism to grow here."[260] Sister Monica Marie Boyle echoed the opinion of many Sisters that the South would never fall to communism when she commented that the Communists were northerners whose language and ideology had little in common with "their Southern Chinese people."[261]

The Communists were not what Maryknollers had expected. Used to the unruly attitude of Nationalist troops, the missioners praised the behavior of the soldiers of the People's Army. "They are models of discipline, they pay for everything; return everything they borrow; if they break something, they repair it; and there is no annoying of the people and the like."[262] They were also pleasantly surprised to note that, except for a few questionings and a house search at the time of the takeover, there was no interference in their mission work. On the contrary, Maryknollers were often congratulated for their "constant efforts in behalf of the people." Moreover, proclamations were posted "guaranteeing not only freedom of religion to the people but also protection and freedom to travel for those propagating religion."[263]

Encouraged by these signs of friendship, several missioners looked for possibilities to continue mission work in ways which could gain the gratitude of the Communist regime. Father John Donovan, for example, optimistically saw a great opportunity for evangelization through education if the missioners could endure the limitations and difficulties of working under the Communists; he felt mission schools would be viewed as indispensable for the modern reconstruction of China.[264] Other Maryknollers, like Father Howard Trube, changed the hours for religious services and catechumen classes to early morning and late evening in order not to interfere with the work in the fields and the meetings held by the Communists.[265]

Yet as 1949 came to an end, most missioners remained circumspect about the coming year. Barred by the Communist policy of preventing foreigners from entering China, half a dozen Maryknollers were stranded in Hong Kong without reentry visas. The prospect of returning looked bleak for those due for furlough or in need of medical attention in Hong Kong or the United States.[266] All over South China, missioners noted that with each passing month Communist officials and soldiers grew more demanding and hostile. They sensed tension in the air and felt the present lull was only a period of transition which would give way to a new era.[267]

Between the spring of 1949 and the summer of 1950, the Communists kept close watch on Maryknollers but did not interfere with their missionary work. There is no doubt that they looked at the foreign-controlled Catholic Church as an enemy of the new regime; the intransigence of Archbishop Riberi, the papal internuncio in China, was in great part responsible for their mounting intolerance toward missioners and their Christian followers, especially the native clergy and sisterhoods. Moreover, the American government's support of Chiang Kai-shek, although half-hearted, added to the Communists' suspicions against Maryknollers.

The Departure of Maryknollers

The standard Communist tactics. In the spring of 1950, the Communists began to unfold a plan to ease missioners out of China by creating an intolerable situation which would leave no alternative to missioners other than departure. The Communists decided to monitor the population's comings and goings in order to isolate remaining pockets of resistance and consolidate their control in the rural areas of South China. Maryknollers were told that because of the danger caused by "bandits," trips beyond their locality of residence had to be approved by the local police. For about six months, the missioners, except in some parts of Kwangsi where the resistance was active, had no difficulty securing permits. The only nuisance was the numerous visits to the police station to fill out applications and submit trip itineraries.[268]

The start of the Korean War in June 1950 gave the Communists a reason to further increase their surveillance of Maryknollers—citizens of a nation at war with China. Between October 1950 and January 1951, almost half of the 99 priests and Brothers and the 38 Sisters in South China were put under house arrest under suspicion of being spies of the American government. The Communists forced them out of their rectories and convents in small rural communities and moved them to other Maryknoll facilities in larger towns where surveillance was easier.[269]

Although not formally charged with crimes, these Maryknollers were confined from one month to over a year. During this time, the Communists tried to wear them down both physically and mentally to make them confess crimes such as harboring arms or hiding radios and transmitters to receive and pass coded messages. The Communists never used direct torture against Maryknollers not formally charged with a crime, but they did use a combination of trying ploys.

The first step was often to group the Sisters in one room of their convent and the Fathers in one room of their rectory and to search the buildings. The Communists usually quartered Maryknollers in the least livable rooms, such as an attic or basement where they suffered the cold of winter and the heat of summer. Privacy was completely denied. Curious people continuously strolled through the house. Day and night guards entered their rooms for inspection or interrogation. The Communists went through missioners' personal property and left them with only necessities such as a few pots and pans and a change of clothes. In some places, Maryknollers were allowed to keep some reading materials, but other possessions, including medicine and supplies, were confiscated.

Money was also taken away, and Maryknollers were given just enough to buy food for a week at a time. Except for a person to buy food, all hired help was dismissed. The Sisters had the responsibility of most of the housework including cooking and laundry. They discovered how exhausting it was to cook over open charcoal firepots, to draw water at a deep well, and to carry pails of water into the house. The Communists also denied special activities: missioners could not exercise by running back and forth; laughing, singing, and sometimes talking were forbidden.

Contacts with the exterior were kept to a minimum. Most letters were withheld, and the only outside news which reached them was through local newspapers given them by their guards. They read of the accusations against themselves along with slander about their sexual promiscuity and immoral behavior. They also learned about the trials and executions of others accused of severe crimes.

The Communists regularly threatened to jail Maryknollers and bring them to trial. Their constant intrusions could be for something insignificant, for another inspection, or worse—for the actual arrest of a priest or a Sister formally charged with a crime. Maryknoll Sisters Mary Paulita Hoffman and Edith (Marion Cordis) Rietz were actually dragged from their room through the streets of Hingning to attend the trial of their pastor, Father Aloysius Au. On the way, a mob jeered at them, stripped them of their veils, and threw dust and stones at them.[270]

The other half of the Maryknollers in South China were never arrested, but after the start of the Korean War, they found travel permits increasingly difficult to secure. By the end of 1950, the Communists told them that "for safety reasons" they should remain in their locality of residence where they could pursue their usual activities between the hours of 8:00 a.m. and 8:00 p.m.[271]

In January 1951, all foreigners were summoned to the county seat of their respective areas to fill out alien registration forms. Many Maryknollers were then submitted to a lengthy interrogation session by the police for the first time. The Communists then inventoried all personal and Church property. Church property was confiscated or locked up until it could be turned over to a Chinese-led Catholic administrative entity. In some cases, the missioners were still allowed the use of one or two rooms; in other instances they were forced to move out of the mission compound and rent housing in the locality. In March, the Communists froze the Church's assets as well as the personal assets of the missioners and banned all financial dealings with banks outside of China. They thought that missioners, forced to rely only on the money they had on hand, would leave when their funds ran out.[272]

Maryknollers, however, had voluntarily decided to stay and were not going to let themselves be easily frightened into leaving. Moreover, they were convinced that the local population, touched by their long-standing works of charity, would not turn against them and would continue to support them, even materially if necessary.

Nonetheless, the Communists were slowly able to isolate the missioners. The campaign usually began with school children who stopped greeting the priests and Sisters; it then spread to the adult population who grew increasingly hostile. Next, the Communists succeeded in turning Catholics away from the mission compounds and prevented them from attending mass. Sister Monica Marie Boyle recalled that "several soldiers stood at the gate [of the Loting compound] and Catholics were afraid to enter. They were scolded and told the church doors were going to be nailed shut and the Christians would all die inside."[273]

In late 1950, the Communists implemented the Agrarian Reform Law in South China. Catechists, hired hands, seminarians, and novices were required to go back to their native village to take part in land redistribution. Moreover, although resistance to the Communists had been crushed, travel restrictions were maintained while land redistribution continued. As a consequence, the Communists informed Maryknollers that since they could not visit their outstations nor ask the Catholics to come to the main church, they should suspend all public services.[274]

By June 1951, most Maryknollers had stopped visiting the Catholics and imposed a voluntary confinement upon themselves when they realized that all those having "connections with the Catholic Church were considered as undesirable people."[275] They suspected that their presence had become more of a liability than a help to the Chinese priests, Sisters, and Catholics who were hard-pressed by the Communists to denounce the missioners. When the Catholics refused, they were singled out for being "valets" of foreigners, put in jail, and brought to trial. All Maryknollers received orders from their ordinaries and their superiors to request exit permits.[276]

Their requests, of course, gave the Communists further reason to investigate missionary activities. It seems that they delayed in issuing an exit permit if there was a hope of charging Maryknollers with a crime; some priests and Sisters, although never formally charged with wrongdoing, were kept waiting for up to 10 months. When the permit was granted, the local newspaper announced the missioner's intention to leave. Anyone who knew of a pending civil or criminal case against the missioner or of any unpaid taxes or debts was urged to register a complaint with the authorities within a week. Once this last obstacle was cleared, the missioner was taken to the Hong Kong border and freed. By December 1951, out of the 137 Maryknollers in South China at the beginning of the year, 103 had already left. Although only 14 had been officially expelled, they all felt they had been forced out by the Communists.[277]

Whenever possible, the Communists brought charges against Maryknollers considered to be key persons in order to discredit the entire group. These missioners were arrested and thrown in jail. In comparison with other Maryknoll territories, the Kweilin prefecture experienced the least inconvenience. Monsignor John Romaniello of Kweilin was the only Maryknoll ordinary who was not arrested, and none of the Maryknoll Sisters under his jurisdiction went to jail.

Imprisonment: the cases of Sisters Thérèse Grondin and Rosalia Kettl. Even though accusations against missioners varied widely, the main purpose of the Communists was to prove that religious activities were a

Table 1

Confinement of Maryknollers in South China, 1951 (Compiled from Maryknoll archival records).

Status	Fathers (97)	Sisters (38)	Brothers (2)
Jailed (1 month +)	20	7	1
Ordered confined to compound	41	18	0
Confined to locality	36	13	1

Table 2

Maryknollers Leaving South China, 1951–1955 (Compiled from Maryknoll archival records).

Year	Deportation			Exit Permit		
	Fathers	Sisters	Brothers	Fathers	Sisters	Brothers
1951	8	6	0	60	27	2
1952	3*	1	0	19	3	0
1953	4	1	0	1	0	0
1954	0	0	0	0	0	0
1955	1	0	0	0	0	0

*Plus Bishop Francis Ford who died in jail.

cover-up for spying. The first pieces of "evidence" were usually found during a house search. Radios, earphones, literature against communism, old Army trousers and shirts, letters, accounting records, small American flags, and even a toy soldier were considered "damaging proof" of espionage. Sometimes a few extra clues were planted to make a stronger case against the missioners. Sister Thérèse Grondin, the novice mistress of the native Sisters of Kaying, recalled the three pieces of "evidence" that led to her imprisonment: Catholic pamphlets and leaflets which proved her connection with anti-Communist propaganda; $350 in Hong Kong currency which proved she was on the American payroll; and, most significant, a box conveniently found in one of her file cabinets containing three bullets said to be manufactured in America.[278] Other Maryknollers were similarly framed. For example, Sister Rosalia Kettl, superior of the Sisters in the Wuchow vicariate, was taken to jail after opium was discovered in her room.

After evidence was "found," a period of imprisonment usually followed while the Communists tried to build a case for a public trial. The search for further evidence continued; accusations were solicited—sometime under coercion—from the population; missioners were kept under terrible conditions and pressured to write confessions. Most of the time the Communists' efforts were to no avail. The story of the imprisonment of Sister Rosalia Kettl is representative of the ordeal suffered by many of the 28 priests, Brothers, and Sisters jailed for on suspicion of spying for the United States.

On December 19,[1950,] we waited until 7:30 a.m. for Mass, but Bishop Donaghy did not come. We had just decided to go upstairs when a group of about fifteen people, some in uniform and some in plain clothes appeared at the door. We were told to assemble in the parlor while they searched our house, taking our cook with them, and questioning her as to where Sister Rosalia's room was.

When the group returned to the parlor, we were told to go to our own rooms. After about ten minutes we noted that they were interested only in Sister Rosalia, so I stepped into her room, just at the time they were telling Sister to move the water buckets in the lavatory off her room.

Immediately one of the officers shouted, "What is that?" and made Sister pick up a package that they had placed there while we had been assembled in the parlor. Several men began to examine this package, saying it was contraband; we did not know what it was until they informed us it was opium. Our cook heard this and immediately said she had heard the buckets being moved when their own men went into that room previously. Sister Rosalia heard the woman say this, and told her to be quiet, otherwise the poor woman probably would have been shot.

Upon leaving Sister Rosalia's room, we saw that they had our radio too, which had been registered twice before. There was still five days' time in which to re-register for the third time. But in our case this was not taken into consideration. . . .

Sister Rosalia was taken to the police station, where she met Bishop and Father Kennedy, and also Doctor Wallace, a Protestant missionary who had often befriended us. Around nine a.m. she was taken inside, and immediately three men rushed at her, and tore her habit from her, taking collars, cuffs, rosary, and everything apart including her bonnet; when they got down as far as her slip, a woman took over and finished up, doing a thorough job. When Sister received her habit and bonnet back again, all the pins were missing. That night Sister was taken into the very inner section of the prison, and she began to realize that she was considered a political prisoner.

That first night was a real hell for her, as she was near the torture rooms and heard all that the water treatment included—the treatment was followed by screams, as gasoline was mixed with the water. Some of these people under torture were never seen again, some were taken back to prison in preparation for further torture, and the next morning the nurse came around and gave medicine needed to heal the wounds.

The worst part for Sister was when they took her out in the wee hours of the morning to be questioned. Sister said she always insisted on a woman coming with her which they allowed, but of course the woman remained outside the door. Sister was tied up, and two or three times gagged. The room for questioning was quite some distance down from her cell, and the passageways pitch black. The room where Sister was questioned was right next door to the torture rooms and during the questioning, it was always inferred that that would be the next step; some articles of torture were always lying around the room. These questions would last from three to four hours and every word was written down. The subjects of questioning were changed constantly and when Sister was completely off her guard, they would tell her what she had said on a previous statement, not the way she had said it, but his own interpretation of it, until she almost forgot what she had said. On looking back, Sister said she thinks they must have had drugs in the questioning rooms; she said when anyone returned from these questionings, it took most of the next day to recover from them, not only because of the terror they instilled, but because of the physical exhaustion and lethargy. Another thing that seems to point to the use of various drugs was the fact that though the prisoner was made to stay in that room four or five hours, the questioners changed every hour or so. Sometimes, they took Sister to a certain section, then made her go on along through unfamiliar passages. She would have to go upstairs alone where a man was waiting for her. The purpose seemed to be to make the prisoner as uncertain of himself as possible. He immediately snatched her cincture from her, just as a means of unnerving her.

Sister was not only questioned on the opium and radio, but on many other subjects which led her to believe she was considered a spy. Favorite subjects were the organization and working of Maryknoll, the "biggest spy ring" in China. They accused her of being the superior, not only of Wuchow, but of all of South China.

All four foreigners, Bishop Donaghy, Father Kennedy, Sister and Doctor Wallace were made to have their pictures taken each with the implement of his "crime." In Sister's case, she was photographed with her package of opium and the radio. The latter, ironically enough, was covered with mold and dust which should have been a proof that it had never been used as a wireless sending set as the authorities claimed.

. . . .

Sister realized she was in a Russian-modeled Communist prison. The room was very small and low; the window was boarded up except for a space of about four inches wide in a shaft form. The ceiling was of red tiles so as to increase the heat. When the warm weather began in April, the tropical sun made the cell like an oven. This was evidently intended as an added torture for the prisoner.

As for light, there was so little that often Sister had to stand directly under the window shaft to be able to say her office. The beds were about a foot off the ground, placed on bricks. On the side there was an aisle about one foot wide, for walking to the toilet. The latter was a hole in the wall, directly open to all the other toilets in that area. (One of the kind acts of the women in her cell was never to allow Sister to take a turn in emptying the toilets, though the guards wanted her to, even though it meant the women had to carry more than the required amount themselves.)

The room was so small that the six women with Sister could just lie on their sides, close to one another. We know how these folks sleep. Sister said that they always had their arms and legs on her person. No matter which way she turned someone's breath was always in her face. Her body was so cramped and tired, that she could not lie, stand or sit. She said they rarely slept, as the screams and wailings kept them on edge all the time; the questionings were always done at night, and everyone would lie awake wondering when his or her turn would come.

The women were questioned as she had been; when they returned they were often hysterical, and often Sister had to comfort them, sometimes holding them all night, trying to bring them out of their hysteria and fright.

All night, at each hour, the guards would pass, flashing bright electric lights for long periods on each one in turn. Prisoners in chains would pass by the door, dragging the chains, and crying, as they knew they were going to be tortured. All in all, Sister said she never had one full night's sleep during the entire period.

. . . .

The day before Sister was released was terrible, as there had been another "purge" the night before, and one hundred and fifty more prisoners were taken (they had numbered seven hundred in that prison before that!). This is one prison, and there are three more prisons in the city. Sister said all night long prisoners were moved around making room for the newcomers, and there was nothing but terror, noise and confusion, and always darkness. A woman chained was thrown into Sister's cell. Towards dawn Sister's number was called. She gathered all her belongings together, and prepared to be executed, the process they knew was in store for those whose numbers were called in the morning. She waited until later in the morning, when she was called a second time, but again the guards after calling her, did not return for her. Sister said this was one of the worst days for her. She cried all day, together with the other women. But it happened to be the storm before the calm.

That night, May 21, she was called and taken to the questioning room, and asked to sign papers saying she had opium in her room, and an unregistered radio. She refused, and was kept there for two hours. They said all she had to do was sign the papers and she would be back in her convent by night. Sister thought the end had come, because she felt she could not sign the paper about the opium, fearing it would involve the Church.

Glances were thrown toward the torture room, and Sister said she was ready for it, and for death also. She told them she must have time to think (to which they answered, hadn't she been thinking these five months?) and she pushed her way out of the room into an open corridor. They let her go, which had never happened before. Her good angel was guiding her, for through an open window she saw the Bishop [Donaghy] in the act of signing the paper for his release. This latter stated that a gun, not his, was found in his house.

Sister had seen just what she needed, so she went back into the room and said she would sign the paper saying the radio was unregistered, but not the one concerning the opium. They agreed, and Sister was free.[279]

As in the example of Sister Rosalia, the Communists were not often able to build a case against the missioners and bring them to a public trial. In some cases, the Maryknollers had to sign token confessions. Among all the terrible crimes she had been charged with, Sister Rosalia had to confess only that she was guilty of harboring an unregistered radio. Some missioners, like those in Loting, were released without having to sign admissions of guilt. After two months in jail, Fathers Robert Kennelly and John Graser, and Sisters Colombiere Bradley and Monica Marie Boyle were told that the People's Government of China had decided to expel them for having broken four rules: (a) teaching religion, which was against the law of the new regime; (b) killing 4,000 babies; (c) having hidden ammunition and guns; and (d) having unregistered American money. Although they never underwent a formal trial, they were deported as undesirable aliens who had betrayed the people of China.[280] Altogether, among the 87 Maryknollers jailed or kept under house arrest in South China for a period of one month or more, only 24 were officially deported.

Trials: the cases of Bishop Francis Ford and Sister Joan Marie Ryan. The Communists were able to gather enough "evidence" of spying or antigovernment activities to justify bringing 20 Maryknollers to a public or court trial. The well-documented case of Bishop Francis Ford reveals how the Communists probed into the past to build incriminating cases of political espionage.[281]

The first sign that the Communists were tightening the noose around the Catholic community in the Kaying diocese came in November 1950, when Father Aloysius Au, the pastor of Hingning, was jailed and Sisters Mary Paulita Hoffman and Edith Rietz were confined to their convent. On December 3, Maryknollers in Kaying city took the news of the arrest of Father Allan Dennis in Yaohang and Father Joseph Van den Bogaard and Sisters Thérèse Grondin and Pauline (M. Paul Thérèse) Sticka in Laolung as a warning that their turn would soon come.

Unknown to the missioners, the police department had recently arrested two Nationalist agents and one "tyrant-landlord" who confessed to having hidden for over a month in the center house. One agent, a member of Tai Li's Blue Shirts, even told Communist detectives that he had joined the organization at the instigation of Bishop Ford. On the morning of December 23, the police investigated the men's catechumenate in Kaying, located in the center house, and arrested four persons without residence permits. When it turned out that these men were rich landlords fleeing Kiangsi, Bishop Ford and Father Paul Lam (who taught in the catechumenate) became suspect. It appeared as if the catechumenate was harboring Nationalist agents and fugitives from the law. In the afternoon, the police returned and thoroughly searched the center house, the parish rectory, and the convent.

Although no incriminating evidence was found at the convent, the five Sisters—Rita Marie Regan, Magdalena Urlacher, Julia Hannigan, Anne (George Marie) McGowan, and Joan Marie Ryan—were kept under house detention. At the parish house, Lam was arrested for disguising the landlords from Kiangsi as catechumens and sheltering them, and also for having a pair of field glasses and a subversive book. He was confined to his room with two guards watching him day and night. Three Maryknoll priests, Fathers James McCormick, James O'Donnell, and Francis White, and one Chinese priest, Father Paul Ts'ia, happened to be at the center house. They were restricted to the house while Ford was immediately put under room detention. An investigation of his office files began at once. In the days which followed, the suspicion of the investigators also fell on Ford's secretary, Sister Joan Marie Ryan. On February 27, she was separated from the other Sisters and put in solitary confinement for having "deceived the government."[282]

During the four-month investigation conducted by a special Bureau of Public Safety, further evidence of Ford and Ryan's alleged spying activities was retrieved from the bishop's files. The bishop and Sister Joan Marie were both subjected to constant harassment and questioning: What was the source of money for the diocese? Who paid the bishop and his agents? Who sent them to China? What did they think of the new Chinese government? What part did the bishop play in the activities of the American military units stationed in the Kaying rectory during the war? Why did American naval personnel visit the bishop so frequently? What was the secret code the bishop used in his correspondence with the American consul and Maryknoll headquarters?

Meanwhile, the Communists organized a portable photo exhibit to inform the people of the bishop's alleged villainy. Photostats of his correspondence with American consuls in Swatow and Shanghai, copies of anti-Communist literature, and pictures of counterrevolutionaries harbored by the bishop were part of this exhibit which was shown in cities, towns, and villages in the entire Hakka territory of Kaying.[283]

In its final report made on April 13, the Bureau of Public Safety presented Ford as a very crafty American secret agent of long experience. It pointed out that in 1925 he was already sharpening his spying skills when he went to Peking to represent the interests of the American Catholic Church at the discussion of extraterritoriality under the Nine-Power Treaty. Having proven himself, he was then promoted to head of the Catholic Church in Kaying because it lay in the mountains of eastern Kwangtung, one of the earliest bases of Chinese communism. Religious activities were but a front for Ford's real mission. According to the report, his house in Kaying was an observation post from which he directed a spy ring in the neighboring districts and spread reactionary propaganda for the American government.

The spying charges brought against the bishop and his secretary fell into four categories. First, they were charged with the original accusation of harboring secret agents and enemies of the government as well as inciting Catholics to join the anti-Communist Blue Shirts. Although the bishop and his secretary were often asked about their relationship with American personnel stationed at the Kaying mission at the end of World War II, the matter was not pursued, probably because at that time America was an ally of China. Evidence zeroed in on more recent incidents. The names of the Nationalist agents and the landlords who had taken refuge in Ford's catechumenate were publicly revealed and their "evil" activities described. Furthermore, Ford was charged with giving asylum and helping in the escape of a Chinese priest wanted for acts of treason against Communist patriots, and for cooperating with the Japanese. Actually, Ford had used the services of Father Hsü Teh for two years before helping him to make his way to Hong Kong in 1949.

The second charge accused the bishop of distributing and writing anti-Communist literature. Many pamphlets and booklets with titles such as *The Anti-Communist Position of the Church* and *A Brief Exposition of Communism* were seized at the parish rectory and the center house as proof that the bishop dealt with imperialistic propaganda and was working to undermine the new government.[284] Ford's files also contained many samples of his anti-Communist writings and conferences, some of these going back to the mid-twenties when the "Reds" first entered the Hakka hills. One piece of incriminating evidence produced was a letter of January 1948 addressed to Jesuit Father R. Harris of the regional seminary in Hong Kong. Ford mentioned that at the request of local government officials he had devised a strategy to wipe out the Red guerrillas in Kwangtung which he had entitled "A Program for the Solution of Communist Disturbance in Kwangtung Province." According to his letter, Ford was pleased to learn from these officials that the provincial governor, T. V. Soong (Chiang Kai-Shek's brother-in-law), had decided to implement his plan. The bishop added also that he had been most careful not to sign the document or indicate in any way that it came from him.[285] The Communists intended to prove not only that the bishop had been distributing and writing subversive literature but that he was also a high-ranking spy working for the Nationalist and American governments. This accusation paved the way for a third round of evidence.

Ford was charged with collecting and passing secret information about

China's military affairs, politics, and economics to the American government during the previous 20 years. These intelligence reports were said to have been concealed in his regular correspondence as well as in the Kaying Church's annual reports and also carried in person by missioners going on furlough to America. Besides these "usual methods," the bishop was accused of using a secret telegraphic code since 1936 to send confidential communications to the American consul in Swatow. The incriminating document was a letter from the consul, Frederick Hinke, which stated: "I am enclosing for your confidential use in communication with the consulate by telegraph a cipher which I have specially devised for this purpose."[286] It did not matter to the investigators that the code was primarily designed to cope with emergency cases such as the capture of Father Harry Bush by bandits in 1935. They had "proof" from the bishop's files that he had furnished intelligence information to the American consulate in Swatow during the previous year and concluded that the code was designed to ensure greater confidentiality.

From the Communist viewpoint, the letters produced clearly revealed the bishop's spy activities. Included in the proof of his spying were three letters of October through November 1929 addressed to the consul which did provide substantial information on Communist troop movements and, to a certain degree, gave the impression that the bishop was a spy eagerly serving his government. On October 30, he opened his report by saying, "I know you wish to obtain word of the situation in this area. I can gladly give you the news up to this moment."[287]

The investigators were even able to find a document which discredited Ford's pro-Chinese activities during the Sino-Japanese War. The letter, dated December 4, 1939, from the consulate in Swatow, asked Ford to submit clearly marked maps and plans of all places where the Catholic Church had personnel and properties. This information was requested by the Japanese forces in Swatow allegedly to ensure the protection of third country nationals in the war areas and was to be transmitted to the Japanese War Department.[288] Of course, the Communists interpreted the document as proof of the U.S. government's treacherous attitude toward China and of Bishop Ford's complicity in providing Japan with crucial intelligence reports.

During the 1940s, the correspondence between the bishop's office and the consulate showed that Ford regularly continued to provide information on the status of the local economy, agriculture, highways, and communications in general which were then relayed to American governmental agencies. Several times the consul was pleased to inform the bishop that in "higher places" his reports were viewed as "interesting and useful."[289]

The fourth charge was that Ford had attempted to incite his Catholics to rise up against communism and to help the Nationalist Party. Of course the Communists emphasized that in 1948 the bishop had declared that every year on the first Sunday of May each parish of his diocese would conduct special ceremonies to pray for "the conversion of Russia and against communism." The bishop had in fact used this day for widespread propaganda against the Chinese Communists and in support of the Nationalists. Using Liu Jen-sheng, a Catholic who had joined Chiang Kai-shek's Blue Shirts, as an example, the investigators even accused Ford of attempting to organize the Catholics into Blue Shirt units. Other evidence of the bishop's counterrevolutionary activities among Catholics included excerpts of letters, reports, and pamphlets in which he mentioned the "steadfast anti-Communist stand of the Catholic Church in Kaying" and denounced the evil of communism. A secret list of his "most reliable local personnel" was produced to prove that he had trained a special force of priests and Sisters to sabotage the newly established Patriotic Movement of the Catholic Church.[290]

On the morning of April 14, 1951, Ford and Sister Joan Marie, both tied like criminals, were taken to the courthouse, pronounced guilty, and sentenced to the provincial prison in Canton as spies against the People's Government. During their four-day trip to Canton, demonstrations and denunciation rallies were staged along the way against the two "American spies." Ford and his secretary were paraded through the main streets of the towns while people marched in front of them, carrying signs describing their crimes. At the mercy of an angry and vociferous crowd who demanded their death, they were beaten with sticks, struck with stones and refuse, and tripped to the ground. Following their imprisonment in Canton, the case was given wide coverage in the newspapers. On April 24, the *South China Daily* of Canton, the official Communist newspaper for all of South China, devoted its entire first page and part of page four to the accusations. The paper provided pictures and translations of several compromising letters and showed some anti-Communist pamphlets found in the bishop's files. Snapshots and short biographical profiles of two of the Nationalist agents concealed by the missioners were added as further proof.

The next day, the local Kaying newspaper, *Hingning-Meihsien Daily*, followed suit by reprinting the lead article of the *South China Daily* on its first page. In addition it also published a one-page article explaining how imperialism had historically made use of Christianity in its aggression against China. In a shorter piece the local branch of the Chinese Patriotic Movement denounced the bishop as a spy and expressed its determination to sever all links with imperialism. On April 26, a full page of the paper carried reproductions of documents similar to those already published in the *South China Daily*. For more than two weeks, articles and letters to the editor continued to appear, denouncing the bishop as a "poisonous snake" and calling for severe punishment.[291]

In Moscow, *Pravda* also jumped on the band wagon, accusing American missioners in China of collecting information for American intelligence agencies and citing a number of cases of alleged espionage activities. The article focused on charges against Bishop Ford, who was presented as one of the leading spies in China.[292] In Canton, a caricature soon began to circulate showing Bishop Ford pretending to read his prayer book while he treacherously kept watch as Sister Joan Marie signaled on a wireless set to American aircraft flying overhead. Finally, in January 1952, a satirical booklet entitled *The Most Evil American Spies* was widely distributed. It combined four caricatural drawings of the bishop and his secretary with a seven-page long popular rhymed version of their alleged crimes.[293]

In the Canton prison, Ford and Sister Joan Marie endured tedious hours of indoctrination and interminable questioning and were told to search their minds to recall the various occasions on which they had spoken or acted against communism. Their trial was repeated many times before different judges with the same accusations and the same verdict. Bishop Ford died in jail from exhaustion and illness in early 1952, at the age of sixty. In early September 1952, Sister Joan Marie was taken to his grave and then ordered out of the country as an undesirable alien who had betrayed the people of China.[294]

Staying at all costs: the case of Bishop James E. Walsh. Bishop James E. Walsh was another Maryknoller brought to trial. His release in 1970 after 12 years in a Communist prison caught the attention of the world press.

After his term of office as superior general of the Maryknoll Fathers and Brothers, Walsh returned to China in 1948 as executive secretary of the newly formed Catholic Central Bureau of China. In 1947, apostolic delegate Archbishop Riberi had expanded the Commission on Schools, Books and Press, which was created in 1924, to about 20 Chinese and foreign priests, and moved it within the Bureau in order to coordinate the Church's missionary efforts throughout the country.

After the fall of Shanghai to the Communists in May 1949, the Bureau came under increasing surveillance. In June 1951, the Shanghai Military Control Council suspended its activities. An investigation was conducted on charges that the Bureau was "the center of activities of imperialistic elements in the Catholic circles." Specifically, the Communists accused the organization of producing and circulating large quantities of "reactionary books," of "slandering the Chinese people and people's government," of opposing the "independent movement of the patriotic Chinese Catholics," and of directing "such reactionary groups as the Catholic Action and the Legion of St. Mary." Two months later, two foreign and two Chinese priests of the Bureau staff were arrested. Following this incident, all

Fig. 4. "The Most Evil American Spies," a caricature of Bishop Francis Ford and Sister Joan Marie Ryan. Source: FARC, Box 37, Folder 3, *Mei-kuo Chien-t'ieh Tsui Eh Ta*, cover page.

members were gradually apprehended and detained.[295]

Only Bishop Walsh was free to move around the city and mingle with the people. Occasionally he met with visiting foreigners who reported news of his well-being. Moreover, with the cooperation of the British consul in Shanghai who made his diplomatic pouch available to them, the bishop was able to exchange messages with Father James Smith of Mary-knoll in Hong Kong until his arrest in 1958.

Since the activities of the Central Bureau were suspended, Walsh occupied himself with writing articles describing the methods of famous missioners. He also spent much time helping foreigners and Chinese who wanted to leave China for Hong Kong. He used his good rapport with the British Consulate to assist in securing the necessary exit permits and visas.[296]

Walsh himself could have left China at any time, and it seems that the Communists wished he would do so. Instead, the bishop became a strong advocate of the position that missioners should remain at their posts even if it meant imprisonment and death. His thesis, based on the idea that the good shepherd remains with his flock, was set forth very forcefully in the June-July 1951 issue of the *China Missionary Bulletin*:

> I think it is the plain duty of all Catholic missionaries, priests, Brothers and Sisters to remain where they are until prevented from doing so by physical force. If internment should intervene in the case of some, or even death, it should simply be regarded as a normal risk that is inherent in our state of life, as a necessity concomitant to our responsibilities, and as a small price to pay for carrying out our duty.[297]

When Maryknoll's General Council expressed concern for the bishop's safety and suggested that he apply for an exit permit, Walsh, who by then was over sixty years old, replied that unless Maryknoll ordered him to leave, he would not give up his commitment to the Chinese people. Then, with a touch of temper, he added, "To put up with a little inconvenience at my age is nothing. Besides, I am a little sick and tired of being pushed around on account of my religion."[298]

Starting with the fall of 1955, the Communists gradually restricted his freedom. He was submitted to occasional house arrests, forced out of the Catholic Central Bureau building, forbidden to say mass in public, and finally arrested in October 1958 and sent to a house of detention. Then followed a period of a year and a half of questioning at any hour of the day or night. Although the Communists never used physical torture, the bishop recalled that this was the most difficult time of his 12 years in prison because of the mental pressure and the harsh living accommodations.[299]

At first the interrogations centered on a financial matter. The bishop was accused of breaking the law by conspiring to import money from Hong Kong into Shanghai. At the request of Bishop Kung P'in-mei of Shanghai who had run out of funds for his diocese, Walsh had indeed sent a message to a bank in Hong Kong to enable a Chinese priest to withdraw money and bring it back to Shanghai. It was obvious to the bishop that the Communists had found a way to read some of his messages in the British diplomatic pouch. He admitted, therefore, that he had broken the law on this point.[300]

Next, the Communists tried to make the bishop confess that he was guilty of spying. Among the evidence produced were two alleged cases of military espionage. He was charged with gaining the confidence of a Chinese in the shipping industry who had told him about the building of a submarine in Shanghai. He was also accused of having received information from a Chinese soldier fighting in the Korean war about the weapons and ammunition used by the Chinese army. For several months, the Communists tried to get the bishop to sign a confession admitting he was a spy, but each time he refused to comply. Walsh's stamina was steadily deteriorating when he finally found a way to satisfy the Communists without compromising his position. At a press conference in Hong Kong in 1970, he recalled how it happened:

> Finally I said "Well, I may have become a spy in the legal sense. I know that you consider all missionaries as spies. You say that your laws provide penalties for these things you allege that make me a spy. Maybe that's true. So I admit I may be a spy in the legal sense." That seemed to satisfy them and the next morning they brought to me [a statement] to sign [which read] "I admit I became a spy in the legal sense." So I thought: Well, my saving clause is in there. I can sign that.[301]

In March 1960, following his confession, Walsh was brought to trial at the Shanghai People's Intermediate Court and received a sentence of 20 years of imprisonment for espionage and conspiracy. After three months' incarceration in a cell of the infamous Ward Street prison, he became ill. He was then transferred to a large airy room of the prison hospital where he remained for the next 10 years, even after his recovery.

On June 8, 1970, he was suddenly told to pack because, owing to his good behavior and the benevolence of the government, he was being taken to the Hong Kong border for release. Three days later, at the age of seventy-nine, he crossed the border and was reunited with Maryknollers.[302]

Conclusion

Throughout the late 1930s, Maryknollers in China simultaneously carried on the evangelization and socio-economic improvement programs while trying not to take sides in Chinese internal politics. As long as there was peace, the missioners, like most of the rural people with whom they lived, cared little about who maintained the peace or how it was maintained. In periods of war and unrest, they sometimes intervened to avoid bloodshed and to save the lives of civilians. Whatever the outcome, they showed equal respect to the continually changing local, civil, and military officials.

Nonetheless, the missioners' presence itself was in fact seen as a sign of political interference. Under the privileges of extraterritoriality, finally abolished in 1943, they enjoyed rights and protection unknown to the Chinese. Despite the fact that Maryknollers rarely called on the American government, and generally kept a low profile when tensions arose and Chinese nationalism flared up, they could not totally cast off their image as pawns of Western imperialism.

The aggressive behavior of Japan toward China also contributed to the politicization of Maryknollers. This politicization was expressed in two quite different ways. As Japan increased her control over Manchuria and missioners could no longer count on the protection of Western nations, Maryknollers claimed that their purpose was entirely religious and nonpolitical. Yet, over the years, Church leaders increasingly cultivated the good will of the Manchukuo government. In order to be allowed to continue to work in the Fushun vicariate, Maryknollers bent over backward to refrain from criticism or actions against the Japanese and the Chinese puppet government. Although they knew some of their Chinese parishioners were engaged in the resistance, they never mentioned resistance fighters in their writings and blamed "bandits" for most of the difficulties. However, in December 1941, all these compromises with the Japanese could not save Maryknollers from arrest as enemies of the regime.

In South China, Maryknollers did not have to compromise with the Japanese. At first, they viewed the Japanese invasion as just another nuisance which disrupted their well-thought-out plans for evangelization. However, with the intensification of the conflict, and sharing the same hardships, Maryknollers developed a special bond with the Chinese people which Sister Richard Wenzel called a "spiritual comradeship." Moreover, the unselfish dedication of missioners to feed and shelter refugees, care for war orphans, and provide medical treatment during epidemics strengthened these bonds and improved the image of the Catholic Church among the non-Christian population. The more Maryknollers in South China shared in the Chinese people's suffering, the more they expressed derogatory views about the Japanese aggressors. Therefore, news of the entry of the United States into the conflict on the side of China was received with great joy and anticipation.

After Pearl Harbor, the decision of several Maryknollers to stay behind enemy lines was a clear departure from Maryknoll's previous policy. The rule so far had been to stay in case of religious persecution but to withdraw in cases involving political reprisals against foreigners. During the Sino-Japanese War, Maryknoll came to realize that the duty of its missioners was to stay at all times with the Chinese people to share their sorrows and their joys and also to pose a political act of opposition to Japanese aggression.

This same idea of opposing Japanese aggression was a reason for other Maryknollers to enroll as contract chaplains and hospital nurses with the American forces in China. After the war, these close relationships between Maryknollers and American Army personnel were used by the Communists as examples of American imperialism. Because of the involvement with the military, previous demonstrations of the missioners' unselfish dedication to the Chinese people were now looked upon with suspicion. Moreover, the Communists questioned the reality of the missioners' commitment to the cause of a strong and free China since many Maryknollers had actually preferred to withdraw rather than stay. Even those who had chosen to stay behind the Japanese lines came under attack and were accused of having gathered information for the American government. According to the Communists, the support of the leadership of the Catholic Church for the corrupt government of Chiang Kai-shek was proof that the missioners did not really care for the Chinese people. All along, it was said, they had been clever spies, whose actions were geared to the enslavement of China by American imperialism.

Most of these accusations were farfetched. The Catholic Church's contributions to Chinese nationalism cannot be easily dismissed: Maryknollers enrolled in the national war effort against Japan and provided modern education, medical care, and social services, all in conformity with Chinese governmental regulations. At the same time, these accusations were not pure invention or without foundation. In fact, Maryknollers had accepted the protection of the unequal treaties. Moreover, Maryknoll's official policy of neutrality led, particularly in Manchuria, to an attitude which, from a Chinese point of view, smacked of compromise with the enemy. From the first antiforeign outburst in 1925 until Pearl Harbor in 1941, it took Maryknoll 16 years to completely abandon this facade of religious neutrality and to realize that the Catholic Church in China would never be culturally integrated if it continued to remain aloof from the Chinese socio-political context.

At that time, two different camps extolled nationalism in China—the the Nationalist government of Chiang Kai-shek and the Communist Party. Since communism was identified by the papal encyclical *Divini Redemptoris* of 1937 as the number one enemy of the Catholic Church, the missioners, of course, could not support it. Chiang, on the contrary, was in power and also happened to be a Christian. Therefore, the leadership of the Catholic Church in China rallied behind him. After the war, many Maryknollers, including Bishop Ford, realized the extent of corruption among the Nationalists. However, since the only alternative was communism, they felt that they had to continue support for the Nationalist government and hope for a change for the better. American governmental and Catholic circles, and certainly Maryknoll headquarters, showed a definite tendency to hide the corruption of the Nationalists behind the figure of Chiang Kai-shek, who was presented as the "ideal Christian leader."

The conflict between the Catholic Church and communism was raised by the Church to the level of an ideological contest between good and evil. Missioners could not have been more vehemently opposed to Communist ideology: the Communists professed atheism, while the missioners preached belief in God. Yet in practice, many policies of the Communists and the charity work of the missioners were both focused on the same goal—improving the living conditions of the Chinese people.

For their part, the Communists raised the conflict with the Church to an ideological contest between the people's cause and imperialist aggression. They charged Maryknollers with being American imperialist spies, and the native clergy and sisterhoods with being their "valets." Yet in practice, through their works of mercy, their community projects and their efforts to establish a self-administered Chinese Church, Maryknollers did pursue the people's cause.

In the end, the Catholic Church's adamant support of the Nationalist government, and silence about the corruption of many government officials, sealed the missioners' fate. The difference in attitude between Maryknollers in China and Maryknollers today is striking. Maryknollers of the late 1940s thought it was preferable to work on the side of a less-than-desirable government for the purpose of resisting the Communist threat. Maryknollers today are often inclined to put aside the question of ideology and firmly denounce practices of corrupt or oppressive governments.

Yet this difference hides a strong resemblance, for example, between Bishop Ford and his niece, Maryknoll Sister Ita Ford, who died some 30 years apart. Bishop Ford was charged with spreading American imperialism in China, and Ita Ford was shot for helping alleged Communist-backed revolutionaries in El Salvador. However, the real reasons for their deaths lie elsewhere—both died because their success in gaining the hearts of the people was viewed as a threat by the respective government.[303] The Communists jailed the bishop because his methods in reaching the people competed with theirs. The Salvadoran soldiers were ordered to kill Sister Ita because she was too close to the families of their victims.

If the theology of Francis Ford, with some of its emphasis on baptism and salvation through the Church, appears outdated by today's standards, his methods, nonetheless, revealed a mission vision which anticipated several reforms of Vatican II by more than a quarter of a century. Bishop Ford's main effort was to foster a self-governing local Church, financially self-reliant and unburdened by Western institutions. His dream was to develop well-educated lay leaders to take positions of responsibility in building modern China. Ford's directives to his missioners, especially the Sisters, were to move out beyond their convents and rectories to meet and live with the people, in order to root the Gospel in the daily lives of those people. In a similar sense, Sister Ita Ford gave her life among the oppressed people of El Salvador, because, 30 years earlier, under the impetus of Bishop Ford, other Maryknoll Sisters in the Hakka hills had paved the way.

During the past four decades, communism in China has also undergone a transformation. Today, Christianity is not necessarily viewed as an imperialist tool which must be destroyed, but rather as a force which can contribute to the people's cause. Nonetheless, the past excesses of communism cannot easily be forgotten. The stories of the mental and physical sufferings of Sisters Rosalia Kettl and Joan Marie Ryan and Bishop Francis Ford are but examples of the ordeal endured at the hands of the Communists by Maryknoll Brothers, Sisters, and priests. These accounts, together with those of other missioners and Chinese priests, Sisters, and countless Christians, will remain a dark moment in the history of China. Many were caught in a clash of ideologies and fell victim to the Communist drive to rid China of all those suspected of being imperialist agents.

In 1950, since her organization, finances, and leadership were still mostly in the hands of missioners, the Chinese Catholic Church, for all practical purposes, remained a foreign institution. When the Communist axe fell on the missioners, the Chinese Catholics were also suspected of being traitors and spies who could not be trusted and who should be punished unless they could prove their patriotism. The Communist takeover forced the Chinese Church to pass suddenly from a state of infancy and almost total dependency on Western Churches to a state of selfhood and self-determination. Since then, it has charted a difficult and courageous course through seas of suffering and oppression.

In many ways, the Church has persevered until today because of its missionary heritage. In spite of many imperfections, the missioners' catechetical programs and training of local priests and Sisters established the native Church on solid foundations. The Chinese Catholic Church has also gained the experience of living dangerously and not relying on outside help. Through constant wars and upheavals, it has developed survival techniques and weathered many storms.

The ambiguous political involvement of missioners resulted in their expulsion by the Communists, but it opened the way for the first truly local Church in modern times. To counter the political involvement of missioners on the side of the Nationalists and their strong ideological opposition to communism, the Church of China felt the need to prove its patriotism. In opting for a course independent of foreign influence and alienating many of its former mentors, some Catholics created the Chinese

Catholic Patriotic Association with the goal of encouraging all Catholics to participate in Chinese national development and progress.

In a letter of admonition to the missionary leaders of China in 1926, Pope Pius XI reminded them that the Church "has always adapted to all kinds of nations and governments and preached respect and obedience to legitimate civil authorities." He also claimed that "the Church has never consented to her missions becoming political tools in the hands of world powers."[304] In reality, however, during most of the nineteenth and early twentieth centuries, the Vatican allowed Western nations to use the missionary enterprise to foster their colonial or imperialistic undertakings. In contrast, the Vatican today refuses to recognize the Chinese Church, suspecting that several leaders of that Church have become tools of communist ideology.

For its part, the Chinese Catholic Church has retaliated by denouncing the Vatican as a tool of imperialism and by ordaining local bishops without the pope's authorization. Recently some dialogue between the two sides has begun, but as yet, neither party seems ready to trust the other. Unless both are convinced that, despite some mistakes, the other has lived by Pope Pius's instruction, forgiveness and reconciliation seem remote.

The experience of the Chinese Church during this century could be a living testimony that Christianity should not only strive to take on different forms to reflect the genius of different cultures, but also that it can adapt and survive under any government or ideology. Furthermore, this experience could give more momentum to the idea that Christianity cannot remain neutral because its message of universal love and liberation of mankind is in itself a political force. When it ceases to denounce injustice for the sake of its own survival, Christianity fails; when it risks everything to defend the poor and the oppressed, it revives and expands. If the Chinese Catholic Church succeeds in remaining steadfast in religious doctrine while encouraging its followers to be model citizens, it will have lived up to Pope Pius XI's instruction, remaining in communion with the Holy See.

PART IV

Introducing China to North America

8

Maryknoll's Influence on American Catholics

James A. Walsh was convinced that to survive, an American foreign mission society needed the widespread support of mission-minded Catholics. He founded the Catholic Foreign Mission Bureau in Boston to stimulate vocations and both spiritual and material backing.

Largely through *The Field Afar*, the literary propaganda of the Mission Bureau provided a favorable climate which eventually led to the founding of Maryknoll. Vocations and financial support grew because, since its beginning, Maryknoll had always considered the nurturing of a missionary spirit among American Catholics as one of its basic tasks and as a condition for its survival. China missioners always played an important role in this work.

James A. Walsh had a special fascination with the Far East. The strong bond which grew between Maryknoll and China was not an accident but rather the result of his careful planning to ensure the successful launching of an American foreign mission society. It also seems probable that Walsh chose a geographic region exactly opposite to the United States in order to emphasize that the American missionary spirit should know no limits. Most significant of all, Walsh's analysis of the international political situation at the beginning of the century, and of Protestant missionary efforts in China, had convinced him that time had come for "Americans to bear the banners of Catholicity . . . in China and elsewhere [and] to persuade people that everything American [was] not Protestant."[1]

More than half of the first issue of *The Field Afar* in January 1907 emphasizes the Far East; news about China alone spread over six of the 16 pages. Walsh left no doubt that he considered China the mission field most likely to arouse the interest of American Catholics and to generate missionary vocations.

> If, as we hope to do, we can place before our readers, in an interesting way, the mission fields of China, the personality of the workers, their hopes, enthusiasms, sacrifices and successes, we feel assured that others will come to feel with us the glory and greatness, the honor and privilege of working together with God, that His kingdom may extend into this vast country.[2]

The magazine achieved what Walsh had expected. In less than six years, an American foreign mission seminary had opened and the Teresians, in Walsh's own words, had become an "incipient [religious] society."[3]

The Use of Mass Media

The Field Afar—Maryknoll Magazine

Long before they met to share their dream of forming an American Catholic foreign mission society, Fathers James A. Walsh and Thomas F. Price were both publishing mission magazines. From its earliest days, therefore, Maryknoll inherited a predilection for the media as a way to promote mission awareness. *The Field Afar* magazine immediately emerged as the main vehicle to draw the attention of American Catholics to China. By the end of its first decade, its circulation had stabilized at around 35,000 subscribers in all 48 states. Walsh, however, was not satisfied; in fact, he was rather disappointed because that number was well below his goal of 50,000 subscribers.

American Catholic missionary consciousness had increased substantially since the turn of the century and was reflected in the growth from $71,000 to over $465,000 in American contributions to the Society for the Propagation of the Faith. Yet, this amount was in no way comparable to the $100 million given annually for the needs of the Church at home. The idea of foreign missions had caught only the peripheral attention of American Catholics. To reach deeper into their wallets, it was necessary to touch people's lives at a more personal level.

The announcement in the June 1918 issue of *The Field Afar* that Maryknoll had found a mission field in China signaled a new growth for the magazine. When reports of the first Maryknollers in Yeungkong began to appear half a year later, thousands of new subscribers joined each month. In 1920, the magazine passed the 75,000 mark. By March 1923, a very satisfied Walsh wrote that with more than 100,000 subscribers and a half-million cover-to-cover readers, *The Field Afar* had a larger circulation than a "certain well-known daily [newspaper] in New York City," undoubtedly referring to the then-popular *New York Evening Telegram.*[4]

In 1924 *The Field Afar* subscription list settled at a new plateau of 125,000,[5] but during the Depression in the United States, the magazine's circulation fell back under 100,000. However it rebounded after 1935. By 1941, *The Field Afar*—renamed *Maryknoll—The Field Afar* in April 1939—had an average circulation of 216,000; ten years later, when most foreigners had been expelled from China, over 600,000 copies were distributed monthly.

The Organization of Mission Circles and Other Activities

To develop a readership actively involved in mission work, *The Field Afar* fostered a number of activities. In January 1916, it officially launched the Mission Circles, which encouraged subscribers to form small groups "to cultivate in themselves and others a knowledge of Catholic foreign missions, to pray for the mission cause, and to help provide for the special needs of Maryknoll at home and in the mission field."[6]

These circles became popular among women from all walks of life who were interested in helping Maryknoll. Except for a few groups which belonged to larger organizations such as the Catholic Daughters of America and the Catholic Women's Benevolent Association, these circles usually grouped mission-minded women of a particular parish. Their immediate aims varied widely but all were of great help to Maryknoll. Members enrolled new subscribers and contacted those who had lapsed; they placed mite boxes among friends and families to collect small change for the missions; they collected funds for Maryknoll's construction needs in the United States and in the Far East; they provided church linens, religious articles, books, and furniture for the Maryknoll preparatory schools, seminary, and the Sisters' novitiate; they paid for the training of many Maryknollers as well as Chinese seminarians, novices, and catechists; they sewed and knitted garments for departing missioners and gathered old clothes for the Maryknoll missions; they adopted Maryknoll missioners in China, sent money for the catechists' salaries, and continually replenished funds for orphans and lepers.

The Field Afar also targeted special audiences among its subscribers and provided information relevant to their interests. One important group was school children. In the first issue, Father John Lane, one of the founders of the Catholic Foreign Mission Bureau, started "Our Young Apostles," a column under the pen name of Father Ignatius which dealt almost exclusively with China. When Lane's precarious health and new responsibilities for the formation of seminarians forced him to give up the column in 1912, articles aimed at young people continued to appear but only sporadically.

In March 1916, Father Ignatius' column reappeared as a four-page supplement called "The Maryknoll Junior"; however, Lane was too sick to continue. In September 1918, under the pen name of Father Chin, Father James A. Walsh managed to revive "The Maryknoll Junior." Father Chin was introduced to the readers: "He has spent a portion of his life in China [and] if he had stayed there longer, he would be called Father China."[7] Father Chin became so successful that in April of the following year, *The Maryknoll Junior* became an independent magazine which reached 15,000 young subscribers by 1924.[8] China remained its primary emphasis.

College students, seminarians in major seminaries, and Sisters in novitiates also received special attention. In April 1913, *The Field Afar* highlighted the academia or mission circle of St. John's Seminary in Brighton which had cultivated the foreign mission spirit among seminarians and contributed funds to both the Society for the Propagation of the Faith and to Maryknoll for more than 15 years. When the Society of the Divine Word launched the Catholic Students' Mission Crusade in 1917, *The Field Afar* gave enthusiastic support and included abundant notes on the organization. Within a few years the Crusade became the main mission-oriented organization for young American Catholics and a most important source of missionary support. *The Field Afar* continuously encouraged Crusade activities under various headings such as "Academia," "For Crusaders," or simply "The Students' Page."[9] With the February 1930 issue, the "Crusade" column became a regular feature.

Starting with the first national convention in Techny, Illinois in July 1918, Maryknollers always attended meetings of the Mission Crusade. Mother Mary Joseph and Fathers Raymond Lane and James Drought addressed the students at the seventh national convention in 1931, and Father James A. Walsh was a guest speaker at the meeting in 1933. Both Mother Mary Joseph's and Father Walsh's talks relied heavily on examples from the Catholic experience in China. To demonstrate "the bravery and endurance, the zeal, the buoyancy, the adaptability of our [American] girls," Mother Mary Joseph told of her Sisters' harrowing experiences at the hands of pirates.[10] Walsh explained that the Church had little face in

China because of the absence of educated Catholics, and urged American students to "give special attention to the educational needs that pressed missioners."[11]

In September 1937, in an effort to reach Catholic youth beyond grade school, the magazine introduced the Maryknoll Pioneers, who were "university, college, and high school young men and women, and seminarians, who, as special friends of Maryknoll, are disposed to forward actively its ideals." The organization also appealed to young people "in professional, business, or home spheres" and started a *Maryknoll Pioneers* bulletin in January 1938 to guide them in missionary activities.[12]

The Beginning of the Maryknoll Bookshelf

Rich with experience gained in Boston, the newly born Catholic Foreign Mission Society of America sponsored and published books on mission. By 1912, *The Field Afar* claimed that James A. Walsh's first book, *A Modern Martyr*, published in 1905, had been read by more than 50,000 Americans. All but one of the nine books offered by The Maryknoll Bookshelf dealt with martyrs in the Far East.[13]

In 1913, a collection of mostly fictitious short stories was published under the title *Field Afar Stories*. About two-thirds of the 15 stories were written by Mary J. Rogers, the future Mother Mary Joseph, and by Father James A. Walsh, under the pseudonym John Wakefield. Each account dealt with an aspect of mission life in China or with the awakening of a missionary vocation to the Far East. Two more volumes of stories appeared in 1915 and 1921. The success of these narratives convinced The MacMillan Company to undertake the publication in 1923 and again in 1927 of two books of selected writings of Maryknollers entitled *Maryknoll Mission Letters—China*.

Meanwhile, James A. Walsh published in book form two accounts he had earlier printed in *The Field Afar*. In 1919, *Observations in the Orient* told of his 1917 search for a mission field. This was followed in 1922 by *In the Homes of Martyrs*, the story of his 1907 pilgrimage to the homes of French missioners martyred in the Far East. Other Maryknollers were also pressed into service to write. Father Patrick Byrne published the *Life of Father Price* in 1923, and in 1924 translated *The Catholic Church in Korea* from the French. The following year, Father John Considine, who had gone to Rome to supervise the construction of Maryknoll's booth at the Vatican Mission Exposition, prepared *A Window on the World*, a book with photographs which described the exposition. In 1926, Father George Powers published a history of the beginning of Maryknoll under the title *The Maryknoll Movement*. By 1927, Maryknoll had published 22 books, most of which focused on the Far East, particularly China.[14]

The Depression years and the Pamphlet Library

During the following decade, the publishing activity of Maryknoll went into eclipse. The combined effects of the Depression and the growing financial needs of the Maryknoll family required concentration on promotional efforts to produce income and to curtail educational activities geared to fostering vocations among American youth. During those ten years, the only new book published was written by Bishop James E. Walsh on the life of Father Daniel McShane in China.

One Maryknoller, however, took it upon himself to perserve in Maryknoll's original commitment to contribute to the missionary education of American Catholics. In 1933, Father Robert Sheridan was reassigned from the Philippines to the United States for what was called at that time promotion work. He viewed his responsibility as not only recruiting new personnel and gathering funds, but also supplying Catholics with good information on the missions. Sheridan had already successfully experimented in the Philippines with booklets dealing with specific items of Catholic doctrine and decided to build up a pamphlet library on mission subjects. These pocket-sized booklets with Mandarin red covers usually were under 40 pages. Meant for widespread distribution, they were priced at five cents.

During his seven-year stay in the United States prior to his return to the Philippines in 1940, Father Sheridan published over 30 different titles, 13 of which he wrote himself. One category contained booklets on the life and customs in various countries of the Far East in relation to Christianity. Apart from four basic pamphlets entitled *Christ in China, Christ in Japan, Christ in Korea,* and *Christ in the Philippines,* China had the lion's share with titles such as *Ten Thousand Questions about China, Schools in China, Marriages in Manchu-Land, The Case for Catholic China,* and *Chinese Proverbs.*

The second category of pamphlets dealt with aspects of mission life. The necessity and the value of prayer were stressed in *Novena to St. Francis Xavier* and *Novena for Mission Vocation.* The training of native personnel was presented in *Chinese Apostles, Native Sisters in the Orient,* and *The Chinese Seminarian.* The charity aspect of mission work appeared in *Missions, Medicine and Maryknoll* and *Lo Pa Hong, Coolie of St. Joseph. Thieves of Paradise* spoke eloquently about orphans, and four other pamphlets told about Maryknoll's work among Chinese lepers. The dangers of mission life were amply expounded in *Forty-Two Days among Chinese Outlaws, Father Jerry Donovan, Captive for Christ,* and *Father Burns among Manchu Bandits.*

The Mission Education Bureau

In January 1937, Father John Considine, by then editor of *The Field Afar*, organized the Maryknoll Mission Education Bureau, refocusing Maryknoll's promotional efforts on mission education. To stress that the task of promoting mission education had been one of Maryknoll's original goals, he liked to quote from a paper entitled "Mission as a Duty," written in 1918 by Father Thomas Price, one of Maryknoll's co-founders, a few months prior to his departure for China:

> I wonder how many of us realize what is contained in the assertion that mission education and training are a necessity, a duty, not a work of supererogation. . . . We belong to a missionary organization established by Our Lord for the sole purpose of teaching all nations. . . . Now the Church cannot, humanly speaking, carry out that mission effectually, except that our people cooperate. . . . But our people cannot possibly give this cooperation unless they are educated to realize the appalling need, and trained to the fullest mission effort. . . .[15]

Gathering Maryknollers, especially Sisters, with literary, dramatic, or artistic talents, he divided the Bureau into five sections: press, reference and research services, literature, entertainment and lectures, and schools.

The press section provided newspapers and magazines with press releases, mission articles, photographs, and a weekly letter written by a Maryknoller on the missions. To encourage members of the press to use this material, the section stressed that it was not heavy reading:

> Although the incidents related by our missioners are human-interest stories, and sometimes reflect the more serious side of life with which they come in contact, more often the Merry-knoller discovers the humorous note, and makes a lively tune with it.[16]

The section also used catchy formulas to get the attention of the press. Since the material was written "Ex-Press-ly for your paper" and to "Im-Press your readers," journalists were told: "When next your paper goes to press, Do not the mission news repress."[17]

The reference and research services provided inquirers with bibliographies, subject reading references, statistics, photographs, and general mission information. Through its Free Lending Library service, individuals could borrow large collections of magazines and books on missions and churches; schools and civic groups also had access to films, slide shows, and records made by Maryknoll.

The literature section took Father Sheridan's enterprise under its wing and encouraged the preparation of books. Father Considine was convinced that Maryknoll's practice of publishing its own books prevented access to a wider readership who did not regularly read religious literature. He favored making arrangements with publishers who would attract the public by the high quality of their reading material:

> We desire these firms' names on our items because we believe they will have greater effectiveness as promotion pieces for the very reason that material published by these firms will not be regarded by the public as promotional.[18]

The first two books prepared under the aegis of the Education Bureau were written by Father Considine and Sister Alma Erhard, the head of the school section. Sister Alma's *Grey Dawns and Red,* a biography of Father Théophane Vénard for young people written under the pen name of Marie Fisher, was published by Sheed & Ward of New York in 1939. The following year Considine wrote another biography. *When The Sorghum Was High,* published by Longmans, Green, and Company of New York, retraced the life of Father Gerard Donovan, the Maryknoll priest captured and murdered by bandits in the mountains of Manchuria.

Following in the footsteps of Father Considine and Sister Alma, Maryknollers wrote about 50 books on foreign missions between 1940 and 1955, more than half of them published by well-known commercial publishers such as Longmans, Green, and Company, Charles Scribner's Sons, Dodd, Mead and Company, and McGraw-Hill.

From Photographs to Moving Pictures and Stage Plays

The entertainment and lecture section of the Education Bureau produced slide shows, films, and plays. James A. Walsh was convinced that the printed or spoken word without the support of an image had little impact on most people. Thus, *The Field Afar* began as an illustrated magazine and some of its first appeals were for "photo-cameras" to send to missioners so that they could provide pictures to go with their letters and articles. In Boston, he often illustrated his lectures with glass slides projected through a stereopticon.

When the Bureau was organized, a stereopticon department was created to help "picture" the missions. By 1922, Maryknoll had a series of six mission lectures consisting of glass slides and manuscripts for loan at no charge: one on Maryknoll at home and in the mission fields, one on Théophane Vénard, two on Japan, one on Lourdes and, by far the most popular

The Maryknoll Bookshelf

holds some choice titbits
for your reading menu—

OUR LATEST

GREY DAWNS AND RED

by Marie Fischer

Fresh and gripping—a new life of the missioner martyr, Blessed Theophane Venard, published by Sheed & Ward.

"Any boy who loves adventure will find that the life of a martyr can be more thrilling than that of a gangster, and girls will follow with sympathetic interest the loving little thread of story about Melanie, Theophane's sister who shared his martyrdom in spirit."
—Blanche Jennings Thompson in "The Pro Parvulis HERALD"

$1.25

Save trouble in ordering—use the coupon on page 256.

books

pamphlets

plays

story leaflets

sound films

Ask for our new

MARYKNOLL BOOKSHELF
CATALOGUE

(Use the coupon on page 256.)

The Maryknoll Fathers

Maryknoll --- New York

Fig. 1. First announcement of *Grey Dawns and Red*. Back cover of *Maryknoll—The Field Afar*, September 1939.

with children, one on San Min, the Chinese boy described in the first story of *Field Afar Stories*.

The number of lectures increased to about 20 by the mid-1930s when Maryknoll released its first successful film. Maryknoll's interest in moving pictures went as far back as its pioneering days in South China. The first motion picture, entitled "Maryknoll on the Hudson and Maryknoll in China," was released in late 1923. The first 800 feet of this 2,000 foot-long movie were shot in South China, showing views of the Yeungkong parish when the first Maryknoll Sisters arrived on November 21, 1922. Some footage was also made a few days later in Hong Kong at a reception given in honor of the visit of Bishop Celso Costantini, first apostolic delegate to China. The second part of the film, made in the United States, depicted Maryknollers in their formative years in the seminary and the novitiate.[19]

The film had little immediate impact, however, because movie projectors were a rarity in Catholic schools and parishes at that time. In 1927 Father Bernard Meyer produced another silent film, "Teach Ye All Nations," with scenes of mission life in Wuchow, which also failed to gain an American audience. However, Maryknollers kept on experimenting with movie cameras and by 1934 had over a dozen 35mm and 16mm mission movies available on loan. That same year, another Wuchow missioner, Father Mark Tennien, produced a four-reel "talkie," "The Missioner's Cross," which remained the most popular movie on Catholic missions for many years.[20]

After viewing the film, Monsignor Griffin, diocesan director for the Propagation of the Faith in Newark, was so enthusiastic that he wrote to the Maryknoll superior in New York: "The picture should do much for the mission cause. It is a presage of greater things which, I am sure, sound pictures will accomplish in bringing the mission idea to the attention of our people."[21] The success of this film confirmed the forward-looking attitude of the Maryknoll leadership toward media: "The day of the 'talkie' is here and what we could teach by the town crier two centuries ago, we must now commit to the reel and the disque to be heralded to the millions through the cinema hall."[22]

Under the leadership of Father Considine, the entertainment section collaborated with the school section to produce World Horizon Films, a film series for young people to open "a window of adventure and sacrifice on the exciting world of mission." In 1940, Maryknoll released "The Hope of the Harvest," the first film in a series which featured departure day at the seminary in New York. Over the next 15 years, 12 more short films were produced on Africa, South America, and the Far East and were lent free of charge through the Maryknoll lending library.[23]

At the same time, trying to reach an ever larger audience, Maryknoll eagerly examined each new form of mass communication. As early as 1929, Maryknoll made a weekly appearance on the Paulist radio station WLWL in New York City. This was the beginning of several Maryknoll radio shows of which "Father Chin's Chin Chats" of the mid–1950s were the most popular.[24]

In the early 1950s, Father Francis Caffrey launched the "Sunday in Hollywood" series of seven long-playing records, featuring talks by well-known personalities of stage, screen, radio, television, and sports, such as Bing Crosby, Loretta Young, John Ford, Perry Como, and Rocky Marciano. A few years, later Maryknollers were on the air with their own radio and television shows.

During the 1930s, prior to establishing the Mission Education Bureau, the Maryknoll Sisters were responsible for the only organized Maryknoll effort to reach young people. As head of what was then known as Mission Education Activities, Sister Alma Erhard had gathered a team of enterprising and creative Sisters who edited *The Maryknoll Junior* and most of the literature appealing to youth. Her associate director, Sister Immaculata Brennan, had a special talent for writing and editing school plays and was later responsible for plays in the entertainment and lecture section of Considine's Education Bureau. Less than a year after the official opening of the Bureau, she had prepared some 25 plays that included directions for staging, costuming, and music. Her plays were written for each part of the liturgical year and accommodated all age groups from primary school children to college students and adults; some were even written for an all-male or all-female cast.[25]

Mission Education of Students

The task of the fifth division of the Mission Education Bureau, the school section, was to provide teaching materials which would "build mission ideals in the hearts of the young people of school age."[26] This section relied heavily on the services of the other four sections. Together with the literature section, it produced *The Maryknoll Junior* and *Maryknoll Pioneers*. With help from the reference and research service, it answered inquiries from schools. The entertainment section assisted in preparing slide series, films and plays geared to children and young adults.

Considine entrusted the direction of the school section to Sister Alma and her team. The group comprised a wide range of talented women who had already proven their ability to reach young people. An accomplished author, Sister Alma wrote extensively for *The Field Afar*, *The Maryknoll Junior*, the play library and the Maryknoll Bookshelf under a variety of pseudonyms, ranging from "S.M.A." and "Marie Fisher" to more exotic names such as "Autumn Fairy" or "Granma Li Li." Sister Chaminade Dreisoerner, who edited the materials, became indispensable as the number of school-oriented publications increased. Sister Louise (Maria Giovanni) Trevisan, a professional illustrator, brought the books alive with her drawings and paintings. In the early 1950s, she also developed several

For your Bulletin Board

FATHER CHIN

OF MARYKNOLL

ON - THE - AIR!

EVERY FRIDAY — 7 P.M.

STATION **WCPO** CINCINNATI

THE NEWEST THING IN RADIO PROGRAMS.

Interesting experiences of Maryknoll Missioners in the Orient; thrilling — exciting — different!

FATHER CHIN'S RADIO CHIN CHATS

Every Friday—7 P.M.—Station WCPO

Sponsored By THE MARYKNOLL FATHERS, Mount Washington, Cincinnati, Ohio

Fig. 2. Announcement sent to all Catholic schools and institutions for the radio series which began November 29, 1935. Maryknoll Fathers Archives.

series of popular teaching cards on the mass, the sacraments, and various mission countries.

As the years went by, several Sister-writers were added to Sister Alma's team; perhaps none more valuable than Sister Juliana Bedier who began in 1937. A veteran of 12 years in the Far East, she had launched a mission art industry in Korea and in Manchuria, supervised by the Maryknoll Sisters. She was also talented in teaching primary and high school students. Moreover, having been a convert at the age of seventeen, she knew from experience how to stimulate non-Christian students to consider the Catholic faith. By the mid–1950s, she had written or co-authored 28 books, 24 filmstrips, and countless articles, mostly for children of kindergarten and primary-school age.

In October 1938, together with Father Considine (who used the pen name Peter Cosmon) and Sisters Alma Erhard and Grace Marian Martel, Sister Juliana launched *Mission Time*. This bi-monthly bulletin was published during the school year to provide Catholic teachers with guidance and inspiration on how to inculcate mission ideals in their students. Each issue offered a mine of information on the missions, as well as lesson plans to give a missionary dimension to catechetical classes, regular courses, and extra-curricular activities.

Sister Juliana's most popular publications were five books in The Loting Series, written from 1940 to 1943 for children between the ages of eight and eleven. In a very lively style, they recounted the adventures of two Chinese children, Thomas and his youngest sister, Anna. The first story, *The Long Road to Lo-Ting*, was a race to escape from a wicked uncle. After a hurried flight in the moonlight, a night in an old pagoda, a ride on a load of turnips, and many more strange experiences, Thomas and Anna arrived safely at Loting. More exciting adventures told of life in Loting: *Little Miss Moses, The Important Pig, Thomas—the Good Thief*, and *A Horse for Christmas*. With the colorful illustrations of Sister Louise, the characters came alive for young readers. Three-year-old Anna appeared as a very gay little girl in a red jacket, while Thomas, who thought himself a man, really looked and acted the part.

After completion of The Loting Series, Sister Juliana prepared a three-volume series on teaching religion in the classroom, entitled *Religion Teacher and the World*. Her first attempt to make mission education more than just a component of religious education resulted in 1943 in *Patterns for Tomorrow* and an accompanying teacher's guide. This unit on agriculture developed many aspects of the Catholic Church's social teaching and applied them to situations in the United States and other countries.

Sister Juliana was also the main driving force behind *The Catholic Geography Series* published by William H. Sadlier for school children in grades three through eight. Between 1948 and 1952, Sister Juliana wrote three volumes and co-authored the others in this nine-volume series. Sister Chaminade, as technical editor, was responsible for unity and continuity of the textbooks and their accompanying workbooks. The Geography Series was widely adopted in Catholic schools throughout the United States. Its blending of Catholic doctrine with geography was favorably described by the superintendent of schools for the diocese of Pittsburgh:

> *The Catholic Geography Series* is Catholic in the sense that it points out the universal oneness of the human family. It stresses religious living and Catholic social living all over the world. . . . Finally it points out our responsibility for all our fellow men as members of the mystical body of Christ.[27]

From 1945 to 1947, Sister Juliana's efforts among young children were continued at the high school level by Sister Mary Just David who produced the *Our Neighbor Series* for social studies classes presenting cultural, economic, and spiritual aspects of the people of China, Korea, Japan and the Andes.

Direct Contact with the Catholics

Although Maryknoll's mission education program relied heavily on the mass media, it was also defined by a deliberate effort to create personal ties between American Catholics and American missioners. Most of the letters and articles in *The Field Afar* were written by American missioners whose places of birth, names, and pictures were well publicized. In the same way, the mission efforts of schools, circles, academia, and junior groups were always well identified by their names and locations.

To further enhance that sense of togetherness in working for the foreign missions, Maryknoll created as many direct contacts as possible between the missioners and American Catholics. During his years as diocesan director of the Society for the Propagation of the Faith, Walsh was a tireless speaker for missions. Even after he assumed responsibility for the Maryknoll seminary, he still put aside time to talk to students in the New York City area. The real soul of this type of apostolate, however, was Thomas Price. Prior to his departure for China in 1919, he traveled for several months at a time to speak about foreign missions and Maryknoll in parishes, schools, and seminaries throughout the northern states east of the Mississippi.[28]

During Maryknoll's first 15 years, seminarians were sent on similar speaking tours during their vacation time, as were priests prior to their overseas assignment. A special corps of Maryknollers, Fathers, Brothers, and Sisters, called "promoters," gradually emerged. Sharing their experiences or those of other Maryknollers on the missions in churches, schools, seminaries, and public auditoriums helped individuals and groups all over the United States feel a part of Maryknoll's work. The public appearance of a missioner in a certain community often brought the world of mission to life. A special bond was created which led people to subscribe to *The Field*

Afar, to support the missions spiritually and financially, and for some, to become a Maryknoll Sister, priest, or Brother.

Mother Mary Joseph and Father James A. Walsh described the work of the promoters as "a mission most important and most difficult."[29] The great value attached to promotion is quite apparent in a letter written by Mother Mary Joseph in 1946 to announce the death of Sister Joan Miriam Beauvais. Instead of recalling Sister Joan Miriam's earlier accomplishments as a missioner in Kaying and at the Shanghai mental hospital, the entire eulogy focused on Sister's last assignment as a promoter.

> Sister Joan Miriam has stimulated mission interest in thousands of souls throughout this country and what is most pleasing to us, is to hear from bishops, priests, and Sisters high words of praise for her intelligent presentation of the mission cause.[30]

However, because Maryknoll's first priority was to send missioners to foreign countries, promoters have always remained a small group whose role is mainly to ignite or rekindle the interest in foreign missions. Nurturing that interest is the responsibility of Maryknoll's media services.

The Impact of China Missioners on Maryknoll Vocations

China and the Growth of Maryknoll

Six years after their arrival on the New York farm in the fall of 1912, the Maryknoll family had grown from 19 to 104. However, it was not until the first four Maryknollers went to China and began to relay their experiences in *The Field Afar* that applications increased considerably. Between 1919 and 1921, Maryknoll membership more than tripled to a total of 329. By 1928, there were 600 Maryknollers worldwide with 48 Maryknollers at work in China. As servants of the American Catholic Church, these missioners brought the reality of foreign missions into the parishes and homes of their fellow Americans and prompted many young people to follow in their footsteps. Maryknoll's presence in China reached its peak in 1942 with 246 missioners.

Over the next decade, although circumstances of war and the Communist expansion brought about the curtailment and finally the withdrawal of all Maryknoll personnel from China, the stories of the missioners' work in the midst of war and persecution continued to attract American youth. When Maryknoll celebrated its fortieth anniversary in 1951, the Maryknoll family had grown to a total of 2,500 members, most of whose vocations were in response to the inspiration of the China missioners.[31]

The Importance of The Field Afar

It was a windy day in Denver. The high school lad hurrying down the street to catch a departing trolley car didn't even take time to throw away the piece of paper that blew against his leg. He just pulled it off and kept running. Once aboard the car and out of the path of the wind, the boy threw himself into a seat. Only then did he realize that he was still clutching the paper that the wind had tossed against him. He opened the paper and smoothed it out. It was a page from a magazine called *The Field Afar*. With the curiosity of youth, he began to read the wrinkled sheet. The page told of the experiences of a priest in China, and the small inset on the page asked that American boys give their lives to the work of the foreign missioners. The high school lad thought about the page, all the way home. That night he wrote to Maryknoll for further information. In a few months' time, he was at Maryknoll.[32]

This Maryknoller's vocation, although a little more dramatic than most, exemplified the role played by Maryknoll's monthly magazine. *The Field Afar*, was undoubtedly the major attraction to Maryknoll. In "The Secret of Maryknoll," an article published in the October 1950 issue of the magazine, the editor wrote:

Every year at Maryknoll we make a survey of our new students to determine the sources of their vocations. Each year the results are the same. Over 60 percent of them were introduced to Maryknoll and had the missions personalized to them by *Maryknoll—The Field Afar*.[33]

A screening of biographies in the Maryknoll archives and of interviews for the Maryknoll China History Project revealed the truth of this statement over many years. In the early 1920s, Father Thomas Kiernan and Sister Mary de Ricci Cain joined Maryknoll because they had read *The Field Afar*. So did Sister Monica Marie Boyle and Father Michael Gaiero in the 1930s and Sister Ann Carol Brielmaier and Father Paul Touchette in the 1940s. Even today in the 1980s, many Maryknollers, such as Father Stephen Booth, ordained in 1986, still attribute their vocations to the Maryknoll magazine. The decisive influence of the magazine was well described by Sister Antonia Maria Guerrieri, who entered the Maryknoll Sisterhood in 1935:

I had wanted to be a religious ever since I was a small girl but I didn't know where or why or how. It was the Maryknoll magazine that my father subscribed to when I was a little girl that decided I was to be a Maryknoller.[34]

It is also interesting to note that even among the 40 percent who were not primarily attracted to Maryknoll by *The Field Afar*, a majority made their decision after reading some form of missionary literature published by Maryknoll. Neither Father John Driscoll who joined in 1920 nor Sister Mary Ruth Riconda who came the following year had read the magazine. Driscoll, who had been thinking about the priesthood, chose Maryknoll after seeing letters of Father Francis Ford in the *Homiletic Review*; Sister Mary Ruth was drawn to Maryknoll after reading *A Modern Martyr*, James A. Walsh's version of the life of Théophane Vénard. As for Father Thomas Nolan, who was only fourteen years old when he went to the Venard in January 1922, it was *The Maryknoll Junior* which set his heart on the foreign missions.[35]

Throughout the 1930s and 1940s the same pattern was evident, and Maryknoll continued to recognize the importance of mass media in awakening mission vocations. In the 1940s, as the movie industry blossomed, Maryknoll stepped up its production of films. Many Maryknollers of that decade attributed their first attraction to mission in part to the viewing of a Maryknoll film. Father John J. Casey remembers watching "The Missioner's Cross" when he was a seventh grader at St. Emydius School in San Francisco. The sight of a white-cassocked priest in a pith helmet plodding through the rice fields of South China convinced him to become a Maryknoll missioner.[36]

By comparison, only a minority of Maryknollers attributed the origin of their vocation to talks given in churches and schools by assigned "promoters." More effective were letters and visits by Maryknollers who were relatives or from the same parish. Almost invariably, these contacts reinforced an attraction to Maryknoll which had already been cultivated by the reading of missionary literature.[37]

Until the late 1940s, the most important characteristic of vocations to Maryknoll was that they included—by an overwhelming majority—the desire to go to China. This attraction was cultivated in great part by *The Field Afar* and other Maryknoll publications which always emphasized China. "*The Field Afar* at that time [1933] was predominantly on China missions," recalled Sister Ignatia McNally, "so of course I felt the urge to go to China."[38]

Moreover, since Maryknoll began its mission work in China and maintained more missioners there than in any other foreign country, its name became almost synonymous with China in the minds of most American Catholics: "When people said 'Maryknoll,'" reflected Sister Virginia Flagg, "at first they thought of China."[39] So it was not surprising for new recruits arriving at Maryknoll to find a Chinese meal on the table: "I thought," said Kathleen Bradley in 1938, "that every meal was going to be like that, that their only interest was China."[40]

All these factors combined to create a mystique around the China missioner which profoundly influenced many young Catholic Americans. Father Robert Sheridan recalled:

> I decided to join Maryknoll because from what I understood, the life of the foreign missionary in China was the most difficult life which you could undertake. . . . We were going to China and never coming back.[41]

Like Father Sheridan, most Maryknollers traced their attraction to Maryknoll to the idea of going to China with statements like "To go to China, that's why you came to Maryknoll," or "I always wanted to go to China," and "There was no place in my heart for anything except China."[42] During their training, Maryknollers had to accept the fact that they might never get to China and would instead be assigned to the United States. After 1923, when Maryknoll began to send missioners to Korea, the Philippines, and Japan, China was still the coveted assignment, and other countries ranked only as second choices.

Even within China, certain missions were more sought after, at least for the newly professed Sisters. Because Kaying offered the possibility of doing direct evangelization, it was always considered the best assignment. Yet disappointments were usually of short duration. Maryknollers were trained to accept their assignments in a spirit of obedience, self-denial, and sacrifice. In most instances, the missioners fell so deeply in love with their assigned locations that they quickly forgot their former dreams. It was only in the 1940s when Maryknoll missioners spread throughout Latin America and started working in Africa that Maryknoll lost its strictly Oriental appeal. As the focus of the magazine and other mass media appeals became more universal, new vocations to Maryknoll were attracted to a large number of countries as well as to China.

Images of China Presented by Maryknoll

The images of China presented to the American public by Maryknoll come alive in the pages of Maryknoll's most widely disseminated and far-reaching means of spreading mission information: *Maryknoll—The Field Afar.* Through thousands of stories and articles aimed at increasing American understanding and generosity toward China, the publication presented a highly favorable but not always accurate picture.

A Great Civilization and a Great People

Perhaps the most prevalent theme found in the magazine was one which extolled the qualities of the Chinese and their civilization, trying to rid American readers of silly misconceptions or sheer ignorance about China. *The Field Afar* presented this list of "don'ts" in 1918:

Don't say "Chink," unless you are trying to make enemies.

Don't imagine that all Chinese women bind their feet or that all Chinese men wear queues. Modern Chinese are discarding these things, just as modern American women are ceasing to wear "hobble skirts" and American men to wear "peg-top" trousers.

Don't ask your Chinese friend whether he eats rats and dogs. It will please him just about as much as it would please an American to ask him if he ate snakes and toads.

Don't try to make persons believe you know all about China just because you have visited Chinatown in San Francisco, Shanghai or Hongkong. They are no more like the real China than the East Side of New York is like America.

Don't think that because one or two Chinese in your city operate laundries all Chinese in China are engaged in the same kind of business.

Don't try to purchase "chop suey" in China. It's a dish prepared by Chinese in America for American consumption and is unknown in China.[43]

Maryknollers liked to instill in their readers respect toward China by reminding them of its ancient civilization:

Chinese civilization was hoary with age when our own European ancestors were barbarians. Her greatest philosophers . . . preceded by generations Socrates, Plato, and Aristotle, as well as the Egyptian [sic] Euclid. . . . China traces her ancestry far back of any Western written record. . . . She developed independently of the West, and when Western empires crashed and were consumed by succeeding waves of civilizations, China rode the storm.[44]

Among the Maryknollers, Francis Ford was without a doubt the most enthusiastic. In presenting the basic differences between Chinese and American civilizations, he had no qualms about tilting the balance in favor of China:

China has much that we have lost in culture. . . . The modern world bases its life on "the survival of the fittest" with the hasty conclusion, as a background, that "every day in every way we are growing better." Chinese life has its roots in the command, "Honor thy father and thy mother," and includes in this the members of the family and the clan, besides ancestors dead or deified. This inculcates reverence and obedience and worship and sinking of self for family solidarity, and reacts on the minute details of daily life. . . . There is, I think, less danger of abnormalities in acting as a family unit than as an individual. Certainly there is less danger of forgetting principles, of losing control of patience, when the restlessness of the individual is checked by tradition.[45]

Ford and other Maryknollers wrote many articles to illustrate this point of view. Ford struck at the core of American lifestyles by claiming that life on the farm and in the city were much more human in China than in the United States. He drew a bleak picture of the lonely and isolated life on American farms and the migration of the rural people to the city. In the American city, according to Ford, most people still lived in isolation despite the physical crowding because of a lack of common interests and family ties. Moreover, he predicted that the "uncrowding" of the cities by spacing homes farther apart would only bring the disadvantages of country isolation to the city. Ford claimed that China, on the contrary, had none of these problems, neither among its huge farming population nor in its large and century-old cities.

Naturally his advice was to look to China for a solution to America's problems. In his opinion, the backbone of the Chinese countryside was the village, which pulled together common yet diverse interests.

The Chinese population is still eighty percent farmers and a nation that can keep its farmers has solved a problem that has stumped the West. . . . Chinese farmers build, it is true, in the valleys near their crops, but they group houses into a village surrounded on all sides by common fields for grazing grounds and hills to supply firewood. . . . The village is alive and a unit and a hive of mutual service. . . . Every inhabitant of an average village is related to all his neighbors at least by marriage, usually on the father's side, so there is found the strongest bond of common interests that reconciles at once the privacy of family life and the need of companionships outside the immediate family.[46]

Ford also blamed rural decline in America on the lack of character of American farmhouses. To him, these box-like structures of unpainted wood and tar-paper roofing did not deserve the name of home. By comparison, the Chinese farm was a building made of several courtyards and rooms clustered around large guestrooms with patios and cool corners. Built and enlarged by its inhabitants as the family grew over several years, it housed several generations under one roof. Ford reported:

Such construction if adopted more generally in America would solve many problems. It would beget a pride in our homes, to counter a restless urge to move; it would focus and thereby intensify the natural instinct in all of us to own something permanent; it would localize and color childhood memories, now dissipated over a dozen dwellings; it would be the expression of a family's united aim and harmonious labor. Morally, it would be a bond between the present and future generations; it would be the loadstone for the restless youth and a safeguard of its communion with parents. Economically, it would prove the solution of financial difficulties for pioneering couples; it would abolish the numerous middlemen who now control house shortage. It is an investment that enhances the land and the stability of its dwellers.[47]

As for the Chinese cities, they were also extremely liveable, according to Ford, because every Chinese was a farmer of one sort or another and kept close to the soil even in the city. A block or two away the country begins—not a dump of discarded scrap iron but in genuine fields where each householder grows his daily vegetables.[48] Explaining that the Chinese word for family was composed of two characters signifying a pig under a roof, Ford asserted that this was still a reality almost everywhere in China. Even in the city, the Chinese house was a miniature replica of village life which avoided many of the evils found in American cities.[49]

Although Maryknollers were aware that China was undergoing drastic changes and entering a new modern order, they did not seem to have understood the depth of the transformation until the early 1930s. They considered the changes merely as a veil over the older civilization; the older civilization was permanent and the modern, a veneer. In 1933, Father Thomas Kiernan was the first Maryknoller to explain that China's transformation was fundamental. In an article in *The Field Afar* entitled "A Matter of Education," Kiernan raised the question of whether or not China, which had always assimilated her conquerors while remaining fundamentally Chinese, would be able to do the same with modern Western learning and culture. His analysis of the situation was that Christian schools, educational reforms, and "returned Chinese students" from universities in America and Europe had irreversibly altered China. His hope was that China would not lose her old way of life while adopting modern Western learning but instead blend the best of the two together into a more nearly perfect civilization.

> We are inclined to think that at last "East and West will meet" and will blend into one common civilization—at least in China—the good of the old supplying what is wanting to the new. . . . Our prophecy is not without suspicion that modernity in China will have its typical and essential dress.[50]

Other Maryknollers followed suit, presenting a very optimistic picture of the transformation of China. In October 1935 Ford likened the change to a spiritual renaissance rather than a mere imitation of Western culture. By importing the best from the West and banning the bad, China held firm to its ancient natural virtue:

> This is a spiritual renaissance that must be sensed rather than it can be proved in black and white—yet recent, continued legislation forbidding cabarets, extravagant banquets, birth control propaganda and certain cinema productions seems to point to serious underlying motives.[51]

Two months later, Father Joseph Ryan pointed out the difference between civilization and modernization: China could not be called uncivilized because it had passed that point centuries before any European nation; by borrowing Western learning and technology, China was becoming modernized. Ryan rejoiced that while retaining certain national traits and customs, Chinese were becoming more and more like foreigners. He dared to predict ". . . before long a traveler in China will find only minor differences such as he would find in any European country."[52]

To counter the muddled mental image of a baffling Confucius and an even more mysterious Fu Manchu so common among Westerners, Maryknoll's writings presented the ordinary human side of the Chinese. In a short article displaying pictures of smiling Chinese children and toddlers and a mother with her baby, *The Field Afar* asked:

> Have you ever stopped to consider that however "queer" the Chinese may appear to us, with their slant eyes, their yellow skin, and their odd clothes, they are after all like ourselves, "just folks." People who joy and suffer, who marry, who bear children, and who, like every one of us, at the end go out alone into eternity. Souls for whom Jesus suffered the death of the Cross.[53]

In many instances, the qualities of the Chinese people were upheld as examples for the West to emulate. Maryknollers described the spartan simplicity of Chinese furnishings and meals as a sign of fortitude. They maintained that these sparse living conditions did not result from poverty but from a conscious choice made by very contented people who knew how to differentiate the important from the superfluous. Describing an average middle-class home, Ford said:

> On entering it, one does not receive an impression of poverty, much less of unhappiness. It looks planned and balanced with deliberate avoidance of a frill or frippery. The Chinese enjoyment of life is in human beings, not in incidentals.[54]

During the hardship of the Sino-Japanese War, Maryknollers regularly emphasized Chinese endurance and discipline. In 1943, Ford wrote:

> It is stamina that has enabled China to thrive on a six-year invasion exhaust-
> ing to her enemy. . . . This stamina is inbred in the Chinese through genera-
> tions of hard living. . . . It has that good-humored element in it of the
> Poverello: smiling hunger, nonchalance in pain, endurance unconscious of
> heroism. It retains zest for adventure even in prosaic daily happenings, and
> keeps the nation supple.[55]

At the end of the war, two years later, Bishop James E. Walsh, superior
general of the Maryknoll Society, made a very similar remark:

> My sadness at the sight of war privation and hardship was tempered by the
> cheerfulness and courage of the Chinese people in breasting their sea of
> troubles. Not even eight years of warfare could daunt them. There was
> misery, everywhere, but there were the same smiles, patience, industry,
> energy. That is China. . . . Its people are surely the most durable human
> beings in all God's creation.[56]

It is important to point out, however, that the daily reality of the war
described in routine correspondence and the diaries of missioners in China
was at odds with the noble image presented by Maryknoll to the American
public. As noted in previous chapters, diaries described bombings and the
ravages of war, caring for the wounded and destitute, feeding refugees—in
sum, the existence of a suffering Chinese people living in inhuman conditions.

A Country Ready for Christianity

The overwhelmingly positive picture of China and its people presented in
the Maryknoll magazine led easily to the conclusion that Christianity was
bound to succeed in such a naturally virtuous civilization. Early articles in
The Field Afar intended to alarm readers—the Catholic Church could miss
wonderful opportunities in China because of *its* lack of missionary spirit.
The magazine warned that Catholic Europe, weakened by World War I,
lacked the manpower and financial resources to sustain mission work in a
China ready for Christianity, and that American Protestants were pouring
into China while American Catholics remained unconcerned. In a diary
published in *The Field Afar* in May 1919, Father Bernard Meyer referred
to the good results of Protestant work and to its terrible consequences for
the Catholic Church:

> Not only have Protestant missionaries established hospitals and brought
> over doctors who are at the same time engaged in propaganda, but they are

training the natives, men and women, and having them trained in America as doctors and, at the same time, disseminators of Protestant teaching. . . . In their education work, the Protestants instill into the minds of thousands and hundreds of thousands of Chinese children, who are bound to be a power, perhaps the power, in the next generation, a deep contempt for the Catholic Church as an out of date institution, a bar to progress. . . .[57]

In later years, appeals to counter the Protestant efforts gave way to the theme of China as a place naturally prepared to receive the Catholic faith. In the article "Holy Week in the Orient" in 1933, Ford showed that life in China, which greatly resembled the Palestine of Jesus' time, made his parables more easily understood:

[It is] a land devoted to simple agriculture with a barefoot people who walk, not ride, who bear the heat of the day and the burdens, who gather the crops by hand and winnow the chaff in the wind, who draw water from the pool, who make bricks with straw and burn the grass of the field; a land whose temples have porticos, and whose cities are girthed with walls, whose blind and lame sit begging at the city gate, and whose lepers are a common sight.[58]

In looking at Chinese civilization, Ford also saw in it traces of the four signs—one, holy, catholic, and apostolic—which characterized the Catholic Church as a perfect society:

Chinese civilization is one—a unified force, evolved from and revolving around filial piety which permeates each action of life. . . . Chinese civilization is holy in that it is rooted in reverence. Its ethics have molded the minds of the youth to uphold the dignity of age. . . . It is catholic, extending to all Chinese, embracing an area twice the size of the United States. . . . And finally it is a traditional civilization above all. Its very essence is derived from ancestry.[59]

The significance of Chinese civilization was also emphasized by James A. Walsh following his fourth visit to the Orient in the early 1930s. He warned American readers not to confuse civilization with Western comfort.

It is a great mistake to think of the Oriental as uncivilized and of ourselves as superior, simply because we have made greater progress. We have added to our comforts and cut corners on time, but this does not prove that we have advanced in the higher things that count for culture and the right philosophy of life.[60]

The proper attitude of American Catholics towards China was indicated by Walsh, quoting counsel he had received from Cardinal Camillus Laurenti, a long-time friend in the Roman Curia: "Warn your missioners not to impose on their converts in Asia the customs of the West. Leave these people as they are so long as what they have and what they like is not harmful to soul or body."[61] This admonition was a reminder of the solemn instruction given by the Propaganda Fide to its first vicars apostolic in 1659, some 300 years earlier: "Do not attempt for any reason whatever to persuade the people to change their rites, customs, and manners, provided they are not openly contrary to religion and good morals."[62] Walsh affirmed that he had never failed to pass on Laurenti's admonition to young Maryknollers.

In contrast to these positive articles on Chinese civilization in general, Maryknoll literature had no words of praise for Chinese religious beliefs until the late 1930s. In accordance with the Catholic soteriology of the time, non-Christian beliefs were superstitious or pagan. Father Ryan's article on Chinese civilization and modernization was very representative of that attitude. While upholding the greatness of Chinese civilization, the article called, in fact, for its demise by advocating not only material modernization, but also spiritual modernization to replace the "ancient superstitions of China." Without using the word "Westernization," Ryan pointed out that modernization, meaning the adoption of modern methods of life from Westerners, would eventually result in accepting their scientific, political, and, of course, religious doctrines:

> The substitution of Catholicity for the ancient superstitions of China is not now a difficult matter for the individual, since the nation as a whole is ready to accept what is foreign, and side by side the material and the spiritual change goes on to form a new China.[63]

Looking into the future, Ryan saw the possibility for China "to become the great central power of the world—the Central Kingdom" and imagined how comforting it would be for the world to find "China [as] a Catholic nation governed by Catholic principles, and carrying on her international relations on the same Catholic principles."[64]

It is important to note, however, that in spite of its disparaging tone toward Chinese beliefs, Maryknoll literature did not convey a negative image of the Chinese people. Rather, it stressed how unfortunate it was for a race endowed with so many beautiful natural virtues to remain ignorant of the Gospel.

In late 1939, *The Field Afar* printed an article entitled "China's Three 'Isms,'" which reflected Rome's changing attitude toward the Confucian rites. In this very positive presentation, Meyer referred to each of China's three great "teachings" as a path which paved the way for Christianity, rather than dismissing them as superstitious.

> We have the Confucian ethics, the Taoist philosophy, and the Buddhist religion, each developed by earnest seekers after the truth, and each contributing to one of the best natural foundations on which to build Christianity. To Confucianism it owes the idea of a personal God, as well as social and family virtues; to Taoism, the concept that man is akin to the infinite and that the highest good is found in mystical contemplation and union with the infinite; to Buddhism, an appreciation of the value of meditation, prayer, and fasting, and a well-developed theory of moral responsibility.[65]

The Faith of Chinese Catholics

The wonders of Catholic faith among "naturally virtuous Chinese" composed another favorite theme of Maryknoll publications. *Maryknoll—The Field Afar* abounded with descriptions and photographs of zealous new converts, exemplary old Catholics, apostolic catechists, and stories of their steadfastness in the midst of war, isolation, and persecutions.

In 1939, Father Aloysius Rechsteiner answered the question, "What kind of Christians do the Chinese make?" with a narrative of his first experience as a young curate just out of language school. He arrived in the parish of Kochow and volunteered to spend the Feast of the Assumption among new Catholics in a small village called Ch'eung Paan.

> I went, saw, and heard, and returned, thanking God for the opportunity of having seen the depth of faith which people can reach. . . . Their eagerness to learn more about God and the doctrine of the Catholic Church has certainly been an inspiration. . . . Ch'eung Paan's faith and good example has spread. A village nearby has caught its spirit and already has laid foundations for its own chapel.[66]

Maryknoll knew that Catholics in America would be moved by such manifestations of faith and highlighted some of these narratives to generate financial contributions. To replenish the catechists' fund, there was the story of Ahman, a native catechist assigned to prepare a little group of catechumens in a distant mountain village of a bandit-infested region.

> Ahman, the catechist chosen by Monsignor Ford, accepted the post gladly, though he knew perfectly the dangers to which he would expose himself. When he had been in the village awhile, the bandits came and ordered Ahman to point out the houses where they could find money. This he refused to do. He was then backed against a wall and nailed there with outstretched hands, while the houses were being searched. He died from the treatment. Greater love than this no man hath that he lay down his life for his friends.[67]

To persuade more American Catholics to give the one dollar necessary to sustain a missioner for a day, the magazine printed the story of a visit by two Maryknollers to a remote Catholic village in the wooded mountains of Manchuria—a village where no priest had gone for 20 years.

> These poor people were overjoyed at the unhoped opportunity of again receiving the sacraments and assisting at Holy Mass. When the Maryknollers started on the long homeward trek, the Christians followed them to the outskirts of the forest, gazing after them with tear-dimmed eyes and calling out, "Come back to us! Do not abandon our souls!"[68]

Besides the lives of exemplary rural Catholics, *The Field Afar* also gave visibility to contributions by the Church and the Chinese Catholic elite to the building of modern China. In the 12 years following the opening of the Catholic University of Peking in 1925, *The Field Afar* had no fewer than 15 articles on that institution, which almost always mentioned its older sister, Jesuit Aurora University in Shanghai. It was also routinely mentioned that Maryknoll's South China missions traditionally supplied students to both universities.[69]

If a local Chinese civil or military official happened to have been educated in a Catholic institution or, better yet, was Catholic, articles always stressed his contributions to social progress and the improvement of relations with the Church. Prominent Catholic laymen, however, were still unusual in China, and *The Field Afar* does not mention many. Among those introduced to Americans was Vincent Ying, co-founder and editor-in-chief of a Tientsin progressive newspaper, *Ta Kung Pao*. In 1912 he became the first Chinese scholar to advocate the idea of a Catholic university in Peking and in 1925 became its first dean.

Also introduced as a "model Catholic layman" was Timothy Yin, a banker from Antung in Manchuria.

> His position brought him in contact with pagans and pagan practices but his faith and personality—especially his gracious smile—touched many hearts. There was no class distinction with Timothy. He was a friend of the lowly coolies as well as the highest official. . . . He was valuable to the Church in his secular position; his charity toward the poor made him a God-given asset to the parish.[70]

He was also described as a man of prayer. His circle of friends reached into the heavens to the company of saints, whose help he counted on to remain a good Catholic and a successful businessman: "I ask the Little Flower [St. Thérèse of Lisieux] to keep me in God's grace, and beg St. Jude to keep me from going broke."[71]

However, the Catholic layman who was given by far the most prominence in *The Field Afar* was Lo Pa-hong, the famous Shanghai entrepreneur and benefactor. Between 1918 and 1938 when he was assassinated, 24 articles in the magazine focused on Mr. Lo, with many others mentioning his name. Lo's impressive titles convinced American readers of his outstanding business acumen: he was director of a Shanghai tramway company, and general manager of the China Electric Power Company of Shanghai, the Chapei Electricity and Water Works Company, the Shanghai Inland Water Works Company, and the Tatung Zung Kee Steam Navigation Company.

These businesses however, were, only part of his activities. His tremendous energy raised funds for the poorest people of Shanghai. On his initiative three important establishments were built for the least privileged. With 2,000 inmates, St. Joseph's Hospice was the largest Catholic charitable institution in China. It sheltered sick people, penniless old folks, wayward girls, orphans, and the sick from the city prisons. Lo also built Sacred Heart Hospital, a 300-bed facility providing free treatment for the poor. Free clinics at the two hospitals treated up to 1,000 outpatients daily. Lo Pa-hong not only built these institutions, but visited them regularly to spend time with the patients. His third outstanding accomplishment was the construction of Mercy Hospital for the mentally ill, the first of its kind in China. He also visited frequently at the Shanghai Municipal Prison, bringing blankets and clothing to prisoners, teaching them doctrine, and baptizing and comforting those about to be executed. In addition to his business titles, Mr. Lo acquired others which better reflected his Christian charity. He liked to refer to himself as the "coolie of St. Joseph" while others called him the "Vincent de Paul of China" and the "chaplain of the brigands."[72]

The Rise of a Patriotic Catholic Church

When Maryknollers arrived in Kwangtung province in 1918, China was in turmoil. The Chinese Revolution of 1911 had not brought peace or unity. For all practical purposes, the country had no government. Warlords still fought each other, bandits were frequently encountered in the hills of South China and in the forests of Manchuria, and pirates made travel perilous along the coast. Maryknollers did not attempt to hide these facts. They gave an accurate portrait of "poor old China" with its "all jumbled political situation." However, they stressed that this "awful muddle" was not the fault of the Chinese—"the most patient people in the world"—but the result of the greed of a few men.

> When it is recalled that the great masses of China's people are peace-loving and industrious, intelligent, and at heart religious, there is every reason to

Fig. 3. Bishop James A. Walsh, with Lo Pa-hong in 1926 when Mr. Lo visited the United States. *The Field Afar*, March 1938, p. 91.

> look for changed conditions soon. . . . We hope and pray that in their country law and order will soon be established, and the wolves, large and small, who prey upon and scatter these helpless human beings, may soon be exterminated.[73]

Maryknollers asked their readers to abstain from passing derogatory judgment on China. They reminded them that the ratification of the Constitution had not changed the United States into a peaceful democratic nation overnight; rather, democratization had been a long process which had included—as in China—the cruel test of civil war.[74]

When antiforeign agitation flared up in the mid–1920s, *The Field Afar* asserted that these manifestations were not antireligious but political. The Soviet Union, it said, was fanning the anger of the Chinese people, and the Western nations were paying the price for their arrogance and their mistreatment of China.

> It is being recognized gradually that China has not had a "square deal" from some of the Powers, and that Soviet Russia has taken advantage of this fact to strengthen herself and to embitter Chinese, especially those of the student class, against the Westerners generally.[75]

Following the Northern Expedition and the Nationalist victory, Maryknollers welcomed quieter times and emphasized how the unhampered and rapid transformation of China into a great modern power went hand in hand with the growth of the Catholic Church. China's economic progress in the fields of communication, industry, and education were continuously, described. During the decade ending in 1937, the Chinese railway network, exclusive of the Japanese-controlled lines in Manchuria, had grown from 4,900 miles to about 8,100 miles. Even more impressive was the construction of highways and bridges which led to much improved transportation. By 1936 the Chinese highway network included 71,736 miles as compared with a mere 620 miles in 1921.

At the same time, urban areas were expanding along these roads and pushing beyond old city walls. The work accomplished by the enterprising young mayor of Kaying and his plans for 1934 were characteristic of the widespread rapid modernization in China. Bishop Ford wrote:

> I complimented him for his energy in recent road building, whereupon he got out maps and showed me his plans for the immediate future. During the past two years, he has built over 100 miles of auto roads leading out of the city in all directions, and connecting with the main arteries of the province. About 20 buses now ply these roads and there is enough business for double the number. He has had torn down about half of the city wall, as the city has long outgrown its limits and has sold the ground for building sites. Within the

past six months new buildings have been erected on this space, all four stories, in cement, with arcaded sidewalks that doubled the width of the streets. Several hundred new buildings have been built this year within the city, while along the auto roads outside dwellings are springing up surprisingly. The buses have in turn caused larger bridges to be built. . . . Our neighbor, Father Constancis, a French missioner with a reputation for his reliable engineering knowledge, consented to draw the plans for the bridge that is to cross the big river; it is a suspension bridge of the fixed bowstring type on 11 piers, 1,600 feet in length and about 30 wide. Already about one-third of the structure is complete. . . . The mayor showed me plans of two other bridges on which work will soon begin.[76]

Maryknollers also mentioned how postal services and telecommunications expanded during the decade: more post offices were created in the rural areas; telegraph lines which had been damaged during the warlord periods were restored and grew to a length of 59,086 miles; long distance telephone lines reached a total of 32,364 miles.

Notable progress in the field of education was also brought to the attention of the American readership. *The Field Afar* described how the Ministry of Education realized the usefulness of private educational institutions and accordingly relaxed some of its policies toward Christian schools. Also mentioned was the Ministry's decision to recognize and extend subsidies to private institutions of higher learning, benefiting the two Catholic universities in Peking and Shanghai and the Industrial and Commercial College in Tientsin.

When the government promoted the New Life Movement in 1934 to revitalize the moral fiber of the people, *The Field Afar* explained its meaning: "Invented by statesmen, conscious of their country's needs, it seeks to inculcate lessons of order, industry, hygiene, civic pride, and mutual charity. . . ."[77]

Of course Maryknollers backed the movement as a worthwhile enterprise, although they felt that unless it was grafted onto Christianity, it could never bring the real "new life" to China: "The New Life Movement is an aim beyond all praise but it lacks motive power. Surely, it is the strangest of all delusions that makes men fancy they can have the fruits of Christ's religion without the tree."[78]

During the decade of 1927-1937, the overall message was that China was making progress, but that China's economy of scarcity was so characteristic of old agricultural conditions and practices that it could not be changed overnight. There was no suggestion that the Nationalist government was not coping with rural problems or not implementing a comprehensive social and economic plan. The Soviets were blamed for trying to discredit the Nationalist government and for fomenting rural discontent rather than helping implement the government's reforms.

In 1937, the widening of the Sino-Japanese war severely disrupted China's development. Railway lines were bombed, bridges blown up, roads cut open, and many factories and universities removed into unoccupied China. In fact, as described by missioners, the China of the late 1930s and the mid–1940s was much like the China they had found in the early 1920s, with shortages of food, displaced people, and lack of communication and electricity. The war had eliminated most of the progress of the previous 25 years.

As mentioned in a previous chapter, for several years *Maryknoll—The Field Afar* refrained from anti-Japanese statements. China was fighting a faceless invader because articles sent by Maryknollers in China and Manchuria were carefully edited in order to not reflect any negative judgment on Japan. It was only in the summer of 1942, when Maryknoll headquarters received word that most interned Maryknollers would soon be repatriated, that the magazine began to develop the theme of a patriotic Chinese Church rallying behind the Christian figures of Generalissimo and Madame Chiang Kai-shek to free China of Japanese invaders. Chinese Catholics were praised for their active participation and leadership in the national war effort. The presidential couple was presented as God's blessing for China. According to *Maryknoll—The Field Afar*, Chiang had grown to understand and respect the Catholic Church and its members, Chinese and foreign. He told his army officers at the Whampoa Academy to model themselves after the Catholic missioners in China. He was "the world's only silent dictator [who] played on no emotions, stirred no throngs with hysterical harangues, [and] appealed to no race hatreds or mob action." Instead, said Bishop Ford, Chiang was like Lincoln because "he sensed in this moment of China's crisis the need of moral principles to found a new nation," and by his integrity "won the reverence of his people."[79]

By 1946, Bishop James E. Walsh has become even more enthusiastic in his praise of the Generalissimo:

> We have almost reached the halfway mark of the twentieth century, and it is safe to predict now that, when the history of our age shall be finally assessed and written, the present leader of China and her people will stand revealed as one of its greatest men. . . . Among the great war leaders, Generalissimo Chiang Kai-shek stands out above all his contemporaries, President Roosevelt and Prime Minister Churchill not excepted.[80]

The magazine also acknowledged Madame Chiang as "the only one person in public life in the world" who matched Chiang's accomplishments and high moral standards. The magazine proudly reprinted one of her speeches praising missionary contributions to China:

> Large numbers of Catholic missioners at the risk of their own lives have

Fig. 4. "Missioners are welcomed in China. The nation's Christian leader, Generalissimo Chiang Kai-shek, has praised the Catholic Church for its service." *Maryknoll—The Field Afar*, April 1946, p. 33.

protected refugees and preserved the honor of terrified and helpless women. . . . Others devoted themselves to the rescue and care of innocent and bewildered children caught in the whirlwind of war. Others continued educational work among the stricken and the destitute. Their lives of self-denial and inner discipline has proved to be a source of inspiring courage to all those they serve and with whom they suffer.[81]

Articles hailed her as the perfect combination of "the Christianity of the Western world with the age-long wisdom, beauty, and graciousness of the Orient." Readers were shown her spirituality through her comments on prayer:

> Prayer is our source of guidance and balance. God is able to enlighten the understanding. I am often bewildered, because my mind is only finite. I question and doubt my own judgments. Then I seek guidance, and when I am sure, I go ahead, leaving the results with Him.[82]

The magazine also presented other Chinese Christian officials who led in the defense and reconstruction of the country. Among them was H. H. Kung, the self-proclaimed seventy-fifth lineal descendant of Confucius, who served as finance minister and vice-president of China's cabinet, the Executive Yuan, under Chiang Kai-shek (and who happened to be his brother-in-law). Today his graft and corruption have been well-documented. At the time, however, Maryknollers seemed unaware of Kung's unscrupulous dealings or unwilling to believe they really took place. Instead, *Maryknoll—The Field Afar* praised Kung for modernizing China's fiscal system and quoted his call to the country's 270 million Confucians to become followers of Christ:

> Confucianism is proposed as an ethic, not a religious system. In my study of religion, I discovered that God is a loving and kindly heavenly father. The Confucianist masses should embrace Christianity in order to perfect their Confucian principles.[83]

Kung proudly announced that in the missioners' preaching of Christian brotherhood he had found the achievement of his ancestor's ideals that "within the four seas, all men are brothers":

> Through the evangelical activities and scientific and literary pursuits of Christian missionaries, the East and West were brought to each other, and humanity moved closer to the Christian ideal of universal brotherhood.[84]

Another prominent person who often appeared in the pages of the Maryknoll magazine was Bishop Yü Pin, vicar apostolic of Nanking, national director of Catholic Action, and a member of the Legislative Yuan, China's parliament. As a prelate, he was presented as "a pillar of the Catholic Church in China"; as a Chinese citizen he was depicted as "an ardent patriot [and] a pillar of his nation."[85] His message to American Catholics was that World War II had helped to reveal the true nature of the Church to the Chinese and especially to its leadership:

> The Catholic Church in China has a rising popularity with the whole nation. The leaders of China, in the past, felt that the Church was too far from national interests. The war has changed all this. . . . [Chinese] Catholics have helped to build homes for the wounded soldiers. We work in military hospitals. We have organized Red Cross groups to go to the front lines and take care of the wounded. We have opened homes to shelter refugee students while they continue their studies. . . . The Catholic people apply their Catholic philosophy to their own lives and environment. This philosophy is simply loyalty to God and country.[86]

A Country Touched by Christian Charity

It was not by pure chance that the Catholic Church assumed an important role in social welfare during the Sino-Japanese War. As already mentioned, the reliance of the Catholic Church on works of mercy was at the core of missionary work. From the days of their arrival in China, Maryknollers were convinced that, with the Chinese in particular, good example could be more persuasive than reason. As far back as January 1919, a page of Meyer's diary reprinted in *The Field Afar* introduced that idea: "The Chinese are a people who can be appealed to only by practical examples set before their eyes and affecting them directly. . . . They are not going to be reasoned into the Church." Then, with the disparaging tone so typical of that time toward nonwhite races, he added:

> Even among races more highly gifted, the "beginnings of faith," the channels of the first graces, have been an act of charity, a good example, a simple devotion that appealed not so much to the intellect as to the heart.[87]

As Maryknoll used works of charity to reach the Chinese, so did Maryknoll's publications use descriptions of them to reach American Catholics. Readers were presented with a thousand and one ways to participate in the works of mercy of Maryknollers in China. Abandoned infants and lepers received the largest coverage. From the beginning, the "saving of Chinese babies" was the charitable work with the most visibility. In the 1930s, a combination of these articles with the presentation of leper work formed a compelling image of China which no reader could forget. The poignant pictures of dying babies and distorted bodies, the happy faces of cared for babies and lepers and the vivid narratives of Maryknollers about their orphanages and the leper colony were skillfully presented to touch both the heart and the wallet of American Catholics.

Monetary appeals for saving Chinese babies, mostly girls, were routinely run. The initial cost was estimated at five dollars and covered the donation made to women who found the children—five cents per child. If the child died, it also defrayed the burial expenses of about 35 cents. Because healthy babies were entrusted to outside "wet nurses" at the cost of one dollar a month, the original offering was spent in less than half a year if a child survived. Although the plea for Chinese babies appealed to the readership of the magazine as a whole, a special emphasis was made in the "Juniors" and "Crusaders" pages to galvanize American youth to donate money for their less fortunate Chinese sisters. Mission activities of many school groups centered on raising funds for Chinese babies; "save a pagan baby" became their slogan.[88]

With the widening of the Sino-Japanese War in the late 1930s, the Maryknoll magazine shifted its readers' attention from the abandoned babies to the drama of the multitude of Chinese "warphans." These children were left alone to fend for themselves. Some had been separated from their relatives in moments of panic and flight and had not been able to find them again. Others had seen their parents killed. All were traumatized children whom readers were asked to help through Maryknoll's programs such as orphanages and boys' towns:

> Imagine that you are six years old, that you live in a good section of a Chinese city, with kindly and wealthy parents. Then imagine that men with guns and planes and tanks come to wreck the city. . . . At night crying, frightened, hungry, you creep out of the ruins. Playmates are lying dead in the streets. All around are fires. Other children join you. . . . Begging, sleeping in ditches, living like animals, you children make your way across country. . . . At last you come to a town where tall, white-faced men in black robes give you food and shelter. . . . You do not understand, but you know they are good people, and you feel sure that their America and their God must be good, too.[89]

The magazine also printed pictures of these children who were not easily forgotten by well-fed and well-dressed Americans. In a five-page photo story on "China's Desperate Millions," focusing mainly on orphans of the war, American Catholics were told "Look at the faces of these Chinese. Study them well. Then turn away if you are able. Then try to forget their grief."[90]

The rapid growth of Maryknoll's leper colony showed that American Catholics were moved by the reports of such work and gave it their seal of approval with generous financial backing. Between 1933 and 1943, the number of lepers sheltered by Maryknollers increased from 20 to 500. The accommodations improved from a few clusters of ramshackle huts to a modern leprosarium.

Although during and after the war the emphasis shifted to the problems of war orphans and refugees in general, the magazine still continued to present the plight of the lepers as one of the biggest needs. The cry was even raised in poetry:

Forced to roam	Lepers, too
Far from here	(Not a few)
Almost nude,	At Ngai Moon
Without food.	Need rice soon,
Refugees—	In Christ's name,
Help them, please?	Feed the same?[91]

At other times the appeal was a lengthy article, such as one by Father John Joyce in November 1947, which retraced 15 years of Maryknoll's work among lepers. The most commonly used form was a short moving entry in the "Want Ads" section of the magazine: "To be a leper anywhere is pitiful. To be one in torn, bleeding, starving China represents about the limit of human misery. Can you spare $5—the price of a month's life—for a Chinese leper?"[92]

After the surrender of Japan, Maryknollers thought the time was ideal to launch an all-out campaign of charitable works. They hoped to capitalize on the good reputation earned during the war by Chinese Catholics and missioners alike. The magazine reiterated that financial support had become even more important and valuable:

> Out of the evil of the war in China, one good thing has come. Many thousands of Chinese, young and old, are ready to accept Christianity. Homeless, ragged, sick and starving, guided by rumor or chance, the Chinese came thronging to the Maryknoll missions through all the years of war. And there they were helped and kept alive by the food and medicine, the clothing and shelter, which American friends of Maryknoll had provided. . . . Chinese understand self-interest but they could not understand why foreign priests were devoted unselfishly to them. . . . Many Chinese are grateful, their hearts are touched, they are curious. If Maryknollers can instruct them now, they will become Catholics. If not, they may be lost to the Church of Christ.[93]

The readers were told that they could participate in the reconstruction of China through the missioners. Most important was to help the estimated 84 million people (in a country of 440 million) who needed relief—food, clothing, shelter, and education.

In one article entitled "The Greatest Opportunity in History," the magazine pointed to the results which could be expected from helping war orphans. "If we can feed them, care for them, keep them alive, bring them somehow through this time of trial, they may be Christians—they, and their children, and other descendants, forever!"[94]

A Country Threatened by Communism

Starting in 1945, the magazine also stressed that there was much more at stake than just seizing or missing an opportunity. It prophesied that if the Church lost that opportunity, the Communists would seize it and capitalize on it. Concerning the care and education of war orphans, the magazine warned American Catholics:

> If these youngsters and others like them are sheltered and fed and trained by Maryknoll missioners, they will grow up as friends; powerful friends in years to come for our country, our Church, our God. If we neglect them—be assured the International Communists will not![95]

In 1946, Bishop James E. Walsh wrote an article calling for "true friends of China" not to be deceived by reports from the press vilifying the Nationalist government. Walsh readily acknowledged that the Chinese government was not perfect and had not been elected by popular vote. On the other hand, however, he described it as:

> . . . a well-intentioned government, one full of plans and reforms for the welfare of the Chinese people . . . [which] respects the rights and preserves the liberties of the people and is the only one that is wanted by the people.[96]

Walsh recognized that the Nationalist Party contained "petty despots, unprincipled opportunists, inefficient officials, and dishonest grafters"; but he maintained that its percentage of bad elements was not larger than that of any other political party in the world. On the contrary, he said, the Nationalist Party, especially its top leadership, had a "preponderance of patriots and statesmen who set the standard and determine the policies to further the welfare of the people and the nation as a whole."[97]

In conclusion, Walsh lashed out at the Communists for not supporting the war effort and for sabotaging national reconstruction.

> The Communist group took advantage of their own people's misery and their own country's extremity, to impose themselves on great sections of the population who despised and feared them, establish a separate state, divide the nation, sabotage the war effort, abstain carefully from fighting the Japanese invaders; and finally, to broadcast around the world the claim that they represent a spontaneous movement of the Chinese people. . . . China

has a good government and will set its house in order; and all true friends of China will be known by their support of that constructive program.[98]

Recent studies on Chiang Kai-shek and his entourage have been critical of Chiang, H. H. Kung, the Soong family, and other prominent Nationalist officials of the government and the military.[99] In the light of these findings, Walsh's article and others written in the same vein appear to have been naive and to have misled the Catholic readership of *Maryknoll—The Field Afar*. Not all Maryknollers, however, were so uncritical of the Nationalists. Some raised serious reservations about their unscrupulous methods and corruption, but these views were never published. These Maryknollers eventually concluded that, as bad as the Nationalist regime was, it was to be supported because, in the eyes of the Church, communism was no alternative.[100]

Obviously, the course of events did not turn out as Maryknollers had expected. Between 1947 and 1951, the Maryknoll magazine opted to remain silent on the changing political situation in China and concentrated instead on the rapid growth of the Catholic Church. Only when Maryknollers themselves were forced by the Communists to leave China did the magazine suddenly explode with numerous stories on the plight of the Chinese Catholics and the missioners at the hands of the "Reds" or "Commies." By the peak of the missionary exodus in 1952 and 1953, 27 articles had been printed on the Communist persecution.

At the same time, Maryknoll published several popular books with accounts of life under the Communist regime in Maryknoll's mission territories. *Nun in Red China* by Sister Mary Victoria (pseudonym of Sister Maria del Ray Danforth) retraced the appalling experiences of Sister Mary Paulita Hoffman and Sister Edith Rietz. *No Secret Is Safe* was the prison diary of Father Mark Tennien. *Calvary in China* told of the jailing, trial, and sentencing of Father Robert Greene. *Bird of Sorrow* by Monsignor John Romaniello depicted the patient endurance, loyalty, and witnessing to the faith of Chinese Catholics.

All these books told stories of arrests on trumped-up charges; of horror-filled months of imprisonment and shocking treatment; of cells that crawled with vermin and so overcrowded that sleeping space was often only two feet wide. Screams issued from torture rooms all night long. Often missioners were awakened in the middle of the night, bound painfully, and subjected to incessant and bullying questioning. The threat of execution always hung over their heads until the Communists finally released them at the Hong Kong border.

However, Maryknoll did not concentrate for long on lamenting the evils of communism; instead Maryknoll began to reflect on the lessons learned by the Catholic Church in China. Already in 1952 in a very perceptive editorial entitled "Failure in Asia," Father John Donovan attempted to explain why the Christian West had failed in China. Donovan opened his analysis of the historical steps which led to the Communist victory in China by quoting the French Catholic philosopher Jacques Maritain:

> The complaints and curses which the East utters against us are inspired not only by hatred but also by profound disillusion. We cannot hear that outcry without quivering for sorrow and shame. . . . Before becoming indignant with our accusers, let us first admit we have sinned against them. . . .[101]

Donovan then proceeded to explain how the Christian West had failed the Chinese through its traders and statesmen, as well as its missioners. In their relentless search for profit, Western traders had introduced nefarious traffic in opium and Western nations supported unjust treaties with gunboats. As for Western missioners, Donovan wrote:

> They too blindly and too complacently accepted the benefits conferred by imperialistic and unjust treaty rights. Today we see the ethical absurdity of gunboat support for Christian missionary endeavors. Today our missioners suffer in silence the horrors of unjust prison terms or house confinement.[102]

If China had turned to communism, said Donovan, it was in great measure the fault of the Christians from the West with whom the Chinese had come in contact. However, his conclusion was quite hopeful. He believed that the abiding faith of Chinese Catholics under persecution would reveal the true face of Catholicism and become an unshakable foundation on which the future Church of China would be built.

Conclusion

Maryknoll's influence on American Catholics appears to have been quite pervasive. Characterized by a bold and imaginative use of mass media, Maryknoll relentlessly sought better ways of reaching American Catholics and was quick to make use of new forms of mass communication.

Maryknoll's originality, however, rested not only in its extensive use of diverse media; it was also displayed by the ability to address a very broad Catholic audience, as well as specific segments of that audience. Within the pages of Maryknoll's magazine, for example, sections appealed more specifically to children, to young men and women, to educators, to medical persons, and to parish groups.

The focus on youth and educators had direct results on the growth of

Maryknoll. Its novitiates and seminaries filled with young people eager to serve on the foreign missions. Even those who did not persevere retained their interest in the missions and swelled the ranks of those Americans who contributed prayers and funds for the success and growth of Maryknoll's work.

At the time of Maryknoll's founding, Americans in general felt a special attraction to the Far East—and to China in particular—which did not exist for any other region of the world. China presented an exotic and mysterious aura for Americans, which Maryknoll cultivated with a wide range of information on China.

The overall characteristic of Maryknollers portrayed in publications and films was that they had a deep love for the Chinese people and a great admiration for their civilization. Francis Ford, by the number and length of his contributions, appeared as Maryknoll's main spokesman for Chinese culture and human qualities. The Chinese were not strange creatures, but ordinary human beings. Their philosophy of life revolved around filial piety—the reverence for older generations—and upheld the good of the family and the country above the needs of the individual. This discipline was behind the simplicity of their life and their virtues of patience, industry, energy, and endurance against all odds.

In their enthusiasm, however, the missioners, and particularly Ford, often gave a portrait of China and its people which lacked balance and bordered at times on fiction. According to Ford, the Chinese simplicity of living was a matter of choice; in times of war and famine it made them bear suffering and hunger with a lightheartedness and a good humor which reminded him of St. Francis of Assisi. Although Ford was from the city and had not experienced farm life, he wrote extensively on the subject. Ford's disparaging description of the American farmhouse as a styleless ugly wooden structure, compared to its idealized Chinese counterpart, showed that his knowledge of the American countryside was very limited. Even the Chinese farmhouse he described, with its several courtyards, rooms, patios, and cool corners, was not a common sight in South China. Most villagers were too poor to maintain such a home. Instead, they lived in small one- or two-room houses which were so dark and humid that tuberculosis was endemic. This "reality" of Chinese life, well depicted in Maryknollers' diaries and letters, was rarely allowed to surface in Maryknoll publications.

In their attempts to prove that Westerners were not morally and culturally superior to the Chinese, Maryknollers often described China as a nearly perfect society nourishing a naturally virtuous people with ancient wisdom. The Maryknoll magazine conveyed a sense of a Chinese state of natural goodness somewhat reminiscent of Rousseau's philosophy or Chateaubriand's writings in *Le génie du Christianisme*.

Maryknollers claimed that China was ideally prepared for Christianity and needed but an introduction. Christianity would incorporate all the goodness of Chinese society and, at the same time, bring about the demise of its superstitions and imperfections—such as the abandoning of baby girls—which were considered marks of the devil. As proof, missioners pointed to the steadfastness and rapid growth of the Chinese Catholic Church with its own priests, Sisters, Brothers, and even its own bishops. Chinese lay people were leaving their mark not only in the countryside but also in the cities and in higher levels of government, business, and education. Maryknollers envisioned a modern China which would enrich and regenerate the splendid wisdom of its ancient civilization by borrowing Christian faith and scientific progress from the West.

Looking into the future, Maryknoll presented American readers with a vision of a great Catholic Chinese nation. All this was but a dream. Certainly the Chinese were rapidly adopting Western methods and discoveries. In the realm of spiritual values, however, most Chinese clung to their own values and viewed Christianity as a foreign and unneeded product of the West.

Most Maryknollers seemed to have been aware of some of these difficulties. Their efforts at adapting the Catholic message, their training of the native clergy and sisterhood, and their development of an apostolic laity were signs that they did realize that China would become Catholic only when Catholicism became Chinese. By the end of the Sino-Japanese War, Maryknollers saw some signs that efforts of the Church to become more Chinese were having results. They felt that the strong patriotism displayed by Chinese Catholics during the war helped to wash away the foreign stigma that Catholicism had always carried in China.

It is ironic to note, however, that at the precise moment when the Chinese Church was being recognized as patriotic, its leadership—both foreign and Chinese—endorsed the Nationalist regime and linked their destinies in the years ahead. This attitude was clearly reflected in the Maryknoll magazine's blind praise of the Nationalist leadership. Because communism was no acceptable alternative in the eyes of the Church, the Communist victory left the Church in the camp of the defeated Nationalist government. As the Communists exposed the widespread corruption of the Western-supported Nationalist government, the entire Chinese Catholic Church also appeared unpatriotic.

Nonetheless, if the Catholic Church had not been so closely linked with the Nationalist government and had limited itself to showing its love for China by relieving misery and helping reconstruction, it still would have faced persecution for religious reasons. However, it would not have had to reestablish its patriotism, and it is also probable that some of the current tension between the Chinese Catholic Church and the Vatican might not exist.

In the wake of the religious persecutions and expulsion of the missioners during the 1950s, the Maryknoll magazine quite naturally published many articles which depicted communism as the worst of all evils. Nonetheless, the Chinese people themselves were always portrayed in a favorable light. Bad attitudes and deeds were attributed to "the Reds," as if by turning Communist, they had lost the admirable traits and virtues of their race and culture.

Since 1972, America's fascination with China is being rekindled by a political rapprochement most visible in the cultural and economic sectors. From a religious point of view, the dream of a Catholic Chinese nation has proven to be an illusion, although the existence of a Chinese Church has become a reality.

Concluding Remarks: "Souls Are People"

Maryknoll has just celebrated its 75th anniversary. It has expanded its presence to 28 countries in Asia, Africa, and the Americas. China, however, was Maryknoll's first mission field and for 35 years remained the foreign country with the largest number of Maryknollers.

The history of Western missioners in China is part of the history of the Church in China but also part of the history of the Churches in the West. Interrelations—difficulties as well as mutual enrichment—link the Western Churches and the Chinese Church. Understanding the weaknesses and strengths of this link is crucial to forging new and better links in the present and in the future.

Contacts with foreigners who lived in Third World countries have been at the core of the transformation of many of these countries. In China, these foreigners included Western missioners who not only preached the Gospel and gained converts, but performed a variety of services. The impact of Christian missions in China forms a much broader subject than even a comprehensive history of Western missioners in China. By establishing extensive factual records, based both on Western and Chinese sources, this history of Maryknoll in China extends beyond its own findings and thus provides opportunities for scholars to study other facets of the influence and effects of both Christian missions and the development of the Catholic Church in China. Such an approach to mission history can be a point of entry into dialogue and cooperation with Chinese historians about China's modern history and the role Christianity played.

Maryknoll set out to save the soul of China and to bring millions of Chinese people into the Catholic Church. In pursuing their goal, Maryknollers encountered a diversity of challenges—to their bodies, their souls, and their work. The physical surroundings in China were not favorable: the climate did not suit North Americans, the terrain was mostly hilly, the means of transportation were slow and unreliable. The social and political conditions also hindered their work: widespread banditry, endemic local feuds, and large-scale wars plagued the country and interfered with long-range plans for evangelization. The difficulty of the Chinese language with its variety of dialects prevented many missioners from communicating effectively with the Chinese people. China's rich cultural heritage and complex philosophical-religious underpinnings permeated Chinese life, from the most important decisions to the simplest daily tasks. Books on Chinese culture, philosophy, and religious beliefs certainly increased the missioners' knowledge and appreciation of China, but study could not make the missioners *become* Chinese. Most Maryknollers did not shy away from the challenges of China; instead, they tried to live with them and overcome them.

Maryknollers arrived in China as eager students of the missionary methods of their French M.E.P. mentors. The young American missioners learned the importance of being in constant touch with the rural people, of mastering the language, of living simply, of reaching out to the people, and of keeping the mission compounds open to visitors. Diaries and letters conveyed the image of the missioners' efforts to share the life, joys, and sorrows of the people. Maryknollers wrote of their travels to visit Catholics or catechumens, to contact non-Christians, to marry young people, to anoint the sick, and to bury the dead. Stories from the war and tales of the work in orphanages, dispensaries, and hospitals presented compassionate missioners who cared for those in direst need.

Through the personal experience of these missioners and their Chinese converts, the goals of Maryknoll in China were contextualized. They became embedded into a historical and human setting of war and peace, good harvests and cataclysms, life and death. The Chinese were not just souls to save for the life hereafter; they were also people who deserved a better existence in this world.

The deep, abiding commitment of Maryknoll today to serve the poor and the oppressed is not a recent development, but is rooted in the personal experience of the first Maryknollers who went to China. In an editorial entitled "Souls Are People" for the September 1939 issue of *Maryknoll* magazine, Bishop James E. Walsh recalled how, years earlier, he had felt the call to such a commitment in a rice field near the Kongmoon mission:

> "I choose you," sang in my heart as I looked at my awkward farmer boy, perfect picture of the underprivileged soul . . . the overworked and overlooked, the forgotten and despised. . . . I choose you and dedicate myself to you and I ask no other privilege but to devote the energies of my soul to such

as you. . . . Shine on, farmer boy, symbol to me of the thousand million like you who drew the Son of God from heaven to smooth and bless your weary anxieties and puzzled brows. . . . Teach me that souls are people. And remind me everlasting that they are magnificent people like you.

Since then, this touching story, retitled "Shine on, Farmer Boy," has been a treasured part of Maryknoll's heritage.[1]

As Maryknollers traveled from one region of China to another, they realized how easily one could identify the nationality of the missioners and their religious background by noting the style of the church building, the devotions most emphasized, and the songs used at mass. Coming from America at a time when each parish often had an ethnic character, Maryknollers were used to such variety; however, in China, they realized that these differences reflected Western influences rather than the local Chinese community. In their own missions, therefore, they worked to establish a type of Catholic Church with more genuinely Chinese characteristics.

Maryknollers were not immediately successful in their endeavors to reach the people or to foster a Chinese Church because they were still imbued with counterproductive Western ideas and prejudices. Diaries and letters record many of these flaws: colonialism, cultural arrogance, rugged individualism. Although most Maryknollers successfully overcame physical hardships, many were never able to rid themselves of a certain lack of sensitivity to Chinese social, cultural, and religious institutions.

Maryknollers also knew that they would never be able to explain the Catholic religion as well as Chinese priests, Sisters, and lay apostles. They realized that eventually the Chinese themselves would have to provide leaders for the Church and leaders who could improve social conditions in the country. As a result, Maryknollers emphasized training for religious and lay leaders. But here, too, they could not escape the prejudices of the missionary community in China at the time. If the effort at promoting a native bishop for Wuchow failed, it seems to have been in great part because several Marykollers did not want to be responsible to a Chinese.

In spite of failures and setbacks, Maryknoll never relented in its effort to make the Catholic Church more Chinese. This drive, more than the conversion movement after World War II or even the success of its missionary methods, constitutes Maryknoll's greatest achievement and contribution to China. In 1918, Maryknoll went to China to save souls and was, in turn, saved from the false belief that everything outside the realm of Christianity and the West was necessarily bad or wrong. Maryknollers became increasingly aware that the Chinese philosophy of life, culture, and traditions compared favorably to those of the Christian West.

This understanding enabled the missioners to reach beyond the appearance, the changes, and the chaos, and to glimpse a perennial China whose set of values rivaled those of the West. These values needed to be preserved and to become part of the patrimony of the Chinese Catholic Church. These values were the fertile ground in which the Chinese Church would flourish. With Francis Ford as one of their most eloquent spokesmen, many Maryknollers believed that the Church of China had no real future unless it was set free from the methods, civilization, and control of the West.

Maryknollers were certainly not the only missioners to think along these lines; other Christian groups—Catholics and Protestants alike—were also actively involved in promoting a Church truly rooted in Chinese culture.

The expulsion of most foreigners after the Revolution of 1949 does not necessarily mean that the missioners failed. In fact, Communist intervention might have been providential because it removed the last signs of Western influence from the Church of China which was then forced to chart its own course.

For the relatively young Maryknoll Society and Congregation, the three and a half decades spent in China were a time of training and enrichment. Their resiliency and adaptability were severely tested. The experience also gave them a sense of identity, a tradition, and a way to look at people and cultures which have set the two communities on the course they follow today.

From their years in China, Maryknollers also learned that Christianity could not be lived and preached in isolation, but was part of the political events taking place around them. They had been branded as co-conspirators in the unequal treaties and unjust concessions imposed by the Western nations on China. They had been implicated in the United States' support of corrupt Chinese Nationalist officials. And yet, they had also experienced a test of their belief that the Christian message of universal love, if lived truthfully, was a political force which transcended all ideologies. It took Maryknoll some time to decipher this mixed legacy and to stand up on the side of the deprived and the exploited for an end to all forms of oppression. Today Maryknoll considers it a part of its mission education to point out the damage caused by some American foreign enterprises as well as to challenge First World Churches to become more globally aware and receptive to the views of their Third World partners. What Maryknoll conveys, therefore, is not just news or ideas about itself and its mission work. It transmits the heartbeat of many peoples from around the world who present the challenges of authentic, indigenous expressions of Christian faith, practices, and theological interpretation.

Perhaps there is no better way to summarize Maryknoll's own development and accomplishments in China than to recall one of Mother Mary Joseph's reflections on Maryknoll: " . . . there is nothing to do but wonder, realizing how little we planned, how little we achieved, and yet how much has been done."[2]

APPENDIX I

Methodology of the Maryknoll China History Project

The methodology of the Maryknoll China History Project was based on a carefully researched "List of Major Categories and Topics." For the oral history part of the project, the list of categories was modified into a standard questionnaire, which served as a guide for interviewers and included one list of questions in English for American missioners, and one in Chinese for Chinese-language interviews.

As the project progressed, the "List of Major Categories and Topics" was refined by analyzing interviews and archival materials. An outline will give an idea of the entire range of topics which were covered by the Maryknoll project and formed the underpinning of this study.

1. The American home base
   The American Catholic Church of that period
   The American socio-political context of that period
2. The making of a missioner
   Family and religious background
   Vocation
   Training for mission
   Personal mission vision
   Changes in images of China and attitudes
3. Theology and missiology: Maryknoll's mission vision
   The original vision
   How the vision changed (from Society/Congregation chapter to chapter)
   Impact of the China experience of Maryknoll vision today
   Changes in theology and missiology
4. Stages in growth, stasis, and retreat: Chronology of Maryknoll missions in China
5. Categories of mission work (by Maryknoll Fathers, Sisters, and Brothers)
   Evangelization and church planting
   Christian nurture
   Social and charitable works (including parish work and outreach, catechumenates, clergy and leader training, orphanages, clinics and hospitals, schools, seminaries, and refugee and relief work)
6. Maryknollers' daily work and living
   Daily schedules
   Sense of vocation
   Spiritual formation and growth
   Cultural adjustment: successes and failures
7. Roles of Maryknoll Fathers and Maryknoll Sisters
   Distinctions in mission tasks
   Relationships and changing roles
   Sisters' role in work with women and families
   Sisters as inspiration to Chinese women
8. The Chinese Church
   Church planting and growth
   Theory and practice of an indigenous Church
   Chinese leadership: religious and laity

Survival of the Church today
9. Chinese Catholics: Clergy, religious, catechists, laity
   Who were they?
   How did they become Christians?
   Their training in the faith and their concept of Christianity
   Their relations with Maryknoll missioners
   Their views and recollections today
10. Reverse mission: American images of China
    How Maryknoll influenced American images of China: *The Field Afar* magazine, letters home, home-leave speaking, books and other published writings
11. The larger history: China and American of that period
    The socio-political context in America, which inspired and supported the China missions
    The socio-political context in China, which affected Maryknoll
12. Biography
    This is a human as well as an institutional history; biographical and anecdotal vignettes, both of Americans and Chinese, are considered essential to document and authenticate this history.
13. Evaluation

The researchers seek to discover lessons learned in the Chinese experience, based on goals, issues, successes and failures, struggles, tensions, and conflicting views based on contemporary reports of the time, as well as on reflections or hindsights for today—by both Maryknollers and non-Maryknollers.

APPENDIX II

Sources and the Retrieval System at Maryknoll

The mention of mission history immediately brings to mind the richness and the multitude of documents often jealously preserved in the archives of some mission institutions. The Maryknoll archives and the photo libraries, both at the Sisters' Center and at the Fathers and Brothers' Center, are well preserved and organized. They contain more than 10,000 photographs and about 90,000 pages of documents related to China. A unique feature of Maryknoll was to require that each mission parish and each Sisters' house maintain a diary of events and activities. Although their quality and content vary greatly according to the diarist, these writings are an invaluable source of information on all aspects of life in China. Altogether, diaries comprise 36,000 pages, or about two-fifths of the total archival documents on China held at Maryknoll.

Of all these documents, only selected and edited pages of the missioners' correspondence and diaries have been published in book form as *Maryknoll Mission Letters* and in *The Field Afar* magazine. *The Field Afar*—later renamed *Maryknoll*—is the official magazine published in common by both Maryknoll societies. It is an important tool, in particular, for looking at the images of China and themselves that Maryknollers were passing on to their American readers and benefactors. An added advantage is the detailed index of the magazine kept in the library of the Maryknoll Fathers and Brothers since its first issue in January 1907.

At the start of the Maryknoll China History Project in 1980, Maryknoll was fortunate to have nearly half of the Maryknoll men and women who served in China still alive. Two hundred missioners, mostly Maryknollers, were interviewed. To complete the story of the development of the Chinese Catholic Church and the role played in it by Maryknoll, researchers also interviewed 56 Chinese priests, Sisters, and laypersons who worked with, were trained by, or were associated with Maryknollers in China before 1952. Interviews were taped, carefully transcribed, and translated into English when needed, according to accepted oral history guidelines. The average transcript is 40 pages long. Releases were secured to allow use of the content for writing the history of Maryknoll.

The oral history component of the project supplemented and enriched the written records preserved in the archives. It gave a broader base of inquiry by allowing missioners and Chinese who were not necessarily skilled or inclined to writing to recount events and experiences, some of them not previously recorded. It also included the reflections of old China hands and Chinese on their lives as missioners, converts, or religious leaders. Conscientiously gathered, carefully processed, and critically examined, oral histories contributed to both the quantity and quality of what is known about the recent past.

Use of the "List of Major Categories and Topics" and a standard questionnaire (see appendix on methodology) ensured that the researchers' inquiries—both in conducting interviews and in reading archival materials—were as thorough and organized as possible. However, the sequence of acts, experiences, or reflections described in the diaries and the interviews did not necessarily follow the patterns of the questionnaire of "List of Topics." A major task, therefore, was to devise a system that permitted easy retrieval of data scattered throughout 10,000 pages of interviews and 36,000 pages of diaries as well as in some 2,000 pages of important correspondence and reports.

For this purpose, Maryknoll China History Project researchers compiled a list of entries by subjects, names of individuals or groups, and locations. Each interview and each archival document was indexed according to this list and entered into a computerized data-retrieval system designed by the staff. This unique system was most useful in writing this book on the history of Maryknoll in China as it helped to detect significant themes and to efficiently retrieve data. It is hoped that it will also facilitate access to Maryknoll sources on China by other researchers in the future.

APPENDIX III

Maryknoll Sisters with Medical Training Who Served in China

Name	Degree	Years of assignment
Boyle, Monica Marie	RN/Medical Technician	1934–1951
Bourguignon, Marie de Lourdes	RN	1923–1927
Conlon, Mary Matthew	Diploma in Nursing	1923–1927
Coveny, Angela Marie	RN	1939–1948
Cusack, M. Mercedes	RN/Training in Surgery/Obstetrics	1925–1942
Foley, Lawrence	Certificate/Ossining Hospital	1921–1937
Guerrieri, Antonia Maria	MD	1941–1951
Hock, Mary	RN	1934–1938
Jaramillo, Maria Corazon	MD	1942–1952
Kelly, Dominic	RN	1937–1945
Lynn, Virginia Marie	RN/Psychiatric Nursing	1935–1937
Maloney, Ann	RN	1949–1951
Marsland, Francis de Sales	RN	1936–1940
McKenna, Mary De Lellis	RN/Specialty in Tropical Diseases	1931–1938
McNally, Ignatia	Nursing Certificate	1936–1938
Moore, Mary Gertrude	RN	1922
O'Leary, Mary Angelica	RN	1934–1940
Rafferty, Agnes Regina	RN	1936–1938
Reynolds, Mary Camillus	RN	1924–1939
Schleininger, Roma	RN	1935–1938
Stitz, Herman Joseph	BS Chemistry/Lab. Technician	1936–1938
Sullivan, Mary Paula	RN	1933–1941
Thyne, Maria	RN	1934–1951
Turner, Dominic Marie	Nursing Certificate Pharmaceutical Degree (2 years)	1936–1953
Urlacher, Magdalena	RN	1935–1951
Vennemann, Espiritu	RN	1936–1938

Summary

22 trained nurses; 1 chemist trained as a laboratory technician. Of the nurses, one had special training in pharmacy, one in surgery and obstetrics, and one in tropical diseases. Two medical doctors.

Source: Prepared from Maryknoll China History Project records.

APPENDIX IV

Mission Statistics: Catholics and Mission Personnel

1. TOTALS FOR CHINA

Year	Catholics	Yearly increase	Priests-F*	Priests-C*	Brothers-F	Brothers-C	Sisters-F	Sisters-C	Cate-chists	Seminarians	Cate-chumens
1928–29	2,486,841	23,091	1,975	1,369	314	466	1,327	2,641	10,446	—	—
1932–33	2,623,560	60,818	2,303	1,595	462	469	1,693	3,419	11,324	784g†	411,184
1933–34	2,702,468	78,908	2,367	1,647	541	607	1,831	3,319	11,833	804g	466,287
1934–35	2,818,839	96,450	2,481	1,734	532	635	1,995	3,418	13,817	302g	495,060
1935–36	2,934,175	115,336	2,636	1,822	574	689	2,120	3,626	13,339	983g/5,992p†	526,673
1936–37	3,018,338	84,163	2,679	1,898	619	762	2,224	3,769	12,595	843g	517,423
1937–38	3,082,894	64,566	2,822	1,941	598	744	2,284	3,781	11,420	1,033g/5,719p	600,560
1938–39	3,182,950	100,056	2,289	2,008	585	677	2,281	3,852	11,407	1,037g/5,114p	654,418
1946–47	3,258,536	–21,277	2,527	3,006	682	421	4,735	2,046	—	957g/2,900p	191,921

Source: Annuaire des Missions Catholiques de Chine, 1928–1948.

*F = foreign, C = Chinese.

†p = petit, or seminarians studying in minor seminary; g = grand, or seminarians studying at a major seminary.

462

Mission Statistics: Catholics and Mission Personnel

2. KONGMOON

Year	Priests-F*	Priests-C*	Brothers-F	Brothers-C	Sisters-F	Sisters-C	Catholics	Catechumens	Male/Female Catechists
1921–22	17	0	2	0	12	—	2,380	2,118	50/30
1923–24	24	0	5	0	23	—	6,333	1,868	58/22
1924–25	20	0	2	0	12	—	7,009	2,010	—
1925–26	23	0	3	0	12	4	7,126	1,907	60/30
1926–27	20	0	3	0	12	3	7,022	437	35/18
1927–28	24	0	3	0	0	6	7,207	1,491	41/24
1928–29	23	0	2	0	0	5	7,318	1,506	46/26
1931–32	24	0	3	0	6	4	8,069	639	61/42
1932–33	27	0	3	0	9	6	8,149	353	57/33
1933–34	20	1	4	0	9	4	8,420	370	—
1934–35	24	1	2	0	10	2	8,535	458	59/44
1935–36	25	1	3	0	9	7	9,022	388	55/48
1936–37	29	1	3	0	10	7	9,560	592	68/58
1937–38	31	1	4	0	8	7	9,755	691	127
1938–39	30	1	4	0	8	7	9,680	655	135
1939–40	26	1	4	0	8	10	10,394	483	126
1940–41	27	3	4	0	8	10	10,760	438	65/50
1941–42	25	4	0	0	8	12	11,051	375	30/25
1942–43	27	6	1	0	6	12	9,418	223	36
1943–44	25	7	0	0	7	16†	9,056	71	19/12
1944–45	21	6	1	0	4	18†	8,820	165	32
1945–46	21	7	0	0	4	22†	8,180	127	13/26
1947–48	17	11	2	0	8	23	7,933	207	22/23
1948–49	27	11‡	2	0	9	28	8,553	350	025/28

Source: Compiled from the Maryknoll Archives.
*F = foreign, C = Chinese. †Two Chinese Sisters were from Canton. ‡Plus two Chinese priests who were refugees.

Mission Statistics: Catholics and Mission Personnel

3. KAYING

Year	Priests-F*	Priests-C*	Brothers-F	Brothers-C	Sisters-F	Sisters-C	Catholics	Catechumens	Male/female Catechists
1926	—	—	0	0	0	—	4,456	—	26
1927–28	—	—	0	0	0	—	5,566	—	14/8
1928–29	12	2	2	0	0	—	7,261	145	—
1929–30	14	2	2	0	0	—	7,732	202	18/9
1930–31	16	2	1	0	0	—	7,707	282	—
1931–32	17	2	2	0	0	—	8,035	545	25/11
1932–33	21	3	2	0	0	—	8,454	544	32/15
1933–34	23	5	—	0	4	—	8,263	585	30/18
1934–35	25	5	—	0	10	—	9,458	1,236	41/27
1935–36	26	6	—	0	12	—	10,451	1,338	87
1936–37	25	6	—	0	14	—	13,411	2,889	—
1937–38	29	7	—	0	13	—	15,915	2,326	—
1938–39	28	1	8	0	8	7	17,718	1,615	80/46
1939–40	—	—	—	0	—	—	18,055	1,703	56/43
1940–41	—	—	—	0	—	—	—	1,218	47/32
1941–42	34	8	—	0	14	—	19,397	310	32/29
1942–43	28	11	—	0	15	—	19,567	143	23/16
1943–44	21	11	—	0	15	—	18,937	148	13/18
1944–45	16	11	—	0	14	—	18,959	747	19/22
1945–46	—	—	—	0	—	—	19,186	—	—
1946–47	19	11	—	0	14	11	19,411	378	30/26
1947–48	18	16	—	0	18	16	19,684	581	25/19
1948–49	24	16†	—	0	20	15	19,691	393	28/22
1949–50	16	19	—	0	—	—	18,924	1,218	47/32

Source: Compiled from the Maryknoll Archives.
*F = foreign, C = Chinese. †Plus six Chinese priests who were refugees from North China.

Mission Statistics: Catholics and Mission Personnel

4. WUCHOW

Year	Priests-F*	Priests-C*	Brothers-F	Brothers-C	Sisters-F	Sisters-C	Catholics	Catechumens	Male/female Catechists
1926–27	2	0	0	0	0	0	322	550	5/4
1927–28	4	0	0	0	0	0	365	702	5/6
1928–29	8	0	1	0	0	0	721	800	7/3
1930–31	14	1	1	0	0	2	1,448	1,335	19/9
1931–32	—	—	—	—	—	—	1,689	1,225	—
1932–33†	17	2	1	0	0	5	2,565	3,063	40
1933–34†	15	1	1	0	0	6	3,306	4,907	—
1934–35†	18	1	1	0	0	8	4,601	2,196	45/33
1935–36†	19	1	1	—	2	8	5,891	3,132	5/34
1936–37†	17	3	1	—	4	8	7,045‡	1,918	—
1937–38	11	2	1	0	6	3	7,493	1,585	51/48
1938–39	13	3	1	0	5§	1§	8,588	1,544	51/52
1939–40	—	—	—	—	—	—	9,745	—	—
1940–41	—	—	—	—	—	—	10,344	753	40/39
1942–43	—	—	—	—	—	—	10,169	385	29/21
1943–44	—	—	—	—	—	—	11,922	156	18/16
1944–45	—	—	—	—	—	—	12,072	162	14/13
1945–46	—	—	—	—	—	—	11,422	56	9/11
1946–47	17	1	0	0	9	5	12,122	7,953	—
1947–48	23	3	1	0	5	10	14,414	7,323	99/77
1948–49	26	0	1	0	7	10	16,805	4,588	153/95
1949–50	25	0	1	0	8	10	19,871	3,811	107/81

Source: Compiled from the Maryknoll Archives.
*F = foreign, C = Chinese. †Combined for Wuchow-Kweilin. ‡Wuchow alone: 6,296. §Two of the foreign Sisters and the Chinese Sister belonged to the Congregation of the Sisters of Our Lady of the Angels and were on loan from the Nanning vicariate.

Mission Statistics: Catholics and Mission Personnel

5. KWEILIN

Year	Priests-F*	Priests-C*	Brothers-F	Brothers-C	Sisters-F	Sisters-C	Catholics	Catechumens	Male/female Catechists
1931-32	—	—	0	0	0	—	410	225	—
1937-38	8	0	0	0	0	5	1,066	225	20
1939-40	13	0	0	0	5	0	1,826	—	—
1940-41	16	0	0	0	5	4	2,750	110	15/13
1941-42	16	0	0	0	6	4	3,194	110	10/8
1942-43	18	0	0	0	6†	7	3,514	189	8/7
1946-47	19	1	0	0	4	9	3,603	600	18/3
1947-48	26	1	0	0	6	9	5,173	325	20/11
1948-49	26	1	0	0	6	9	7,595	2,000	35/20
1949-50	—	—	—	—	—	13‡	8,539	—	—

Source: Compiled from the Maryknoll Archives.
*F = foreign, C = Chinese.
†Plus 4 Chinese Sisters who were refugees.
‡3 of these Chinese Sisters were in Macao.

Mission Statistics: Catholics and Mission Personnel

6. FUSHUN

Year	Priests-F*	Priests-C*	Brothers-F	Brothers-C	Sisters-F	Sisters-C	Catholics	Catechumens	Male/female Catechists
1930-31	14	5	0	0	5	—	5,000	550	42 (9/33)
1932-33	17	5	2	0	12	7	4,367	3,073	—
1933-34	17	5	2	0	12	7	4,567	3,073	—
1935-36	24	5	2	0	25	3	7,475	3,596	—
1936-37	26	5	2	0	27	2	7,751	3,377	69
1937-38	28	5	2	0	31	2	8,646	3,377	87 (49/38)
1938-39	29	5	2	0	29	2	9,460	2,385	89 (51/38)
1939-40	30	5	2	0	33	0	10,332	2,805	90
1940-41	32	5	2	0	27	1	11,033	1,916	—
1941-42	—	—	—	—	—	3	—	—	—
1942-43	—	—	—	—	17	—	—	—	—
1946-47	—	5	2	0	—	16	11,000	—	—
1948-49	0	11	0	0	0	20	—	—	—

Source: Compiled from the Maryknoll Archives.
*F = foreign, C = Chinese.

APPENDIX V

Maryknoll Mission Works

1. KONGMOON	1929	1939	1949
Pastoral			
Area in square miles	15,500	15,500	15,500
Population (approximate)	6,000,000	6,000,000	5,000,000
Stations or parishes	15	20	23
Outstations	195	263	180
Catholics	7,318	9,680	8,553
Catechumens	1,506	655	350
Baptisms of adults	176	515	192
Baptisms of children of Catholics	173	241	191
Baptisms, danger of death/adults	29	58	39
Baptisms, danger of death/children	1,259	3,542	2,225
Confirmations	107	118	201
Marriages	43	83	73
Communions	37,959	110,170	120,028
Extreme unctions	83	—	77
Formation of clergy and Sisters			
Chinese seminarians/major	2	8	5
Chinese seminarians/preparatory	42	64	22
Chinese novices	0	3	2
Chinese postulants	12	17	11
Educational			
Chinese teachers employed	27	36	42
Primary schools	42	10	20
Primary students: male/female	1,319m/226f	538m/110f	834m/260f
Secondary schools/students	0	0	0
Vocational schools/students	0	0	1/5
Hostels/students	0	0	0
Medical			
Hospitals/beds	0	1/22	1/50
Leprosaria/lepers	1	1/271	1/139
Dispensaries/treatments	6/17,724	17/40,000	21
Charitable			
Orphanages/older orphans	3/—	7/195	7/259
Babies brought in	—	3,501	—
Babies sent to nurses for care	—	106	—
Homes for the aged/persons	1/—	1/10	1/10
Homes for the blind/females	1/—	1/20	1/23

Source: Compiled from the Maryknoll Archives. Data on social and relief works were too sparse to be tabulated.

Maryknoll Mission Works

2. KAYING	1929	1939	1949
Pastoral			
Area in square miles	8,400	8,400	8,400
Population (approximate)	2,625,000	2,625,000	2,625,000
Stations or parishes	7	22	26
Outstations	149	326	331
Catholics	7,261	17,718	19,691
Catechumens	—	1,615	393
Baptisms of adults	116	2,225	784
Baptisms of children of Catholics	245	472	554
Baptisms, danger of death/adults	18	277	121
Baptisms, danger of death/children	17	78	112
Confirmations	4	—	173
Marriages	89	153	178
Communions	55,118	217,627	197,849
Extreme unctions	79	—	443
Formation of clergy and Sisters			
Chinese seminarians/major	3	7	5
Chinese seminarians/preparatory	32	40	60
Chinese novices	0	9	4
Chinese postulants	15	9	10
Educational			
Chinese teachers employed	29	34	39
Primary schools	6	11	30
Primary students: male/female	461m/131f	517m/157f	1,186m/262f
Secondary schools/students	0	0	1/90*
Vocational schools/stduents	0	0	0
Hostels/students	—	4	7/145
Medical			
Hospitals	0	0	0
Leprosaria/lepers	0	0	0
Dispensaries/treatments	1	0	0
Charitable			
Orphanages/older orphans	1	0	0
Homes for the aged/persons	0	1/15	0
Homes for the blind	0	0	0

Source: Compiled from the Maryknoll Archives. Data on social and relief works were too sparse to be tabulated.
*Includes 60 seminarians.

Maryknoll Mission Works

3. WUCHOW	1929	1939	1949
Pastoral			
Area in square miles	—	13,185	13,185
Population (approximate)	3,000,000	3,550,000	3,550,000
Stations or parishes	3	8	14
Outstations	46	181	30
Catholics	721	8,588	16,805
Catechumens	800	1,644	4,588
Baptisms of adults	304	1,028	2,380
Baptisms of children of Catholics	35	192	466
Baptisms, danger of death/adults	0	77	18
Baptisms, danger of death/children	7	236	100
Confirmations	—	467	1,029
Marriages	—	49	153
Communions	2,086	88,822	100,085
Extreme unctions	—	163	195
Formation of clergy and Sisters			
Chinese seminarians/major	0	3	5
Chinese seminarians/preparatory	7	60*	35*
Chinese novices	0	4	4
Chinese postulants	0	—	6
Educational			
Chinese teachers employed	13	9	57
Primary schools	13	2	10
Primary students: male/female	231m/11f	62m/33f	969m/347f
Secondary schools/students	0	0	0
Vocational schools/students	0	0	0
Hostels/students	1/10	1/22	0
Medical			
Hospitals	0	0	0
Leprosaria/lepers	0	0	0
Dispensaries/treatments	1/1,831	9/89,983	14/150,750
Charitable			
Orphanages	—	0	0
Homes for the aged	—	0	0
Homes for the blind	—	0	0

Source: Compiled from the Maryknoll Archives. Data on social and relief works were too sparse to be tablulated.
*Includes seminarians from Kweilin.

Maryknoll Mission Works

4. KWEILIN	1929*	1939	1949
Pastoral			
Area in square miles	—	12,500	12,500
Population (approximate)	—	2,500,000	2,500,000
Stations or parishes	—	5	9
Outstations	—	23	71
Catholics	—	1,562	7,595
Catechumens	—	—	2,000
Baptisms of adults	—	210	2,265
Baptisms of children of Catholics	—	10	226
Baptisms, danger of death/adults	—	0	13
Baptisms, danger of death/children	—	36	0
Confirmations	—	130	774
Marriages	—	12	77
Communions	—	11,910	105,746
Extreme unctions	—	8	—
Formation of clergy and Sisters			
Chinese seminarians/major	—	0	1
Chinese seminarians/preparatory	—	2	24
Chinese novices	—	0	6
Chinese postulants	—	18	12
Educational			
Chinese teachers employed	—	9	5
Primary schools	—	1	1
Primary students: male/female	—	19f&m	—
Secondary schools/students	—	0	0
Vocational schools/students	—	0	0
Hostels/students	—	0	0
Medical			
Hospitals	—	0	0
Leprosaria/lepers	—	0	0
Dispensaries/treatments	—	7/34,900	9/274,250
Charitable			
Orphanages/older orphans	—	0	1/165
Homes for the aged	—	0	0
Homes for the blind	—	0	0

Source: Compiled from the Maryknoll Archives. Data on social and relief works were too sparse to be tabulated.
*No report available. Kweilin was part of Nanning vicariate until 1932, then part of Wuchow prefecture until 1938.

Maryknoll Mission Works

5. FUSHUN	1929	1939	1949
Pastoral			
Area in square miles	—	37,500	37,500
Population (approximate)	—	5,950,000	5,500,000
Stations or parishes	10	21	20
Outstations	—	33	33
Catholics	4,226	9,460*	—
Catechumens	—	—	—
Baptisms of adults	65	694	—
Baptisms of children of Catholics	279	364	—
Baptisms, danger of death/adults	0	417	—
Baptisms, danger of death/children	116	1,249	—
Confirmations	—	377	—
Marriages	—	111	—
Communions	—	191,467	—
Extreme unctions	—	256	—
Formation of clergy and Sisters			
Chinese seminarians/major	0	1	8
Chinese seminarians/preparatory	29	51	30
Chinese novices	0	0	8
Chinese postulants	8	44	0
Educational			
Chinese teachers employed	—	36	—
Primary schools	5	11	—
Primary students: male/female	—	667m/316f	—
Secondary schools/students (male/female)	0	1/123m/17f	0
Vocational schools/students (male/female)	0	2/10m/25f	—
Hostels/students	0	0	0
Medical			
Hospitals	0	0	0
Leprosaria/lepers	0	0	0
Dispensaries/treatments	—	8/46,130	—
Charitable			
Orphanages/older orphans	—	9/99	—
Homes for the aged/persons	—	9/102	—
Homes for the blind	—	0	—

Source: Compiled from the Maryknoll Archives. Data on social and relief works were too sparse to be tablulated.
*The Catholic population was composed of 8,413 Chinese, 574 Japanese, 443 Korean and 30 people of other nationalities.

APPENDIX VI

Maryknoll Personnel in China

Maryknoll Fathers and Brothers Who Served in China

Ahern, Maurice F.
Ashness, Bertin
Barry, Cornelius F. (Bro. Benedict)
Barry, Martin F. (Bro.)
Batt, Norman P.
Bauer, George H.
Bauer, Thomas J.
Becka, Frederick J.
Bowers, Lawrence J. (Bro.)
Boyd, Anthony (Bro.)
Brack, Thomas J.
Brennan, Warren
Brennock, John L. (Bro. Gregory)
Bridge, Francis A.
Briggs, Arthur J.
Buckley, John F.
Burke, Martin J.
Burns, Constantine F.
Burns, J. Clarence
Bush, Harry M.
Buttino, James V.
Cairns, Robert J.
Callan, John B.
Chatigny, Donat W.
Churchill, Mark A.
Coffey, John
Comber, John W.
Conley, Lawrence A.
Connors, Francis J.
Cosgrove, Joseph G.
Cotta, Anthony
Cunneen, Arthur J.
Curran, John F.
Daley, Timothy J.
Daly, George M.
Daubert, Francis J.
Davis, J. Leo
Dempsey, Arthur F.
Dennis, Allan J.
Dietz, Frederick C.
Donaghy, Frederick A.
Donnelly, Francis T.
Donnelly, Jude (Bro.)
Donnelly, Patrick J.

Donovan, Gerard A.
Donovan, John F.
Donovan, Joseph S.
Donovan, Thomas R.
Dorsey, John (Bro.)
Downey, Richard E.
Downs, William J.
Drew, John J.
Driscoll, John J.
Drought, James M.
Duchesne, Paul J.
Duffy, Maurice J.
Early, Joseph E.
Eckstein, Cody
Edmonds, Stephen B.
Eggleston, William J.
Elliott, Herbert V.
Elwood, John J.
Escalante, Alonso
Farnen, Joseph L.
Fedders, Albert V.
Feeney, Maurice A.
Felsecker, Henry J.
Fisher, John A.
Fitzgerald, Frederick E.
Fitzgerald, James E.
Flanagan, George P.
Fletcher, William A.
Flick, George H.
Foley, J. Leo
Ford, Francis X.
Franco, Rocco P.
Gaiero, Michael R.
Gallagher, John D.
Gaspard, Raymond A.
Geselbracht, Howard C.
Gilbert, Sylvio R.
Gilleran, Thomas F.
Gilligan, George N.
Gilloegly, J. M.
Gilmartin, Gregory J.
Glass, Lloyd I.
Gleason, Maurice P.
Graser, John L.

Greene, Robert W.
Haggerty, George D.
Hahn, Joseph A.
Hanrahan, Raymond L.
Hater, Louis H.
Heemskerk, John C.
Henry, J. Michael
Herrity, Peter (Bro.)
Hessler, Donald L.
Hewitt, Leo W.
Hilbert, Charles P.
Hirst, Cyril
Hodgins, Anthony P.
Hogan, Michael J. (Bro.)
Hohlfeld, Raymond C.
Jacques, Armand J.
Jones, Leo J.
Joyce, John E.
Joyce, John H.
Karlovecius, Anthony J.
Kaschmitter, William A.
Keelan, Francis X.
Kelliher, Francis G.
Kennedy, Justin B.
Kennelly, Robert P.
Kent, Mark L.
Kiernan, Thomas V.
Killion, William R.
Kneuer, Rudolph G.
Knotek, Wenceslaus F.
Krock, George L.
Krumpelmann, Edward L.
Kupfer, William F.
Lacroix, Arthur C.
Lane, Raymond A.
Langley, Thomas S.
Lavin, Joseph P.
Le Prelle, Edward F.
Lenahan, Daniel F.
Lenahan, John F.
Lima, John E.
Lynch, P. Francis
MacRae, Francis
Madigan, Henry J.
Madison, Anthony L.
Malone, Patrick F.
Malone, Thomas J.
Manning, Edward J.
Manning, James T.
Manning, James V.
McCabe, Edwin J.
McCarthy, Leo F.
McCarthy, Michael J.

McClarnon, James P.
McCormack, Joseph P.
McCormick, James A.
McDermott, James E.
McDonald, Joseph A.
McGinn, John A.
McGinn, Joseph P.
McGurkin, Edward A.
McKeirnan, Michael J.
McKenna, William T.
McKernan, Hugh C. (Bro. Augustine)
McLaughlin, James E.
McLoughlin, John M.
McShane, Daniel L.
Meehan, Joseph A.
Mershon, Richard D.
Meyer, Bernard F.
Mihelko, John J.
Moffett, Edward
Moore, John
Morrissey, William J.
Mueth, Edward V.
Mulcahy, William P.
Mullen, Francis E.
Mulligan, Francis J.
Murphy, Albert J.
Murphy, Charles
Murphy, Francis G.
Murphy, J. Maynard
Murray, John H.
Murrett, John C.
Neary, William (Bro.)
North, William P.
Nugent, Irwin D.
O'Brien, William M.
O'Connell, Michael H.
O'Day, James F.
O'Donnell, James J.
O'Donnell, John R.
O'Mara, John B.
O'Melia, Thomas A.
O'Neill, Francis J.
O'Shea, William F.
Paschang, Adolph J.
Paulhus, Anthony J.
Petley, Bernard G. (Bro. Anselm)
Pheur, William F.
Pouliot, Francis J.
Price, Thomas F.
Pulaski, Joseph
Putnam, George N.
Quinn, Carroll I.
Quinn, Raymond

Quirk, Thomas N.
Rauschenbach, Otto A.
Reardon, Joseph M.
Rechsteiner, Aloysius J.
Regan, Joseph W.
Reilly, Peter A.
Revers, Thomas H. (Bro. Thaddeus)
Rhodes, Richard B.
Romaniello, John
Rottner, James J.
Ruppert, John E.
Ryan, Edmond L.
Ryan, Joseph P.
Schmidt, Charles J.
Schmidt, J. O.
Schrubbe, Joseph H.
Schulz, William F.
Sheridan, Robert E.
Sherman, Daniel J.
Siebert, Ralph
Slattery, Dennis J.
Smith, James F.
Smith, John F.
Sprinkle, R. Russell
Staubli, Albert (Bro.)
Sullivan, John J.
Sweeney, Joseph A.
Tackney, John
Taggart, Philip A.

Teat, John W.
Tennien, Mark A.
Tibesar, Leopold H.
Tierney, John J.
Toomey, Edmund A.
Toomey, John J.
Toomey, Patrick C.
Troesch, John C.
Trube, Howard D.
Van den Bogaard, Joseph E.
Vogel, Alphonse S.
Walker, Charles A.
Walsh, James E.
Walsh, John F.
Walsh, John J. (Kelly)
Walsh, Vincent W.
Walter, Leo J.
Weber, Arthur
Weis, Edward A.
Welch, Bernard T.
Welty, P.
Wempe, Theodore, F. (Bro. Francis)
White, Francis J.
Wieland, Bernard E.
Winkels, Robert H.
Wiseman, George
Wolotkiewicz, Constantine F.
Youker, Edward C.
Ziemba, Stanislaus T.

Lay Persons

Bagalawis, Dr. Artemio I.

Blaber, Dr. Harry

Maryknoll Sisters Who Served in China

Babione, Mary Jude
Basto, Candida Maria
Baumann, Marie Elise
Beauvais, Joan Miriam
Bedier, M. Juliana
Bourguignon, Marie de Lourdes
Boyle, Monica Marie
Brachtesende, Mary Amata
Bradley, M. Colombiere
Bradley, Kathleen (M. Jane Imelda)
Bresnahan, Mary Thomas
Brielmaier, M. Ann Carol
Burke, Mary Eva
Cain, Mary de Ricci
Carney, Veronica Marie
Carvalho, Cecilia Marie

Cavagnaro, Maria Ynez
Cazale, Agnes (Maria Petra)
Chau, Agnes
Chin, Rose
Clements, Anne (M. Famula)
Collins, M. Cornelia
Comber, M. Rita Clare
Conlon, Mary Matthew
Coughlin, Mary Patricia
Coupe, M. Eucharista
Coveny, Angela Marie
Cruickshank, Mary Cecilia
Cruise, Mary Dolores
Cunningham, Henrietta Marie
Cusack, M. Mercedes
Davis, Mary Francis

Debrecht, Rose Duchesne
De Felice, Rosemary
Devlin, Agnes (Gabriel Marie)
Dicks, Mary Jean
Diggins, Mary (M. John Karen)
Dillon, Mary Catherine
Doelger, Marie (M. Magdalen)
Doherty, Grace (M. Tarsicius)
Doherty, Rose (Rose Thomas)
Donnelly, M. St. Bernard
Duggan, Mary Peter
Evans, Ruth (M. Margaret Veronica)
Farrell, Ann Mary
Flagg, Virginia (Stella Marie)
Flanagan, Eleanor Marie
Flynn, M. Berchmans
Fogarty, Irene (M. Francis Jogues)
Foley, Mary Lawrence
Froehlich, Mary Barbara
Fuhr, M. Godfrey
Furey, M. Christella
Gallagher, Mary Gerard
Gallagher, Rose Bernadette
Gardner, Frances Marion
Geist, Marie Antoinette
Gonyou, Mary Fabiola
Grondin, Thérèse (Marie Marcelline)
Guerrieri, Antonia Maria
Guidera, M. Dominic
Hall, M. Frederica
Hanan, Rose Benigna
Hannigan, Julia (Mary Julia)
Harrington, Mary Raphael
Hatsumi, Marie Barat (Agatha)
Hayden, M. St. Teresa
Healy, Marie Antoine (Helen Marie)
Heaney, M. Dolorita
Herrgen, Mary Corita
Higgins, Agnes Virginia
Hock, Mary (Mary Augusta)
Hoffman, Mary Paulita
Hollfelder, Teresa (M. Claudia)
Jackson, M. Rachel
Jaramillo, Maria Corazon
Jung, Margaret Marie
Kane, Joseph Marie
Karlon, M. Madeline Sophie
Kelly, M. Dominic (St. Dominic)
Kettl, M. Rosalia
Killoran, Theresa (M. Mark)
Kim, M. Margaret
Kroeger, Louise (Miriam Louise)

Kuper, Mary Augustine
Lechthaler, Miriam Carmel
Lee, Catherine Mary
Leifels, Mary Rose
Leonard, M. Doretta
Ling, Joan
Logue, Mary Luke
Lucier, Jessie (M. Francisca)
Lynn, Virginia Marie
Mahoney, Joseph Marian
Makra, Mary Lelia
Maloney, Ann (Maura Magdalen)
Manning, Santa Maria
Marsland, M. Francis de Sales
Martin, Mary Louise (Regina Marie)
McGowan, Anne (George Marie)
McKenna, Mary de Lellis
McKenna, Mary Paul
McNally, M. Ignatia
Mersinger, Barbara (Rose Victor)
Meyer, M. Beatrice
Moffat, Mary Monica
Moore, Mary Gertrude
Moss, Anna Mary
Mug, Miriam Xavier
Murphy, Ellen Mary
Murphy, Frances (Maria Regis)
Nakamura, M. Sabina
Nakata, Rose Ann
O'Connor, Maura Bernadette
O'Hagan, M. Joan Catherine
O'Leary, Mary Angelica
O'Neill, M. Cecile
Oberle, Mary Dolorosa
Puls, M. Carolyn
Quinlan, Mary Liguori
Quinn, Mary Clement
Rafferty, Agnes Regina
Reardon, Mary Regina
Regan, Rita Marie
Reynolds, Mary Camillus
Riconda, Mary Ruth
Riehl, Moira
Rietz, Edith (Marion Cordis)
Rizzardi, Mary Gonzaga
Rost, Marie Corinne
Rowe, Catherine (M. Michael Elizabeth)
Rubner, Dorothy (Barbara Marie)
Ryan, Joan Marie
Schafers, Mary (M. Scholastica)
Schleininger, M. Roma (Frances)
Schmitt, Miriam

Seiler, Mary Andre
Sexton, M. St. Anne
Shalvey, Xavier Marie
Shanahan, Rosana (Miriam Jogues)
Shea, Kathleen Marie
Shea, Mary Gemma
Sheehan, Mary Coronata
Sheridan, Mary Imelda
Silva, Mary Reginald
Skehan, Rose Olive
Stapleton, Beatrice (Matthew Marie)
Steinbauer, Jean Theophane
Sticka, Pauline (M. Paul Therese)
Stitz, Herman Joseph
Sullivan, Mary Paula
Sullivan, Mary Teresa
Tam, Mary Bernadette
Thyne, Maria

Tibesar, Miriam Agnes
Tolan, Mary Eunice
Turner, Dominic Marie
Unitas, Anthony Marie
Urlacher, M. Magdalena
Veile, M. Luella
Venneman, Clara (Mary Albert)
Venneman, M. Espiritu
Vonfeldt, Mary Cordula
Wagner, M. Gloria
Walsh, M. Dorothy
Weber, Mary Rosalie
Wenzel, M. Richard
Werner, Celine Marie
Wilson, M. Edward Marmion
Wittman, M. Xaveria
Xavier, M. Chanel
Yamagishi, Maria Talitha
Yeung, Maria Teresa

Notes

Introduction

1. Today the Society also admits associate lay missioners. However, since they did not officially begin until June 1975, they do not fall within the scope of this study.

2. Between 1781 and 1783 Leonard Neale worked as a young priest in British Guinea. He later became the second archbishop of Baltimore.

3. From author's notes taken during the address given by Father James Hennesey, S.J., president of the American Catholic Historical Association, on the occasion of Maryknoll's 75th Anniversary Symposium in San Francisco, November 22, 1986.

4. FARC, Box—Miscellaneous, Constitutions, "General Rule of the Catholic Foreign Mission Society of America," I, 1-2.

5. SARC, Box—Constitutions, "Tentative Constitutions, circa 1917," I, 1.

6. Gerard A. Arbucle has made a very good analysis of the Church theology of evangelization from its beginning as a Judaic sect until the post-Vatican II era; see "Inculturation and Evangelization: Realism or Romanticism?" in *Missionaries, Anthropologists, and Cultural Change* (Williamsburg, VA: College of William and Mary, Studies in Third World Societies, 1985), pp. 171-214.

7. One of the promoters of this type of history has been French historian, Jean Delumeau, who, with the collaboration of 33 other historians, published a two-volume study in 1979 entitled *Histoire vécue du peuple chrétien* (Toulouse: Privat, 1979). See also Francesco Chiovaro, "History as Lived by the Christian People: Hypothesis for a New Methodic Approach to Christian History," in *Church History in an Ecumenical Perspective*, edited by Lucas Vischer, (Berne: Evangelische Arbeitsstelle Oekumene Schweiz, 1982).

8. *Ad Gentes*, Decree on the Missionary Activity of the Church, Vatican II, 1965: 2.

9. FARC, Box—Miscellaneous, China Research, Father John Cioppa, "Introduction," *The Society Response to China, 1983-1985* (Maryknoll, 1983), p. 1.

PART I—Maryknoll in Context

1. Walbert Bühlmann, *God's Chosen Peoples* (New York: Orbis Press, 1982), pp. 242–243, 247–248.

2. In historical studies, the Sacred Congregation for the Propagation of the Faith is often referred to in short as Propaganda or Propaganda Fide. After the Vatican II Council, however, its offical name was changed into the Sacred Congregation for the Evangelization of Peoples. It is a department of the Vatican administration charged with supervising the spread of the Catholic faith and legislating ecclesiastical affairs in mission territories. Its role in a particular country ends usually when the local Church is organized on a regular basis with dioceses and resident bishops. In the meanwhile, Propaganda divides mission territories into three types according to their stage of development. An independent mission is the lowest level of ecclesiastical organization. It is divided into various mission stations and is headed by a priest who does not have episcopal power. A prefecture apostolic is similar, except that it is headed by a prefect apostolic who is rarely a bishop but who has wide episcopal powers and acts as the direct representative of the pope. With an increased number of converts and a fuller development of Catholic life, the prefecture is erected into a vicariate apostolic. It is administered by a vicar apostolic who is usually a bishop also directly responsible to the pope. For all practical purposes, however, a vicariate is equivalent to a diocese.

3. *Ad Gentes*, Decree on the Missionary Activity of the Church, Vatican II, 1965: 4–6. *Evangelii Nuntiandi*, apostolic letter of Pope Paul VI on Evangelization in the World Today, 1975: 14–16.

Chapter 1—The Coming of Age of American Foreign Missioners

1. Robert Sheridan, ed., *Discourses of James Anthony Walsh, 1890–1936* (Maryknoll Fathers, 1981), "Walsh to the Novices Crusade Unit," March 4, 1924, p. 128.

2. *The Field Afar*, May 1907, p. 2.

3. Sister Jeanne Marie Lyons, *Maryknoll's First Lady* (New York: Dodd, Mead & Co., 1964), p. 34.

4. *Ibid.*, pp. 39–41. Mary Coleman, ed., *Discourses of Mother Mary Joseph Rogers, 1912–1955* (Maryknoll Sisters, 1982), IV, "Mother Mary Joseph, History Talk of January 1948," p. 1459.

5. Quoted in John C. Murrett, *Tar Heel Apostle* (New York: Longmans, Green, 1944), pp. 48–49.

6. *Discourses of James Anthony Walsh*, "Address to the Conference of Missionaries to Non-Catholics," Washington, 1904, p. 9.

7. J. G. Snead-Cox, *The Life of Cardinal Vaughan* (St. Louis, MO: B. Herder, 1912), I, p. 167–170, 179–180.

8. The original letter is in Baltimore Cathedral Archives. It was also reprinted by Monsignor John Tracy Ellis in *The Catholic Historical Review*, October 1944, pp. 290–298.

9. FARC, 18, Letters of Importance, 1901–1911, Letter of Cardinal Gibbons to the Archbishops of the United States, March 25, 1911, p. 232.

10. *Ibid.*, p. 231.

11. *The Field Afar*, June-July 1911, p. 2. See also further proof of confidence in

Maryknoll expressed by another letter of the American archbishops at their next meeting the following year: *The Field Afar*, June 1939, pp. 180–181.

12. *The Field Afar*, December 1912, p. 9. FARC, Box—Miscellaneous, Non-Maryknoll Societies, Folder—Mill Hill Fathers, 1905–1929, Letter of Father Henry to Father James A. Walsh, February 24, 1905. See also letter of September 8, 1905.

13. *The Sacred Heart Review*, August 19, 1905, p. 123. Letter of Vaughan to Gibbons, October 28, 1889, *The Catholic Historical Review*, October 1944, p. 298.

14. *Discourses of James Anthony Walsh*, "Address to the Conference of Missionaries to Non-Catholics," Washington, 1904, p. 9. Letter of Vaughan to Gibbons, pp. 292–293.

15. *Ibid.*

16. *Discourses of James Anthony Walsh*, "Walsh to the Novices Crusade Unit," March 4, 1924, p. 129.

17. *Annales de la Propagation de la Foi* (Lyon and Paris: Oeuvre de la Propagation de la Foi): Annual reports of contributions for the years 1833–1907. John V. Tracy, "The Catholic Church in the U.S. and Mission Work," *The Ecclesiastical Review*, July 1906, pp. 1–14. James A. Walsh, "The Society for the Propagation of the Faith in the Archdiocese of Boston," *The Ecclesiastical Review*, January 1904, pp. 9–19.

18. George Powers, *The Maryknoll Movement* (New York: Catholic Foreign Mission Society of America, 1926), pp. 28–30. *Annals of the Propagation of the Faith* (Baltimore: Society for the Propagation of the Faith), 1903, pp. 47–48.

19. *Annals of the Propagation of the Faith*, May-June 1903, May-June 1906: Receipts from diocesan contributions. FARC, Box—Miscellaneous, U.S. Offices and Agencies, Folder—Society for the Propagation of the Faith, 1900–1923: Annual Reports for the Archdiocese of Boston, 1901–1907. *The Field Afar*, February 1908, p. 11.

20. *Discourses of James Anthony Walsh*, "Address to the Second Washington Conference of the Catholic Missionary Union," June 1904, p. 3.

21. *Discourses of Mother Mary Joseph Rogers*, IV, "Mother Mary Joseph, History Talk of January 1948," p. 1418.

22. *Discourses of James Anthony Walsh*, "Address to the Second Washington Conference of the Catholic Missionary Union," June 1904, p. 8. FARC, Annual Reports for the Archdiocese of Boston, January 1907, p. 5.

23. *Discourses of James Anthony Walsh*, "Address to the Second Washington Conference of the Catholic Missionary Union," June 1904, p. 3.

24. FARC, Annual Reports for the Archdiocese of Boston, January 1906.

25. FARC, Box—Development-Promoters, Folder—The Missioner Promoter, "An Apology for Missions by Father James Anthony Walsh," 1906, p. 17. See also *The Field Afar*, January 1957, p. 26 and July-August 1961, pp. 40–41.

26. *Discourses of James Anthony Walsh*, March 2, 1927, p. 201.

27. FARC, 18, Letters of Importance, 1901–1940, Father James A. Walsh to Alexander Guasco, March 3, 1906, p. 80. See also *Discourses of James Anthony Walsh*, p. 131.

28. FARC, 18, Letters of Importance, 1901–1940, "First Meeting of the Catholic Foreign Mission Society at Boston," p. 91; see also p. 131. *The Field Afar*, June-July 1911, p. 2.

29. *The Field Afar*, January 1907, pp. 8, 11–12.

30. *The Field Afar*, March 1907, pp. 6, 12.

31. *The Field Afar*, January 1907, p. 1.

32. *The Field Afar*, January 1907, p. 2.

33. *The Field Afar*, March 1907, p. 3. Bishop Raymond Lane, third superior

general of the Maryknoll Fathers and Brothers, recalled that James A. Walsh continuously dissected and analyzed each issue of the most popular magazines such as *Life* and *Literary Digest* to keep *The Field Afar* abreast of the times, and was critical of the dull, poorly printed; and badly reproduced *Annals of the Propagation of the Faith*, in *The Early Days of Maryknoll* (New York: David McKay Co., 1951), pp. 36–37.

34. *Discourses of James Anthony Walsh*, March 2, 1927, p. 201. By 1927 there were at least 22 Catholic foreign mission magazines in the United States. A discussion of the growth and impact of *The Field Afar* may be found at the beginning of Chapter 8.

35. *Discourses of James Anthony Walsh*, March 2, 1927, p. 201. In his book *The Missionary Mind and American East Asia Policy, 1911–1915*, James Reed states that until 1915, Roman Catholics "had virtually no interest in foreign missions" and that "there were no—that is zero—American Catholic foreign missionaries" (p. 14). These assertions are incorrect. During the early years of the century, there already were some American Catholic missioners abroad. In China there were at least seven: two Sisters of Charity, Catherine Buschman and Joanna O'Connell; and five Franciscans, Bishop Athanasius Goette and Fathers Capistran Goette, Agnell Blesser, Juniper Doolin, and Sylvester Espelage; see *The Field Afar*, March 1907, p. 8; June 1908, p. 13; April-May 1910, p. 8. At the same time, a rapidly growing segment of the American population began to realize the duty of the American Catholic Church toward foreign missions. In the years 1907–1908 alone, three Catholic missionary magazines—*Catholic Missions*, *The Field Afar*, and *The Good Work*—were successfully launched. In 1911 the Catholic Foreign Mission Society of America was born. By 1915 the Catholics of the United States had become the world's largest financial supporters of the Society for the Propagation of the Faith.

36. In the parlance of the Catholic Church, Maryknoll priests are labeled "secular" priests and the Brothers "lay Brothers" to distinguish them from "religious" priests and Brothers. Religious, like the Jesuits, the Franciscans, the Dominicans, or the Vincentians, are members of organizations called orders or congregations, while the Maryknoll Fathers and Brothers belong to a foreign mission society. Among the many differences between religious organizations and foreign mission societies, one is important for understanding this study. A religious community is usually international in character; therefore, in each country where it does mission work, it attempts to establish a local Church and it also recruits local members. On the contrary, the Catholic Foreign Mission Society of America—the official name of the Maryknoll Fathers and Brothers' organization—recruits only in the United States. It always encourages Third World nationals to join the local clergy and sisterhoods of their native countries. In contrast to the Fathers and Brothers, the Maryknoll Sisters are religious women and therefore have many Third World members.

37. FARC, 18, Letters of Importance, 1901–1940, Petition of Fathers James A. Walsh and Thomas F. Price, June 1911, pp. 348–350; "Words of Cardinal Gotti on June 29, 1911," pp. 351–352. FARC, Box—Maryknoll Chronicle, June 19, 1911.

38. FARC, 18, Letters of Importance, 1901–1940, letter of Father Thomas Price to Cardinal Gibbons, July 5, 1911, p. 356. FARC, Box—Maryknoll Chronicle, July 1, 1911. Leonard McCabe, ed., *The Spiritual Legacy of the Co-Founders* (Maryknoll: 1950), I, p. 22.

39. *The Field Afar*, June-July 1911, pp. 2–3; March 1913, p. 2; January 1916, inside front cover; August 1918, pp. 130–131; October 1918, p. 173. See also October-November 1912, p. 6 and May 1923, p. 132.

40. Sister Jeanne Marie Lyons, p. 45.

41. *Discourses of Mother Mary Joseph Rogers*, IV, "History Talk of January 1948," pp. 1420, 1426.

42. *The Field Afar*, December 1911, p. 4; February-March 1912, p. 7; November 1913, p. 12.

43. *Discourses of Mother Mary Joseph Rogers*, II, June 29, 1922, p. 435. *The Field Afar*, June 1913, pp. 8, 13; July 1913, p. 12; November 1913, pp. 12–13.

44. *Discourses of Mother Mary Joseph Rogers*, IV, "More of Maryknoll History, January 17, 1948," pp. 1427–1428. *The Field Afar*, November 1913, p. 13.

45. *The Field Afar*, November 1913, pp. I-II.

46. SARC, Box—Diary Excerpts, October 15, 1914; see also October 15, 1913.

47. SARC, Mother Mary Joseph Collection, File 3, Folder 15, letter of Mother Mary Joseph to Father John T. McNicholas, January 24, 1916. *Discourses of Mother Mary Joseph Rogers*, II, June 29, 1922, p.435.

48. *The Field Afar*, March 1920, p. 51; May 1922, p. 153. See also article written by Mother Mary Joseph in *The Field Afar*, June 1931, pp. 176–178. For details on the development of the Maryknoll Sisters from secretaries to religious women, see Marie Therese Kennedy, "A Study of the Charism Operative in Mary Josephine Rogers (1882-1955), Foundress of the Maryknoll Sisters," Ph.D. dissertation, St. Louis University, 1980), pp. 44–70.

49. *The Field Afar*, April 1920, p. 76; July-August 1931, p. 219. *Discourses of Mother Mary Joseph Rogers*, III, "Retreat Conference," August 4, 1940, p. 1199; III, "Conference," September 28, 1940, pp. 1202–1204; IV, "The Maryknoll Ideal," 1950, pp. 1514–1515. *The Spiritual Legacy of the Co-Founders*, I, p. 23. See also chapters on "Admission and Dismissal" in Maryknoll Constitutions in FARC, Box—Miscellaneous, Constitutions and SARC, Box—Constitutions.

50. TS10, Sister Mary Paul McKenna, pp. 7–8; TS24, Sister Grace Doherty, p. 16; TF32, Father Leo McCarthy, p. 2.

51. TF03, Father Thomas Kiernan, pp. 4–8; TF39, Father Joseph Early, p. 6; TF58, Father Thomas Brack, pp. 34–35; TF04, Father Francis Daubert, p. 10; TS63, Sister Ignatia McNally, p. 6; TS78, Sister Doretta Leonard, p. 7; TS24, Sister Grace Doherty, p. 16; TS21, Sister Mary Louise Martin, p. 9.

52. See, for instance, *The Field Afar*, January 1914, pp. 11–12.

53. SARC, Mother Mary Joseph Rogers Collection, File 3, Folder 15, Letter of Father James A. Walsh to Father John T. McNicholas, March 5, 1919.

54. *Discourses of Mother Mary Joseph Rogers*, II, June 29, 1922, pp. 435–436.

55. *The Field Afar*, December 1912, pp. 5–6. See also February 1913, p. 13 and March 1913, p. 11. Except for morning duties and manual labor, the daily schedule of the Maryknoll seminarians and Brother-candidates was similar to that followed in other Catholic seminaries of the United States. With a few minor variations over the years, it was as follows:

Daily Horarium
5:30 Rise
5:55 Prime (Morning Prayers), Meditation, Angelus
6:30 Mass
7:20 Breakfast
7:40 Morning Duties
8:00 Free Time
8:15 Tidy Rooms
8:25 Study
9:25–10:15 Class or Study

10:20–11:10 Class or Study
11:15–12:05 Class or Study
12:00 Remission (i.e., free silent time)
12:20 Particular Examen, Hymn, Angelus
12:30 Dinner
1:10 Manual Labor
2:10 Recreation
3:05 End of Recreation
3:30 Class or Study
4:25 Class or Study
5:15 Rosary
5:30 Conference or Spiritual Reading
6:00 Supper, Free time
7:15 Study
9:20 Compline (Night Prayers)
10:00 Lights Out

Because the Seminary was viewed as a house of prayer and study, silence was observed everywhere in the building and on the property, except during recreation, free time, and manual labor. (FARC, Box 27, Maryknoll Houses—Center Rector, Folders, Schedules 1920–1949.)

Similarly, with a few minor variations over the years, the daily schedule at the Sisters' novitiate was as follows:

Sisters' Horarium
5:30 Morning Prayers
6:00 Meditation
6:30 Mass
7:20 Breakfast, Morning Duties
9:00–12:00 Assigned Work (office, kitchen, sewing room)
12:00 Particular Examen, Noon Prayers, Lunch, Free Time (including a spiritual reading and a visit to the Blessed Sacrament)
2:00–5:00 Assigned Work/Classes
5:00 Vespers, Rosary
5:30 Supper
6:00–7:00 Recreation
7:00–9:00 Compline, Salve Regina (and other prayers), Free Time
9:00 Profound Silence

The Sisters observed silence during the daytime except for a work break in the morning and afternoon, lunch, and the period after supper. They also practiced perpetual adoration in front of the Blessed Sacrament with each person assigned a half-hour period. (Oral interview with Sister Virginia Thérèse Johnson on January 22, 1987.)

56. James E. Walsh, *Maryknoll Spiritual Directory* (New York: Field Afar Press, 1947), p. 27.

57. TF 58, Father Thomas Brack, p. 6.

58. TF38, Father Robert Greene, p. 40; TF82, Father William Eggleston, p. 3; TF 57, Father Lloyd Glass, pp. 29–30; TF 58, Father Thomas Brack, p. 7; TF49, Father Donat Chatigny, p. 4; TS97, Sister Santa Maria Manning, p. 9; TS89, Sister Amata Brachtesende, p. 3; TS80, Sister Veronica Marie Carney, p. 7; TS101, Sister Antonia Maria Guerrieri, p. 8; TS63, Sister Ignatia McNally, p. 6.

59. TF05, Father John Driscoll, p. 8. See also TS23, Sister Rose Duchesne Debrecht, p. 8; TF04, Father Francis Daubert, p. 10.

60. TS21, Sister Mary Louise Martin, p. 9.

61. TF01, Father Robert Sheridan, p. 9.

62. *Discourses of James Anthony Walsh*, July 1, 1928, p. 269; June 29, 1928, p. 266; June 29, 1927, p. 230.

63. *Discourses of James Anthony Walsh*, July 1, 1928, pp. 269–270.

64. FARC, Box—James A. Walsh, "Notes Written by Father General 1936," p. 2. In 1950 Father Leonard McCabe rearranged this 54-page document into chapters and supplemented it with other writings by James A. Walsh. This compilation forms the first part of the book called *The Spiritual Legacy of the Co-Founders*, see pp. 2, 20, 23.

65. *Ibid.*, p. 28.

66. "Description of a Missioner" was first written in 1937 and has been reprinted many times. See entire text in *Maryknoll Spiritual Directory*, pp. 249–266. The actual quote is on p. 261.

67. *Maryknoll Spiritual Directory*, p. 55.

68. FARC, Box—James E. Walsh Letters, letter of Bishop James E. Walsh to Council Members, June 19, 1939.

69. *Maryknoll Spiritual Directory*, pp. 72–73.

70. James E. Walsh, "Christmas Letter of 1942," *Zeal for Your House* (Huntington, IN.: Our Sunday Visitor Press, 1976), pp. 86–88, 91.

71. *Maryknoll Spiritual Directory*, p. 156.

72. Nine conferences by Mother Mary Joseph with a major emphasis on the Maryknoll spirit have been preserved; see *Discourses of Mother Mary Joseph Rogers*, II, October 2, 1932, pp. 627–631; August 4, 1930, pp. 882–886; III, February 14, 1936, p. 1117; March 15, 1940, p. 1184; August 4, 1940, pp. 1197–1200; December 9, 1943, p. 1313; IV, May 7, 1951, pp. 1574–1578; circa 1929, pp. 1699–1702; no date, p. 1703.

73. *Discourses of Mother Mary Joseph Rogers*, IV, "The Maryknoll Sisters' Spirit," circa 1929, p. 1699; II, "Dominican Spirit—Maryknoll Spirit," October 2, 1932, pp. 6–7; "Maryknoll Spirit," August 4, 1930, p. 882; III, "Retreat Conference," August 4, 1940, p. 1197.

74. *Discourses of Mother Mary Joseph Rogers*, IV, "Talk Given to Senior Novices," May 7, 1951, p. 1515; III, "Conference for the New Year," December 9, 1943, p. 1313.

75. *Discourses of Mother Mary Joseph Rogers*, III, "Chapter Talk," March 15, 1940, p. 1184; see also II, "Maryknoll Spirit," August 4, 1930, p. 882.

76. *Discourses of Mother Mary Joseph Rogers*, II, "Maryknoll Spirit," August 4, 1930, p. 883; III, "Retreat Conference," August 4, 1940, p. 1198.

77. *Discourses of Mother Mary Joseph Rogers*, IV, "The Maryknoll Sisters' Spirit," circa 1929, p. 1700.

78. *Discourses of Mother Mary Joseph Rogers*, II, "Maryknoll Spirit," August 4, 1930, p. 882. See other instances of the quotation in I, p. 366; II, p. 627, III, pp. 1087, 1197, 1201; IV, p. 1532, 1702, 1703.

79. *Discourses of Mother Mary Joseph Rogers*, II, "Maryknoll Spirit," August 4, 1930, p. 883. See also III, "Retreat Conference," August 4, 1940, pp. 1197–1198.

80. *Discourses of Mother Mary Joseph Rogers*, III, "Retreat Conference," August 4, 1940, p. 1199. See also II, "Dominican Spirit—Maryknoll Spirit," October 2, 1932, p. 628; III, "Conference," September 28, 1940, pp. 1203–1204; IV, "The Maryknoll Ideal," 1950, pp. 1514–1515; "Our Vocation," (no date), p. 1707.

81. *Discourses of Mother Mary Joseph Rogers*, II, "Maryknoll Spirit," August

4, 1930, pp. 885. See also III, "Retreat Conference," August 4, 1940, p. 1199.

82. *Discourses of Mother Mary Joseph Rogers*, IV, "Talk Given to Senior Novices," May 7, 1951, p. 1574.

Chapter 2—Maryknoll in the Chinese Environment

1. Evariste R. Huc, *Le Christianisme en Chine, en Tartarie, et au Thibet* (Paris: Gaume Frères, 1857), pp. 42–51, 67–70, 106–107). Pasquale M. D'Elia, *Fonti Ricciane* (Rome: La Libreria Della State, 1942), I, p. 190–199.

2. Adrien Launay, *Histoire des Missions de Chine: Mission du Kouang-Tong* (Paris: Téqui, 1917), pp. 7, 10, 15–16, 18, 28, 35, 37, 149. *Lettres édifiantes et curieuses des missions étrangères* (Toulouse: N. E. Sens and A. Gaude, 1811), Vol. 17, pp. 72, 240, 324–327.

3. Briefly stated, the controversy had to do with the translation into Chinese of the term for God and the permission given by the Jesuits to Chinese Christians to continue the performance of ancestral and Confucian honors in accordance with the customs of their country. For more on Rome's condemnation of the Jesuit experiment, and the later developments, see George Minamiki, *The Chinese Rites Controversy* (Chicago: Loyola University Press, 1985).

4. *Annales de la Propagation de la Foi* (Lyon: J. B. Pélagand and Co., 1825–1890), 20 (1840), pp. 405; 22 (1850), pp. 454–455; 30 (1858), pp. 343–355. Kenneth Scott Latourette, *A History of Christian Missions in China* (London: The Macmillan Co., 1929), pp. 158–166.

5. Launay, *Kouang-Tong*, p. 123, 151, 191.

6. Launay, *Kouang-Tong*, pp. 7, 10, 13, 25, 37, 152, 156, 191, 206. Manuel Teixeira, *Macau e sua diocese no ano dos centenarios de fundacao e restauracao* (Macao: Tipographia do Organado Salesiano, 1956–1963), Vol. 3, p. 94.

7. Lü Shih-ch'iang, *Chung-kuo kuan shen fan chiao ti yuan yin, 1860–874* (The cause of anti-missionary attitudes among the Chinese officialdom and gentry) (Taipei: Chung Yang Yen Chiu Yuan, 1966), pp. 90–102. Louis Wei Tsing-sing, *La Politique missionnaire de la France en Chine, 1842–856* (Paris: Nouvelles Editions Latines, 1960), pp. 446–469, 528–555.

8. Edmund S. Wehrle, *Britain, China, and the Antimissionary Riots of 1891–1900* (Minneapolis: University of Minnesota Press, 1966), pp. 200–209.

9. Latourette, pp. 548–549.

10. Louis Wei Tsing-sing, *Le Saint-Siège et la Chine de Pie XI à nos jours* (Paris: Editions A. Allais, 1968), pp. 83–85, 91–98.

11. Launay, *Kouang-Tong*, p. 3. M. M. Planchet, *Les Missions de Chine et du Japon* (Peking: Imprimerie des Lazaristes, 1919), 1919, pp. 262–267.

12. See the extensive collection of letters between James A. Walsh and non-Maryknollers in the Maryknoll Fathers Archives (FARC).

13. James A. Walsh, *Observations in the Orient* (Ossining, NY: The Catholic Foreign Mission Society of America, 1919), p. 184.

14. For instance, letters of Bishop Dennis J. Dougherty of Jaro, Philippine Islands, September 29, 1911; Bishop Jules Chatron of Osaka, Japan, September 11, 1911; Bishop Mutel of Seoul, Korea, May 1912 in FARC, 18, Letters of Importance, 1901–1940. See also FARC, Box—James A. Walsh, George Power's manuscript of biography of James A. Walsh (1938), p. 235.

15. FARC, 18, Letters of Importance, 1911–1940, letters of Bishop Albert

Faveau to Walsh, February 24, 1912; Bishop Jean-Marie Mérel to Walsh, September 12, 1912.

16. FARC, 45-1, letters of Bishop de Guébriant to J. A. Walsh, October 22, 1914; and de Guébriant to Father Gavan Duffy, September 25, 1915.

17. George C. Powers, *The Maryknoll Movement* (New York: Catholic Foreign Mission Society of America, 1926), p. 159. *The Field Afar*, September 1915, p. 139; December 1915, pp. 188–189.

18. FARC, 18, Letters of Importance, 1911–1940, Father James A. Walsh to Bishops of China, October 30, 1915.

19. FARC, Box—Miscellaneous C, Prospective Missions, 1913–1920, letters of Father Kennelly to Father James A. Walsh , May 2, 1914 and October 8, 1914; Father James A. Walsh to Father Kennelly, January 17, 1916. See also FARC, 18, for instance, answers of Bishops Francis Geurts of Eastern Tchely, December 5, 1915; Stanislaus Jarlin of Peking, January 8, 1916; and Paul Marie Reynaud of Ningpo, November 17, 1916.

20. FARC, 18, Letters of Importance, letter of Bishop Paul Dumond to Walsh, December 5, 1915; FARC, Box—Miscellaneous C, Bishop Prosper Paris to Father James A. Walsh, January 10, 1916; FARC, Box—Miscellaneous N, Non-Maryknoll Societies, letter of Father James A. Walsh to Père Robert, April 24, 1916.

21. FARC, 45-01, letter of Sister Mary Angeline to Father James A. Walsh (January or February), 1916; FARC, 29-01, letters of Sister Mary Angeline to Father James A. Walsh, June 13, 1916 and July 4, 1917. See also *The Field Afar*, December 1916, pp. 177–178.

22. FARC, 18, Letters of Importance, letter of Bishop Adolphe Rayssac to Father Gavan Duffy, March 15, 1916.

23. FARC, Box—Maryknoll Houses, Rome, Correspondence Society Propaganda Fide, 1911–1933, letter of James A. Walsh to Cardinal Van Rossum, June 4, 1918. *The Field Afar*, February 1917, p. 17; September 1917, p. 141; March 1918, p. 45; July 1918, p. 111.

24. Robert Sheridan, ed., *Discourses of James Anthony Walsh, 1890–936* (Maryknoll Fathers, 1981), p. 48.

25. FARC, Box—Miscellaneous N, letter of Père Robert to Father James A. Walsh, April 12, 1912; December 12, 1915; March 18, 1916, March 1, 1917. *The Field Afar*, April-May, 1912, pp. 8–9.

26. FARC, Box—Miscellaneous N, letter of Father James A. Walsh to Pere Robert, April 24, 1916.

27. FARC, 45-01, letter of Father James A. Walsh to Bishop de Guébriant, August 16, 1916; and de Guébriant to Walsh, October 12, 1916.

28. FARC, Box—Miscellaneous N, letter of Père Robert to Father James A. Walsh, October 18, 1916.

29. FARC, Box—Miscellaneous N, Robert to Walsh, February 4, 1917.

30. James A. Walsh, *Observations*, p. 184.

31. Ibid.

32. Ibid., p. 196.

33. James A. Walsh. *Observations*, p. 196. See also *Les Missions de Chine (1919)*, pp. 260, 263.

34. FARC, 45-01, letter of Bishop de Guébriant to Father James A. Walsh, July 3, 1918. These districts, also known as subprefectures or counties, were Watlam, Tinpak, Sunwui, Loting, Maoming (Kochow), Wanfow, Sunning (Toishan), Yeungkong, Sunyi, and Chikkai.

35. The 14 districts of Wuchow were Tsangwu (Wuchow), Waitsap, Tengyun, Pingnam, Shumkai, Jungyun, Paklow, Luchwan, Pokpak, Yaoshan, Sintu, Chaop-

ing, Mengshan, and Watlam. Later, two more districts, Kweiping and Hingip, were also given up by Nanning vicariate. The 16 districts of the Kweilin prefecture were Kweilin, Chuanhsien, Kwanyang, Yangso, Hingan, Lungsheng, Lingchwan, Ining, Kuhwa, Yungfu, Laipo, Pinglo, Kungcheng, Fuchwan, Chungshan, and Hohsien.

36. The nine districts of the Kaying vicariate were Meihsien, Taipu, Pingyun, Hingning, Lungchun, Chiuling, Hoping, Linping, and Ngwa.

37. These 21 districts were Fushun, Penki, Hailung, Tsengyuan, Hingking, Liuho, Kinchwan, Hweinan, Antung, Chwangho, Siuyen, Fengcheng, Kwantien, Hwanjen, Tunghwa, Tsian, Linkiang, Fusung, Changpai, Kwantung, and the territory of the South Manchuria Railway.

38. FARC, Box 33-Folder 2; Box 37-Folder 2; Box 38-Folder 2. In November 1921, Father James A. Walsh and Bishop Stanislas Jarlin signed a preliminary agreement which would have detached five districts from the vicariate of Peking to form a Maryknoll mission territory. The idea was opposed, however, by the superior general of the Vincentians in Paris. See FARC, Box—Foreign Dioceses, Folder Peking, 1921–1922.

39. TF56, Father James McLaughlin, p. 22.

40. SARC, unpublished manuscript by Sister Mary Imelda Sheridan, "A Brief History of the South China Region," (1959), p. 5. TS10, Sister Mary Paul McKenna, pp. 15–16.

41. "A Brief History," p. 6.

42. *Ibid.*, p. 7. See also, TS10, Sister Mary Paul McKenna, pp. 15–16; TS32, Sister Mary Paul McKenna, pp. 11–16; TS82, Sister Mary Rosalie Weber, pp. 2–5, 12–14; *The Field Afar*, February 1930, p. 40.

43. TS74, Sister Kathleen Shea, pp. 2–6, 18–20; TS16, Sister Herman Joseph Stitz, pp. 1, 7–8, 11, 14; TS102, Sister Herman Joseph Stitz, pp. 16–18.

44. *Collectanea Commissionis Synodalis* (Peking), May 1928, p. 2. *China Missionary*, June 1949, pp. 607–614. *The Field Afar*, December 1932, p. 333; January 1933, p. 12. FARC, William A. Kaschmitter, *The Story of a Hobo* (Maryknoll Fathers, n.d.), pp. 78–82. TF50, Father William Kaschmitter, pp. 5, 25–27. In 1948, *Lumen News Service* became *Hua Ming News Service*.

45. FARC, 3-10, Sancian Diary, April 15, 1941.

46. Robert Sheridan, *Bishop James E. Walsh as I Knew Him* (New York: Maryknoll Publications, 1981), pp. 71–78.

47. *China Missionary*, May 1948, pp. 250–251; October 1948, p. 575 and June-July 1951, p. 527. TF31, Father Paul Duchesne, pp. 5–8. U.N.R.R.A. aid stopped when the organization was dismantled in the fall of 1947.

48. See the interviews of these two priests: TF02 and TF30.

49. FARC, 45-03, 45-04, 45-05.

50. See, for instance, a short account in Albert J. Nevins, *The Meaning of Maryknoll* (New York: McMullen Books, 1954), pp. 275–282.

51. FARC, 1-01, Yeungkong Diary, Father Ford, July 19, 1922.

52. SARC, 43-10, Kaying City, August 18, 1937; October 5–6, 1937.

53. FARC, 42-04, Yungfu Diary, October-November 1946.

54. FARC, 26-02, Chongpu Diary, Father Maurice Duffy, November 26, 1939.

55. FARC, 42-04, Yungfu Diary, January-February 1947; Box 3-Folder 4, Kaochow Diary, January 7, 1921.

56. FARC, 4-01, Yeungkong Diary, February 5, 1919. SARC, 42-04, Laohukow Diary, January 8–27, 1945: Very cold wave which even froze papayas. See also SARC, 42-03, Laohukow, January 7–10, 1943.

57. FARC, 23-12, Pingnam Diary, Father Thomas Kiernan, July 19, 1930.

58. FARC, 3-04, Kaochow Diary, January 7, 1920.

59. FARC, 23-05, Pingnam Diary, October 1946.

60. FARC, 23-12, Pingnam Diary, May-June 1927; 26-01, Chiuling Diary, March 9, 1941; 42-04, Yungfu Diary, October-November 1946; 23-05, Pingnam Diary, January 22, 1947. TF40, Father James Smith, p. 7. SARC, 52-09, Maryknoll Convent, Kweilin/Laipo, November 6, 1947.

61. FARC, 23-10, Pingnam Dairy, September 21, 1932; see also FARC 26-02, Chongpu Diary, July 18-29, 1939; and SARC, 43-06, Siaoloc Diary, July 20, 1934.

62. FARC, 23-03, "Kwangsi Bamboo Leaves," December 1928-April 1929; 23-05, Paksha Diary, April 1946. For famine in Kongmoon territory, see SARC, 49-09, Loting Diary, November 30-December 6, 1936.

63. FARC, 25-15, Linkiang Diary, November 1940; SARC, 44-03, Dairen Convent Diary, February 12, 1941; SARC, 54-12, Tunghwa Diary, January 20, 1941; SARC, 55-13, Fushun Honan Convent Diary, February 3, 1947.

64. FARC, 25-02, Chakow Diary, July 30, 1931; SARC, 54-05, Dairen Maryknoll Academy Diary, July 4, 1941.

65. FARC, 25-16, Erhpatan Diary, June 22, 1927.

66. FARC, 4-01, Yeungkong Chronicle, Mary 25, 1919.

67. FARC, 8-04, Sancian Diary, March 27, 1934. See also FARC, 26-02, Chongpu Diary, February 19, 1928 and November 30, 1939.

68. FARC, 4-01, Yeungkong Diary, August 4-September 1921.

69. TS18, Sister Mary Paul McKenna, p. 2.

70. FARC, 4-01, Yeungkong Diary, May 10, 1921. See also 26-01, Chiuling Diary, March 9, 1941.

71. Ibid., Yeungkong Diary.

72. FARC, "The Manchu-Knoller," Vol. 2, No. 8, August 1927.

73. SARC, 54-03, Dairen, Japanese Parish Diary, September 16, 1939; 54-05, Dairen Maryknoll Academy Diary, September 22, 1939; 55-02, Dairen Convent Diary, September 27, 1939; October 6, 1937; September 13, 1939. SARC, unpublished manuscript by Sister Mary Eunice Tolan, "Manchuria, Book 3," n.d., pp. 104-105.

74. TS18, Sister Mary Paul McKenna, p. 2; TS11, Sister Mary Paul McKenna, pp. 2-3; Tolan, "Manchuria, Book 3," pp. 105-106.

Part II—The Evangelization of Non-Christians

1. Mark 16:15.

2. Pope Paul VI, Evangelii Nuntiandi, Apostolic Exhortation on Evangelization in the Modern World (Washington, DC: U.S. Catholic Conference, 1976, Nos. 27-28 and 34).

3. FARC, Box—Miscellaneous, Constitutions, "General Rule of the Catholic Foreign Mission Society of America," I, 1; SARC, Box—Constitutions, "Tentative Constitutions, Circa 1917," I, 1.

4. William Frazier, "Guidelines for a New Theology of Mission," World Mission, Vol. 18, No. 4, Winter 1967-1968, p. 18.

5. In the early post-apostolic era, Justin Martyr, Origen, Clement of Alexandria held the view that God's saving purpose was not confined to his covenant with the Hebrews and spoke of the Divine Word "seminally" present and active in the world even before the coming of Christ. Clement went even further and refused to accept the opinion that paganism was an invention of the devil. His positive approach, however, was soon overshadowed by an emphasis on the reality of sin

and of the role of the Church in salvation; see Henry Chadwick, *Early Christian Thought and the Classical Tradition* (New York: Oxford University Press, 1966), pp. 2-31, 40-45; Walbert Bühlmann, *God's Chosen People* (New York: Orbis Press, 1982), p. 95.

6. *Acta Apostolicae Sedis* (Rome: Typis Polyglottis Vaticanis), Vol. II, December 1, 1919, p. 446.

7. Joseph Schmidlin's *Katholische Missionlehre im Grundriss*, first published in 1919, was printed in English in 1931 under the title, *Catholic Mission Theory* (Techny, IL: Techny Mission Press, 1931); see in particular pp. 42-48, 78-79, 260-265.

8. Kenneth Scott Latourette, *A History of Christian Missions in China* (New York: Macmillan, 1929), pp. 557-559, 729. Joseph Schmidlin, *Catholic Mission History* (Techny, IL: Techny Mission Press, 1933), p. 617. Jacques Leclercq, *Thunder in the Distance: The Life of Père Lebbe* (New York: Sheed and Ward, 1958), pp. 115, 146-147. *Maryknoll—The Field Afar*, May 1946, pp. 44-45.

9. FARC, 21-01, Diary of First Departure Group, 1918, p. 43

10. FARC, 10-10, "Notes to Father Ford" by Father Auguste Gauthier, December 22, 1920, pp. 2-3.

11. James E. Walsh, *Mission Manual of the Vicariate of Kongmoon* (Hong Kong: Nazareth Press, 1937), pp. 92-119. TS76, Sister Rose Bernadette Gallagher, pp. 2-3, 8-10. TF46, Bishop Edward McGurkin, p. 34.

Chapter 3—The Direct Apostolate

1. FARC, 10-14, letter of Father Francis Ford to Maryknoll, April 11, 1921, p. 5.

2. Father Bernard Meyer, *Mission Methods of the Prefecture Apostolic of Wuchow* (n.p., 1936), p. 23.

3. *The Field Afar*, January 1921, p. 6; September 1922, p. 266; January 1924, p. 4.

4. FARC, 10-10, "Notes to Father Ford," p. 1; FARC, 4-01, Yeungkong Diary, December 11, 1919.

5. TC27, Bishop John Baptist Wu, pp. 21-22; see also Adrien Launay, *Histoire des Missions de Chine, Missions du Kouang-Tong* (Paris: Téqui, 1917).

6. Father Bernard Meyer, *Mission Methods*, p. 23; FARC, 10-10, "Notes to Father Ford," pp. 1-3; FARC, 4-01, Yeungkong Diary, January 22, 1919.

7. FARC, 4-01, Yeungkong Diary, December 11, 1919; Father Bernard Meyer, *Mission Methods*, p. 23.

8. Bernard Arens, *Handbuch der Katholischen Missionen* (Freiburg im Breisgau: Herder, 1920), p. 162-163. J. M. Planchet, *Les Missions de Chine et du Japon* (Peking: Imprimerie des Lazaristes, 1916), p. 28; see also 1917, p. 301. *Digest of the Synodal Commission* (Peking: December 1929), p. 957.

9. FARC, 12-46, letter of Father Thomas Price to Father James A. Walsh, March 12, 1919.

10. FARC, Box—Father Bernard Meyer (Articles), letter of Father Bernard Meyer to Bishop Austin Dowling, December 16, 1918; FARC, 10-12, letter of Father Bernard Meyer to Father James A. Walsh, May 30, 1919; FARC, 12-25, letter of Father Bernard Meyer to Father James A. Walsh, August 3, 1919.

11. FARC, 10-12, letter of Father Bernard Meyer to Father James A. Walsh, March 25, 1919; FARC, 12-46, letter of Father Thomas Price to Father James A. Walsh, March 12, 1919.

12. FARC, 5–10, Tungchen Diary, September 7–21, 1919; FARC, 39–02, letter of Father Bernard Meyer to Father James A. Walsh, April 11, 1922.

13. FARC, 3–04, Kochow Diary, October 1920-April 1921; FARC, 39–02, letter of Father Bernard Meyer to Father James A. Walsh, March 12, 1922. *The Field Afar*, October 1930, pp. 282–283; July-August, 1936, p. 219.

14. *The Field Afar*, October 1930, p. 283; see also May 1920, p. 108 and July-August 1936, p. 219.

15. FARC, 3–04, Kochow Diary, February 10 and March 5, 1920; *The Field Afar*, June 1921, p. 159.

16. FARC, 10–12, letter of Father Bernard Meyer to Father James A. Walsh, March 25, 1919; FARC, 39–03, letter of Father Bernard Meyer to Father James A. Walsh, March 11, 1923; FARC, 39–02, letter of Father Bernard Meyer to Father James A. Walsh, March 12, 1922; *The Field Afar*, May 1918, p. 73.

17. FARC, Box—Father Bernard Meyer (Articles), letter of Father Bernard Meyer to Father James A. Walsh, April 4, 1923; FARC, 39–02, letters of Father Bernard Meyer to Father James A. Walsh, March 12, April 11 and December 10, 1922. FARC, 5–10, Tungchen Diary, February 17 and June 6, 1922: Father Bernard Meyer was particularly impressed by the type of school run by Vincentian Father Cyprien Aroud at Wenchow in the vicariate of Ningpo; in his writing, he often mentioned it as the ideal to pursue.

18. *The Field Afar*, November 1923, p. 312; FARC, 3–04, Kochow Diary, December 11–31, 1922; FARC, 8–06, Kochow Diary, July 30, 1923; FARC, 12–25, "Questions for Written Exams."

19. FARC, 8–06, Kochow Diary, June-July 1924.

20. FARC, 39–03, letter of Father Bernard Meyer to Father James A. Walsh, March 11, 1923.

21. FARC, 23–10, letter of George Wiseman to Maryknollers, October 26, 1923; FARC, 13–16, reports of Pingnam, September 1, 1924; letter of Father George Wiseman to Father James A. Walsh, October 22, 1924. *The Field Afar*, March 1924, p. 74.

22. *The Field Afar*, May 1924, p. 146.

23. *The Field Afar*, May 1923, p. 134; May 1924, p. 147. FARC, Box—Father Bernard Meyer (Articles), Father Bernard Meyer's report of December 1922.

24. *The Field Afar*, May 1920, p. 108; January 1927, p. 32; January 1929, p. 31.

25. FARC, 23–06, letter of Father Bernard Meyer to Father James A. Walsh, October 11, 1930; FARC, 18—Letters of Importance, "Instruction of Fall 1929 Regarding Missioners' Allowance," pp. 663–664 and letter of Father James A. Walsh to Missioners of August 30, 1930, p. 669. FARC, Box—First General Chapter, 1929, "Appendix to Minutes of the Chapter: Viatique." TF03, Father Thomas Kiernan, p. 107; TF58, Father Thomas Brack, p. 47.

26. Conversation of Father Robert Sheridan with the author, February 20, 1986.

27. FARC, 39–06, letter of Father Bernard Meyer to Father James A. Walsh, January 11, 1928; see also letter of April 21, 1928.

28. FARC, 33–01, report of James E. Walsh, August 10, 1929, p. 7.

29. FARC, Box—Second General Chapter, 1936, "Figures Taken From Copies of Annual Reports to Rome, 1924–1935." FARC, 35–02, letter of Father Francis X. Ford to Father James A. Walsh, July 17, 1932; FARC, 37–01, Kaying Financial Report, 1937. FARC, 33–02, Kongmoon Financial Report, 1937. FARC, 39–05, letter of Father Joseph Ryan to Secretarial General of the Society for the Propagation of the Faith, July 17, 1933. SARC, Box—Sister Mary Paulita Hoffman's Collection of Talks by Bishop Ford, Foundation Day Report on Kaying Mission, June 29, 1939.

30. FARC, 32–07, letters of Bishop James E. Walsh to Father James Drought, August 24 and September 1, 1935.

31. FARC, 35–02, Monsignor Francis X. Ford's Confidential Letter to Kaying Missioners on the Budget, 1933. FARC, 32–06, letter of Father James A. Walsh to Bishop James E. Walsh, January 15, 1932. FARC, 33–02, Kongmoon Report of 1932, p. 11. FARC, 35–02, letter of Father James A. Walsh to Monsignor Francis X. Ford, January 13, 1932; Francis X. Ford to Father James A. Walsh, April 13, 1932; letters of Monsignor Francis X. Ford to his clergy, April and July-August 1933. FARC, 35–03, "The Past Year at Kaying," August 19, 1934. FARC, 39–07, letter of Father James A. Walsh to Monsignor Bernard Meyer, January 15, 1932. TF03, Father Thomas Kiernan, p. 107. The Field Afar, April 1932, May 1932, back covers.

32. FARC, 33–01, Kongmoon Report of August 10, 1929. FARC, 38–08, Wuchow Report of June 1935. FARC, 23–03, "Kwangsi Bamboo Leaves," November-December 1931. FARC, 23–10, Pingnam Diary, March 8–30, 1932. FARC, 35–03, "The Past Year at Kaying," August 1934. FARC, 37–01, Kaying Report of June 1934. FARC, 16–01, Fushun Center Diary, December 1, 1932. The Field Afar, June 1930, p. 169; November 1931, p. 311; February 1932, pp. 35–36.

33. Monsignor Bernard Meyer, "Launch out into the Deep," Digest of Synodal Commission, June 1937, p. 573. The Field Afar, January 1936, p. 9. See also FARC, Box—Kiernan (Articles), "Catechists, Catechumens and Catechumenates," 1934, p. 6. FARC, 23–10, March 8 and 30, 1932: The two-year course was not established before 1935 and had to be shortened during the Sino-Japanese War.

34. "Launch out into the Deep," pp. 574–580. FARC, 23–01, Wuchow Bulletin, November 1, 1931. FARC, 23–10, Pingnam Diary, April 24–30, 1932; March 1, 1933. FARC, 39–06, letter of Father Bernard Meyer to Father James A. Walsh, April 21, 1928.

35. TF45, Father Russell Sprinkle, pp. 8–9.

36. FARC, 4–01, Yeungkong Diary, February 3, 1920; January 26, 1921; FARC, 12–25, letter of Father Bernard Meyer to Father James A. Walsh, August 3, 1919; FARC, 39–02, letter of Father Bernard Meyer to Father James A. Walsh, March 12, 1922. TF03, Father Thomas Kiernan, p. 54. The Field Afar, November 1920, pp. 248–250.

37. The Field Afar, December 1932, p. 356.

38. Sister Thérèse (Marcelline) Grondin, Sisters Carry the Gospel (Maryknoll: Maryknoll Publications, 1956), pp. 75, 110. SARC, Box—Sister Mary Paulita Hoffman's Collection of Talks by Bishop Ford, "Sisters and Local Women Catechists," Kaying Conference of 1939. See also TS79, Sister Julia Hannigan, p. 29; TS44, Sister Rosalia Kettl, pp. 25–26; TS80, Sister Veronica Marie Carney, p. 31; TF52, Father Edward Weis, pp. 15–17; TF20, Father Sylvio Gilbert, p. 72.

39. FARC, 8–07, "The Toishan Torch," July 1934. For more on the institution of Chinese Virgins, see Echos de la Rue du Bac (Paris), July 1982, pp. 217–221 and Collectanea Commissionis Synodalis, July-August 1941, pp. 642–649. See also TC38, Sister Leatitia Lee, pp. 5–8; TC21, Sister Catherine Mary Lee, p. 10; TC01, Father Paul Pang, pp. 8–9.

40. FARC, 23–03, "Kwangsi Bamboo Leaves," May-June 1931. FARC, 38–07, report of Maryknoll in Wuchow, July 1, 1931-July 1, 1932. SARC, 51–01, Pingnam Convent Diary, September 16, 1935.

41. FARC, Box—Kiernan (Articles), "Catechists, Catechumens and Catechumenates," 1934, p. 6. See also The Field Afar, January 1935, p. 20.

42. FARC, 38–07, Wuchow Reports of June 1931, June 1933 and June 1936.

43. The Field Afar, April 1934, p. 107; July-August 1938, p. 201; February 1950, p. 34. See also "Launch out into the Deep," p. 555; The Field Afar, January 1936,

pp. 8-11; February 1936, pp. 40-43.

45. Shumkai Chronicle, p. 5.

46. FARC, 23-05, Shumkai Chronicle, June-December 1947, pp. 4-5.

47. Monsignor Bernard Meyer, *Mission Methods*, pp. 27-32. See also *The Field Afar*, April 1934, p. 107.

48. Father Mark Tennien, "My Man Friday," *Maryknoll—The Field Afar*, May 1948, p. 15.

49. FARC, 23-05, Shumkai Chronicle, June-December 1947, p. 4.

50. TS22, Sister Dorothy Rubner, p. 21.

51. Father Mark Tennien, "D-Day in Shumkai," *Maryknoll—The Field Afar*, March 1949, pp. 1-5; "The Miracle of Blue Cloud County," January 1948, p. 3.

52. FARC, 23-05, Shumkai Chronicle, June-December 1947, p. 7.

53. Shumkai Chronicle p. 2.

54. TS22, Sister Dorothy Rubner, pp. 24-25, 28.

55. "Launch out into the Deep," pp. 17-24. FARC, 23-10, Pingnam Diary, March 1, 1943, p. 3. FARC, 23-05, Shumkai Chronicle, June-December 1947, pp. 7-8. Monsignor Bernard Meyer, *Mission Methods*, pp. 31-33.

56. SARC, Box—Sister Mary Paulita Hoffman's Collection of Talks by Bishop Ford, "July 1940 Annual Mission Conferences to the Maryknoll Sisters—Visit to Pagan Homes," p. 18.

57. By contrast, Protestant missionary women in China had already engaged in direct evangelization for a long time; it seems, however, that Ford's idea developed independently.

58. SARC, Box—Sister Mary Paulita Hoffman's Collection of talks by Bishop Ford, "1941 Foundation Day Conferences to Maryknoll Fathers—A Mission Policy," p. 23.

59. SARC, Box—Sister Mary Paulita Hoffman's Collection, "1941 Foundation Day Conferences to Maryknoll Fathers—The Ideal Missioner," pp. 17-18.

60. SARC, Box—Sister Mary Paulita Hoffman's Collection, "1941 Kaying Sisters Mission Conference—The type of Sister for Direct Evangelization." pp. 1, 4.

61. SARC, Box—Sister Mary Paulita Hoffman's Collection, "1941 Foundation Day Conferenced to Maryknoll Fathers—Why Stand Ye All the Day Idle?—Applied to Catechists," pp. 6-7. SARC, Box—Bishop Ford's Conferences, "The Catechist," Local Conference of March 25, 1949, pp. 1-4.

62. "Why Stand Ye All the Day Idle?," p. 5.

63. Letter of Father Francis X. Ford to Father James A. Walsh, February 20, 1924, quoted in *Sisters Carry the Gospel*, p. 18. SARC, Regional Correspondence ChP20F1A, letter of Sister Mary Paul McKenna to Mother Mary Joseph, May 5, 1922.

64. Letter of Monsignor Francis X. Ford to Father James A. Walsh, March 13, 1924, quoted in *Sisters Carry the Gospel*, p. 17.

65. SARC, 48-03, Yeungkong Convent Diary, March 15, 1924.

66. SARC, 48-03, Yeungkong Convent Diary, March 17-22, 1924.

67. SARC, Regional Correspondence, CHP21F2A, letter of Sister Mary Paul McKenna to Mother Mary Joseph, April 5, 1934 and letter of Monsignor Francis X. Ford to Sister Mary Paul McKenna, March 17, 1934.

68. SARC, Regional Correspondence, CHP21F2A, letter of Mother Mary Joseph to Monsignor Francis X. Ford, February 1, 1935.

69. TS46, Sister Louise Kroeger, p. 1-3.

70. SARC, Regional Correspondence, CHP21F2A, letter of Mother Mary Joseph to Monsignor Francis X. Ford, September 10, 1936.

71. SARC, Sister Mary Imelda Sheridan, "A Brief History of the South China Region, 1921-1958," quoting a letter of Peter Cardinal Fumasoni-Biondi to Mother

Mary Joseph, Rome, March 30, 1939, pp. 30–31.

72. SARC, Box—Sister Mary Paulita Hoffman's Collection, June 29, 1939, "Foundation Day Report on Kaying Missions," p. 5.

73. Since she came out of China in September 1951, Sister Rosalia Kettl has continued to be a herald of the direct apostolate both in Hong Kong and on the island of Taiwan.

74. SARC, Box—Sister Mary Paulita Hoffman's Collection of Talks by Bishop Ford, "July 1940 Annual Mission Conferences to the Maryknoll Sisters—Direct Evangelization." SARC, 7-04, letter of Bishop Francis X. Ford to Sister Mary Imelda Sheridan, October 10, 1942. SARC, Box—Ford's Conferences, "The Sisters' Activities According to the Kaying Synodal Decree, July 1943," p. 72

75. TS58, Sister Madeline Sophie Karlon, p. 25.

76. SARC, 42-02, Pettochai Convent Diary, January 1-June 30, 1939.

77. TS51, Sister Mary Paulita Hoffman, pp. 16–18.

78. TS58, Sister Madeline Sophie Karlon, p. 71.

79. The Divine Office is the official prayer of the Roman Catholic Church for the different periods of the day such as matins and compline.

80. TS44, Sister Rosalia Kettl, p. 19. See also TS30, Sister Jean Theophane Steinbauer, p. 5.

81. SARC, Box—Constitutions, "Operating Constitutions of Maryknoll Sisters of St. Dominic, May 1985," p. 14.

82. Sister Thérèse Grondin, "Contemplative Prayer and Mission Activity," in "Maryknoll—Taiwan, Mission Forum," special issue of September 1982. See also TS29, Sister Thérèse Grondin, p. 23.

83. TF53, Father Dennis Slattery, pp. 26–27.

84. TS44, Sister Rosalia Kettl, pp. 19–20. See also SARC, 42-11, Pettochai Convent Diary, January 26, 1939.

85. SARC, Box—Sister Mary Paulita Hoffman's Collection, "July 1940 Annual Mission Conferences to the Maryknoll Sisters—Catechumenates at the Mission," pp. 1, 71. See also Summer Rally of July 1938, "Catechumenates for Women," p. 18.

86. TS99, Sister Frances Murphy, pp. 22–23. See also FARC, 35-02, Letter of Monsignor Francis X. Ford to Bishop James A. Walsh, July 20, 1934 and SARC, Box—Sister Mary Paulita Hoffman's Collection of Talks by Bishop Ford, "July 1940 Annual Mission Conferences to the Maryknoll Sisters—Catechumenates at the Mission," pp. 4–5.

87. TC18, Mrs. Cheuk Yee-chiu, pp. 15–16. See also TC42, Mr. Liu Hon-ching, p. 17.

88. TC40, Peter Chum, p. 10.

89. SARC, 42-10, Pettochai Convent Diary, December 31, 1939; SARC, 42-11, Pettochai Convent Diary, January 5, 1940; SARC, 42-12, Pettochai Convent Diary, May 8 and June 8, 1941. Sister M. Rosalia Kettl, "An Appeal for the Direct Apostolate" in *China Missionary Bulletin*, February 1952, p. 93.

90. SARC, Box—Sister Mary Paulita Hoffman's Collection, "July 1940 Annual Mission Conferences to the Maryknoll Sisters—Catechumenates in Villages," p. 10.

91. TS51, Sister Mary Paulita Hoffman, p. 19. Grondin, *Sisters Carry the Gospel*, p. 102.

92. TS30, Sister Jean Theophane Steinbauer, pp. 3–4.

93. TS51, Sister Mary Paulita Hoffman, pp. 19–20.

94. Grondin, *Sisters Carry the Gospel*, p. 103.

95. TF08, Father Allan Dennis, p. 68.

96. TF53, Father Dennis Slattery, pp. 30–31. See also FARC, 37-03, Letter of Bishop Francis X. Ford to Bishop James E. Walsh, April 10, 1946 and TS65, Sister

Irene Fogarty, p. 20.

97. Grondin, *Sisters Carry the Gospel*, pp. 95, 102.

98. Grondin, *Sisters Carry the Gospel*, p. 110. SARC, Box—Sister Mary Paulita Hoffman's Collection, "1939 Kaying Conference—Sisters and Local Women Catechists."

99. TS86, Sister Agnes Cazale, p. 22. See also TS47, Sister Mary Diggins, p. 20–21.

100. TS76, Sister Rose Bernadette Gallagher, p. 2.

101. TS22, Sister Dorothy Rubner, pp. 3–4. TS39, Sister Barbara Mersinger, pp. 7, 31, 36.

102. FARC, 42-20, Kweilin Prefecture Mission Directive, 1946, pp. 4–5; 42-06, letters of Monsignor John Romaniello to Bishop Raymond Lane, February 12 and March 22, 1947.

103. TS33, Sister Cornelia Collins, p. 4.

104. TS101, Sister Antonia Maria Guerrieri, p. 22.

105. TS33, Sister Cornelia Collins, pp. 5–6. See also TS39, Sister Barbara Mersinger, pp. 35–37.

106. TC06, Sister Joan Ling, pp. 14–15. See also TC43, Sister Agnes Chau, p. 15; TS39, Sister Barbara Mersinger, p. 65; and *Maryknoll—The Field Afar*, February 1948, pp. 30–31.

107. TC43, Sister Agnes Chau, pp. 15–16.

108. TS39, Sister Barbara Mersinger, p. 26.

109. TS80, Sister Veronica Marie Carney, pp. 14, 24–25; TS53, Sister Celine Marie Werner, pp. 4, 7.

110. TF46, Bishop Edward McGurkin, p. 32. See also TF52, Father Edward Weis, p. 31; TF20, Father Sylvio Gilbert, p. 34; TF21, Father Francis Mullen, pp. 29–30.

111. TS93, Sister Ann Carol Brielmaier, pp. 49–50. See also TC07, Sister Joseph Lam, pp. 21–22.

112. TS68, Sister Colombiere Bradley, pp. 11, 13; TS43, Sister Candida Maria Basto, pp. 12–16.

113. TS43, Sister Candida Maria Basto, p. 26.

114. These underlying principles are often reiterated in *The Field Afar*; see, for instance, September 1932, p. 236; January 1936, p.40; February 1936, p. 40; December 1941, p. 15.

115. TC15, Dr. David Tse, p. 9.

116. TC04, Father Thomas Lau, p. 2; TC06, Sister Joan Ling, p. 4.

117. TF11, Father Joseph Van Den Bogaard, p. 11. See also TF12, Father Francis Murphy, p. 8; TC04, Father Thomas Lau, pp. 7, 11–12; TC39, Father Peter Ma, p. 12; TC40, Mr. Peter Chum, pp. 7–8.

118. The most important papal writings of that period on Catholic Action are Pius X's encyclical *Il Fermo Proposito* of 1905, and Pius XI's encyclicals *Ubi Arcano* of December 23, 1923 and *Non Abbiamo Bisogno* of June 29, 1931. For texts, see Claudia Carlen, *The Papal Encyclicals, 1903-1939* (Wilmington, NC: McGrath Publishing Company, 1981), pp. 37–44, 225–240, 445–458. See also "Letter of Pius XI to Cardinal Bertram, Archbishop of Breslau, of November 13, 1928 on the Origin of Catholic Action" in Odile M. Liebard, *Official Catholic Teachings: Clergy and Laity* (Wilmington, NC: McGrath Publishing Company, 1978), pp. 30–34.

119. First Council of China, Decree 573, quoted by Bishop Francis X. Ford in SARC, Box—Ford's Conferences, "The Sisters' Activities According to the Kaying Synodal Decree, July 1943," p. 72.

120. Father Bernard Meyer, *Like to Leaven* (Hong Kong: Catholic Truth Society, 1950), p. 205. Outstanding Catholic Action groups in China in the late 1930s were those organized by Father Vincent Lebbe in Ankuo and Mr. Lo Pa-hong in Shanghai.

121. SARC, Box—Ford, Summer Rally of July 1938, p. 39. *Maryknoll—The Field Afar*, January 1940, p. 18.

122. TS44, Sister Rosalia Kettl, p. 15. See also TS65, Sister Irene Fogarty, pp. 24, 49; TS45, Sister Rita Marie Regan, p. 9; TS51, Sister Mary Paulita Hoffman, p. 34; TS80, Sister Veronica Marie Carney, p. 28; TF55, Father Henry Felsecker, pp. 12-13. SARC, 55-11, Fushun-Honan Convent Diary, July 1941.

123. FARC, Box—Kiernan (Articles), "It Can Be Done," September 25, 1940. FARC, Box—Meyer, Letter of Monsignor Bernard Meyer to Bishop James E. Walsh, April 29, 1941. See also SARC, Box—Ford, Summer Rally of July 1941, p. 9.

124. TF20, Father Sylvio Gilbert, p. 61.

125. FARC, 25-01, Letter of Father Sylvio Gilbert to Maryknoll Seminary, November 20, 1929. TF20, Father Sylvio Gilbert, pp. 27-28.

126. *The Field Afar*, September 1935, p. 245. TF46, Bishop Edward McGurkin, p. 35; TF20, Father Sylvio Gilbert, p. 28.

127. TF20, Father Sylvio Gilbert, p. 61. FARC, 25-23, Tunghwa Diary, July 1935.

128. TF20, Father Sylvio Gilbert, p. 61. FARC, 25-22, Tunghwa Diary, December-March 1932, p. 2. FARC, 25-22, Letter of Father Sylvio Gilbert to Father James A. Walsh, August 6, 1933. FARC, 47-05, Conference Bulletin, January 22, 1934. FARC, 47-11, Annual Report, Fushun, 1937-1938.

129. TF20, Father Sylvio Gilbert, p. 70.

130. Ibid., p. 71.

131. FARC, 25-09, Fushun Center Diary, March-April 1939.

132. FARC, Box—Gilbert, "Christian Doctrine Sunday," March 27, 1939, pp. 2-3.

133. Ibid. See also *Maryknoll—The Field Afar*, January 1940, pp. 18-19.

134. FARC, 25-09, Fushun Center Diary, January 1939. FARC, Box—Gilbert, "Christian Doctrine Sunday," March 27, 1939, pp. 3-4. FARC, 47-11, Annual Reports, Fushun, 1938-1941.

135. *The Official Handbook of the Legion of Mary* (Louisville, KY: Publishers Printing Company, 1952), pp. 1-2.

136. TS65, Sister Irene Fogarty, p. 49; TS71, Sister Pauline Sticka, p. 19; TS99, Sister Frances Murphy, p. 25; TS51, Sister Mary Paulita Hoffman, p. 34. See also Meyer, *Like to Leaven*, p. 204.

137. Quoted in *China Missionary Bulletin*, December 1951, "The Scapegoat: The Legion of Mary," p. 827. See also TF83, Father Edwin McCabe, p. 7; TF60, Father Russell Sprinkle, p. 62. Father Robert Greene, *Calvary in China* (New York: J. P. Putnam Sons, 1953), p. 163.

138. TF83, Father Edwin McCabe, p. 10.

139. *Calvary in China*, pp. 22-23.

140. *Ibid.*, pp. 44-45.

141. *The Field Afar*, June 1935, p. 177.

142. FARC, 33-01, 33-02, 37-01, 37-02, 38-07, 42-09: Mission Reports.

143. *China Missionary Bulletin*, September 1950, p. 732.

144. Monsignor Bernard Meyer, "The Lay Vocation," *China Missionary Bulletin*, June 1949, p. 644. TF10, Father Albert Fedders, p. 20.

145. Meyer, *Like to Leaven*, p. vi.

146. TS45, Sister Rita Marie Regan, pp. 9-10.

147. Letter of Léon-Joseph Cardinal Suenens to Sister Marcelline (Sister Thérèse Grondin), June 28, 1957, quoted in Sister Mary Ann Schintz, "An Investigation of the Modernization Role of the Maryknoll Sisters in China," unpublished dissertation, University of Wisconsin-Madison, 1978, p. 132. See also the English translation of Suenen's book, *The Gospel to Every Creature* (Westminster, MD: The Newman Press, 1957), pp. 83–112.

148. Gregorio Petro Cardinal Agagianian, "New Horizons on the Missionary Apostolate," *Christ to the World,* 13:1, 1968, pp. 63–64.

Chapter 4—Corporal Works of Mercy

1. TF28, Father Peter Reilly, p. 4. See also TF15, Father James Smith, pp. 3 and 7.

2. Bishop James E. Walsh, *Mission Manual of the Vicariate of Kongmoon* (Hong Kong: Nazareth Press, 1937), pp. 96, 109–110.

3. TF49, Father Donat Chatigny, p. 13.

4. SARC, Box—Maryknoll Sisters, Mercy Hospital, Account by Sister Herman Joseph Stitz, p. 16. See also *Maryknoll—The Field Afar*, December 1941, p. 15.

5. FARC, Box—Maryknoll Chronicle, p. 227. *The Field Afar*, April 1914, p. 14; February 1915, p. 29; May 1921, p. 124; February 1922, p. 38; June 1924, p. 188.

6. TF15, Father James Smith, p. 6; TF53, Father Dennis Slattery, p. 4; TF16, Father Howard Trube, p. 4; TF03, Father Thomas Kiernan, pp. 5–6; TS94, Sister Mary Gerard Gallagher, p. 13; TS16, Sister Herman Joseph Stitz, p. 5.

7. *The Field Afar*, February 1923, p. 60.

8. FARC, Box—James A. Walsh, Miscellaneous, Folder—Catholic Medical Mission Bureau, Letter of Father James A. Walsh to Dr. Flagg, July 30, 1914.

9. *The Field Afar*, March 1914, p. 4; May 1914, p. III; July 1914, p. 13; August 1914, p. 13; December 1914, p. 15; *Maryknoll*, May 1966, pp. 17–19. See also FARC, Box—James A. Walsh, Miscellaneous, Folder—Catholic Medical Mission Bureau, pamphlet published by Catholic Medical Mission Society (1916).

10. *The Field Afar*, October 1923, pp. 291, 294; January 1924, p. 12. See also SARC, 48–23, letter to Mother Mary Joseph, September 3, 1923.

11. FARC, 14–01, letters of Brother John Dorsey to Maryknoll, May 10, 1923; March 3 and April 10, 1923. *The Field Afar*, October 1923, p. 291.

12. *The Field Afar*, June 1922, p. 184.

13. See interviews of Maryknoll Sister-nurses: TS02, Sister Monica Marie Boyle; TS37, Sister Angela Marie Coveny; TS12, Sister Agnes Regina Rafferty; TS66, Sister Magdalena Urlacher; TS50, Sister Mary DeLellis McKenna; TS17, Sister Mary Paula Sullivan; TS16, Sister Herman Joseph Stitz. *The Field Afar*, November 1923, p. 324.

14. FARC, 8–05, letter of Father Robert Cairns to Bishop James A. Walsh, April 30, 1937.

15. TF21, Father Francis Mullen, p. 46; TF68, Father Edward Mueth, p. 24; TF12, Father Francis Murphy, p. 8; TS65, Sister Irene Fogarty, p. 15. FARC, 37–02, Kaying Reports, August 19, 1945 and November 1, 1949.

16. TF31, Father Paul Duchesne, pp. 30–31.

17. TS33, Sister Cornelia Collins, pp. 15–16.

18. TS37, Sister Angela Marie Coveny, p. 4.

19. TF26, Father Bernard Wieland, pp. 9–10; TF38, Father Robert Greene,

p. 3; TF77, Father Cyril Hirst, p. 15; TF15, Father James Smith, p. 7; TF25, Father Raymond Gaspard, p. 18; TF78, Father Joseph McGinn, p. 11; TS36, Sister Francis de Sales Marsland, pp. 6–7; TS02, Sister Monica Marie Boyle, pp. 7, 13–14; TS26, Sister Mary Angelica O'Leary, pp. 7, 15, 19.

20. TS02, Sister Monica Marie Boyle, p. 16.

21. TS63, Sister Ignatia McNally, p. 11. See also TS65, Sister Irene Fogarty, p. 14; TF72, Father Timothy Daley, p. 14.

22. TS02, Sister Monica Marie Boyle, p. 16.

23. TF12, Father Francis Murphy, p. 18; TS41, Sister Rita Clare Comber, p. 7.

24. TS37, Sister Angela Marie Coveny, p. 4.

25. TS41, Sister Rita Clare Comber, p. 8.

26. TC04, Father Thomas Lau, pp. 7, 11, 43; TC43, Sister Agnes Chau, p. 36; TC06, Sister Joan Ling, p. 6.

27. TS68, Sister Colombiere Bradley, pp. 4–5; TS02, Sister Monica Marie Boyle, p. 16; TS56, Sister Eucharista Coupe, p. 22; TC38, Sister Laetitia Lee, p. 41. SARC, 48–15, Yeungkong Convent Diary, August 4, 7, 1940; 48–22, Yeungkong Convent Diary, August 20, 1950. SARC, 49–03, Loting Convent Diary, June 16, July 9, 1926; 49–08, Loting Convent Diary, June 10, 1935; 49–09, Loting Convent Diary, October 16, December 23, 1936. FARC, 4–01, Mission Diary of Father Bernard Meyer, November 30, 1918.

28. SARC, 48–18, "The Maryknoll Sisters' First Mission in the Interior of South China," January 1944, p. 1.

29. FARC, 4–01, Yeungkong Chronicle, January 6, 14, 1919.

30. FARC, 4–01, Yeungkong Diary, April 10, 1921. *The Field Afar*, July 1920, p. 154.

31. FARC, 4–02, letter of Father Francis X. Ford to Father James A. Walsh, January 24, 1923.

32. *Ibid.*

33. TC26, Sister Philomena Chan, p. 14. Father Robert Sheridan, *Thieves of Paradise in China* (New York: Maryknoll Publications, 1933), p. 24. SARC, 48–02, Yeungkong Convent Diary, February 27, March 13, 1923; 48–09, Yeungkong Convent Diary, December 1, 1934; 48–11, Yeungkong Convent Diary, September 30, 1936; 48–23, "Methods of Our Orphanages in Yeungkong and Loting," 1938, pp. 1–2. SARC, 49–13, Loting Convent Diary, June 30, 1940. *The Field Afar*, April 1937, p. 104.

34. FARC, 4–02, Yeungkong Diary, November 3, 1922.

35. *The Field Afar*, May 1924, p. 141. See also Statistics for December 1924 in SARC, 48–03, Yeungkong Convent Diary.

36. SARC, 49–01, Loting Convent Diary, September 1924; 49–04, Loting Convent Diary, June 4–12, 1927; August 9–11, 1927. FARC, 3–02, Letter of Father Otto Rauschenbach to Father James A. Walsh, June 7, 1927. James E. Walsh, *Father McShane of Maryknoll* (New York: Catholic Foreign Mission Society of America, 1932), pp. 214–221.

37. SARC, 49–05, Loting Convent Diary, September 8–15, 1932. FARC, 9–10, letter of Father Philip Taggart to Father James A. Walsh, April 25, 1929; letter of Father James McDermott to Father James A. Walsh, December 8, 1929.

38. *The Field Afar*, September 1934, p. 252. SARC, 49–06, Loting Convent Diary, October 31, 1933. SARC, Box—Chronicles, South China, 1931–1949, Folder 4.

39. SARC, 48–06, Yeungkong Convent Diary, March 26, 1931; 48–23, "Methods of Our Orphanages in Yeungkong and Loting," 1938, p. 2. SARC, 49–03, Loting Convent Diary, June 15, 1926. *The Field Afar*, November 1931, p. 311; April 1933,

p. 108. TS11, Sister Mary Paul McKenna, p. 5.

40. SARC, 49-10, Loting Convent Diary, June 11-16, July 19, August 1-4, 1937. SARC, 48-15, August 27-29, 1940; 48-16, July 14, 1941. TS56, Sister Eucharista Coupe, pp. 26-27; TS43, Sister Candida Maria Basto, pp. 25-26. *Maryknoll—The Field Afar*, June 1948, p. 5.

41. *China Missionary Bulletin*, May 1951, p. 442.

42. TS43, Sister Candida Maria Basto, p. 27.

43. SARC, 48-18, "The Maryknoll Sisters' First Mission in the Interior of South China," p. 12. *Maryknoll—The Field Afar*, July-August 1942, p. 33; July-August 1944, p. 22.

44. Father Henry Madigan, "Catholic Orphanages in Communist China," *China Missionary Bulletin*, June-July 1952, p. 449. Sheridan, *Thieves of Paradise*, p. 18.

45. SARC, Box—Chronicles, South China, 1931-1949, Folder 2, Loting Chronicles; Folder 4, Yeungkong Chronicles. SARC, 49-06, Loting Convent Diary, July 31, August 31, October 31, 1933; 49-11, Loting Convent Diary, September 30, October 31, November 30, 1938. SARC, 48-10, Yeungkong Convent Diary, September 21, 1935; 48-15, Yeungkong Convent Diary, November 30, December 31, 1940.

46. SARC, 48-09, Yeungkong Convent Diary, December 23, 1934; 48-10, Yeungkong Convent Diary, September 20, 1935; 48-12, Yeungkong Convent Diary, August 20-December 15, 1937; 48-18, Yeungkong Convent Diary, June 1944. TS43, Sister Candida Maria Basto, pp. 2-3.

47. SARC, 49-01, Loting Convent Diary, December 8, 1924. See also 49-11, Loting Convent Diary, November 7, 1938; SARC, 48-05, Yeungkong Convent Diary, September 12, 1930; 48-09, Yeungkong Convent Diary, November 15, 1934; TS68, Sister Colombiere Bradley, p. 6.

48. SARC, 49-02, Loting Convent Diary, May 25, June 1, June 18, 1925; 49-03, Loting Convent Diary, April 8, 27, 1926. Sheridan, *Thieves of Paradise*, p. 28.

49. SARC, 49-04, Loting Convent Diary, February 16-20, 1927.

50. SARC, 48-05, Yeungkong Convent Diary, September 13-26, 1930. TS02, Sister Monica Marie Boyle, p. 2; TS56, Sister Eucharista Coupe, pp. 21, 25.

51. SARC, 49-03, Loting Convent Diary, May 7, August 20, December 9, 1926; 49-10, Loting Convent Diary, January 17, July 29, 1937.

52. TS68, Sister Colombiere Bradley, pp. 17, 38. SARC, 49-03, Loting Convent Diary, October 24, 1926. *Maryknoll—The Field Afar*, June 1948, pp. 3-4.

53. TC38, Sister Laetitia Lee, p. 43. SARC, 49-03, Loting Convent Diary, May 16, 1926.

54. SARC, 49-03, Loting Convent Diary, September 2, 1926.

55. SARC, 49-03, Loting Convent Diary, April 11, 1926.

56. TC23, Sister Maureen Au, pp. 2-3.

57. SARC, 49-03, Loting Convent Diary, April 11-25, August 20-26, September 1-6, October 1-6, 1926; 49-10, Loting Convent Diary, August 8, 1937.

58. SARC, 49-03, Loting Convent Diary, August 28-September 1, September 7, 1926; 49-10, Loting Convent Diary, June 11-August 4, 1937. *The Field Afar*, May 1938, p. 136.

59. SARC, War Years, File 2, Drawer 3, Iron Curtain Diaries and Accounts, Sister Mary Dolorosa Oberle, "Memories of Yeungkong."

60. *China Missionary Bulletin*, June-July 1952, p. 451. TC44, Sister Rose Chan, p. 51.

61. FARC, 44-07, press release, Father Maurice Feeney, "Two Years under the Chinese Reds," pp. 2-3.

62. SARC, War Years, File 2, Drawer 3, Iron Curtain Diaries and Accounts, Chinese clippings of *Wen Hui Pao*, late December, 1951, no exact date. *China Missionary Bulletin*, May 1951, p. 458. TC44, Sister Rose Chan, pp. 46–51.

63. *China Missionary Bulletin*, April 1952, p. 307; June-July 1952, p. 451; August-September 1952, pp. 591–592. Released on the same day were Father Maurice Feeney, pastor of Taikau and Sister Rose Chan, a native Sister of the Immaculate Heart of Kongmoon, who had also been detained in Yeungkong since November 1950. Father Feeney was expelled and Sister Rose was given permission to go to Kongmoon to work as a seamstress.

64. FARC, 44–05, "Father Kennelly's Story"; 44–06, Father John Graser's press release, "Inside Communist China." FARC, 33–06, Letter of Father Thomas Malone to Bishop Raymond Lane, June 25, 1951. SARC, War Years, File 2, Drawer 3, Iron Curtain Diaries and Accounts, Sister Monica Marie Boyle, "Behind the Curtain in Loting." TS02, Sister Monica Marie Boyle: see the various newspaper clippings attached to her transcript.

65. *The Field Afar*, March 1922, p. 88; May 1922, p. 146; June 1922, p. 184; July 1922, p. 210; August 1922, p. 242; September 1922, p. 284; October 1922, p. 316; November 1922, p. 348; December 1922, p. 380; June 1923, p. 190.

66. FARC, 8–07, article by Fathers Francis Connors and Joseph Sweeney, of June 1934 published in *The Field Afar*, October 1934, p. 266.

67. FARC, 12–49, letter of Father Otto Rauschenbach to Father James A. Walsh, November 23, 1930. See also FARC, 32–05, letter of Bishop James E. Walsh to Father William O'Shea, February 25, 1930; 32–07, letter of Bishop James E. Walsh to Father James Drought, July 1, 1935. *The Field Afar*, May 1931, p. 141; September 1931, pp. 236–237.

68. FARC, 8–07, "The Toishan Torch," March 1934. FARC, 30–07, article by Father George Haggar published in *The Boston Pilot*, October 12, 1935, *The Catholic Transcript* of Hartford, Connecticut, October 24, 1935, and the *Denver Register*, n.d.

69. FARC, 30–07, article by Father George Haggar.

70. FARC, 8–07, Toishan Diary, April 19, 1934. *Fides News Service*, July 24, 1937, p. 587. TF76, Dr. Artemio Bagalawis, p. 5. *The Field Afar*, March 1936, p. 82.

71. *The Field Afar*, October 1934, p. 269; June 1937, pp. 174–175. FARC, 30–07, letter of Dr. Harry Blaber to Bishop James E. Walsh, January 30, 1937. See also article in *The Boston Pilot*, October 12, 1935.

72. TF76, Dr. Artemio Bagalawis, p. 4. FARC, Father Francis O'Neill's autobiography, "Entre Nous," book 2, p. 54. *The Field Afar*, October 1934, p. 269.

73. *The Field Afar*, November 1944, pp. 18–20; January-February 1945, p. 35. *Maryknoll Mission Letters*, Vol. II, 1944 (New York: Field Afar Press), letter of Father Joseph Lavin from Hoingan, pp. 16–17. FARC, Father Francis O'Neill's autobiography, "Entre Nous," book 2, pp. 54, 57–60.

74. SARC, Box—South China, Kaying, Kongmoon, Kweilin, Wuchow, Folder 6, "Toishan Hospital: Information about the Hospital." TC38, Sister Laetitia Lee, pp. 28–30. *Maryknoll—The Field Afar*, April 1949, pp. 1–3.

75. SARC, 40–18, Sacred Heart Hospital Diary, January 6–11, December 20–26, 1948; 40–19, Sacred Heart Hospital Diary, May 17–23, June 4, October 20, November 3, 1949. SARC, Box—South China, Kongmoon, Kaying, Kweilin, Wuchow, Folder 6, "Toishan Hospital: Monthly Medical Report." SARC, War Years, File 2, Drawer 3, Iron Curtain Diaries and Accounts, Sister Dominic Marie Turner, "Toishan under Red Rule," p. 2.

76. SARC, 40–17, Sacred Heart Hospital Diary, April-May 1947; 40–19, Sacred Heart Hospital Diary, September 1–8, 1949.

77. SARC, War Years, File 2, Drawer 3, Iron Curtain Diaries and Accounts, Sister Dominic Marie Turner, "Toishan under Red Rule," pp. 1–46; Sister Magdalena Urlacher's account, pp. 1–5. TC38, Sister Laetitia Lee, p. 32.

78. Besides Sister M. Roma Schleininger, the other nurses were Sisters Mary Augusta Hock, M. Espiritu Venneman, M. Mercedes Cusack and Virginia Marie Lynn, the superior of the group. Sister M. Antoinette Geist was in charge of occupational therapy and Sister Herman Joseph Stitz ran the hospital laboratory. In 1936, some Sisters were replaced and the number increased to nine; however, three nurses and the laboratory technician in the original group, stayed until the Maryknoll Sisters withdrew in November 1938.

79. SARC, Box—South China, History, Shanghai Hospital, Folder 2—Shanghai History; File 2, "Maryknoll Sisters' Work at Shanghai Mercy Hospital, 1935–1938" by Sister Herman Joseph Stitz, n.d., pp. 1–4.

80. SARC, 53–01, Shanghai Mercy Hospital, July 16–19, 1935. Stitz, "Maryknoll Sisters' Work at Shanghai Mercy Hospital, 1935-1938," p. 5. TS16, Sister Herman Joseph Stitz, pp. 1–4; TS12, Sister Agnes Regina Rafferty, p. 6.

81. SARC, 53–02, Shanghai Mercy Hospital, "Interview with Sister Virginia Marie Lynn," November 16, 1937.

82. TS16, Sister Herman Joseph Stitz, p. 10. SARC, 53–02, Shanghai Mercy Hospital, August 30, 1936; 53–03, Shanghai Mercy Hospital, December 17, 1937.

83. TS102, Sister Herman Joseph Stitz, pp. 9–10; TS16, Sister Herman Joseph Stitz, pp. 7–8.

84. SARC, Box—Chronicles, South China, 1931–1949, Folder 14, Shanghai Hospital Chronicles, August 13-November 15, 1937. SARC, 53–03, Shanghai Mercy Hospital, August 13-November 10, 1937. SARC, Box—South China, History, Shanghai Hospital, Folder 1, "Shanghai Silhouettes," August 3-November 10, 1937.

85. SARC, Box—South China, History, Shanghai Hospital, Folder 1, "Shanghai Silhouettes," September 11, 1937. See also SARC, Box—South China, History, Shanghai Hospital, File 2, "Maryknoll Sisters' Work at Shanghai Mercy Hospital, 1935–1938," p. 13.

86. SARC, 53–03, Shanghai Mercy Hospital, September 9, 1937. SARC, Box—South China, History, Shanghai Hospital, Folder 1, "Shanghai Silhouettes," August 16, November 23, 1937.

87. SARC, 53–03, Shanghai Mercy Hospital, November 12, 1937.

88. TS74, Sister Kathleen Marie Shea, p. 27.

89. TS102, Sister Herman Joseph Stitz, pp. 20–22. SARC, 53–03, Shanghai Mercy Hospital, November 12-24, 1937. See also Sister Maria Del Rey, *No Two Alike* (New York: Dodd, Mead, & Co., 1965), pp. 153–177.

90. TF102, Sister Herman Joseph Stitz, pp. 3, 31. SARC, Box—South China, Stitz, "Maryknoll Sisters' Work in Shanghai Mercy Hospital," pp. 13–14.

91. TS74, Sister Kathleen Marie Shea, pp. 14–16.

92. SARC, Box—South China, History, Shanghai Hospital, Folder 1, Shanghai Mercy Hospital Report of 1938.

93. FARC, 21–01, First Departure Diary, December 10, 1918. FARC, 15–06, letter of Brother Michael Hogan to Father James A. Walsh, July 11, 1926. FARC, 3–01, Loting Mission Diary, February 27, 1926.

94. *The Field Afar*, March 1933, pp. 67–69; October 1933, p. 275; July-August 1934, p. 200.

95. Fathers Joseph Sweeney and Francis Connors, *Maryknoll Lepers* (New York: Maryknoll Publications, 1934), pp. 15–17. See also *The Field Afar*, October 1934, p. 269.

96. FARC, 32–06, letter of Father James A. Walsh to Bishop James E. Walsh, November 25, 1933 and letter of Father Joseph Sweeney to Father James A. Walsh, November 10, 1933.

97. *The Field Afar*, July-August 1934, pp. 200–201; September 1934, p. 249; October 1934, p. 269. *Maryknoll Lepers*, pp. 18–21, 26–27. Fathers Joseph Sweeney and Francis Connors, *Gate of Heaven Leper Asylum* (New York: Maryknoll Publications, 1938), p. 14. FARC, Box—Joseph Sweeney, letter to Brother Henry Corcoran, March 7, 1934. FARC, 32–07, letter of Bishop James E. Walsh to Father James A. Walsh, January 19, 1934.

98. Quoted in Sweeney and Connors, *Gate of Heaven*, pp. 31–32. See also *The Field Afar*, January 1936, pp. 14–15; April 1936, p. 116.

99. Perry Burgess, *Born of Those Years* (New York: Henry Holt & Co., 1951), "Recollections of a Cemetery," p. 116.

100. FARC, Box—Sweeney, "Our Lepers Are Preparing Christmas," October 1934. *The Field Afar*, April 1935, pp. 104, 106; April 1936, pp. 116–117. *Gate of Heaven*, pp. 20–21, 26–28.

101. FARC, 8–08, Sunwui Diary, August 29, 1937. *The Field Afar*, July-August 1937, p. 202; September 1938, p. 249. *Gate of Heaven*, p. 34. See also FARC, 33–02, press release of 1949 by Father Albert Nevins, "Leper Colony in China Faces Third Closing," also published in *Daily Herald* of New Britain, CT, July 22, 1949.

102. James Keller and Meyer Berger, *Men of Maryknoll* (New York: Grosset and Dunlap, 1943), pp. 25–26. *Gate of Heaven*, pp. 34–35.

103. *Maryknoll—The Field Afar*, May 1943, p. 27; July-August 1944, pp. 30–32; November 1947, pp. 18–20. FARC, 5–03, Chikkai Diary, September 1941. FARC, 33–02, Kongmoon Reports, June 30, 1941, June 30, 1942, June 30, 1944. FARC, Box—Sweeney, "News Transmitted by the Chinese International Broadcasting Station XGOY," December 31, 1941; letter of Father Joseph Sweeney to Miss Dillon, September 30, 1942; letter of Father Joseph Sweeney to the Director of the Hartford Branch of the Society for the Propagation of the Faith, Columbus Day, 1942; letter of Father Joseph Sweeney to his mother, June 13, 1943. TF66, Father John Joyce, pp. 8, 10.

104. *Maryknoll—The Field Afar*, September 1945, p. 1.

105. TF66, Father John Joyce, pp. 10–14. FARC, Box—Sweeney, letter of Father John Joyce to Father Joseph Sweeney, July 6, 1945. *Maryknoll—The Field Afar*, July-August 1946, pp. 7–8; November 1947, pp. 20–21.

106. FARC, 33–02, Father Albert Nevins, "Leper Colony in China Faces Third Closing," p. 3. FARC, Box—Sweeney, clipping of the *Daily Herald* of New Britain, CT, July 22, 1949.

107. TF63, Father Carroll Quinn, p. 1.

108. FARC, 40–02, diary of Father Thomas Malone, May 1951, November 1951, January 1952, August 1952, September 1952. FARC, 33–06, diary of Father Thomas Malone, January 1953; letter of Father Thomas Malone, May 11, 1953. FARC, Box—Sweeney, letter of Father Thomas Malone to Father William Dwyer, August 2, 1952; newspaper clippings, *The Catholic Transcript*, Hartford, Connecticut, December 17, 1953, p. 18; *The Hartford Times*, May 7, 1954; *New Britain Herald*, May 7, 1954, p. 1. TF63, Father Carroll Quinn, pp. 1–2.

109. SARC, 40–07, Kongmoon Convent Diary, August 14, October 27–30, 1938; July 1, 1940. SARC, 43–15, Kaying Convent Diary, June 20, 1942; 48–14, Yeungkong Convent Diary, June 2, 1939.

110. FARC, 3–09, Kongmoon Diary, may 1939; TS84, Sister Chanel Xavier, pp. 25–26; TC07, Sister Joseph Lam, p. 24.

111. FARC, 23–04, Wuchow Center Diary, August 1, 1939.

112. FARC, 8-08, Sunwui Diary, April 1940. FARC, 8-06, Kochow Diary, July 1940.

113. SARC, 40-07, Kongmoon Convent Diary, May-October 1940, October 25, 1941. FARC, 3-09, Kongmoon Diary, May 1940, November 1941.

114. FARC, 8-08, Sunwui Diary, December 8-11, 1939; 42-18, "Kweilin News Bulletin," April 19, 1943. FARC, Box—Joseph Sweeney, letter to Margaret, March 15, 1943.

115. SARC, 49-12, letter of Sister Mary Francis Davis to Mother Mary Joseph, November 22, 1942. In that same year, cases of cannibalism were also mentioned by Father Edward Mueth in Sunchong: TF68, p. 22 and by Father Joseph Sweeney around Sunwui: FARC—Box Joseph Sweeney, letter to Miss Dillon of September 30, 1942 and letter to the director of the Hartford (CT) branch of the Society for the Propagation of the Faith, Columbus Day 1942, p. 8.

116. *Maryknoll—The Field Afar*, November 1944, pp. 18-20. *Maryknoll Mission Letters*, Vol. II, 1944 (New York: Field Afar Press), letter of Father Joseph Lavin from Hoingan, pp. 16-17.

117. *Maryknoll—The Field Afar*, February 1947, pp. 46-47.

118. FARC, 8008, Sunwui Diary, May 24, 1940.

119. *Maryknoll—The Field Afar*, October 1944, Sister Rose Victor (Barbara Mersinger), "In League with Mars," pp. 32-34. *Maryknoll Mission Letters*, Vol. I, 1945, Letter of Father Lloyd Glass, p. 2. Tennien, *Chungking*, pp. 180-185.

120. *Maryknoll Mission Letters*, Vol. I., 1946, pp. 22-23.

121. Tennien, *Chungking*, p. 187.

122. TF38, Father Robert Greene, pp. 5-6, 13-15. TS42, Sister Henrietta Marie Cunningham, pp. 41-45. FARC, 30-05, Letter of Father James Smith to Father John Considine received at Maryknoll on December 29, 1944. Tennien, *Chungking*, pp. 185-191. *Maryknoll—The Field Afar*, March 1945, p. 38.

123. FARC, 37-02, Kaying Report, August 19, 1945, pp. 2 and 4; see also Kaying Report, June 17, 1944, pp. 4-5 and Report of Meihsien International Relief Committee, August 1, 1944. SARC, 42-03, Lahukow Novitiate, May 22, 1944. *Maryknoll—The Field Afar*, September 1944, p. 21. In 1944-45 in Kaying, the rate of exchange between the Chinese and the U.S. dollar was 60 to 1.

124. *Maryknoll—The Field Afar*, March 1945, p. 3.

125. *Maryknoll Mission Letters*, Vol. I, 1946, pp. 20-21. FARC, 42-18, letter of Father Edwin McCabe to Bishop James E. Walsh, October 19, 1945. *Maryknoll—The Field Afar*, March 1945, pp. 4-5.

126. FARC, 49-01, letter of Father Edward McGurkin to Father John Comber, February 15, 1946. TS75, Sister Margaret Kim, pp. 41-43. *Maryknoll—The Field Afar*, September 1946, p. 8.

127. FARC, 23-05, Pingnam Mission Diary, January-March 1947; 42-06, letter of Bishop Raymond Lane to Monsignor John Romaniello, January 17, 1947. TF38, Father Robert Greene, pp. 16, 20-21. *China Missionary*, June 15, 1948, pp. 251-252. *Maryknoll—The Field Afar*, February 1947, p. 3.

128. FARC, 42-19, Chuanhsien Mission History, 1947-1949, p. 2; 42-19, Kweilin Center Diary, October 1948, p. 6.

129. FARC, 42-19, Chuanhsien Mission History, 1947-1949, p. 2; 42-19, Chuanhsien Diary, April 1949. *Maryknoll—The Field Afar*, December 1948, pp. 1-3. TF83, Father Edwin McCabe, p. 11; TF57, Father Lloyd Glass, pp. 38-39.

130. FARC, 42-19, Chuanhsien Mission History, 1947-1949, p. 2.

131. FARC, 3-04, Kochow Diary, December 19, 1919; March 1, 1921; December 11-31, 1922. FARC, 8-02, Sancian Diary, November 1926-January 1927.

132. FARC, 5-08, Chiklung Diary, October 8, 1939.

133. *Maryknoll—The Field Afar*, November 1940, p. 23.

134. FARC, 23-05, Pingnam Mission Diary, April 1947.

135. FARC, 42-19, Chuanhsien Mission History, 1947-1949, pp. 3-4. FARC, 23-05, Pingnam Mission Diary, January-April 1947.

136. *Digest of the Synodal Commission*, January 1938, pp. 19-24. For more information on government-sponsored Chinese cooperatives, see *Digest*, February 1940, pp. 249-251; *Far Eastern Review*, February 1940; and *Chinese Recorder*, March 1940.

137. FARC, 8-06, Kochow Diary, July, August and October 1940; January 1941.

138. TF31, Father Paul Duchesne, p. 12; TF62, Father Richard Downey, p. 10. FARC, 5-11, Tungchen Diary, September 1938; FARC, 23-05, Pingnam Mission Diary, March 1947. *Maryknoll—The Field Afar*, June 1951, p. 2.

139. FARC, 42-19, Chuanhsien Mission History, 1947-1949, p. 3.

140. FARC, 5-08, Chiklung Diary, March 1939; March-April 1940. See also letter of Father John Smith to Bishop James E. Walsh, March 20, 1940.

141. TF31, Father Paul Duchesne, pp. 11-12. FARC, 5-08, Chiklung Diary, October 8, 1939; FARC, 23-05, Pingnam Seminary Diary, April 1947.

142. FARC, 23-05, Pingnam Mission Diary, March 1947. *Maryknoll—The Field Afar*, June 1951, pp. 3-4. TF62, Father Richard Downey, p. 10.

143. *Maryknoll Mission Letters*, Vol. I, 1946, pp. 21-22. Father Edwin McCabe also bought many of these shoes with his own money for the poorest families of his station during the winter months (FARC, 42-19, "Making the Rounds," April 12, 1946, pp. 3-4).

144. TF38, Father Robert Greene, pp. 16-17.

145. TF66, Father John Joyce, pp. 28-29.

146. FARC, 37-02, Kaying Report, August 19, 1945, pp. 12-13.

147. Joseph Schmidlin, *Catholic Mission Theory* (Techny, IL: Mission Press, 1931), pp. 407-410.

148. FARC, 4-02, letter from Father Francis X. Ford, copied at the Maryknoll Center on August 17 and October 5, 1922.

149. FARC, 4-01, Yeungkong Chronicle, February 20, 1919.

150. Father Adolph Paschang, *Schools in China* (New York: Maryknoll Pamphlet Library, 1935), pp. 25-26. See also *The Field Afar*, May 1926, p. 127; June 1926, p. 155.

151. Kenneth Scott Latourette, *A History of Christian Missions in China* (New York: Macmillan Co., 1929), pp. 698-699. Lu-dzai Djung, *A History of Democratic Education in Modern China* (Shanghai: The Commercial Press, 1934), pp. 171-178. Maryknoll Library Vertical Files, Drawer—China, Folder—Education, letter from Maryknoll to Justin McGrath, Director of NCWC News Service, March 2, 1925. Bishop James E. Walsh, *Mission Manual of the Vicariate of Kongmoon*, pp. 69-73.

152. FARC, 38-07, Wuchow Report, July 1929, p. 8; see also Report, July 1931, p. 4. FARC, 5-03, Chikkai Diary, March 5-6, 1939.

153. FARC, 8-06, Kaochow Diary, August-October 1923, June 8-October 15, 1925. *The Field Afar*, February 1924, p. 40; April 1924, p. 107; November 1925, p. 302; June 1926, pp. 154-155.

154. SARC, 48-06, Yeungkong Convent Diary, March 2, 29, 31, June 8, 1931; 48-12, Yeungkong Convent Diary, February 8, 19, 20, 23, March 12, April 3, 16, May 3, June 3, October 4, 14, 15, November 16, 17, 1937; 48-13, Yeungkong Convent Diary, May 5, 1938. The New Life Movement started in 1934 by Chiang K'ai-shek aimed at the moral revitalization of the people through the cultivation of the ancient Chinese virtues of propriety, right conduct, honesty and self-respect.

155. FARC, 38-07, Wuchow Reports, July 1929, pp. 7-8; July 1931, p. 5.

156. SARC, 48–05, Yeungkong Convent Diary, June 8, 1931. SARC, 3–07, Hoingan Diary, September 14, 1936; May 31, 1937. *The Field Afar*, April 1929, pp. 113–114. TF05, Father John Driscoll, pp. 21, 25, 34; TC20, Mr. Cheuk Chiu-Yin, p. 7.

157. *The Field Afar*, March 1935, p. 71; September 1935, p. 235. TC37, Mr. Andrew Cheung, pp. 1–2; TC25, Mr. Jong Kin-shum, p. 3.

158. Sister Marcelline (Therese Grondin), *Sisters Carry the Gospel* (New York: Maryknoll Publications, 1956), p. 55.

159. *Ibid.* p. 75. TS83, Sister Mary Hock, pp. 76–77; TC08, Mrs. Yau Chun Yuen, pp. 7–8; TC25, Mr. Jong Kin-shum, p. 10. See also TS58, Sister Madeline Sophic Karlon, pp. 19–20, and *Maryknoll—The Field Afar*, December 1944, pp. 32–34.

160. SARC, 55–06, Fushun-Honan Convent Diary, March 4, July 10–11, 1933. FARC, 25–02, Chakow Diary, June 1931; February 13, March 3, 1937. FARC, 25–17, Erhpatan Diary, October 9, 1935; 25–23, Tunghua Diary, October 1, November 8, 1935; 25–18, Shanchengtze Diary, March 7, 1940; 25–22, letter from Father Sylvio Gilbert to Bishop James A. Walsh, August 6, 1933. *The Field Afar*, April 1935, pp. 106–107.

161. SARC, 54–01, Dairen Convent Diary, April 8, May 15, June 30, 1930; February 22, July 27, August 3, 21, 29–31, September 16–28, 1931. SARC, unpublished manuscript by Sister Mary Eunice Tolan, "Manchuria, Book 1," n.d., pp. 21–23. TS62, Sister Mary Corita Herrgen, p. 14.

162. SARC, 54–02, Dairen Convent Diary, April 28, June 15, 1934; June 17, 1935; December 15, 1936. SARC, 54–06, Maryknoll Academy Reports, June 1932. Tolan, "Manchuria, Book 1," pp. 25-26. TS62, Sister Mary Corita Herrgen, p. 16.

163. SARC, 54–06, Maryknoll Academy Reports, June 1932, April 1937, July 1937. Tolan, "Manchuria, Book 1," pp. 26–27. See also SARC, 54–02, Dairen Convent Diary, May 24, July 2, 1934; July 2, August 21, 1935; July 1, 1936. TS49, Sister Mary Eunice Tolan, pp. 3, 5; TS88, Sister Virginia Flagg, p. 2.

164. TS31, Sister Rose Benigna Hanan, p. 8; Sister Mary Corita Herrgen, p. 18. SARC, 54–02, Dairen Convent Diary, May 13, 1936; 54–06, Maryknoll Academy Diary, October 11, 1939.

165. SARC, 54–02, Dairen Convent Diary, September 3, 1936; 54–06, Maryknoll Academy Report, April 1937. TS31, Sister Rose Benigna Hanan, pp. 7, 22; TS05, Sister Virginia Flagg, pp. 9–10. Tolan, "Manchuria, Book 1," p. 26.

166. Tolan, "Manchuria, Book 1," p. 29. See also SARC, 54–06, Maryknoll Academy Diary, June 27, 1941.

167. SARC, 54–06, Maryknoll Academy Diary, May 25–27, 1941.

168. The population of Dairen was reported in one of the local newspapers to be 1,227,942 on March 8, 1938. The city was 85 percent Manchu and Chinese; the other inhabitants were 181,411 Japanese, 4,714 Koreans and 1,763 foreigners. SARC, 54–04, Fushimi-Dai Diary, March 8, 1938; 54–06, Maryknoll Academy Report, April 1937.

169. SARC, 54–01, Dairen Convent Diary, May 10, 1930, May 10, 1931, May 8–10, 1933; 54–02, Dairen Convent Diary, May 10, 1934; 54–03, Maryknoll Academy Diary, May 30, 1941; 54–04, Fushimi-Dai Diary, May 10, 1938; 54–06, Maryknoll Academy Diary, May 10, 1938.

170. SARC, 54–06, Maryknoll Academy Diary, May 30, 1941. For ceremonies involving more Catholic boys, see TS05, Sister Virginia Flagg, p. 9.

171. SARC, 54–06, Maryknoll Academy Diary, May 1, 1941.

172. SARC, 54–06, Maryknoll Academy Diary, April 19–26, May 12, September 6–15, 1939. Tolan, "Manchuria, Book 1," p. 27.

173. Tolan, "Manchuria, Book 2," pp. 58–59. TS27, Sister Marie Elise Baumann, pp. 8, 11; TS75, Sister Margaret Kim, p. 33.

174. Letter of Sister Marie Elise Baumann quoted by Tolan, "Manchuria, Book 2," p. 61.
175. Letter of Bishop Raymond Lane quoted by Tolan, "Manchuria, Book 2," pp. 60–61.
176. SARC, Box—Ford's Conferences, "The Sisters' Activities According to the Kaying Synodal Decree, July 1943," pp. 33–35.

PART III—The Building of the Native Church

1. FARC, Box Miscellaneous—Constitutions, "General Rule of the Catholic Foreign Mission Society of America," I, 2. SARC, Box Constitutions, "Tentative Constitutions, ca. 1917," I, 1; "First Constitutions, 1925," I, 1; "Constitutions, 1931," XXI, 325/326/328.
2. Pasquale D'Elia, *The Catholic Missions in China* (Shanghai: Commercial Press, 1941), p. 72. J. M. Planchet, *Les missions de Chine et du Japon* (Peking: Imprimerie des Lazaristes, 1920), pp. 402–403.
3. D'Elia, *The Catholic Missions in China*, pp. 58–59, 73–74; *Mémoires de la Congrégation de la Mission en Chine*, Nouvelle édition, Tome III (Paris: Procure de la Congrégation de la Mission, 1912), pp. 241–242.
4. Louis Kervyn, *Méthode de l'apostolat en Chine* (Hong Kong: Imprimerie de la Société des Missions Etrangères, 1911), pp. 592–598.
5. Archives Vincent Lebbe, Fonds I, IIe, Section 2c: carnet bleu, Louvain University, Belgium.
6. *Acta Apostolicae Sedis*, Volume 11, 1911 (Rome: Typis Polyglottis Vaticanis), No. 13, December 1, 1919, pp. 445–446.
7. Ibid.

Chapter 5—The Indigenization of the Clergy and Sisterhoods

1. FARC, 4-03, Yeungkong Diary, December 15, 1924. FARC, 9-06, "Kongmoon Mission, Preparatory Seminary," Father T. V. Kiernan, December 3, 1930. James E. Walsh, "The Kongmoon Seminary—An American Catholic Venture in China," *The Ecclesiastical Review*, July 1927, p. 50.
2. SARC, 48-03, Yeungkong Convent Diary, December 1924.
3. *The Field Afar*, March 1936, "Gateway to a Million Families," pp. 76–77.
4. FARC, 9-15, letters of Father Francis X. Ford, Kaying, June 3, 1926; October 2, 1926.
5. FARC, 23-03, "Kwangsi Bamboo Leaves," July-August 1931. FARC 23-01, "The Wuchow Bulletin," June 1931. FARC, 23-10, Pingnam Diary, July 3, 1931; August 17-18, 1931; March 1, 1933.
6. TF04, Father Francis Daubert, pp. 30–31; TC13, Fathers Simeon To and John Yeung, pp. 35–36.
7. FARC, "The Manchu-knoller," September 1928, February 1929, June 1929. FARC, 16-01, Fushun Center Diary, November 4, 1931. FARC, 25-03, Fushun-Hopei Seminary, January 28, 1940. TC22, Father Protase Pai, p. 9; TF46, Bishop Edward McGurkin, p. 19.
8. Carl H. Becker, M. Falski, P. Langevin, R. H. Tawney, *The Reorganisation of Education in China* (Paris: League of Nations, Institute of Intellectual Cooper-

ation, 1932), pp. 68–69, 77, 85, 98. Father Adolph Paschang, *Schools in China* (New York: Maryknoll Pamphlet Library, 1936), p. 13.

9. *The Field Afar*, March 1933, p. 88; October 1935, p. 286. Father Raymond P. Quinn, *The Chinese Seminarian* (New York: Maryknoll Pamphlet Library, 1935), p. 21.

10. TF46, Bishop Edward McGurkin, p. 40; TF21, Father Francis Mullen, p. 26; TF52, Father Edward Weis, p. 31. See also note 12 below.

11. FARC, 26–14, Tsungkow Diary, Father Dennis Slattery, September 1938.

12. Quinn, *The Chinese Seminarian*, pp. 21–22. FARC, 25–13, Fushun-Hopei Seminary, February 15, 1941. TC01, Father Paul Pang, pp. 12, 16. *The Reorganisation of Education in China* provides the following curriculum for a standard Chinese junior middle school—Principles of Kuomintang (Nationalist Party) and Civics, Chinese, Foreign Language, History, Geography, Mathematics, Nature Study, Physical Training, Physiology and Hygiene, Drawing, Music, Labor (i.e., Manual Work), Vocational Subjects; for the senior school—Principles of Kuomintang and Civics, Chinese, Foreign Language, Mathematics, Chinese History, Foreign History, Chinese Geography, Foreign Geography, Physics, Chemistry, Biology, Military Training, Physical Training, Elective Subjects. In the state of Manchukuo, the fundamentals of Confucianism were studied in place of the Principles of the Kuomintang, and the Japanese language was required.

13. Quinn, *The Chinese Seminarian*, p. 25.

14. TC27, Bishop John Wu, p. 41; TC04, Father Thomas Lau, p. 36; TC40, Peter Chum, p. 5; TF06, Father Allen Dennis, pp. 13–15.

15. *The Field Afar*, June 1927, p. 153; January 1928, pp. 18–19.

16. FARC, 25–12, Fushun Hopei Seminary, March 1933 and September 1, 1933; 25–13, January 7, 1939 and May 27, 1940.

17. TC05, Father John Tse, p. 16; TC02, Father Paul Pang, p. 2; TC27, Bishop John Wu, pp. 40–44. FARC, 26–06, Hwangtang Seminary, August 6, 1940. John F. Donovan, *The Pagoda and the Cross* (New York: Charles Scribner's Sons, 1967), pp. 96–97.

18. Quinn, *The Chinese Seminarian*, p. 21. TF77, Cyril Hirst, p. 9. FARC, 26–14, Tsungkow Diary, Father Dennis Slattery, September 1938.

19. FARC, unpublished manuscript by John F. Donovan, "Maryknoll's Wuchow Mission, Kwangsi," p. 158.

20. FARC, 5–05, Fachow Diary, August 31, 1941.

21. TC40, Peter Chum, p. 5; TC16, Paul Lei, pp. 5–6.

22. TF23, Father Albert Fedders, addenda, p. 2. FARC, 9–16, "Hakka Howls," October 1927.

23. TC16, Paul Lei, p. 5; TC27, Bishop John Wu, p. 7; TC13, Father Simeon To, p. 78; TF77, Cyril Hirst, p. 10.

24. FARC, 26–06, Kaying St. Joseph Seminary, Father Francis T. Donnelly, January 15–16, 1939.

25. TC41, Robert Tse, pp. 28–29, 31–32.

26. TF10, Father Albert Fedders, p. 15. FARC, 25–12, Fushun-Hopei Seminary, October 1932. *The Field Afar*, June 1927, p. 153.

27. Quinn, *The Chinese Seminarian*, p. 26. FARC, 26–14, Tsungkow Diary, September 1938.

28. *The Field Afar*, June 1927, pp. 152–153.

29. TC27, Bishop John Wu, p. 41.

30. TC27, Bishop John Wu, p. 41–44; TC01, Father Paul Pang, pp. 11, 16–18. FARC, 25–08, Fushun Center Diary, October 20, 1930. FARC, 25–13, Fushun-Hopei Seminary, March 2, 1940. FARC, 9–16, "Hakka Howls," September 8, 192. FARC, 3–09, Kongmoon Diary, June 1939.

31. *Maryknoll—The Field Afar*, November 1948, "Seminary Candidates," p. 46. FARC, 4-03, Yeungkong Diary, Father Paulhus, December 15, 1924, p. 5.

32. Quinn, *The Chinese Seminarian*, pp. 5-6. TC19, Father Peter Chum, p. 21. *Maryknoll—The Field Afar*, June 1944, "Anthony Arrives," p. 18.

33. TC27, Bishop John Wu, pp. 10-11; TC37, Father Peter Ma, p. 19; TS51, Sister Mary Paulita Hoffman, p. 57.

34. TC19, Father Peter Chum, p. 19. SARC, unpublished manuscript by Sister Mary Eunice Tolan, "The Pai Family" in "Manchuria, Book 3."

35. FARC, 26-12, Tsiahang Diary, Father Francis T. Donnelly, September 1, 1940.

36. FARC, 23-04, Wuchow Newsletter, July 8, 1937. TC27, Bishop John Wu, p. 9.

37. TC27, Bishop John Wu, pp. 8-10; TC40, Peter Chum, pp. 4-5.

38. Planchet, *Les missions de Chine, 1936-1937* (Shanghai: Procure des Lazaristes, 1938), p. 404. FARC, 3-08, "Kongmoon Bulletin," June 1938.

39. Planchet, *Les missions de Chine, 1938-193*9 (1940), p. 407; *1940-1941* (1942), p. 416. FARC, 3-09, Kongmoon Diary, November 1938.

40. TC19, Father Peter Chum, p. 21; TC27, Bishop John Wu, pp. 8-10; TC13, Father Simeon To, p. 55.

41. TC27, Bishop John Wu, p. 7. FARC, 5-05, Fachow Diary, August 31, 1941. *The Ecclesiastical Review*, September 1923, letter of Father Paschang from Kochow, p. 295.

42. TF77, Cyril Hirst, pp. 9-10. FARC, 25-12, Fushun-Hopei Seminary, August 24, 1940; 25-13, February 15, 1941. FARC, 3-09, Kongmoon Diary, November 1938.

43. TF21, Father Francis Mullen, p. 21; TF46, Bishop Edward McGurkin, pp. 40-44. FARC, Manchu-knoller, September-October, 1937. FARC, 49-06, letter from Father Simon Pai, January 22, 1981. *Maryknoll News* (Newspaper of the Maryknoll Fathers & Brothers), July 1984, pp. 1, 3.

44. TC39, Father Peter Ma, pp. 3-10. *UCA News* (Hong Kong), August 27, 1986, pp. 16-17. *Maryknoll News*, October 1986, pp. 1-2.

45. FARC, 23-09, Pinglo Diary, June 1933; 23-10, Pingnam Mission Diary, June 4, July 6, July 16, 1933.

46. TF23, Father Albert Fedders, pp. 2-3. FARC, 23-04, account about Evacuation of Wuchow, Cyril Hirst, September 28, 1944.

47. FARC, 23-04, Cyril Hirst, account, September 1, 1944-October 1, 1944. TF10, Father Albert Fedders, pp. 13-14; TF23, Father Albert Fedders, pp. 3-7; TF04*, Father Charles Daly, pp. 1-3; TC16, Paul Lei, pp. 1-3; TC39, Father Peter Ma, pp. 3-5.

48. TC13, Father Simeon To, p. 18. FARC, 23-06, Pingnam Seminary Diary, September 6, 1948. Albert J. Nevins, *The Meaning of Maryknoll* (New York: Macmillan Books, 1954), pp. 117-119. FARC, 44-05, "The Case of the Seminary of Wuchow Diocese," account by Father Frederick Becka, pp. 1-2. Father Joseph Laai was on loan from the Kongmoon diocese.

49. TF28, Father Peter Reilly, introduction and p. 1. FARC, 38-08, Wuchow Report, February 11, 1952. Priests ordained in Hong Kong after 1952 for Wuchow: Thomas Lau, Peter Chum, Matthew Liang. Priests for Kweilin: Simeon To, John Yeung, Stephen Liang.

50. *Maryknoll—The Field Afar*, February 1943, pp. 8-9.

51. TC01, Father Paul Pang, pp. 14, 16-18; TF05, Father John Driscoll, p. 36. *Asia Focus* (Hong Kong), January 2, 1987, pp. 1, 7. SARC—Box Bishop Francis X. Ford, Folder "Kaying Bulletin," May 1, 1949. SARC, 43-24, letters of Bishop

Francis Ford, June 9 and October 5, 1949. FARC, 37–04, Chinese Clergy, letters and reports, 1952–1986. John F. Donovan, *The Pagoda and the Cross*, pp. 96–98.

52. FARC, 3–04, Kochow Diary, Father O'Shea, August 1, 1921. FARC, 5–06, Hoingan Diary, Father Dietz, October 1924.

53. SARC, Box—Native Novitiates, General, File—Native Sisters: letter of Father Bernard F. Meyer, July 8, 1923; letters of Sister Mary Paul McKenna, July 9, 1923 and January 26, 1925.

54. SARC, 40–01, Sister Mary Patricia Coughlin, Kongmoon Candidates, 1926–1930. TC07, Sister Joseph Lam, pp. 8–12. FARC, 7–03, Hoignan Diary, Father Robert Sheridan, October-December 1926. *The Field Afar*, March 1933, p. 88.

55. SARC, Box—Novitiate, Kongmoon, File—2. SARC, 40–01, Immaculate Heart Sisters Novitiate, December 12, 1931; SARC, 40–02, October 3, 1933; SARC, 40–05, February 11, 1936. TC07, Sister Joseph Lam, p. 19. *The Field Afar*, May 1928, "Kongmoon Plans a Novitiate," pp. 149–150.

56. SARC, 40–06, 07, 08, 09, Immaculate Heart Sisters' Novitiate; 40–11, August 15, 1946. SARC, 49–14, Loting Convent Diary, December 17–23, 1941; 49–15, January 5, 1942 and February 11, 1942; 49–16, November 28, 1943; 49–24, letters of October 20, 1943 and May 30, 1944. TC44, Sister Rose Chan, pp. 14, 18–28; TC07, Sister Joseph Lam, pp. 34–38; TC38, Sister Laetitia Lee, pp. 27–28; TS56, Sister Eucharista Coupe, p. 3.

57. SARC, 40–11, Immaculate Heart Sisters' Novitiate, February 2–13, 1946; 40–12, August 6–15, 1947; 40–13, August 15, 1948 and September 9, 1948; 40–14, March 1, 1949 and August 15, 1949.

58. TC38, Sister Laetitia Lee, pp. 30–37; TC44, Sister Rose Chan, pp. 32, 44–44, 52; TC23, Sister Maureen Au, p. 19. *Maryknoll—The Field Afar*, December 1981, pp. 51–54.

59. SARC, Box—Novitiate, Wuchow, History of the Congregation of the Sisters of the Charity of the Sacred Heart; An Account of the First Profession; Letter of Official Foundation by Monsignor Meyer, July 1, 1937. SARC, 51–01, Pingnam Convent Diary, September 2–7, 1935; 51–02, August 18, 1936; 51–03, February 18, 1937 and July 1, 1937; 51–04, January 6, 1938; 51–06, January 6, 1940. SARC, 50–03, Sacred Heart Sisters' Novitiate, July 6, 1949. SARC, 40–01, Immaculate Heart Sisters' Novitiate, Sister Mary Patricia Coughlin, Kongmoon Candidates, 1926–1930. FARC, 23–03, Bamboo Leaves, January-February 1931. FARC, 23–10, Pingnam Diary, May 31, 1932; June 13, 1932, March 1, 1933. FARC, 42–15, Tanchuk Diary, January 6, 1940, and Tanchuk Seminary Diary, January 6, 1940. TC07, Sister Joseph Lam, p. 7.

60. SARC, Box—Novitiate, Wuchow, letters of Sister Moira Riehl, November 30, 1942 and October 15, 1943. SARC, 51–05, October 23-December 4, 1939; 51–06, November 25–30, 1940; 51–09, January 6, 1943.

61. SARC, Box—Novitiate, Wuchow, History of the Congregation of the Sisters of the Charity. SARC, 50–08, Father Peter Reilly, Diary Digest, December 1946, p. 9. SARC, 51–12, January 10, 1946.

62. SARC, 50–04, Sacred Heart Sisters' Novitiate, June 30-July 1, 1950. SARC, Box—South China, Kaying, Kongmoon, Kweilin, Wuchow, Folder 8, "History of Wuchow Vicariate," p. 4. TC46, Rose Lam, pp. 13, 18–20, 23–25, 27; TS96, Sister Moira Riehl, p. 26; TS21, Sister Mary Louise Martin, pp. 47–51.

63. SARC, 51–03, Pingnam Convent Diary, February 18, 1937. SARC, 52–01, Laipo Convent Diary, February 3–27, 1939. FARC, 42–14, Laipo Diary, March 8, 1937.

64. SARC, 52–01, Laipo Convent Diary, September 12, 1939. SARC, Box—Novitiate, Kweilin, Kweilin Convent Personal History Cards of the Sister Cate-

chists. FARC, 42-14, Laipo Diary, March 19, 1941.

65. SARC, 52-06, Laipo Convent Diary, April 1944; 52-07, September 19-27, 1945; 52-08, September 6-7, 1946. TS09, Sister Miriam Carmel Lechthaler, pp. 6-7.

66. SARC, 52-08, Laipo Convent Diary, September 29, 1946; SARC, 52-23, Kweilin Maryknoll Convent Diary, May 30-31, 1950; TC06, Sister Joan Ling, pp. 25-26.

67. SARC, 43-01, Kowloon Hakka Apostolic School, October 2-December 31, 1930. SARC, 43-05, Siaoloc Hakka Apostolic School, October 18-November 30, 1933. FARC, 35-02, Kaying Letter, June 1930, October 1933, November 1933. *The Field Afar*, March 1933, "Native Sisterhoods in the Making," p. 88; June 1934, "Convent Beginnings in Hakkaland," p. 166.

68. SARC, 43-11, Rosary Convent Diary, February 11, 1938 and September 12, 1938. SARC, 47-03, Holy Child Convent, Tungshek, July 29-31, 1940. SARC, 42-03, Our Lady of China Novitiate, Laohukow, February 11, 1943.

69. TS83, Sister Mary Hock, p. 52; TS51, Sister Mary Paulita Hoffman, pp. 12-13. SARC, 47-04, Holy Child Convent, February 8-9, 1941, September 11, 1941, and September 16-20, 1941.

70. SARC, 42-01, Laohukow Novitiate, Sister Catechists of Our Lady, April 21, 1948, p. 1. *Maryknoll—The Field Afar*, February 1943, p. 9.

71. SARC, Box—Novitiate, Kaying, File—2, Sister Catechists of Our Lady, October 8, 1949; March 25, 1950; File—3, Vocational Inquiry, September-November 1950; Personnel List, June 6, 1949. SARC, 42-01, July 18, 1941; August 21, 1941; March 10, 1942.

72. SARC, Box—Novitiate, Kaying, File—1, My Chinese Sisters by Sister Catherine Mary Lee. TC21, Sister Catherine Mary Lee, pp. 17-18.

73. SARC, Box—Novitiate, Kaying, File—2, Sister Catechists of Our Lady, October 8, 1949, pp. 1, 4.

74. *The Field Afar*, February 1939, "Bibiana" by Bishop Lane, p. 41; March 1942, "Boxer Martyrdom Bears Fruit" by Sister Fabiola (Gonyou), pp. 24-25.

75. TS40, Sister Mary Lelia Makra, p. 24. SARC, 55-09, Fushun-Honan Convent, Coal Dust, September 8, 1939. SARC, 54-08, Fushun-Hopei Convent, September 8, 1939. SARC, Sister Mary Eunice Tolan, "Manchuria, Book 3," pp. 88-89.

76. SARC, 55-11, Fushun-Honan Convent, December 8-14, 1941; 55-12, February 11, 1942; March 21, 1942; Easter 1942. Tolan, "Manchuria, Book 3," pp. 90, 97; "Book 4," pp. 150-155; "Manchuria, Supplement," pp. 20-21.

77. Tolan, "Manchuria, Book 3," pp. 94, 97; "Book 4," pp. 159-160. SARC, 55-13, Fushun-Honan Convent, June 5, 1947; June 19, 1947; December 6, 1947. TS27, Sister Marie Elise Baumann, pp. 8, 29.

78. Tolan, "Manchuria, Book 3," pp. 90-95, 99; SARC, Box—Statistics and Current Information, China, Native Novitiates, Letter from Sister Mary Celine Ch'en to Sister Celine Marie Werner,; Letter from Sister Christine Ortis, January 4, 1987; Letter from Sister Rose Guercio to Sister Luise Ahrens, January 2, 1987. Information on Sister Andrew Wen of Fushun given to the author by Sister Veronica Marie Carney, January 26, 1987. FARC, 49-06, letter of seminarian Protase Pai to Bishop Raymond Lane, December 12, 1952. *Maryknoll News*, July 1984, pp. 1, 3. TC23, Father Protase Pai, p. 20.

79. TF52, Father Edward Weis, p. 18; TS57, Sister Agnes Devlin, pp. 17, 20; TS39, Sister Barbara Mersinger, p. 65; TS09, Sister Miriam Carmel Lechthaler, pp. 3-4; TC43, Sister Agnes Chau, p. 8.

80. FARC, 5-06, Hoingan Diary, Father Dietz, October 24, 1924. FARC, 3-07, Hoingan Diary, Father Bauer, August 10-11, 1935; Father Weber, September 8,

1936. FARC, 23–09, Pinglo-Pantien Diary, Father Regan, June 1933. SARC, Tolan, "Manchuria, Book 3," p. 100.

81. *The Field Afar*, July-August 1936, "Chinese Sisters," by Father Thomas V. Kiernan, p. 208. See also Father Robert Sheridan, *Native Sisters in the Orient* (New York: Maryknoll Pamphlet Library, 1936), pp. 13–15. TC44, Sister Rose Chan, pp. 2, 3; TC46; Rose Lam, p. 9; TC06, Sister Joan Ling, pp. 7–8; TS87, Sister Margaret Marie Jung, pp. 31–32; TS39, Sister Barbara Mersinger, p. 64. SARC, 52–01, Laipo Convent Diary, February 3, 1939.

82. FARC, 23–05, Szwong Diary, July 19, 1947.

83. SARC, Box—Novitiate, Wuchow, Pre-Novitiate Training, Outline of Work to be Begun at Pingnam in August 1935, Monsignor Bernard Meyer; Box—Novitiate, Manchuria, Constitutions, Article 54; Box—Novitiate, Kaying, File 2, Sister Catechists of Our Lady, Kaying, October 8, 1949, p. 5. SARC, 43–08, Rosary Convent Diary, February 21, 1935; September 1, 1935; 43–09, September 1, 1936. SARC, 40–07, Immaculate Heart Sisters' Novitiate, February 14, 1938.

84. TC07, Sister Joseph Lam, pp. 10, 13–16, 21. SARC, 40–05, Immaculate Heart Sisters' Novitiate, January 16, 1936 and February 27, 1936. 40–13, September 9, 1938. SARC, 47–01, Tungshek Diary, January 25, 1935. SARC, 51–12, Pingnam Convent Diary, January 9, 1946. *The Field Afar*, April 1938, "Oriental Sisters in the Making," pp. 124–125. FARC, 03–08, "Kongmoon Bulletin," February 1936.

85. SARC, 40–11, Immaculate Heart Sisters' Novitiate, January 7, February 16, September 6, October 8, 1946; 40–12, February 11, August 31, September 4, 1947; 40–13, September 9, 1948. SARC, 50–02, Wuchow Convent Diary, July 6–9, 1948. SARC, 51–12, Pingnam Convent Diary, January 9, 1946. SARC, Box—Novitiate, Kaying, File 3, letter of Bishop Ford to Mother Mary Columba, September 7, 1948; Box—Novitiate, Wuchow, Sisters of Charity of the Sacred Heart, July-August 1946, p. 1 and History of the Sisters of the Charity of the Sacred Heart, 1947, p. 3; Box—Novitiate, Kweilin, Congregation of the Sister Catechists of the Blessed Mother, June 1947, nos. 7 and 19. TS57, Sister Agnes Devlin, pp. 11, 23–24; TS96, Sister Moira Riehl, p. 6; TS86, Sister Agnes Cazale, p. 6; TS53, Sister Celine Marie Werner, pp. 5, 25–26; TC44, Sister Rose Chan, p. 28–29.

86. SARC, Box—Novitiate, Kweilin, Nos. 8 and 18; Box—Novitiate, Wuchow, Sisters of Charity, pp. 1, 4. Sheridan, *ibid.*, pp. 13, 15; *The Field Afar*, July-August 1936, "Chinese Sisters," p. 208.

87. SARC, Box—Novitiate, Kweilin, Nos. 9 and 13; Box—Novitiate, Wuchow, Pre-Novitiate Training, 1935. SARC, 40–07, Immaculate Heart Sisters Novitiate, May 12, 1938; September 13, 1938. SARC, 51–01, Pingnam Convent Diary, September 9, 1935; 51–03, January 15, 1937. SARC, Tolan, "Manchuria, Book 3," pp. 88–89, 98. TS49, Sister Mary Eunice Tolan, p. 12; TS50, Sister Mary De Lellis McKenna, p. 10; TS93, Sister Ann Carol Brielmaier, p. 3; TS87, Sister Margaret Marie Jung, pp. 31–33; TC44, Sister Rose Chan, pp. 11–12.

88. SARC, 52–05, Laipo Convent, September 9, 1943. SARC, 51–12, Pingnam Convent, January 10, 1946. SARC, 50–08, Wuchow Convent, February 17, 1946. SARC, Box—Novitiate, Wuchow, Letter of Sister Margaret Marie to Mother Mary Joseph, Pingnam, March 20, 1944.

89. SARC, Box—Novitiate, Kaying, File 2, "Review of Our Novitiate Work, Kaying Vicariate, June 1946-February 1947," Part 3, p. 2.

90. *Ibid.*, pp. 3–5.

91. SARC, Box—Novitiate, Wuchow, Constitutions, p. 2; Box—Novitiate, Kweilin, No. 8. TS09, Sister Miriam Carmel Lechthaler, p. 4.

92. SARC, Box—Novitiate, Wuchow, Sisters of Charity, p. 2–3; History of the Congregation, pp. 5–6; Box—Novitiate, Kweilin, Nos. 15, 16; Box—Novitiates,

Kaying, File 2, Sister Catechists of Our Lady, Kaying, October 8, 1949, pp. 7–8. SARC, 55–12, Fushun-Honan Parish, Report of Sister Mary Lelia (Makra), "Native Novitiate and Aspirants, October 1943." SARC, 42–02, Laohukow Novitiate, December 28, 1942; 42–03, May 7 and 17, 1944; 42–06, December 28, 1948.

93. SARC, Box—Novitiate, Kaying, Review of Novitiate Work, Part 4, p. 4; Box—Novitiate, Wuchow, Sisters of Charity, p. 2–3.

94. Box—Novitiate, Kaying, File 2, Sister Catechists of Our Lady, Kaying, October 8, 1949, p. 8. SARC, 42–01, Laohukow Novitiate, March 14, 1942; 42–02, September 10–12, 1942 and October 20, 1942; 42–03, January 24–25, 1943. SARC, 40–03, Immaculate Heart Sisters' Novitiate, January 23, 1934 and March 21, 1934; SARC, 51–02, Pingnam Convent Diary, June 26, 1936. *The Field Afar*, July-August 1936, "Chinese Sisters," p. 208. FARC, "The Manchu-knoller," May-June 1934, p. 1. TS79, Sister Julia Hannigan, p. 2.

95. SARC, 42–02, Laohukow Novitiate, July 24–26, 1942 and August 2, 1942.

96. SARC, Box—Novitiate, Wuchow, Sisters of Charity, pp. 2–3; History of the Congregation, p. 6.

97. SARC, Box—Novitiate, Wuchow, Sisters of Charity, pp. 2–3; Box—Novitiate, Kweilin, The Congregation, nos. 14, 16.

98. SARC, Box—Novitiate, Fushun, Constitutions, Part 3, no. 95; Box—Novitiate, Kweilin, The Congregation, no. 12; Box—Novitiate, Wuchow, Constitution, Part 6, no. 41; Box—Novitiate, Kaying, File 2, Sister Catechists, October 8, 1949, p. 4.

99. SARC, Box—Novitiate, Wuchow, History of the Congregation, p. 4; Box—Novitiate, Kaying, File 2, Review of Our Novitiate Work, June 1946-February 1947, Part 4, pp. 4–5; Box—Novitiate, Kaying, File 2, Sister Catechists, October 1949, p. 9; Box—Novitiate, Kweilin, Bulletins of the Sister Catechists by Sister Rose Victor (Mersinger), October, December 1949. SARC, 42–03, Laohukow Novitiate, February 2, March 3, April 5 and June 1, 1943; 42–04, July 23-August 6, 1945; SARC, 51–08, Pingnam Convent Diary, February 5–8, 1942; March 6, 1942; May 1, 1943.

100. FARC, 30–06, Constitutions of the Kongmoon Sisters. SARC, Box—Novitiate, Kweilin, The Congregation, nos. 4, 20; Box—Novitiate, Wuchow, Sisters of Charity, July-August 1946, p. 1; Box—Novitiate, Kaying, File 2, Our Novitiate Work, April 10, 1948, no. 2; Congregations of the Sister Catechists, June 1946-February 1947, Part 1, p. 1.

101. See Chapter 3 on The Direct Apostolate.

102. SARC, Box—Novitiate, Kaying, File 2, Our Novitiate Work, April 10, 1948, nos. 3, 4.

103. SARC, 40–05, Immaculate Heart Sisters' Novitiate, May 20, 1936; 40–14, March 1, 1949. SARC, 51–03, Pingnam Convent Diary, February 9, 1937. SARC, 55–05, Fushun-Honan, Coal Dust, February 3 and March 10, 1932; 55–06, July 6, 1935. TC06, Sister Joan Ling, p. 8.

104. SARC, 40–01, Immaculate Heart Sisters' Novitiate, Kongmoon Candidates by Sister Mary Patricia Coughlin, 1926–1930; 40–02, December 21, 1932 and October 3, 1933; 40–05, February 11, 1936.

105. SARC, 55–05, Fushun-Honan, Coal Dust, December 31, 1931; February 21, 1932; 55–09, September 8, 1939; 55–12, February 11, 1942. SARC, 51–02, Pingnam Convent Diary, August 18, 1936; 51–03, February 18, 1937; 51–04, January 6, 1938; 51–06, January 6, 1940. SARC, Box—Novitiate, Wuchow, History of the Congregation, p. 2.

106. SARC, 43–11, Kaying Rosary Convent Diary, February 11, 1938 and September 12, 1938. SARC, 42–02, Laohukow Novitiate, November 21, 1942; 42–03, September 19 and November 21–23, 1944. SARC, 47–03, Tungshek Holy Child

Convent, September 12, 1939; 47–04, September 16, 1941; SARC, Box—Novitiate, Kaying, Review of Our Novitiate Work, June 1946-February 1947, Part 1, pp. 2–3.

107. TF65, Father Frederick Fitzgerald, p. 25; TF67, Father Robert Winkels, p. 5.

108. TF06, Father Allan Dennis, pp. 71–72. See also TC46, Bishop Edward McGurkin, p. 47.

109. FARC, 4–01, Kongmoon-Yeungkong Diary, August 23, 1919 and April 29, 1921; FARC, 7–03, Hoingan Diary, November 24 December 11, 1923; FARC, 15–03, Hoingan Diary, May 4, 1924; FARC, 3–04, Kochow Diary, February 3, 1920; FARC, 4–01, Yeungkong Chronicle, August 23, 1919 and April 29-May 2, 1921.

110. TF46, Bishop Edward McGurkin, p. 45. Also FARC, 25–24, letters of Father Joseph McCormack to Father James A. Walsh, November 2 and December 12, 1926.

111. TF01, Father Robert Sheridan, p. 10.

112. TF46, Bishop Edward McGurkin, pp. 39, 44; TF32, Father Leo McCarthy, pp. 18–19.

113. TC39, Father Peter Ma, pp. 22–23, 37–38; TC01, Father Paul Pang, p. 13; TC19, Father Peter Chum, pp. 40–41; TC27, Bishop John Wu, pp. 25, 27, 46–47, 82, 84. Mark Tsai, "Bishop Ford, Apostle of South China," *The American Ecclesiastical Review*, October 1952, pp. 241–247.

114. TC13, Father John Yeung, pp. 50–51; TC13, Father Simeon To, p. 19; TC27, Bishop John Wu, pp. 77–80. Father Francis X. Ford, "Maryknoll Mission Letters," *The Ecclesiastical Review*, November 1926, pp. 538–540.

115. *The Field Afar*, June 1927, "Maryknoll's First Seminary in China," p. 152. See also February 1920, "The Native Priest Idea," p. 304; January 1928, "The Making of Chinese Priests in the Hakka Mission," p. 18.

116. TC13, Father John Yeung, pp. 44; TC13, Father Simeon To, pp. 14–17, 30–33, 66–72.

117. TC13, Father Simeon To, pp. 16–17, 24–28, 65–66; TC19, Father Peter Chum, pp. 43–44.

118. TC11, Sister Rose Chin, pp. 2–3, 8.

119. *Ibid.*, pp. 2, 4, 10.

120. TC11, Sister Rose Chin, pp. 8, 9; TC23, Sister Maureen Au, pp. 9–11; TC46, Rose Lam, p. 12. TC26, Sister Philomena Chan, p. 22, recalls that she did not join the community of the Kongmoon Sisters because she heard that their rules prescribed that they had to report if they did not empty their bowels daily.

121. TC43, Sisters Agnes Chau, pp. 10–11; TC46, Sister Joseph Lam, pp. 4–5, 13–16, 42, 55.

122. TC11, Sister Rose Chin, p. 17; TC43, Sister Agnes Chau, p. 12. TS09, Sister Miriam Carmel Lechthaler, p. 6.

123. TC43, Sister Agnes Chau, pp. 37–39; TC44, Sister Rose Chan, pp. 75–76.

124. TC11, Sister Rose Chin, pp. 17–20.

125. TC06, Sister Joan Ling, pp. 31, 34–35; TC11, Sister Rose Chin, p. 25.

126. TC43, Sister Agnes Chau, pp. 12–14.

127. *Ibid.*, p. 39.

128. TC21, Sister Catherine Mary Lee, pp. 19–22.

129. FARC, 31–05, letter of Father James E. Walsh to Father James A. Walsh, May 31, 1922.

130. M.E.P. Archives-K59, letter of Bishop Adolphe Rayssac to Bishop de Guébriant, July 23, 1924. FARC, 31–06, letter of Monsignor James E. Walsh to Father James A. Walsh, June 8, 1924; letter of Father James A. Walsh to Monsignor James E. Walsh, July 11, 1924.

131. FARC, 31–07, letter of Bishop de Guébriant to Father James A. Walsh,

November 11, 1924; 16–04, letter of Bishop Jean-Marie Blois to Father James A. Walsh, February 29, 1924, February 12, 1925 and August 7, 1925.

132. M.E.P. Archives–555R, No. 85, letter of Bishop Antoine Fourquet to Bishop de Guébriant, October 11, 1924. FARC, 31–07, letter of Monsignor James E. Walsh to Bishop Adolphe Rayssac, January 12, 1925.

133. FARC, 45–02, letter of Bishop Antoine Fourquet to Father James A. Walsh, January 13, 1925; 31–07 and M.E.P. Archives–555R, No. 101, letter of Monsignor James E. Walsh to Father James A. Walsh, January 6, 1925.

134. FARC, 45–02, letter of Father James A. Walsh to Bishop Antoine Fourquet, February 28, 1925; letter of Bishop Antoine Fourquet to Father James A. Walsh, March 26, 1925.

135. FARC, 31–07, letter of Monsignor James E. Walsh to Bishop Adolphe Rayssac, January 12, 1925; letter of Monsignor James E. Walsh to Father James A. Walsh, January 6, 1925; 45–02, letter of Bishop Antoine Fourquet to Father James A. Walsh, January 13, 1925.

136. FARC, Miscellaneous N-Paris Foreign Mission, 1922–1923: letter of Bishop de Guébriant to Father James A. Walsh, February 25, 1925; letter of Father James A. Walsh to Bishop de Guébriant, March 9, 1925; 31–07, letter of Father James A. Walsh to Monsignor James E. Walsh, March 16, 1925.

137. FARC, 31–07, letter of Monsignor James E. Walsh to Father William O'Shea, February 5, 1925, February 21, 1925. M.E.P. Archives–555R, No. 100, letter of Monsignor James E. Walsh to Bishop Antoine Fourquet, January 12, 1925; No. 103, letter of Monsignor James E. Walsh to Bishop Antoine Fourquet, January 22, 1925.

138. M.E.P. Archives–555R, No. 112, letter of Bishop Antoine Fourquet to Bishop de Guébriant, March 23, 1925. FARC, 45–02, letter of Bishop Antoine Fourquet to Monsignor James E. Walsh, March 24, 1925.

139. FARC, 31–07, letter of Monsignor James E. Walsh to Father James A. Walsh, March 28, 1925; letter of Father William O'Shea to Monsignor James E. Walsh, June 1, 1925.

140. *The Field Afar*, February 1927, p. 45.

141. FARC, 31–08, letter of Monsignor James E. Walsh to Father John Considine, September 30, 1926.

142. FARC, 39–09, Bishop James E. Walsh, "Report to Cardinal Prefect of Propaganda," May 24, 1938, pp. 2–3.

143. *Ibid.*, pp. 4, 7.

144. FARC, 39–09, letter of Bishop James E. Walsh to Father James Drought, May 28, 1938.

145. FARC, 39–09, letter of Bishop James E. Walsh to Father James Drought, June 23, 1938, p. 1.

146. *Ibid.*, pp. 2–4.

147. FARC, 39–09, Bishop James E. Walsh, "Report on Visitation of Wuchow Vicariate, November 10–30, 1938," December 10, 1938, p. 4.

148. FARC, 39–09, letter of Father James Drought to Bishop James E. Walsh, July 30, 1938, pp. 5–6.

149. Bishop James E. Walsh, "Report on Visitation," p. 4.

150. Ibid., pp. 5–7. See also TC19, Father Peter Chum, pp. 6–7.

151. James E. Walsh, "Report on Visitation," pp. 7–8. FARC, 35–04, letter of Bishop Francis X. Ford to Bishop James E. Walsh, March 13, 1939.

152. James E. Walsh, "Report on Visitation."

153. FARC, 39–10, letter of Bishop James E. Walsh to General Council, March 4, 1939 quoted in letter of Father John Considine to Cardinal Fumasoni-Biondi,

pp. 1–2; letter of Bishop James E. Walsh to Archbishop Zanin of April 10, 1939, pp. 1–2; letter of Bishop James E. Walsh to Cardinal Fumasoni-Biondi, May 22, 1939, pp. 1–3.

154. FARC, 39–10, telegram from Rome to Maryknoll, July 21, 1939.

155. Monsignor James E. Walsh, "Report on Visitation," p. 9.

156. *Ibid.*, pp. 8–9; 30–03, letter of Father Bernard Meyer to Father James A. Walsh, January 4, 1925.

157. *The Field Afar,* September 1932, p. 236.

158. SARC, Box—South China, Kaying, Kongmoon, Kweilin, Wuchow, Folder 9, Wuchow Vicariate, "Our Relations with the Chinese Sisters," Bishop Frederick Donaghy, August 1949, p. 1.

Chapter 6—Adaptation and Accommodation

1. TF28, Father Peter Reilly, p. 4.

2. James E. Walsh, *Mission Manual of the Vicariate of Kongmoon* (Hong Kong: Nazareth Press, 1937), p. 146. Since the Manual was meant primarily to be a priest's handbook, Bishop Walsh always referred to the missioner as "he," although in sections like this one, he certainly included the Maryknoll Sisters as well.

3. *Ibid.*, p. 147.

4. *Ibid.*, pp. 148–149.

5. *Ibid.*, pp. 149–150.

6. *Ibid.*, pp. 153–154, 173.

7. FARC, 16–04, letter of Bishop Blois to Father Patrick Byrne, June 14, 1926.

8. James E. Walsh, *Mission Manual*, pp. 21, 54. FARC, 8–04, Sancian Diary, March 27, 1934. TC04, Father Thomas Lau, p. 14.

9. TF37, Edward Youker, p. 17. James Smith, *Maryknoll Hong Kong Chronicle, 1918–1975* (Maryknoll: Maryknoll Fathers, 1950), p. 65.

10. TS13, Sister Mary Schafers, p. 8; TS12, Sister Agnes Regina Rafferty, pp. 8–10.

11. TS18, Sister Mary Paul McKenna, p. 2.

12. TF25, Father Raymond Gaspard, p. 41; TS05, Sister Virginia Flagg, p. 13; TC12, Michael Tsa, p. 2; TC44, Sister Rose Chan, p. 69; TC47, Cheuk York Mong, pp. 3–8. SARC, 48–12, Yeungkong Convent Diary, August 10, 1949.

13. TF03, Father Thomas Kiernan, pp. 72–73.

14. TC26, Sister Philomena Chan, p. 28.

15. TC20, Cheuk Chiu Yin, p. 21; TC44, Sister Rose Chan, pp. 69–70.

16. TC13, Father John Yeung, p. 57.

17. TC04, Father Thomas Lau, pp. 16–17. See also TC20, Cheuk Chiu Yin, p. 21; TC49, Peter Wong, p. 19; TS05, Sister Virginia Flagg, p. 13; TS83, Sister Mary Hock, pp. 57–58.

18. FARC, 35–05, letter of Bishop Francis Ford to Superior General, October 25, 1943, p. 3.

19. *Ibid,* p. 4. TS36, René Koo, pp. 24–25.

20. TS65, Sister Irene Fogarty, p. 54.

21. TF03, Father Thomas Kiernan, p. 9. *Collectanea Sacrae Congregationis De Propaganda Fide* (Rome: Typis Polyglottis Vaticanis, 1907) I, p. 312, n. 504; II, pp. 187–188, n. 1606.

22. FARC, unpublished manuscript by Father William Downs, "The Kaying Diocese—A Historical Sketch," 1962, p. 56.

23. FARC, 3-04, Kochow Diary, Father William O'Shea, July 10, 1920; 9-04, letter of Father John Heemskerk to Father James A. Walsh, September 18, 1927. TF01, Father Robert Sheridan, pp. 1, 61, 76-80; TF03, Father Thomas Kiernan, pp. 14-16; TF68, Father Edward Mueth, pp. 17-18.

24. *The Field Afar*, July 1926, p. 184; March 1928, p. 77; April 1928, p. 117; June 1928, p. 179. FARC, 9-05, letter of Father Thomas McDermott to Father James A. Walsh, January 30, 1928; letter of Father Frederick Dietz to Father James A. Walsh, February 14, 1928. FARC, 4-03, Yeungkong Diary, November 19, 1927.

25. FARC, 23-01, "Kwangsi Bamboo Leaves," February 15, 1930 and March 1, 1930; 23-13, letter of Father John Buckley to Father James A. Walsh, November 10, 1929 and letter of Father Frederick Dietz to Father James A. Walsh, March 14, 1929.

26. *The Field Afar*, February 1927, p. 43; November 1931, p. 344. Father William Downs, "The Kaying Diocese," p. 56?RCR

27. FARC, 52-09, Father Thomas O'Melia, July 16, 1939, pp. 1-14; Father Thomas O'Melia, September 1937, pp. 1-11.

28. FARC, 27-03, 04, Maryknoll House Diary, August 3, 1935, August 19, 1940, February 1941.

29. *Maryknoll Hong Kong Chronicle*, 1918-1975, pp. 13-14, 39, 43, 149, 156. FARC, 52-09, letter of Father William Downs to Father James Drought, May 3, 1940. TF58, Father Thomas Brack, pp. 9-10; TF73, Francis Pouliot, pp. 17-19.

30. *Maryknoll Hong Kong Chronicle*, pp. 146, 150-151. FARC, 9-19, Siaoloc Diary, March 1948, p. 1; 23-05, Pingnam Language School Diary, September-November 1947; 59-09, The Kaying Vicariate Five-Year Language Course, May 19, 1943. TF82, Father William Eggleston, p. 8; TF32, Father Leo McCarthy, pp. 4-5; TF17, Father Irvin Nugent, pp. 10-11; TF63, Father Carroll Quinn, p. 1.

31. FARC, 12-17, letters of Father Joseph McCormack to Father James A. Walsh, November 2, November 12, 1926. TF36, Bishop John Comber, p. 4; TF20, Father Sylvio Gilbert, pp. 21a-22; TF46, Bishop Edward McGurkin, p. 45.

32. FARC, 11-45, letter of Father Sylvio Gilbert to Father James A. Walsh, February 5, 1928; 48-01, letter of Father Raymond Lane to Father James A. Walsh, August 2, 1926. FARC, 49-07, letter of Father Joseph McCormack to Maryknoll Headquarters, February 27, 1940; Father John O'Donnell, Report on Language School, January 1946; Father Joseph McCormack, Report to 1946 Chapter on Language School, July 1946. TF33, Father Edward Manning, pp. 10-12; TF50, Father William Kaschmitter, pp. 21-22. *The Field Afar*, June 1928, p. 181; November 1934, p. 290.

33. FARC, 16-01, Fushun Diary, April 1930; 49-27, Fushun Mission Language Students, n.d. TF31, Father Henry Felsecker, p. 1; TS40, Sister Mary Lelia Makra, p. 12. *The Field Afar*, July-August 1932, p. 203; June 1934, p. 173; December 1934, p. 348.

34. TS10, Sister Mary Paul McKenna, pp. 1, 6-7; TS82, Sister Mary Rosalie Weber, p. 25. SARC, Sister Mary Imelda Sheridan, "A Brief History of the South China Region, 1921-1958," Part I, p. 6.

35. TS08, Sister Joseph Marie Kane, pp. 2, 6; TS20, Sister Marie Corinne Rost, p. 8.

36. TS05, Sister Virginia Flagg, p. 3.

37. TS12, Sister Agnes Regina Rafferty, pp. 4, 10; TS74, Sister Kathleen Marie Shea, p. 5.

38. TS02, Sister Monica Marie Boyle, p. 1; TS68, Sister Colombiere Bradley, pp. 3-4, 12.

39. TS34, Sister Teresa Hollfelder, p. 3.

40. Sister Mary Imelda Sheridan, "A Brief History," Part II, p. 4.

41. TS58, Sister Madeline Sophie Karlon, pp. 57, 69. SARC, 47–01, December 29, 1934, April 26, 1935. FARC, Father William Downs, "The Kaying Diocese," p. 94.

42. TS46, Sister Louise Kroeger, pp. 7–11, 31; TS44, Sister Rosalia Kettl, pp. 6–7; TS30, Sister Jean Theophane Steinbauer, pp. 8–9. SARC, Box—South China Histories, File—Tungshek Language School.

43. TS51, Sister Mary Paulita Hoffman, pp. 21–23; TS46, Sister Louise Kroeger, p. 12; TS07, Sister Julia Hannigan, p. 9; TS58, Sister Madeline Sophie Karlon, pp. 40–41; TS44, Sister Rosalia Kettl, pp. 20–21.

44. Sister Mary Imelda Sheridan, "A Brief History," p. 28. TS23, Sister Rose Duchesne Debrecht, p. 20.

45. TS21, Sister Mary Louise Martin, pp. 11–13; TS22, Sister Dorothy Rubner, pp. 15–16; TS47, Sister Mary Diggins, pp. 2, 9–10; TS93, Sister Ann Carol Brielmaier, pp. 2–3; TS76, Sister Rose Bernadette Gallagher, pp. 20–21; TS86, Sister Agnes Cazale, pp. 1–2.

46. SARC, 54–01, 1930. TS14, Sister Mary Gemma Shea, pp. 5–6; TS26, Sister Mary Angelica O'Leary, p. 3; TS01, Sister Mary Jude Babione, pp. 5, 9. *The Field Afar*, December 1935, p. 351.

47. SARC, unpublished manuscript by Sister Mary Eunice Tolan, "Manchuria, Book 3," pp. 77–78. TS26, Sister Mary Angelica O'Leary, p. 16; TS36, Sister Francis de Sales Marsland, pp. 1–2; TS41, Sister Rita Clare Comber, p. 9; TS53, Sister Celine Marie Werner, pp. 3–5; TS40, Sister Mary Lelia Makra, p. 11.

48. TS41, Sister Rita Clare Comber, p. 9.

49. TF40, Father James Smith, p. 9; see also TC04, Father Thomas Lau, p. 15.

50. TS47, Sister Mary Diggins, p. 10.

51. *Ibid.*, p. 38.

52. TC04, Father Thomas Lau, p. 15; TC44, Sister Rose Chan, pp. 71–72; TC11, Sister Rose Chin, p. 18; TC12, Michael Tsa, pp. 2–3; TC13, Father John Yeung, p. 44; TC05, Father John Tse, p. 14; TC41, Robert Tse, p. 17; TS41, Sister Rita Clare Comber, p. 9; TS49, Sister Mary Eunice Tolan, p. 49; TF25, Father Raymond Gaspard, p. 46; TF80, Father James T. Manning, p. 33; TF38, Father Robert Greene, pp. 82–83.

53. TC06, Sister Joan Ling, p. 41.

54. TC25, Jong Kin Shum, p. 25; TF05, Father John Driscoll, p. 48.

55. TF56, Father James McLaughlin, pp. 37–38.

56. TF11, Father Joseph Van den Bogaard, pp. 13–14, 19.

57. TC06, Sister Joan Ling, p. 40; TC49, Peter Wong, p. 8.

58. TS35, Kathleen Bradley, p. 18.

59. TF20, Father Sylvio Gilbert, p. 91; TF33, Father Edward Manning, p. 49.

60. TC12, Michael Tsa, p. 3; TC49, Peter Wong, pp. 8–9, 19–21; TF54, Father William Pheur, p. 18.

61. TF28, Father Peter Reilly, pp. 3–6.

62. TS39, Sister Barbara Mersinger, pp. 44–45; TF59, Father Joseph Early, p. 12.

63. TC44, Sister Rose Chan, p. 71.

64. TS93, Sister Ann Carol Brielmaier, p. 44; TF28, Father Peter Reilly, p. 3.

65. TS15, Sister Mary Gemma Shea, p. 16.

66. FARC, 31–03, letter of Father James A. Walsh to Father James E. Walsh, September 20, 1920.

67. "Letter of the Apostolic Delegate to China Addressed to the Very Reverend James E. Walsh and Edward J. Galvin, April 23, 1923," *The Ecclesiastical Review*, September 1923, pp. 288–293.

68. FARC, 31-07, letter of Monsignor James E. Walsh to Father James A. Walsh, June 8, 1925.

69. FARC, 5-05, Fachow Dairy, September 21, 1924.

70. FARC, 8-10, Sunchong Diary, February 27-August 1, 1926, pp. 1-4; see also November 1, 1923.

71.FARC, 31-07, letter of Monsignor James E. Walsh to Father James A. Walsh, June 8, 1925.

72. TF07, Father Francis MacRae, pp. 48-49.

73. *Ibid.*, pp. 49-50.

74. FARC, 4-01, Yeungkong Chronicle, January 30, 1919; 4-03, letter from Father Ford, October 1, 1924, p. 7.

75. FARC, 4-03, letter from Ford, p. 8.

76. John F. Donovan, *The Pagoda and the Cross* (New York: Charles Scribner's Sons, 1967), pp. 165-169. *The Field Afar*, December 1940, "Cathedral in Adobe," pp. 24-25.

77. FARC, 48-01, letter of Father James A. Walsh to Father Raymond Lane, April 21, 1927. Letters of Father Raymond Lane to Father James A. Walsh, July 20, 1926; January 24, 1927; March 7, 1927; May 27, 1927. Cablegram of Father James A. Walsh to Father Raymond Lane, April 20, 1927.

78. *The Field Afar*, July-August 1932, p. 202.

79. FARC, 40-01, letter of Father Raymond Lane to Father James A. Walsh, June 13, 1927.

80. *The Field Afar*, July-August 1932, p. 203.

81. *Maryknoll*, August 1963, "Journey's End for Mr. Oka," p. 12. FARC, 25-06, letter of Father John Swift to Father James A. Walsh, February 2, 1928.

82. *Maryknoll*, August 1963, p. 12.

83. *The Field Afar*, May 1927, p. 124.

84. *The Field Afar*, October 1929, p. 284.

85. TC13, Father Simeon To, pp. 56-57.

86. TF07, Father Francis MacRae, p. 14. SARC, 40-05, Pakkai Convent Diary, July 16, 1936. FARC, 4-01, Yeungkong Chronicle, January 13, 1919, p. 45.

87. *Collectanea Commissionis Synodalis* (Peking), November 1928, pp. 438-448. These pages give a list of 95 catechisms in print at the time but the bibliography is incomplete; unlisted are those published by the Scheut Fathers at their printing house of Siwantzu in Inner Mongolia.

88. *Collectanea Commissionis Synodalis*, March 1929, pp. 253-254; July-August 1934, pp. 611-612.

89. The difference between the Mandarin version and the Cantonese version is immediately apparent. The first question, "Why are you in this world?", in Mandarin is 你為什麼生在世上? [Ni wei-shih-ma sheng tsai shih-shang?] appears in Cantonese as 你為乜緣故生在世上呢? [Nei wai mat uen-koò shaang tsoì shai sheŭng ni?]

90. FARC, 23-01, February 1, 1930.

91. FARC, 23-01, December 1, 1930; June 15, 1931.

92. See bibliographic reference in *Collectanea Commissionis Synodalis*, November 1928, p. 440; March 1929, pp. 247-248.

93. *Collectanea Commissionis Synodalis*, February 1929, pp. 155-156; April 1929, pp. 324-325.

94. FARC, 3-08, "Kongmoon Bulletin," January 1939; FARC, 23-04, Wuchow Notes, January 1937; Wuchow Newsletter, July 8, 1937. FARC, 3-08, "Kongmoon Bulletin," January 19, 1937. Monsignor Bernard F. Meyer, "Launch into the Deep," *Collectanea Commissionis Synodalis*, June 1937, p. 152. Monsi-

gnor Bernard F. Meyer, *Mission Methods, Pastoral Instructions to the Clergy of the Prefecture Apostolic of Wuchow* (n.p., 1936), p. 40.

95. Monsignor Bernard Meyer, "Launch into the Deep," pp. 557, 569; *Fides News Service*, February 6, 1937, p. 563.

96. *Yaoli Wenda* (Hong Kong: St. Louis Industrial School, 1939, 1946, 1947, 1951).

97. Monsignor Bernard Meyer, *Mission Methods*, p. 18.

98. Monsignor Bernard Meyer, "Launch into the Deep," pp. 557–558. *Our Holy Religion Series, Course I, Study Book* (Hong Kong: Catholic Truth Society, 1937, 1939), inside cover and Lesson 1; *Course I, Teacher's Manual* (1939), Lesson 1, pp. 1–9.

99. Monsignor Bernard Meyer, *Mission Methods*, p. 19; "Launch into the Deep," p. 558. Monsignor Meyer acknowledged that he borrowed ideas for his catechism for children from *A Course in Religion for the Elementary School*, a catechism written by Reverend Alexander Schorsch, C.M. and Sister M. Dolores Schorsch, C.S.B., published first by the Archdiocese of Chicago in 1935. See Preface to the teachers' edition of *Our Religion Series, Course I, Teacher's Manual* (1949); see also FARC, 8–06, Tungchen Diary, September 1938.

100. FARC, 23–04, Wuchow Notes, September 9, 1938. In 1949 Meyer completed the *Our Holy Religion Series* by offering an illustrated *Preparatory Course* for inquiries; it came in two volumes, a study book and a manual of brief explanations.

101. Monsignor Bernard Meyer, *Mission Methods*, pp. 18, 29. Introduction to *Our Religion Series, Course II*(a) (1940).

102. *Mission Methods*, p. 19.

103. This catechism called in Cantonese *Shing kaaù iù leĩ mân taàp* was published by the M.E.P. Nazareth Press in Hong Kong in 1923.

104. Reverend Charles Rey, M.E.P., *Hãc kā t'où t'âm yáo lĩ lioc chôt, Explications du Catéchisme* (Hong Kong: Nazareth Press, 1912).

105. TS51, Sister Mary Paulita Hoffman, p. 20.

106. TS44, Sister Rosalia Kettl, pp. 20–21.

107. TS51, Sister Mary Paulita Hoffman, p. 21.

108. *Ibid.*, pp. 22–23; see also TS58, Sister Madeleine Sophie Karlon, pp. 40–41.

109. FARC, Box—Sister Anna Mary Moss—Catechism, *Preaching the Catholic Doctrine in the Local Dialect*, Book 13, pp. 6–10.

110. TS51, Sister Mary Paulita Hoffman, p. 23.

111. *Collectanea Sacrae Congregationis De Propaganda Fide* (Rome: 1907), I, pp. 130–141. For a detailed study of the Rites controversy, see Reverend George Minamiki, S.J., *The Chinese Rites Controversy from its Beginning to Modern Times* (Chicago: Loyola University Press, 1985).

112. Sven Hedin, *Chiang Kai-shek: Marshal of China* (New York: The John Day Company, 1940), p. 81; Robert Payne, *Chiang Kai-shek* (New York: Waybright and Talley, 1969), p. 163.

113. TF03, Father Thomas Kiernan, p. 61.

114. TF07, Father Francis MacRae, pp. 30–32; TC45, Wu Pak Seng, pp. 13–14.

115. TS30, Sister Jean Theophane Steinbauer, p. 7; TS09, Sister Miriam Carmel Lechthaler, p. 12; TC06, Sister Joan Ling, pp. 21–22.

116. TF03, Father Thomas Kiernan, p. 60.

117. TF68, Father Edward Mueth, p. 48.

118. TF20, Father Sylvio Gilbert, p. 27.

119. The text of these three important documents can be found in *Acta Apostolicae Sedis* (Rome), October 15, 1936, pp. 406–409; and *Collectanea Commissionis Synodalis*, October 1936, pp. 868–869; January 1940, pp. 125–126. See also *The*

Rock (Hong Kong), March 1940, pp. 107–112.

120. TC21, Sister Catherine Mary Lee, p. 6.

121. TC45, Wu Pak Seng, pp. 12–13. See also TS65, Sister Irene Fogarty, pp. 50–51.

122. TS51, Sister Mary Paulita Hoffman, pp. 43–44.

123. TC45, Wu Pak Seng, p. 14.

124. TS01, Sister Antonia Maria Guerrieri, p. 45.

125. *Maryknoll—The Field Afar*, March 1949, pp. 1–6.

126. TC43, Sister Agnes Chau, p. 33.

127. TS19, Kathleen Bradley, pp. 5–6.

128. TS76, Sister Rose Bernadette Gallagher, p. 13.

129. FARC, unpublished manuscript by Father John Donovan, "Maryknoll's Wuchow Mission, Kwangsi," p. 439.

130. TS76, Sister Rose Bernadette Gallagher, p. 13.

131. "Letter of Francis X. Ford," *The Ecclesiastical Review*, October 1923, p. 417.

132. *Ibid.*, p. 418.

133. *Collectanea Sacrae Congregationis De Propaganda Fide, I*, No. 135, pp. 42–43. The whole text is translated by Father James E. Walsh in his *Maryknoll Spiritual Directory* (New York: The Field Afar Press, 1947), pp. 60–63.

134. Father James E. Walsh, *Manual of the Vicariate of Kongmoon*, pp. 150, 153.

135. Monsignor Bernard Meyer, *Mission Methods*, pp. 14, 19.

136. SARC, Box—South China, Kaying, Kongmoon, Kweilin, Wuchow, Folder 9, Wuchow Mission Meeting, August 1949, p. 1.

137. SARC, Box—Ford's Conferences,"The Sisters' Activities According to the Kaying Synodal Decree," July 1943, pp. 33–35.

138. TS29, Sister Thérèse Grondin, pp. 1–2.

139. TS30, Sister Jean Theophane Steinbauer, p. 16.

140. FARC, 5–05, Fachow Diary, June 27, 1924.

141. "Maryknoll Mission Letters," *The Ecclesiastical Review*, February 1927, p. 195.

142. *Ibid.*, p. 196.

143. TS76, Sister Rose Bernadette Gallagher, pp. 16–17.

Chapter 7—Maryknoll and Politics

1. Immanuel C. Hsü, *The Rise of Modern China* (New York: Oxford University Press, 1975), pp. 584–588, 629–631; Diana Lary, *Region and Nation, The Kwangsi Clique in China Politics, 1925–1937* (Cambridge: Cambridge University Press, 1974), pp. 32–63, 138–162. Martin C. Wilbur, *Sun Yat-sen, Frustrated Patriot* (New York: Columbia University Press, 1976), Chapters 3 to 9.

2. FARC, 3–04, Kochow Diary, December 1920.

3. SARC, 48–02, Yeungkong Diary, July 28, 1923.

4. FARC, 1–03, Kochow Diary, October-December 1920, pp. 213–214, 221–229; 23–01, Wuchow Diary, November 16–17, 1920; 5–10, letter of Bernard Meyer to James A. Walsh, October 11, 1920; also *Maryknoll Mission Letters*, Vol. I, pp. 318–320.

5. FARC, 3–04, Kochow Diary, November 16–17, 1920 and June 23-July 10, 1921; 23–01, Wuchow Diary, May 20–23 and June 20–30, 1921; 23–10, Pingnam

Diary, December 28, 1921-January 20, 1922.

6. FARC, 4–02, letter of Father Francis Ford to Maryknollers, August 3 and August 24, 1922. See also 23–10, Pingnam Diary, May 1922, p. 4.

7. FARC, 23–10, letter of Father George Wiseman to Maryknollers, October 26, 1923, pp. 4–6; 23–12, letter of George Wiseman to Father James A. Walsh, June 5, 1925; 3–01, letter of Father John Toomey to Father James A. Walsh, November 20, 1925; 35–01, letter of Father Francis Ford to Father James A. Walsh, November 20, 1925; 5–10, Tungchen Chronicle, October 17-November 19, 1925.

8. FARC, 23–10, letter of Father George Wiseman to Maryknollers, October 26, 1923; 4–02, Yeungkong Chronicle, March 10–12, 1923; 4–02, Sancian Diary, September 1924-February 1925, pp. 4–5. FARC, 5–10, Tungchen Diary, July 31, 1922; January 7–10, 1923; July 21, 1923 and October 23-November 11, 1923. FARC, 3–01, Loting Diary, October and November 1925. SARC, 48–02, Yeungkong Diary, January 12-February 27, 1923; July 28, 1923; November 26-December 4, 1923. *The Field Afar*, May 1923, pp. 140–141.

9. FARC, 23–12, letter of Father John Ruppert to Father James A. Walsh, January 15, 1927.

10. FARC, 4–03, Yeungkong Diary, December 1927.

11. FARC, 9–08, Tungchen Diary, June 17, 1929; 23–03, Pingnam Diary, May-June 1929. FARC, Box—Kiernan, letter to Father James A. Walsh, April 28, 1929; also Wuchow Diary, April 8-June 26, 1929, pp. 4–12. See also Canton consular correspondence in National Archives, RG59, Department of State Decimal File 1910–1929, 393.11/955, 11/1029, 11/1032.

12. FARC, 23–13, letter of Father Thomas Kiernan to Maryknollers, October 11, 1929; 23–12, letter of Father Thomas Kiernan to Maryknollers, March 19, 1930.

13. FARC, 23–12, letter of Father Thomas Kiernan to Maryknollers, March 19, 1930; letters of Father Mark Tennien to Maryknollers, April 1930, pp. 3–4 and May 14, 1930, pp. 1–3.

14. FARC, 23–20, Pingnam Diary, January-March 1930; 23–12, letter of Father Thomas Kiernan to Maryknollers, April 2, 1930 and letter of Father Mark Tennien to Maryknollers, April 1930, pp. 1–3; 23–13, letter of Brother Francis Wempe to Maryknollers, October 20, 1929; 39–06, letter of Father Bernard Meyer to Father James A. Walsh, April 6, 1930; 13–11, letter of Father Mark Tennien to Maryknollers, May 16, 1930.

15. FARC, 23–13, letter of Father Joseph Ryan to Maryknollers, October 12, 1929, pp. 2–3.

16. FARC, 4–02, letter of Father Francis Ford to Maryknollers, August 3, 1922, p. 3.

17. FARC, 31–05, letter of Father James E. Walsh to Father James A. Walsh, August 3, 1922, p. 3.

18. FARC, 4–02, letter of Father Francis Ford to Maryknollers, August 24, 1922.

19. FARC, 4–02, Yeungkong Chronicle, March 10, 1923. See also FARC, 5–10, Tungchen Chronicle, October 24–25, 1923.

20. FARC, 5–10, Tungchen Chronicle, November 10–11, 1923; 39–03, letter of Father Bernard Meyer to Father James A. Walsh, September 14, 1924.

21. FARC, 4–02, Sancian Diary, September 1924-February 1925, pp. 4–5; 39–03, letter of Father Bernard Meyer to Father James A. Walsh, January 4, 1925.

22. FARC, 20–02, Father Philip Taggart, "Essay on the Present Anti-Christian Movement in China," May 15, 1925, pp. 2–3.

23. FARC, 23–13, letter of October 11, 1929 by unidentified Maryknoller.

24. FARC, 23–12, letter of Father Mark Tennien to Maryknollers, April 1930, p. 2.

25. SARC, 48-02, Yeungkong Diary, January 12-February 3, 1923 and July 4, 1923.

26. SARC, 48-02, Yeungkong Diary, January 27, 1923.

27. FARC, 23-01, Wuchow Diary, June 23, 1921. See also FARC, 3-04, Kochow Diary, December 1920 and *The Field Afar*, May 1923, p. 140.

28. FARC, 5-10, letter of Father Bernard Meyer to Father James A. Walsh, October 11, 1920, p. 2; 31-05, letter of Father James E. Walsh to Father James A. Walsh, October 3, 1922, p. 2; 23-01, Wuchow Chronicle, June 27, 1921 and June 30, 1921. SARC, 48-02, Yeungkong Diary, February 5, 1923. *The Field Afar*, June 1922, p. 181 and May 1923, pp. 140-141.

29. SARC, 48-02, Yeungkong Diary, January 22, 1923.

30. FARC, 5-10, letter of Father Bernard Meyer to Father James A. Walsh, October 11, 1920, p. 2; 23-10, letter of Father Joseph Ryan to Maryknollers, October 12, 1929, p. 2.

31. FARC, 3-04, Kochow Diary, June 1921, pp. 105-107; 23-10, Pingnam Diary, January 4, 1922.

32. FARC, 3-04, Kochow Diary, June-July 1921, pp. 105-111. For other instances, see FARC, 23-10, Pingnam Diary, December 29, 1921-January 20, 1922 and letter of Father George Wiseman to Maryknollers, October 26, 1923, pp. 4-5.

33. FARC, 1-03, Kochow Diary, November-December 1920, pp. 224-226; 23-01, Wuchow Chronicle, June 24, 1921.

34. FARC, 31-05, letter of Father James E. Walsh to Father James A. Walsh, January 4, 1922. See also FARC, 3-01, Loting Diary, July 9, 1925.

35. *The Field Afar*, March 1925, p. 76.

36. FARC, 8-06, Kochow Diary, May 1924; 9-03, letter of Brother John Dorsey to Father James A. Walsh, October 25, 1925.

37. FARC, 23-12, letter of Father Thomas Kiernan to Maryknollers, April 2, 1930, p. 1.

38. FARC, 23-10, Pingnam Diary, January 5-11, 1922.

39. *Ibid.*, January 20-22, 1922.

40. Raymond Kerrison, *Bishop Walsh of Maryknoll* (New York: Lancer Books, 1962), p. 98.

41. FARC, 9-08, Tungchen Diary, June 17, 1929, p. 2; 4-02, letter of Father Francis Ford to Maryknollers, August 3, 1922, pp. 1-4; 10-12, letter of Father Bernard Meyer to Father James A. Walsh, February 12, 1919, pp. 4-5.

42. FARC, 31-05, letter of Father James E. Walsh to Maryknollers, August 3, 1922, p. 2.

43. *Ibid.*, p. 2.

44. Immanuel C. Hsü, *The Rise of Modern China*, pp. 642-643, and Edward John Michael Rhoads, "Lingnam's Response to the Rise of Chinese Nationalism: The Shakee Incident (1925)," in Kwang-ching Liu, ed., *American Missionaries in China*, Papers from Harvard Seminary (Cambridge: Harvard University Press, 1966), pp. 183-214. For an account through Maryknollers' eyes, see FARC, 5-05, Fachow Diary, August 2, 1925.

45. FARC, 5-05, Fachow Diary, August 1, 1925; 3-01, Loting Diary, July 1, 1925.

46. SARC, 49-02, Loting Convent Diary, June 30, 1925; "Chi Knoller," July 1, 1925.

47. FARC, 4-03, letter of Father James Drought to Maryknollers, August 17, 1925, pp. 5-6.

48. FARC, 23-01, Maryknollers' translation of the circular from Wuchow city, 1925:

IMPORTANT CIRCULAR

A. Capitalists in Shanghai and Tsingtao shot Chinese laborers.

B. British constables massacred Chinese undefended demonstrators.

C. Americans occupied the Wan Koi (lit. cloud-covered) Hill in Wuchow by force.

D. China will shortly be absorbed by foreigners.

1. Assist our wounded and killed fellow-countrymen in Shanghai and Tsingtao!

2. Get back the Wan Koi Hill in Wuchow!

3. Get back the educational power!

4. Get back all Foreign Settlements in China!

5. Cancel Extra-territoriality in China!

6. Abolish all unequal treatment in treaty rights!

7. Overthrow imperialism!

8. Effect republican revolutions everywhere!

Object of the Demonstration:

1. To request the Commissioner of Foreign Affairs in Shanghai to lodge a protest with the consular body there.

2. To prompt the Japanese mills to declare they will move their factories to Japan.

3. To request students to lecture everywhere. The more persons arrested the more lectures to be given. The last step we should take is to strike.

4. To boycott British and Japanese goods and to sever financial connections with them.

The above for your information and patriotic guidance. From the Students General Union of Kwangsi,

(Signed) The Propaganda Bureau of the Executives of the Kuomintang, Wuchow.

See also FARC, 23–12, letter of Father Joseph McGinn to Father James A. Walsh, June 14, 1925.

49. FARC, 3–01, Loting Diary, June 20-July 13, 1925; 5–05, letter of Father Robert Cairns to Father James A. Walsh, August 1, 1925. See also consular correspondence in National Archives, RG59, Department of State Decimal File 1910–1929, 393.11/371 and 893.00/6264.

50. FARC, 4–03, letter of Father James Drought to Maryknollers, August 17, 1925, pp. 1–11; 31–07, letter of Father James E. Walsh to Father James A. Walsh, July 11, 1925. SARC, 48–04, account by Sister Marie de Lourdes Bourguignon, July 1, 1925; "Chi Knoller," July 1, 1925. See also Douglas Jenkins' correspondence in National Archives, RG59, Department of State Decimal File 1910–1929, 393.11/379.

51. FARC, 31–07, letters of Father James E. Walsh to Father James A. Walsh, July 11, 1925 and August 24, 1925; 4–03, letter of Father James Drought to Maryknollers, August 17, 1925, p. 1.

52. SARC, 49–02, Loting Convent Diary, July 2, 1925.

53. FARC, 31–07, letter of Father James A. Walsh to Father James E. Walsh, August 28, 1925; 31–07, letters of Father James E. Walsh to Father James A. Walsh, September 9 and October 24, 1925; 32–01, letter of Father James A. Walsh to Father James E. Walsh, June 22, 1926; 32–02, letter of Father James E. Walsh to Father James A. Walsh, March 3, 1927.

54. FARC, 31–07, letter of Father James A. Walsh to Father James E. Walsh, November 5, 1925. See also Jenkins' reports in RG59, 393.1111/1–1111/5.

55. FARC, 8–10, Sunchong Diary, July 13–19, 1926; 31–07, letter of Father James E. Walsh to Father James A. Walsh, October 24, 1925; 32–01, letter of Father James E. Walsh to Father James A. Walsh, May 20, 1926; *The Field Afar*, January 1927, p. 4; February 1927, p. 45; March 1927, p. 84. TC26, Sister Philomena Chan, pp. 5–9.

56. SARC, 49–02, Loting Convent Diary, March 21–29, 1926; 49–03, Loting Convent Diary, April 5 and August 9, 1927.

57. FARC, 20–02, Father Philip Taggart, "Essay on the Present Anti-Christian Movement in China," pp. 2–3; 31–07, letter of Father James E. Walsh to Father James A. Walsh, August 24, 1925.

58. FARC, 31–07, letter of Father James E. Walsh to Father James A. Walsh, August 24, 1925.

59. FARC, 3–01, Loting Diary, October-November 1925.

60. FARC, 20–02, Father Philip Taggart, "Essay," p. 2.

61. *Ibid.*, p. 3.

62. *Ibid.*, p. 4.

63. *Ibid.*, p. 4.

64. FARC, 35–01, letter of Father Francis Ford to Father James A. Walsh, November 27, 1925.

65. FARC, 35–01, letter of Father Francis Ford to Father James A. Walsh, August 10, 1925.

66. FARC, 35–01, letter of Father Francis Ford to Father James A. Walsh, November 20, 1925.

67. FARC, 35–01, letter of Father Francis Ford to Father James A. Walsh, August 10, 1925.

68. FARC, 35–01, letter of Father Francis Ford to Father James A. Walsh, November 27, 1925.

69. FARC, 35–01, letter of Father Francis Ford to Father James A. Walsh, November 20, 1925.

70. FARC, 31–07, letter of Father James E. Walsh to Father James A. Walsh, July 11, 1925.

71. FARC, 3–01, Loting Diary, October-November 1925.

72. FARC, 31–07, letter of Father James E. Walsh to Father James A. Walsh, August 24, 1925.

73. FARC, 35–01, letters of N.C.W.C. to Father James A. Walsh, October 6 and 12, 1925; and letter of N.C.W.C. to Father Francis Ford, October 12, 1925.

74. FARC, 9–04, letters of Father Adolph Paschang to Maryknollers, January 24 and February 12, 1927.

75. FARC, 5–05, Fachow Diary, January 1, 1926; 9–04, letter of Father Adolph to Father James A. Walsh, December 11, 1926; 4–03, letter of Father Frederick Dietz to Father James A. Walsh, December 25, 1926; 23–13, letter of Father John Murray to Father James A. Walsh, June 24, 1926; 9–15, letter of Father Francis Ford to Maryknollers, June 1, 1926. TC49, Mr. Peter Wong, pp. 2–4.

76. FARC, 12–25, letter of Father Bernard Meyer to Father James A. Walsh, December 17–30, 1926, p. 3; 8–02, Sancian Diary, February 1927; 9–04, letter of Father Adolph Paschang to Father James A. Walsh, February 12, 1927; 5–01, Chikkai Diary, February 12-July 2, 1927; 5–06, Hoingnan Diary, April 1927.

77. FARC, 32–02, letters of Father Charles Walker to Father James E. Walsh, March 25 and 26, 1927; and "Dispatch from the Acting Chinese Minister of Foreign Affairs," April 30, 1927. FARC, 5–05, Fachow Diary, January 1928.

78. FARC, 32–02, "Dispatch from the Acting Chinese Minister of Foreign Affairs," April 30, 1927.

79. The three reports are found in FARC, 32–02, letter of March 25, 1927 and

Dispatch from the Acting Chinese Minister of Foreign Affairs, April 30, 1927, pp. 1-2; FARC, 5-05, Fachow Diary, January 1, 1928; *The Field Afar*, February 1928, pp. 40-42.

80. FARC, 42-02, letter of Father Charles Walker to Mr. Jenkins, May 28, 1927.

81. FARC, 32-02, Father James E. Walsh, "Note on the Report of the Acting Minister of Foreign Affairs," June 1, 1927.

82. FARC, 32-02, letters of Father James E. Walsh to Mr. Jenkins, March 31 and April 12, 1927.

83. FARC, 32-02, "Dispatch of the Acting Chinese Minister of Foreign Affairs," pp. 4-5.

84. *The Field Afar*, February 1928, pp. 40-42.

85. FARC, 32-02, letter of Father James A. Walsh to Father James E. Walsh, May 25, 1927.

86. FARC, 32-02, letters of Father James E. Walsh to Father James A. Walsh, June 1 and August 1, 1927.

87. FARC, 32-02, letters of Father James A. Walsh to Father James E. Walsh, May 25, and September 6, 1927; Clipping of *Catholic Universe Bulletin* (Cleveland, Ohio), August 5, 1927.

88. FARC, 32-02, letter of Father James A. Walsh to Father James E. Walsh, September 6, 1927. See also *The Field Afar*, February 1923, p. 46.

89. FARC, 32-02, letter of Father James E. Walsh to Father James A. Walsh, October 25, 1927.

90. FARC, 39-04, letter of Father Bernard Meyer to Father James A. Walsh, December 21, 1926.

91. FARC, 39-04, letter of Father James A. Walsh to Father Bernard Meyer, February 8, 1927.

92. FARC, 39-04, letter of Father Bernard Meyer to Father James A. Walsh, November 27, 1927.

93. FARC, Box—Fletcher, letter of Father Frederick Dietz to Father James A. Walsh, November 25, 1927; 32-02, letter of Brother Michael Hogan to Father James A. Walsh, November 23, 1927; letter of Father James E. Walsh to Father James A. Walsh, November 25, 1927; 4-03, Yeungkong Diary, November 1927; TF01, Father Robert Sheridan, pp. 45-46.

94. FARC, 32-02, letter of Father James E. Walsh to Father James A. Walsh, November 25, 1927.

95. FARC, 32-02, letter of Father James E. Walsh to Father James A. Walsh, November 25, 1927; 32-03, letter of Father James E. Walsh to Father James A. Walsh, February 26, 1928.

96. Rodney Gilbert, *What's Wrong with China* (New York: Frederick A. Stokes Company, 1926). O. D. Rasmussen, *What's Right with China, An Answer to Foreign Criticisms* (Shanghai: Commercial Press, 1927).

97. TF03, Father Thomas Kiernan, pp. 85-86; TF01, Father Robert Sheridan, pp. 20-21.

98. FARC, Box—Kiernan, letter of Father Thomas Kiernan to Father James A. Walsh, November 17, 1929. See also FARC, Box—Meyer, Articles, "Acquisition of Property in China for Mission Work—Extrality": Meyer, rather than favoring the abolition of extraterritoriality, thinks in terms of a new treaty to ensure that the foreigners' right to buy property in China will be protected from "squeeze" and antiforeign or anti-Christian sentiment.

99. FARC, 12-11, letters of Father Thomas Kiernan to Father James A. Walsh, December 9 and 16, 1928; 23-01, Wuchow Chronicle, May 20-23, 1921. FARC, 23-02, Wuchow Diary, December 14-15, 1928; February 23-24, 1929; June 25, 1929; February 1, 1930. FARC, Box—Kiernan, letter of Father Thomas Kiernan to

Father James A. Walsh, February 24, 1929.

100. FARC, 31-07, letter of Father James E. Walsh to Father James A. Walsh, August 24, 1925; TF03, Father Thomas Kiernan, p. 102.

101. *Collectanea Commissionis Synodalis* (Peking), September-December 1943, p. 726. See also *Digest of the Synodal Commission* (Peking), July 1928, p. 205.

102. *Digest*, July 1928, pp. 200-205 and September 1928, pp. 231-236. *Maryknoll—The Field Afar*, July-August 1942, p. 16. See also Thomas F. Ryan, S.J. *China Through Catholic Eyes* (Cincinnati: Catholic Students Mission Crusade, 1942), p. 147.

103. For instance, the book *Le Triple Démisme de Suen Wen* (Zikawei: Imprimerie des Jésuites, 1929) was a translation with annotations and commentaries by Pascal M. D'Elia of Sun Yat-sen's *San Min Chu-i*. It carried approval of the Jesuit order, the local bishop and the apostolic delegate. See *Collectanea Commissionis Synodalis* (Peking), February 1929, pp. 156-157 and March 1929, pp. 251-252.

104. FARC, 5-10, Tungchen Chronicle, December 29, 1925; 31-05, letter of Father James E. Walsh to Father James A. Walsh, August 3, 1922, p. 2.

105. *The Field Afar*, October 1929, p. 279 and November 1934, p. 302.

106. SARC, 48-12, Yeungkong Convent Diary, February 19-20, 1937 and May 3, 1937.

107. FARC, 47-04, letters of Monsignor Raymond Lane to Father James A. Walsh, February 23, and December 23, 1932.

108. FARC, 25-08, Fushun Center Diary, June 22, 1931.

109. FARC, 25-08, Fushun Center Diary, October 1-13, 1930; 25-01, letter of Father Albert Murphy to Father James A. Walsh, October 15, 1931. For other instances, see FARC, 16-01, Fushun Center Diary, August 20, 1929 and FARC, 25-20, Hsinpin Diary, December 25, 1931.

110. FARC, 25-16, letter of Father Thomas Quirk to Father James A. Walsh, August 5, 1932, p. 2.

111. FARC, 25-08, Fushun Center Diary, March 1 and 11, 1932.

112. FARC, 25-20, letter of Father Gerard Donovan to Father James A. Walsh, November 22, 1931; 25-22, letter of Father John Comber to Father James A. Walsh, May 20, 1932.

113. FARC, 25-22, letter of Father John Comber to Father James A. Walsh, May 20, 1932.

114. FARC, 25-15, Father Walter Coleman, "Stirring Events on the Upper Yalu," June 22, 1932; 47-04, letter of Monsignor Raymond Lane to Father James A. Walsh, February 23, 1933.

115. See, for example, the flyer of October 14, 1932 in FARC, 47-04.

116. FARC, 25-16, letter of Father Thomas Quirk to Father James A. Walsh, August 5, 1932, p. 2; 25-15, "Stirring Events," p. 3. TC22, Father Protase Pai, p. 7.

117. FARC, 25-20, Hsinpin Diary, June and October 1932; 25-15, "Stirring Events."

118. SARC, Box—Correspondence, Mother Mary Joseph, letter of Sister Mary Eunice Tolan to Mother Mary Joseph, Fushun, October 27, 1932; FARC, 25-20, letter of Father Gerard Donovan to Father James A. Walsh, October 19, 1932.

119. FARC, 11-19, letter of Father John Comber to Father James A. Walsh, November 15, 1932; 25-20, letter of Father Gerard Donovan to Father James A. Walsh, October 19, 1932; letter of Father Alonso Escalante to Father James A. Walsh, October 20, 1932; 47-04, letter of Monsignor Raymond Lane to Father Patrick Byrne, October 20, 1932.

120. SARC, 54-01, Dairen Tenshudo Diary, September 15, 1932.

121. FARC, 47-04, letter of Monsignor Raymond Lane to Father James

A. Walsh, September 9, 1932.

122. FARC, 47–03, clippings from the *Peking Times* and the *Tientsin Times* of September 17, 1931.

123. FARC, 47–03, letter of Father Joseph McCormack to the Editor, September 30, 1931; letter of Father Joseph McCormack to Father James A. Walsh, October 8, 1931.

124. FARC, 47–04, letters of Monsignor Raymond Lane to Father James A. Walsh, February 24 and October 20, 1932.

125. FARC, 47–04, letter of Monsignor Raymond Lane to Father James A. Walsh, February 23, 1933.

126. FARC, 47–04, letters of Monsignor Raymond Lane to Father Patrick Byrne, October 20, 1932 and letters of Monsignor Raymond Lane to Father James A. Walsh, February 23 and November 23, 1933.

127. FARC, 47–04, letter of Monsignor Raymond Lane to Father James A. Walsh, December 23, 1932.

128. FARC, 47–04, letter of Monsignor Raymond Lane to Father James A. Walsh, December 23, 1932 and letter of Monsignor Raymond Lane to Father Patrick Byrne, October 20, 1932.

129. FARC, 47–04, letter of Mr. Edward Hunter to Monsignor Raymond Lane, December 16, 1932 and letter of Monsignor Raymond Lane to Father James A. Walsh, February 23, 1933.

130. FARC, 47–04, letter of Monsignor Raymond Lane to Father James A. Walsh, November 23, 1933.

131. FARC, 47–04, articles in *Sheng-ching Shih-pao*, *Hoten Mainichi Shimbun*, *Manshū Nippō*, and *Ta-lien Hsin-pao* of November 21, 1933.

132. FARC, 47–04, letter of Monsignor Raymond Lane to Father James A. Walsh, November 23, 1933 and accompanying "Summary of Action in Reference to the *Sheng-ching Shih-pao* Article."

133. FARC, 47–04, letter of Monsignor Raymond Lane to Father James A. Walsh, December 13, 1933.

134. TF52, Father Edward Weis, p. 25; TF46, Bishop Edward McGurkin, p. 19; TF20, Father Sylvio Gilbert, p. 42.

135. SARC, 55–06, Fushun Convent Diary, March 1, 1934; 54–02, Dairen Tenshudo Diary, March 1, 1934.

136. SARC, 54–02, Dairen Tenshudo Diary, September 15, 1934; FARC, 47–07, letters of Monsignor Raymond Lane to Father James A. Walsh, September 24 and November 23, 1934; *The Field Afar*, September 1935, p. 241.

137. SARC, 55–08, Fushun Hopei Convent Diary, February 23, 1940. FARC, 25–09, Fushun Center Diary, December 1937; 25–12, Fushun Hopei Diary, June 9, 1938; 25–02, Chakow Diary, May 5, 1937.

138. FARC, 25–02, Chakow Diary, November 15, 1936; 25–15, Linkiang Diary, February 10, 1938.

139. FARC, 47–05, letter of Monsignor Raymond Lane to Father James A. Walsh, April 10, 1934.

140. FARC, 25–15, Linkiang Diary, September 17-October 25, 1934.

141. FARC, 25–21, Hsinpin Diary, April 1935. See also Chong-Sik Lee, *Revolutionary Struggle in Manchuria, 1922-1945* (Berkeley: University of California Press, 1983), pp. 271-275.

142. FARC, 25–21, Hsinpin Diary, April 1935; 25–15, Linkiang Diary, October 1934; 25–23, Tungchen Diary, September 1935; 25–02, Chakow Diary, August-October 1936.

143. *The Field Afar*, February 1939, Monsignor Raymond Lane, "The Church

in Manchu-Land," p. 35.

144. SARC, 55-05, Fushun-Honan Convent Diary, February 28-29, July 12, 1932; 55-07, Fushun-Honan Convent Diary, July 21, August 24, October 7, 1936 and October 7, December 3, 1937; 54-08, Fushun-Hopei Convent Diary, July 16-25, 1936 and October 5, 1937.

145. FARC, 25-15, Linkiang Diary, December 1934, p. 3 and January 7, 1938.

146. TF20, Father Sylvio Gilbert, Follow-up Interview, August 12, 1985.

147. TF20, Father Sylvio Gilbert, Appendix, clipping of *Worcester Telegram*, n.d., "Webster Priest Describes Thrilling Experiences in Bandit-ridden Manchuria."

148. TF20, Father Sylvio Gilbert, pp. 35-38.

149. *Ibid.*, pp. 41-42.

150. SARC, Sister Mary Eunice Tolan, "Banditry," in unpublished manuscript "Manchuria, Book 4", p. 142.

151. TF52, Father Edward Weis, p. 29.

152. TF20, Father Sylvio Gilbert, p. 46.

153. FARC, 48-04, Father John O'Donnell, "Report for Bishop James E. Walsh, August 22, 1942," p. 1; TF46, Bishop Edward McGurkin, pp. 19 and 58.

154. FARC, 25-21, Hsinpin Diary, July 1935; 25-02, Chakow Diary, March 23, 1935 and August-September 1937; TF46, Bishop Edward McGurkin, pp. 61-62.

155. TS53, Sister Celine Marie Werner, p. 9.

156. TF52, Father Edward Weis, p. 25.

157. For more information about Wang Feng-ko and the guerrilla groups in Manchuria, see Chong-Sik Lee, *Revolutionary Struggle in Manchuria*, pp. 214, 220, 240, 316.

158. Father Clarence Burns, *Bandits Surrounded Him* (New York: Maryknoll Pamphlet Library, 3rd ed., 1941).

159. TF52, Father Edward Weis, p. 26; TF46, Bishop Edward McGurkin, pp. 61-62. See also *Father Jerry Donovan, Captive for Christ* (New York: Maryknoll Pamphlet Library, 1939) and Sister Kathleen Kelly, "Maryknoll in Manchuria, 1927-1947: A Study of Accommodation and Adaptation" (unpublished dissertation, University of Southern California, December 1982), p. 446.

160. Quoted in Tolan, "Manchuria, Book 4," p. 143.

161. Burns, *Bandits*, pp. 12-13; FARC, Box—Burns, article by Father Clarence Burns in *Boston Sunday Post* of January 31, 1937.

162. SARC, 55-07, Fushun-Honan Convent Diary, July 21 and August 24, 1936; FARC, 25-02, Chakow Diary, October 1, 1937; TS80, Sister Veronica Marie Carney, p. 47.

163. These Maryknollers were Fathers John Lenahan, Leo Hewitt, and Edmond Ryan; Brother Benedict Barry; Sisters Mary Peter Duggan, Mary Jean Dicks, Mary Gerard Gallagher, Rachel Jackson, Mary de Lellis McKenna, Mary Fabiola Gonyou, Rose Benigna Hanan, Mary Luke Logue, Stella Marie Flagg, Mary Corita Herrgen, and Xavier Marie Shalvey. See FARC, 47-10, letter of Bishop James E. Walsh to Archbishop A. G. Cicognani, Apostolic Delegate, April 8, 1943.

164. FARC, 48-04, Father John O'Donnell, "Report from Bishop James E. Walsh, August 1942," p. 3. SARC, Box—Manchuria, War Years, ID2, account by Sister Angela Marie Coveny, and ID3, account by Sister Mary Lelia Makra. TS37, Sister Angela Marie Coveny, pp. 10-13; TF46, Bishop Edward McGurkin, pp. 19-20; TF33, Father Edward Manning, p. 56.

165. Sister Jeanne Marie Lyons, *Maryknoll's First Lady* (New York: Dodd, Mead, and Company, 1964), p. 241. FARC, O'Donnell, "Report," pp. 5-6. TS44, Sister Rosalia Kettl, p. 48.

166. These Maryknollers were Sisters Mary Lelia Makra, Maria Thyne, Celine Marie Werner, Gloria Wagner, Carolyn Puls, Mary Eva Burke, Dominic Guidera, Mercedes Cusack, and Mary Paula Sullivan; Fathers John O'Donnell, Joseph McCormack, Albert Murphy, Joseph Early, J. Michael Henry, George Haggerty, John J. Walsh, George Flick, Edward Manning, Francis Mullen, Stanislaus Ziemba, Raymond Hohlfeld, and James Rottner. See Tolan, "Manchuria, Supplement K" and also Sister Mary de Paul Cogan, *Sisters of Maryknoll, Through Troubled Waters* (New York: Charles Scribner's Sons, 1947), pp. 158-161. TS53, Sister Celine Marie Werner, p. 11; TF46, Bishop Edward McGurkin, p. 20; TF33, Father Edward Manning, p. 57.

167. FARC, 48-04, O'Donnell, "Report," pp. 9-10. For an eyewitness account of the repatriation on the *Asama Maru* and the *Gripsholm* by non-missionary personnel, see Max Hill, *Exchange Ship* (New York: Farrar & Rinehart, Inc., 1942).

168. The pope's letter is referred to in FARC, 47-09, letter of Father James E. Drought, Vicar General, to nearest of kin of Maryknoll Fathers and Brothers in Manchuria, April 28, 1942, and in Cogan, *Sisters of Maryknoll*, p. 157. See also SARC, Box—Manchuria, War Years, ID2, account by Sisters Mercedes Cusack and Mary Peter Duggan. Tolan, "Manchuria, Book 2," pp. 56-59. TS94, Sister Mary Gerard Gallagher, pp. 15-28.

169. The Maryknollers repatriated from Fushun were: Sisters Ellen Mary Murphy, Veronica Marie Carney, Rita Clare Comber, Miriam Schmitt, and Angela Marie Coveny; Fathers Sylvio Gilbert, John Sullivan, John Fisher, John Comber, Howard Geselbracht, Thomas Quirk, Norman Batt, William Pheuer, and John Coffey. See FARC, 47-10, letter of Bishop James E. Walsh to Archbishop A. G. Cicognani, Apostolic Delegate, April 8, 1943. See also Tolan, "Manchuria, Supplement K." TS41, Sister Rita Clare Comber, pp. 11-13. Repatriated from Shanghai were Sisters Mary Jean Dicks, Mary Peter Duggan, Mary Gerard Gallagher, Virginia Flagg, Rose Benigna Hanan, Mary Luke Logue, Rachel Jackson, Mary Corita Herrgen, Xavier Marie Shalvey, Mary de Lellis McKenna, and Mary Fabiola Gonyou; Fathers Leo Hewitt, John Lenahan, and Edmond Ryan; and Brother Benedict Barry.

170. Tolan, "Manchuria, Book 2," pp. 56-70 and "Book 4," p. 156; TS27, Sister Marie Elise Baumann, pp. 8-9, 11, 15, 28-29; SARC, Box—Manchuria, War Years, ID1, War Diary of Sister Marie Elise Baumann, May 1943-September 1946.

171. TS75, Sister Margaret Kim, cover page and p. 42; TS31, Sister Rose Benigna Hanan, p. 15..

172. Quoted in Tolan, "Manchuria, Book 2," p. 59. See also *Maryknoll—The Field Afar*, September 1946, p. 8.

173. John Paton Davies, Jr., *Dragon by the Tail* (New York: W. W. Norton & Co., 1972), pp. 180-181.

174. TF33, Father Edward Manning, p. 51-52.

175. *Ibid.* pp. 55-56.

176. FARC, 3-08, "Kongmoon Bulletin," December 1936 and February 1937.

177. *Ibid.*, August 1937.

178. *Ibid.*, October and November 1937. FARC, 23-04, Wuchow Center Diary, February 19, 1939.

179. The instruction urged the bishops of China to observe absolute neutrality vis a vis the Sino-Japanese conflict, "Nec ad dexteram nec ad sinistram declinantes," *Collectanea Commissionis Synodalis*, May 1939, p. 454. See also Louis Wei Tsing-sing, *Le Saint Siège et la Chine de Pie XI à nos jours* (Sotteville-lès-Rouen: Editions A. Allais, 1968), p. 142.

180. SARC, 48-12, Yeungkong Convent Diary, August 19, 1937; 48-13, Yeung-

kong Convent Diary, October 1938; 49-11, Loting Convent Diary, October 17, 1938. FARC, 3-09, Kongmoon Diary, September 18, 1937.

181. SARC, Sister Mary Imelda Sheridan, "A Brief History of the South China Region, 1921-1958," p. 25. FARC, 3-09, Kongmoon Diary, December 14, 1937; 32-09, Letter of Bishop Adolph Paschang to Bishop James E. Walsh, December 11, 1937. TS43, Sister Candida Maria Basto, p. 1; TS02, Sister Monica Marie Boyle, pp. 7-11.

182. FARC, 3-09, Kongmoon Diary, January 1939; TS84, Sister Chanel Xavier, pp. 28-30.

183. SARC, 49-12, Loting Convent Diary, February 25-27, 1939; 51-05, Ping-nam Convent Diary, October 23-November 19, 1939.

184. SARC, 49-12, Loting Convent Diary, February 25, 1939. FARC, 3-02, Letters of Father Robert Kennelly to Japanese Consulate, February 26, 1939 and to American Consul General, December 19, 1939; see also in same folder a newspaper clipping related to the incident. Father John Considine, *Across a World* (New York: J. J. Little and Ives Company, 1942), p. 197.

185. FARC, 8-05, Sancian Diary, March 22, 1941, pp. 1-3. TF66, Father John Joyce, pp. 19-20. Albert Nevins, *The Meaning of Maryknoll* (New York: MacMullen Books, 1954), p. 72. *Maryknoll—The Field Afar*, May 1943, p. 27.

186. FARC, 5-03, Chikkai Diary, September 3, 1941; TF66, Father John Joyce, pp. 7-8; *Maryknoll—The Field Afar*, November 1947, pp. 18-20.

187. FARC, 3-09, Kongmoon Diary, August-October 1939 and September 1941; 8-08, Sunwui Diary, July 12-30 and September 1-20, 1939. TS84, Sister Chanel Xavier, pp. 32-35.

188. TF66, Father John Joyce, pp. 8-9; Nevins, *The Meaning*, p. 73.

189. One priest, Father Maurice Feeney, was with the Maryknoll Sisters in Kowloon at the time of the Japanese takeover of Hong Kong. He managed to get a special pass as an American of Irish descent to return to free China. Five Sisters were not interned: Sisters Chanel Xavier, Cecilia Marie Carvalho, Candida Maria Basto, and Maria Corazon Jaramillo were third country nationals, and Sister Maria Teresa Yeung was Chinese.

190. SARC, Regional Correspondence ChP21F2F, letter of Sister Mary Paul McKenna to Mother Mary Joseph, June 15, 1942. Sister Mary Imelda Sheridan, "A Brief History," pp. 34-38. Repatriated in June 1942 were: Sisters Mary Regina Reardon, Mary Liguori Quinlan, Mary Reginald Silva, Mary Camillus Reynolds, Mary Gonzaga Rizzardi, Santa Maria Manning, Joseph Marie Kane, Rose Olive Skehan, Mary Amata Brachtesende, St. Bernard Donnelly, Frances Marion Gardner, and Matthew Marie Stapleton. Among the 16 other Maryknoll Sisters, Sisters Anne Clements, Maria Teresa Yeung, Maria Corazon Jaramillo, and Ann Mary Farrell went to Macao; Sister Frances Murphy rejoined her mission in Kaying; Sisters Henrietta Marie Cunningham and Chanel Xavier made their way to Wuchow, Sister Candida Maria Basto to Yeungkong, and Eucharista Coupe to Loting; Sisters Cecilia Marie Carvalho, Mary Clement Quinn, Christella Furey, Dominic Kelly, Mary de Ricci Cain, and Dorothy Walsh were in Kweilin with Sister Mary Paul McKenna.

191. Father James Smith, *Maryknoll Hong Kong Chronicle, 1918-1975* (Maryknoll: Maryknoll Fathers, 1958), pp. 49-140. Repatriated in June 1942 were: Fathers Arthur Allie, Raymond Quinn, John Callan, Joseph Reardon, Vincent Walsh, and George Bauer; Brothers Michael Hogan, Lawrence Bowers, Anselm Petley, and William Neary. Fathers who reentered China in January 1943 included: John Toomey, John Troesch, William Downs, Francis Keelan, Ralph Siebert, Leo Walter, Wenceslaus Knotek, John Tackney, Anthony Madison, John Moore, Michael McKeirnan, Michael Gaiero, Michael O'Connell, and Brother Thaddeus Revers.

192. FARC, 3–09, Kongmoon Chronicle, December 1941, pp. 1–3.

193. FARC, 42–01, letter of Bishop James E. Walsh to Monsignor John Romaniello, March 25, 1942; Box—Council Minutes, 1942, pp. 950 and 990. SARC, Regional Correspondence ChP21F2F, letters of Sister Mary Paul McKenna to Mother Mary Joseph, June 15, 1942, September 10, 1942, and October 28, 1942; letter of Sister Mary Columba Tarpey to Sister Mary Paul McKenna, March 19, 1943. *Maryknoll—The Field Afar*, January 1945, p. 33.

194. SARC, 50–06, Wuchow Convent Diary, September 3–6, 1943. TS84, Sister Chanel Xavier, pp. 45–48. FARC, 38–04, letter of Bishop Frederick Donaghy to Bishop James E. Walsh, September 13, 1943; TF45, Father Russell Sprinkle, pp. 27–28. *Maryknoll—The Field Afar*, March 1944, pp. 2–4, 38–39.

195. SARC, 48–18, Yeungkong Convent Diary, June 5, 1944; TS43, Sister Candida Maria Basto, p. 5.

196. SARC, 48–18, Yeungkong Convent Diary, June 8-September 13, 1944; 56–08, Kweiyang Diary, July 1-December 2, 1944. TS56, Sister Eucharista Coupe, pp. 4–11; TS97, Sister Mary de Ricci Cain, pp. 12–14; TS43, Sister Candida Maria Basto, pp. 4–6; TS68, Sister Colombiere Bradley, pp. 9–11. TS42, Sister Henrietta Marie Cunningham, pp. 45–54. *Maryknoll—The Field Afar*, November 1944, p. 4; March 1945, pp. 36–38.

197. TF38, Father Robert Greene, p. 14; Father Albert Nevins, *The Meaning of Maryknoll*, p. 154. *Maryknoll—The Field Afar*, June 1945, pp. 10–13.

198. FARC, 30–05, letter of Bishop James E. Walsh to Mr. William P. Langdon, American Consul in Kunming, January 17, 1945; letter of Bishop James E. Walsh to Father John Considine, December 14, 1944; cable from Father John Considine to Bishop James E. Walsh, December 29, 1944. FARC, 37–03, "Wartime Slate of Kaying Mission Superior," January 12, 1945.

199. TF66, Father John Joyce, pp. 10–13; *Maryknoll—The Field Afar*, November 1947, pp. 18–21. These units were responsible for gathering intelligence reports on Japanese-held territory.

200. FARC, Father Francis O'Neill's autobiography, "Entre Nous," Book 2, pp. 54–55. Father Mark Tennien, *Chungking Listening Post* (New York: Creative Age Press, 1945), p. 63.

201. FARC, 33–06, letter of Bishop Adolph Paschang to Bishop James E. Walsh, June 6, 1945 and letter of Bishop James E. Walsh to Bishop Adolph Paschang, June 22, 1945; *Maryknoll—The Field Afar*, September 1945, p. 7.

202. FARC, 30–05, letter of Bishop James E. Walsh to Mr. William P. Langdon, American Consul in Kunming, January 17, 1945; TF48, Father Leo Walter, p. 3.

203. Sister Mary Imelda Sheridan, "A Brief History," pp. 28, 32–33.

204. FARC, 30–05, letter of Bishop James E. Walsh to Maryknollers, February 1, 1945.

205. FARC, 3–09, Kongmoon Diary, May 1939.

206. *Maryknoll—The Field Afar*, March 1944, p. 2. See also *Maryknoll—The Field Afar*, September 1942, p. 1. TF25, Father Raymond Gaspard, pp. 20–22.

207. SARC, 42–03, Laohukow Novitiate, May 21–23, 1944; 43–17, Kaying Convent Diary, May 22–25, 1944; 44–10, Shuichai Convent Diary, March 2, 1945. *Maryknoll—The Field Afar*, September 1942, p. 1; January 1943, p. 1; March 1943, pp. 16–17; October 1943, pp. 46–47; March 1944, p. 19; April 1944, p. 9; December 1944, pp. 16–18; March 1945, p. 12; November 1945, pp. 40–42.

208. Father John F. Donovan, *The Pagoda and the Cross* (New York: Charles Scribners' Sons, 1967), pp. 148–149.

209. FARC, 30–05, letter of Bishop James E. Walsh to Mr. William P. Langdon, American Consul in Kunming, January 17, 1945; *Maryknoll—The Field Afar*, July-

August 1945, "Contract Chaplains," pp. 38–41.

210. *Maryknoll—The Field Afar*, November 1944, p. 35; FARC, 36–04, Father Cody Eckstein, "Kaying Vicariate Report, 1936–1946 for the Maryknoll General Chapter," p. 3.

211. FARC, 37–02, Kaying Report, August 19, 1945, p. 5; FARC, 9–19, letter from Father John Donovan, September 16, 1945; Donovan, *The Pagoda and the Cross*, p. 149.

212. John K. Fairbank, *Chinabound, A Fifty-Year Memoir* (New York: Harper & Row, 1982), p. 220.

213. FARC, 47–04, letter of Monsignor Raymond Lane to Father James A. Walsh, February 24, 1933.

214. *The Field Afar*, August 1932, p. 102.

215. FARC, 47–07, letter of Monsignor Raymond Lane to Bishop James E. Walsh, April 1938 and December 30, 1938. *The Field Afar*, July-August 1938, p. 205; February 1939, p. 6.

216. *The Field Afar*, February 1939, p. 71; *Maryknoll—The Field Afar*, September 1939, p. 248.

217. *The Field Afar*, April 1939, pp. 100–101, 112–113, 123; *Maryknoll—The Field Afar*, June 1939, pp. 170–171. Articles in other years are similar in keeping silent on the Japanese role in the conflict; see article on war orphans in February 1941 issue, p. 9.

218. See for instance FARC, 3–09, Kongmoon Center Diary, November 1938-May 1940 and FARC, 42–17, Kweilin-Chuanchow Diary, October 1940.

219. FARC, 3–02, letter of Father James Drought to Father Robert Kennelly, March 13, 1940; 33–04, letters of Bishop James E. Walsh to Bishop Adolph Paschang, January 18, 1940 and April 19, 1940.

220. Gu Changsheng, *Chuanjiaoshi yu jindai Zhongguo* (Missioners and Modern China) (Shanghai: Shanghai People's Publishing Company, 1981), p. 395.

221. FARC, Box—Drought, letter of Father James Drought to the Foreign Policy Association President, August 28, 1934.

222. FARC, 3–02, letter of Father James Drought to His Excellency Kensuke Horinouchi, March 7, 1939.

223. FARC, Box—Drought, "Walsh's Remarks at the Luncheon of the Pan-Pacific Club of Tokyo," December 20, 1940.

224. FARC, Box—Drought, "Secret Document" and "Confidential Memorandum to the Honorable Secretary of State Cordell Hull." The proposal that reached Hull on April 9, 1941 can be found in U.S. Congress, *Papers Relating to the Foreign Relations of the United States: Japan, 1931–1941* (Washington, DC: 1943, Vol. II), pp. 398–402.

225. *Papers Relating*, p. 403.

226. The role of Drought and Walsh in trying to bring Japan and the United States to terms has been studied in detail by R. J. C. Butow, *The John Doe Associates, Back Door Diplomacy for Peace, 1941* (Stanford: Stanford University Press, 1974). See also G. W. Prange, *At Dawn We Slept* (New York: McGraw Hill, 1981), pp. 116–118 and Jonathan G. Utley, *Going To War with Japan, 1937–1941* (Knoxville: University of Tennessee Press, 1985), pp. 138–143.

227. *Maryknoll—The Field Afar*, April 1942, p. 16.

228. *Maryknoll—The Field Afar*, June 1942, pp. 2–3, 6–8.

229. *Maryknoll—The Field Afar*, July-August 1942, pp. 14–16; October 1943, p. 2.

230. *Maryknoll—The Field Afar*, July-August 1942, p. 16; January 1942, p. 22; March 1942, p. 26; March 1943, p. 30; April 1943, p. 22; January 1944, p. 37; April

1944, pp. 8-9; July-August 1945, p. 4; September 1945, pp. 2-3; January 1946, pp. 20-21; April 1946, p. 33.

231. *Maryknoll—The Field Afar*, March 1943, p. 30.

232. *Maryknoll—The Field Afar*, December 1944, pp. 20-24; see also September 1945, p. 3.

233. *Maryknoll—The Field Afar*, November 1941, "The Blessings of War," p. 2.

234. Hsü, *The Rise of Modern China*, pp. 667-669, 672. Harrison E. Salisbury, *The Long March, The Untold Story* (New York: Harper & Row, 1985), pp. 7-8, 29.

235. FARC, 9-24, Siaoloc Diary, June 6 and 20, 1929; 9-25, letters of Father William Downs to Father James A. Walsh, November 18, 1931.

236. FARC, 9-24, Siaoloc Diary, June 20, 1929; 9-25, Siaoloc Diary, November 9-15, 1931. FARC, 15-10, letter of Father William Downs to Maryknollers, October 29 and November 8, 1929; letters of Father Patrick Malone to Maryknollers, November 1 and 12, 1929; letter of Father William O'Brien to Maryknollers, November 5, 1929.

237. FARC, 9-23, letters of Father Patrick Malone to Maryknollers, May 1929. See also FARC, 35-02, letter of Monsignor Francis X. Ford to Kaying missioners, May 1, 1930.

238. FARC, 15-10, letter of Father William Downs to Maryknollers, December 28, 1929; 9-23, letter of Father Patrick Malone to Maryknollers, February 28, 1930; 9-25, letter of Father William Downs to Father James A. Walsh, November 18, 1931 and letter of Father Charles Hilbert to Father James A. Walsh, December 9, 1931; 9-25, Siaoloc Diary, December 1931 and April 1932; 9-22, letter of Father Maynard Murphy to Father James A. Walsh, March 25, 1930. FARC, 26-14, Tsungkow Diary, July 25, 1931; 9-27, letter of Father John Gallagher to Father James A. Walsh, June 29, 1930. *The Field Afar*, July-August 1930, pp. 204-207; April 1931, p. 99; March 1932, p. 67.

239. FARC, 23-12, letter of Thomas Kiernan to Maryknollers, March 19, 1930; letters of Father Mark Tennien to Maryknollers, April 1930 and May 14, 1930.

240. FARC, 42-18, Kweilin Diary, November 10-December 7, 1934. *The Field Afar*, July-August 1935, pp. 201-202. TF72, Father Timothy Daley, pp. 8-9. Salisbury, *The Long March*, pp. 91-104.

241. TF04, Father Francis Daubert, pp. 36 and 38; see also TS65, Sister Irene Fogarty, p. 34.

242. TS39, Sister Barbara Mersinger, p. 50.

243. FARC, 37-02, Kaying Report, August 19, 1945, pp. 5-6, 9.

244. FARC, 48-07, letter of Father Joseph McCormack to Bishop Raymond Lane, June 29, 1947 and letter of Father George Haggerty to Bishop Raymond Lane, July 15, 1947.

245. FARC, 48-07, letters of Father George Haggerty to Bishop Raymond Lane, August 16, 1947 and June 29, 1947; letter of Father Joseph McCormack to Bishop Raymond Lane, August 14, 1947.

246. FARC, 48-07, letter of Father Joseph McCormack to Father Thomas Walsh, December 28, 1947; 48-08, letter of Father Joseph McCormack to Thomas Walsh, January 8, 1948. SARC, 55-13, Fushun-Honan Convent Diary, October 23, 1947.

247. FARC, 48-08, letter of Father Joseph McCormack to Father Thomas Walsh, February 20, 1948.

248. FARC, 48-08, letters of Father Joseph McCormack to Bishop Raymond Lane, March 18, May 18, July 8 and August 10, 1948; *Maryknoll—The Field Afar*, October 1948, p. 4.

249. FARC, 48-08, letter of Father Joseph McCormack to Bishop Raymond Lane, October 8, 1948.

250. See correspondence of Father Joseph McCormack in FARC, 48-08 and 48-09, and also in *Maryknoll—The Field Afar*, March 1959, pp. 22-27.

251. *Maryknoll—The Field Afar*, October 1948, p. 4.

252. SARC, 40-13, Kongmoon Convent Diary, May 7, 1948; FARC, 23-06, Szwong Diary, May 2, 1948. See also the pope's Easter Sunday address on the danger of communism, exhorting all Christians to be vigilant and to pray, in *China Missionary*, June 1948, pp. 248-249.

253. FARC, 37-03, Official Letter of Bishop Ford to His Clergy, Easter 1948.

254. SARC, 47-08, Tungshek Convent Diary, May 16, 1948.

255. SARC, 43-21, Kaying Convent Diary, May 2, 1948.

256. SARC, 42-05, Laohukow Novitiate, May 18, 1947; 42-06, Laohukow Novitiate, March 26, 1948; 42-07, Laohukow Novitiate, June 22, 1949.

257. Quoted in SARC, Box—Francis X. Ford Correspondence, Kaying Letter, January 1949, p. 3.

258. FARC, 23-06, Wuchow Diary, December 1949, pp. 3, 6. SARC, Regional Correspondence, ChP22F3E, letter of Sister Mary Imelda Sheridan to Mother Mary Columba Tarpey, November 14, 1948 and letter of Father Raymond Lane to Father Thomas Malone, December 15, 1948. TS21, Sister Mary Louise Martin, p. 50; TS22, Sister Dorothy Rubner, pp. 2-3; TF57, Father Lloyd Glass, p. 44. Statistics are compiled from annual reports in FARC, 39-02, 37-02, 38-07, 42-09 and *Maryknoll Hong Kong Chronicle, 1918-1975*, pp. 150-175.

259. FARC, 5-07, Lintaan Diary, December 1948.

260. FARC, 23-06, Szwong Diary, Late Fall 1949, p. 3; TS98, Sister Agnes Virginia Higgins, pp. 34-35. See also TS47, Sister Mary Diggins, p. 39; TF69, Father Joseph Pulaski, p. 32.

261. TS02, Sister Monica Marie Boyle, p. 16; TS93, Sister Ann Carol Brielmaier, pp. 30-31; TS22, Sister Dorothy Rubner, pp. 7, 43.

262. FARC, 23-06, Szwong Diary, Late Fall 1949, p. 3. See also TS96, Sister Moira Riehl, pp. 20-21; TS47, Sister Mary Diggins, p. 41; TF71, Father John Drew, pp. 16-17.

263. FARC, Box—Communist Period, account by Father Howard Trube, pp. 3-4. See also account by Father Joseph Regan, pp. 1-2 and SARC, Box—South China, War Years, Iron Curtain, account by Sister Dominic Marie Turner, p. 1. On September 1, 1949, the Chinese People's Political Consultative Conference adopted a sort of provisional constitution called the Common Program which stipulated that "the people of the People's Republic of China shall have freedom of thought, speech, publication, assembly, . . . and religious belief." (Article 5); see Harold C. Hinton, ed., *The People's Republic of China, 1949-1979—A Documentary Survey, Vol. I* (Wilmington, DE: Scholarly Resources, Inc., 1980), p. 51-55.

264. Father John F. Donovan, "Schools Count in China," *The American Ecclesiastical Review*, November 1951, pp. 377-379. See also Father John F. Donovan, *China Learns* (Detroit: Maryknoll Publications, 1951), pp. 13-14. Similar views are expressed in TS21, Sister Mary Louise Martin, p. 47.

265. FARC, Box—Communist Period, account by Father Howard Trube, pp. 3-4.

266. *Maryknoll Hong Kong Chronicle*, pp. 164, 167-171.

267. FARC, 23-06, Szwong Diary, December 21-25, 1949. TS21, Sister Mary Louise Martin, pp. 46-47.

268. FARC, Box—Communist Period, Accounts by Fathers Joseph Regan, p. 2; Edwin McCabe, p. 3; James Fitzgerald, p. 1. TS47, Sister Mary Diggins, p. 40;

TS101, Sister Antonia Maria Guerrieri, pp. 55–56.

269. For instance, Sisters Joan Catherine O'Hagan and Rose Doherty were removed from Shekhang to Ngwa in the Kaying vicariate, Fathers John Drew and John Joyce from Sancian to Toishan in the Kongmoon vicariate, and Fathers Howard Geselbracht and Herbert Elliot from Pinglo to Kweilin city in the Kweilin prefecture. See SARC, Box—South China, War Years, Iron Curtain, account by Sister Dominic Marie Turner, p. 6; FARC, Box—Communist Period, account by Father George Bauer, p. 3.

270. TS54, Sister Edith Rietz, pp. 28–32. See also accounts in SARC, Box—South China, War Years, Iron Curtain, accounts by Sisters Mary Paulita Hoffman, Magdalena Urlacher, Monica Marie Boyle, and Thérèse (Marcelline) Grondin. Many interviews contain several pages on the detention of Maryknollers by the Communists.

271. SARC, Box—South China, War Years, Iron Curtain, account by Sister Barbara (Rose Victor) Mersinger, p. 5. TS21, Sister Mary Louise Martin, pp. 50–51; TS86, Sister Agnes Cazale, p. 32.

272. SARC, Box—South China, War Years, Iron Curtain, account by Sister Dominic Marie Turner, pp. 7–8. FARC, Box—Communist Period, accounts by Monsignor John Romaniello, p. 2; Father James McCormick, pp. 3–5; Father George Bauer, p. 3; Father Howard Trube, pp. 16–18. TF70, Father Charles Schmidt, p. 11.

273. SARC, Box—South China, War Years, Iron Curtain, Sister Monica Marie's account "Behind the Curtain in Loting," p. 2. See also TS47, Sister Mary Diggins, p. 36; TS84, Sister Chanel Xavier, p. 50; TS21, Sister Mary Louise Martin, p. 50; TS90, Sister Ann Maloney, p. 8; TS99, Sister Frances Murphy, p. 3; TF71, Father John Drew, p. 12; TF41, Father Stephen Edmonds, p. 17; TF69, Father Joseph Pulaski, p. 23.

274. FARC, Box—Communist Period, accounts by Fathers Richard Rhodes, p. 3; Edward Youker, p. 1; Edwin McCabe, p. 4. FARC, 53–02, letter of Father Frederick Becka to Father Thomas Malone, November 2, 1951. TF70, Father Charles Schmidt, pp. 11–12. SARC, Box—South China, War Years, Iron Curtain, account by Sister Dominic Marie Turner, p. 7. TS96, Sister Moira Riehl, p. 23.

275. TC20, Mr. Cheuk Chiu-yin, p. 16.

276. SARC, Regional Correspondence ChP22F3I, letter of Sister Mary Imelda Sheridan to Mother Mary Columba Tarpey, February 3, 1951. SARC, 48–22, Yeungkong Diary, January 21, 1951. TS65, Sister Irene Fogarty, pp. 40–41; TS96, Sister Moira Riehl, p. 23; TS21, Sister Mary Louise Martin, pp. 39, 50–51; TS86, Sister Agnes Cazale, p. 38; TS76, Sister Rose Bernadette Gallagher, p. 24. TF80, Father James Manning, pp. 23, 29; TF82, Father John Eggleston, p. 26; TF62, Father Richard Downey, p. 22; TF70, Father Charles Schmidt, p. 24. FARC, Box—Communist Period, accounts by Fathers Howard Trube, p. 19, Gregory Gilmartin, p. 9, Joseph McGinn, p. 1.

277. See clippings of Chinese newspapers in SARC, Box—South China, War Years, Iron Curtain. Also SARC, 42–14, Shekhang Sisters' Diary, July 1951; 43–23, Kaying Convent Chronicle, May 30, 1951, p. 6. *Maryknoll Hong Kong Chronicle, 1918–1975*, p. 168. In accounts written at the time as well as in later interviews, most Maryknollers, although acknowledging they received orders from their superiors and ordinaries to leave, considered that they had been expelled by the Communists.

278. SARC, Box—South China, War Years, Iron Curtain, Sister Marcelline's accounts, "Under Communism in China" and "Fifteen Weeks in Prison."

279. SARC, Box—South China, War Years, Iron Curtain, account of the imprisonment of Sister Rosalia Kettl written by Sister Moira Riehl.

280. SARC, Box—South China, War Years, Iron Curtain, account by Sister Monica Marie Boyle.

281. Eighteen belonged to South China; the two others, Father Joseph McCormack and Bishop James E. Walsh, were sentenced in Shanghai. Sources for Bishop Ford's case are: FARC, 37-03, *Nan Fang Jihpao* (South China Daily), April 24, 1951, pp. 1, 4; *Hsingmei Jihpao* (Hsingning-Meihsien Daily), April 25 and 26, 1951; letters of Father Thomas Malone to Father Thomas Walsh, January 8 and April 26, 1951; *Meikuo Chien-t'ieh Tsui Eh Ta* (The Most Evil American Spies), (Canton: South China People's Publishing Company, 1952). Also SARC, 43-23, Kaying Convent Chronicle, December 1, 1950-June 6, 1951.

282. SARC, 43-23, Kaying Convent Chronicle, February 27, 1951.

283. FARC, Box—Communist Period, account by Father Howard Trube, p. 30.

284. *Kung-chiao fan-kung chih li-ch'ang* and *Kung-ch'an-tang ti chi-lüeh*. For more samples of this type of literature published by the Catholic Truth Society of Hong Kong and the Catholic Church in Kaying, see SARC, Box—Correspondence of Bishop Francis X. Ford.

285. *Nan Fang Jihpao*, pp. 1, 4: "Kwangtung-sheng kung-luan chieh-chüeh pan-fa." Also mentioned in FARC, Box—Communist Period, account by Father Howard Trube, p. 28.

286. *Nan Fang Jihpao*, p. 1: letter of American Consul to Bishop Francis Ford, April 18, 1936.

287. *Nan Fang Jihpao*, p. 1: letter of Bishop Francis Ford to American Consul, American 30, 1929.

288. *Nan Fang Jihpao*, p. 4: letter of American Consul to Bishop Francis Ford, December 4, 1939.

289. FARC, 37-03, *Nan Fang Jihpao*: letters of American Consul to Bishop Francis Ford, September 4, 1940, October 19, 1940 and July 21, 1941.

290. FARC, 37-03, *Nan Fang Jihpao*, p. 4. See also Jean Lefeuvre, *Shanghai: les enfants dans la ville* (Paris: Casterman, 1957), pp. 42-45, 328-336.

291. *Hsingmei Jihpao*, April 25, 1951, pp. 1-2. FARC, Box—Communist Period, accounts by Father Howard Trube, pp. 27-29 and Father James McCormick, pp. 8-9.

292. FARC, 37-03, Father Albert Nevins, "American Bishop in China Called Spy by Moscow Paper," May 1951; Father John Donovan, *The Pagoda and The Cross*, p. 191.

293. FARC, 37-03, *Meikuo Chien-t'ieh Tsui Eh Ta*.

294. *The Pagoda and the Cross*, pp. 196-203. FARC, 35-01, Father William Downs, "The Kaying Diocese, a Historical Sketch, 1845-1961," pp. 184-185, 203-208.

295. FARC, 43-03, clippings of *Hong Kong Standard*, June 18, 1951, September 14, 1951; *The Shanghai News*, June 27, 1951, p. 4.

296. *Maryknoll Hong Kong Chronicle*, pp. 207-208. Bishop James E. Walsh, *Zeal for Your House* (Huntington, IN: Our Sunday Visitor, 1976), p. 179.

297. *China Missionary Bulletin*, June-July 1951, pp. 491-492. See also *China Missionary Bulletin*, October 1948, pp. 581-586.

298. Quoted in "Biography," *A Missionary for All Seasons* (New York: Maryknoll Publications, 1981). See also Father Robert Sheridan, *Bishop James E. Walsh as I Knew Him* (New York: Maryknoll Publications, 1981), p. 75 and *Maryknoll Hong Kong Chronicle*, p. 210.

299. *Zeal for Your House*, p. 172, 177; *Maryknoll Hong Kong Chronicle*, p. 210.

300. *Zeal for Your House*, p. 172.

301. *Ibid.*, p. 175.

302. *Ibid.*, pp. 171-172, 176-177; *Maryknoll Hong Kong Chronicle*, p. 230;

Father Robert Sheridan, *Bishop James E. Walsh as I Knew Him*, pp. 74–78.

303. On December 2, 1980, four American women were killed in El Salvador: Maryknoll Sisters Ita Ford and Maura Clarke, Ursuline Sister Dorothy Kazel and Lay Missioner Jean Donovan.

304. Letter *Ad Ipsis Pontificatus* of Pope Pius XI, quoted in *Digest of the Synodal Commission* (Peking), September-December 1943, p. 726.

PART IV—Chapter 8—Maryknoll's Influence on American Catholics

1. *The Field Afar*, October-November 1912, p. 3. See also January 1907, p. 2; June-July 1912, p. 2.

2. *The Field Afar*, January 1907, p. 10.

3. SARC, Box H–3.3 (1), Diary Excerpts, January 29, 1913.

4. *The Field Afar*, February 1913, p. 3; January 1914, p. 2; September 1917, p. 131; January 1918, p. 2; September 1920, p. 194; October 1922, p. 292; March 1923, p. 92.

5. *The Field Afar*, July-August 1924, p. 231.

6. *The Field Afar*, January 1916, p. 16; November 1922, p. 350.

7. *The Field Afar*, April 1918, p. 136.

8. *The Field Afar*, March 1916, pp. I-IV; July 1918, p. 116; August 1918, p. 136; September 1918, pp. 145–148; March 1919, pp. 44, 51; May 1924, p. 145; September 1926, p. 222. For lack of funds *The Junior* was again reunited with *The Field Afar* from September 1926 to August 1935 when it resumed as a separate publication.

9. *The Field Afar*, April 1913, p. 5; December 1917, p. 179; September 1918, p. 139; November 1918, p. 180; February 1930, p. 60; August 1931, p. 252; January 1932, p. 28.

10. Mary Coleman, ed., *Discourses of Mother Mary Joseph Rogers, 1912–1955* (Maryknoll Sisters, 1982), II, pp. 470–471.

11. Robert Sheridan, ed., *Discourses of James A. Walsh, 1890–1936* (Maryknoll Fathers, 1981), pp. 434, 436.

12. FARC, Box—Maryknoll Publications, Folder 3, "Maryknoll Pioneers." *The Field Afar*, September 1937, p. 258; January 1938, p. 30.

13. *The Field Afar*, February-March 1912, p. 15.

14. *The Field Afar*, April 1926, p. 110; November 1926, p. 285; December 1927, p. 322. FARC, Box—Pamphlets, Maryknoll, *American Youth and Foreign Missions* (New York: Catholic Foreign Missions of America, 1925).

15. FARC, Father George C. Powers, [Biography of Father Thomas Frederick Price], untitled and unpublished manuscript, 1943, p. 176. FARC, Box—Maryknoll Publications, Folder 5, *Mission Time*, I:1, October 1938, p. 1.

16. *Maryknoll—The Field Afar*, May 1939, p. 159.

17. *Ibid.*

18. FARC, Box—Development—Correspondence, 1924-1950, Folder 1940-1944, "Cultivation Section: 1941-1942 Program," November 26, 1940.

19. *The Field Afar*, October 1922, p. 312; February 1923, p. 65; June 1923, p. 188; January 1924, p. 6; February 1924, pp. 50, 58; June 1933, inside back cover. FARC, Box—New York Archdiocese, letter from Eastern Film Corporation, September 27, 1923. TS11, Sister Mary Paul McKenna, p. 6.

20. *The Field Afar*, April 1927, p. 108; October 1934, p. 288; November 1934, p. 297; December 1934, p. 329; May 1935, pp. 148-149; April 1938, p. 127.

21. *The Field Afar*, May 1935, p. 149.

22. *Ibid.*

23. *The Field Afar*, January 1937, p. 31; *Maryknoll—The Field Afar*, November 1940, p. 329. SARC, Box—Catalogues—Maryknoll Publications, catalogue of Maryknoll Free Lending Library, c. 1955, pp. 42–45.

24. *The Field Afar*, March 1929, p. 71. See also reproduction of advertisement for Father Chin's Radio Chin Chats on Station WCPO out of Cincinnati.

25. *The Field Afar*, October 1936, p. 290; November 1936, p. 325; January 1937, p. 30; February 1937, p. 62; March 1937, p. 95; April 1937, p. 126; May 1937, pp. 158–159; June 1937, p. 191; September 1937, p. 259; November 1937, p. 323.

26. *The Field Afar*, January 1937, p. 31.

27. SARC, Box—Catalogues—Maryknoll Publications, catalogue of Maryknoll Free Lending Library, c. 1955, p. 41.

28. *The Field Afar*, March 1913, p. 13; February 1917, p. 18; April 1917, p. 60.

29. FARC, Box—Development Correspondence, 1924–1950, Folder 1937–1939, "The Missionary Promoter: Counsels of Bishop James A. Walsh," p. 2. SARC, *Discourses of Mother Mary Joseph Rogers*, I, p. 328.

30. *Discourses of Mother Mary Joseph Rogers*, I, p. 328.

31. *The Field Afar*, October-November 1912, p. 6; March 1918, inside front cover, p. 45; September 1921, p. 245; March 1928, p. 86. FARC, Box—Departures, Folder—Departure Leaflets, 1940 ff.

32. *Maryknoll—The Field Afar*, October 1950, p. 40.

33. *Ibid.*

34. TS101, Sister Antonia Maria Guerrieri, p. 1; TF03, Father Thomas Kiernan, pp. 2–3; TS95, Sister Mary de Ricci Cain, p. 3; TS02, Sister Monica Marie Boyle, p. 1; TF84, Father Michael Gaiero, p. 2; TS93, Sister Ann Carol Brielmaier, p. 3. FARC, Necrology, Father Paul Touchette. These findings are corroborated by Sister Joan Chatfield's analysis of a carefully selected sample of 250 Maryknoll Sisters in "First Choice: Mission: The Maryknoll Sisters, 1912–1975," (Ph.D. diss., Graduate Theological Union, Berkeley, 1983). "One of every five women joining Maryknoll would list the Maryknoll magazine as one of the most important factors in the development of her decision to enter. Only one out of 33 persons answering the questionnaire said it had not had any influence on them" (p. 10).

35. TF05, Father John Driscoll, p. 2; TS91, Sister Mary Ruth Riconda, pp. 1, 4. FARC, Necrology, Father Thomas F. Nolan. See also Sister Joan Chatfield's "First Choice," p. 139.

36. *Maryknoll*, June 1986, p. 78.

37. TS28, Sister Ann Mary Farrell, p. 1; TS71, Sister Pauline Sticka, pp. 2–3; TF78, Father John McGinn, pp. 1–4; TF67, Father Robert Winkels, p. 1. See also the column "How It Came" on mission vocation in *The Field Afar*, February-November 1932. See also Sister Joan Chatfield's "First Choice," p. 139.

38. TS63, Sister Ignatia McNally, p. 3.

39. TS88, Sister Virginia Flagg, p. 4.

40. TS19, Sister Kathleen Bradley, p. 12.

41. TF01, Father Robert Sheridan, p. 9.

42. TS02, Sister Monica Marie Boyle, p. 1; TS53, Sister Celine Marie Werner, p. 2.

43. *The Field Afar*, May 1918, p. 68.

44. *The Field Afar*, September 1933, p. 234.

45. *The Field Afar*, March 1925, p. 81.

46. *Maryknoll—The Field Afar*, February 1942, pp. 5–6.

47. *Maryknoll—The Field Afar*, September 1942, p. 23.

48. *Ibid.*, p. 5.
49. *Maryknoll—The Field Afar*, February 1942, p. 6.
50. *The Field Afar*, September 1933, p. 235.
51. *The Field Afar*, October 1935, p. 228.
52. *The Field Afar*, December 1935, p. 344.
53. *The Field Afar*, June 1933, p. 192.
54. *Maryknoll—The Field Afar*, July-August 1943, p. 30.
55. *Ibid.*, pp. 30, 32.
56. *Maryknoll—The Field Afar*, September 1945, p. 2.
57. *The Field Afar*, May 1919, p. 95.
58. *The Field Afar*, April 1933, pp. 99–100.
59. *The Field Afar*, April 1925, p. 103.
60. *The Field Afar*, May 1933, p. 133.
61. *Ibid.*
62. For entire text, see *Collectanea Sacrae Congregationis De Propaganda Fide* (Rome: Typis Polyglottis Vaticanis, 1907), I, No. 135: "Instruction of the Sacred Congregation of Propaganda Fide, A.D. 1659."
63. *The Field Afar*, December 1935, p. 345.
64. *Ibid.*
65. *Maryknoll—The Field Afar*, September 1939, p. 241.
66. *Maryknoll—The Field Afar*, November 1939, p. 301.
67. *The Field Afar*, January 1933, p. 32.
68. *The Field Afar*, February 1933, p. 64.
69. *The Field Afar*, January 1926, p. 24; June 1927, p. 157.
70. *Maryknoll—The Field Afar*, September 1939, p. 246.
71. *Ibid.*
72. *The Field Afar*, May 1933, p. 132.
73. *The Field Afar*, May 1919, p. 86; June 1919, p. 111. See also *The Field Afar*, June 1918, p. 81; August 1918, p. 117; August 1919, p. 163; October 1919, pp. 206–207; March 1921, p. 52.
74. *The Field Afar*, May 1918, p. 68.
75. *The Field Afar*, November 1925, p. 311. See also *The Field Afar*, July-August 1923, p. 196; October 1925, p. 284; February 1926, p. 40; March 1926, p. 68.
76. *The Field Afar*, February 1934, pp. 42–43. See also Immanuel Hsü, *The Rise of Modern China* (New York: Oxford University Press, 1975), pp. 682–684.
77. *The Field Afar*, December 1934, p. 355. See also May 1933, p. 131; January 1937, p. 26.
78. *The Field Afar*, December 1934, p. 355.
79. *Maryknoll—The Field Afar*, June 1943, p. 25. See also July-August 1942, pp. 15–16; October 1943, p. 2.
80. *Maryknoll—The Field Afar*, April 1946, p. 36.
81. *Maryknoll—The Field Afar*, July-August 1942, p. 16. See also April 1946, pp. 36–37.
82. *Maryknoll—The Field Afar*, June 1943, inside front cover.
83. *Maryknoll—The Field Afar*, May 1943, p. 2.
84. *Maryknoll—The Field Afar*, January-February 1945, inside front cover.
85. *The Field Afar*, January 1937, p. 26.
86. *Maryknoll—The Field Afar*, June 1943, p. 32. See also October 1943, pp. 2-3.
87. *The Field Afar*, May 1919, p. 95.
88. *The Field Afar*, June 1930, p. 189; November 1930, p. 321; *Maryknoll—The Field Afar*, November 1945, p. 48.

89. *Maryknoll—The Field Afar,* December 1945, p. 21.

90. *Maryknoll—The Field Afar,* November 1947, pp. 23–27. See also November 1943, pp. 14–16; January-February 1945, p. 20; June 1945, p. 48; March 1946, p. 48; February 1947, pp. 34–35; April 1947, p. 48.

91. *Maryknoll—The Field Afar,* September 1943, p. 48.

92. *Maryknoll—The Field Afar,* July-August 1945, p. 48; November 1947, pp. 18–21. See also January-February 1945, p. 48; June 1945, p. 48; October 1945, p. 48; November 1945, p. 48; June 1946, p. 48; October 1947, p. 48; December 1947, p. 48; February 1948, p. 48.

93. *Maryknoll—The Field Afar,* July-August 1946, p. 45.

94. *Maryknoll—The Field Afar,* December 1945, p. 21. See also March 1945, pp. 3–5.

95. *Maryknoll—The Field Afar,* January-February 1945, p. 20.

96. *Maryknoll—The Field Afar,* April 1946, p. 35.

97. *Ibid.,* p. 36.

98. *Ibid.,* p. 37.

99. Jean Chesneaux, Françoise Le Barbier, Marie-Claire Bergère, *China, From the 1911 Revolution to Liberation* (New York: Pantheon Library, 1977), pp. 198–199, 269–270, 272, 325. Brian Crozier, *The Man Who Lost China* (New York: Scribner, 1976), pp. 242–244, 258–259, 279, 394–395. William Morwood, *Duel for the Middle Kingdom* (New York: Everest House, 1980), pp. 308, 310, 355–358. See also Sterling Seagrave, *The Soong Dynasty* (New York: Harper & Row, 1985).

100. TF04, Father Francis Daubert, pp. 36–39; TS65, Sister Irene Fogarty, p. 34.

101. *Maryknoll—The Field Afar,* October 1952, p. 52.

102. *Ibid.,* p. 53.

Concluding Remarks

1. *Maryknoll—The Field Afar,* September 1939, pp. 238–239; see also July-August 1942, p. 12 and July 1980, pp. 48–49. For Maryknoll's most recent official statements of solidarity with the poor, see "Statements of Mission Vision and Mission Directions, Eighth General Chapter 1984," Maryknoll Fathers and Brothers, pp. 15–17; and "Proceedings of the Twelfth General Assembly, October 9-November 26, 1984," Maryknoll Sisters, internal document, pp. 1 and 4.

2. Mother Mary Joseph, 1936, in "Proceedings of the Twelfth General Assembly, October 9-November 26, 1984," Maryknoll Sisters, internal document.

Glossary of Locations in China*

Maryknoll Spelling	Pinyin Romanization	Characters
AMOY	Xiamen	廈門
ANTUNG	Andong	安東
AUPOE	Yaobei	凹背
BINGTSUEN	Bingcun	丙村
BLUE CLOUD	Lüyun	綠雲
CANTON	Guangzhou	廣州
CHAKOW	Chagou	岔溝
CHANGPAI	Changbai	長白
CHANGSHA	Changsha	長沙
CHAO-T'UNG	Zhaotong	昭通
CHAOPING	Zhaoping	昭平

*Locations for which Chinese characters could not be found are not listed.

CHAOYANGCHEN	Chaoyangzhen	鎮府
CHENGTINGFU	Zhengdingfu	
CHENPING	Zhenping	
CHIKAI	Chixi	
CHIKLUNG	Zhigong	
CHINCH'ENGCHIANG	Jinchengjiang	江
CHIULING	Jiaoling	
CHONGLOK	Changle	
CHONGPU	Changpu	
CHUANHSIEN	Chuanxian	
CHUKTAOSHIN	Zhutoushen	神
CHUNGSHAN	Zhongshan	
CHUNGSUN	Zhongxin	
CHWANGHO	Zhuanghe	
DAIREN	Dalian	
DOSING	Ducheng	
ERHPATAN	Erbadan	石
FACHOW	Huazhou	
FAHSIEN	Huaxian	
FAYANG	Huayang	
FENGCHENG	Fengcheng	

FENGTIEN	Fengtian	奉天
FUCHOW	Fuzhou	福州
FUCHWAN	Fuchuan	富川
FUKIEN	Fujian	福建
FUSHUN	Fushun	撫順
FUSUNG	Fusong	撫松
HAILUNG	Hailong	海龍
HAINAN	Hainan	海南
HAMAHO	Hamahe	哈馬河
HANGCHOW	Hangzhou	杭州
HANKOW	Hankou	漢口
HARBIN	Haerbin	哈爾濱
HEILUNGKIANG	Heilongjiang	黑龍江
HINGAN	Xingan	興安
HINGIP	Xingye	興業
HINGKING	Xingjing	興京
HINGNING	Xingning	興寧
HO T'IN	Hetian	河田
HOHSIEN	Hexian	賀縣
HOIFUNG	Haifeng	海豐
HOINGAN	Haiyan	海晏

HOIPING	Kaiping	
HOKSHIHA	Haoshixia	
HONAM	Henan	
HONAN	Henan	
HONG KONG	Xianggang	
HOPEI	Hebei	
HOPING	Heping	
HSIAOSHIH	Xiaoshi	
HSINKING	Xinjing	
HSINPIN	Xinbin	
HUNAN	Hunan	
HUPEH	Hubei	
HWANGTANG	Huangtang	
HWANJEN	Huanren	
HWEINAN	Huinan	
INING	Yining	
JUICHIN	Ruijin	
JUNGYUN	Rongxian	
KANCHINGTZE	Ganjingzi	
KANCHOW	Ganzhou	
KAOYAO	Gaoyao	

開鶴河河香河和小新新湖湖黃桓光輝義瑞容甘贛高

平市南南港北平市京賓南北塘仁南寶金縣井州要

下

子

KAPSHUI	Heshui	合水
KAYING	Jiaying	嘉應
KIANGNAN	Jiangnan	江南
KIANGSI	Jiangxi	江西
KIAOTOW	Qiaotou	橋頭
KIENTCHANG	Jianchang	建長
KINCHWAN	Jinchuan	金川
KIRIN	Jilin	吉林
KOCHOW	Gaozhou	高州
KONGCHOWWAN	Guangzhouwan	廣州灣
KONGMOON	Jiangmen	江門
KOPI	Gaopo	高陂
KUHWA	Guhua	古化
KUKONG	Gujiang	曲江
KUNGCHENG	Gongcheng	恭城
KUNMING	Kunming	昆明
KWANGHOI	Guanghai	廣海
KWANGSI	Guangxi	廣西
KWANGTUNG	Guangdong	廣東
KWANTIEN	Kuandian	寬甸
KWANTUNG	Guandong	關東

KWANYANG	Guanyang
KWEICHIANG	Guijiang
KWEICHOW	Guizhou
KWEILIN	Guilin
KWEIPING	Guiping
KWEIYANG	Guiyang
LAANTIEN	Lantian
LAIPO	Lipu
LAITSUI	Lizui
LAOHUKOW	Laohukou
LAOLUNG	Laolong
LIAONING	Liaoning
LIAOTUNG	Liaodong
LINGCHWAN	Lingchuan
LINGNAM	Lingnan
LINKIANG	Linjiang
LINPING	Lianping
LINTAAN	Liantan
LIUCHOW	Liuzhou
LIUHO	Liuhe
LOKING	Luojing

LOTING	Luoding	羅定
LUCHWAN	Luchuan	陸川
LUICHOW	Leizhou	雷州
LUK YAM	Lüyun	綠雲
LUMCHAI	Linzhai	林寨
LUNGCHOW	Longzhou	龍州
LUNGCHUN	Longchuan	龍川
LUNGSHENG	Longsheng	龍勝
LUNGWOH	Longwo	龍窩
MACAO	Aomen	澳門
MANCHUKUO	Manzhoukuo	滿州國
MAOMING	Maoming	茂名
MENGSHAN	Mengshan	蒙山
MOYAN	Meixian	梅縣
MUKDEN	Shenyang	瀋陽
NAAM YEUNG	Nanyang	南洋
NAMFUTONG	Nanhutang	南湖堂
NANCH'ANG	Nanchang	南昌
NANFEN	Nanfen	南分
NANKING	Nanjing	南京
NANNING	Nanning	南寧

NGAIMOON	Haimen	海門
NGWA	Wuhua	五華
NINGPO	Ningbo	寧波
PAKHOI	Beihai	北海
PAKKAI	Beijie	北街
PAKLOW	Beiliu	北流
PAKSHA	Baisha	白沙
PANTIEN	Bantian	湴田
PAOTINGFU	Baodingfu	保定府
PATPO	Babu	八步
PEI-CH'IAO	Beiqiao	北橋
PEKING	Beijing	北京
PENKI	Benxi	本溪
PETTOCHAI	Beitouzhai	北斗寨
PINGLO	Pingluo	平樂
PINGNAM	Pingnan	平南
PINGYUN	Pingyuan	平遠
POHAI	Bohai	渤海
POKPAK	Bobai	博白
POSE	Baise	百色
PUCHI	Puqi	蒲圻

SAINING	Xining	西寧 河 壩
SAMHOPA	Sanheba	三河
SAMSHUI	Sanshui	三水
SANCIAN	Shangchuan	上川
SANUK	Xinwu	新屋
SHAANIU	Shanyao	山腰
SHAHOKOU	Shahekou	沙河 口
SHAKCHIN	Shizheng	石正
SHANCHENGTZE	Shanchengzi	山城 子
SHANGHAI	Shanghai	上海
SHE SHAN	Sheshan	佘山
SHEKKOO	Shigu	石固
SHENYANG	Shenyang	瀋陽
SHEUNG YEUNG	Shangyang	上洋
SHEUNGSHAN	Shangshan	上山
SHIUHING	Zhaoqing	肇慶
SHUICHAI	Shuizhai	水寨
SHUICHOW	Shaozhou	韶州
SHUMKAI	Cenqi	岑溪
SIAOLOC	Soule	叟樂
SINTU	Xindu	信都

SIUYEN	Xiuyan	巖子街
SIWANTZU	Xiwanzi	灣平昌口算會宜頭旺八埔灣慶竹安山坑隸縣津
SSUPINGKAI	Sipingjie	
SUNCHONG	Xinchang	
SUNGKOW	Songkou	
SUNNING	Xinning	
SUNWUI	Xinhui	
SUNYI	Xinyi	
SWATOW	Shantou	
SZWONG	Siwang	
TAIPATHU	Dibaxu	岫西四新松新新信汕思第大大德丹坦斗粘直藤天
TAIPU	Dapu	
TAIWAN	Dawan	
TAKHING	Deqing	
TANCHUK	Danzhu	
TANON	Tanan	
TAUSHAN	Doushan	
TCHAMHANG	Zhankeng	
TCHELI	Zhili	
TENGYUN	Tengxian	
TIENTSIN	Tianjin	墟

TIN TOW	Tiantou	田頭
TINGCHOW	Tingzhou	汀州
TINMOON	Tianmen	天門
TINPAK	Dianbai	電白
TOISHAN	Taishan	台山
TONGSHUNCHAI	Tangchunzhai	塘唇寨
TOPONG	Dubang	都榜
TOUNTEOUHONG	Duntouxiang	墩頭鄉
TSANGWU	Zangwu	蒼梧
TSIAHANG	Yukeng	畬坑
TSIAN	Jian	輯安
TSINGTAO	Qingdao	青島
TSINGTUITZE	Qingduizi	青堆子
TSINGYUAN	Qingyuan	清源
TSUITUNG	Shuidong	水東
TUNGAN	Tongan	同安
TUNGCHEN	Dongzhen	東鎮
TUNGHWA	Tonghua	通化
TUNGON	Dongan	東岸
TUNGSHEK	Dongshi	東石
TZUNIHANG	Zinikeng	緇泥坑

VONGNAITONG	Huangnitang
VONGTIEN	Huangtian
VOONAI	Wuni
WAICHAU	Huizhou
WAITSAP	Huaiji
WANFOW	Yunfu
WATLAM	Yulin
WATNAM	Yunan
WUCH'ANG	Wuchang
WUCHOW	Wuzhou
WUNIHANG	Wunikeng
YANGSO	Yangshuo
YANPING	Enping
YAOHANG	Jiaokeng
YAOSHAN	Yaoshan
YENKI	Yanji
YEUNGKONG	Yangjiang
YUNGCHOW	Yongzhou
YUNGFU	Yongfu
YUNGHUI	Rongxu
YUNNAN	Yunnan
ZIKAWEI	Xujiawei

塘

泥田坭州集浮林南昌州泥朔平坑山吉江州福墟南家

黃黃烏惠懷雲鬱樹鬱武梧烏陽恩焦猺延陽永永戎雲徐

坑

滙

*Glossary of Chinese Terms and Personal Names**

Au, Maureen   歐修女

Chai, Longinus   蔡靜山

Chan, Rose   陳玫瑰

Chang Hsüeh-liang   張學良

Chang Tso-lin   張作霖

Chau, Agnes   周依搦斯

Ch'en Chiung-ming   陳炯明

Chen, Joachim   陳梅福

Ch'en, Mary Celine   陳賽理納

Chen, Pierre   陳德啟

Cheuk Chiu-yin   卓超然

Cheuk Yee-chiu   卓二招

*Terms and names for which Chinese characters could not be found are not listed.

553

Cheuk York-mong	卓謙權
Cheung, Andrew	張世博
Cheung, Paul	張立文
Chiang Kai-shek	蔣介石
Chin, Rose	秦羅撒
ching t'ang	經堂
Choi, Benedict	蔡秀峰
Choo, Paul	朱有正
chuchiati	住家的
Chu Teh (Zhu De)	朱德
ch'u teng	初等
Chum, Peter (Father)	覃文華
Chum, Peter (Mr.)	覃彼得
Chung Kwok-kwan	鍾國群
Hon, Paul	韓時欣
Huang Shao-hsiung	黃紹雄
Hung Hu-tzu	紅鬍子
Jong Kim-shum	莊建尋
kao teng	高等
Koo, René	古求敏
Kung, H.H.	孔祥熙
Kung P'in-mei	龔品梅

Laai, Joseph 賴咸瑟榮

Lam, Joseph 福祕榮珍

Lam, Paul 林初國碧修

Lam, Rose 藍國文喜德

Lau, Thomas 林碧尚漁

Lee, Laetitia 劉文德助

Lei, Simon 李喜賢秀撇

Leung Kit-fong 李尚宗仁

Li, Joseph 梁德次庭

Li Tsung-jen 李賢玉華

Liang, Stephen 梁宗貞德

Liao, Peter 廖次漢槙

Ling, Joan 凌玉壬生

Liu Hon-ching 廖貞棟

Liu Jen-sheng 劉漢伯鴻藻

Liu, Paul 廖壬文樞廷

Lo Pa-hong (Joseph) 陸棟中樞魂

Lo Wenzao 羅伯榮廷東

Loo, Luke 盧文思魂

Lu Jung-t'ing 陸中澤東

Ma, Thomas 馬榮

Mao Tse-tung (Zedong) 毛思澤

Pai, Alexis	白	景崇雲惠波西景錦儀潤民中刀笠以神小赫成任煜大	山禧中民羅滿恒華端主山會

Pai, Alexis 白

Pai Ch'ung-hsi 白

Pai, Martin 白

Pai, Maurus 白

Pai, Protase 白

Pai, Simon 白

Pan, Antoine 潘

Pei, John 貝

Puyi 溥

Qiu Runduan 丘

San Min Chu I 三

Sun Yat-sen 孫

Ta Tao Hui 大

Tai Li 戴

Tang, Dominic 鄧

Tao, Thomas 陶

Teng Hsiao-p'ing (Deng Xiaoping) 鄧

Ting, Mary Herman 丁

To, Simeon 陶

Tsai, Mark 蔡

Tsang, Mark 曾

Tse, David 謝

Tse, Eileen	謝漪漣
Tse, John	謝鳴之
Ts'ia, Paul	謝德祿
Tsoc, Anthony	卓正賢
Tsong, Paul	張洪康
Tsui, Paul	崔保祿
t'u t'am	土談
Von-fouc Ma-li-a	萬福瑪利亞
Wang Ching-wei	汪精衛
Wang Feng-ko	王鳳閣
Wong, John	黃卿孫
Wong, Linus	王理諾
Woo Pei Fu	吳佩孚
Wu, John	胡振中
Xu Simeng	許思孟
Yeung, John	楊慶松
Yi Shih-pao	益世報
Yip, Epiphanius	葉先生
Yü Pin (Paul)	于斌
Yü Tso-po	俞作柏
Yüan Shih-k'ai	袁世凱

Working Bibliography

ARCHIVES

Archives of the Catholic Foreign Mission Society of America: letters, diaries, minutes, reports, bulletins, and newspaper clippings related to China. Maryknoll, New York.

Archives of the Congregation of the Foreign Mission Sisters of St. Dominic: photographs, letters, diaries, reports, and newspaper clippings related to China. Maryknoll, New York.

Archives des Missions Etrangères de Paris, Paris.

Interviews of missioners and Chinese people conducted by the Maryknoll China History Project and preserved in both Maryknoll archives.

National Archives, Department of State Decimal File, 1910–1951, Washington, DC.

Photographic archives of the Catholic Foreign Mission Society of America related to China.

PRINTED COLLECTIONS, PERIODICALS, AND NEWSPAPERS

Acta Apostolicae Sedis. Rome: Typis Polyglottis Vaticanis, 1909-.

Annales de la Propagation de la Foi. Lyon & Paris: Oeuvre de la Propagation de la Foi, 1926 and following.

Annals of the Propagation of the Faith. Baltimore: Society for the Propagation of the Faith, 1903 and following.

Annuaire de l'Eglise catholique en Chine, 1948. Shanghai: Bureau Sinologique de Zi-ka-wei.

Annuaire des missions catholiques de Chine. Shanghai: Bureau Sinologique de Zi-ka-wei, 1924–1940.

Annuaire des missions catholiques du Manchoukuo. 5 vols. Moukden: Imprimerie de la Mission Catholique, 1935–1939.

The Boston Evening Transcript. 1903–1907.

The Boston Pilot. 1903–1907 and 1935.

The Boston Sunday Post. 1937.

The Catholic Transcript. Hartford, CO: 1935 and 1952–53.

China Christian Yearbook, 1938–1939. N.p.; n.d.

The Chinese Recorder. Shanghai: 1935–1941.

Christianity and the New China. Continuation of China and Christian Responsibility: A Symposium. South Pasadena, CA: Ecclessia, 1974.

Collectanea Sacrae Congregationis de Propaganda Fide, I and II. Rome: Typis Polyglottis Vaticanis, 1907.

Daily Herald. New Britain, CO: 1949 and 1955.

Denver Register. 1935.

Digest of the Synodal Commission (1928–1957). Title was changed several times to *Collectanea Commissionis Synodalis, China Missionary, China Missionary Bulletin,* and *Mission Bulletin.*

The Ecclesiastical Review, known since 1944 as *The American Ecclesiastical Review.* Philadelphia and Washington, DC: 1904–1953.

Fides News Service. Rome: 1927–1957.

The Field Afar, 1907 to present. This magazine has had various publishers and places of publication. In 1911 it became the official organ of the Catholic Foreign Mission Society of America. There have been several title changes: *The Field Afar—Maryknoll* in November 1918; *The Field Afar—The Magazine of Maryknoll* in January 1937; *Maryknoll—The Field Afar* in May 1939; and finally *Maryknoll* in January 1957.

The Hartford Times. Hartford, CO: 1954.

Hong Kong Standard. June 18 and September 14, 1951.

Juris Pontificii de Propaganda Fide, I. Rome: 1897.

Lettres édifiantes et curieuses des missions étrangères. Toulouse: N. E. Sens and A. Gaude, 1811 and following.

The Maryknoll Junior. Maryknoll: Maryknoll Publications, 1919–1926 and 1935–1949.

Maryknoll Mission Letters. 2 vols. New York: Macmillan Co., 1923, 1927.

Maryknoll Mission Letters. 10 vols. Maryknoll: The Field Afar Press, 1942–1946.

Maryknoll News. November 1980–April 1987. Newspaper of the Maryknoll Fathers and Brothers.

Mémoires de la Congrégation de la Mission en Chine. Nouvelle édition. Tome III. Paris: Procure de la Congregation de la Mission, 1912.

Missiones Catholicae cura S. Congregationis de Propaganda Fide descriptae statistica, anno 1922, anno 1927. Rome: Typis Polyglottis Vaticanis, 1922, 1930.

Missions, séminaires, oeuvres catholiques en Chine (1928–1929). Shanghai: Bureau Sinologique de Zi-ka-wei.

Peking Times. September 17, 1931.

Primum Concilium Sinense, Anno 1924. Zi-ka-wei: Typographia Missionis Catholicae, 1929.

The Rock. Hong Kong: 1936–1940. Monthly publication of the Jesuit Society in Hong-Kong.

The Sacred Heart Review. Boston: August 19, 1905.

Le siège apostolique et les missions. Textes et documents. Instruction de 1659. Paris: Union Missionnaire du Clergé, n.d.

Shanghai News. June 27, 1951.

Stories from Field Afar. Maryknoll, vol. 1, 1913; vol. 2, 1915; vol. 3, 1921.

Tientsin Times. September 17, 1931.
UCA News. Hong Kong: 1985–86.

BOOKS, ARTICLES, AND UNPUBLISHED RESEARCH WORKS

Alexandre, Noël. *Apologie des dominicains missionnaires de Chine*. Cologne, 1700.

Allen, Yorke. *A Seminary Survey*. New York: Harper, 1960.

American Jesuits in Shanghai. *Portraits of China*. New York: Herder, 1950.

Anderson, Gerald H. *The Theology of the Christian Mission*. London: SCM Press, Ltd., 1961.

Anderson, Gerald H. and Stransky, Thomas F., eds. *Crucial Issues in Mission Today*. New York: Paulist Press, 1974.

Arens, Bernard. *Handbuch der katholischen Missionen*. Freiburg im Breisgau: Herder & Company, vol. 1, 1920; vol. 2, 1925.

Austin, Alvyn J. *Saving China: Canadian Missionaries in the Middle Kingdom, 1888–1959*. Toronto: University of Toronto Press, 1986.

Ball, J. Dyer. *Cantonese Made Easy*. 4th ed. Hong Kong: Kelly & Walsh, 1924.

Ballou, Earle Hoit. *Dangerous Opportunity; The Christian Mission in China*. New York: Friendship Press, 1940.

Barnett, Suzanne Wilson and Fairbank, John King, eds. *Christianity in China—Early Protestant Missionary Writings*. Cambridge: Harvard University Press, 1985.

Barrett, William E. *The Red Lacquered Gate*. New York: Sheed & Ward, 1967.

Beckmann, Johannes. *Die katholische Missionsmethode in China in neuester Zeit (1842–1912)*. Immensee, Switzerland: Missionhausen Bethlehem, 1931.

Bergeron, Marie Ina. *Le Christianisme en Chine: approches et stratégies*. Lyon: Chalet, 1977.

Bertreux, Henri. *Au pays du dragon*. Paris: Maisonneuve, 1922.

Bezzenberger, Günter. *Mission in China: d. Geschichte l. Chines*. Kassel: Kurhessen-Waldeck, 1979.

Bigo, Pierre. *The Church & Third World Revolution*. Translated by Sr. Jeanne Marie Lyons. Maryknoll: Orbis Books, 1977.

Bortone, Fernando. *I gesuiti alla corte di Pechino (1551–1813)*. Rome: Desclee, 1969.

Bosch, David. *Witness to the World. The Christian Mission in Theological Perspective*. Atlanta: John Knox Press, 1980.

Bühlmann, Walbert. *God's Chosen Peoples*. Maryknoll: Orbis books, 1982.

Burke, Thomas J. J. *Catholic Mission: Four Great Missionary Encyclicals*. New York: Fordham University Press, 1957.

Butow, Robert J. C. *The John Doe Associates: Backdoor Diplomacy for Peace, 1941*. Stanford: Stanford University Press, 1974.

————. *Kwangsi, Land of the Black Banners*. Translation and supplement by George F. Wiseman. St. Louis: Herder, 1942.

Campbell, Carrie Lee. *Mission Methods*. Richmond, VA: Richmond Press, 1923.

Campbell, Robert E. *The Church in Missions*. Maryknoll: Maryknoll Publications, 1965.

Carlen, Claudia. *The Papal Encyclicals, 1903–1939*. Wilmington, NC:

McGrath Publishing Company, 1981.

Cary-Elwes, Columba. *China and the Cross, A Survey of Missionary History.* New York: P. J. Kenedy & Sons, 1957.

————. *China and the Cross, Studies in Missionary History.* New York: Longmans, Green & Company, 1957.

Caterer, Helen. *Foreigner in Kweilin; The Story of Rhoda Watkins, South Australian Nursing Missionary.* London: Epworth Press, 1966.

Chadwick, Henry. *Early Christian Thought and the Classical Tradition.* New York: Oxford University Press, 1966.

Chao, Jonathan T'ien-en. *Bibliography of the History of Christianity in China.* Waltham, MA: China Graduate School of Theology, 1970.

Chen, Theodore H. E. "Education in China, 1927-1937" in Paul K. T. Sih, ed., *The Strenuous Decade, China's National Building Efforts, 1927-1937.* Jamaica, NY: St. John's University Press, 1970.

Chesneaux, Jean, Le Barbier, Françoise, and Bergère, Marie-Claire. *China, From the 1911 Revolution to Liberation.* New York: Pantheon Books, 1977.

Chiang Mei-ling (Soong). *Christianity in China's National Crisis.* Hankow: n.p., 1938.

Chu, Clayton H. *American Missioners in China: Books, Articles, and Pamphlets Extracted from the Subject Catalogue of the Missionary Research Library.* Cambridge: Harvard University Press, 1960.

Cohen, Paul A. *China and Christianity, The Missionary Movement and the Growth of Chinese Antiforeignism, 1860-1870.* Ann Arbor: University of Michigan Press, 1963.

Costantini, Celso. *Against Hope in Hope.* New York: Society for the Propagation of the Faith, 1931.

————. *L'Arte Cristiana Nelle Missioni.* Rome: Tipografia Polyglotta Vaticana, 1940.

Covell, Ralph R. *Confucius, The Buddha, and Christianity. A History of the Gospel in Chinese.* Maryknoll: Orbis Books, 1986.

Cronin, Archibald Joseph. *The Keys of the Kingdom.* Boston: Little, Brown & Company, 1941.

Cronin, Vincent. *The Wise Man from the West.* New York: Dutton, 1955.

Crozier, Brian. *The Man Who Lost China.* New York: Scribner, 1976.

Cuenot, Joseph. *Au pays des pavillons noirs.* Hong Kong: Imprimerie de Nazareth, 1925.

Cuming, G. A., ed. *The Mission of the Church and the Propagation of the Faith. Papers of the Meeting of the Ecclesiastical History Society.* London: Cambridge University Press, 1970.

D'Arcy, Paul F. *Constancy of Interest Factor Patterns within the Specific Vocation of Foreign Missioners.* Washington, DC: Catholic University of America Press, 1954.

Daly, C. *Cantonese Missionary Handbook.* Hong Kong: Nazareth Press, 1941.

Davies, John Paton, Jr. *Dragon by the Tail.* New York: W. W. Norton Co., 1972.

De Korne, John Cornelius. *Chinese Altars to the Unknown God (with Reactions to Them of Christian Missionaries).* Grand Rapids, MI: Christian Reformed Board of Missions, 1926.

D'Elia, Pasquale M. *Catholic Mission in China.* Shanghai: Commercial Press, 1941.

————. *Catholic Native Episcopacy in China, Being an Outline of the Formation and Growth of the Chinese Catholic Clergy, 1800–1926.* Shanghai: Tousewei Press, 1927.

————. *Fonti Ricciane.* Rome: La Libreria Della State, 1942. 3 vols.

————. *Le Triple Démisme de Suen Wen.* Zikawei: Imprimerie des Jésuites, 1929.

————. *The Triple Demism of Sun Yat-sen.* Wuchang: Franciscan Press, 1931.

Dehergne, Joseph. "L'Eglise catholique en Chine en ces 25 dernières années. *Bulletin de l'Université de l'Aurore,* juin 1949.

Djung Lu-dzai. *A History of Democratic Education in Modern China.* Shanghai: Commercial Press, 1934.

Duperray, Edward. *Ambassadeurs de Dieu à la Chine.* Tournai: Casterman, 1956.

Ellis, John Tracy. "A Challenge to the American Church on its One Hundredth Birthday," *The Catholic Historical Review,* October 1944, pp. 290–298.

————. *Documents of American Catholic History.* Milwaukee: The Bruce Publishing Co., 1956.

————. *Perspectives in American Catholicism.* Baltimore: Helicon, Benedictine Studies, 1963, see pp. 52–53.

Fairbank, John King, ed. *The Missionary Enterprise in China and America.* Cambridge: Harvard University Press, 1974.

————. *Chinabound, A Fifty-Year Memoir.* New York: Harper & Row, 1982.

Flynn, George Q. *Roosevelt and Romanism: Catholics and American Diplomacy, 1937–1945.* Westport, CT: Greenwood Press, 1976.

Foote, George William [Ah Sin]. *Letters of a Chinaman to English Readers on English and Chinese Superstitions and the Mischief of Missionaries.* London: The Pioneer Press, 1903.

Foster, John. *The Church and China.* London: Edinburgh House Press, 1943.

Frédéric-Dupont, Edouart. *La mission de la France en Asie.* Paris: Ed. France-Empire, 1956.

Gaver, Alain Van. *J'ai été condamné à la liberté.* Paris: Le Centurion, 1953.

Gibson, John Campbell. *Mission Problems and Mission Methods in South China.* Edinburgh, London: Oliphant, Anderson, & Ferrier, 1901.

Gilbert, Rodney. *What's Wrong with China?* New York: Frederick A. Stokes Company, 1926, 1932.

Goodrich, L. Carrington. "A Decade of American Catholic Missions in China," *International Review of Missions,* 15 (1929): 97–101.

Goyau, Georges. *L'Eglise en marche; Etude d'histoire missionnaire.* 4 vols. Paris: Ed. Spes, 1930–1934.

————. *La Femme dans les missions.* Paris: Ed. Flammarion, 1933.

Graham, Robert A. *Vatican Diplomacy, A Study of Church and State on the International Plane.* Princeton: Princeton University Press, 1959.

A Guide to Catholic Shanghai. Shanghai: Tousewei Press, 1937.

Guiot, Léonide. *La mission du Su-tchuen au XVIIIème siècle. Vie et apostolat de Mgr. Pottier, son fondateur.* Paris: Téqui, 1892.

Habig, Marion A. *Pioneering in China.* Chicago: Franciscan Herald Press, 1930.

Hagspeil, Bruno. *Along the Mission Trail.* Techny, IL: Mission Press S.V.D., 1925–1927, Vol. 4.

Hallack, Cecily. *The Legion of Mary.* 5th ed. London: Muller, 1950.

Harvey, Van A. *The Historian and the Believer—The Morality of Historical*

Knowledge and Christian Belief. New York: Macmillan, 1966.

Hayward, Victor Evelyn W. *Christians and China.* Belfast: Christian Journal, 1974.

Hearon, William C. "The Confrontation: American Catholicism and Chinese Communism, 1945–1962." B.A. thesis, Vassar, 1975.

Hedin, Sven. *Chiang Kai-shek: Marshal of China.* New York: The John Day Company, 1940.

Heininger, Janet E. "The American Board in China: The Missionaries' Experiences and Attitudes, 1911–1952." Ph.D. dissertation, University of Wisconsin-Madison, 1981.

Hennesey, James, S.J. *American Catholics: A History of the Roman Catholic Community in the United States.* New York: Oxford University Press, 1981.

Hockin, Katherine. *Servants of God in People's China.* New York: Friendship Press, 1962.

Hodgkin, Henry Theodore. *Living Issues in China.* New York: Friendship Press, 1932.

Hong, Silad. *The Dragon Net: How God Has Used Communism To Prepare China for the Gospel.* Old Tappan, NJ: Revell, 1976.

Hill, Max. *Exchange Ship.* New York: Farrar & Rinehart, Inc., 1942.

Hinton, Harold C., ed. *The People's Republic of China, 1949–1979—A Documentary Survey.* 4 vols. Wilmington, DE: Scholarly Resources, Inc., 1980.

Hsü, Immanuel, C. Y. *The Rise of Modern China.* New York: Oxford University Press, 1975.

Huang, Philip, C. C.; Bell, Linda Schaefer; and Walker, Kathy Lemons. *Chinese Communists and Rural Society, 1927–1934.* Chinese Research Monographs, No. 13. Berkeley: Center for Chinese Studies, 1978.

Huc, Evariste R. *Le Christianisme en Chine, en Tartarie et au Thibet.* Paris: Gaume Frères, 1957.

Jones, Philip Hanson. *The Steps of a Good Man; a Missionary's Life Among the Mountain Bandits of Southern China.* New York: Exponkio Press, 1967.

Kearney, James F. *The Four Horsemen Ride Again.* Portraits of China Series. Shanghai: Imprimerie de T'ou-se-wei, 1940.

Krahl, Joseph. *China Missions in Crisis. Bishop Laimbeckhoven and His Times: 1738–1787.* Rome: Gregorian University Press, 1964.

Langlais, Jacques. *Les Jésuites du Québec en Chine (1918–1955).* Québec: Les Presses de l'Université Laval, 1979.

Laracy Hugh. *Marists and Melanesians: A History of the Catholic Missions in the Solomon Islands.* Honolulu: University Press of Hawaii, 1976.

Lary, Diana. *Region and Nation: The Kwangsi Clique in Chinese Politics, 1925–1937.* New York: Cambridge University Press, 1974.

Latourette, Kenneth Scott. *A History of Christian Missions in China.* London: Society for Promoting Christian Knowledge, 1929.

Launay, Adrien. *Histoire des Missions de Chine: Mission du Kouang-Si.* Paris: Téqui, 1903.

———. *Histoire des Missions de Chine: Mission du Kouang-Tong.* Paris: Téqui, 1917.

Leclercq, Jacques. *Thunder in the Distance: The Life of Père Lebbe.* New York: Sheed & Ward, 1958.

Lee Chong-Sik. *Revolutionary Struggle in Manchuria: Chinese Communism and Soviet Interest, 1922-1945*. Berkeley: University of California Press, 1983.

Lefeuvre, Jean. *Shanghai: les enfants dans la ville*. Paris: Casterman, 1957.

Liang Si-ing. *La rencontre et le conflit entre les idées des missionnaires chrétiens et les idées des Chinois en Chine depuis la fin de la dynastie des Ming*. Paris: Domat, 1940.

Liebard, Odile M. *Official Catholic Teachings—Clergy and Laity*. Wilmington, NC: McGrath Publishing Company, 1978.

Liu Kwang-ching, ed. *American Missionaries in China: Papers from Harvard Seminars*. Cambridge: Harvard University Press, 1966.

————. *Americans and Chinese, A Historical Essay and a Bibliography*. Cambridge: Harvard University Press, 1963.

Lutz, Jessie Gregory. *China and the Christian Colleges, 1850-1950*. Ithaca: Cornell University Press, 1971.

————, ed. *Christian Missions in China*. Boston: D. C. Heath and Co., 1965.

Maxwell, Grant. *Assignment in Chekiang: Scarboro Missions in China, 1901-1954*. Scarborough, Ont.: Scarboro Mission Society, 1982.

May, Malcolm Vivian. *Failure in the Far East, Why and How the Breach Between the Western World and China Began*. London: N. Spearman, 1957.

McGoey, John H. *Nor Script, Nor Shoes*. Boston: Little Brown, 1958.

McGrath, William Cecil. *The Dragon at Close Range*. Scarboro Bluffs, Ontario: St. Francis Xavier Seminary, 1937.

McQuaide, Joseph. *With Christ in China*. San Francisco: O'Connor, 1916.

Metzler, Joseph, ed. *Sacrae Congregationis de Propaganda Fide Memoria Rerum, 1622-1972*. Vol. III/2, 1815-1972. Rome: Herder, 1976.

Miller, Basil William. *Twenty-four Missionary Stories from China*. Kansas City, MO: Beacon Hill Press, 1948.

The Mission among the Higher Classes in China, or a Prospectus of the International Institute of China. New York: Press of Eatong Mains, 1910.

Moidrey, Joseph de. *La hiérarchie catholique en Chine, en Corée, et au Japon 1307-1914*. Variétés sinologiques No. 38. Shanghai: Zikawei, 1914.

Morwood, William. *Duel for the Middle Kingdom*. New York: Everest House, 1980.

Nanteuil, Jacques. *L'épopée missionnaire de Théophane Vénard*. Paris: Bloud & Gay, 1950.

Nemer, Lawrence. *Anglican and Roman Catholic Attitudes on Missions. An Historical Study of Two English Missionary Societies in the Late Nineteenth Century (1865-1885)*. St. Augustin, West Germany: Steyler Verlag, 1981.

The Official Handbook of the Legion of Mary. Louisville, KY: Publishers Printing Company, 1952.

Oldham, Joseph H. *Christianity and the Peace Problem*. New York: George H. Doran Co., 1924.

Palmer, Gretta. *God's Underground in Asia*. New York: Appleton-Century, 1953.

Papers on China, East Asian Research Center, Harvard University, 1847-1971.

Paton, David. *"R.O."—The Life and Times of R. O. Hall of Hong Kong*. Cincinnati, OH: Forward Movement Publications, 1985.

Payne, Robert. *Chiang Kai-shek*. New York: Weybright and Talley, 1969.

Pichon, Charles. *The Vatican and its Role in World Affairs*. (Translated from

French). New York: Dutton, 1950.

Planchet, J. M. *Les Missions de Chine et du Japon*. Peking: Imprimerie des Lazaristes, 1916-1933, 10 vols. After 1933 published as *Les Missions de Chine* in Peking by the Imprimerie des Lazaristes, 1935-1937, 3 vols.; in Shanghai by the Willow Pattern Press, 1938-1940, 2 vols., and by the Pax Publishing Company, 1942, 1 vol.

Pollio, Gaetano. *Le calvaire de l'église dans la Chine nouvelle*. Paris: Téqui, 1962.

Potvin, Raymond H. and Suziedelis Antanas. *Seminarians of the Sixties: A National Survey*. Washington, D.C: CARA, 1969.

Prange, G. W. *At Dawn We Slept*. New York: McGraw Hill, 1981.

Price, Francis Wilson. *The Rural Church in China, A Survey*. New York: Agricultural Missions, 1948.

Rabe, Valentin H. *The Home Base of American China Missions, 1880-1920*. Harvard East Asian Monographs, No. 75. Cambridge: Harvard University Press, 1978.

Rasmussen, O. D. *What's Right with China, An Answer to Foreign Criticism*. Shanghai: Commercial Press, 1927.

Ray, Rex. *Cowboy Missionary in Kwangsi*. Nashville: Broadman, 1964.

Rea, Kenneth W., ed. *Canton in Revolution: The Collected Papers of Earl Swisher, 1925-1928*. Boulder, CO: Westview Press, 1977.

Reed, James. *The Missionary Mind and American East Asia Policy, 1911-1915*. Cambridge: Harvard University Press, 1983.

Renaud, Rosario. *Suichow, diocèse de Chine*. Vol. I, 1882-1931. Montréal: Bellarmin, 1955.

———. *Le diocèse de Suchow (Chine), Champ apostolique des jésuites canadiens de 1918 à 1954*. Vol. II. Montréal: Bellarmin, 1982.

Rey, Charles. *Dictionnaire Chinois-Français-Dialecte Hac-Ka*. Hong Kong: Nazareth Press, 1926.

Roberts, Paul. *Lo Pa Hong, "Coolie of Saint Joseph"*. Maryknoll: The Maryknoll Pamphlet Library, 1938.

Rousseau, Michel. *Mission et formation des catéchistes dans un monde en développement*. Brussels: Lumen Vitae, 1967.

Rowbotham, Arnold H. *Missionary and Mandarin: The Jesuits at the Court of China*. Berkeley: University of California Press, 1942.

Ryan, Thomas. *China Through Catholic Eyes*. Cincinnati, OH: Catholic Students Mission Crusade, 1942.

Salisbury, Harrison E. *The Long March, The Untold Story*. New York: Harper & Row, 1985.

Salotti, Carlo. *Sister Mary Assunta, the Seraphic Flower of the Franciscan Missionaries of Mary*. North Providence, RI: Franciscan Missionaries of Mary, 1931.

Schmalz, Norbert. *Shen-Fu's Study: The Memoirs of Two American Missionaries of Yesteryear*. Chicago: Franciscan Herald Press, 1966.

Schmidlin, Joseph. *Catholic Mission History*. Trans. and ed. by Matthias Braun. Techny, IL: Mission Press, 1933.

———. *Catholic Mission Theory*. Techny, IL: Mission Press, 1931.

Scherer, James A. *Missionary Go Home!* Englewood Cliffs, NJ: Prentice Hall, 1964.

Sih, Paul Kwang Tsien. *Decision for China: Communism or Christianity*. Chicago: Regnery, 1959.

Smith, Arthur Henderson. *China and America Today*. New York, Chicago: F. H. Revell Co., 1907.

———. *China in Convulsion*. New York, Chicago: F. H. Revell Co., 1901.

———. *Chinese Characteristics*. 2d ed. New York, Chicago: F. H. Revell Co., 1894.

———. *A Manual for Young Missionaries in China*. Shanghai: Christian Literature Publishing House, 1918.

———. *Rex Christus, an Outline Study of China*. New York: Macmillan Co., 1903.

———. *The Uplift of China*. New York: Young People's Missionary Movement, 1907.

———. *Village Life in China; a Study in Sociology*. New York, Chicago: F. H. Revell Co., 1899.

Snead-Cox, John G. *The Life of Cardinal Vaughan*. St. Louis, MO: B. Herder, 1912, 2 vols.

Suhard, Emmanuel. *The Church Today*. Chicago: Fides Publications, 1953.

Teng Szu-yü and Fairbank, J. K. *China's Response to the West: A Documentary Survey, 1839–1923*. Cambridge: Harvard University Press, 1954.

Teixeira, Manuel. *Macau e sua diocese no ano dos centenarios de fundaçao e restauraçao*. Macao: Tipographia de Organado Salesiano. 1956–1963. 3 vols.

Tracy, John V. "The Catholic Church in the U.S. and Mission Work." *The Ecclesiastical Review* (January 1906): 1–4.

Utley, Jonathon G. *Going to War with Japan, 1937–1941*. Knoxville: University of Tennessee Press, 1985.

Van Dorn, Harold Archer. *Twenty Years of the Chinese Republic—Two Decades of Progress*. New York: Alfred A. Knopf, 1932.

Varg, Paul A. *Missionaries, Chinese and Diplomats, the American Protestant Missionary Movement in China, 1890–1952*. Princeton: Princeton University Press, 1958.

Vriens, Livinus. *Critical Bibliography of Missiology*. Translated from the Dutch by Deodatus Tummers. Nijmegen: Bestelcentrale der V.S.K.B. Publ., 1960.

Weber, Elizabeth Josephine. *Celestial Honeymoon*. New York: Benziger, 1950.

Wehrle, S. Edmund. *Britain, China, and the Antimissionary Riots of 1891–1900*. Minneapolis: University of Minnesota Press, 1966.

Wei, Louis Tsing-sing. *La politique missionnaire de la France en Chine, 1842–1856*. Paris: Nouvelles éditions latines, 1957.

———. *Le Saint Siège et la Chine de Pie XI à nos jours*. Paris: Editions A. Allais, 1968.

Wiest, Jean-Paul. "Catholic Activities in Kwangtung Province and Chinese Responses, 1848–1885." Ph.D. dissertation, University of Washington, 1977.

Wilbur, C. Martin. *The Nationalist Revolution in China, 1923–1928*. New York: Cambridge University Press, 1985.

———. *Sun Yat-sen, Frustrated Patriot*. New York: Columbia University Press, 1976.

Williams, Bascom Winton. *The Joke of Christianizing China*. New York: Peter Eckler, 1927.

Wolferstan, Bertram. *The Catholic Church in China from 1860 to 1907*.

St. Louis: Herder, 1909; London and Edinburgh: Sands & Co., 1909.

Yip Ka-che. "The Anti-Christian Movement in China, 1922–1927, With Special Reference to the Experience of Protestant Missions." Ph.D. dissertation, Columbia University, 1970.

PUBLICATIONS AND MANUSCRIPTS BY OR ABOUT MARYKNOLLERS

American Youth and Foreign Missions. Maryknoll: Catholic Foreign Mission Society of America, 1925.

Barry, Peter J. "A Brief History of the Missionary Work of the Maryknoll Fathers." M.A. thesis, National Taiwan University, Taipei, June 1977.

Bauer, Thomas J. *The Systematic Destruction of the Catholic Church in China.* Maryknoll: World Horizons Report, No. 11, 1954.

Bedier, Juliana. *Long Road to Loting.* The Loting Book Series. New York: Longmans, Green, & Co., 1941.

———. *Thomas the Good Thief.* The Loting Book Series. New York: Longmans, Green, & Co., 1942.

———. *The Important Pig.* The Loting Book Series. New York: Longmans, Green, & Co., 1942.

———. *Little Miss Moses.* The Loting Book Series. New York: Longmans, Green, & Co., 1943.

———. *A Horse for Christmas.* The Loting Book Series. New York: Longmans, Green, & Co., 1943.

Betz, Eva K. *To Far Places; The Story of Francis X. Ford.* New York: Hawthorne Books Inc., 1962.

Bradshaw, Sue. "Religious Women in China: An Understanding of Indigenization." *The Catholic Historical Review* (January 1982): 28–45.

Breslin, Thomas A. "American Catholic China Missionaries, 1918–1941." Ph.D. dissertation, University of Virginia, Charlottesville, 1972.

———. *China, American Catholicism, and the Missionary.* University Park: Pennsylvania State University Press, 1980.

———. "The Disordered Society: American Catholics Look at China, 1900–1937." M.A. thesis, University of Virginia, Charlottesville, 1969.

Byrne, Patrick J., ed. *Father Price of Maryknoll.* Maryknoll: Catholic Foreign Mission Society of American, 1923.

Chatfield, Joan. "First Choice: Mission—The Maryknoll Sisters, 1912–1975." Ph.D. dissertation, The Graduate Theological Union, 1983.

Christman, Ralph F. "A Bibliography of the Works by or about the Maryknoll Fathers, 1937–1958." M.L.S. thesis, Catholic University, Washington, DC, 1958.

Churchill, Mark. *Unto Every Creature, Verses from the Field Afar.* Maryknoll: Maryknoll Publications, n.d.

Cogan, M. de Paul. *Sisters of Maryknoll through Troubled Waters.* New York: Charles Scribner's Sons, 1947.

Coleman, Mary, ed. *Discourses of Mother Mary Joseph Rogers, M.M.,1912-1955.* 4 vols. Maryknoll: Maryknoll Sisters, 1982; Index, 1983.

Colligan, James P. *Maryknoll and Japan.* 2 vols. Tokyo: n.p., 1983.

Considine, John J. *Across a World.* New York: J. J. Little and Ives Company, 1942.

————. *March into Tomorrow*. Maryknoll: The Field Afar Press, 1942.

————. *The Maryknoll Story*. New York: Doubleday & Co., 1950.

————. *The Vatican Mission Exposition: A Window on the World*. New York: The Macmillan Company, 1925.

————. *When the Sorghum Was High*. New York: Longmans, Green & Co., 1940.

Cosgrove, Joseph G. *Accent on Laughter*. New York: McMullen, 1952.

Danforth, Maria del Rey. *Dust on My Toes*. New York: Charles Scribner's Sons, 1959.

————. "Five on the Floor." Chapter 11 in *No Two Alike: Those Maryknoll Sisters*. New York: Dodd, Mead and Co., 1965.

————. [Sister Mary Victoria]. *Nun in Red China*. New York: McGraw-Hill, 1953.

David, M. Just. *China–1925: A Mission Investigation*. Cincinnati: Catholic Student Mission Crusade, 1926.

————. *Our Neighbors the Chinese*. Maryknoll: World Horizon Reports, 1944.

David, M. Just and Kent, Mark. *The Glory of Christ*. New York: Bruce Publishing Co., 1955.

Dease, Alice. *Bluegowns*. Maryknoll: Catholic Foreign Mission Society of America, 1927.

Delaney, Joan. "A Survey of Religious Women in the Diocese of Macao." Paper prepared for the Association of Major Superiors of Religious Women, 1976.

Donovan, John F. *China Learns*. Detroit: Maryknoll Publications, 1951.

————. *The Pagoda and the Cross, the Life of Bishop Ford of Maryknoll*. New York: Charles Scribner's Sons, 1967.

————. *A Priest Named Horse*. Huntington, IN: Our Sunday Visitor, 1977.

————. "Principal Events of the Maryknoll's Wuchow Mission, Kwangsi." Maryknoll: 1976.

————. "Schools Count in China," *The American Ecclesiastical Review*, November 1951: 377–379.

Downs, William. *Beginning Hakka*. Hong Kong: Nazareth Press, 1948.

————. "Enforced Silent Night: The Kaying Diocese, A Historical Sketch, 1845–1961." Unpublished manuscript, Maryknoll, New York, 1962.

Drought, James M. *Introduction to Hakka*. Hong Kong: Nazareth Press, 1926.

Erhard, Alma [Marie Fisher, pseud.]. *Grey Dawns and Red*. New York: Sheed & Ward, 1939.

Flanagan, Maureen. *Women in Mission: Maryknoll Sisters Today*. Maryknoll: Maryknoll Sisters, 1977.

Ford, Francis X. *Come, Holy Ghost*. New York: McMullen Books, Inc., 1953; Maryknoll: Orbis, rev. ed., 1976 as *Come, Holy Spirit*.

Greene, Robert W. *Calvary in China*. New York: G. P. Putnam's Sons, 1953.

[Grondin], Mary Marcelline. *Sisters Carry the Gospel*. Maryknoll: World Horizon Reports, No. 15, 1956. (Author also known as Sr. Thérèse Grondin)

Hogan, Mary Elizabeth. "Breaking Down the Walls of Tradition: The Maryknoll Sisters in Mission, 1920–1980." B.A. thesis in History, Princeton University, 1985.

Hunt, Darryl. *Go Tell It Everywhere*. Maryknoll: Maryknoll Publications, 1965.

Kaschmitter, William. *The Story of a Hobo*. Maryknoll Fathers, n.d.

Keelan, Francis X. *Spoken Chinese—First Year*. Hong Kong: Catholic Truth Society, 1947.

————. *Short Vocabulary of Religious Terms—Southern Mandarin—Kweilin*. Hong Kong: Salesian Printing Press, n.d.

Keller, James G. and Meyer Berger. *Men of Maryknoll*. New York: C. Scribner's Sons, 1943.

Kennedy, Mary Therese. "A Study of the Charism Operative in Mary Joseph Rogers (1882–1955), Foundress of the Maryknoll Sisters." Ph.D. dissertation, St. Louis University, 1980.

————., [under name of Camilla Kennedy]. *To the Uttermost Parts of the Earth—The Spirit and Charism of Mary Josephine Rogers*. Maryknoll: Maryknoll Sisters, 1987.

Kerrison, Raymond. *Bishop Walsh of Maryknoll, A Biography*. New York: Lancer Books, 1962.

Kettl, Rosalia. *One Inch of Splendor*. Maryknoll: Afield Afar Press, 1941.

Kittler, Glenn D. *The Maryknoll Fathers*. New York: World Publishing Co., 1961.

Kress, William Stephen. *Maryknoll at Ten*. Maryknoll: Catholic Foreign Mission Society of America, n.d..

Krock, George L. *Stop Killing Dragons. Letters to a Roman Knight from a Maryknoll Missioner*. New York: McMullen Co., 1947.

Lane, Raymond A. *The Early Days of Maryknoll*. New York: David McKay Co., 1951.

————. *Stone in the King's Highway: Selections from the Writings of Bishop Francis Xavier Ford (1892–1952)*. New York: McMullen Co., 1953.

Logan, Frances Louise. *Maryknoll Sisters, A Pictorial History*. New York: E. P. Dutton, 1962.

Lyons, Jeanne Marie. *Maryknoll's First Lady*. New York: Dodd, Mead, & Co., 1964.

————. *Means of Fostering the Missionary Vocation in the Catholic Primary and Secondary Schools*. Baltimore: J. H. Furst Co., 1941.

MacEoin, Gary. *Agent for Change: The Story of Pablo Steele*. Maryknoll: Orbis, 1973.

Makra, Lelia. *The Hsiao Ching*. Translation. Jamaica, NY: St. John's University Press, 1961.

Martin, John M. *Around the World in More than 80 Days: A Visit to Maryknoll Missions in Many Lands*. Maryknoll: Maryknoll Publications, n.d.

Martin, Mary Lou and MacInnis, Donald. *Values and Religion in China Today, A Teaching Workbook and Lesson Series*. New York: Orbis Books, 1985.

Maryknoll, A Short Account of the American Seminary for Foreign Missions. Maryknoll: Catholic Foreign Mission Society of America, 1916.

Maryknoll's First Seminary in China. Hong Kong: Nazareth Press, 1925.

McCabe, Leonard. *The Spiritual Legacy of the Co-Founders*. Maryknoll: Maryknoll Fathers, 1950 and 1956.

McShane, John F. *My Brother—The Maryknoll Missioner*. St. Meinrad, IN: Abbey Press, 1932.

Meyer, Bernard, F. *A Catechism of Social Action*. Maryknoll: Maryknoll Publications, 1968.

————. *Christian Communities in the Third World*: Maryknoll: 1969.

————. *The Christian Family in Action*. Pittsburgh: St. Joseph's Protectory Press, 1949.

————. *The Illustrated Catechism*. Hong Kong: Nazareth Press, 1942.

————. "Launch out into the Deep." Reprint from *Digest of the Synodal Commission* of June 1937.

————. *Lend Me Your Hands*. Chicago: Fides Publishing Company, 1955.

————. *Like to Leaven: Mission Methods in China*. Hong Kong: Nazareth Press, 1950.

————. *Mission Methods; Pastoral Instructions to the Clergy of the Prefecture Apostolic of Wuchow, Kwangsi, China*. N.p., 1936.

————. *Mr. and Mrs.* Maryknoll: Maryknoll Bookshelf, 1952.

————. *The Mystical Body in Action*. The Center for Men of Christ the King. New York: Ferris Printing Company, 1947.

————. *Our Family Catechism*. 1955.

————. *Teachers' Books of the Illustrated Catechism*. Hong Kong: Nazareth Press, 1941.

————. *Two Lives. A Laymen's Manual of the Catholic Religion*. Bombay/Calcutta: St. Paul Publications, 1960.

————. *The Way to Happiness: A Missionary Manual of Catholic Doctrine*. Maryknoll: Maryknoll Bookshelf, 1958.

————. *The Whole World Is My Neighbor*. Notre Dame, IN: Fides Publishing Company, 1964.

————. *Your Life To Share*. Allahabad: St. Paul Publications, 1962.

Meyer, Bernard F. and Wempe, Theodore F. *The Student's Cantonese-English Dictionary*. Hong Kong: St. Louis Industrial School Printing Press, 1935. 3d ed. reprinted by Maryknoll, 1947.

A Missionary for All Seasons. New York: Maryknoll Publications, 1981.

Moss, Anna Mary. *Course in Hakka*. Mimeographed course of study. Tungshek, China: Holy Child Language School, 1939.

Motte, Mary and Lang, Joseph, eds. *Mission in Dialogue; The Sedos Research Seminars on the Future of Mission*. Maryknoll: Orbis, 1982.

Murrett, John C. *Tar Heel Apostle*. New York: Longmans, Green & Co., 1944.

Nagle, Mary Theresa. "Maryknoll in Print: A Dictionary Catalog of the Writings and Audio-visual Materials by and about the Maryknoll Fathers and Sisters, 1911–1961." M.L.S. thesis, Catholic University, Washington, DC, 1961.

Nevins, Albert J. *Adventures of Men of Markyknoll*. New York: Dodd, Mead and Co., 1957.

————. *The Maryknoll Book of People*. New York: John J. Crawley & Co., 1959.

————. *The Maryknoll Book of Treasures*. Maryknoll: Maryknoll Publications, 1968.

————. *The Maryknoll Golden Book*. New York: H. Wolff, 1956.

————. *The Meaning of Maryknoll*. New York: McMullen Books, 1952.

O'Halloran, James V. "A Bibliography of the Works by and about the Maryknoll Fathers, 1911–1936." M.L.S. thesis, Catholic University, Washington, D.C., 1957.

O'Melia, Thomas. *First Year Cantonese*. Hong Kong: Caritas Printing Training Centre, 1938, 1965.

————. *First Year Cantonese Revised*. Hong Kong: Catholic Truth Society, 1965.

————. *Teaching Chinese Script to Foreigners*. Hong Kong: Wing Tai Cheung Printing Company, n.d.

O'Neill, Francis. "Entre Nous (with no holds barred)," unpublished manuscript, n.p., n.d.

Powers, George C. [The Biography of Father Thomas F. Price.] Untitled manuscript. Maryknoll: Maryknoll Fathers & Brothers, 1943.

————. *The Maryknoll Movement*. Maryknoll: Catholic Foreign Mission Society of America, 1926, (4th ed.. 1941, under title of *The Maryknoll Story*).

Reid, Richard and Edward J. Moffett. *Three Days to Eternity*. Westminster, MD: Newman Press, 1956.

Richardson, William J., ed. *China and Christian Responsibility: A Symposium*. Maryknoll: Maryknoll Publications, 1968.

————. *China Today*. Maryknoll: Maryknoll Publications, 1969.

————., ed. *The Modern Mission Apostolate: A Symposium*. Maryknoll: Maryknoll Publications, 1965.

Rogers, Mary James. *Music in the Maryknoll Mission Field; the Problem and Our Efforts To Meet It*. Maryknoll: Maryknoll Sisters, 1938.

Romaniello, John *Bird of Sorrow*. New York: P. J. Kenedy, 1956.

Roy, Marya. "The Impact of Christianity on China with Concentration on the Time of the Jesuits." M.A. thesis, University of Hawaii, 1973.

Ryan, Joseph P. "America's Contribution to the Catholic Missionary Effort in

China in the Twentieth Century." *The Catholic Historical Review*, July 1945: 171–180.

Sargent, Daniel. *All the Day Long*. New York: Longmans, Green, & Co., 1941.

Schintz, Mary Ann. "An Investigation of the Modernizing Role of the Maryknoll Sisters in China." Ph.D. dissertation, University of Wisconsin, Madison, 1978.

Sheridan, Mary Imelda. "A Brief History of the South China Region, 1921–1958." Unpublished manuscript, Maryknoll Sisters, 1959.

Sheridan, Robert E. *Bishop James E. Walsh as I Knew Him*. Maryknoll: Maryknoll Publications, 1981.

————. *The Founders of Maryknoll*. New York: Catholic Foreign Mission Society of America, 1980.

————., ed. *Bishop James Anthony Walsh, A Tribute by Maryknollers*. Maryknoll: Maryknoll Fathers, 1953.

————., ed. *Collected Letters of Thomas Frederick Price, M.M.* Maryknoll: Maryknoll Fathers, 1981.

————., ed. *Discourses of James Anthony Walsh, 1890–1936*. Maryknoll: Maryknoll Fathers, 1981.

————., ed. *Profiles of Twelve Maryknollers*. Maryknoll: Maryknoll Fathers, 1983.

————., ed. *Very Rev. Thomas Frederick Price, M.M. Co-founder of Maryknoll, A Symposium*. Brookline, MA: Brothers Novitiate, 1956.

Smith, James. *Maryknoll Hong Kong Chronicle, 1918–1975*. Maryknoll: Maryknoll Fathers & Brothers, 1978.

Surface, Bill and Hart, Jim. *Freedom Bridge: Maryknoll in Hong Kong*. New York: Coward-McCann, 1963.

Sweeney, Joseph. *Maryknoll among Chinese Lepers*. Maryknoll: Maryknoll Fathers, 1934.

Tennien, Mark. *Chungking Listening Post*. New York: Creative Age Press, Inc., 1945.

————. *No Secret Is Safe*. New York: Farrar, Straus, & Young, 1952.

Tolan, Mary Eunice. "Manchuria, Books 1–5." Unpublished manuscript, Maryknoll Sisters, n.d.

Tsai, Mark (Chai). "Bishop Ford, Apostle of South China." *The American Ecclesiastical Review* 127 (October 1952): 241–247.

Unsworth, Virginia. "American Catholic Missions and Communist China, 1945–1953." Ph.D. dissertation, New York University, 1976.

Vitcavage, Mariel. "Some Elements of Truth Reflected in Chinese Religious Beliefs." B.A. thesis, Manhattanville College, 1939.

Walsh, James A. *Maryknoll Mission Letters, China.* New York: Macmillan Co., vol. 1, 1923; vol. 2, 1927.

———. *In the Home of Martyrs.* Maryknoll: Catholic Foreign Mission Society of America, 1922.

———. *Observations in the Orient by a Maryknoller.* Maryknoll: Catholic Foreign Mission Society of America, 1919.

———. "The Society for the Propagation of the Faith in the Archdiocese of Boston." *The Ecclesiastical Review,* January 1904: 9–19.

Walsh, James E. *Blueprints of the Missionary Vocation.* World Horizon Report No. 19. Maryknoll: Maryknoll Publications, 1956.

———. *The Church's World Wide Mission.* New York: Benziger Brothers, 1948.

———. *Father McShane of Maryknoll; Missioner in South China.* Maryknoll: Catholic Foreign Mission Society of America, 1932.

———. *The Man on Joss Stick Alley.* New York: Longmans, Green, & Co., 1947.

———. *Maryknoll Spiritual Directory.* Maryknoll: The Field Afar Press, 1947.

———. *Mission Manual of the Vicariate of Kongmoon.* Hong Kong: Nazareth Press, 1937.

———. *Tales of Xavier.* New York: Sheed & Ward, 1946.

———. *The Young Ones.* New York: Farrar, Straus & Cudahy, 1958.

———. *Zeal for Your House.* (Robert E. Sheridan, ed.) Huntington, IN: Our Sunday Visitor Press, 1976.

MARYKNOLL PAMPHLETS AND CHINA

An American Sisterhood for Foreign Missions	July 1927
A Centenary—The Story of Blessed Théophane Venard	1929
Maryknoll Brothers	June 1930
Maryknoll on the March	December 1933
Maryknoll Lepers	1934
Novena to St. Francis Xavier	1934
Shall I Be a Maryknoller?	June 1934
Maryknoll among Chinese Lepers	September 1934
Christ in China	December 1934
The Maryknoll Story	1934?
Marriage in Manchu Land	March 1935
Ten Thousand Questions about China	March 1935
Missions Medicine and Maryknoll	May 1935
Shall I Be a Maryknoll Sister?	May 1935
The Case for Catholic China	June 1935
Secrets of Chinatown	August 1935
Schools in China	August 1935
42 Days among Chinese Outlaws	September 1935
Christ in Korea	October 1935
Christ in the Philippines	Post-1935

The Chinese Seminarian	1935
Novena to St. Francis Xavier	1935?
The Maryknoll Story (2d. ed.)	1936
Chinese Apostles	March 1936
Native Sisters in the Orient	May 1936
Fr. Burns among Manchu Bandits	January 1937
Thieves of Paradise in China	November 1937
Lo Pa Hong, Coolie of St. Joseph	April 1938
Christ in Japan	October 1938
Gate of Heaven Leper Asylum	November 1938
Chinese Proverbs	December 1938
Fr. Jerry Donovan, Captive for Christ	April 1939
Fr. Connors, Priest among Lepers	May 1939
Daily Prayer for Mission	March 1940
Novena for Mission Vocations	May 1940
Novena of Grace (to St. Francis Xavier)	ca. 1940
Bandits Surrounded Him	1941
42 Days among Chinese Outlaws (revised edition)	June 1941
Ahoy, the Story of a Chin Boy, His Brother & His Boat	June 1941
Fr. Winthrop and a Message	October 1941
Recipe to Make a World	September 1941
Knight without Armor (Digest of Fr. Gerard Donovan)	December 1941
Novena—St. Francis Xavier—For Young People	January 1942

CATECHETICAL MATERIALS IN CHINESE USED IN THIS STUDY

Chau nìn Chúe yât chim laĭ shĭng king, 週年主日瞻禮聖經 (*New Testament Readings for the Sundays and Feast Days of the Year*) by Father Mark Tennien. Hong Kong: Catholic Truth Society, 1940, 1947.

Chien-yen yao-li, 簡言要理 (*Abridged Catechism*). Yenchowfu: Typografia Missionis Catholicae, 1934.

Hâc kã t'oû t'âm yaó li lioc chôt (Hakka romanization only), *Explication du Catéchisme* by Father Charles Rey. Hong Kong: Nazareth Press, 1912.

Iù leĭ mân taàp, 要理問答 (*Catechism of Catholic Doctrine*) by Salesian Fathers. Hong Kong: St. Louis Industrial School, 1939, 1946, 1947, 1951.

Iù leĭ mân taàp, 要理問答 Chinese (*Catechism of the Catholic Religion for the Use of the Chinese*), with Cantonese romanization and translation in English and French by Fathers M. Callaghan and H. Montanar. Hong Kong: Nazareth Press, 1914.

Kaó li moún tâp, 教理問答 ([*Official*] *Catechism*) by Bishop Francis Ford. Kaying: 1937.

Kaó yoū chĭn tchĭn, 教友神珍 (*Spiritual Treasures for Christians*) by Bishop Francis Ford. Kaying: 1936.

Ngŏh-moōn-tik Shĭng-kaau 我們的聖教 (also *Women ti Sheng-chiao*), (*Our Holy Religion Series*) by Father Bernard Meyer. Hong Kong: Catholic Truth Society. The Series includes:
> *Preparatory Course*; For inquirers or beginning catechumens (adults), also for the sick, etc. a) 我們的聖教小引 Necessary truths and prayers to be learned, with drawings. b) 我們的聖教小引講解 A brief explanation of these truths and prayers.

Course I. For children preparing for the Sacraments, either in schools or special classes. a) 我們的聖教第一集兒童班 讀本 Study book, with pictures and verses, according to the method of St. Francis Xavier. 1937, 1939, 1947, 1949, 1952. b) 我們的聖教第一集兒童班 教授法 Teacher's Manual, according to modern methods. 362 pages in 12-0. 1937, 1939, 1947, 1949, 1952.

Course II. For catechumens, or students in schools. a)我們的聖教第二集 像帖問答讀本 Illustrated study text; it is the Shanghai Council catechism arranged according to the method of St. Augustine. 1938, 1940, 1947, 1949, 1951, 1958. b) 我們的聖教教授法第二集 (上下冊) Teacher's Manual, Comprising complete instructions on the catechism, a real treasure for catechists and teachers. 2 vols., 1938, 1940, 1947, 1949, 1951, 1958.

Course III. For use by lay apostles, more advanced classes in schools, catechumens studying privately, or Christian families, 我們的聖教第三集像解問答略註. The text is the same as Course II(a), with explanations added. 1938, 1940, 1947, 1949, 1951, 1958.

Preaching the Catholic Doctrine in the Local Dialect, 白話道理宣講. Sister Anna Mary Moss's catechetical series in three different dialects: Hakka, Cantonese, and Taiwanese. N.p., n.d.

Sing kaaù iù leĭ mân tạàp, 聖教要理問答 1) *Catechism in Use in Hong Kong and Swatow*, Hong Kong: Nazareth Press, 1923. 2) *Catechism in Use in Canton*, Hong Kong: Nazareth Press, 1923. 3) *Catechism in Use in Manchuria*, Hong Kong: Nazareth Press, ca. 1921–23.

Uêt-uĕ kaán-ìn iù-leĭ, 粵話簡言要理 (*Abridged Catechism in Cantonese Language*) by James E. Walsh. Hong Kong: Nazareth Press, 1937.

Wen-ta hsiang-chieh, 問答像解 (*Illustrated Catechism*) by Father Leo Van Dyk. Tientsin: Procure of the Scheut Fathers, n.d.

Yao-li hsiang-chieh, 要理像解 (*Illustrated Catholic Doctrine*). Translation by Father Peter Tcheng of French catechism published by La Bonne Press. Peking: Librairie des Lazaristes, 3d ed., 1922; 4th ed., 1929.

Yao-li Wen-ta, 要理問答 (*Catechism of Catholic Doctrine*). Yenchowfu: Typografia Missionis Catholicae, 1934.

Yao-li Wen-ta, 要理問答 (*Catechism of Catholic Doctrine*). Translated in English from the New Chinese Catechism published by the Synodal Commission. Hong Kong: Catholic Truth Society and Nazareth Press, 1936.

OTHER CHINESE AND JAPANESE LANGUAGE PUBLICATIONS

Gu Changsheng, 顧長声. *Chuanjiaoshi yu jindai Zhongguo*. 傳教士与近代中国 (*Missioners and Modern China*). Shanghai: People's Publishing Co., 1981.

Hoten Mainichi Shimbun, 奉天每日新聞 (Fengtien Daily), November 21, 1933.

Hsingmei Jihpao, 興梅日報 (Hsingning-Meihsien Daily News), April 25–26, 1951.

Kung-ch'an-tang ti chi-lüeh, 共產黨的集略 (*A Brief Exposition of Communism*). Hong Kong: Catholic Truth Society, n.d.

Kung chiao fan-kung chih li-ch'ang, 公教反共之立場 (*The Anti-Communist Position of the Church*). Hong Kong: Catholic Truth Society, n.d.

Lo Kuang 羅光. *Chiao-t'ing yü Chung-kuo shih-chieh* 教廷與中國使節 (*A History of Diplomatic Relations between the Holy See and China*). Tai-chung: Kuang-ch'i Press, 1961.

Lü Shih-ch'iang, 呂實強. *Chung-kuo kuan-shen fan-chiao ti yuan-yin, 1860–1874,* 中國官紳反教的原因 (*Causes of the Chinese Gentry-Officials' Hostility towards Christianity, 1860–1874*). Taipei: Institute of Modern History, Academia Sinica, 1966.

Manshū Nippō, 滿州日報 (*Manchuria News*), November 21, 1933.

Mei-kuo Chien-t'ieh Tsui Eh Ta, 美國間諜罪惡大 (*The Most Evil American Spies*). Canton: South China People's Publishing Company, 1952.

Nan Fang Jihpao, 南方日報 (*South China Daily News*), April 24, 1951.

Sheng-ching Shih-pao, 盛京時報 (*Shengking Times*), November 21, 1933.

Ta-lien Hsin-pao, 大連新報 (*Dairen News*), November 21, 1933.

Wen Hui Pao, 文滙報 (*Hong Kong Daily News*), December 15–31, 1951.

Index

Acculturation, 200-01, 213, 215, 233, 246, 258, 260-61, 270, 273, 275, 278-81, 308, 311-17, 408
  of architecture, 281-96
  of Christian practices, 308-13, 339
  lack of, 148-49, 195, 197, 203-04, 246-48, 250-51, 258, 264, 309, 313, 339, 445, 456
  as part of Maryknoll's heritage, 262-64, 314, 433, 454-56
  of spoken and written message, 275-76, 296-308
Ad Gentes, 7
Ad Ipsis Pontificatus Primordiis, 340, 408
Adjustment and lack of, 263, 280-81, 313
  in Chinese seminaries and novitiates, 211, 238-40, 248, 258
  in clothing, 264-66
  in diet, 266-68, 316
  to other people's sensitivity, 148-49, 195, 197, 245, 247-48, 250-51, 455
  to physical surroundings, 69-71, 78, 102, 106-07, 129, 247, 317, 455
Agagianian, Gregorio Petro, 130
Agriculture, 66-68, 112, 173-74, 177, 432, 439
  and cooperatives, 182-86
André, Gabriel, 11, 19
Annals of the Holy Childhood, 22
Annals of the Propagation of the Faith, 22, 24
Antiforeignism, 102, 141, 151, 188, 190, 340, 359. *See also* Antireligious incidents
  demonstrations, 328, 331-34, 336-38
  fueled by May 30th Incident, 327-29
  staged by Communists, 340, 438
Antireligious incidents, 188-89, 329, 331, 341. *See also* Antiforeignism
  fueled by missioners' behavior, 333-338, 339
Antung, 122, 272, 343, 358

Apostasy, 88-89, 91, 334
Apostolate. *See* Evangelization
Au, Aloysius, 389, 395
Au, Maureen, 148
Axis alliance, 376, 381

Babies
  abandonment of, 137, 138-39, 143, 179, 443-44
  baptisms of, 141, 143, 146
  deaths of, 138-139, 143
Bagalawis, Artemio, 153, 154-56, 164, 167, 169, 200
Baldit, Pierre, 335
Banditry
  in Manchuria, 39, 342-45, 352-55, 436
  in South China, 225-26, 330, 369, 388, 436
Barry, Benedict, 343
Basto, Candida Maria, 118, 142, 151, 362, 367
Bauer, George, 163, 334, 337
Baumann, Marie Elise, 198-99, 357
Beauvais, Joan Miriam, 157, 228, 423
Becka, Frederick, 221
Bedier, Juliana, 193, 276, 420-24
Bibiana, 230
Big Sword Society, 343-44, 354
Blaber, Harry, 152-54, 163-65, 167, 200
Blois, Jean-Marie, 59, 230-31, 253-54, 264, 311
Blue Cloud Village, 90, 92
Blue Shirts, 372, 395, 397, 399
Bolsheviks, 322, 332-34, 340-341
Bonne Presse, 296
Booth, Stephen, 424
Boston Evening Transcript, 21, 24
Boston Pilot, 21
Bowers, Lawrence
Boxer uprising, 46, 205, 230, 327, 329, 343, 359

Boyd, Anthony, 279
Boyle, Monica Marie, 136, 137, 151, 362–63, 367, 424
  under communism, 386, 389, 395
Boys Town, 179–80, 444
Brack, Thomas, 35
Bradley, Colombiere, 151, 395
Bradley, Kathleen, 279, 426
Brennan, Immaculata, 419
Brennock, Gregory, 153, 163
Brétenières, Just de, 23
Brielmaier, Ann Carol, 118, 234, 424
Briggs, Everett, 356
Brothers of Charity of Trier, 52, 157, 159–61
Bruneau, Joseph, 23
Buddhism and Taoism, 197, 289, 434
Burgess, Perry, 165
Burns, Clarence, 354–55, 358
Bush, Harry, 355, 398
Byrne, Patrick, 374, 413

Cain, Mary de Ricci, 424
Cairns, Robert, 62, 69, 135, 273, 282, 316, 328, 362
  disappearance of, 364
Caffrey, Francis, 419
Calcutta, 367
Campbell, W.K., 182
Canadian Sisters of the Immaculate Conception, 50, 150–51, 162
Canadian Missionary Sisters of Our Lady of Angels, 381, 465
Canton, 54, 244, 273
  antiforeignism in, 328–29, 331, 334
  Canton-Honam, 63
  Canton-Lingnam, 63
  relief work in, 63, 179
  Sun Yat-sen in, 52, 318–320
  under communism, 340, 399
  under the Japanese, 169, 173
Canton incident, 328–29,
Canton Commune, 320
Capture of missioners
  by bandits and pirates, 39, 330, 345, 352, 354–55, 369
Carney, Veronica Marie, 230
Casey, John J., 425
Catechists. *See also* Chinese Virgins; Yip, Epiphanius; Ue Chi Cheung
  categories of, 81, 85, 111, 127
  female, 81, 86–87, 106
  importance of, 78–79, 83, 127
  male, 81, 100, 106
  recruitment of , 79, 86, 92, 114
  salary of, 83–84, 85
  statistics about, 80, 83–84, 87, 89, 127

training of, 79–81, 83–85, 92. 97, 99, 104, 114, 126
  tribute to, 126–27, 434
  work by, 85–88, 91–97, 99–100, 109, 117–18, 123, 137, 175, 187, 189, 296, 303, 310
Catechumenates
  and burning of ancestral tablets, 310
  in Fushun mission, 117, 122–24
  in Kaying mission, 104, 106, 109–11, 114
  in Kongmoon mission, 118
  in Kweilin mission, 116–17
  post-, 97
  in Wuchow, 67, 89–96, 115
Catholic Action, 62, 120–21, 123–24, 128, 129, 361, 400, 700. *See also* Evangelization; Legion of Mary; Sodalities
Catholic Central Bureau, 63, 400–02
Catholic Church in China, *See also*, Acculturation; Evangelization; Mission methods
  accusations against, 91, 145, 241, 331,342,407, 432
  under communism, 217–23, 225–29, 231, 387, 405–08, 450–51, 456
  ideological difference with communism, 406–07
  indigenization of, 203, 205, 207, 241, 244–46, 253, 255–57, 259–61, 280, 313, 379, 450, 455
  lay leaders in, 80, 126, 435–37, 450, 455
  missionary heritage of, 407, 447–48
  patriotism within, 360–61, 380, 399–400, 405, 407–08, 440, 442–43, 450
  post-1918, 75, 205, 261, 311, 380, 404–05, 447
  pre-1918, 45–48, 74–75, 186, 204, 308–09, 322
  relations with Nationalist government, 341–42, 360–61, 378, 382, 385, 405–06, 440
  rise of a local, 204–05, 222, 228, 230, 244–47, 252–57, 261, 281, 314, 340, 450
  and rites controversy, 45–46, 74–75
  self governing, 205, 222, 245, 254, 260, 340, 407
  self-sufficient, 181, 201, 226
  self-supporting, 181–82
  statistics, 78–79, 126–28, 204, 359
Catholic Foreign Mission Bureau, 23, 409
Catholic Foreign Mission Society of America. *See* Maryknoll
Catholic Mission Medical Board, 134
Catholic Missionary Union, 13, 18, 21
Catholic Missions, 24
Catholic Students' Mission Crusade, 412
Catholic Synodal Commission, 62

Cazale, Agnes, 115
Chakow, 68, 215, 233, 351
Chan, Anthony, 218
Chan, Louis, 153, 154
Chan, Mary, 148, 223
Chan, Philomena, 227
Chan, Rose, 280, 500n.63
Chang Hsüeh-liang, 344
Chang Tso-lin, 343 44
Chao, Peter, 218
Chao-t'ung, 367
Chaoyangchen, 123
Charles, Pierre, 32
Chateaubriand, François, 449
Chatigny, Donat, 132
Chau, Agnes, 117, 228, 251, 312
Ch'en Chiung-ming, 52, 319–22, 331–33
    missioners' opinion of, 312–22, 333
Chengtingfu, 50
Chennault, Claire, 371
Cheuk Chiu-yin, 390
Cheuk Yee-chiu, 110
Chiang Kai-shek, 318, 320–21, 340, 361, 376,
    441, 447
    anti-Communist drive by, 380
    Madame, 440–42
    missioners' opinion of, 322, 326, 440
    missioners' support of, 360–61, 373, 377–
        79, 381–82, 405–06, 450
Chiklung, 163, 181–83
Chin, Pius, 216
Chin, Rose, 228, 248, 250
China National Relief and Rehabilitation
    Administration. *See* Welfare.
China Press, 188
China Weekly Review, 188
Chinch'engchiang, 175–76
Chinese bishops, 246, 256, 283
    search for, 252–257, 259
Chinese clergy, 215, 245. *See also*, Relation-
    ships between; Seminaries in China
    under communism, 217–23, 383–84, 387,
        395–96
    education of, 204–05, 209, 218, 260
    evaluation of missioners by, 246–47, 259,
        268
    under the Japanese, 224, 350, 357, 379, 397
    missionors' opinion of, 218, 245–46, 257,
        259
    ordinations of, 217–218, 221–22, 244
    responsibilities of, 85, 87, 204–05, 222, 245–
        46, 400
Chinese rites, 74, 308–13, 433, 486n.3. *See
    also* Catholic Church in China
Chinese sisterhoods, 204, 223, 225, 227, 230.
    See also Novitiates

as catechists, 87, 96, 223
under communism, 218, 225, 227–29, 384,
    387
constitutions of, 236–37, 248
and direct evangelization, 229–30, 237,
    251–52
education of, 233–34, 250
evaluation of missioners by, 248, 250–51,
    252, 259
in Fushun mission, 123, 177, 230–31, 357–
    58
in Hong Kong, 225, 250
under Japanese, 224–26, 357–58, 364, 367,
    379
in Kaying mission, 111–12, 228–30, 251–52
in Kongmoon mission, 118, 154, 219, 224–
    25, 250–51, 364
in Kweilin mission, 117, 126, 227, 250–51
as nurses, 154–55, 231, 232
self-governing, 226, 231, 250
self-sufficient, 226–27, 236, 250, 252
in Wuchow mission, 115, 220, 225–27
responsibilities of, 85, 98, 129, 175, 226,
    231, 236
Chiu, Uelaia, 224
Choi, Benedict, 218, 221, 244
Chongpu, 65, 190
Chu Teh, 380
Chuanhsien, 175, 179–80, 182, 183
Chum, Peter (Mr.), 110, 211
Chung, Anthony, 222
Chungking, 367, 369, 370
Cioppa, John, 7
Clements, Anne, 194
Clerical tasks, 28, 30, 33–34, 43, 176
Climate, 265, 266, 454
    drought, 67–68,
    flood, 64–65, 67, 351
    in Manchuria, 68
    in South China, 64–68
    typhoons, 64–65, 168, 351
Closeness to Chinese people, 201, 279–81,
    323, 359, 406
    under communism, 386, 402
    lack of, 296, 454
    during war with Japan, 362–63, 366–67,
        369, 371, 378–79, 404, 405
Collins, Cornelia, 116, 136, 227
Comber, John, 345
Comber, Rita Clare, 137, 277
Commonwealth, 338
Communists. *See also* Life under com-
    munism
    land reform by, 221–22, 390
    and Legion of Mary, 125
    missioners' opinion of, 382, 385–87, 405,

446–47
and orphanages, 149
pre–1945, 228, 320–22, 330–33, 336, 340–41, 354–55, 360, 376, 380–82
religious policy of, 125, 342, 381, 386–87, 390, 395, 438–39, 450, 534 n. 263
tactics of, 387–90,
takeover by, 128, 149, 156, 193, 198–99, 217, 221, 222, 276, 386–88
Confucian ethics and Christianity, 309–10, 427–28, 432, 434, 442, 449. *See also* Chinese rites.
Conley, Lawrence, 369
Connors, Francis, 80, 163, 169
Considine, John, 255 ,413, 415–16, 418–19, 421
Constancis, Joseph, 439
Construction, 100, 438–39
of churches, 282–90
of houses, 287–89, 291–96
of leper colonies, 164, 168–69
of Maryknoll headquarters, 84, 281
of Venard seminary, 289, 292, 294
Conversions, 5, 74–76, 78, 91, 305, 308, 311–12
and corporal works of mercy, 131, 136, 168, 172, 201, 443
and direct apostolate, 128
and extraterritoriality, 326
and number of catechists, 87–89, 127–28
and schools, 186, 187, 195–96
of social units, 85–86, 119
after World War II, 313, 379, 382, 445
Cooperatives, 182–85, 200–01
Costantini, Celso, 47, 281–83, 296, 340, 346, 418
Cotta, Anthony, 36, 43, 205
Coughlin, Mary Patricia, 224–25, 365–66, 385
Coupe, Eucharista, 225, 365, 367
Coveny, Angela Marie, 136, 356
Cruise, Mary Dolores, 228
Culion, 165
Customs, Chinese, 138–39, 143, 214, 232, 247, 259, 314

Daley, Timothy, 381
Danforth, Maria del Rey, 447
Dairen, 68, 286, 288, 291, 343–44, 358, 505n.168
academy in, 193, 195, 198–99, 273, 357
Chinese parish in, 231, 357
Japanese parish in, 193, 276, 289, 356–57
Daubert, Francis, 382
David, Mary Just, 422
Davies, John Paton, 350, 358
Davis, Mary Francis, 144, 174, 225, 322

Dempsey, Arthur, 221
Dennis, Allan, 112, 395
Devlin, Agnes, 116, 227, 249
Dickson, Ellsworth, 162
Dietz, Frederick, 62, 270, 319, 323
Diggins, Mary, 277
Diseases, 69–70, 136, 173, 367, 404, 449,
in Fushun mission, 177
in Kongmoon mission, 134, 138, 143, 171, 175
in Kweilin mission, 176
in Wuchow mission, 173
Divini Redemptoris, 405
Dobson, W. H., 162, 163
Doelger, Marie, 274, 322
Doherty, Rose, 535n.269
Dominicans, 380–81
Donaghy, Frederick
and acculturation, 315
and Chinese priests and Sisters, 260
under communism, 392–94
vicar apostolic, 55, 115, 218, 226, 257
Donahoe's Magazine, 21
Donnelly, Francis, 211, 216
Donnelly, Patrick, 272
Donovan, Gerard, 39, 352, 354–55, 358, 374, 416
Donovan, John, 176, 371–72, 387, 448
Donovan, Joseph, 325
Donovan, Mary Angeline, 50
Dorie, Henri, 23
Dorsey, John, 134–35, 325
Downs, William, 269–71, 365, 381
Dreisoerner, Chaminade, 419, 421
Drew, John, 535n.269
Driscoll, John, 36, 190, 425
Drought, James, 256, 267–70, 275, 328, 412
in U.S.-Japan relations, 375–77
Dubourg, Louis, 19
Duchesne, Paul, 63, 136, 179, 183
Ducoeur, Maurice, 54, 81
Duffy, Gavan, 50
Duggan, Mary Peter, 194
Dumond, Paul, 49
Dwyer, Mary, 28–29

Ecclesiastical Review, 21–22, 316
Education in China, 75, 96, 186, 188–89, 341, 429, 439. *See also* Schools.
of women, 112, 192
Elliott, Herbert, 535n.269
Erhard, Alma, 32, 416–17, 419, 421
Erhpatan, 230, 233, 344
Evangelization. *See also* Catechists; Catholic Church in China; Mission methods; Mission work

under communism, 387
and corporal works of mercy, 131–32, 137,
    141, 153, 168, 172–73, 175, 177, 181,
    201, 311, 443, 445
of countryside, 76, 305–06
direct, 76, 78, 88, 97, 99–100, 103, 112, 115–
    18, 120, 121, 128–30, 426
and educational work, 186–88, 196
history of, 74–75, 453
by lay apostolate, 119–24, 128, 200, 435–36,
    450
opportunity for, 445–46
and religious protectorate, 46–47, 205, 260
and social work, 186
theology and strategy for, 5, 7, 10, 74, 119,
    131, 139, 197, 201, 204–05, 261, 281, 305,
    308–09, 314–15, 341, 433, 489n.5
of urban areas, 75, 116, 190
and westernization, 4–5, 9–10, 75, 200, 260–
    61, 455
of women by Sisters, 101–05, 107, 111, 112,
    114–15, 118, 128–29, 200, 306
Ex Quo Singulari, 308–11
Extraterritoriality, 321, 322–26, 333, 338–39,
    343–45, 396, 404

Fachow, 182, 189, 282
    antiforeignism in, 334–37
Fairbank, John K., 372
Famine, 67, 445. *See also* Welfare and relief
    in Kaying mission, 176
    in Kongmoon mission, 171, 173
    in Kweilin mission, 175–76, 179
Farnen, Joseph, 169, 171, 369
Faveau, Albert, 48
Feasts, Catholic, 92–93, 97, 122, 181–82, 197,
    312, 434
Fedders, Albert, 213, 218, 220–21
Feeney, Maurice, 146, 500n.63, 530n.189
Field Afar, 12, 23–24, 27–28, 409–13, 416,
    424–26
    images of China in, 426–51
Financial support by American Catholics,
    84, 199, 200, 409, 411, 422–43, 435, 449
    of catechists, 434
    of construction, 84
    of educational work, 187
    of leper work, 163, 443–44
    of medical work, 134
    of orphanages, 443–44
    of seminarians and novices, 209, 220
    of welfare, 445
First Plenary Council of China, 62, 120, 186,
    252, 296
Flagg, Paluel, 132–34, 152, 200
Flagg, Virginia, 133–34, 198, 273, 425

Fletcher, William, 336–37
Fogarty, Irene, 268
Foley, Mary Lawrence, 101–02, 322
Ford, Francis
    and acculturation, 268, 306, 313–16
    and architecture, 285–86, 292
    arrest of, 395–401, 406
    and catechetical materials, 305
    and center catechumenate, 109–10
    and Chinese priests and Sisters, 207–08,
        211, 221–22, 228–29, 237, 244–45,
        251, 257, 260
    and educational work, 186, 190, 192
    and language study, 275, 306
    legacy of, 99–100, 259–60, 406–07
    and Maryknoll Fathers, 100, 246
    and Maryknoll Sisters, 99–105, 108, 130,
        260, 306, 315, 322
    portrait of the Chinese by, 427–32, 449
    and primacy of direct evangelization, 99–
        100, 260
    and relief work, 176–77
    and social work, 185–86
    and sodalities, 121, 125
    support of Nationalists by, 381–82, 385,
        397–99, 438–40
    during 1925 unrest, 332
    vicar apostolic, 55, 84, 253
    and village catechumenate, 111
    in Yeungkong, 77, 139–41, 208
Ford, Ita, 406–07
Foreign Mission Sisters of St. Dominic. *See*
    Maryknoll.
Fourquet, Antoine, 50, 62, 87, 253–54, 329
Francis Xavier, St., 36, 45, 274
Franciscan Fathers, 482n.35
Franciscan Missionaries of Mary, 235
Franciscan Sisters of Mercy (Luxemburg),
    62, 162
Frazier, William, 74, 489
French Protectorate, 46–47
Freri, Joseph, 22–23, 24
Froehlich, Mary Barbara, 322
Fuchow, 334
Fukien, 380–81
Fumasoni-Biondi, Pietro, 103, 255–56, 257,
    311
Furey, Christella, 365
Furuya San, 198
Fushun city, 177, 188, 217, 230–31, 286, 346,
    349–50, 352, 356–58, 383
    language school in, 272, 276
Fushun massacre, 346, 349
Fushun vicariate, 58–59, 192, 208, 217–18,
    244–46, 342–60, 383–84
    work among Chinese in, 272

work among Japanese in, 193, 273
work among Koreans in, 273

Gaiero, Michael, 424
Gallagher, Rose Bernadette, 115, 312–13, 317
Galvin, Edward, 281
Gaspais, Ernest, 350, 356
Gauthier, Auguste, 76, 77–78
Geist, Marie Antoinette, 160
Geselbracht, Howard, 351, 535n.269
Gibbons, James, 14, 16–17, 19
Gilbert, Rodney, 338
Gilbert, Sylvio, 122–24, 279, 311, 352–54
Glass, Lloyd, 179–80, 183
Gleason, Maurice, 102
Gotti, Girolamo Maria, 25, 48
Gould, Frederick, 133
Graser, John, 152, 395
Greene, Robert, 126, 175, 185, 447
Grondin, Thérèse, 108, 129, 228–29, 234, 240, 251, 260
  under communism, 386, 391, 395
Guébriant, Jean-Baptiste Budes de, 47, 48, 51, 206, 253–54
Guerrieri, Antonia Maria, 116, 175, 424
Guerrillas, 169, 171, 344–45, 351–54, 359, 364, 369, 380
Guidera, Dominic, 116

Hainan, 54
Hall, R.O., 176
Halpern, Fanny, 157,
Han, Joseph, 63
Hanan, Rose Benigna, 198
Hangchow, 50
Hankow, 50, 175, 334, 361
Hannigan, Julia, 396
Haouisée, Auguste, 161–62, 275
Happy Life and Death Societies, 181–82. *See also* Cooperatives
Harris, R., 397
Heilungkiang, 342
Hennesey, James, 4
Henry, Francis, 17
Henry, Michael, 68
Herrgen, Mary Corita, 198
Hessler, Donald, 365
Higgins, Agnes Virginia, 386
Hilbert, Charles, 222
Hingning, 106, 222, 389, 395
Hinke, Frederick, 398
Hirst, Cyril, 211
Hock, Mary, 192, 228
Hodgins, Anthony, 37, 69
Hoffman, Mary Paulita, 106, 112, 306–08,

389, 395, 447
Hogan, John Baptist, 11
Hoingan, 174–75, 197, 223–24, 233
Hollfelder, Teresa, 274
Holy Childhood Society, 84
Homes for the Blind and the Crippled, 141–42, 149–50
Homiletic Review, 425
Hong Kong, 51, 63, 169, 171, 247, 328–29, 386
  internment in, 365
  under the Japanese, 271, 276, 363–65
  language school in, 270–72, 273, 275
  seminary in, 208, 217–18, 220–21
  Sisters in, 60–61, 224, 228, 273–74
Hospitals, 365, 367
  doctors' salaries in, 152
  fees, 153, 155–56, 158
  in Ngaimoon, 169, 172
  Protestant, 152
  in Shanghai, 61–62, 132, 157–62, 200, 274, 501n.78
  statistics about, 153, 155, 156, 158, 159, 169
  in Toishan, 153–57, 175, 199
  in Tungon, 152–53
Hoten Mainichi Shimbun (Mukden), 349
Housekeeping tasks, 30, 33–34, 43, 198, 388
Hsingning-Meihsien Daily, 399
Hsinking, 217, 350
Hsinpin, 192, 345, 351
Hsü, Ambrose, 210, 272, 277
Huang Shao-hsiung, 320, 321
Hull, Cordell, 376
Hunan, 381
Hunter, Edward, 349
Huntington, Edwin, 133

Images of China presented by Maryknoll, 426–48
Illustrated Catholic Missions, 23, 24
Impact of Maryknoll on US, 199, 200, 431, 447, 448–51
  through appeal for dying babies, 443–44
  through direct contact, 422–23, 425
  educators, 421–22
  through leper work, 163, 414, 444–45
  through medical mission, 133–34, 152
  through mission education, 317, 409–22, 425, 456
  women, 411
  young Catholics, 412–13, 416, 418–26, 444

Jackson, Rachel, 198
Jacques, Armand, 357
Jaramillo, Maria Corazon, 155, 156
Jenkins, Douglas, 329, 335

Jesuit Fathers, 75, 526n.103
  Irish, 214, 221
Jong, Peter, 222
Journal of the American Medical Association, 132
Joyce, John H., 171, 174, 185, 363, 369, 535n.269
Juichin, 380

Kanchow, 55, 333
Karlon, Madeline Sophie, 104, 106-07, 275
Kaschmitter, William, 62, 353
Kaying city, 55, 176, 190, 192, 222, 228-29, 245, 286, 371
  Communists in, 380-81, 385, 395-99
Kaying vicariate, 55, 57, 102, 176-77, 215, 228-31, 244-46, 255, 259-60, 370-81, 385-86, 426
  statistics for, 190, 208, 222
Keelan, Francis, 271, 365
Kelly, Dominic, 227
Kennedy, Justin, 226, 392-93
Kennelly, M. (S.J.), 49
Kennelly, Robert, 151-52, 363, 374-75, 395
Kettl, Rosalia, 228, 370
  and catechetical materials, 306-07
  and direct evangelization, 104, 107, 108, 115, 121, 251, 260
  imprisonment of, 226, 391-95, 407
  and language study, 276,
Kiangsi, 55, 380-81
Kiernan, Thomas, 266, 269, 310, 424, 429
Kim, Margaret, 198, 357
Kirin, 59, 218, 342
Kit, K.S., 286
Knotek, Wenceslaus, 182
Kochow, 80, 207, 223, 434
  antiforeignism in, 328, 334
  cooperatives in, 182
  local wars around, 319, 323-25
  schools in, 81, 188-89
Kongchowwan, 183-84
Kongmoon city, 54, 173. *See also* Pakkai
Kongmoon vicariate, 54, 56, 174-75, 188, 199, 207, 218, 223-25, 245, 360-70
Konoye, 377
Korean War, 388-89
Kozlenko, Helen, 198
Kroeger, Louise, 103
Krumpelmann, Edward, 136
Kukong, 222
Kung, H.H., 442, 447
Kung P'in-mei, 402
Kunming, 176, 220, 367, 369, 370
Kwangtung and Kwangsi
  pre-1936 socio-political situation, 46, 52,

188, 309, 318-27, 333-34, 338, 340, 439, 454
  post-1936, see Sino-Japanese War; World War II; Communists
Kwantung Army, 342, 344-45
Kweichow, 175, 367
Kweilin city, 175-76, 185, 272
Kweilin prefecture apostolic, 55-56, 179-80, 208, 218, 227-28, 366-72
  statistics for, 89, 216
Kweiyang, 176, 367

Laai, Joseph, 221
Laipo, 85, 208, 227
Lam, Joseph, 234
Lam, Paul, 222, 385, 395-96
Lane, John, 23, 412
Lane, Raymond, 412
  and architecture, 286
  and Chinese priests and Sisters, 210, 230, 245
  dealings with local authorities, 345-57, 373-74
  and language study, 272-73
  superior general, 383
  tribute to Sisters, 199, 358
  vicar apostolic, 59, 117, 122-23
Language
  English, 210, 235-36, 239
  Latin, 209, 211, 218, 235, 238-39
  proficiency in, 210, 215, 263, 269, 270, 275, 277-79, 454
  study of, by missioners, 80, 269-80, 365
Laohukow, 229, 237, 238, 240
Laolung, 395
Lau, Thomas, 120, 138, 268
Laurenti, Camillus, 433
Lavin, Joseph, 144, 174-75, 369
League of Nations, 182
Lebbe, Vincent, 36, 75, 205
Lechthaler, Miriam Carmel, 116, 227
Lee, Catherine Mary, 112, 229, 311
Lee, Raymond, 154
Legion of Mary, 125-26, 400
Lei, Simon, 244, 256
Leifels, Mary Rose, 101-02, 224, 322
Leong, Paul, 222
Lepers, 162-65, 168, 171-73. *See also* Ngaimoon
  statistics, 163, 164, 168-69
  colonies of, 154, 162, 164-73, 200, 363-64, 369, 445
Lerner, Joseph, 198
Li Tsung-jen, 319-20
Liang, Stephen, 244
Liao, Peter, 222

Liaoning, 342
Life, 23
Life under communism, 447, 450–51. *See also* Communists
accusations, 150–52, 156, 172, 227, 327, 360, 372, 384, 388–400, 402–03, 405–07
brutalities, 156–57, 198–99, 389, 392–94, 399
deaths, 383, 394, 400
deportations, 150, 152, 156, 173, 390, 395, 400, 403, 535n.277
exit permits, 149, 156, 157, 390
forced labor, 220
harassment, 150, 156, 172–73, 227, 388–90, 396
house arrests, 149, 156, 226, 388–89, 396
imprisonment, 221, 225, 228, 384, 390–95, 399–403
since 1980, 217–18, 225, 231, 407–08
trials, 152, 156, 390–91, 395, 399–400, 403
Ling, Joan, 117, 126, 228, 278–79
Lingnam. *See* Canton
Linkiang, 68, 192, 344, 351
Liu, Antonius, 257
Liu Jen-sheng, 399
Liu, Paul, 218, 219
Luichow, 221
Lo, Francis, 161
Lo Pa-hong, 61–62, 157–61, 436–37
Lo Wenzao, 255
Logue, Mary Luke, 198
Loking, 225
Long March, 381
Los Angeles, 194
Loting, 52, 174, 224–25, 286
antiforeignism in, 329, 333
lepers in, 162
orphanage in, 118, 139, 141–42, 145–46, 148–52, 267, 330, 367
schools in, 187
during war with Japan, 363, 367, 374–75
Lourenço Marques, 356
Lu Jung-t'ing, 318–20
Lu, Mary Rose, 231
Luichow, 54
Lumen News Service, 62
Lungchow, 321, 381
Lynn, Virginia Marie, 158

Ma, Aloysius, 256
Ma, Peter, 218
Ma, Thomas, 218
MacRae, Francis, 285
Macao, 54, 228, 365–66
Mahoney, Joseph Marian, 105, 111
Malone, Patrick, 380–81

Manchuria (Manchukuo), 59, 289
Catholic Church in, 350, 360
Japanese occupation of, 342–45, 351, 354, 376
Maryknollers in, 342–60, 404
pre-1932, 177, 188–89, 193
puppet government of, 344–45, 349–52
resistance movement in, 343–44, 351–55, 358–60
Manning, Edward, 359
Manshū Nippō (Dairen), 349
Mao Tse-tung, 380
Maoming. *See* Kochow
Marco Polo Bridge incident, 361
Maritain, Jacques, 448
Martel, Grace Marian, 421
Martin, Mary Louise, 276
Maryknoll Academy, 193–99, 273
Maryknoll Junior, 412, 419, 425
Maryknoll magazine. *See Field Afar*
Maryknoll mission territories. *See also* Kaying, Kongmoon, Fushun vicariates; Kweilin prefecture apostolic
Catholics in, 128–29
finances of, 61, 83, 84, 88, 127, 220–21, 226, 234, 236, 370
location of, 52–59
search for, 48–52
Maryknoll Pioneers, 413, 419
Maryknoll Society and Congregation, 482n.36. *See also* Impact of; Spirituality in practice
assignment of personnel by , 32, 43, 103, 250, 423, 426
constitutions of, 4, 33, 203, 248, 258, 264
finances of, 33, 82–84, 162, 414
goals and purposes of, 4, 43, 155, 180, 187, 190, 192, 199, 203–05 207, 244–46, 250, 258, 260, 262, 316–17, 359, 379, 409, 453
greatest achievement by, 455–56
and indigenization, 252–57, 258–59, 260
influence in the U.S. of, 4, 373–78, 410–26
influenced by China, 7, 409–10, 425–26, 449, 456
nowadays, 406–07, 454, 456, 540n.1
opinions concerning, 16–17, 40
origin of, 3, 11–30, 42–43, 48, 410
recruitment by, 28, 31, 200, 409–10, 414, 422–26, 449
spirituality and spirit of, 33–44, 107, 246, 250, 262, 414, 426, 454
statistics about, 27–29, 49, 50, 362, 423–25
training in, 31–44, 133–35, 140, 185, 250, 258, 262–64, 314, 338, 418, 426, 433, 454–55
Matsuoka, Yosuke, 375–77

Maximum Illud, 36, 47, 74, 206, 261, 340
May Fourth Movement, 327
May 30th Incident, 328
McCabe, Edwin, 125, 179, 184
McCormack, Joseph, 231, 245, 346, 383–84
McCormick, James, 184, 196,
McDermott, James, 86,
McGinn, Joseph, 386
McGowan, Anne, 390
McGurkin, Edward, 122, 231, 357
McKeirnan, Michael, 385
McKenna, Mary de Lellis, 230
McKenna, Mary Paul, 71
  and direct evangelization, 102–03
  and language study, 273–74
  superior in China, 61, 223, 362
  during World War II, 365–367
McLaughlin, James, 59
McLoughlin, John, 372
McNally, Ignatia, 137, 425
McShane, Daniel, 37, 139, 141, 148, 414
Medical work, 91–92, 116, 134, 136, 169, 199,
  324, 369, 371. *See also* Hospitals
  and conversions, 136–37, 168
  through dispensaries, 117, 135, 137, 146,
    153, 155, 169, 172, 175, 199, 363
  fee for, 137, 199
  by Protestants, 162
  and training of Chinese nurses, 137, 142,
    153–55, 201
Meihsien. *See* Kaying
M.E.P. *See* Société des Missions Etrangères
  de Paris
Mérel, Jean-Marie, 48, 50
Mersinger, Barbara, 116, 117, 227, 237, 280,
  382
Meyer, Beatrice, 149, 225, 365–66
Meyer, Bernard, 418, 431–32, 525n.98
  and acculturation, 267–68, 299, 303, 305,
    315, 433–34
  and architecture, 285, 292
  in Canton, 63
  catechetical materials by, 297–305
  and catechists, 79–81, 83–88, 97, 99, 126,
    255, 257
  and Catholic Action, 121, 128
  and Chinese priests and Sisters, 87, 208,
    225, 227, 257
  and corporal works of mercy, 443
  and educational work, 187, 189, 190
  internment of, 365
  and U.S. intervention in China, 337
  and language study, 269–71
  legacy of, 88, 126
  and Maryknoll priests, 257, 310
  not ordained bishop, 255–57

peace efforts by, 322–24, 361
prefect apostolic, 55, 257
and village catechumenate, 89–99
Mill Hill Foreign Mission Society, 14, 17
Mission. *See* Evangelization
Mission methods. *See also* Evangelization
  acculturation in, 310, 312
  in catechetical materials, 299–308
  in center catechumenates, 99, 109–10, 116,
    117
  toward Chinese women, 85–87, 112, 115,
    200
  city vs. countryside, 75–76
  under communism, 387
  direct vs. indirect, 76, 99–100, 103, 115,
    118
  and lay apostolate, 119–21, 122–24, 128,
    200
  and team approach, 114, 117, 120, 129
  in village catechumenates, 90, 97, 111–12,
    116
Mission work. *See also* Mission methods
  end of, 205
  organization of, 59–60, 67, 75, 359
  priorities of, 199
  reports, 74, 221–22, 257, 262
Missions Catholiques, 22
Missions de Chine et du Japon, 79
Modernization in China, 75, 192, 200–01,
  429–30, 438–40, 450
Moore, Mary Gertrude, 37, 134–35, 322
Morrissey, William, 386
Moss, Anna Mary, 275, 305–08
Moyan. *See* Kaying
Mueth, Edward, 311
Muiluk, 335
Mukden, 50, 59, 195, 209, 217, 231, 356
Mukden incident, 342, 345
Murphy, Albert, 343
Murphy, Ellen Mary, 194
Murphy, Frances, 110
Murphy, Maynard, 111, 278
Murray, John, 81
Murrett, John, 351

Nakamura, Sabina, 198, 357
Nakata, Rose Ann, 198, 357
Nanking, 50, 159, 160, 320, 334, 340
Nanning, 55, 312
National Catholic Welfare Conference of
  America, 333
National Geographic, 353
Nationalism, Chinese, 205, 317–20, 326, 327–
  33, 338–42, 360, 404–05
Nationalist regime, 182, 190, 337, 340, 376,
  439, 447

fight against Communists, 372, 380, 382–83, 395–96, 397
  prior to Sun's death, 320, 331–33
  religious policy of, 188, 193, 340, 439
  support of, 361, 385, 405–06, 439, 446–47, 450
Neale, Leonard, 3
New Life Movement, 190, 341, 439, 504n.154
Ngaimoon, 164, 168–73
Ningpo, 50
Nine-Power Treaty, 327, 332–33, 396
Nolan, Thomas, 425
North, William, 365–66
Northern Expedition, 319–20, 333, 340, 380, 438
Novitiates in China, 207, 223–41, 248, 250–52, 258, 484n.55
  apostolic training in, 229, 230, 235, 237, 252
  attrition in, 240–42
  between 1936 and 1949, 224–27, 229, 231, 367
  under communism, 225–31, 383–84, 390
  curriculum in, 224, 235–36, 239–40
  education in, 224, 226, 228–30, 233–36, 237, 250–52
  spiritual training in,. 224, 234–37, 240, 248, 252
  post novitiate training, 237, 250
  vocation for, 142, 223, 230, 233, 243, 248
  vows in, 224–28, 231, 236–37, 240

Oberle, Mary Dolorosa, 149, 150, 274, 367
O'Donnell, James, 396
O'Donnell, John, 356
Office of Strategic Services, 369
O'Hagan, Joan Catherine, 535n.269
Ohmann, Daniel, 36
Oka, Joseph, 286, 288–89
Old Folks Home, 141, 352
O'Leary, Mary Angelica, 193, 276–77
O'Melia, Thomas, 270–71, 276, 321, 330
O'Neill, Francis, 63, 154, 174, 362, 369
Opinions about Maryknollers
  from Chinese priests and Sisters, 245–50, 268, 279
  from non-Christian Chinese, 294, 296, 325–26, 331, 339, 359, 362
  from other missioners, 49
  during war with Japan, 362–63, 369, 371, 404
Opium, 68, 331
Opium War, 46
Orphanages, 118, 138–52, 179, 199–200, 365. *See also* War orphans
  under communism, 149–52
  difficulties with relatives, 146, 148–49

finances of, 140, 142
foster nurses for, 140, 146
Maryknoll Sisters in, 140–42, 144–45, 146, 367
prejudices against, 145, 146
during Sino-Japanese War, 143–45
statistics about, 141–42, 143
young adults leaving, 142
O'Shea, William, 254, 319, 323–25, 356

Pai Ch'ung-hsi, 320
Pai, Martin, 245
Pai, Maurus, 383
Pakkai, 54, 286, 385. *See also* Kongmoon city
  language school in, 270
  novitiate in, 224–25
  relief work in, 173–74
  seminary at, 207, 216–18
  during World War II, 365
Paklow, 92
Paksha, 220
Pan, Antoine, 245
Pantien, 217, 233, 294–95
Pardy, James, 356
Paris, Prosper, 49
Parish life, 120
  division of tasks in, 100–01, 105, 114, 117, 123
  nurture of Christians in, 97, 105–06, 119–20, 122, 124, 357, 360
  traditional tasks of Sisters in, 101, 103, 118, 187
Paschang, Adolph
  during Japanese occupation, 364–66, 369
  in Kochow, 188
  vicar apostolic, 54, 154, 155, 362
Paulhus, Anthony, 211, 212, 365–66
Paulist Fathers, 418
Pearl Harbor, 198, 231, 245, 364, 373–74
Pei-ch'iao, 157, 159–60
Peking, 50, 62, 217, 340, 383–84
Peking Times, 346
Peng Yang (Korea), 59
Pettochai, 78, 105, 111
Pingnam, 67, 182, 190, 266, 325
  antiforeignism in, 334
  language school in, 270, 272
  novitiate in, 225–26, 237
  seminary in, 221
Plane Compertum Est, 311–12
Political role of missioners, 407–08
  accused of subversive activities, 149, 151, 156, 327, 348–50, 352–53, 357–58, 380, 384, 388, 391–93, 395–400, 403, 405
  advocating neutrality, 319, 324, 342, 349, 358–62, 373–74, 378, 403–05

as foreign nationals, 339, 343–45, 349, 354–
59, 456
legacy of, 456
during local wars, 319–20, 322–27
in Manchuria, 342, 344–56, 358–60, 404
in Shanghai, 401–02,
in South China, 360–65, 367, 369–71, 385,
397–98, 404–05
in support of Nationalist regime, 190, 192,
367, 373, 377–78, 382–83, 385, 397–99,
405–06, 440, 442, 456
in U.S.-Japan relations, 375–77
and use of U.S. protection, 329, 335–36,
338–39, 350, 358, 362–63, 367, 371, 374,
404–05
Port Arthur, 342
Pose, 321, 381
Poverty, 138, 155, 179, 449
Powers, George, 413
Pravda, 400
Press in Manchuria, 346, 348–51
Price, Thomas
and catechists, 79
death of, 37, 52
and founding of Maryknoll, 16–17, 25, 27,
48
mission education by, 415, 422
in North Carolina, 13–14, 410
Propaganda Fide. *See* Sacred Congregation
for the Propagation of the Faith
Protestant missionaries, 47, 162–63, 176,
186, 188, 328, 331–32, 380, 409, 431–32,
456, 493n.57
American Presbyterians, 162, 345
under communism, 392
held for ransom, 381
Publications by Chinese Communists, 125,
150, 399–400
Publications by missioners in China
articles, 79, 128, 135, 163, 255, 289, 316,
331, 336, 338, 373–74, 378, 384, 402,
425–48
against communism, 397
language, 269–71, 272, 275, 276
in the press, 62, 75, 275
religious, 62, 112, 121, 126, 131, 262, 271,
272, 296–308, 518n.87
Putnam, George, 63
Puyi, 342, 350

Quinlan, Mary Liguori, 32
Quinn, Carroll, 172–73, 370
Quinn, Raymond, 209–10, 213
Quirk, Thomas, 343–44, 383

Rafferty, Agnes Regina, 274

Rasmussen, O.D., 338
Rauschenbach, Otto, 153, 294, 330, 369
Rayssac, Adolphe, 50, 55, 252–55
Rechsteiner, Aloysius, 149–50, 434
Red Beards, 343, 352, 354
"Reds," 320, 332, 340, 354
Regan, Joseph, 279, 381
Regan, Rita Marie, 129, 385, 396
Reilly, Peter, 131, 262, 280
Relationships between. *See also* Political
role
Chinese Sisters and local people, 236, 248,
250–51
Maryknoll Fathers: and Chinese seminar-
ians, 212–14; and Sisters, 33–34, 112,
114, 117, 118, 129
Maryknoll Sisters and Chinese students,
195–96
Maryknollers: and Chinese Catholics, 122,
172, 278–79; and the Chinese military, 176, 179, 198–99, 221, 323–26; and
Chinese priests, 241, 244–47; and Chinese Sisters, 238–44; and civil officials,
145–46, 148, 179, 195, 198, 361; and Nationalist authorities, 341, 378, 382, 385,
397, 399, 405; and non-Catholics, 134–
35, 137–38, 140, 148–49, 171, 180, 201,
221, 267, 278, 323, 369; and Manchukuo
authorities, 345–59
Relief work. *See* Welfare
Religious instruction of Chinese
Catholics, 97, 189, 190
children, 105–06, 187–89
students, 190, 192, 195, 197
Rerum Ecclesiae, 340
Rey, Charles, 270, 296
Riberi, Antonio, 125, 384, 386–87, 400
Ricci, Matteo, 6, 45, 145
Rice Christians, 110, 116
Riconda, Mary Ruth, 425
Riehl, Moira, 225–26, 236–37
Rietz, Edith, 390, 396, 447
Rizzardi, Mary Gonzaga, 225–27
Robert, Léon, 50–51
Rogers, Mary Josephine (*also* Mother Mary
Joseph), 456
and architecture, 286
and direct evangelization, 101–02, 103
and the founding of Maryknoll, 27–30
and medical work, 135, 157
Miss, 12, 27–30, 413
promoting American missionary spirit, 12,
412–13, 423
and repatriation, 356, 366
spirituality of, 41–42, 107
and the training of Sisters, 32–33, 40–42,

107
Romaniello, John
  under communism, 390, 447
  and native Sisters, 227-28
  prefect apostolic, 55, 116, 257
  and relief work, 175-76,
  during World War II, 367-68
Roosevelt, Franklin Delano, 375-76
Rubner, Dorothy, 97, 115
Ruggieri, Michele, 45, 296
Ryan, Joan Marie, 176-77, 192
  arrest of, 396-97, 399-401, 407
Ryan, Joseph, 32, 430, 433

SACO, 372
Sacraments, 74, 97, 112, 196, 280, 303, 435
  baptism, 5, 96, 111, 143, 146, 308, 311, 314
  confirmation, 364
Sacred Congregation for the Propagation of
  the Faith (Propaganda Fide), 11, 18, 25,
  48, 74, 88, 103, 211, 255, 257, 270, 311,
  314, 480n.2
Sacred Heart Review, 17, 20-21
Salesian Fathers, 81, 300, 303
Sancian, 45, 69, 174, 185
  during Sino-Japanese War, 362-64
Scheut Fathers, 81, 518n.87
Schifer, Wilhelm, 198
Schleininger, Roma, 157
Schmidlin, Joseph, 32, 74
Schmitt, Miriam, 356
qs s84-binSchool Sisters of St. Francis, 367
Schools, 186-87, 193, 200, 332, 365, 367. *See
  also* Education; Maryknoll Academy;
  Student hostels
  accusation against Christian, 188, 196
  and evangelization, 186-87
  kindergarten, 61, 187
  industrial, 61, 117, 179-80, 223, 421
  orphanage, 141, 142
  primary, 61, 179, 186-90, 192-93, 328, 341
  registration of, 188-93
  and rural literacy, 187-88, 200
  secondary, 61, 117, 192, 193, 195, 273, 365
  universities, 63, 75, 190, 194, 435, 439
  on U.S. west coast, 30, 194
  and vocations, 186
Seattle, 276
Seminaries in China, 205, 207-222, 245, 250,
  258, 289, 292-93, 483-84n.55
  attrition in, 211, 215-17
  under communism, 217, 221-22, 384, 390
  curriculum in, 209-13, 217, 220, 222, 383-84
  spiritual training in, 213, 215
  statistics about, 208, 216-18, 220, 221
  vocations in, 207-08, 215-17, 218, 245

during World War II, 218-21
Shakchin, 380-81
Shalvey, Xavier Marie, 198
Shanchengtze, 192-93
Shanghai, 61, 63, 157-62, 178, 274, 383-84
  antiforeignism in, 328
  Communists in, 400-03
Shanghai Foreign Press, 158
Shea, Margaret (*also* Sister Mary Gemma),
  28-29, 193, 276, 281
Shea, Nora, 27, 28-29
Sheehan, Mary Coronata, 193, 276
Sheklung, 162-63, 169
Sheng-ching Shih-pao (Mukden), 349
Sheridan, Mary Imelda, 108, 114, 224, 275,
  370
Sheridan, Robert, 37, 83, 414, 415, 426
Sherry, John J., 165, 169
She Shan, 222
Shiuhing, 234
Shortcomings of Maryknollers, 148-49,
  202, 246-48, 251, 259, 277, 296, 340, 360,
  455
Shumkai, 91-92, 312
Siaoloc, 184, 215, 222, 270, 272, 380-81
  antiforeignism in, 334
Simla, 368
Sino-Japanese War, 193, 313, 341, 361-73,
  381, 404, 440. *See also* World War II;
  Manchuria
  endurance of Chinese people during, 431
  in Kaying mission, 192-93, 221, 228, 370,
  398
  in Kongmoon mission, 143-45, 154, 169-71,
  173-75, 184, 217, 218, 224-25, 250,
  360-64
  in Kweilin mission, 175-76, 227
  in Wuchow mission, 173, 218, 220-21, 225-
  26, 361
  in Shanghai, 159-61
Sister Catechists of Our Lady of
  Kaying, 228
Sister Catechists of the Blessed
  Virgin Mary of Kweilin, 227
Sisters of Charity, 482n.35
Sisters of Charity of the Sacred
  Heart of Wuchow, 225
Sisters of the Holy Family of
  Nanning, 227
Sisters of the Immaculate Con-
  ception of Canton, 223, 225
Sisters of the Immaculate Heart
  of Kongmoon, 223-24
Sisters of the Sacred Heart of
  Jesus of Fushun, 230
Slattery, Dennis, 112, 209

Smith, Arthur H., 270, 273
Smith, James, 277, 365–66, 379, 402
Smith, John, 181, 183–84
So, Phillip, 218
Société des Missions Etrangères de Paris, 45–47, 86, 181, 218, 220, 253–54, 315, 336, 381
   catechetical materials by, 297, 306, 519n.103
   and corporal works of mercy, 162, 181, 183
   diminishing ranks in, 47, 50
   influence of, on Maryknoll, 77–78, 204, 208, 241, 243, 264, 454
   role of, in local wars, 319, 325, 327
Society for the Propagation of the Faith, 19–23, 82, 84, 410, 412, 418
Society of the Divine Word Fathers, 412
Sodalities, 106, 121–25, 128. *See also* Catholic action; Legion of Mary
Soong, T.V., 397, 447
South China Daily (Canton), 399
South Manchuria Railway, 342
Soviet Union, 195, 198–99, 330–31, 333, 439
Soviets
   in Kiangsi, 380–81
   in Kwangsi, 320–21, 381
Spirituality in practice, 454–55. *See also* Maryknoll Society and Congregation
   of Maryknoll Fathers, 132, 402
   of Maryknoll Sisters, 107–08, 111, 132, 134, 228, 274, 393–94
Sprinkle, Russell, 85, 182, 366, 371
Ssupingkai, 357, 383–84
Stanton, James, 23
Staubly, Albert, 168–70, 282–83, 285
Steinbauer, Jean Theophane, 111
Steyl Fathers, 81
Sticka, Pauline, 395
Stitz, Herman Joseph, 132, 158–60
Student Antireligious Movement, 331
Student hostels, 190, 192, 193, 200, 234
Suenens, Léon-Joseph, 129
Sullivan, Sara, 28–29
Sun Yat-sen, 52, 318–22, 324, 331, 338
   missioners' opinions of, 321–22, 333, 341
Sunchong, 283–84
Sunning. *See* Toishan
Sunwui, 163–68, 169, 174–75, 361
Sunyi, 54
Superstitions. *See* Babies, abandonment of; Customs; Traditional religious beliefs
Swatow, 50, 55, 252
Sweeney, Joseph, 162–65, 168–73, 363–64
Sweet, C.C., 133
Synodal Commissions, 62, 296, 400

Szechuan, 48
Szwong, 197, 277, 385

Taggart, Philip, 289, 321, 331–32, 341
Ta Kung Pao (Tientsin), 435
Tai Li, 372, 395
Taiwan, village of, 220, 285
Taiwan, island of, 307
Ta-lien Hsin-pao (Dairen), 349
Tam, Mary Bernadette, 224
Tam, Thomas, 218
Tanchuk, 208, 218, 220, 225–26, 292, 371
Tanguen, 372
Tao, Thomas, 85, 218, 221, 244
Tcheng, Peter, 297
Tennien, Mark, 90–92, 379, 447
   catechetical materials by, 296
   movie by, 418
   in Shumkai, 92–96, 137, 312–13
Tibesar, Leopold, 193, 276, 289
Tientsin, 50, 75, 383
Tientsin Times, 346
Tierney, John, 175
Ting, Mary Herman, 231
Tingchow, 55
Tinmoon. *See* Ngaimoon
To, Simeon, 217, 294
Toishan, 86, 153–57, 163, 164, 174–75, 199, 225
   during war with Japan, 362, 369
Tolan, Mary Eunice, 193, 230, 276, 353
Toomey, John, 156, 331, 365
Topong, 220–21. 226
Touchette, Paul, 424
Towle, Anna, 28–29
Tracy, Joseph, 19
Traditional religious beliefs, 93, 95, 310–13, 428, 433, 450. *See also* Buddhism and Taoism
Transportation, 70, 107, 153, 266, 280, 354, 367, 438, 440, 454
Travels, 101, 111, 266, 280, 343, 345, 352. *See also* Transportation; Visits
   under the Communists, 388–89
   under the Japanese, 364, 370
Treaties, unjust
   impact of, 46, 75, 322, 448, 456
Trevisan, Louise, 419, 421
Troesch, John, 365
Trube, Howard, 387
Truman, Harry, 383
Truth, 13–14
Tsa, Michael, 279
Tsai, Mark, 256
Tsang, Mark, 218, 221, 244
Tse, David, 119

Tse, John, 215
Tse, Robert, 212
Tsia Hang, 381
Ts'ia, Paul, 396
Tsoc, Anthony, 215
Tsong, Paul, 215, 222
Tsui, Paul, 217
Tungan, 126
Tungchen, 80, 134, 207, 325
Tunghwa, 122–24, 136, 192, 352
Tungon, 152, 163, 294–95
Tungshek, 227–28, 273–74, 385
Turner, Dominic Marie, 155–57

Ue Chi Cheung (Big Six), 91–92, 137
Unitas, Anthony Marie, 228
Urlacher, Magdalena, 133, 156, 396

Van den Bogaard, Joseph, 120, 279, 395
Van Dyk, Leo, 297–99, 306
Vaughan, Herbert, 14–18, 23
Veile, Luella, 105, 111
Vénard Théophane, 11, 21, 416
Venneman, Clara, 111, 370
Venneman, Espiritu, 158
Village life, 111–12, 267, 428–29
Vincentian Fathers, 36, 81, 380, 488n.38
Virgins, 86–87, 142, 223, 230
Visits by Maryknoll Fathers
  under the Communists, 388, 390
  of the sick, 137, 352
  of villages, 77–78, 97, 102, 106, 267, 280,
    352, 364
Visits by Maryknoll Sisters
  under the Communists, 388, 390
  and Kaying method, 99, 103–07, 108, 112,
    115, 116, 129–30
  of the sick, 136–37, 155
  of villages, 97, 99, 102, 106–07, 109, 111–13,
    116–19, 230, 267, 354, 367

Wagner, Gloria, 230
Walker, Charles, 334–35, 337
Wallace, William, 392–93
Walsh, James A., 330, 333, 437. *See also* Society for the Propagation of the Faith
  and architecture, 281, 286
  in Boston, 11–13, 17, 19–24, 416, 422
  and the founding of Maryknoll, 16–17, 25,
    27–30, 48
  influenced by Cardinal Vaughan, 17–18
  and medical work, 133–35, 152
  and the printed media, 20–24, 416, 482n.33
  promoting American missionary spirit,
    409–13, 422–23
  relationship with Maryknollers, 83

and the training of Maryknollers, 32, 35–
    38, 433
  and U.S. intervention in China, 335–36
  visits to China, 48–52, 253, 336, 373, 413,
    432
Walsh, James E.
  and acculturation, 262–64, 273, 311, 314
  and architecture, 281, 283
  arrest of, 330, 402–03
  catechetical material by, 297
  and corporal works of mercy, 131, 162–63
  head of Catholic Central Bureau, 63, 384,
    400–02
  and indigenization, 246, 252–57
  and language study, 270
  legacy of, 454–55
  during local wars, 321, 325, 332–33
  and the native Sisters, 223–24, 237
  request for U.S. intervention by, 329, 335–
    37
  and the training of Maryknollers, 35, 38–
    40, 337
  tribute to catechists by, 126–27
  in U.S.-Japan relations, 375–77
  and withdrawal of missioners, 329–30, 337,
    366, 402
  during World War II, 370, 378–79, 431, 440,
    446
Walter, Leo, 175
Wang Ching-wei, 320, 376
Wang Feng-ko, 354–55
War orphans, 143, 179, 404, 441, 444–46
Warlordism, 52, 188, 318–26, 340, 343, 436,
    438
Wedemeyer, Albert, 383
Weis, Edward, 353–54
Welfare and relief, 177, 180, 371, 374, 379,
    382, 404, 445
  from Catholic Welfare Committee, 63, 155,
    177–78, 332
  from civil organizations, 63, 143, 155, 174,
    175–77, 179, 182, 184
  from religious organizations, 62–63, 176,
    361
  in Fushun mission, 68, 122, 177, 344–45,
    351
  in Kaying mission, 176–77
  in Kongmoon mission, 132, 154, 155–56,
    169, 171, 173–75, 361
  in Kweilin mission, 175–76, 179–80
  in Shanghai, 160–61
  in Wuchow mission, 324–25
Wempe, Francis, 271
Wen Hui Pao (Hong Kong), 150
Wenzel, Richard, 138, 143, 366–67, 404
Werner, Celine Marie, 32, 354

White, Constance, 154
White, Francis, 396
Whiteright, John Sutherland, 272, 276
Wholean, Mary Louise, 28-29
Williams, John J., 19, 23
Wiseman, George, 81, 319, 323-26
Withdrawal of missioners
in 1925, 329-30
during World War II, 356-57, 366-67, 369, 370, 404-05
after Communist takeover, 383, 386, 387, 390, 423, 447, 535n.277
Witnessing of faith
by Chinese Catholics, 434-36
under duress, 125-26, 150, 172-73, 230, 434, 447-48
Womanhood, 200
Wong, John (of Swatow), 256
Wong, John (of Kaying), 222
Wong, Linus, 218, 224
Woo Pei Fu, 321
Work of St. Peter the Apostle Society, 84
Working Boys' Magazine, 21
World War II. *See also* Sino-Japanese War
internment of missioners during, 198, 355-58, 365, 377
Maryknollers during: in contact with U.S. army, 367, 369-72, 396, 405; in Fushun mission, 198-99, 231, 357; in Kaying mission, 370-72, 396; in Kongmoon mission, 225, 365-70; in Kweilin mission, 227, 366-72; repatriation of, 356-57, 366-67, 369, 370; in Wuchow mission, 220-21, 226, 366-72
Wu, John, 78, 213, 215-17

Wuch'ang, 218
Wuchow city, 75, 226, 323, 325, 366
antiforeignism in, 328, 522n.48
Communists in, 391-95
Wuchow vicariate, 54-56, 184, 199, 213, 226-27, 245, 255-57 366-72, 418
statistics for, 87, 88-89, 208, 218

Xavier, Chanel, 234, 366

Yamagishi, Maria Talitha, 198, 357
Yaohang, 395
Yeh, Francis, 379
Yenki, 59
Yeung, John, 267
Yeung, Maria Teresa, 61, 223-24
Yeungkong, 50, 52, 64, 69, 141, 208, 225, 285, 322-23 366, 418
antiforeignism in, 328-29, 334, 337-38
catechists in, 80
lepers in, 162
orphanage in, 139-42, 145-46, 149-50
schools in, 187, 190, 341
Sisters' work in, 101-02, 118, 134, 138, 139-50, 187, 190, 274, 330
Yi Shih-pao (Tientsin), 75
Yim, Dominic, 256
Yin, Timothy, 435
Ying, Vincent, 435
Yip, Epiphanius, 80, 81, 84, 324-25
Yü Pin, Paul, 256, 257, 442-43
Yü Tso-po, 320
Yunnan, 367

Zanin, Mario, 177, 256, 257, 361, 381